The Comprehensive Guide to Careers in Sports

Glenn M. Wong

Professor and Attorney
Department of Sport Management
Isenberg School of Management
University of Massachusetts
Amherst, Massachusetts

JONES AND BARTLETT PUBLISHERS

Sudbury, Massachusetts

BOSTON   TORONTO   LONDON   SINGAPORE

World Headquarters

Jones and Bartlett Publishers
40 Tall Pine Drive
Sudbury, MA 01776
978-443-5000
info@jbpub.com
www.jbpub.com

Jones and Bartlett Publishers Canada
6339 Ormindale Way
Mississauga, Ontario L5V 1J2
Canada

Jones and Bartlett Publishers International
Barb House, Barb Mews
London W6 7PA
United Kingdom

Jones and Bartlett's books and products are available through most bookstores and online booksellers. To contact Jones and Bartlett Publishers directly, call 800-832-0034, fax 978-443-8000, or visit our website www.jbpub.com.

Substantial discounts on bulk quantities of Jones and Bartlett's publications are available to corporations, professional associations, and other qualified organizations. For details and specific discount information, contact the special sales department at Jones and Bartlett via the above contact information or send an email to specialsales@jbpub.com.

Production Credits
Acquisitions Editor: Shoshanna Goldberg
Associate Editor: Amy L. Flagg
Editorial Assistant: Kyle Hoover
Production Manager: Julie Champagne Bolduc
Production Assistant: Jessica Steele Newfell
Marketing Manager: Jessica Faucher
V.P., Manufacturing and Inventory Control: Therese Connell
Composition: Lynn L'Heureux
Cover Design: Brian Moore/Kristin E. Parker
Cover Image: © Peafactory/ShutterStock, Inc.
Printing and Binding: Courier Stoughton
Cover Printing: Courier Stoughton

Photo Credits
Adonis Jernolds, Courtesy of Janis Ori; Barney Hinkle, Courtesy of Philip Shoulberg; Buffy Filipell, Courtesy of Mount Union Sport Sales Workshop; Dennis Mannion, © Los Angeles Dodgers, LLC; Gene DeFillipo, Courtesy of Boston College Media Relations; Jeff Price, Courtesy of Alvin Lee; John Calipari, Courtesy of Joe Murphy; John Wentzell, Courtesy of Janis Ori; Josh Berlo, Courtesy of Patricia Herrity; Matt Keator, Zdeno Chara, and Blake Wheeler, Courtesy of Matthew Keator; Mike Tamburro, Courtesy of Michael Gwynn and Pawtucket Red Sox; Mike Tannenbaum and Curtis Martin, Courtesy of New York Jets; Patty Viverito, Courtesy of Jeremiah Ingram; Peter Luukko and Edward Snider, Courtesy of Len Redkoles; Rick Ensor, Courtesy of Stephen Nowland/NCAA Photos; Sandy Barbour, Courtesy of Joan Tiefel, NACDA; Shaun White, Courtesy of Bo Bridges Photography; Wade Martin, Courtesy of AST, LLC.

Library of Congress Cataloging-in-Publication Data
Wong, Glenn M.
    The comprehensive guide to careers in sports / Glenn M. Wong.—1st ed.
    p. cm.
    Includes index.
    ISBN 978-0-7637-2884-7 (pbk. : alk. paper)
    1. Sports—Vocational guidance—United States. 2. Physical fitness—Vocational guidance—United States.
    3. Sports personnel—Employment—United States. I. Title.
    GV734.3.W66 2009
    796.02'3—dc22

                                                                                        2008043192

6048

Printed in the United States of America
12 11 10 09 08   10 9 8 7 6 5 4 3 2 1

For Paula, E. Glenn, and Gary.

Contents

Foreword

All my life I wanted to be a professional footballer (soccer player). Growing up in Liverpool, England, during the era of the Beatles, it was only natural for a Liverpudlian boy to want to be a footballer, a musician, or a comedian (as you had to have a sense of humor to live in that tough, blue-collar, high-unemployment city). Reality set in about age 16 when a couple of try-outs with professional teams revealed that, although I could definitely make it semi-professionally (AAA), I'd never be in the majors. The burning passion, of course, never went away—I spent my latter high school days organizing a local soccer league made up of teams from guys at my school because at St. Mary's we were forced to play rugby, and football (soccer) was not allowed. I acted as the commissioner, putting the schedules together, printing up the standings and scoring statistics, and even writing the game stories. In whatever spare time I had, I sketched out the design for the "perfect" football (soccer) stadium and even designed uniforms. Can you guess what profession I was destined to be in? Boy do I wish this book was in print back in those days!

Despite my all-consuming passion for sport, it was many years later before I had external confirmation of why I belonged in sport management. One of the first things I learned as a professor at the University of Massachusetts in the late 1970s and early 1980s about career counseling for our business and sport management students was to ask them this poignant question: "What three things did you love to do the most in your high school years?" I ask the reader to take the time right now to answer this question. Seek input if need be from your family and friends, or those who know you well. Then write these three things down; as Nike would say, "Just Do It!"—right now.

So what did you find out about yourself? This simple question can reveal a lot about you, and if channeled appropriately, this perspective should help frame your thinking as you read this text. Hopefully it will also help you to formulate strong opinions about the type of position and the industry in which your interests will be best utilized. Let me use an example to show you just how this works. My best friend in high school meandered in his career for almost 10 years after college graduation working as a middle-school teacher and part-time musician. On a trip back to England shortly after I'd learned about the "three-things question," this same friend was soul-searching, so I asked him the three-things question and helped him fill in his blanks. We each readily knew the answers for him: (1) art/something creative; (2) music; and (3) comedy/humor, because he was always telling jokes and sketching cartoons. Soon afterwards my friend decided to go back to university, but this time as an advertising major. Until recently, he headed up the advertising giant Ogilvey and Mather's Direct Marketing Division in London, where for many years he created award-winning print and radio ads with jingles and clever double entendres that used his wry humor. Bingo—all three "loves" encapsulated in one career. The result: a lifetime of satisfaction in his work!

Because I was so focused on playing football in high school, my grades suffered. All I cared about was my beloved Everton FC (English Premier League) and playing football as often as I could. Slowly the realization that I would never be a professional footballer set in, aided by my father making me stay in school until I got passing grades so that I could get into college. Yet, all this time while my father was giving me the "tough love" I needed ("You'll never make any money as a footballer!"), he admitted that he hated his own job as a life insurance salesman. So my father would tell me privately, "Son, do what you love, and you'll love what you do!" As a result, I never ever gave up on my professional sports dream. I just realized it in a different way, and a lot later in life. I played semi-professional soccer while going to both undergraduate and graduate business schools, then after almost a decade as a university professor and a consultant, I finally became a professional team sports executive. Since that time, I can honestly say that I have never had to "work" a day in my life.

Working in sports is, without a doubt, the most amazingly challenging, exhilarating, and yet sometimes frustrating career that anyone can have. When our team wins, it's awesome. When we lose, its agony. You frequently work 7 days a week and then go to the stadium, ballpark, or arena at night. In short, it's a job that you eat, sleep, and drink, but you love it. In entry-level and mid-management positions, invariably you are not well paid because there are so many people who want those jobs. Every major sports organization receives thousands of résumés, many from candidates who are very well qualified for entry-level positions. As a consequence, most sports organizations don't feel the need to pay competitively compared to the rest of the market. In the early days of teaching sport management students, I would sarcastically joke, "Don't worry about the lousy pay, you never have time off to spend the money you don't make!" When you finally get to the top, however, the pay can be outstanding, and the ride up is amazing. The keys to getting in this industry and moving up the ladder are the same: determination and persistence. If you want to get into this industry badly enough and are committed and set out about finding a position in the right way, then you will succeed. This text is all about helping you to get in by going about it the right way. It can be a long, slow road, so you have to be patient, but the rewards are that you will love what you do and always have the feeling that you do not have to "work" another day in your life.

This extremely insightful text, *The Comprehensive Guide to Careers in Sports*, written by my former colleague and business partner, Professor Glenn Wong, provides you with an amazing perspective that few people in this world are qualified to give. For 30 years, Glenn has been at the forefront in placing some of the best students in the world into this industry at the most prestigious sports organizations, and across all sectors of this industry (professional, collegiate, Olympic, or amateur; spectator and participant sports; in retail sporting goods, sport management, sports marketing and event management firms, sport associations, community facilities and programs, etc.). His view of this industry—the opportunities, the skills necessary to get in, and then what it takes to move up and sustain that success—is second to none. In short, this text is an invaluable aid not only to successful entry into this exciting industry, but also to learning what it takes to really succeed. Of course, this text by itself is not enough.

In business today, education, skill, and experience are no longer sufficient. The level of competition for the best jobs in every industry worldwide is so far beyond what we could conceive when my business school class graduated in the early 1970s. Businesses today demand a total commitment from their executives and middle managers that not every applicant for a position is willing to give. Hence in sports business, without a doubt the most competitive of all businesses

in the world, only paralleled by the TV, movie, and entertainment businesses, your passion, backed by your total commitment, will likely be the deciding factors in not only getting that first step on the ladder, but also shooting up the career development track to the CEO's office. But here again, it has to be well-channeled passion and disciplined commitment. Simply stated, *it has to be passion with a purpose and focused discipline.*

This text outlines what Professor Wong and all of us in the profession believe are the critical factors to success in breaking into the sports business and maintaining a successful upward progression. His perspective comes from watching so many of his students progress to the top positions at those very organizations where you most likely want to work. Over the years, as senior executives, we have built League Job Fairs at the NBA and recruited at the best universities. We have worked with the top head-hunting firms in the industry to find the right candidates. In my former life in education working with Professor Wong, we placed thousands of students. I personally have hired hundreds of people in sport management and in every case I selected those with the aptitude, experience, and necessary skills to do the job, but the deciding factor was always their hunger and passion that made them stand out from the crowd.

And therein lays the oxymoron of job seeking in sports. Most professionals in the industry lament about how hard it is to find good qualified candidates for anything above an entry-level job. Job seekers lament that they cannot find any good jobs. So let's look at what's causing this dichotomy.

SUPPLY AND DEMAND FOR SPORT MANAGEMENT JOBS

For the job seeker today, it has become critical to take whatever opportunity is available as the entry point into this industry. Your desired entry-level position may well be unavailable at that time. There are, of course, a couple of caveats that go with this statement:

1. If you are not qualified for the job, don't take it.

2. If you are not fully committed to doing that job 100% for at least 2 years, don't take it.

There are plenty of presidents/CEOs who started in the mailroom or in telemarketing (inside sales), who initially wanted a marketing position or a PR position. But when they took that entry-level job, they committed to being the best mailroom person or the best telemarketer that organization ever had. Even if the only position you are offered is as custodial host (janitor), if you've been looking to break into sports, take it and be the best at it that you can be. If you do this, then I guarantee you that from there you will eventually get the position you want.

For the employer, hiring someone with a law or graduate business degree as a receptionist, administrative assistant, or even in telemarketing is scary, because you know the candidate will bolt for a legal, marketing, or PR job at the first opportunity, and then you will have to train someone all over again. So, you may well be told that you are overqualified and you'll have to work through that. One solution that most sports organizations (who know what they are doing) employ today is to start everyone in telemarketing (inside sales). Sales becomes the sole or major entry point for all business positions, not just those for which marketing or sales makes sense. Butts in seats and sales revenue drive almost all segments of the sports industry. Today many organizations hire all entry-level people, including graduate students, using a 6-month "up or out," "you sell or you leave" philosophy. Specifically, the telemarketing agent has 6 months to hit a specified target (say $100,000 in sales), and only then are they eligible to fill a full-time representative spot. If they fall short of this target, they are released. In this way, the entire organization builds a sales and customer service culture, recognizing that in sports, "butts in seats" (or as they say down under, "bums in seats") is the lifeblood of the business. In return, these organizations then generally fill every marketing, promotions, advertising, and sponsorship sales position from this telemarketing talent pool.

You may have dreamed all your life about working in college athletics, but if the only job available is at an Olympic sport governing body—take it and make a name for yourself as a great worker. You can switch segments later. You may want to work in the major leagues but the only job is in the minors—take it and make a name for yourself as a great worker. You'll be a better candidate for major league jobs with your minor league experience. Consider the lesson pointed out in the two sets of triangles shown below. The first set reflects the supply (number of available jobs) by sport industry segment, and the demand

(interest) by graduates who want those positions. The second set reveals a similar imbalance in the functional areas of the business where jobs are available on a department by department basis (supply) and where candidates want to work (demand). Both sets of triangles reveal that where the jobs are and what candidates want are in sharp contrast with one another.

Job Availability by Sport Industry Segment

Supply
(Organizations having entry-level positions available)

Pro Teams

Olympians and NGB's

Intercollegiate Athletics

All Other Segments

Demand
(Candidates wanting positions in those organizations)

Pro Teams

Intercollegiate Athletics

Olympians and NGB's

All Other Segments

As if the above "inverse pyramid" phenomenon did not provide enough of a challenge, now let's look at the functions of business departments that students/graduates and candidates seek and which organizations have vacancies to fill.

Job Availability by Functional Skills

Supply by Department
(Positions available to be filled)

Demand by Department
(Candidates wanting those positions)

Suffice to say, the job openings are not where the candidates want them to be, so be prepared to be flexible and develop new skills. And remember, working in another function will help you when you hit the executive office because you will have a broader base of understanding of the entire organization.

One piece of good news is that the size of sports organizations' business front offices and college athletic department staffs have grown exponentially as the need to generate revenues has increased. When Professor Wong and I were first placing UMass students in internships in the late 1970s and early 1980s, there were very few business positions at all sports organizations. Jeff Twiss, the long-time VP, public relations, for the Boston Celtics, joined the club during that time as one of seven full-time business staff. Today the Celtics have more than 70 business front-office staff.

YOUR QUALIFICATIONS

Remember, it will be your education, skill, and experience that qualify you to be interviewed for a position. It will be your passion and commitment that will get you the job over other qualified applicants because it sets you apart during the interview process; however, it will be your work habits that will set you apart in your future. Do you come to work early? Do you stay late when necessary? Do you get every assignment done on time? On a budget? And do you add a few of your own creative touches to it? Are you a team player? Or are you totally out for yourself? Do you communicate well verbally and in writing? Can you think on your feet? Can you keep information confidential? And do you stay away from the water-cooler gossip? Do you present yourself well and dress like a future executive? Will you start to dress and act like the best CEO candidate even before you become the CEO? How are your presentation skills in front of 100 people? How about presenting in front of the Board of Governors, or the Board of Directors, or the Board of Trustees? These skills that come from within are the factors that will distance you from the rest of the organization and will most likely be the factors that lead you to the top in this most challenging and most absorbing of businesses.

I'd like to say that the days of discrimination and the glass ceiling are gone for women and minorities in the sports business, but that is untrue. However, nearly every sports organization now affirmatively seeks to broaden the diversity among its staff. The overall situation, in my experience, is getting better every year, certainly in the public sector and intercollegiate athletics. There are fewer and fewer cases of nepotistic hiring of the owner's son or daughter, or worse, their neighbor's son. For the organizations using telemarketing as the sole or preeminent entry point, this garbage is effectively eliminated. Any candidate not up to par gets weeded out quickly. Yes, the owner's son or daughter still frequently gets hired at a level where they may not be competent, but with today's level of razor-edge competition and focus on instantaneous production of results, owners, boards, and decision makers rarely tolerate such "passengers" on the bus to greatness.

In short, this book firmly places the responsibility for finding the right position in this industry on your own shoulders, or in your own hands. Rightfully, that is where it should be. This text, however, is also an excellent road map showing what to do, what not to do, where the successes can be found, and where the potholes are. The lessons from this outstanding text can, I believe, be synthesized by the old story of the student who was learning from a world-renowned guru. Rather than taking everything he or she could from the guru and then processing it with his or her own thoughts, this particular student chose instead to always try to test the guru. One day this student created what he or she believed to be the ultimate test for the guru. The student took a dove in his or her hands and put it behind his or her back. The student asked the guru a question: "Guru, I have a dove in my hands, is it alive or is it dead?" The guru thought for a moment, and realized of course that the question was a trick. If the guru said "Alive," the student would break the dove's neck and reveal it as dead. If the guru said "Dead," the student would reveal it as alive. So instead, the guru said, "My student, that dove's life is in your hands!" In the same way, your life in sport management is in your own hands—this text is the road map, the what to do and the what not to do; however, your career is like a dove: don't crush it, don't kill it, instead nurture it carefully by following the plans and heeding the advice outlined in this book. Then and only then can you set that dove free to soar at the highest level, just like your own career will soar.

— Dr. Bernard (Bernie) Mullin
Principal, The Aspire Group

Preface

The Comprehensive Guide to Careers in Sports contains my thoughts, insights, and experiences about careers in the sports industry. This book's aim is to help readers understand the sports industry and its various jobs as well as to help individuals decide whether they have the *potential* to work in the industry. Currently, there are very few resources available as this is a relatively young industry. This book provides information, raises questions for people to consider, and acts as a starting point for future research. The goal is to provide the tools so that the reader can determine whether he or she should pursue a career in the sports industry. For those who decide to pursue a career in the sports industry, this book will act as a guide for the selection of the right industry segment, and answer questions about the educational and work experience necessary for the particular jobs in which they are interested.

ABOUT THE BOOK

Much of the information collected and the thought processes and analyses that have gone into this book are from my various experiences, including my own work with students. I would like to thank many of my former students whom I have stayed in touch with over the years who provided a great deal of information for this book.

Section 1 of this book, "The Job Search in the Sports Industry," provides the big picture overview of employment in the sports industry, along with the planning process, educational path, and career considerations.

Section 2 is titled "The Sports Industry: Segment Descriptions." The goal of this section is to provide the range of possible sports industry sectors for the reader to consider. I found that people have different interests in the sports industry and often know certain segments of the sports industry very well, but they are quite unfamiliar with other areas of the industry. Some of the areas of the sports industry are discussed in "long segments," which means they provide an in-depth analysis along with a historical timeline. These are supplemented by "short segment" descriptions, which focus on areas of the sports industry that are smaller, less popular, and on a smaller scale financially. The purpose of the short segments is to let the reader know about a sport or a league as a potential career opportunity. From here, the reader can research areas further. This differentiation is not a value judgment on the importance, viability, or potential of that league or segment of the industry.

It should be noted that the revenues of the sports enterprise have been used as a general indication of the number of positions in that organization. Simply stated, the more dollars involved, the more employees usually required. So the fledgling new league with no television or radio contracts, a small fan base, and no season ticket sales will generally have a smaller operation with fewer employees. While it does not mean that there are no jobs, it usually means that there are fewer jobs—on a positive note, it also may mean that there is less competition for those jobs.

Section 3, "Career Tracks of Executives in the Sports Industry," examines the career paths of many of today's leaders in this industry, providing a detailed analysis of how people in the industry have achieved success and what routes have led them there. This section is especially important because the sports industry does not have any type of an accreditation agency that prepares one for a career in the field.

For most jobs in the sports industry, you will find that executives have a wide variety of qualifications, skills, educational backgrounds, and experience. However, there often are certain characteristics that these executives share. The career tracks section is designed to look for these common characteristics. The educational backgrounds, athletic backgrounds, and work experience of these people were collected, compiled, organized, and analyzed. For most jobs in the sports industry, there often is more than one career track to that job.

How can the career tracks section be helpful? It can help with self-assessment. Compare your résumé with the backgrounds of those who hold positions similar to those in which you are interested. Which career track matches up best with your background? If you are deficient somewhere, can you make it up? This section should enable you to put together both a short-term plan and a long-term plan to reach your targeted position.

Section 4, "Organizational Charts," contains the organizational charts of several sports organizations. There are a wide variety of organizational charts for professional teams and college athletic programs. For college athletics, there is a range of schools, from large (Division I) to small (Division III) organizational charts. There also are organizational charts for league offices, college conference offices, and some "cottage industries."

The organizational charts are important for a couple of reasons. One is that they show the various functions of an organization. Most people know about general managers and ticket sales, but they may not know about corporate sponsorship sales or compliance offices. Second, the organizational charts show the reporting lines; this also represents a possible career path.

Section 5 is titled "Job Announcements." Most of the announcements in this section are the actual job advertisements for the position; for example, job advertisements for positions such as director of marketing partnerships for the National Basketball Hall of Fame and the director of compliance for the Big 12 Conference are included. The job announcements provide readers with a description and/or the responsibilities of the particular job. The job advertisements typically provide the educational requirements as well as the types and lengths of experience preferred or required for the job. The job advertisement also may mention the skills and abilities required.

How can a job description help a reader determine his or her path in the sports industry? For one thing, it should assist the reader in determining whether he or she would like the job. It also will help the reader determine whether he or she is qualified in terms of education, experience, and abilities. If the reader does not meet the various job qualifications, it will help the reader determine what he or she needs to do to be a candidate for this type (and level) of job. For the sport management student, the job descriptions can help guide one in deciding on whether to attend graduate school (and what type of graduate school), and the types of jobs he or she has to have to build up the requisite experiences and skills needed. Finally, the job advertisements may provide the salary range so that the reader can get a realistic sense of compensation.

It should be noted that the same job title may differ in terms of not only the job duties, but also the education, experience, and skills required for the job. Therefore, where available, there may be more than one job advertisement. There also are some positions where advertisements are not readily available (mostly in privately owned teams and organizations, such as professional sports). In these situations, position descriptions have been included. These focus on responsibilities and may not include salary range, education, skills, or experiences required.

One final note: gender-neutral pronouns have been used as much as possible. In cases where gender-neutral pronouns are not used, the intent is to include both "he" and she."

Many people working in the sport industry enjoy a successful and extremely fulfilling career in the field. It is my hope that this book will assist others in finding their own place in the sports industry, as well as their own success. Although there is no single path to success in the sports industry, hopefully this book will provide the necessary tools and information to begin to map out a career plan and help with career choices.

ACKNOWLEDGMENTS

There are many people who worked directly on this project (which took much longer than originally planned). These include various research assistants at the University of Massachusetts. They provided research, writing, fact-checking, editing, and the student perspective: Brian Sharkey, Jeff Wagner, Mark Scialabba, Ryan Jonas, Ted Sherburne, Kevin Kristof, Steve Gibbs, Dave Quinn, and Dominic Rivers.

There also are many other people who helped to provide information, research assistance, and answers to questions. A number of these people work in the sports industry, so thank you for helping the next generation of sports managers. There are so many people who have helped along the way that I may have omitted a few. My advanced apologies; all mistakes and omissions will be corrected in the next edition: Ken Sheirr, Liz Hogenson, Hunter Lochman, Beth Robertson, Dan Hauser, Amy Baker, Brett Tillett, Jennifer Pierce, Jason Dennard, Jeff Elliot, John Wentzel, Joseph Lawler, Regan Waters, Mike Tannenbaum, Mark Brumbaugh, Jeff Price, Gene DeFillipo, Kenneth Fuchs, Richard Ensor, Jeffery Twiss, Dennis Curran, Tricia Turley, Greg Cannella, Jay Gladden, Matt Finlayson, Mark Bergeron, Mike Demars, Vivian Chang, David Tyler, Dana Bisordi, Lauren Laio, Jen Hughes, Melissa Hylton, Carol Szymkowicz, Maureen Kocot, Lynda Vasallo, Dr. Louis Jenis, Wade Martin, Judy Dixon, Zach Simmons, Dick Bresciani, Michael Davis, Michael Goldstein, and Chris Deubert.

The publisher has been very patient while waiting for this manuscript, which took five years to complete. The staff at Jones and Bartlett Publishers did an outstanding job handling the editing and preparation of this text. I would like to thank various people at Jones and Bartlett, including the people I most directly worked with: Shoshanna Goldberg, Jacqueline Geraci, Kyle Hoover, Jess Newfell, and Jessica Faucher. They provided timely and excellent guidance, support, and recommendations—always with a smile. There were many more people "behind the scenes" who worked hard to make this proposal a reality.

Thank you also to the reviewers of this edition. Their voices, criticism, and support have truly made this a better text: Danielle Mincey White, PhD, Claflin University, and Patrick J. Clemens, MSS Instructor, Cardinal Stritch University.

I would like to thank the various people and organizations who authorized the use of photos along with photographer: Janis Ori, Richard Ensor, Ed Clinton, Wade Martin, Peter Luukko, Ike Richman, Edward M. Snider, Cheryl Arnao, Mike Tamburro, Michael Gwynn, Bernie Mullin, Jeff Price, Theresa Fitzpatrick, Sandy Barbour, Ashley Gurling, Patty Viverito, John Calipari, Lamar Chance, Mike Tannenbaum, Curtis Martin, Zdeno Chara, Blake Wheeler, Buffy Fillpell, Dennis Mannion, Kathryn Kuykendall, Shaun White, Barney Hinkle, Josh Berlo, John Wentzell, Adonis (Sporty) Jernolds, Matt Keator, Gene DeFillipo, Beth Mahoney, Bob Boone, Mike Rizzo, Dana Brown, and Mark Scialabba.

Thank you also to my career-long friend and colleague, Dr. Bernard (Bernie) Mullin for his terrific "foreward." Thanks to the administration and my colleagues at the University of Massachusetts for their interest and support of both this project and my career.

Finally, thank you to the outstanding students and people whom I have had the privilege and honor of working with for many years. I had the good fortune to work with some of the best and brightest people in the sports industry. It has been a pleasure to watch them progress in their careers, grow both personally and professionally, and rise to leadership positions in the field of work and in their community. A special thanks to the many who have kept in touch with me over the years, and who appreciated the help they have received and continue to talk about their careers. Several times when I talk about the career tracks to leadership positions in the book, I am referring to some of these former students. Some were the first to create a new and unique career path, and I congratulate them for their spirit, determination, and success in a fascinating, challenging, and interesting industry.

— Glenn M. Wong
Amherst, Massachusetts

About the Author

Glenn M. Wong is a professor in the Sport Management Program in the Isenberg School of Management at the University of Massachusetts. He has been a faculty member at the University of Massachusetts since 1979. He served as Department Head from 1986 to 1997. In 1992–1993, he served as Interim Director of Athletics and Acting Dean of the School of Physical Education. He is currently the Faculty Athletics Representative for the University of Massachusetts to the National Collegiate Athletic Association, a role he has served since 1993. He has taught courses in sport law, sport finance and business, college athletics, amateur sports law, and labor relations in professional sports. Professor Wong also is one of the original faculty members with the Sports Management Institute (1990).

In 2007, Professor Wong was named one of "The 100 Most Influential Sports Educators in America" by the Institute for International Sport at the University of Rhode Island. In 2006, Wong received the Academic Achievement Award in Sport Management, presented by the International Conference on Sport and Entertainment Businesses, University of South Carolina. In 2003, he earned the Distinguished Teaching Award from the University of Massachusetts. In April 2001, he received the Distinguished Faculty Award from the University of Massachusetts Alumni Association. In April 1999, he gave a presentation entitled "The Impact of the Law on the Development of Sports" in the University of Massachusetts Distinguished Faculty Lecture Series where he received his second Chancellor's Medal of Honor.

Professor Wong has authored several books and more than 100 sport law articles. He is the author of *Essentials of Sports Law, Fourth Edition* (2009). He has co-authored *Law and Business of the Sports Industries*, Volumes I and II, and *The Sport Lawyer's Guide to Legal Periodicals* (1995). He has also contributed chapters in several books. His articles have appeared in the *Seton Hall Legislative Journal*, The American Bar Association's *Entertainment and Sports Lawyer*, *Athletic Business*, *Detroit College of Law Review*, *Gonzaga Law Review*, *Entertainment and Sports Law Journal*, *The Arbitration Journal,* and *Nova Law Review*. In addition, Professor Wong wrote a monthly column for ten years, entitled the "Sports Law Report" for *Athletic Business* magazine.

Professor Wong is a frequent speaker on sports law and negotiation topics and has made more than 100 presentations. He has been a speaker at the Sports Lawyers Association, the Knight Commission on College Athletics, the Seton Hall Sport Law Symposium, Practicing Law Institute, the American Bar Association, the Athletic Business Conference, the National Association of Collegiate Directors of Athletics Management Institute, the Sports Management Institute, National Association of Collegiate Directors of Athletics, The National Association of Academic Advisors for Athletics, the National Association of Student Personnel Administration, the International Health, Racquet and Sportsclub Association, and others.

Professor Wong also has served as a lawyer or consultant for a number of organizations within the sports industry including, among others, *Sports Illustrated*, Reebok, the National Collegiate Athlete Association, the United States Olympic Committee, U.S. Triathlon, U.S. Biathlon, and Major League Baseball. In addition, he served as an expert witness in sport cases involving liability issues and damages. He has also worked with universities starting sport management programs, the sports insurance industry, heath/fitness clubs, trading card manufacturers, and NCAA conferences. He has served as an arbitrator in cases involving the United States Anti-Doping Agency and Major League Baseball. Also, Professor Wong worked as outside counsel for the Boston Red Sox in salary arbitration cases from 1997–2003.

Professor Wong is a member of the Massachusetts Bar. He is currently a member of the board of directors for the Sports Lawyers Association, where he has served for 10 years. He has also been a member of the Arbitration Panel of the Court of Arbitration for Sport.

He received a Bachelor of Arts degree in economics and sociology at Brandeis University, where he co-captained the basketball team, and a Juris Doctorate degree from Boston College Law School. He has received a distinguished alumnus award from Brandeis University.

Section 1

The Job Search in the Sports Industry

What Is It Really Like to Work in the Sports Industry?

"Success is not the key to happiness. Happiness is the key to success. If you love what you are doing, you will be successful."

—Albert Schweitzer, theologian, philosopher, and winner of the 1952 Nobel Peace Prize

"Dictionary is the only place that success comes before work. Hard work is the price we must pay for success. I think you can accomplish anything if you're willing to pay the price."

—Vince Lombardi, former head coach of the Green Bay Packers and member of the National Football League Hall of Fame

"For a typical 7:00 pm game, I arrive at 9:00 am. I first bring press passes to the security gate where the media will be arriving. I then begin making copies around 10:00. Assuming the copy machine does not jam, they are usually completed by 3:30. Next, I bring most of the copies to the pressroom, where media personnel meet with one another and have dinner. I then bring 50 copies of game notes and statistics to the ninth floor press box. While in the press box, I distribute the seating charts so that people will know where to go come game time. At 4:30, I cut out newspaper articles and place them in their respective folders and scrapbooks. At 5:30, I eat dinner in the pressroom. At 6:15, I make my way to the press box for my game night duties."

—An entry-level media relations employee for a National Hockey League franchise

If you are reading this book, you are most likely considering a career in the sports industry. You've seen the glitz and glamour of the sports headlines and are wondering, "What's it like to work in the sports industry?" As a job seeker, you should be aware of a few generalizations. Working in the sports industry can be exciting, but also extremely challenging. In talking to many people who currently work in the sports industry, it is typical to find very high job satisfaction. This is not a scientific observation, but is based on various conversations and feedback. This seems to sharply contrast with other fields, such as the legal profession, where a low job satisfaction is expressed in many different surveys and studies. However, remember that this is a generalization and that many people in the sports industry are not satisfied with their jobs, just as many in the legal industry are very satisfied with their jobs. Here are some more generalizations about the sports industry: internships are relatively easy to come by, but jobs are hard to come by. Upward mobility in the sports industry can be very slow or difficult because there are few positions and little turnover of high-ranking executives. Generally speaking, it is also an industry that does not pay well, at least from entry-level to mid-level positions, and a lot of this can be traced to the economic principle of supply and demand. There is a high demand from people who want to work in the sports industry, and there is a limited supply of jobs.

The following story of a National Basketball Association (NBA) team helps illustrate the type of job environment commonly found in sports. (Note: The team name is not disclosed for confidentiality purposes.) One of the favorite activities of the team's executives is to read the unsolicited letters from people looking for jobs with the team. Many times, the letters go like this:

I am a successful businessperson with an MBA (or a law degree), and I do not like my job. I would be willing to do anything for the team. I love sports; money is not a big factor for me, and I am not looking for a salary commensurate with my educational background or work experience.

The executives, who may have less educational background and/or work experience, typically laugh as they deposit the letter in the circular file (trash). The bottom line is that a lot of people, many of whom are qualified or possibly overqualified, are interested in working in the sports industry. This type of demand drives down compensation levels, resulting in low-paying or unpaid internships, and low-paying entry- to mid-level positions. In addition to the impact on compensation, it also makes it more difficult to obtain positions in the sports industry.

"Being a professional is doing the things you love to do, on the days you don't feel like doing them."

—Julius Erving, member of the
Basketball Hall of Fame

There are two polar opposite views commonly shared by employees working in the sports industry. Viewpoint A is that it is great to work with LeBron or Tiger every day. Employees who share this view get satisfaction from working with premier athletes and the "magic" of sports. Viewpoint B is that the sports aspect of a job wears off pretty quickly, and, after a few years in the business, it is no different from any other job. For many, the magic of the sports industry can wear off after one sees how the product is produced. This is similar to the "sausage factory" analogy—if your favorite food is sausage, don't take a job in a sausage factory because seeing how the product is made will likely cause you to never eat sausage again.

Although every job is different and every person is different, the reality probably falls somewhere in between viewpoints A and B. The first sentiment is usually from someone who does not know much about the industry. This person may have stars in his eyes and may be attracted to the industry because of an interest in a particular athlete, a group of athletes, a particular sport, or a team. He may have been a fan or a participant in sports. He may think he is qualified because of his background. For the most part, the industry is an exciting and interesting place to work; however, the interesting is interspersed with the routine and the mundane.

Working in sports does have some cachet in that people are interested in what someone working in sports does. *Sports* is a fairly universal language. It may be common for people at cocktail parties to pay more attention to a person working in the sports industry, due to their fascination with that person's job. (The irony is that with the long hours people in the sports industry work, they may not spend much time at cocktail parties.)

In addition, the people involved in sports such as athletes and coaches are generally interesting people and gifted in their profession. So if the job seeker loves sports, he will be working in an interesting area. He will also have the opportunity to work with people with similar interests.

"Working in sports can be a very difficult profession. The advice I give to people is, if you can live without it, do not get into sports—go work in business, something outside of sports. You have to truly be willing to put in the hours, the 60- to 70-hour workweeks. You have to be unable to live without it to make it in this industry."

—Gene DeFilippo, Athletic Director at Boston College

SPORTS ORGANIZATIONS AS EMPLOYERS

Sports organizations do not rank highly on the "best places to work" surveys, and this ranking may be justifiable. It is important for the prospective employee to understand not only what causes this perception, but also why sports organizations do not find it necessary to change their current practices.

In 2008, *BusinessWeek* published an article entitled, "Best Places to Launch a Career." Scanning the list of the top 50 companies, the likes of Disney, Lockheed Martin, and Deloitte & Touche appear; however, you will not find a single sports organization (though you will find larger companies that have sports organizations within them). Why do you suppose this is the case? The article indicates that favorable organizations offer "entry-level employees more variety and challenges, providing senior-level mentoring, and giving them opportunities to work for causes they believe in."[1] This includes "granting more competitive pay and benefits, faster career advancement, and greater responsibility."[1] Recruiting, retention, and training practices also play a large role. For the most part, sports organizations fall well short of the ideal in all of these areas.

One reason is that sports organizations generally do not have problems attracting and retaining employees using their current practices. This is largely due to the aforementioned supply and demand issues. The number of people who wish to work in the sports industry is far greater than the number of available positions. This creates an environment in which sports organizations find it unnecessary to provide competitive compensation packages (particularly for entry-level positions). After all, why pay someone more than you have to? Given the relatively low-paying nature of the industry, even if a sports organization had a terrific work environment (in terms of providing variety, challenging work, etc.), the organization would still have a difficult time making *BusinessWeek's* list. One can predict that should sports organizations ever begin to experience difficulty finding viable applicants, they would need to improve their compensation levels. However, such a move seems rather unlikely given the overabundance of job seekers in the market.

Another reason for sports industry organizations not making the list of the "Best Places to Launch a Career" is the relatively small size of the organizations. For the most part, sports organizations have considerably fewer employees than the companies listed in the *BusinessWeek* article. This makes it more difficult to build variety and flexibility into jobs. It also makes it difficult for employees to quickly move up the corporate ladder—there just are not enough open positions to move into. And it is possible that the people in the middle- and upper-level positions stay in their positions, and therefore there are fewer turnovers. This is something sports organizations have little power to change. Additionally, most sports organizations must work around schedule constraints, which often call for night and weekend games. This can often lead to long hours and little time off during the season. For the most part, organizations have little control over the schedule and timing of games, so there is no easy way around this problem—the games must be played.

Long hours, low pay, little development, and few advancement opportunities all play a part in the typical sports organization's work environment. In addition, marketplace forces do not currently dictate that sports organizations change their practices. As a prospective employee in the sports industry, you should anticipate encountering similar circumstances upon entering the industry.

LACK OF JOB SECURITY

Job security within sports organizations is not very good compared to other nonsport organizations, particularly for those working in professional sports. At any point in time, a team can be sold and the ownership change may have a dramatic impact on the personnel. There is a common saying: "a new broom sweeps clean," meaning the new ownership group may decide to remove the existing management team in favor of a new group of people. Although this typically does not happen with every ownership change, it is possible

you could be subjected to this type of change even if you are an outstanding employee. Jeffrey Loria's acquisition of the Florida Marlins and Daniel Snyder's acquisition of the Washington Redskins, two of the more extreme examples of employee turnover, are described in Box 1-1.

The ownership changes of Jeffrey Loria and Daniel Snyder are somewhat unique situations, but you should be aware that this type of mass turnover does take place. Keep in mind, though, there have been many other ownership changes that were far less extreme. Even so, ownership changes can happen unexpectedly, creating a stressful work environment and higher than normal employee turnover.

DISPELLING THE MYTH: SPORTS ORGANIZATIONS ARE NOT AS LARGE AS YOU THINK

Because of the amount of media attention the sports industry receives, most people assume sports entities are rather large organizations. This perception is further compounded by the exorbitant player salaries and franchise sales prices reported by the media. In reality, sports organizations are somewhat small in comparison to a typical business. Many people find this to be surprising.

The size of an organization is generally dictated by the amount of revenue the organization produces, so here are some numbers. The average per-team revenues for the four major professional sports leagues are as follows:

- *National Football League (NFL)*: $192.5 million (for the 2005–2006 season)[3]
- *Major League Baseball (MLB)*: $170.4 million (for the 2006 season)[4]
- *National Basketball Association (NBA)*: $112.2 million (for the 2005–2006 season)[5]
- *National Hockey League (NHL)*: $75.6 million (for the 2005–2006 season)[6]

Box 1-1   New Owner, New Employees

The winter of 2002 was an interesting one for Jeffrey Loria. He sold his ownership stake in the Montreal Expos to Major League Baseball and then proceeded to purchase the Florida Marlins. Upon completing the purchase of the Marlins, Loria fired 60 of the team's employees. The firings were mostly isolated to the player development staff, including scouts, administrators, minor league managers, and minor league coaches. The move allowed Loria to bring in about 50 employees who had previously worked for him at the Montreal Expos. This type of mass turnover with an ownership change should not be unexpected. Owners want employees with whom they are comfortable,

with whom they have experience working. Essentially, in its simplest form, owners want their people in important positions. Interestingly, though, most of the Marlins' business employees were able to keep their jobs.[2]

A similar situation occurred with Daniel Snyder's purchase of the Washington Redskins in 1999. Within days of completing the sale, Snyder fired around 25 Redskins employees, some with 20-plus years of experience. The Marlins and Redskins situations provide excellent examples of the lack of job security that may be found in the sports industry. If a team is sold, and the new owner wants to insert his or her guy into your position, there is very little you can do no matter how good you are at your job.

Seem like pretty significant numbers, right? Well consider this—your average Costco store generates $121 million in sales each year (per store).[7] This makes a typical Costco, financially speaking, larger than your average NBA or NHL franchise, and reasonably close to the size of your average NFL and MLB team. This means that in a large number of cases, more money flows through your local shopping center than your local sports franchise. This catches most people off guard. They expect sports franchises to be monstrous organizations because they are not only in the newspaper and on the evening news, but also have their own sections of the newspaper specifically devoted to them. Additionally, sports franchises drive other media outlets such as ESPN, regional sports networks, and a large number of Internet sites.

This phenomenon is not isolated to professional sports. As an additional point of comparison, the Ohio State University athletic department brought in $101.5 million of revenue during the 2005–2006 fiscal year, more than any other college athletic program.[8] From a revenue generation standpoint, this places the largest college athletic department $20 million behind a Costco store.

A similar comparison can be made at the league level. Total revenues for recent seasons for the four major professional sports leagues in North America were as follows:

- NFL: $6.1 billion (for the 2005–2006 season)[3]
- MLB: $5.1 billion (for the 2006 season)[4]
- NBA: $3.3 billion (for the 2005–2006 season)[5]
- NHL: $2.2 billion (for the 2005–2006 season)[6]

To get a real sense of the relatively small financial size of the leagues, compare these amounts to the total revenues of the following prominent companies:[9]

- American Airlines: $22.5 billion (for 12 months, ending December 31, 2006)
- Apple Computer: $19.3 billion (for 12 months, ending September 30, 2006)
- Ford Motor Company: $160.1 billion (for 12 months, ending December 31, 2006)
- Google: $10.6 billion (for 12 months ended December 31, 2006)
- General Electric: $163.3 billion (for 12 months, ending December 31, 2006)
- Walt Disney Company: $34.3 billion (for 12 months, ending September 30, 2006)

This should give you a better idea of how sports leagues stack up against corporate America. From a revenue standpoint, all of these companies are larger than the NFL, North America's most financially successful sports league.

What does this mean for you as a job seeker in the sports industry? This comparison provides an indication as to why it may be easier to find a job in business than in the sports industry. Jobs usually follow the money. Thus because there is more money in corporate America, there are typically many more job opportunities. The more opportunities, the better your odds of landing a job. So, in light of the relatively small size of sports organizations and a strong demand by those seeking to enter the industry, be prepared for a highly competitive scramble for the scarce positions found in the sports industry.

Endnotes

1. Gerdes, L. (2006, Sep. 18). The Best Places to Launch a Career. *BusinessWeek*. Retrieved September 4, 2008, from http://www.businessweek.com/magazine/content/06_38/b4001601.htm.

2. Loria Fires 60 Employees. (2002, Feb. 16). CBC Sports. Retrieved August 8, 2007, from http://www.cbc.ca/sports/story/2002/02/16/marlinsfire020216.html.

3. Badenhausen, K., Ozanian, M., and Roney, M. (2006, Aug. 31). The Business of Football. *Forbes*. Retrieved July 20, 2008, from http://www.forbes.com/lists/2006/30/06nfl_NFL-Team-Valuations_land.html.

4. Badenhausen, K., Ozanian, M., and Settimi, C. (2007, Apr. 19). The Business of Baseball. *Forbes*. Retrieved July 20, 2008, from http://www.forbes.com/2007/04/19/baseball-team-valuations-07mlb-cz_kb_0419baseballintro.html.

5. Badenhausen, K., Ozanian, M., and Settimi, C. (2007, Jan. 25). The Business of Basketball. *Forbes*. Retrieved August 4, 2008, from http://www.forbes.com/business/2007/12/06/nba-team-valuations-biz-07nba-cz_kb_mo_cs_1206nba_land.html.

6. Ozanian, M., and Badenhausen, K. (2006, Nov. 9). The Business of Hockey. *Forbes*. Retrieved July 20, 2008, from http://www.forbes.com/lists/2006/31/biz_06nhl_NHL-Team-Valuations_land.html.

7. Greenhouse, S. (2005, July 17). How Costco Became the Anti-Wal-Mart. *New York Times*. Retrieved July 20, 2008, from http://www.nytimes.com/2005/07/17/business/yourmoney/17costco.html.

8. Ohio State's Athletic Revenue Tops $100 Million. (2006, Aug. 18). *USA Today*. Retrieved July 20, 2008, from http://www.usatoday.com/sports/college/2006-08-18-ohio-state-revenue_x.htm.

9. Yahoo! Finance. Retrieved August 8, 2007, from http://finance.yahoo.com.

Preparation, Preparation, Preparation

"The will to win is important, but the will to prepare is vital."

—Joe Paterno, head football coach of the Penn State Nittany Lions

"Luck is what happens when preparation meets opportunity."

—Darrel K. Royal, former head football coach at the University of Texas and member of the College Football Hall of Fame

Many people are interested in working in the sports industry without really knowing a great deal about the types of career options that are available. They see the flashy headlines in the newspaper and watch ESPN's *SportsCenter*, and, like a large number of Americans, their passion for sports is undeniable. But, how do you convert this passion into a fulfilling career in the industry? The first step in this process is preparation—in order to find success in the industry, you must first learn about what the industry provides (and, almost as importantly, what it does not provide).

HOMEWORK

By doing a little homework, you can learn a lot about the business side of the sports industry. A number of resources are readily available that provide financial and business information. The following are a few of the better sources to examine. This is not an exhaustive list, but it should provide a good start and an idea about the types of information to look for.

SportsBusiness Journal

Any person considering a career in the sports industry needs to read *Street and Smith's SportsBusiness Journal*. Largely known throughout the industry as *SBJ*, it is the most important trade journal for the sports industry. As advertised on the *SBJ* website:

Street & Smith's SportsBusiness Journal *is a national weekly trade magazine, and the flagship publication for the Street & Smith's Sports Group. Since its launch in 1998 it has become the undisputed authority on the business of sports and a must read for top executives in every segment of sports business—properties, sponsors, media, facilities, finance, and professional services.*[1]

In addition, the publication's mission is stated as:

Each week, SportsBusiness Journal *provides the critical news and information sports industry executives need to be successful in the fast paced world of sports business. Every issue features coverage of the latest and most important stories, in-depth reports on important trends, original research and up-to-date industry statistics, and profiles of key executives, plus regular columns on the critical areas of sports business management including marketing, finance, media, and facilities.*

SBJ provides a great deal of information, particularly on the less-publicized business side of sports. The magazine provides in-depth industry knowledge that readers cannot find anywhere else, and it accurately reflects what is happening in the industry. It is recommended reading for people considering, studying in, or working in the sports industry.

SBJ offers a 4-week free trial to potential subscribers. If you are contemplating making a move into the sports industry, you should take advantage of this offer. Read the free issues and get a sense of what the industry is all about. If you are still intrigued, excited, and curious about what you have read, then the sports industry is likely a viable option for you. If you find the material boring and dull, that should raise a red flag that maybe this industry is not the one for you.

Newspapers and Magazines

It also is important to stay current on sports business stories found in the popular press. Quite often, publications such as the *Wall Street Journal*, *Forbes*, or *BusinessWeek* publish articles pertaining to the sports industry. Such stories are meant to appeal to a large number of people both inside and outside the sports industry, so the subject matter is likely to represent significant trends and major happenings within the industry. The sports pages of *USA Today* also can be a useful resource.

Books

Although they may not possess the most current information available, books on the sports industry can be a valuable resource. For example, if you are interested in working in player personnel, it is highly recommended you read the book *Moneyball* by Michael Lewis. This highly publicized book created some controversy within the player personnel field, so it is important to understand what the book is about and why it was controversial. Lacking this knowledge could be somewhat embarrassing in an interview or networking opportunity. Another good example of a must-read book is *License to Deal* by Jerry Crasnick. This book provides an inside perspective on the world of sports agent Matt Sosnick and should be read by anyone interested in working in the sports agent industry. If you have a particular interest in a segment of the sports industry, investigate what prominent books have been published recently on the topic.

Organizational Information

Another good source for information within the sports industry is the organizations themselves. This is an age of information overload, so make sure to take advantage of the resources available to you. Particularly good items to consider include an organization's:

- Website
- Press releases
- SEC filings (if the organization is publicly traded)
- Blog or social networking site (if sponsored by the organization)
- Media guide and yearbook (for professional and college teams)

Conferences

If you are interested in a particular field, see if there is a conference pertaining to that field. If there is (and most fields do hold conferences of some sort), look for a conference brochure and consider attending. A typical conference has speaker panels, which usually address a variety of topics currently affecting that industry. There is no better way to learn what is happening in your desired field than to listen to presentations by professionals in that particular industry. Many conferences also are excellent networking opportunities.

Associations

Similar to conferences, associations are an excellent source of information for people who have an interest in a particular field; for example, anyone interested in sports law should seriously consider joining the Sports Lawyers Association (SLA). In addition to holding an annual conference, the SLA also publishes a journal and a newsletter and, on its website, provides recent legal cases, contracts, and collective bargaining agreements. Other examples of sports-related associations are the Sporting Goods Manufacturers Association (meant to appeal to people working in or interested in the sporting goods industry) and the Sports Marketing Association (meant to appeal to sports marketers). Similar associations exist for people interested in other facets of the sports industry, including facility management and college athletics.

INFORMATIONAL INTERVIEWS

Your homework should provide you with some ideas about the types of careers that may be most interesting to you. The next step in the process is to conduct informational interviews to find out more information and to help you gauge your interest and fit. In fact, it would be extremely difficult for a person to fully learn about a position in the sports industry without first completing an informational interview of someone currently (or previously) employed in that position. After all, there is no better way to learn about the sports industry than to talk to professionals with industry experience—this may provide you with insights that are not available anywhere else.

So what is an informational interview? The term *job interview* implies that a position is open or is expected to be open in the near future. In contrast, an *informational interview* is one where the person is trying to gather information about a particular job, career, and/or organization (rather than applying for a specific job). The information gathered in informational interviews can be extremely helpful because it supplies an insider's account of the industry. Conducting informational interviews can have important networking implications—for more information on the importance of building a network, please read Chapter 6, *Networking*. As an added bonus, the person providing the informational interview may be able to give you job leads, information sources, and/or personal contacts.

The advantage of informational interviews is that they are excellent opportunities to gain valuable information in a relatively low-stress environment. Although it may be difficult to set up an informational interview, many industry professionals enjoy imparting their knowledge and industry insights to the next generation of sports professionals. Your likelihood of obtaining an informational interview increases tremendously when you have a particular reason to conduct the interview or a contact with the person. The following are examples of situations that may increase your success rate:

- Conducting a class project
- Conducting a research project (not associated with a particular class)
- Contacting an alumnus of your high school, college, or university
- Contacting a friend of the family
- Being referred by a former employer
- Being referred by a faculty member from your high school, college, or university

Remember to treat every informational interview like gold. It is best to prepare extensively for any informational interview you obtain. You should know who the person is and what they have done in their career. Most people dislike being asked questions about information that is public knowledge. For example, questions such as, "How long have you been at *X*?" or "Did you go to *X* law school?" are questions that often could be answered easily by looking, for example, at their media guide biography. By doing the preparation, you can show that you are diligent, prepared, serious, and respectful of the time you have been given. Questions such as, "What classes did you take at *X* law school that have really helped you in your career?" or "How did you obtain your current position at IMG after working at Proctor & Gamble?" are examples of the types of questions you can ask if you are prepared.

It is important to tailor each informational interview for the person you are meeting with. Nonetheless, in general, you can use the following list of sample questions as a guide to get the most out of your informational interviews:

1. What are your daily responsibilities?
2. What do you like about your job? What do you dislike?
3. How did you get to your current position?
4. What are your future career aspirations?
5. How can someone best prepare himself or herself for a career in the sports industry?
6. What types of opportunities should someone look for as an initial internship or job in the sport industry?
7. What are some of the trends occurring in your industry, or across the sports industry?
8. Overall, how do you feel about your quality of life?
9. Are you able to balance work and family demands?
10. Can you recommend any other industry professionals for me to contact? If so, can I use your name in contacting the person, or would you be willing to set up a meeting?

The last question is quite important. If you have successfully built a good rapport with the interviewer, they may be able to provide you with the names of contacts they believe may be of help to your situation. This is an excellent opportunity for you to expand your network, so use it. Remember to treat every interaction with industry professionals, including informational interviews, in a professional manner. Chapter 12 discusses interview preparation, dress, and interview follow-up, all which apply to both job interviews and informational interviews. Please read these sections and prepare accordingly.

As you go through the preparation process, keep in mind the following two questions:

1. Is there a particular segment of the industry that is appealing to you?
2. Are you interested in a particular type of work?

Doing your homework and conducting informational interviews should help you to begin to answer these key questions. From here, you can begin to think about what types of careers interest you. The next step in the process is to take a look at what you bring to the table. This is discussed in the following chapter.

Endnotes

1. About Us—Company History. (n.d.). *Street & Smith's SportsBusiness Journal*. Retrieved August 22, 2007, from http://www.sportsbusinessjournal.com/index.cfm?fuseaction=page.feature&featureId=45.

CHAPTER THREE 3

The Assessment Process

*"Always bear in mind that your own resolution to suc-
ceed is more important than any one thing."*

—Abraham Lincoln

*"Knowledge of the self is the mother of all knowledge.
So it is incumbent on me to know my self, to know it
completely, to know its minutiae, its characteristics,
its subtleties, and its very atoms."*

—Kahil Gibran, *The Philosophy of Logic*

SELF-ASSESSMENT

In the sports industry, you will find that a passion for sports is not nearly enough to warrant an employer giving you a job. Most employers assume that if you are applying for a job in the sports industry, you are passionate about sports. They are typically looking for something more that you can bring to the organization. For example, you may have an educational background and/or work experience in marketing, sales, or information technology. Whatever it may be, you have to have skills and abilities that extend beyond an interest in sports. You should conduct a self-assessment to determine what this "something else" is for you.

A self-assessment is a process in which one closely examines what it is they do well, what they enjoy, and what they are qualified to do. This process often involves a great deal of introspective study. One way to go about a self-assessment is to answer these questions and prepare an inventory of the significant findings. The ultimate goal should be to find a combination of things (such as marketing, finance, or operations) that you are good at *and* passionate about. The key then is to find a way to connect your competency and passion to a position and a segment of the sports industry.

During the self-assessment process, you need to weigh how important it is for you to work in a specific segment of the industry against how important it is for you to do a specific type of job (such as community relations or finance). For example, is it more important that you work in football

or in marketing? This assessment can vary considerably from person to person. If you are a former college football player, working in football may be of the utmost importance to you, and you may be willing to work in any of several different job types to work in football. On the other hand, if you are someone who likes football, but also likes baseball or basketball, you may not be as determined to find employment strictly within football; the type of job may hold greater importance to you. Or, you may have a particular expertise, such as accounting, and it does not matter which segment of the sports industry you are in. More flexibility in regards to industry segment will create more job opportunities because you can apply for positions across multiple industry segments. The key point is to give some thought to your situation. What is more important—industry segment or type of job? In answering this question, you are likely to find yourself in one of three general categories:

- I want to work in a specific industry segment, such as soccer, and I am flexible as to the type of position.

- I want to work in a specific type of job, such as public relations, and I am flexible as to the specific industry segment.

- I want to work in sports, and I am flexible as to the industry segment and the type of position.

Understanding where your true career interests lie *before* you start looking for a job will allow you to be more focused in your job search. This will greatly enhance your chances of finding a job in sports that is of interest to you.

How Will an Employer Look at Me?

"Athletics is not brain surgery. In looking at candidates, I look for certain characteristics, such as a great person, an unbelievable work ethic, and an ability to communicate with people and to get along. Working in athletics reveals your true character, so I look closely at character qualities."

—Gene DeFilippo, Athletic Director at Boston College

A key part of the self-assessment process is analyzing how a potential employer will look at you as a job candidate. A good way to do this is to look at your résumé and view it from an employer's perspective. An employer looking to fill a ticket sales position is likely to be uninterested in your ability to memorize statistics or in how good you are at fantasy football. All they care about is your ability to sell. If you can sell, you are more likely to be hired. In conducting this process, ask yourself the following questions:

- What can I contribute to an organization right away? Is this effectively communicated on my résumé?
- What special skills, abilities, or experiences do I bring to the table?
- What will catch the interest of the employer and convince him or her to consider hiring me?

At this stage in the game, you shouldn't necessarily worry about the quality of your answers to these questions. Instead, focus on making a reasonable assessment of where you stand—know what you have and also what you may be lacking. Chapter 12, *The Presentation*, will address what you can do to improve the quality of your skills, abilities, and experiences. This assessment also may help you decide whether you need to further your education (see Chapter 5, *The Educational Path*).

Boston College's Athletic Director, Gene DeFillipo, stands on the sidelines during a recent BC football game. DeFillipo led BC's transition from the Big East Conference to the Atlantic Coast Conference. DeFillipo, who was hired at BC in 1997, was previously the director of athletics at Villanova University.

There are a number of important skills that may or may not come across on your résumé, such as interpersonal skills, how hard you work, how you interact with supervisors, how you interact with co-workers, how effective you would be as a supervisor, your organizational skills, your physical appearance, your communication skills, and how you act under pressure. Most of these are very important considerations for *all* employers, but many of these are crucial to particular jobs in the sports industry. You should take the time to learn your strengths and weaknesses in these particular areas and to improve on these where possible so they can be reflected in your résumé and/or cover letter.

EXTERNAL ASSESSMENTS

In addition to your self-analysis, it also may be helpful to seek assessments from other parties. It is very helpful to have a sounding board during your assessment process

---

Box 3-2   The Self-Assessment Process

As an example of how the self-assessment process can play out, let's take a look at someone with a desire to work in media relations. To begin with, communication skills are extremely important in most media relations jobs. So, if you do not have good communication skills and you want to be a media relations director, perhaps you should consider either working in another department, working on your communication skills, or working at a job within a media relations department that does not prioritize communication skills. For example, although a person with suboptimal communication skills may not be the best fit for the top media relations job, he may be a better fit for an assistant's job dealing with publications or Internet matters.

Undergoing this assessment of skills that you possess and skills required by a particular job is extremely helpful in setting career expectations and establishing a career plan. In addition to the self-assessment and informational interviews, the job descriptions found in Section 5 of this book will help you to ascertain which skills and experience are necessary for particular positions within the sports industry.

---

because it is often difficult to make entirely accurate self-assessments. More than one opinion may also prove to be very helpful. External assessments can be obtained from parents, friends, professors, employers, mentors, and/or search firms. Ideally, one or more of your external assessments should come from people affiliated with or knowledgeable about the sports industry. You can also obtain valuable external assessments from people in business and people who are involved in hiring and/or personnel issues. Such external assessments can help you establish a realistic self-assessment, which may then direct you to a realistic job level and appropriate sports industry segment.

COMPUTER EVALUATIONS AND PSYCHOLOGICAL TESTS

Computer evaluations and psychological tests also are available to assist students and job seekers in narrowing their career searches. Two computer-based tests, Discover and SIGI-plus, are available to students at some universities and secondary schools. Some tests also can be accessed via the Internet. Examples include Ansir's 3 Sides of You Self Perception Profiling System and the Campbell Interest and Skill Survey. Keep in mind that the scope of these tests can vary; for example, some tests are geared toward people looking to begin their professional careers, whereas others focus more on people looking to make career changes. Before completing a test, particularly if there is a fee associated with it, make sure the test's purpose fits your personal situation.

Professionally administered psychological examinations, such the Myers-Briggs Type Indicator, may be helpful to job seekers. The results of such tests provide insight into the types of jobs that have traditionally been a good fit for people with similar personalities and interests.

It is important to note that the value received from computer evaluations and psychological tests will vary from person to person. Some people find the results very helpful in choosing a career path, whereas others do not. If you are the type of person who likes to receive confirmation and validation from outside sources before making a decision, then you may want to look into any computer evaluation and psychological testing opportunities that may be available to you.

ANALYZING OTHER FACTORS

Another key part of the self-assessment process is analyzing other factors that may influence your ability to pursue a particular job and/or career. These could be financial considerations, geographic considerations, and/or personal considerations, such as family, significant others, children, and the like. It can be rather difficult to begin a career in the sports industry, so try to minimize as many of these other factors as possible. The fewer restrictions you place on your job hunt, the more likely you are to successfully find employment. Nonetheless, you need to keep these factors in mind as you consider jobs and your chosen career path.

Show Me the Money!

The general rule, as discussed in Chapter 1, is that a job in the sports industry pays much less than a comparable non-sports job. This differential begins at the internship and entry-level positions, and goes through middle management, though it decreases (and is sometimes eliminated) at the top levels of management. The main reason for this is economics—significantly more people want to work in the sports industry than most other industries, and there are relatively few jobs.

Box 3-3   Compensation

Prominent sports agent Leigh Steinberg employs only 13 people at his sports agent business. However, he receives 5,000 resumes each year from people who want to work for him.[2] This type of competition throughout the sports industry works to suppress compensation levels for industry professionals. If you are unwilling to do a job for X dollars, the sports organization can easily find someone else who is. This is simply the nature of the industry.

Keep in mind, however, that the demand is not constant throughout the industry. Some jobs and segments are better known and more popular, and consequently are more in demand; for example, there is a lot of interest in working for a professional sports team. There is less demand to work in the segment of facility management. Consequently, one can advance more quickly and move to a leadership position (and be paid more money) if he decides to pursue the career path of general manager of a facility, instead of general manager of a National Football League team.

It is important to note that the compensation for high-level executives seems to be changing. As reported in the *Wall Street Journal*, "The pay gap for MBA-level jobs in and out of sports narrows as professionals climb the ladder."[3] This type of pay structure often is referred to as a hockey stick: "Salaries are flat at lower levels of sports organizations and then shoot up."[2]

You need to be realistic about money. How important is it to you? What do you need to earn at various stages of your career and life to be satisfied? You must weigh the cost (in reduced earnings) against the love of the sport and the career and other additional benefits of working in sports. These benefits may include tickets, access to other sporting events, rubbing shoulders with well-known people, and having an interesting job to talk about.

In evaluating these "other" factors, answering the following questions may be helpful:

1. What level of compensation do you need to live comfortably? Is this sufficient to meet any debt requirements (such as student loans, car loans, or credit cards) that you currently have?

2. Are you willing to relocate, and if so, to what cities/areas of the country? This may mean living far away from family members and friends.

3. Are you prepared to work long hours, often during nontraditional business hours such as nights and weekends? This will likely reduce the amount of time you have to spend with family, friends, children, and others.

All of these factors must be considered when determining what career options are available to you. For example, if you require an annual salary of $50,000 to cover your living expenses and to pay off your student loans, this may greatly limit the number of positions you can pursue in the sports industry (or eliminate the industry entirely). However, if you can stay with friends or family members (to cut down on living expenses) or if you have financial support from your parents or relatives then you may not require as large of a starting salary.

Benefits

As you might imagine, given the immense supply of interested workers and the limited availability of positions, sports organizations often provide less than exceptional benefits. In fact, particularly with internships and some entry-level positions, not all positions include basic benefits such as health insurance. However, positions in the sports industry are likely to come with nontraditional benefits, such as tickets and access to high profile people. For example, depending on the specific role within an organization, working in the sports industry may require interaction with athletes and other celebrities affiliated with the team (who may attend a sporting event as either a fan or part of a team's entertainment program). These types of nontraditional benefits can, for some, carry significant personal value. As you begin thinking about what is important for you, keep this in mind. If these extras are important for you now, think about whether they will be important for you in a few years.

Endnotes

1. Catching up with Cardinals VP and GM John Mozeliak (2008, Apr. 1). *Street and Smith's SportsBusiness Daily*. Retrieved July 20, 2008, from http://www.sportsbusinessdaily.com/article/119657.

2. Gangemi, J. (2006, Feb. 3). A Hot Ticket for Sports-Biz Rookies. *Business Week*. Retrieved July 20, 2008, from http://www.businessweek.com/bschools/content/feb2006/bs2006023_5104_bs001.htm.

3. Fatsis, S., and Keating, P. (2006, Sep. 16). The Business of Sports: Getting in the Game. *The Wall Street Journal*, p. R.1.

CHAPTER FOUR 4

Mapping the Plan

"I never did anything by accident, nor did any of my inventions come by accident; they came by work."

—Thomas Edison, American inventor

"Setting a goal is not the main thing. It is deciding how you will go about achieving it and staying with that plan."

—Tom Landry, former head coach of the Dallas Cowboys and member of the National Football League Hall of Fame

STARTING BIG

Certain people are passionate about pursuing a job in one particular industry, one particular sport, or even one particular company/team. Others have several different possibilities, but they are fairly certain they know what is right for them. They may seek advice about how to reach their goals, but they believe they need little advice about *what* their goals should be. Individuals should never be discouraged from following their dreams. Such focus can be a positive thing, causing the individual to work harder than those around him or her. However, such individuals should be careful of not developing tunnel vision and failing to follow up on other opportunities that might be presented to them. This is not to say *necessarily* that someone who is interested in public relations should accept a faster-track or more lucrative job offer in, say, sales. However, it is common for people not to realize that:

- There are more ways for them to reach their goals than they can imagine.

- There are different jobs and/or industry segments that can make them happy.

- Goals should be re-evaluated constantly, and they may change.

Anyone pursuing a career in the sports industry should step back and take a look at the entire sports industry, keeping an open mind about other sports industry segments and other jobs. This is referred to as *starting big*. Of course, this should be done in conjunction with your self-assessment.

The combination of one's interests and abilities, along with available opportunities, may help someone find a career path that has a higher likelihood of success. For example, a person may initially be interested in marketing for the National Basketball Association because the person is a fan of the NBA; however, the person's self-assessment leads him to conclude that his real interest is marketing, and that he is open to sports marketing in any industry segment. He does his research and informational interviews, and arrives at three possibilities:

1. An NBA club

2. Marketing for a facility

3. *Sports Illustrated*

He is still interested in basketball, so he will continue to pursue work with an NBA club. He also realizes and considers how difficult this may be.

The second option, sports marketing for a facility, has many more positions because there are many more facilities than teams. Often such positions are considered less glamorous, so there may not be as much competition. This job does not have the "cocktail party appeal" of an NBA job, so that must be considered. However, the likelihood of getting a job, moving up to the director level, and receiving better compensation packages are advantages of pursuing a position in marketing for a facility.

The third option is to consider pursuing a position at *Sports Illustrated*. *Sports Illustrated* (*SI*) has recently put a significant emphasis on marketing and, for the first time, hired a chief marketing officer. Much of the work involves new technologies, such as putting *SI* content on cell phones and providing content on the Internet. *SI* provides several advantages, such as that this is a growth area for *SI*, meaning the company is placing a great deal of emphasis on this area, which might lead to a larger number of available positions, greater amounts of responsibility, and an ability to conduct work that the magazine considers important. A second advantage is the fact that the development and implementation of new technology-based marketing initiatives is a growth area for the sports industry as a whole. If he gets experience at *SI* in this area, he becomes attractive for other companies, thus increasing his ability to make a career shift to an NBA team (or any number of other options) at a later point in his career.

As you can imagine, and as this example shows, there is no simple answer here. But, by expanding your focus, you can greatly increase the number of opportunities available to you, which will, in turn, increase your likelihood of successfully finding employment within the industry.

Some people have trouble looking big, while others look big only after their first choice(s) have not worked out. The danger of waiting to look big is that some of your contacts may not be as accessible (e.g., a student may no longer be in school and may not have the same access to faculty members). It is strongly recommended that you look big from the start, if only to set up your contingency plan.

Hopefully, this book will serve as a starting point to help you start big. A number of resources throughout this book will help you research possible areas of interest:

- Section 2, *The Sports Industry: Segment Descriptions*, provides a summary and history of the most prominent areas of the sports industry. Read this section and keep an eye out for any new areas that may interest you.

- Section 3, *Career Tracks of Executives in the Sports Industry*, provides career paths for executives employed within the industry. Reading this section will provide you with examples of how people went about obtaining the positions they currently hold. The most important piece of advice this section provides is that there is not a standard career path for many jobs and careers. The people presented in this book obtained their positions by following any number of different career paths. This demonstrates that, in order to obtain your dream job, you do not have to start with any one particular position within the industry—further emphasizing the value of starting big. You can use the information from this section to begin to map out multiple potential career paths.

- Section 4, *Organizational Charts*, contains organizational charts from a number of sports organizations across a variety of industry segments. The organizational charts provide a visual representation of the types of positions available in the industry. This will give you a better idea of the types of positions that are available in your field(s) of interest and also the progression as one advances.

- Section 5, *Job Announcements*, is a collection of actual job descriptions and job postings. These are real-life examples of positions in the industry, and will provide you with an idea about what types of skills, abilities, and experiences are required for specific positions. This section also can be used to learn about positions that you may not have otherwise considered. For example, say you are interested in marketing and really think that a position in the ticketing department is the way for you to go. Read all of the marketing job postings to see if there are other areas close to marketing, such as sponsorship or new business development, that may be as attractive to you.

To reiterate the discussion from previous chapters, the information collected on the sports industry segments, career tracks, and job announcements should be considered and analyzed in combination with your self-assessment (both personal and external), and then should be followed up with informational interviews. Use all of this information to identify things you are (or might be) good at and things you are passionate about. If you do so, it will play an important role in helping you choose an appropriate career path.

In addition to position flexibility, candidates should also remain geographically flexible. As Buffy Filippell of TeamWork Online, a sports-recruiting company that helped leagues fill 2,200 sports openings in a recent 15-month period, noted, "The jobs might be in North Dakota, but if you're 22 and movable, you should be able to find a job in the sports business."[1] This is very good advice: If you limit your options to certain geographic locations, you greatly limit your chances of obtaining that elusive first job in the industry. For example, you will find more opportunities (because there are many more employers) if you look at the entire United States versus only looking in one major metropolitan area, such as Chicago. Furthermore, by taking a better position in a less desirable location, you will likely gain more valuable work experience. You then will likely be able to leverage this experience into obtaining a better position in a more desirable location. Remember, it is not only about where you start, but also where you finish. As long as it helps you meet your ultimate end goal, try to remain flexible with your starting point. If you have a preferred geographic area, it may be better to make it a goal to get there at some point in the future. It will be much more difficult to work up the corporate ladder while staying the entire time in the same geographic area.

NARROWING

"When you come to a fork in the road, take it."

—Yogi Berra, former catcher for the New York Yankees and member of the Baseball Hall of Fame

Not everyone knows exactly what they want to do; these people can be considered "blank canvases." They are open to a plethora of ideas for their long-term career goals, and are thus amenable to more and different internships and jobs in the short term. However, being too open can be just as dangerous as being too focused. If you simply want to work in sports, but do not particularly favor any one industry segment or type of job, you will likely encounter difficulty in your career development. If you find yourself in such a situation, you are likely in need of some narrowing (as opposed to expanding, which the previous section was all about) in your career focus.

If you need to narrow your future, try to avoid *limiting* your opportunities. For example, if you limit your job search to New York City, you will reduce the number of potential job opportunities. This type of narrowing is not ideal and should be avoided, if at all possible. Narrowing should instead be about focusing. Instead of saying, "I want to work in sports," a more focused approach would be something like, "I want to work in sports marketing" or "I want to work in baseball." By focusing your efforts, it will be easier to conduct your job search and to make valuable connections with industry professionals.

The *ideal* way to approach your job/internship search is to figure out what you are interested in and what you are good at, rather than reflexively approaching your favorite sport or your favorite team (in other words, do not be a fan). Use your personal assessment and external assessments to determine what it is you want to pursue, and make sure this coincides with the job skills you can provide. This focus will make it easier for you to map out a career path.

Figure 4-1 demonstrates that some jobs are helpful only to particular industries (e.g., compliance in college athletics), whereas other jobs are highly needed in every industry (e.g., marketing and general legal counsel).

PRIORITIZE

At some point, it is important to prioritize. As an example, here is a potential dilemma. Let's say that a person has decided to take the job type approach, and she is interested in sports marketing. She has six jobs that she has applied for in sports marketing, which are listed below in priority order:

1. NBA club
2. Facility
3. *Sports Illustrated*
4. Major League Soccer (MLS) club
5. NASCAR
6. Gatorade

She receives an offer from NASCAR and they would like an answer within 2 weeks. Her immediate reaction is that she has not heard back from the NBA club, which is her top choice and is her dream job. Her dilemma is that she will not hear from the NBA club for at least 2 weeks.

So she has the choice of accepting the NASCAR job and wondering if she would have received the NBA job. Or, she can turn down the NASCAR job, but she may not get an NBA offer. She also has not heard from the facility, *Sports Illustrated*, and the MLS club. In addition, her mentor, who made a call on her behalf to NASCAR, may not be happy (which means she may be less likely to receive help from him in the future).

One way to avoid this problem (or at least reduce the likelihood of it occurring) would be to stagger the applications and apply to the highest priority positions first. So if the NBA is #1, then apply there first. If an NBA club position is not offered, the person can move to priority #2, and so on, and have no doubts.

Even with this planning, you may still run into the dilemma outlined above. You may not be able to follow this strategy if organizations have certain application deadlines. Or some organizations may make decisions quicker than other organizations. So, what should you do? Start early, do your best planning, and hopefully you will get your top choices first. What if choice #1 gets slowed down, and you get an offer for your second choice, but the offer is only good for 48 hours? You should call your first choice and discuss the situation. If you act delicately and sincerely, you should be able to do so without offending or jeopardizing your chances of receiving an offer. Let the employer know that it is your first choice, but you have been offered a position in a different organization that you consider less attractive and you only have 48 hours to make a decision. It is completely acceptable to politely ask if there is any possibility that a decision can be made on your first choice within the 48-hour time period. If the decision on your first choice cannot be sped up, try to ascertain from the conversation whether the employer considers you a strong candidate. If you believe that you are a strong candidate, call the second-choice employer to see if there is any flexibility in the 48-hour deadline. In doing so, do not indicate that you are waiting on another opportunity—simply state that you find the offer attractive and there are many

	INDUSTRIES					
JOBS	Professional Teams and Leagues	Professional Individual Sports and Tournaments	College Athletics	Agents and Agency Firms	Footwear and Apparel	Corporations Sponsoring Sporting Events
Tickets	X	X	X			
Marketing	X	X	X	X	X	X
Sales	X	X	X	X	X	
Public Relations/Media	X	X	X	X	X	X
Community Relations	X	X				
Development			X			
Facility Management	X	X	X			
Event Management	X	X	X	X		
Compliance			X			
Corporate Sponsorship						X
Broadcasting	X	X	X			
Licensing	X	X	X	X	X	
General Legal Counsel	X	X	X	X	X	X
Information Technology	X	X	X	X	X	X
Accounting/Finance	X	X	X	X	X	X
Human Resources	X	X	X	X	X	X

Figure 4-1   Jobs by Industry

things to consider. If luck is on your side, the second-choice employer will grant you the flexibility you need. If this is not the case, you have two options:

1. Accept the offer from the second organization and do not look back. Having doubts thinking about "what if" will merely detract from your happiness and your ability to give top performance at choice #2.

2. Wait for choice #1 to make a decision and decline the offer from organization #2. If you do not get choice #1, move on to choices #3, #4, and so on.

This really becomes a personal value judgment. If you perceive there to be very little difference between your top choice and your second choice, your best choice may be to

When I sit down with a student or someone who is interested in the sports industry, the first thing I do is try to find out as much as I can about the person. This is what I call the assessment stage. If the person has a résumé, I want to see a copy of it. I look to see where the person has gone to school (undergraduate and graduate), how the person has performed in school, the person's history as an athlete and/or a coach, the person's work experiences, and presentation and special skills and abilities that this person might have. If the person is still in high school, our discussion will involve colleges, majors, and also the possibility of graduate school. If the person has already completed his or her undergraduate education, then the discussion will involve graduate school options and/or obtaining work experience first. These issues will be discussed in more detail in Chapter 5, *The Educational Path*.

The next important matter that I like to ascertain is what the person would like to do. The following is a dramatization of a common exchange that occurs when a student comes into my office hours to discuss their career:

Me: Where do you want to be 10 years after graduation?

Undergraduate Student: (Dressed in a David Ortiz jersey and backwards Red Sox cap) I would like to be general manager of the Boston Red Sox.

Me: Have you given any consideration to becoming an astronaut?

Undergraduate Student: No. That would be wicked hard.

Me: Are you aware that in most of the past 15 years, 30 or more astronauts per year have gone on U.S. space shuttle missions,[2] while only a handful of slots open up each year for the 30 Major League Baseball GM positions?

Undergraduate Student: But . . . but . . . Theo [Epstein] was only 28, and I'm only 21.

Me: I don't want to discourage you from pursuing your goals in life. I just want you to go in with your eyes open and to know the odds of getting this sort of position. I also encourage you to develop a backup plan, just in case.

Obviously, I have selected one job in one industry. However, this is indicative of the approach that I recommend taking in helping a young man or woman determine his or her ultimate goal. Having a goal is great, but you need to take the necessary steps to make sure you have a reasonable chance of achieving your goal. What this student needs to do is to look at the potential career paths for general managers, which can be found in Section 3.

simply accept the offer for your second choice. However, if you perceive there to be a large gap between your top choice and your second choice, and possibly only a small difference between your second choice and your third choice, it may be worth taking the risk to see if you get your top choice. If you do not, there is only a small drop-off from your second choice to your third choice. In addition, you must also factor in how likely you are to receive an offer from your third, fourth, or fifth choices. There are no hard and fast rules here—you must decide what is best based on the options available to you and your career goals. If you aspire to be a top-level manager, you will have to make these types of tough decisions often. If you make a reasonable decision based on information, it will be a good start to a career filled with tough decisions.

HOW HAVE OTHERS REACHED THE JOB I WANT?

The key to developing any good career plan is to know where you are, where you want to go, and what you need to do to get there. From the assessment process, you should have a good idea about where you currently are, and the homework, industry segment descriptions, organization charts, and job descriptions have hopefully given you an indication of where you would like to go. So, how do you get there? A number of useful resources have been included

in this book to help out in this process. To begin with, the career paths in Section 3 provide examples of how other people have reached top positions.

If Section 3 contains your dream job, take the time to closely study the types of experiences and education the people currently working in that position hold. Although there is usually not one prototypical career path, there may be several different career paths. This will give you ideas about what type of path is more likely, and what type of path you may choose to take. You can find more analysis on this topic in Section 3.

If Section 3 does not include the specific job that interests you, you can still learn a great deal from the information provided. For example, take note of the variety of career paths found throughout each position presented. This supports the theory that there is not one prototypical career path. You will find this is rather consistent across most industry segments. You can then research and do you own analysis of career tracks for the position you would like to obtain.

In addition, resources included in this book (such as the organizational charts and job descriptions) provide information that you can use to map out a career plan. Take a look at the organizational charts to learn the titles of positions within organizations. As you move up the organizational hierarchy (and it is easier to move up through the same area), there is an increased demand on skills and abilities, as well as increased responsibilities. Use the organizational charts to identify positions that interest you. You can then match them up with job descriptions (found in Section 5) for the various levels in your desired field (entry level, 2 years' experience, 5 years' experience, 10 years' experience, etc.). This will give you an indication of the types of skills and abilities that are required as you progress to higher levels within an organization. If your goal is to obtain one of these higher-level positions, you will need to devise a strategy on how to obtain the requisite skills and abilities over the next 2, 5, or 10 years.

Endnotes

1. Fatsis, S., and Keating, P. (2006, Sep. 16). The Business of Sports: Getting in the Game. *The Wall Street Journal*, p. R.1.

2. See Mission Archives at www.nasa.gov for a detailed account of all shuttle missions.

The Educational Path

"A winner is someone who recognizes his God-given talents, works his tail off to develop them into skills, and uses these skills to accomplish his goals."

—Larry Bird, former NBA star and member of the Basketball Hall of Fame

Completing a sport management education program can be critical to getting a job. However, it is not uncommon to find industry professionals in similar positions with vastly different types of degrees (sport management vs. nonsport management) and different levels of degrees (bachelor's vs. master's). Getting a job does not rest solely on one's ability to get into and complete a sport management education program. It is a function of other qualities, such as experience, presentation, and abilities. The decision of whether to pursue sport management education is different for each person, depending on the individual's grades, standardized test scores, finances, existing experiences, strengths, weaknesses, and goals.

Once a student identifies his or her goals and backup plans, it is common that additional education will be necessary to reach those goals. A number of options are available. The following sections provide important points to consider in making decisions about sport management education. They show some of the alternatives available—a starting point to ask key questions and to collect information so each person can make the best decision possible.

SPORT MANAGEMENT EDUCATION

Sport management education is a relatively new field of study, experiencing tremendous growth in the last 30 years. As the *Wall Street Journal* reported in September 2006, "In the 1970s, the list pretty much began and ended with Ohio University and the University of Massachusetts. Today, some 300 universities offer everything from sports-management MBAs and doctorates to continuing-education certificates."[1] Ultimately, prospective students have the following sport management education options available:

- Bachelor's degree in sport management
- Bachelor's degree in a field other than sport management in conjunction with a specialization in sport management
- Master's degree in sport management
- MBA with a specialization in sport management
- PhD in sport management
- Continuing education certificates

Most sport management programs are located in the United States, but the North American Society for Sport Management (see Box 5-1) lists international programs located in places such as Canada (12 programs), Europe (14), Australia (8), New Zealand (4), India (1), and Africa (1). Each year, more and more schools introduce new programs of study in sport management, both in the United States and internationally. Additionally, online programs are becoming more prevalent and run the gamut from degree-granting programs to certificate programs.

EVALUATING SPORT MANAGEMENT PROGRAMS

The quality and depth of programs can vary significantly from school to school. From the names of the programs, to basic philosophies, to areas of emphasis—there is much more variation than in many other professional programs, such as law, medicine, or even business. There are many

> *Box 5-1* ***The North American Society for Sport Management***
> The North American Society for Sport Management (NASSM) is actively involved in supporting and assisting professionals working in the fields of sport, leisure, and recreation. The purpose of NASSM is to promote, stimulate, and encourage study, research, scholarly writing, and professional development in the area of sport management—both theoretical and applied aspects.

reasons for this, but the most logical is that this is a new field of study, and, as occurs with all new disciplines, it is going through the normal growth period, along with a determination and evaluation of what is important.

Key areas of difference include location of the program on campus (within various departments or schools); creation of a separate department; areas of specialization; size (in terms of both students and faculty); number of required courses within sport management; and the number of courses that are outside of the sport management department. The following sections discuss some of the more significant differences among programs.

Position of the Program Within the University or College

In the early years, sport management programs were primarily located in physical education departments or schools (i.e., the academic unit on campus). As the industry has evolved and moved closer to business, sport management education has changed along with it. The trend in the last 10 years has been to place more sport management programs in business schools. However, not all programs are in business schools; some still reside in schools of physical education, kinesiology, communication, education, and others. In gauging the quality of any sport management program, it is important to find out whether the program is an academic unit and what implications this creates. Sport management programs residing in business schools are going to provide more business-oriented courses than in a communications school. However, if it's your goal to work in the television side of the sports industry, then attending a sport management program that is housed in a communications academic unit may be quite beneficial to you.

Separate Sport Management Departments

A number of schools have sport management programs that are part of other departments, such as the business school. Some programs have a separate department dedicated solely to the study of sport. Such programs show a greater commitment to the field, usually in the financial commitment to the program, and often have a greater number of dedicated, full-time faculty (faculty who spend 100% of their time working

in the field of sport). Having a separate department for sport management increases the likelihood of the program's continuation in the future.

Areas of Emphasis

Some programs develop sport managers with a broad-based skill set (enabling students to work in any number of sports industry segments), while other programs emphasize a particular segment of the sports industry or a particular job type. For example, some programs emphasize facility management whereas others emphasize marketing. When comparing schools, it is important for prospective students to understand the strengths of a particular program and make sure that it fits their interests. If a student knows with great certainty the specific part of the industry in which she wants to work, then the student should strongly consider schools specializing in that area. If the student is less sure about the particular industry of choice, then a less specialized program may be better.

Program Size

Another area of difference in sport management education is the size of programs, which can be a factor in the quality of education received. A smaller class size may be advantageous because students have an opportunity to obtain more personalized attention from faculty members. There will also be less internal competition for internship and/or job opportunities. However, programs with a larger student body may have more alumni working in the industry (because there have been more graduates of the program), which can make it easier to secure internship and/or job opportunities. It may mean more faculty and more courses to select from.

The number of students in the program is not the only measure to look at, though. It also is important to look at the student–faculty ratio. More favorable ratios potentially mean more faculty interaction and greater accessibility for students to receive class and career help. Professors often play a key role in both advising students and helping students build contacts within the industry (with both alumni and personal contacts of the faculty member), so a better student–faculty ratio may increase a student's opportunities to develop a solid network while in school.

It is also important to look at the number of dedicated, full-time faculty. A greater number of full-time faculty indicates a greater dedication and commitment to the program (and likely also to research) on the part of the school. (This is in addition to the separate department status discussed previously.) Furthermore, sport management faculty who focus on the sports industry should be more informed on the industry than faculty in other fields who might teach part-time in a sport management program. This usually allows full-time faculty to do more student advising, provides more opportunities for faculty to develop industry-relevant projects and examples for their classes, and might enable the faculty members to have stronger industry contacts.

Some schools have upwards of 12 full-time faculty, dedicated exclusively to the teaching, study, and research of sport management. If you compare such a school to one with only one or two full-time faculty members, then you can begin to understand some of the advantages of attending a program with a larger full-time faculty. For example, a student attending a program with 12 sport faculty members will have more opportunities to gain industry-specific knowledge across a wider variety of topics than a student attending a program with only a few sport faculty members. With a larger faculty, there is a greater chance that a faculty member will be an expert in a particular student's area of interest. This creates opportunities for the student to work on individual projects with a faculty member in his or her area of expertise. This should not only improve the student's educational experience, but it also increases the chance of that student finding a job in his or her area of interest (such as through better industry contacts or focused education).

In assessing the size of a school's sport management faculty, consider what the impact would be if one or two faculty members decided to leave. Would the program still grade as high, particularly in your desired field of study? On the flip side, you may also want to see whether the school has any plans to increase the size of its faculty prior to your planned term of enrollment.

Quality of the Faculty

In addition to the size of the faculty, the quality of the faculty can vary significantly from program to program. It is important to look at how many faculty members have terminal degrees, which means that they have a doctorate or a law degree. You also may want to examine the subject matter of the degrees to make sure they match your areas of interest, and you also may want some diversity in their areas of expertise. Another important element to look at is the faculty's practical industry experience. This includes any

positions the faculty may have held within the sports industry, as well as any consulting projects they have conducted on behalf of sports organizations (while working as a professor). The real-world work experience of the faculty adds depth to the information they convey in class, but also increases the number of industry contacts that a student may be able to use to generate job and internship leads. Most schools post faculty biographies on the programs' websites. This is a good place to start researching.

You should also be aware of any full-time faculty members who split time between different departments on campus. For example, rather than hire a dedicated full-time sport management professor, a program may share a professor with the sociology department to teach a sports sociology class. Such situations result in the faculty member having teaching and/or research responsibilities in other departments, which may reduce their availability to students studying sport management. Consequently, the faculty member may not have as much time to advise sport management students or to oversee independent studies. In addition because the faculty member spends a significant amount of time in another department, he may have contacts and/or industry experience that are better suited toward helping students in another department and may have fewer sport management contacts and/or experiences.

You also may encounter part-time faculty who split their time between academia and industry, commonly referred to as practitioners or off-campus faculty. Although such individuals may not have teaching backgrounds as extensive as full-time professors, they may have valuable industry experience to contribute to the classroom. Depending on the part-time faculty member's position in the industry, he also may have very good industry contacts to share with students.

In evaluating different programs, it would be reasonable to ask about any part-time faculty at a program (both on-campus and off-campus) and to gather information to better understand the specific circumstances of the situation.

Box 5-2   The Study of Sports

Jeff Price, president of *Sports Illustrated Digital*, can relate to the struggles of finding a professor willing to oversee a sports-related project. In finishing coursework for a history degree at his undergraduate institution, Jeff wanted to complete a thesis dealing with sports and history. He proposed a topic examining such things as the role of sports in society and the impact the Industrial Revolution had on the development of sports in the United States. Jeff's request for a thesis topic dealing with sports was denied, and he was told there was no real educational value in studying sports. Forced to pick a nonsports topic for his thesis, Jeff never forgot the situation. Years later, he noticed when

A. Bartlett Giamatti, late commissioner of Major League Baseball, published an extended essay entitled, "Take Time for Paradise: Americans and Their Games." This essay dealt with the very same thesis topic that Jeff had hoped to examine. Looks like there was merit in the topic after all.

The study of sport management is an emerging field that is not yet fully embraced by everyone in the academic community. Jeff's story demonstrates the difficulty and resistance students can encounter at institutions that are not supportive of sports-related projects. In order to fulfill his desire for educational work in sports, Jeff completed the sport management master's degree program at the University of Massachusetts.

In addition, if you find you are drawn to a particular school because of one specific faculty member (either full-time or part-time), it is advisable to ask the institution about the faculty member's teaching schedule and any planned sabbaticals that may reduce your opportunities to take classes from that professor.

Age of the Program

More established programs have inherent advantages over newer programs. To begin with, the faculty at established programs may be more experienced, which should result in a larger number of industry contacts. In addition, established programs may have a larger alumni base, creating greater networking opportunities for students. Finally, an established program, particularly one that has been successful, may have a solid reputation within the industry.

This is not to say newer programs are not as good as the established programs. It may very well be the case that a newer program has excellent contacts within a student's desired field or that the program is led by highly respected people in the industry. Newer programs may be very ambitious and energetic with rising star faculty members. Some new departments are a priority of a university, which usually means a commitment of resources. Some colleges will have alumni who are in the sports industry (but not a graduate of sport management) who will support the new sport management program. These are all factors a student should learn about and consider when evaluating a school.

Types of Degrees Offered

The types of degrees offered also can vary tremendously from school to school. Some schools offer bachelor's degrees, others offer master's degrees, and still others offer doctoral degrees. Additionally, some schools offer all three, whereas others offer only one or two degree options.

Adding even greater complication, some programs offer certificates in sport management and others provide an opportunity to obtain a specialization in sport in conjunction with another degree (for example, an MBA with a specialization in sport management or a BS in business administration with a concentration in sport management). Concentrations and specializations in sport do not always appear on degree certificates, though. Quite often, in fact, the university granting the degree makes no such distinction on diplomas. However, students who complete such programs are able to indicate the concentration/specialization on a résumé, which is what an employer is more likely to see.

Later in this chapter, the Master's Degrees section discusses the merits of various degree options, particularly as they relate to graduate degrees.

Curricula

Some programs require students to take only a handful of sport-specific courses, whereas others require a great deal more. For example, one program may require students to take business law, while another requires sports law. The same often applies to marketing, finance, and management as well. By taking a greater portion of classes within the context of sport, students have a greater opportunity to work on sport-specific projects and examples. Depending on the student's previous experience(s) in the sports industry, this may greatly enhance the depth of the student's education. See the website for this book, http://health.jbpub.com/sportscareers, for three sample curricula for different types of sport management programs, both undergraduate and graduate levels. This will help display the differences in terms of number of required courses, as well as the breadth or variety of courses offered in the field.

In addition to the names of courses in a program, it is useful to look at the underlying substance of courses. One good way to examine this is through course syllabi. Some professors make syllabi available on class websites. If this is not the case, or if you do not have access to the class website, ask if you can review the course syllabi when you visit the school.

It is also advisable to ascertain if upper level courses are available to the general student population, or if they are available only for students within the sport management major. Restricting classes to students within the major should enhance the learning environment and elevate the value received from the class.

Internship Programs

Most schools have established internship programs as part of their curriculum, and many require that the student enroll in this class. When examining different schools, make sure to ask whether the school has an internship program. If it does, learn how it works. The following questions are good to ask to ascertain the quality of the internship program:

1. How many students are in the sport management program?
2. How many students go out on internship each year? What percentage of sport management students complete an internship?
3. In what fields, at what companies, and at what types of organizations are students obtaining internships?
4. How do students go about getting an internship? Do they have to find the internship on their own, or does the school provide assistance in placing students in internship positions?
5. What is the interaction between internship employers and the school? Do employers make regular visits to the school?
6. Who runs the internship program? Is the person full-time or part-time?

7. What individual advising does the internship director or faculty member do?

8. What type of supervision is provided by the school?

9. Are the internships done for credit? Are they paid or unpaid?

10. Is there an internship contract?

11. How long has the internship program been in existence?

12. What do alumni think about their internship experiences?

13. What are the requirements to be part of the internship program? Are there costs associated with this? Are there academic requirements?

14. Is there an opportunity to complete more than one internship as part of the internship program?

Alumni

A sport management program is greatly enhanced by a successful and loyal alumni base. Alumni are a key source of networking contacts as well as internship and job leads. Given the valuable nature of a school's alumni, it is important that schools take steps to foster relationships with their alumni. Some schools do a very good job of this, whereas others seem to struggle. As you look at a particular school, ask yourself whether it is evident that the program maintains contacts with its alumni through networking events or reunions. Sometimes this information can be ascertained through the department's website. If the information is not readily available, this is an appropriate question to ask on a school visit.

Guest Speakers

Guest speakers are another key aspect of sport management programs. Interacting with guest speakers is an effective way to help build your network. When considering a school, determine whether the school brings in guest speakers in your areas of interest—look not only at the number of speakers, but also the quality. Programs often have a professional seminar class in which guest speakers are invited specifically to talk about careers in the sports industry. The information provided in such classes can be invaluable to your search for internships and jobs. It's worth asking to see whether the schools you are considering include such a class.

Practicum Courses

Practicum courses are an excellent opportunity to obtain real-world experience and also receive some course credit. As an example, the University of Massachusetts provides students an opportunity to plan, create, and execute an event of significant size. In previous years, the class managed a 3-on-3 basketball tournament with over 1,500 participants. For the last several years, the class organized a grass roots soccer tournament with over 100 teams. Such classes allow students to build marketing, tournament operations, and sponsorship sales skills—all important aspects that employers look for in job seekers. Not all schools offer such courses, so be sure to ask whether a school you are considering has any.

Student Success Rate

When evaluating any program, it is important to look at the success rate the school has at placing students in full-time sport management positions. This is the true measure of quality for any program. The success rate may differ significantly between undergraduate and graduate students. Look at both internship placement and full-time job placement. In addition, you should look not only at the most recent graduates, but also people who graduated 5 to 10 years ago. As an example, take a look at the positions held by BS graduates from 6 years ago from the University of Massachusetts:[2]

- Assistant director of communications for a BCS college conference
- Inside sales manager for an NBA team
- Marketing and events manager for a sports agency
- Promotions coordinator for an NFL team
- Senior account representative for an MLB team
- Account executive for an MLB team
- Account manager-new business development for a sports marketing agency

MS graduates from 6 years ago hold positions such as:
- Marketing manager for a major footwear and apparel company
- Director of new media business development for a league office
- Assistant director of community relations at an NFL team

BS graduates from 11 years ago currently hold positions such as:
- Director of sales for an NBA team
- Group sales account executive for an MLB team
- Account manager at a sports marketing company
- Sponsorship sales manager for an NBA team
- Assistant athletic director at a mid-size college athletic program
- Director of ticket sales at a minor league baseball team
- Event manager for an NFL team
- Director of event services for an NBA team

MS graduates from 11 years ago currently hold positions such as:

- VP of baseball operations for an MLB team
- Director of player development for an MLB team
- Director of community relations for an NBA team
- CFO of an NFL team
- Director of college scouting for an NFL team
- Associate director of partnership marketing for an Olympic governing body

Although these lists are not exhaustive, they do provide good insight into the types of jobs and the level of jobs graduates from the University of Massachusetts hold beyond graduation. Closely examine the track record of whatever school(s) you are considering, and make sure there are graduates in jobs that interest you.

GENERAL ACCEPTABILITY OF DEGREES IN THE FIELD

The acceptability of sport management degrees within the industry is not uniform. Given the relatively new nature of programs, this is understandable. However, more employers are starting to understand and believe in the merits of sport management degrees, as demonstrated by the increased number of job descriptions that include a requirement and/or preference for candidates with sport management education. This trend is likely to continue in the future.

ONLINE PROGRAMS

Online sport management programs are the newest addition to the portfolio of options. In comparison to more traditional programs, online programs are in their early stages of development.

Although the industry is still trying to figure out how online degrees should be viewed, there are benefits to completing such a program. For example, if a student successfully completes the program, he will receive a sport management education and degree. In addition, the student might possibly gain some contacts in the industry. The student can list the program on a résumé, showing both education and interest in the field. Finally, the opportunity costs of such a program are generally quite low because the student can maintain his or her current employment while completing the program and the student does not have to move to attend the program.

Before enrolling, students also should be aware of the potential negative factors of online programs. For example, an online program may not offer as many courses as a more traditional on-site program. This is most likely to result in fewer electives being offered. With fewer electives, a student has less ability to customize the program to meet his or her interest and content needs. Therefore, the student should conduct a thorough examination to determine how much he will gain from the program—what are the breadth and depth of courses?

Another important consideration is faculty interaction, which will be much different in online courses. It may be difficult for the professor to truly get to know his or her students to help with things like career guidance. In addition, the student's interaction with faculty members will be limited to only those professors from whom the student is taking classes, limiting the student's ability to create a relationship with other faculty members.

Interaction with classmates also is very different. According to students, one of the best aspects of completing an on-site sport management program is the built-in network they develop among classmates. Students often stay in touch with fellow members of their class throughout their professional careers, developing relationships that last over 20 years. Building such a network with classmates in an online program would be rather difficult.

You should also consider an online program's alumni base. Are the alumni committed to helping current students? Do students have access to alumni, and if so, what types of relationships are they able to build with them? A program's alumni are a key source of industry contacts, so if this is one aspect you are seeking from a program, make sure to ask these types of questions before enrolling.

A number of people currently working in the sports industry have turned to online programs as a means of advancing their careers. Such people typically do not need many of the benefits found in classroom-based programs, such as networking opportunities because they have industry connections by working in the industry. Some of these individuals aspire to move higher within their current field, but need additional education to do so. A good example of this is someone working in college athletics who wants to become an athletic director (AD). Most AD positions require candidates to hold a graduate-level degree, so anyone without such a degree is in need of additional education to even be considered for the position. Some online programs are geared toward providing this advanced level of education, and they allow industry professionals to obtain the desired level of education without having to give up their current jobs.

Not all online programs are designed to provide advanced levels of education, though. In fact, many programs are specifically designed to help newcomers to the industry. Such programs may be beneficial for someone looking to obtain an entry-level position, but may not be as helpful to someone looking at more advanced positions, such as someone wanting to move up within the industry or make a career change into the industry. It is important to closely scrutinize any program to make sure it meets your specific needs. If you need education sufficient to obtain a mid-level or advanced position, make sure the online program can deliver this specific level of education. Look at both the content of the program and what type of degree you will receive upon completing the program.

In addition to online programs, executive MBA programs are another viable source of advanced education available to industry professionals. Such programs typically meet on weekends and/or evenings for several hours, thus allowing the student to complete the program while continuing to work.

A distinction should be made between online *degree* programs and online *certificate* programs. Although a certificate program may provide a sufficient amount of knowledge for someone looking for an entry-level position, it may not be enough for someone looking at more advanced positions. For example, in certain fields, an online certificate may not meet the minimum requirements for certain jobs. This is often the case in college athletics, where the standard requirement is a graduate degree.

In comparison to traditional programs, online programs take less time and may be less expensive (particularly when factoring in opportunity costs), but you may be getting less. Given the newness of such programs, it is difficult to gauge the acceptance and perception of online programs in the eyes of employers.

SPORT MANAGEMENT PROGRAM ACCREDITATION

The North American Society for Sport Management (NASSM) began an accreditation process of sport management programs in the 1990s. NASSM now works in conjunction with the National Association for Sport and Physical Education (NASPE) to set standards to review and approve sport management programs. The most recent standards, established in 2000, are under review for possible revisions.

WHERE TO FIND INFORMATION ABOUT SCHOOLS

So you read the information so far in this chapter, and you concluded that sport management education is an appropriate path for you. What now? Once you reach the decision to pursue an undergraduate sport management degree, it is important to thoroughly research the schools. A very comprehensive list of programs can be found on the NASSM website, which contains links to programs in the United States, Canada, and abroad. Although this list is comprehensive, it may not be exhaustive.

New, innovative, and competitive undergraduate programs could emerge at any time; all it would take is some initiative on the part of a university, a commitment of

---

Box 5-3   Finding the Right Program

In narrowing down your list of schools, here are some important factors to investigate and consider:

1. What courses are available? What courses are required? How many students make up a typical class?

2. Are the courses sports-specific, or are they general business/management courses that require the student to make the transition into sport?

   Is the program located in a school of business, physical education, or exercise science?

3. Does the school have a separate department for its sport management program, or is the program lumped in with other departments?

4. How many of the faculty members are full-time faculty members in the sport management program?

5. What is the average class size?

6. Are the classes (at least the upper level classes) for majors only?

7. Does the school have an internship program? If so, what is the quality of the program?

8. Is it evident that the program maintains contacts with its alumni through networking events or reunions?

9. What quality of guest speakers does the department attract? Are they in your desired field?

10. Does the program offer any practicum courses?

11. What is the success rate of students?

12. Does the department offer any assistance with jobs in the sports industry, after one has graduated from the sport management program?

13. What is the recent record of the school's placements of internships? Are students being placed in organizations that might interest you?

14. Are any students compensated for their internships or are they all no pay? (Sometimes no pay internships are the best internships, due to high demand; however, it is good to know what you might be in for.)

15. What is the percentage of students who went from an internship to a job in the sports industry?

16. What are the graduates from 3 to 5 years ago doing now? How about those from 8 to 10 years ago? Are they still in the sports industry?

university resources and/or a couple of wealthy benefactors, and some faculty hires of "connected" industry or ex-industry people with good teaching skills. Therefore, prospective students might want to continue to research for additional sport management programs. In order to do so, start with an Internet search, using a good search engine like Google, and searching by terms such as "sports business programs," "sports administration programs," or "sport management programs." In addition, *Street & Smith's SportsBusiness Journal* publishes an annual summer issue on sport management programs. This publication can be ordered online, and back issues are available at some libraries.

If you are fortunate enough to be accepted into more than one program, here are some questions you might want to ask the programs' faculty and staff in order to narrow down your search.

STUDENTS LOOKING TO TRANSFER INTO SPORT MANAGEMENT PROGRAMS

Often, students are interested in either transferring schools or transferring majors to enroll in a sport management program. There are three common types of transfer students:

- Students who are at a community college and looking to transfer to a 4-year undergraduate school with a sport management program
- Students wishing to transfer from one 4-year school to another 4-year school with sport management in mind
- Students who are looking to transfer majors within a university from a different major into a sport management major

Typically a student must meet specific academic requirements in order to complete the transfer successfully, and these requirements may vary significantly by school and the type of transfer being sought. As an example, the University of Massachusetts Sport Management program currently requires the following, *at a minimum*, of those who wish to transfer into the sport management major:

- Satisfactory *overall* grade point average
- One introductory-level sport management class with a grade of B or higher
- Satisfactory grade point average in the following four courses: microeconomics, statistics, computer science, and precalculus or calculus
- The requirements obviously vary from school to school, but as sport management programs continue to become more popular and competitive, the standards for transferring into these programs will be high.

It is important to keep in mind that transferring into a sport management program may extend the total amount of time that a transfer student will be in school. For example, depending on the timing of the transfer and the number of credits the student is ultimately able to transfer, the student may need an additional semester or two to complete the sport management program. This is particularly true the further along the transfer student is in his or her current program. If you are considering transferring into a sport management program, but taking additional time to complete your schooling is not feasible, an alternative to consider is to complete the program you are currently in and then plan on applying to a graduate sport management program in the future.

MASTER'S DEGREES

Many people considering making a move into the sports industry often ask if they should obtain a graduate degree in sport management. There is no one definitive answer to this question because it really depends on the person's particular situation. There are three things that should be closely examined and considered:

- The person's career goals
- The person's past experiences
- What will help the person the most, in terms of education, to reach those career goals

The following discussion of sport management education at the graduate level will center around this basic framework.

With the growing interest in sport management, in 20 years will someone without an advanced degree still be able to obtain a leadership position? The answer to this question is probably yes, although it is more likely in some fields (such as facility management) and less likely in others (such as college athletics). Generally speaking, looking towards the future, an applicant without an advanced degree will be at a competitive disadvantage, especially as one applies for higher-level positions and more so for some jobs than others.

It is important to note, though, that an advanced degree is not a guarantee of success; it just gives a person one more asset to put in play. Along these same lines, obtaining a degree from a particular program with a strong reputation is also not a guarantee for success. You need to take advantage of the aspects of the program (such as a strong alumni base) that have helped build the program's reputation. This often requires hard work and initiative on the part of the graduate student. Lastly, attending a new or lightly regarded program does not mean that you cannot be successful. It just means that you may have to work harder to achieve success.

In today's educational environment, a prospective sport management student faces a multitude of degree options. Should I obtain a Master of Science in Sport Management? Should I get an MBA? Should I get a law degree? The following sections discuss the benefits of the most prevalent options offered today. Hopefully this information will help you to decide which option is best for your particular situation.

Those who are considering a master's degree in sport management or a joint program with an MBA and a master's degree in sport management should read the beginning sections of this chapter about what to look for when considering a sport management program. Not all of the top undergraduate sport management programs have master's degree programs and vice versa. However, the resources (such as NASSM and *SportsBusiness Journal*) and procedures for identifying such programs are similar.

Master of Science Degrees in Sport Management

Master's programs in sport management are a crash course in the sports industry. Students can complete the program in a year, so they can obtain a master's degree in a relatively short period of time. This helps minimize the opportunity cost of attending school. Alumni connections are, for many, an important consideration in the selection of a sport management education program. By attending a 1-year master's program, the student should have adequate opportunity to enhance his or her network through the school's alumni network. A potential downside to obtaining a master's degree in sport management, without combining this degree with an advanced business degree such as an MBA, is that the student may not receive all the necessary business skills necessary to become an executive in the industry. This really depends on the particular person and their background. For example, a person with strong business skills may not need additional graduate-level business education. In this case, a master's degree in sport management may be sufficient.

Joint Degrees in Sport Management

Joint degree MBA/MS Sport Management programs provide students with both in-depth sports industry expertise and a strong business education. The sport management portion of such programs provides a student with an opportunity to work exclusively on sports-specific projects. In addition, the depth of sports academic content may be deeper and more enriched by the dual sports/business nature of the programs. At the University of Massachusetts, students learn business skills in their MBA classes and then draw upon this knowledge to complete more comprehensive sports-related projects in their sport management classes. For instance, in previous years:

- Students have utilized knowledge gained in their MBA statistics courses to complete market research projects for sports entities.
- Students have utilized knowledge gained from their MBA economics courses to complete ticket pricing analyses for sports entities.

- Students have utilized knowledge gained from their MBA marketing courses to complete sports marketing consulting projects.

Such projects would be difficult to implement in the sport management classes if the students had not previously completed their MBA coursework.

By completing an MS in Sport Management in conjunction with an MBA, a student will develop a greater level of specialization in sports while still obtaining a traditional business school education. Students attending such programs are also able to interact with classmates who all aspire to work in sports, and can typically do so in larger classes with 10–25 students. This not only expands the student's future network, but also may enhance the overall learning environment by improving classroom dynamics. Additionally, given their propensity to be older, more established programs, such programs often have a larger alumni base. Typically, such programs require a 2-year, full-time commitment on the part of the student.

MBA with a Specialization in Sport Management

Many MBA programs now allow students to obtain a specialization in sport management. This differs from the joint degree programs in that only one degree, an MBA, is awarded (i.e., a separate master's degree in sport management is not awarded). The MBA with a sport management specialization should be considered after the joint degree. Granted, much of this depends on the particular program, but although it can be better preparation than a straight MBA (with no sport specialization), it may not offer as much as a joint degree MBA/MS in Sport Management. One of the benefits of the MBA with a sports specialization include an overall general acceptance that sports is an acceptable field to study. This makes it more likely that the student will be able to gain faculty support for sports-related projects in the traditional MBA courses. However, the depth of sports-specific education students receive may not be as rich as in an MS program. Also, be aware of smaller programs that have only recently been established. Such programs likely have fewer alumni contacts and may be one- or two-person operations. If you come across this situation in researching schools, carefully consider the longevity and continuity of the program. In an industry that's driven by who you know, you can never be too cautious about such matters. It may be that a school has a small program (with a small number of students and/or alumni), but it may have a relatively large number of contacts at a particular organization or have a program director who is well-respected within a field that is of interest to you. Just make sure to do your homework and make sure there is a good fit before signing on.

MBA with No Sport-Specific Specialization or Joint Degree

The third MBA option available to prospective students is to obtain an MBA from a traditional business school, which does not have any sport specialization. This may be the most viable option for students looking to attend school in a specific geographic location, or students with previous sports industry experience, particularly if the student already has a well-established network. In addition, it is generally not recommended that a person who obtained an undergraduate degree in sport management pursue a graduate degree in the same field. Instead, such people should consider obtaining an MBA with no sport specialization, or a law degree. This gives the student a more diversified educational background.

One benefit of obtaining a traditional MBA is, should the student's attempt to break into the sports industry be unsuccessful (or if the student decides that sports is not the best area to be working in), it may be easier for the student to find work outside the sports industry. This is particularly the case for high profile business programs, where the job placement record is very good. It's also important to keep in mind the ever-changing landscape that is sports. More and more, organizations are looking for employees with well-established business skills and they are becoming more receptive to candidates from traditional MBA programs. For example, a number of league offices and other sports organizations are turning more and more to graduates of highly regarded academic institutions (with no sport management education program) to find their new hires. If your career aspirations are to work in a league office, it would be beneficial to examine what type of education current league employees have. This type of information can sometimes be found on a league's website. Again, it helps if the student has an understanding of where they want to go in their career, and then finds programs that have helped students in similar situations achieve those goals.

Advice for Those Wanting Both a Juris Doctor (JD) and a Master's in Sport Management

Some people ask, "I've decided to get both a JD and a master's in sport management or administration. Should I get a JD or a sport-related master's degree first?" No single answer is best for everyone. Sometimes the best answer is to get the master's degree first and sometimes the best decision is to get the law degree first. Some of it depends on what you want to do—do you want to be a sports lawyer or a sports administrator? The following are some of the advantages of pursuing the master's degree first:

- The academic work in a master's programs will be more challenging than most undergraduate programs, but less challenging than most law programs, so it is a logical step in one's academic progression.

- One can establish contacts in the sports industry and use those contacts to help secure summer and/or part-time employment while in law school.

- A master's program in sport management provides an understanding of the sports industry. As a result, if there is an opportunity to be involved in law review, writing, independent study projects, or sport law society or clubs, a student will be able to rely on their work and knowledge from the master's degree in sport management.

- The initial financial burden may be less significant. Law programs are typically more expensive, especially if you attend a private or an out-of-state law school. Opportunities for teaching assistantships, research assistantships, and tuition remissions are more likely in sport management programs. The average law or medical student graduates with over $70,000 in debt—of course, some have significantly more debt. By comparison, the average MBA student graduates with about $30,000 to $40,000 in debt, while graduate students in general average between $24,000 and $28,000 of debt.[3] There are no studies specifically focused on the indebtedness of the average MS in Sport Management student, but it is likely to be significantly below the $24,000 to $24,000 average of the typical graduate student.[3] The point in discussing all these numbers is to mention some of the financial considerations of this choice. It may become necessary after law school to work for a few years in more lucrative nonsports-related fields in order to reduce the student's debt. Nevertheless, during this time, graduates can maintain and possibly increase networking connections from their years as a sport management student, and work their way toward sports-related legal positions.

It can be difficult to place JD-to-MS degree people on internships. Internships are usually low paying (or nonpaying) and involve a fair bit of menial labor, so employers are sometimes reluctant to hire lawyers for an internship. This is known as the "fear of the OQ" (overqualified). Some employers may be concerned that lawyers will become bored on an internship, or will be reluctant to do grunt work. But even if you can find an employer who doesn't fear the OQ, what can you do on an internship as a JD-to-MS? How will this mesh with your career goals? One option is to find an internship practicing sports law, but such internships are rare and competition for these positions is high.

The advantage of doing the JD first is that the master's degree program may be able to provide some of the contacts or leads in the sports industry, at a time when the graduate can stay on the internship or job.

Which Law School Is Best?

The question sometimes comes up as to whether a prospective law school applicant should select a law school based on the academic reputation of the law school or based on courses, journals, and/or a specialization in sports law. The reason this question is raised is that law schools have varying approaches to the study of sports law. Some law schools do not even offer a course in sports law. Other law schools may offer a course or two in sports law. In addition, there are several law schools with a "specialization" in sports law. Marquette University Law School is one such program. Students graduating from the university's law program have an opportunity to earn a Sports Law Certificate from the National Sports Law Institute, which is in the law school. In order to receive the certificate, students must successfully complete the following requirements:

- Two introductory sports law courses, Amateur Sports Law and Professional Sports Law

- One sports law workshop, choosing from the following available options:
  - Amateur Sports Law Workshop
  - Representing Professional Athletes and Coaches
  - Sports Industry Legal and Business Practices
  - Sports Venues: From Election Day to Game Day

- Sports law research paper

- Topics in Advanced Legal Research: Sports Law

- One of the following:
  - Alternative Dispute Resolution
  - Arbitration Workshop
  - Mediation Workshop
  - Negotiation Workshop

- One or more of the following substantive law courses that significantly impact the sports industry:
  - Antitrust Law
  - Business Associations
  - Constitutional Law 2: Speech and Equality
  - Disability Law
  - Education Law
  - Federal Income Taxation of Individuals
  - Intellectual Property Law
  - Labor Law

- Marquette Sports Law Review staff position for a full academic year

- A one-semester National Sports Law Institute–sponsored volunteer sports law internship

This is just one example of a law school with a specialization in sports law. Other law schools with a specialization and/or journals in sports law classes are Tulane University Law School, Florida Coastal School of Law, and Seton Hall University School of Law, to name a few.

In addition to looking for schools with designated sports law programs, you can also search for schools that are actively involved in sports law associations or that publish a sports law journal (for example, the University of Virginia's *Virginia Sports & Entertainment Law Journal* or Villanova University's *Villanova Sports and Entertainment Law Journal*). Publishing such a journal is a strong indication that the school supports the study of sports law. It may be worth a phone call or Internet search to see whether such schools offer sports law classes, certificates, and/or conferences.

There are a few things to keep in mind with sports law education, though. To begin with, most schools are likely to have only one faculty member interested in and available to teach sports law, particularly schools that offer only a course or two rather than a specialized program or certificate. Such professors are often in high demand, so if another university hires these people away, the school may not continue to offer classes in sports law.

It also is important to consider the school's academic reputation, both inside the sports law industry and outside. A school with a strong sports law reputation will naturally help in the pursuit of a job within the sports industry. What happens if this pursuit is unsuccessful, though? If the school does not have as strong of a reputation outside the sports industry, a person may have greater difficulty finding employment outside of the sports industry than if the person had attended a school with a stronger reputation as a law school. Not everyone who sets out to work in sports law ultimately stays in the sports industry, so it is important to consider this.

For schools that teach only one or two sports law courses, be wary of the fact that such courses may not be offered every year. This is because the faculty member may be on sabbatical or handling administrative duties, or the faculty member who is capable of teaching the course(s) may be assigned to a different course. Sports law courses often take a low priority from the law school's perspective. Also, be aware that adjunct or part-time professors may not have the same availability as full-time professors. Therefore, they may not have time to help or to supervise extra work or special projects in your field of interest, such as an independent study.

For schools that offer courses in sports law, it may be useful to learn about the sports law background of the

---

Box 5-4   *Key to Success*

In completing my own sports law education at Boston College Law School, I took sports law and completed two independent study projects with Robert C. Berry, a full-time faculty member and a pioneer in the field of sports law. Finding one good professor who has the time and is willing to help may be the key to successfully completing a sports law education program.

faculty member. The faculty member who has had experience in sports law may have a former student or students who are working in the sports law field, and can be helpful to future students for career information and possibly job leads. A faculty member may also be an important career advisor, especially if he has contacts and/or dealings in the sports industry.

Sports law is often taught from the perspective of the professor, who will usually cover and teach the course to his area of expertise. Therefore, a professor who specializes in labor law may focus the course more heavily on labor law issues, whereas a tort law professor may focus his sports law class on tort liability. This is not meant to be a criticism of any professor; however, it may be useful information for a prospective student.

For any school that offer sports law "specializations" or certificates, take a look at the school's placement records. Are graduates obtaining jobs in sports law, or are they primarily working outside the sports industry? Make sure to ask not only about recent graduates, but also about graduates from 5 years ago (or more if the program existed then). How many of these people are currently working in the sports law field? Where are some of these people now? This should give you an indication of the likelihood that you will be able to find successful employment within sports law should you choose to attend the program.

Another consideration is geographic location. Some cities where sports law is more likely to be practiced lend themselves to the possibility of work during the school year. It is also more convenient for the law school student to work in the geographic location where he is going to school. Some of the cities where sports law is more likely to be practiced include New York; Washington, DC; Boston; Chicago; Los Angeles; San Francisco; Indianapolis; and Colorado Springs.

The choice of what law school to attend is a very personal decision. There are many factors to consider, some of which have been addressed in this chapter; others include finances (scholarship and financial aid availability), family situations, personal matters, and geographic preferences. People will weigh these factors differently, so there is no one right answer for everyone.

SCHOOLS FOR SPECIALIZED CAREERS

Although much of the focus of this chapter has been on sport management degrees, MBAs, and law degrees, there are other possible degree options. A good sport management program, in particular, can provide you with a valuable understanding of the sports industry as a whole, and can expose you to a variety of contacts and experiences that you might not otherwise find. However, for certain specialized careers, different specialized degrees might be warranted.

A handful of graduates from sport management programs go on to work in high profile sports broadcasting jobs; however, most of the sports broadcasters you see on cable, local, and national noncable television typically have a broadcasting degree, a journalism degree, a liberal arts degree, or a combination of two of the three. The top broadcasting schools have a much different academic program from the top sport management schools. The internships and jobs are also much different. Some, but not all, of the work and education positions are transferable to sport management positions. Those who are interested in broadcasting should ask questions such as:

- Am I interested in sports broadcasting exclusively, or other forms of broadcasting as well?

- Do I speak well and read well? Do I present myself well?

The career path for a broadcaster is very different from the career path for a sport manager, meaning there may be little transferability between the two. How committed am I to a career in sports broadcasting? If it doesn't work out, am I willing to start over?

Likewise, those who aspire to obtain coaching jobs should consider an academic program focused on the particular skills and abilities needed to become a successful coach. Keep in mind, the same lack of transferability also applies to coaching.

ADVICE WHILE ATTENDING SCHOOL

If a job seeker does not have practical work experience, employers evaluate two important factors when comparing candidates with only an undergraduate degree—the quality and reputation of the undergraduate institution and how the person performed in school. Keep this in mind when selecting a school for undergraduate work.

If you do not have plans for any graduate work, your grades may or may not be critical in gaining employment. However, in such a case, it may be important for you to select a major that is an asset for the types of jobs that interest you. For example, if you wish to work in marketing for a sports entity, a sport management major may be of more use than a psychology major, although success may be found with either major.

If you have any designs on graduate school, in either the near term or the long term, grades and academic performance can be crucial in the admissions process. To a certain extent, in most situations, although the passage of time can slightly reduce the emphasis on grades, it will not eliminate them as a factor in the admissions process for graduate school. So make sure you get good grades!

In addition to performing well in school, remember grades are not the only reason you attend school—the ultimate goal is to get a job. Keeping this in mind, take advantage of every opportunity your program provides. If there is a guest speaker, make every effort to attend and do so in a professional manner. This means you should not show up in jeans and a t-shirt with a baseball cap. Look like someone who is ready for a job, and not your typical college student. Even if the guest speaker is not in a field you are currently considering, attend anyway. You never know who the person knows or what type of previous experience he may have had. For example, maybe the person works in corporate sponsorship at MasterCard, but you really want to get into marketing for a professional team. Even though the person does not currently work in your desired field, the person may have started out in sales for the New York Mets. Through his previous work experience, he may be able to provide you with contacts such as former colleagues, friends, or former classmates who work in marketing for a pro sports team. Chances are, if the person is taking the time to come and speak to students, he has an interest in helping students. Take advantage of this. You will find difficulty duplicating such opportunities on your own. This is also an easy way to expand your network, which is discussed in the following chapter. Remember to always follow up with guest speakers by sending a thank you note, and including your business card, if you have one.

Endnotes

1. Helyar, J. (2006, Sep. 16). Failing Effort: Are Universities' Sport Management Programs a Ticket to a Great Job? Not Likely. *Wall Street Journal*, p. R5.

2. Information obtained from the University of Massachusetts Sports Management Program Alumni Database.

3. NASFAA.org. (2004, Mar. 1). Law, Dental, and Medical School Graduates Leave with Substantial Loan Debt, SOGAPPP Results Reveal. Retrieved July 28, 2008, from http://www.nasfaa.org/publications/2004/rnsogappp030104.html.

Networking

"Luck is the residue of design."

—Branch Rickey, former MLB executive best known for helping to break the color barrier in baseball by signing Jackie Robinson

"The harder I work, the luckier I get."

—Samuel Goldwyn, former Hollywood producer and film mogul

"Get out and meet people face to face. Paper résumés are worthless in this industry. People only hire individuals who they know, so the best thing to do is call people up and ask them if they have time to talk in person. Either ask if you can do a personal interview at their office, shadow them for a day, or offer to buy them lunch. Whatever you can do to make yourself memorable is important."

—Community relations coordinator for an NFL franchise

The sports job/internship market is more competitive than those found in most other industries. Finding one's first sport management job or internship can be a daunting task; however, some job/internship seekers make the process more difficult than it needs to be. People working in sports (or people trying to do so) limit their prospects of success by failing to recognize all of the resources available to them. This chapter will explore some sport-specific employment and internship services that are available through the Internet, print media, and private businesses. But before addressing these resources, job/internship seekers should first assess whether they can expect any assistance from colleagues, friends, relatives, and acquaintances.

Six degrees of separation—the notion that you can connect someone you know to virtually anyone important via six people or fewer—is becoming a bit of a cliché in popular culture. However, major players in sports business may be *less* separated from you than you realize. You may know somebody who knows somebody, but do not even know it.

An exhibit in Section 3, *Career Tracks of Executives in the Sports Industry*, shows that *at least* two of the current general managers (GMs) in Major League Baseball are sons of former GMs and/or prominent baseball executives. Several others knew family members or close acquaintances working in the game of baseball. These individuals already had some type of network built for them. Most readers of this book, however, are not so fortunate and must create their own network.

The first step in building a network is to perform an inventory of your resources. In this case, your inventory will consist of *people* whom you have met and *institutions* with which you have been associated. Although some of this may sound obvious, it is easy for even the most thorough job seeker to neglect one of these resources.

Here are some questions to ask yourself when you perform a networking inventory:

- Do I have any family members working in the sports or entertainment industries?

- Do I have any friends working in the sports or entertainment industries?

- Do I have any friends of friends (acquaintances) working in the sports or entertainment industries? (Count the degrees of separation.)

- Do my parents have any friends, colleagues, former classmates, or professional contacts working in the sports or entertainment industries?

- (If you are a college graduate or matriculating under-graduate) Does my undergraduate institution have a career placement or alumni contact program? If so, have I looked for people who are connected to the sports industry?

- Does my high school have a career placement or alumni contact program? If so, have I looked for people who are connected to the sports industry?

- (If you are an athlete) Can the coach and/or assistant coaches be of any assistance?

- (If you are an athlete) Can my athletic director be of any assistance?

- Can my teachers (high school and college) be of any assistance?

- (If you have a graduate or law degree or are a matriculating graduate student or law student) Does my undergraduate and/or graduate institution have a career placement or alumni contact program? If so, have I looked for people who are connected to the sports industry?

MAKING CONTACTS WITH INDUSTRY PROFESSIONALS

In an ideal world, job and internship seekers could crack open the want ads of their local newspaper every morning and see dozens of new sports-related job openings. In the real world, this does not usually happen. Although Chapter 7, *Resources for Job and Internship Seekers*, can direct you to sports-specific job postings on the Internet and in print media, job and internship seekers need to be more proactive than just applying for jobs. Job seekers need to find a way to meet people and build their network. If you can make a connection with people in the sports industry, even an informal one, it may pay off in the future.

Take the following example. Joan Barno, human resources specialist for baseball's Cleveland Indians, says, "We have people from, I am not kidding you, all over the world apply for jobs." She says the team recently received 412 online applicants for a 32-hour-a-week community-outreach assistant. "And that's nothing," she adds. Last year, the Indians got 1,500 applications for 6 internships.[1] Given the large number of applicants, how do you suppose a team determines who is a viable candidate and who is not? Often it comes down to knowing the right people, in addition to being strong on paper (i.e., having a good résumé). Candidates who have developed networking connections are more likely to rise to the top of the stack of résumés, thus greatly enhancing the likelihood they will receive an invitation to interview.

How does one go about making such connections, though? It is sometimes difficult to get past the gatekeepers in the sports organizations, in order to talk with upper-level executives. In other cases, especially in the less glamorous positions (think non-general manager or non-athletic director jobs), it may be easier to track such individuals down. Regardless, most industry professionals, at either the top or the bottom, do *not* like to receive unsolicited calls asking for a job. So how does one make contact with someone in their chosen industry, especially at times when organizations in this industry are not accepting résumés? Particularly for individuals who are nervous about cold-calling industry professionals, it is helpful to have a reason (or an excuse) to call such people.

One strategy that is *sometimes* effective for students is to conduct some type of research project about the organization. At the University of Massachusetts, master's level students are required to write a career paper in their second semester of coursework. The career paper has three parts. In one part, a student writes an analysis of the industry and position that she currently favors (such as compliance in college athletics, public relations in the NFL, facility management for an arena, etc.). Students are required, in this section of the paper, to interview professionals in their chosen niche of the sports industry. In another part of the career paper, the students perform a self-analysis and are given the Myers-Briggs personality test by someone trained to administer the test (see "Self-Assessments" in Chapter 3, *The Assessment Process*, for a description of self-assessments). Finally, the students reconcile their self-analysis and personality with their chosen future profession. One goal of this project is for students to discover whether their chosen profession is right for them before committing to an internship or a job in that field.

The fringe benefit to the career paper is that it provides students with an opportunity to contact industry professionals under less intimidating circumstances. Instead of figuratively holding out their hats and begging for a job or internship, students have the opportunity to contact high-level individuals with a much more manageable request: "I'm a student at University of X. I am conducting an academic writing project about media relations directors in Division I-A sports [or insert whatever segment is appropriate]. I was wondering if you could please answer a few questions. Your answers will not be published, and are strictly for academic purposes."

Not every academic program requires its students to conduct this type of project; however, it is fairly common for students in business programs, sport management programs, and other programs to at least be assigned some open-ended academic projects that would allow them to write a paper of this nature. This is an opportunity to contact and possibly meet some important people, while earning academic credit in the process. Each year, certain students thrive in this project, and make pivotal connections for their careers. Unfortunately, other students fail to see the opportunity in the project, and view it as a burdensome academic episode—like any other paper they have to turn in.

Will every industry professional agree to be interviewed? Certainly not. The success rate seems quite high, though, especially when students contact an alumnus of the program and/or school. (Be sure to check with your academic institution to see whether any alumni are working in the industry you are targeting.) As mentioned previously, some people generally enjoy talking about themselves and what they do for a living while others realize that they received some help along the way. Some industry professionals speak frankly—much more frankly than they would to a member of the media—while others speak in clichés or with extreme caution. Regardless of their demeanor and openness, you can make a positive lasting impression by asking good questions, listening attentively, interacting in a friendly and professional manner, and following up with a thank you note.

Months later, when it comes time for you to resume or initiate your job/internship search, you can start your cover letter by saying "Please allow me to *re*-introduce myself" as opposed to "Please allow me to introduce myself." Especially if that person's company is soliciting résumés at the time, you are certain to set yourself apart from the competition somewhat, if you have had some previous contact with the hiring party.

In addition to the research project described here, there are other opportunities to make industry connections. For example, sport management programs often bring prominent sport management executives to campus to lecture as guest speakers. Make sure to attend all such programs and to introduce yourself to guest speakers after the lecture. Then follow up these meetings with an e-mail or phone call. In doing so, it's advisable to jog the lecturer's memory; for example, "I was the guy/woman in the blue blazer who asked the question about *X*." Sometimes, schools will set up designated times for students to interact with guest speakers on a one-on-one basis, or the guest speaker may even conduct internship interviews while on campus. If your school provides any such opportunities, take advantage of them.

Another way to build your network is by attending events that executives are likely to attend, such as conferences, trade shows, and job fairs (for example, baseball's winter meetings). Chapter 7 provides additional information about sports-related career/job fairs.

Under whatever pretense you engage in conversation, it is strongly encouraged that all prospective sport management professionals contact people currently employed in the

---

INTERNSHIP STORY

Networking is one of the most important things you can do to help break into the sports industry. The following story highlights the networking approach taken by one successful student in terms of networking.

Coming into the sport management program at the University of Massachusetts, I had some sports industry contacts from working at ESPN, but I knew this would not be enough to open doors to the type of work I wanted to do, which is sports marketing. During my time at University of Massachusetts, I made it a point to talk to as many alumni and industry professionals as possible, and I started this process literally from day one of the program.

Contacting the school's alumni made the whole networking process easier. In general, the alumni have great pride in the school and are more than willing to help out. I think they realize how difficult the industry can be and they remember how they may have struggled to gain a foothold in the industry. This makes them more responsive to inquiries from students. The University of Massachusetts tie was also a nice icebreaker to initiate conversations.

What I didn't do was call up alumni and immediately ask for a job. I found the best approach was to view this as a process—make an initial contact, build a rapport over time, and then later ask about job opportunities. No one likes to be called by a stranger who immediately asks for a job. To be successful at networking, I believe you have to take the time for the person to get to know you.

The initial conversations were informational in nature. I would try to find out what the person does, how they got their job, what they think of the industry, and what current industry trends they consider important. These conversations typically lasted anywhere from a half-hour to an hour. I always made sure to end every call by asking if the person was willing to share any of their personal contacts with me. This enabled me to expand my network beyond University of Massachusetts alumni. I contacted everyone I was referred to, no matter who the person was or what organization they worked for.

I think my success in networking was due in large part due to my willingness to talk to anyone. Even if the person worked for an organization I had no particular interest in, I talked to them anyway on the off chance that they may have worked previously for, or they might be able to refer me to someone at an organization that did interest me. In this industry, you cannot be timid about contacting complete strangers. It is the nature of the industry—the more people you know (and the more people who know you) the better off you will be.

industry. Talking to sports professionals is an excellent opportunity to gain valuable insights into the industry. Through these conversations, you should be able to quickly learn what it is truly like to work in the industry. Such conversations are also likely to help better determine an appropriate career path given your talents, skills, preferences, and interests.

When tracking down a sports executive of any stature, it is imperative that the job/internship seeker is prepared with intelligent questions. Some good informational interview questions are provided near the end of this chapter. Additionally, treat every encounter in a highly professional manner. The write-up on "Interview Preparation" (Chapter 12) provides advice on how to do this.

CONFERENCES, ASSOCIATIONS, AND PROFESSIONAL MEETINGS

Many organizations have conferences, association meetings, and/or professional meetings. Most conferences have an open registration policy and you do not have to be a member of that organization to attend. Many sports-related conferences have a student rate, so if you are a student, you should ask about a student registration rate.

Many association or professional meetings allow non-members to participate. So, for example, members and non-members can attend the Annual Sports Lawyers Association Conference. This is a 2 1/2-day conference offering panel discussions, speeches, and lunches and receptions. This is an excellent opportunity to learn about sports law and the current issues in sports law, and to meet other sports lawyers. There is also the opportunity to join as a student member, which in addition to the conferences gives access to the members-only section of the website, which contains legal documents, cases, and contact information for other members of the organization.

Some organizations, such as the National Collegiate Athletic Association (NCAA) and MLB, also offer job fairs in conjunction with their meetings.

INFORMATIONAL INTERVIEWS AND INFORMAL CONTACTS

When approaching a friend of a friend, an acquaintance, or someone you do not know particularly well, it's generally not advisable to start a conversation with, "Can I have a job?" or "Can I have an internship?" It is usually better to ask for more general advice about the area of the sports industry in which this person works. People generally do *not* like to be asked about employment, but will talk about their jobs. Asking intelligent but sincere questions is a good way to strike up a conversation with an individual and to develop a positive rapport with her. Make sure you listen carefully to what the individual has to say, and note any names of other contacts that she mentions. (These contacts might be people whom you will want to approach later, thus increasing your network.) Once you sense that this person has given you as much time as she is going to give you, then it is acceptable to mention that you are in the internship/job market. Perhaps say something like: "I really appreciate you taking the time to speak with me. I would love to work for your company if you ever have any openings. Here is my résumé [and business card if you have one]." If you developed a good rapport with this person, it is possible that she will say something like "I enjoyed meeting with you too. We aren't looking for anyone with your qualifications right now. But please keep me informed of your job/internship search. Feel free to contact me in the future."

Box 6-1   Building and Maintaining Your Network

The hardest part of networking is building your network. A great deal of time and effort go into making the initial contact and building a meaningful relationship with members of your network. That being said, the easiest part of networking should be maintaining the contacts you have already developed. Take the time to periodically reach out to your network—let your contacts know what you have been up to and how things are going. This is particularly easy in the age of e-mail. Although this may seem relatively straightforward, many people overlook the importance of maintaining their network.

Box 6-2   Networking Tip

People will generally take an interest in you if you take an interest in them. It's human nature—people like to feel important or helpful. Keeping this in mind, a very helpful networking tip is to call upon the interests of those with whom you are trying to make contact. For example, if you are trying to develop a contact with a prominent executive of a sports marketing agency, and you happen to notice that the person was quoted in a recent *SportsBusiness Journal*, use this to get your foot in the door. Make a copy of the story or clip the story out and send it to the person. Include a note that explains why the story has importance to you, but also use this as an opportunity to introduce yourself. If you have business cards, which are worth investing in, make sure to include one in the mailing as well. This shows initiative and can make a positive impression on the person. Always follow up with the person after a few weeks to see if they are willing to meet for an informational interview.

Clipping articles is also a good way to stay in contact with the people who are already in your network. Doing so proves you value your connection to the person, and that person is more likely to remember you when it comes time to fill an open position.

If or when someone makes this offer, *take them up on it*! You have now officially increased your network. Make a note in your calendar to write this person an e-mail in a couple months (or if the person suggests an interval of time, adhere to it). Even if you happen to find a great job in the interim, write them back anyway, saying something like this:

Please allow me to re-introduce myself. My name is X. Thank you for your assistance a couple months ago. During our meeting, you encouraged me to let you know how I was doing in my career search. I wanted to let you know that I have found an internship with X.

I also recommend that job and internship seekers keep a journal. If you are starting at a point where your network is small, this may sound like a useless task; however, you might become surprised by how quickly your network can grow after you have made a few contacts. It becomes easy to forget about people whom you met, or to whom you were referred, several months after the contact.

Endnotes

1. Fatsis, S., and Keating, P. (2006, Sep. 16). The Business of Sports: Getting in the Game. *The Wall Street Journal*, p. R.1.

Resources for Job and Internship Seekers

"We are all capable of infinitely more than we believe. We are stronger and more resourceful than we know, and we can endure much more than we think we can."

—David Blaine, American magician and entertainer

Job seekers often ask where to look for job and internship opportunities. This chapter lists some helpful resources related to this topic. One disclaimer, though: Although the list provided here is extensive, it is by no means meant to be exhaustive, and the resources are constantly changing. Job seekers should use the Internet, career officers at their schools, and the advice of friends and colleagues to find additional job search resources. The information provided here is not meant to be an evaluation or endorsement of any job site, but provides an example of the types of sites available. However, it is important to point out one website, TeamWork Online because it is a well-established and comprehensive site providing both job postings and career advice free of charge. Many in the industry recognize it as a leader.

JOB AND INTERNSHIP LISTINGS: VARYING EXPERIENCE LEVELS

The following web-based resources, listed **in alphabetical** order, may be helpful in locating job and internship opportunities. Some of the sites require subscription or payment to access job information, whereas others are free. The level of job category (e.g., internship, full-time position, entry-level position, executive position) can vary significantly from site to site. URLs tend to change over time, so addresses are not provided here. Conduct an Internet search using a search engine such as Google or Yahoo! to locate specific web addresses.

Chronicle of Higher Education

- Top news source for college and university administrators, faculty members, and staff. The site includes a comprehensive job listing section that includes available sport/athletic positions in higher education (e.g., faculty positions in sport management, athletic administration positions such as athletic directors).

- Job database available online free of charge and in print for a fee. Print subscriber rates range from $45 print/$40 online for 6 months to $199 print/$179 online for 3 years.

- Enables applicants to search for available positions by keywords (e.g., sport management, athletics).

- Includes detailed profiles on colleges, universities, and other employers.

IEG (International Events Group) Job Bank

- This site is part of sponsorship.com, which offers fresh news and analysis of the sponsorship industry. IEG's purpose is to establish sponsorship as the fourth arm of marketing, alongside advertising, promotion, and public relations. It serves sponsors, sponsored properties, and agencies in sports, entertainment, event, cause, and association marketing.

- Free online listing of available sponsorship and marketing positions. Registration is required, but there is no charge.

- Allows job seekers to post their résumé and search available positions, and allows employers to search for talent or post positions.

JobsInSports.com

- Internet-based employment service dedicated to helping members find jobs in the sports industry.

- Subscribers have access to four main aspects of the website:
  - Job databases listing full-time employment opportunities
  - Internship center specifically listing sports internships for job seekers looking to gain experience
  - Sports and industry contacts, including names and contact information for prominent sports organizations
  - Résumé posting, allowing employers to review the résumés of job seekers

- The job databases list all levels of job opportunities in a variety of segments within the sports industry, including internships, entry-level, management, and executive positions.

- Jobs are organized into six categories: sports marketing/events/promotions, sports media, sports administration and management, health/fitness/recreation, sales, and computer/tech jobs.

- The job database is updated daily, and job openings remain in the database for 30 to 90 days.

- Subscription rates range from a 1-week trial membership for $9.95 to 1 year at $99. Month-to-month and 6-month memberships also are available.

- The site also provides a free newsletter containing advice on how to prepare for a career in the sports industry.

National Association of Collegiate Directors of Athletics (NACDA)

- Job listing for members of NACDA and its affiliate associations: National Association of Collegiate Marketing Administrators (NACMA), National Association of Athletic Development Directors (NAADD), International Collegiate Licensing Association (ICLA), National Association for Athletics Compliance (NAAC), College Athletics Business Management Association (CABMA), Football Championship Subdivision Athletics Directors Association (FCS ADA), Division II Athletics Directors Association (DII ADA), National Alliance of Two Year College Athletic Administrators (NATYCAA), and Minority Opportunities Athletics Association (MOAA).

- Positions focus on athletics administration and fall under the categories of athletics director (including associate and assistant positions), commissioner (including associate and assistant positions), executive director/president, marketing/promotions, development/fund raising, licensing, compliance, and business manager.

- Jobs range from internship and entry-level to executive positions.

- Jobs are posted for 30 days or until the deadline date. Job postings are updated daily.

- There is no fee for job seekers to view and respond to posted positions.

National Collegiate Athletic Association (NCAA)

- Lists employment opportunities in college athletics. Positions are located at member schools and the NCAA national office. Job postings are updated daily.

- Website has résumé posting capabilities.

- Available online free of charge.

- Employment opportunities in college athletics are organized by geographic region and job category (including type of position and sport). An e-mail notification service is available.

- Student-athletes benefit from NCAA CareerCoach, a job search, résumé posting, and career planning resource powered by Monster.com. This service also provides information for student-athletes on grants and scholarships.

- Employment opportunities at the NCAA national office are posted as they become available. The NCAA national office does not accept unsolicited résumés to keep on file.

- Jobs range from internship and entry-level to executive positions.

National Sports Marketing Network

- Provides job-matching services for both job seekers and employers. Both parties must be members of the National Sports Marketing Network.

- Services include a résumé bank, job board, and one-on-one career appointments.

- Student memberships cost $50 and individual memberships cost $100. Both types of memberships last 12 months.

- Positions are primarily sports marketing in focus and range from professional teams to agencies to media (among others).

- Most jobs are mid- to executive-level, with some entry-level positions also listed.

OnlineSports.com: Career Center

- Job bank for applicants interested in sports-related career opportunities.

- Résumé bank for sport and recreation employers.

- Links to jobsinsports.com.

PrecisionHire Sports

- Online applicant tracking system designed specifically to cater to the hiring needs of employers in the sports industry.

- Through an online team job board, job seekers are able to view and apply for open jobs free of charge.

- Job seekers also are able to make their résumés available for employers to search by creating a free PrecisionHire account.

- Job seekers can receive e-mail notifications of positions matching their desired criteria.

- Positions range from entry-level to executive.

SportsCastingJobs.com

- Provides job search and résumé posting for individuals interested in the sports broadcasting industry. Specializes in on-air positions, but there are also listings for sports production jobs, as well as editor, producer, and photographer listings.

- The site also allows multimedia résumés (incorporating audio and video files) as an additional service.

- Subscription rates for the job listing service range from $4.99 for a 10-day trial to $49.99 for a year. Membership fees for the multimedia database range from $9.99 for 1 month to $79.99 for 1 year. Members who elect to join both the multimedia database and the job listing service receive a bundled discount.

- Job listings are updated daily and posted for up to 60 days.

- Caters to all levels of experience.

SportsJobBoard.com

- Job board with listings from the Big Four, auto racing, MLS, minor league teams, colleges and universities, professional tennis, professional volleyball, professional golf, sporting goods organizations, sports marketing agencies, league offices, and more. Job postings include both the business (sales, marketing, media relations) and athletic side (coaching, scouting, trainers) of sport.

- Subscriber rates range from $9.95 for a 3-day trial to $79.95 for 3 months.

- Positions range from entry-level to top-level executive.

- Job postings are updated constantly and remain on the site until the position is filled.

SportsJobsUsa.com

- Subscriber-based online job site dedicated to the sports industry.

- Members have access to job listings, an internship database, and professional sports team contact information.

- Subscriber rates start at $9.95 for a weekly trial and range up to $29.95 on a per-month basis.

TeamWork Online

- Online recruiting software that resides on sports organizations' websites. Each organization has its own database, which ensures that applicants are specifically interested in that particular organization. Since its creation, TeamWork claims it has filled over 12,000 positions.

- Powers job boards of the Big Four, MLS, Arena Football League (AFL), and the WNBA, as well as sports conglomerates Mandalay, Comcast, AEG, Palace Sports, and many more.

- Job seekers have access to job listings free of charge. Participating sports organizations pay a fee to license the software. Free access by job seekers broadens the available pool of applicants.

- Caters to applicants seeking entry-level to middle-management positions.

- Job seekers can apply for a specific job with a specific organization or apply to receive future notifications via e-mail.

- The site also includes advice for job seekers in the sports industry, including interviews with sports executives (discussing what they seek in job candidates), executive stories, and career help from the site's founder, Buffy Filippell, in a section called "Ask Buffy." This material is an excellent complement to the information found in this book.

Buffy Filipell speaks to students at Mount Union College about careers in the sports industry. She is the founder and president of TeamWork Online, a sports executive search firm that has placed 350 executives in its 20-year history.

Women Sports Jobs

- Online job board with a particular focus on women and "helping women achieve their career dreams in the sports industry." Services include a job database, résumé preparation, career counseling, and interview preparation.

- Subscription rates vary by service. The job database can be accessed for $24.99 for a 1-month subscription and $69.99 for a 1-year subscription. Résumé preparation services are $129.99, while one-on-one sports career consultation costs $149.99. Job applicants purchasing multiple services receive a bundled discount. College career centers, sport management departments, and college libraries can access the job database for $179 per year. Applicants can post their résumé to the résumé bank free of charge.

- Caters to applicants seeking entry-level to mid-level positions, with a particular focus on mid-level positions.

- Job postings are updated daily and typically listed for 30 days.

- While the site provides a special focus for women and is committed to helping women achieve their career dreams in the sports industry, it is happy to provide its services to men as well.

WorkInSports.com

- Job board and employment resource available online. Nonmembers can post résumés, search jobs, and receive limited job notifications. Members can do these things as well as search contact information for over 300 key contacts in 22 leagues and sport-related categories (including all NFL, NBA, MLB, and NHL teams), view entire job descriptions, apply for jobs, receive career and résumé advice, and receive advance job notifications.

- Job listings range from internships to executive-level positions.

- Subscription rates range from $9.95 for a 1-week membership to $89.95 for 6 months.

- The website also includes a Resources section, which features career spotlights of dozens of prominent sports executives from a wide variety of professional sports and college athletic organizations. The spotlights talk about current industry trends and general career advice.

TEAM AND ORGANIZATION WEBSITES

Another extremely valuable resource to utilize in conducting a search for job or internship opportunities is the actual websites of professional teams and other sports organizations. Spending a little time on such sites will reveal that most sites link to a job or career opportunities page. For example, every MLB team website has a link at the bottom of the page called "Job Opportunities." It is common to find such links on most NFL, NBA, and NHL team pages. Although the jobs posted on these sites often may also be found on one or more of the employment sites detailed in the previous section, this is not always the case. Sometimes a team will choose to bypass the employment sites and post positions directly (and exclusively) on the team's website. Therefore, if you are interested in working for a team in a particular sport, it may be beneficial to visit each team's website and check the job/career links. Some employment links are not easily accessed, so it may take a bit of work to find the appropriate link. Common places to look include the bottom of the webpage, under a "contact us" page, or within links to information about the front office. Although not all sites will have an employment link, it still may be worth spending a few minutes on each site—you never know what you will find. Remember to check out league websites as well.

This same process will likely yield job opportunities in other sports organizations, such as facility management organizations, agencies, media outlets, and athletic supply companies (e.g., Nike, Adidas). It also can be helpful to conduct an Internet search using the organization's name and such terms as "jobs" or "careers." As an example, a Google search of "ESPN and jobs" will lead you to ESPN's job website. With a little bit of work and some creativity, you should be able to track down the job opportunities an organization has posted on its website.

WEBSITES OF SPORT MANAGEMENT PROGRAMS

Many sport management education programs host websites that link to information that may be helpful to job or internship seekers. For example, the University of Massachusetts Sport Management website includes links to the following categories of information: college sports; sports business; sports news; sports commentary; stadiums and arenas; leagues and entities; the Olympics; and job sites. It also is common to find links to sports associations on such sites. Sport management program websites provide an additional resource to use in gathering information about the industry, as well as searching for job and internship opportunities. Some of these websites may be available only to certain people, however, such as alumni and current students.

CAREER AND JOB FAIRS

Teams and leagues host an increasing number of job or career fairs each year. At a typical team-sponsored job fair, the team will gather professionals from a variety of local sports organizations and from various fields within those organizations. Attendees will be charged a fee somewhere around $25 to $35, which includes admission to the career fair, as well as a ticket to a game generally held immediately following the career fair.

As an example, a Boston Celtics Sports Career Fair (held February 28, 2007) advertised that representatives of the Boston Celtics, Boston Red Sox, and Fox Sports New England would be on hand. Fair attendees had access to professionals working in public relations, marketing, sales, broadcasting, finance, ticket office, journalism, and advertising. Attending such an event can be invaluable because you gain access to several industry professionals in an organized setting.

Career fairs can vary depending on who is hosting the event and organizational needs at that particular point in time. At a minimum, career fairs are an opportunity to make contacts and to conduct informal informational interviews to learn about various aspects of the industry. Sometimes it is best to treat them as an information-gathering mission. You will also find that some career fairs will be more job-oriented and will have an interview process scheduled into the agenda. Most likely, the types of positions you will find at this type of a career fair will be at the entry level, such as internships, volunteer, and part-time positions. Depending on the particular career fair, you also may be able to find some full-time job opportunities. You likely should not expect to find your dream job at a career fair, but it is possible to develop the necessary contacts at a career fair that might one day lead to obtaining your dream job. The best approach is to use career fairs to build your network, gather information, and learn about opportunities in the industry.

> *"Preparation is key to career fair success: 'A lot of people think you can show up, see who's there and wing it on the spot. That's a big mistake.'"*
>
> —Tory Johnson, CEO of New York-based
> Women for Hire

In an environment filled with job seekers, you must work to separate yourself from the other attendees. This is done through preparation. If possible, before the event, try to obtain a complete list of organizations that will be in attendance (even better would be the names of the actual organization representatives scheduled to attend). Similar to preparing for an interview, research the organizations that are of interest to you, and use this knowledge when talking to the organization's representatives. The more you know about the organizations (or individuals) beforehand, the more polished and professional you will appear. Along with building your confidence, this also will help you stand out from the other job seekers in attendance.

Typically, your interaction with any one organization at a career fair will be brief, so you will want to make the most of it. One way to do this is to have a well-rehearsed "elevator" pitch prepared. This is your 30-second personal commercial that communicates who you are, what you are looking for, and, most importantly, sells someone on why they should be interested in talking to you. Smoothly delivering such a pitch takes practice. The best advice is to have a clear understanding of what it is you want to get out of the career fair (and what you want in a career), and make sure you are able to deliver this message in a clear, concise manner. Your pitch is likely to be what the representative remembers about you once you walk away, so take the time to make sure it accurately portrays who you are and what you are all about.

It is important to have a professional appearance at career fairs, so make sure to dress as you would for an interview. Bring plenty of copies of your résumé and business cards and be prepared to pass them out. Remember to follow up with thank you notes to everyone you had a meaningful interaction with at the event.

SEARCH FIRMS SPECIALIZING IN EXECUTIVE RECRUITMENT

For those with a more substantial athletic employment history, some firms specialize in the recruitment and/or placement of athletic directors, head coaches, and other high-level sport management positions. Again, the following list is not meant to be exhaustive, but it provides an idea of the types of executive recruitment firms that exist in the sports industry. The organizations are listed in alphabetical order. One word of caution: executive search firms typically deal only with experienced candidates. Consequently, such firms should *not* be used to help land your first job or internship. They are really meant to aid in mid-career moves.

- *Carr Sports Associates:* A consulting firm that specializes in leadership placement and program advancement for intercollegiate athletic programs.

- *Executive Sports Placement:* Positions cover major league teams, minor league teams, sports marketing agencies, colleges and universities, and corporations with sports marketing divisions.

- *Parker Executive Search:* Executive search firm with specialized expertise in placing leaders at all levels of intercollegiate sports, including athletic administrators and coaches.

- *TeamWork Consulting:* A retained executive search firm, focusing on mid- to senior-level positions in the sports and live event industry. Past clients include NFL, MLB, NHL, NBA, NASCAR, and PGA Tour, among many others. Sister organization of TeamWork Online.

- *Alden and Associates:* An executive search firm for colleges and universities that specialize in athletic administrators and head coaches.

Endnotes

1. Mello, J. (2003, Oct. 12). Maximizing Opportunity at Job Fairs. *Boston Sunday Globe.*

The Internship: Getting Started

"The biggest limitation to the internship with basketball operations is the downtime. There are significant periods of time when there is not much work ... I took it upon myself to take advantage of the downtime to prove myself. Recognizing that I had some time on my hands, I decided to create a project for myself. The department was considering developing a fantasy basketball camp concept in which each camp would be given one set of official [NBA team] game-worn gear including warm-ups, shooting shirts, jerseys, and shorts. The department received several boxes of gear from the equipment manager. The 19 or so boxes included game gear worn from the last two seasons ... I created a spreadsheet to track the number of shorts, jerseys, shooting shirts, and warm-ups by size and by style (e.g., home, away, alternate uniforms). This allowed me to show the entire department my willingness to work hard, my organizational skills, and my initiative."

—Basketball operations intern with an NBA team

"If you're not making mistakes, then you're not doing anything. I'm positive that a doer makes mistakes."

—John Wooden, legendary UCLA men's basketball coach

"For future students seeking employment, I would recommend getting the best experience possible after completing course work. It may mean selecting a lower paying internship over a higher paying job, but it's important to keep things in perspective and think long-term."

—Marketing promotions associate for a major athletic footwear corporation

"There have been a few negatives to the internship. As with any internship, I have been asked to do a lot of the tedious work such as copying, faxing, and filing. The one limitation that I have had so far is that I have not been asked to write for publications. Instead of actually writing, I have been asked to edit a lot of other people's writing. The only other negative I have seen is that the employees of [the MLB franchise] are always busy. This does not give people a lot of time to sit down and explain why things are done the way they are done. In some instances, staff members would rather just do what they have to do quickly, rather than take the time to show you how to do things."

—A public relations intern with an MLB franchise

Generally speaking, deciding whether to complete an internship is a personal choice, but it is strongly recommended. There are basically three options you need to consider regarding internships:

1. Completing an internship for academic credit
2. Completing an internship that's *not* for academic credit
3. Not doing an internship

Why do an internship? An internship is an excellent way to gain experience and learn in a business environment. This is an opportunity to get your foot in the door, to show what you can do, and to make contacts to add to your network. Most likely, if it comes down to hiring someone who has successfully completed an internship versus someone who has not had one, an employer will choose the person with the internship experience. This doesn't mean that the person will do a better job than the person without the internship, but this is likely how it will play out. Consequently, option #3 is not an advisable path for you to take. Make every effort to do sevearl internships before entering the job market in search of full-time positions.

If you do plan on taking an internship, you can typically do so in one of two ways—either for academic credit or not for academic credit. Some organizations will not allow you to have an internship unless you do it for academic credit. This may be done for legal reasons; for example, if you are working for credit, organizations may not be under state minimum wage laws and worker's compensation laws. In fact, many internships for academic credit are unpaid—the student's compensation takes the form of the academic credit earned. If you are interested in internships for credit, planning a time for your internship within the framework of your academic career is very important.

It also is important to plan your internship during the proper season. Summer internships are fine in some industries, but if you're interested in baseball, you might need to do either a spring internship or one for spring, summer, and fall. Ideally, you will conduct your internship work during a time in which the organization is busiest. In college athletics, the institution may want you for the academic year (typically September to May) or the entire calendar year. Just be aware that the time period can vary tremendously by sport, industry, segment, and, sometimes, the position. For example, some marketing and sales work is done before the season, whereas operations work is done during the season.

You may want to consider taking an internship during the typical academic school year (approximately August/September to May). Most students plan to do their internships during the summer months, when they are not enrolled in classes. This creates greater competition for internship positions because there are more candidates looking to obtain internships. If you look for an internship in either the spring or fall, you may find reduced competition.

When selecting an internship, you should take the "best" internship available, in terms of experience, contacts, and future job possibilities. These should be the clear priorities, ahead of internship compensation and geographic location. Some students have insisted that they need to make a certain amount of money on the internship and/or be in a particular geographic location or region. This reduces the internships that this individual can consider and therefore the person may not get the best internship position. Granted, sometimes family, financial, and personal issues become factors; however, if they are not, you should focus on the quality of the internship. There may be only one internship opportunity for academic credit, meaning some people take no more than one internship. Consequently, the goal of the internship should be to find the very best one.

There are a number of items to consider in planning your internship search:

- What type of experience are you looking for? Do you want experience in a particular sport (such as football or baseball), or is it better to gain experience in a particular field (such as marketing or public relations)? This choice comes down to your career goals. Take the internship that is best suited to help you advance toward those goals.

- In what cities can you do the internship? Most internships are either unpaid or low-paying, so geographic location can play a large part in which internship opportunities are viable for you. If you do not have the financial resources available to you, focus your internship search on cities where you have relatives or friends who you can stay with during the internship. If no such options exist for you and you are doing your internship during the summer, consider cities or towns with large college student populations. In most college towns, it is rather easy to sublet a furnished apartment for the summer at a relatively reduced cost. Some colleges, such as Columbia University in New York City, rent their housing to students on summer internship. It may not be the most luxurious accommodations and you may have to share a room with someone else, but considering such housing options can greatly expand the number of geographic locations in which you can complete your internship. With a little hard work and creativity, you can find viable housing in many cities.

- Do you have the resources to do an internship and not get paid? For some people, doing an unpaid internship is not too troublesome. They can receive financial support from family and/or friends to help offset the lack of paid compensation. For others, this is simply not the case. They have to find a way to pay for rent, food, and car insurance and other living expenses. It is advisable to make a determination prior to starting your internship search as to what you can afford. If an unpaid or low-paying internship is not financially possible, focus on internships that are paid. It is important to note that some schools award internship "scholarships" to help offset a student's internship costs. If you do not have the financial means to cover the costs of an unpaid or low-paying internship, make sure to ask about any such funding opportunities at your institution. Another possibility is to plan ahead and put money aside to cover your internship costs. If you are receiving academic credit for the internship, there is also the possibility of obtaining student loans to help cover your costs.

THE QUALITY OF INTERNSHIP EMPLOYERS

One reality of the sports industry is that some organizations value their interns more than others. For example, some organizations work to create both a learning and a work envi-

---

INTERNSHIP STORY

You need to consider many factors when selecting the best internship opportunity. The following story is an example of the decision-making process one student undertook.

When deciding where to intern the summer between my two years of graduate school there were four major issues that I considered—location, compensation, company, and duties. To put myself in the best position possible, I talked to as many people as possible as early in the process as possible. This process began almost immediately upon arriving at school in September. Having said that, I didn't wind up getting any offers or having to make any decisions until late April. I was definitely surprised by how long the process took and by the general unresponsiveness and informality of the process.

My fiancée was in law school at the time and was also in need of a summer job and ideally, we wanted to be together. However, if we both had terrific jobs in different cities, we could deal with the situation for the summer. Geographically, I targeted Boston, Chicago, and the greater New York City/Connecticut area. I could live for free in Boston, or New York City, or Connecticut, and all of these cities were places my fiancée would be willing to move to after we graduated. Plus all three cities had multiple companies doing what I was interested in (sports marketing) and were places I had contacts.

Compensation was an issue—I wanted to get paid, although I would have been much more willing to take an unpaid internship if I could live for free in that particular location. I felt like the most important piece of the internship was the company I would work for and the duties I would have all summer. Ideally, I wanted to work for a big-name company with cachet, be given real, legitimate work for the summer, and get to meet as many people as possible. This would put me in the best position possible to get a full-time job with either the internship company or elsewhere in the industry after I graduated the following year.

I wound up with three offers. One offer was from a small company in Chicago that I was not particularly interested in (but was an offer nonetheless). The second offer was from the AST Dew Tour in Chicago, and the third offer was with Octagon out of their Washington, DC/Virginia office. My fiancée also had an offer in each of these locations, so it was pretty much my decision as to which job would be best for me and my career development.

It was a very tough decision for me. The Dew Tour offered a very substantial workload/project for the summer, it paid decently for a sports internship, and I would get to travel a bit, which was nice. The work was primarily market research in focus, and would allow me to develop important skills I could use as a sports marketer. The Dew Tour President and CEO also is a University of Massachusetts sport management alum, which would create a great networking opportunity. Octagon, on the other hand, was a bigger name and would have had more cachet moving forward. The Octagon offer was also unpaid and I would have not been able to live for free. Additionally, the Octagon work would be more focused on public relations than actual sports marketing.

In the end, I decided to go with the Dew Tour. While not quite the name recognition as an Octagon internship, the Dew Tour internship was more closely related to the type of work I hoped to be doing upon graduation. I just felt the market research experience would put me on a better career path than working in a public relations capacity for the summer. As an added bonus, the compensation was nice, and Chicago was ultimately my fiancée's first choice as well. Looking back a year later, I have no regrets about my decision. I had a worthwhile experience with the Dew Tour, met some good people and feel my time there will help me moving forward in my career.

This former student now works for Octagon in the company's sports marketing/consulting division.

---

ronment for interns. They value the work the interns provide, but they also accept a responsibility to provide a learning experience for the interns in return. This may be accomplished by rotating the intern through a variety of positions, holding regular meetings between the intern and the supervisor, and setting up meetings with the intern and other company employees. All of these measures are meant to provide the best possible learning experience for the intern.

In contrast, other organizations use interns primarily as low-paid, but necessary labor. Often needing the services of a full-time employee, some organizations will instead turn to an intern or interns. For example, instead of hiring an assistant media relations director at $35,000, an organization can pay an intern $12,000 to complete the same work. To ensure the intern is productive, the organization might give the intern only limited duties or some time-intensive responsibilities. Although this may save the organization money, it greatly limits the intern's opportunity for growth and development.

"Internships are no pay or low paid labor, but we all went through it."

—Highly ranked executive in a college athletics department

Although there are many stories of interns doing nothing but making copies or getting coffee, employers do not always set out to be poor internship employers. Often it is a matter of poor planning, lack of execution, and/or lack of good supervision. Employers set out with good intentions to create a rewarding and positive internship experience, but then the demands of work set in, and the quality of the intern's experience is neglected in order to meet the demands of the business. This is where an established internship program comes in handy. Organizations with a strong history of working with and managing interns are likely to be more capable of providing a suitable internship environment because they have years of experience to learn from.

WHAT TO LOOK FOR FROM INTERNSHIP EMPLOYERS

Internships can vary greatly from organization to organization, so it is very important to carefully decide which organization you choose to do your internship with. In analyzing the organization, first look at the nature of the organization's internship program. Does the organization have an established internship program? If so, is there an opportunity to speak to past interns to assess their satisfaction with the internship? If so, ask about their experiences on the internship. Were they given a variety of responsibilities? Were they given direction and feedback? Although every internship has a certain amount of gopher work, did at least a *portion* of the internship give the person some responsibility and, possibly, the opportunity to learn on the job? It is also useful to examine the size of the internship "class." If an organization brings in 25 interns a year, this increases the competition among interns and may make it more difficult for you to stand out; however, the camaraderie among interns may be strong, thus creating a more enjoyable internship environment. Competition among interns will be addressed in greater detail in Chapter 9, *Internships: Be Prepared for Bumps in the Road.*

Another important aspect to consider is the nature of work the interns do. Is the internship a rotational position (meaning, will you have an opportunity to work in more than one area of the organization)? Participating in a rotational internship program is an excellent opportunity to learn about the various functions and departments of sports organizations. Experiencing multiple areas during your internship may help you decide what type of position you would most like when seeking full-time employment.

I also recommend students examine an organization's track record with past interns. In particular, what has happened to the interns who worked for this organization? Were any of them hired after they completed their internships? Some organizations make it a practice or at least a priority to hire interns when positions become available. For those interns who were not hired by the organization, has the organization been helpful in assisting them with their full-time employment/job search? Be careful of becoming too

critical of the organization here because sometimes an organization will not support its former interns because the organization feels that the former intern did not do an adequate job. The best advice is to do such a good job on the internship that the organization hires you, and if not, will pick up the phone and support you when you are looking for a job somewhere else in the sports industry.

Many schools require students to submit an internship report as part of the school's internship program. It's advisable that students do as much homework about an internship employer as possible, and one good resource for such homework is the internship reports. Students should review the reports of employers they are targeting to ascertain what life is like as an intern at the organization. It is also good if a student can review more than one internship report from the same employer. This allows the student to look at the scope of responses and to see multiple points of view. Reading the reports may also provide ideas on what types of internships you should be looking for, particularly for those who are struggling with their internship search. Although not all programs have such reports, it's well worth the effort to find out whether your school does.

GETTING THE MOST OUT OF YOUR INTERNSHIP

"Go hard or go home. Focus, don't fold. Be committed, not just involved. Will power over won't power. Contribute, don't contaminate. Warriors act and fools react!"[1]

—Dennis Mannion, COO of the Los Angeles Dodgers and former senior vice president of business ventures of the Baltimore Ravens

The sports industry has changed. In the early 1980s, internships were viewed as part of the academic experience. Students would go into an internship, learn about the job, and learn about what it would take to help the organization. In the 1990s, the philosophy for the University of Massachusetts changed to reflect industry changes. Although students should still learn from the internship, they must be prepared to make a contribution to the organization in the early stages of their internship. By making early contributions to the organization, the student would

Dennis Mannion is the chief operating officer of the Los Angeles Dodgers. He has worked in all four league sports: Major League Baseball (Dodgers and Philadelphia Phillies), National Football League (Baltimore Ravens), National Hockey League (Colorado Avalanche), and National Basketball Association (Denver Nuggets).

In the early 1980s, a student in the master's program here at University of Massachusetts, who was a longtime fan of a particular NBA franchise, asked me to advise him about whether to pursue an internship with that franchise. I discouraged him. I told him that I know you're a big fan, I know you are a good student, and you look like you have plenty of potential, but the last eight or nine interns we've sent to this team have not been offered jobs at the end of the internship. (This was true.) Therefore, I encouraged him to pursue something else.

Well, like many wayward young people, this person did not take the advice of his elder (me). And it is a good thing he didn't. Sure enough, at the end of his internship, this NBA team needed some assistance running its facility. Now, 25+ years later, this person is still with the same team as a vice president.

The bottom line is that I cannot in good conscience tell students *not* to follow their hearts, but I can advise them of probabilities. For every one person like this one who pursues an internship in a high-risk high-reward position, there will be several qualified individuals who will end up with nothing to show for it. Positions are hard to come by in attractive organizations because people don't leave very often.

---

then be given more responsibility, and would be able to make a tangible contribution to the organization. At the end of the internship, the organization would have a much better understanding of what the individual could contribute, and possibly would realize that the person had become indispensable. Now, how does a person put him- or herself in a position to make a contribution early in the internship? There are three ways to do this:

- Get experience during the school year in a sports organization on campus, such as the athletic department, radio station, school newspaper, local newspaper, or local sports organization.

- Volunteer or work during the summers prior to the internship.

- Get involved in any experiential learning opportunities your school may provide, such as a practicum class. Please refer to Chapter 5 for additional information on such classes offered in sport management programs. If your school provides similar opportunities, take full advantage of the offerings.

Case Study   *Life as a Minor League Intern: Promotions Operations for the Durham Bulls*

The week surrounding the Fourth of July is typically a busy time for minor league baseball teams. Crowds are larger than normal with the holiday and nightly fireworks shows—it never fails to amaze me as to how powerful fireworks are in attracting people to minor league baseball games. At the Durham Bulls, the fireworks are launched very close to the field, so after the show there is a sizeable amount of debris on the field. For whatever reason we did not have blowers for the first couple of shows, so we had to literally rake left and center field to get all the junk off the field. This was a job for the entire front office, including the general manager!

July 3 was particularly crazy because one of the promotions assistants called in sick, and there was some miscommunication from his replacement, leaving me with just one promotions assistant for the on-field games. It was definitely not an ideal situation because we had a sold-out crowd. Any mistakes would look especially bad. Luckily, everything went off without a hitch. I viewed the situation as a great opportunity to practice some crisis-management skills.

The Durham Bulls played a game on July 3 and then headed out on a road trip. To bring in additional revenue over the July 4th holiday, the team hosted four exhibition games between the USA Baseball National Team and the Japanese Collegiate National Team. The Japan team's presence attracted about 100 Japanese media members, so the Bulls secured a sponsorship deal with PENTAX for the series because of the company's Japanese roots. There were PENTAX signs everywhere and their name was even watered into the infield—definitely a lesson in creative sponsorship.

For the last game of the Team USA–Japan series, I got to run the entire show for promotions operations without the aid of a supervisor. This required me to write the game script, pick the promotional games, and direct everything from the press box. Many of the events centered around the Japanese team, including drummers performing between innings, 30 kids who went on the field pregame with the Japanese team, and 10 kids who did the public address announcements for the Japanese at-bats. This was my first real interaction with the Japanese culture, so it was a little stressful. In the end, everything went smoothly, and I can now say I have legitimate promotions operations experience with some international cultural experience as an added bonus.

By using these opportunities to develop your skills and abilities, you will be in a much better position to make early and meaningful contributions to the internship organization.

You should also maintain a professional attitude throughout your internship experience. Invariably, you will be assigned some work that you feel is tedious. It is important that you do not project an "I'm bored" persona while completing this work. Consider the internship to be one long job interview, and act accordingly. In addition, do not ask for more work or different work, unless you have completed what was already assigned to you.

For help in finding internship opportunities, please refer to Chapters 6 and 7 of this book.

Endnotes

1. What I Like . . . Dennis Mannion. (2007). *Street & Smith's SportsBusiness Journal*, vol. 10, issue 17, p. 42.

Internships: Be Prepared for Bumps in the Road

"You have to perform at a consistently higher level than others. That's the mark of a true professional."

—Joe Paterno, head football coach for the
Penn State Nittany Lions

"Don't compromise yourself. You're all you've got."

—Betty Ford, former First Lady
of the United States

Although an internship is highly recommended and can have many positive features, some internships are less than perfect with a number of problems. It is important to remember that an internship—like any job—will have aspects that are frustrating and troublesome, some more than others. This chapter examines some of the most common problems that you may face as an intern. Hopefully, it will help you make more informed decisions during your search

for an internship and leave you better prepared to face similar problems.

One problem that many interns face is the lack of financial compensation or benefits. When searching for an internship, one should be aware that many are unpaid and offer few monetary benefits. Some companies will do their best to lessen financial strain of their interns by providing housing, meals, and access to part-time jobs. Another frustration

Case Study   *Bait and Switch*

The following case study is taken from an actual report filed after a student internship. The names have been changed.

The biggest drawback of my work experience was the handling and organization of the internship program. Originally, when Ann Smith interviewed me on campus, I was asked to rank my top seven internship position choices. I then talked to her about my top two choices, and she said I would surely get one of those positions in the rotation. When I arrived on the first day of work, I found out that these two positions were year-round and not part of the regular rotation. I then was informed that I did not get either of these placements. I was not pleased with the situation because my main reason for taking this internship was to obtain experience in one of my top two choices, team operations. Additionally, Ann had told me there was a good chance that a portion of the intern's housing would be subsidized. In talking with her a month before I arrived in town,

she mentioned that the housing was almost in place. I then received a phone call from her 2 weeks before I left and she said everything had fallen through (i.e., I would have to find my own housing). The timing of the whole ordeal was what made me angry. I didn't mind paying for housing, but I had been told that the organization would help interns with their living expenses. In addition to this, Ann Smith left the organization shortly after the interns arrived, and the program was turned over to the human resource manager. This further complicated the rotation as everyone was left in the dark about his or her upcoming placements. We were never given a choice on where we would like to work or a new starting date. We were only told we would receive an e-mail sometime in mid-October with our new assignments, and everyone would start at these positions on the following day. Overall, I just felt everything was organized poorly.

among interns can be the lack of responsibility given to them. As an intern, one should expect to do a fair share of busy-work (such as making copies or getting coffee), but one also should be given projects that will help develop into useful, professional experience. One should always make sure to inquire about the level of responsibility that accompanies the position when applying for an internship. An additional problem that many interns face is that of an unsatisfactory supervisor. If possible, you should try to get learn about the person who you will be working under before committing to the position. A great internship position can be greatly hampered by a poor supervisor. Finally, it is not uncommon for interns to feel as if they are "second class citizens" within the company because of their position on the bottom rung of the company ladder. Obviously, these problems and issues do not arise in every internship, but it is important to be aware of them during your internship search.

The following Case Studies have been provided to give you a first-hand account of other common problems that can arise during an internship. Hopefully, these stories will help you better prepare for the bumps in the road, as well as understand the importance of knowing the details of a job ahead of time.

For some placements, there may be only one student intern in the entire organization. In others, there may be

Case Study   *Intern Competition*

The following case study is taken from an actual report filed after a student internship with a major multipurpose athletic facility.

Since there were two other interns also in the marketing department, I couldn't always take the best jobs … Another limitation was the relationship I had with one of the other interns. She was always trying to compete with me and lost. I simply did a better job and was put in charge of more important tasks. This burned her up, but who cares. I was there to showcase my talents and not to make someone else look better.

interns in various departments throughout the organization. In still other situations, there are many interns in the same department. For example, some organizations will hire 10 to 12 student interns to sell tickets. At the end of the internship, the organization will hire the top one or two salespeople. So, except for the first situation, there can be competition among interns because the interns realize that most of them are not likely to be hired. This can lead to some rather difficult situations. Make sure you do your due diligence and

Case Study   *Bigger Isn't Always Better*

The following case study is taken from an actual report filed during a student internship with a major Division I-A college athletic department. The names of persons, facilities, and organizations that would identify the author have been changed.

It's not at all what I expected. While I was at Small-Time University, I was a sports information intern, but I felt like I was working with the entire department and learned what everyone did. At Big-Time University, I felt like a member of the sports information staff, not the athletic department staff. People were not especially friendly, and only really talk to you if they need you to do something. I did not necessarily feel like a part of the department. The benefits were nonexistent. As staff members, we did not get complimentary tickets to anything, we did not get to use the facilities, and we had to pay for parking. I guess employment at Big-Time University is such a desirable thing, they do not have to provide these benefits to their employees.

The internship really made me question what I want to do for a career. Being surrounded by big-time college athletics on a daily basis has shown me what it is all about. I know for a fact now that sports information is not the path I want to take. I am way too impatient to put up with the lazy and impatient members of the media. When I was working

at Small-Time University, I worked hard trying to get them interested. Now that I'm in a place where the media are interested, I have no interest in helping them. I cannot tell you how many stupid questions I have answered. Unfortunately, I don't have a lot of patience, so when someone calls with a dumb question, I get annoyed. Hopefully, when school starts and students start working in the office, they'll answer the phones and I won't have to deal with it.

One of the reasons I got into the sports information world was an attempt to promote athletes who don't normally get publicity for their hard work. I've been working at Big-Time University with the defending NCAA champion [nonmajor sport] team, which includes an Olympian and four All-Americans, and still no one cares. It has taught me that there are limitations to what I can do in sports information. No matter how hard I work, and how good the team is, the big sports are going to get all the publicity. That's great—they work hard and deserve to be recognized for it. But I was hoping that the other hard-working athletes would be recognized in the local media, too. I get frustrated when my hard work does not yield the results that I am hoping for, and it frustrates me that my hard work for [aforementioned nonmajor sport] does not create exposure for the hard-working athletes.

Case Study　*Gaining the Competitive Advantage?*

One of my students described a situation she encountered with one of her fellow interns. Turns out, her fellow intern took the competitive nature of the internship to a very interesting level. As a means to stand out from the other interns, he became friends with the parking lot security guard. In doing so, he made arrangements for the security guard to call him whenever the GM came into the office during the weekend. This intern would then get in his car and drive to the office and look like an overly industrious workaholic. Unfortunately, his fellow interns and some full-time employees found out about this arrangement, and he was ostracized. This story clearly demonstrates that sports are extremely competitive, both on and off the field.

understand the situation. Ask how many interns will be in the department that you are interviewing with and how many interns will be in the organization. If you have a problem during your internship, you have limited options. One is to consult with your internship supervisor. Within the organization, you could consult with the supervisor of internships at your academic program.

Sometimes, a student will discover during the internship that a particular industry is just not a good fit for him or her. Although you should certainly not strive for this situation, and should do as much research as you can about the industry and organization in advance, sometimes you can only unearth your feelings about something by actually doing it. If this happens, it is important to be realistic and look on the bright side. This is the advantage of an internship. It is temporary. You are more than welcome to walk away from the experience after completing it, without burning any bridges with your supervisors. Even if you dislike the nature of the work, it is quite possible to emerge from the internship with contacts, who will provide you with good references, counsel, or even friendship in the future.

CHAPTER TEN

The Big Step: Internship to First Job

"It is a rough road that leads to the heights of greatness."

—Seneca, Roman dramatist, philosopher, and politician

"I learned to take the first job that you have in the business that you want to get in to. It doesn't matter what the job is; you get your foot in the door."

—Wes Craven, American film director

"In my opinion, there are several key factors to consider when attempting to secure a position in professional sports:

Be willing to work for free.

Be willing to work anywhere in the country.

Be the first in the office, the last to leave.

Make a positive impression on someone.

Attempt to make yourself indispensable in some phase of the job.

Take on as much responsibility as the organization will give you.

Be courteous and get along with people."

—A then-intern with a Major League Baseball club, now (6 years later) assistant general manager of a different MLB club

The step from internship to first job often is more difficult than the step from school to the internship. Many sport management majors drop out of the sports industry after their internship and do not get a full-time job. One of the primary goals of the internship is to get a job at the end of it, either at the organization that sponsors the internship or at another organization.

FULL-TIME JOB OR SECOND INTERNSHIP?

Finding employment after an internship can be quite difficult, and many people struggle with this. Consequently, people often ask for advice as to what they should do if they are unable to obtain a full-time sports position following the internship. If you cannot find full-time employment,

spending all of your time looking for a full-time position may not be the best solution. In general, it is recommended that a person should stay involved in the sports industry, even if it is only through an internship. The advantage of staying in an internship in the sports industry is that the person is more likely to be called to fill a full-time position when one becomes available. It also provides an opportunity to meet new people and to expand your network. However, each situation is different. Each person has different circumstances and priorities. Thus, you must weigh all of the costs/benefits and opportunity costs of a second internship. In addition to taking a second internship, part-time work (see "Part-Time Work" later in this chapter) may provide a viable alternative because it allows you to stay connected to the industry while you are looking for full-time employment.

THE BEST TIME TO LOOK FOR A FULL-TIME POSITION

You will find there is no typical "hiring season" when looking for employment in the sports industry. For the most part, organizations practice what is called "just-in-time hiring," meaning an organization does not simply hire for the sake of hiring, but waits until there is a legitimate business need before hiring an employee. A business need can be created either by an employee leaving the organization (requiring the organization to replace that employee) or through business growth sufficient to warrant adding a new position. Therefore, you generally will not find an organization in the sports industry hiring X number of new college graduates each and every year as a matter of practice. There is simply not a need to do so. In contrast, such a practice is somewhat common in the nonsports business world, particularly with larger companies.

As a job-search tip, when it comes to the sports industry, often the best time to look for a full-time position is during the organization's off-season, if there is one. This is usually because employees leave after the busy time (for example, in colleges, in May or June at the end of the academic year). Although positions do sometimes open up during the season, it is much more common to find opportunities once a season has ended. Ultimately, though, when it comes to finding full-time employment opportunities, it is all about being in the right place at the right time—you never know when an opportunity may arise.

PART-TIME WORK

There are many benefits to working part-time in the sports industry. For example, a part-time position may be sufficient to satisfy your need to be involved in the sports industry. Upon working part-time, you may discover that working in the sports industry is not your ultimate dream. Part-time positions also help you to gain a better understanding about the organization and the types of full-time positions there. This should place you in a better position to learn about new full-time openings as they arise. Lastly, part-time positions are an excellent way to build connections. You will undoubtedly make connections with those you work with directly, but you may also have an easier time gaining access to higher-level executives for informational interviews.

Ethics

If you are ready to commit to an internship or a job, and you give a verbal or e-mail indication that you are going to accept the internship offer, then you should do everything possible to honor that commitment. And this certainly applies if you sign an internship contract. Make sure that all the paperwork for the actual contract gets done, in order to make sure that the parties are in agreement on all the details. The internship contract will formalize the agreements, and will hopefully prevent misunderstandings about the responsibilities, expectations, compensation, expenses, and so on.

So what happens if another internship or job offer comes in after you have committed to an internship? It is important that you still honor the commitment to the organization; however, there are a couple ways to avoid this situation. One is not to commit to the internship until you have checked on the status of any other internship or job application that you have pending. So, for example, if there is an internship or job that might be more attractive to you, but you have not yet heard from the organization, you should feel free to contact the organization and let them know that you have another opportunity, but would like to consider this organization if a decision is going to be made within the

---

Case Study   *Career Transitions*

The following story is an account of how one high-level sports media executive first broke into the sports industry. The person's name has been changed.

Ken Fuchs is the vice president and general manager of Golf.com and FanNation.com for *Sports Illustrated*. He began his professional career as a corporate attorney working in Chicago. After practicing law for 3 years, Ken decided he wanted to make a transition into business. He started contacting investment banking firms and media companies, but was having difficulty finding a position to his liking. Ken also applied to and got into business school. However, already armed with one advanced degree, Ken decided that obtaining a second advanced degree was not in his best interest. Unable to find a company willing to take a chance on him, Ken

chose to follow a much less conventional route—he offered to work for *Sports Illustrated* for free. *Sports Illustrated* accepted his offer. Working at a business manager level, Ken completed various projects and performed so exceptionally that he was offered a job after only 1 month. Ken has gone on to a rewarding career in business development and operations, working for both *Sports Illustrated* and Fox Interactive Media. He credits three attributes to his success: knowledge of new media, good contacts in the industry, and an ability to adapt and learn quickly. More than anything, Ken's story goes to show that sometimes you have to be creative and do whatever it takes to land that elusive first job. Offering to work for free is a rather bold move; however, once Ken got his opportunity, he did everything he could to capitalize on it.

near future. If the organization is not going to make a decision within the time frame you need, then you should probably thank the organization and ask that you no longer be considered. For more advice on this topic, see the section entitled "Prioritize" in Chapter 4, *Mapping the Plan*.

If you do receive a job offer early in the internship—for example a couple weeks into a 3-month internship—you have two choices: one is to thank the organization that's made the offer to you and say that you feel obligated to complete the internship, and would be very interested if the offer is still there at the end of the internship (or that you can commit to the job now, but cannot start work until your internship commitment has been fulfilled). The second choice is to tell them that you're currently in an internship, and you'll have to check with your current supervisor (then check with the employer, but if they won't release you, you probably shouldn't leave). It is important when you sit down with your supervisor to ask permission to leave that you stress:

- You did not solicit this opportunity during the internship.

- You're committed to fulfilling the internship and would only leave with the blessing of the organization.

However, it is important to begin your job search before the internship ends. It takes weeks (and sometimes more) to land a job. Generally, it's advisable that about halfway through the internship, the intern needs to begin considering what's going to happen 6–7 weeks down the road. Set up a meeting with the internship supervisor to discuss your situation. The reason for doing it this early is that, if you (as an intern) are going to be leaving the organization, you need some time to look for an opportunity. During your meeting, the internship supervisor might say, "Thank you, but we don't have any job opportunities, nor can we extend the internship." This may or may not be related to your performance on the job. The organization may also offer you a full-time job; if so, you certainly want to get all the details about the job. For many people, it is recommended that they take the job, because coming out of an internship they are unlikely to have many job opportunities. However, if you are fortunate enough to have other opportunities, you should

communicate effectively with your internship supervisor, so you can clearly understand how long an offer is on the table and decide which offer you should accept.

One other scenario sometimes arises. The organization may offer to extend the internship. There are a few things to consider here. First, what are the terms and conditions (e.g., is it the same rate of compensation or does it change)? Second, check with the university internship director to see whether it is okay to extend the internship. Third, you need to weigh the alternatives and opportunity cost of extending the internship. Are there other jobs and internships available? Or should you not extend the internship so you can stay at home and focus on the job search, and be more available for job searches and interviews? Or should you take a higher paying job that's not in the sports industry?

If your internship employer does not have an opening for a full-time employee, and they do not have the ability or desire to extend the internship, ask whether they know about any opportunities in other organizations. Doing so communicates your preferences for the type of work or type of jobs you prefer. You are more likely to find work of the same type (because you now have some experience). Most employers understand how difficult it can be to break into the industry and are willing to help out interns who have performed exceptionally well for an organization during their internship. If you have a good relationship with your internship employer, there is nothing wrong with soliciting his help in your job search.

A word of caution about searching for other employment opportunities. Employers want people who are committed to their job (even if the job is merely an internship), and are likely to look unfavorably on someone seeking opportunities at other organizations at the wrong time. Be discrete in your search for post-internship employment, and avoid job searching on company time. If you do need to request time off from your internship for job search activities (such as an interview in another city), offer to make up the lost time as a courtesy to your current employer. This will help to preserve the good relationships you have built during your internship experience.

Mentors

"Hitch your wagon to a star."

—Ralph Waldo Emerson, American author, poet, and philosopher

"Many receive advice, only the wise profit from it."

—Harper Lee, Pulitzer Prize-winning American author

Successful people sometimes do not make it to the top entirely on their own. They often find someone who will support, push, and motivate them to succeed. It is common for such coaches to be labeled mentors.

One definition for the word *mentor* is "a wise and trusted counselor or teacher."[1] A mentor can be very helpful to a young person entering the field of sport management, and in fact may be helpful to the person throughout his career. There are numerous stories both within sports and outside of sports of a highly placed, experienced, and usually older person guiding, helping, and advising a person throughout a person's career. If a person has a mentor who can serve in this role, it can significantly increase his chances of success in the field. Many times the first mentor a young person has, as the definition suggests, is a teacher or faculty member. Many sport management faculty members spend a great deal of time and take delight in mentoring their students. Sometimes this assistance occurs only in the initial phases of the person's career. In other instances, teachers and professors continue to guide and open doors for former students as they progress through their careers.

Another place where a mentor can be found is at the place of employment or within the industry where he is working. Sometimes a young person can find an experienced older person, within the organization or within the industry, who is willing to offer help and guidance. In other situations, mentors may be personal friends or friends of the family, and therefore may have an interest in helping the young person.

Is every person of stature a mentor to someone? No. Some people do not mentor at all; others mentor a little, and a few (often in academia) do quite a bit of mentoring.

For those who mentor, why do they do it? There are many different reasons—sometimes it is because of a friendship with the family or a business associate; sometimes it is because the person to be mentored shows great potential; sometimes it is because the mentor just likes the individual; and for teachers and faculty, some view it as part of the job. Teachers and faculty often derive a great deal of satisfaction from a former student's career success. They want to do everything they can to help them get started, and later, help them make the right decisions so they can continue their career progress.

Mentors can provide an objective, experienced, usually unbiased opinion on the considerations (both positive and negative) a person needs to weigh. Some of the questions mentees commonly ask mentors include:

- Which internship should I take?
- Should I extend my internship or take a full-time job outside of the sports industry?
- Should I leave my internship or job, which would enable me to spend more time looking for my next job?
- Should I leave my job after only 1 year to take another job?
- Is this job enough of a move up, or should I wait for something better?
- Should I sign a covenant not to compete?
- There's going to be change in the ownership of the organization. How can I protect my position in the organization?
- Can you contact organization *X* to let them know that I'm interested in a position? I cannot personally do it because they might interpret it as disloyal to my current employer.

- My company has asked me to sign a legal document to protect its trade secrets. Should I sign it?

- What compensation, terms, and employment conditions should I be asking for?

These are only some of the many questions a person might face during his career. There are certainly many places to seek answers to and opinions regarding these questions, including family, friends, colleagues, and former classmates. It also may be important to seek several opinions. However, it can be very helpful to have a mentor to rely on who is knowledgeable, experienced, unbiased, and has only *your* best interest in mind.

For those of you who do not have mentoring relationships with a teacher or friend of the family, how does one find and/or establish a mentoring relationship? Often a mentoring relationship starts when the mentor, in recognition of some "potential," offers you some advice. Other times, it starts with your seeking out a potential mentor to ask a question or have an informational interview. From there, a mentoring relationship may develop. Some people choose to mentor someone after they see an aspect of themselves in that person. Others simply look for smart people, who conduct themselves professionally, and whom they think would appreciate the advice, time, and effort the mentor is willing to give them. In most cases, a mentor looks for someone who has a great potential to succeed, someone that he likes personally, and someone who is a willing and able listener (although not necessarily doing everything that the mentor suggests). And sometimes, finding a mentor is beyond your control.

It is very important for the person who wants to keep this mentoring relationship going to stay in touch with the mentor on some sort of periodic basis. What can detract from a relationship is when a mentee does not acknowledge the help that he has received. Another way of losing a relationship with a mentor is when the mentee *only* contacts the mentor when he needs something. Although there is nothing wrong with seeking the help of a mentor in a time of need, this should not be the only time a mentee contacts the mentor. The relationship must be one of give and take and must be built up over time. Showing a genuine interest in a mentor can go a long way toward building a lasting and meaningful mentor/mentee relationship.

Mentoring should not be viewed as an all out quid pro quo. Just because a mentor offers you advice doesn't mean you have to take it. Additionally, just because a mentor does you a favor does not mean you should feel obligated to reciprocate in an excessive fashion. Mentors typically have different degrees of contact with those whom they have mentored. Some relationships are very personal, with mentees going as far as to invite their mentors to special occasions such as their weddings. In such mentor/mentee relationships, mentees are likely to correspond with their mentors quite frequently. Other relationships are not as personal, with less frequent correspondence. Both of these scenarios can work quite well. Mentees should simply utilize common courtesy, and keep their mentors informed at reasonable intervals. Mentors do not necessarily have to be among your closest friends, but they should also not be viewed as an employment agency. As a way to reciprocate the mentor/mentee relationship, it is also nice to provide mentors with feedback on any advice or help they have given.

Although not typical, sometimes people have more than one mentor. This can be helpful to get different perspectives, particularly if the mentors are in different organizations. However, having more than one mentor from the same organization could create complicated situations and difficulties, particularly if the mentors feel as if they are in competition with one another. Generally, it is advisable for people to avoid having more than one mentor working in the same organization.

If you do have two or more mentors, it can become difficult to adequately reciprocate in the mentor/mentee relationship. The cultivation of a good mentoring relationship involves a large investment in one-on-one time, and it can be difficult to maintain connections with multiple mentors, while also maintaining a good level of productivity in your job and/or studies. Also, good mentors have numerous mentees to choose from. Good mentors are hard to come by, so if you find one, stay with him.

Please do not misinterpret this to mean that you should limit your *network* to only one person. You should treat *everyone* with respect, and maintain as large a network of contacts as you can. Sometimes people, other than your mentor, have a particular area of expertise from which you can benefit when investigating a particular subject. But a mentor is someone who is your *main* go-to person whom you will rely upon in most circumstances. This can create some confusing situations. For example, what if your mentor is the vice president of the company that you work for, but you spend a significant amount of time reporting to a middle manager that works under him? Obviously, in this case, you should be careful not to undermine the authority of your middle manager boss by spending an inordinate amount of time communicating with the vice president. Perhaps, unless he is a close friend of the family or someone with whom you've already cultivated a great relationship, this vice president may not be your ideal mentor. Although sometimes it is unavoidable, you want to avoid creating nasty office politics situations or being perceived as a "brown-noser."

Sometimes people have mentors early in their career, and not later. Some people have mentors throughout their entire career. Sometimes people find their mentors later in their career. Must you have a mentor to be successful? No. It is certainly not a precondition to success. However, if a mentoring relationship is established, it can be mutually satisfying and beneficial to both parties.

Endnotes

1. Dictionary.com. Retrieved July 20, 2008, from http://dictionary.reference.com/browse/mentor.

Presenting Yourself

"If you knew how much work went into it, you wouldn't call it genius."

—Michelangelo, Italian Renaissance painter, sculptor, architect, poet, and engineer

RÉSUMÉS

People can improve their résumés in two ways:

1. Be *perfect*—no mistakes with good organization and presentation
2. Pursue experiences and opportunities that beef up the résumé

This section will help the reader in both areas. However, you should be aware that numerous additional resources are available to assist job seekers in the first point (such as books on how to construct a résumé). Many, if not most, of the general principles of résumé construction are the same in the sports industry as they are in any other sector of business. Therefore, you are encouraged to consult one or more books that cover résumé construction. For your convenience, a number of these books are listed at the end of this chapter. Also, if you are in a school setting, you should consult your campus career center and/or a professor who may have some résumé writing expertise.

It is important to remember that a good résumé will *not* necessarily get you a job. Typically, employers look at each individual résumé for only a short period of time, often 30 seconds or less per résumé. During this review, employers look for reasons to either keep or dismiss the person from the applicant pool. A good résumé simply keeps you in the applicant pool, which may get you an interview. However, a bad résumé *can* lose you a job, by preventing you from getting an interview in the first place.

It also is important to realize there is no such thing as a perfect résumé format. The judgment of résumés is a somewhat subjective process. One employer may be very impressed with your résumé, while another might not like its composition and will take you out of the applicant pool on the spot. Although it is important to obtain as many opinions about your résumé as possible, know that the ideal résumé is the one that gets you an interview, and this can change dramatically from employer to employer.

Presentation and Organization

As mentioned previously, there is no one perfect way to write a résumé; however, there are a number of generally accepted practices.

One Page or Two Pages?

The general rule is that a résumé should be one page for people in the early stages of their career. If you are a recent college graduate, your résumé should be no more than a page long. For persons with more work experience and in the middle stages of their career, opinions in the business and sports business worlds differ on the importance of keeping your résumé at one page. There are numerous stories of executives who automatically throw a résumé in the trash if it is longer than a page; however, this may be nothing more than urban folklore. In general, there are exceptions to the one-page rule, especially in situations where your work experience is particularly applicable to the job. However, if you are a borderline case (perhaps 5 or 10 years out of college with a great deal of disparate work experiences), it is especially important to scrutinize the information on your résumé. For example, you do not want to bump your résumé from one page to two pages, just so you can include your fast-food jobs in high school or your spelling bee championships in elementary school.

Résumé Organization

Another question that sometimes arises is the order in which to present information on your résumé. There are primarily two schools of thought here—chronological and functional. For the most part, résumés are presented in reverse chronological order, and many employers are accustomed to this presentation. However, such a presentation may not emphasize your most pertinent experience, particularly if that experience is not your most recent. In such cases, it may be beneficial to follow a functional structure, placing the most relevant information at the top of your résumé. Just be aware that some employers may not prefer this method (whereas others may). Another alternative is to present your résumé in reverse chronological order and then draw attention to your experience in a cover letter. (See "Cover Letters" later in this chapter for more information.) This would help to avoid confusion from employers expecting to see a résumé in reverse chronological order.

Absolutely No Typos, Grammatical Errors, or Faux Pas

It is common for your résumé to be just one in a pile of résumés sitting in front of a potential employer. This means that the employer is searching for a reason, *any* reason, to throw your résumé in the trash and move on to the next one in the pile. It is not uncommon for large sports organizations to discard thousands of résumés every year because of seemingly minor typos and grammatical errors. This is why it is essential that you eliminate all spelling and grammatical errors before distributing your résumé. Be sure to have a friend, parent, and/or colleague peer review the drafts of your résumés and cover letters. If possible, have some people who work in that industry and/or job type review the résumé as well. If you are a student, utilize your career office for help in drafting and/or reviewing the résumé. This is part of what you (or your parents) are paying for with tuition dollars—experts on campus for job placement and career advice. Often these offices also offer services to alumni in the field. Utilize them!

Finally, instead of running off 100 copies of your résumé, run off just a few at a time, and then change your résumé (if necessary) to cater to particular jobs. If you can, check to see whether there are any do's, don'ts, and/or preferences for the particular job or company to which you apply. For example, if you apply to a very conservative sports company, it might be advisable to delete the entry about the death-metal band that you played in during college. On the other hand, if you are applying to a media company or extreme sports company, this might show your creative side and should therefore be included.

Make Your Résumé Stand Out Visually

It is not necessary to be overly ostentatious with fonts, bolding, layout, and text sizes. A simple layout that is easy to read and free of mistakes is certainly preferable to a highly creative layout that is confusing and/or mistake-ridden. However, it is not advisable to distribute a résumé that is made from the standard résumé templates found on most word processing programs (e.g., Microsoft Word's Résumé Wizard). This application is fine, and perhaps helpful, to use for your first draft, but consider changing the fonts, sizes, margins, and spacing for your final version. The final version should look good to you, your advisor, and potential employers.

Stick to standard fonts (e.g., Times New Roman), so if you e-mail it, the reader will see the same thing you see. Also, be cautious about using font sizes under 10 points. It is possible that the person viewing your résumé has vision worse than yours, and you do not want to give him a reason to throw your résumé in the trash and move to the next one in the pile.

In constructing your résumé, don't forget your awards and accomplishments—both athletic and academic. These can separate you from your competition, displaying your character and work ethic. Additionally, unless the employer asks for it, avoid putting your grade point average on your résumé unless you have at least a B+ or A– average.

Keywords

For the most part, employers are looking for a good match when examining résumés of candidates for a particular position. They are not necessarily looking for individualism. To improve your chances of looking like a match, incorporate as many keywords from the job description into your résumé as appropriate. For example, if the job description mentions such things such as "sales skills" or "communication skills," specifically address these in your résumé (and your cover letter). Another tip is to look at multiple listings for similar positions. If each of the listings contains similar language and requirements, these are likely to be the most important aspects of the job. Make sure your résumé highlights your ability to cover any such items.

Beefing Up Your Résumé

"You are what you are."

—Bill Parcells, responding to a comment that the New England Patriots team he was coaching at the time was in fact better than its record

Some of you who are reading this book are looking for an internship or job right now; others of you are trying to put yourself into a position to get an internship, a job, or a *better* job in a year, 2 years, or maybe 4 years. For *all* readers, but especially those in the latter group, it is never too late to look for opportunities to beef up your résumé.

- Seek out internship or job opportunities that expand the scope of your capabilities. Look for opportunities that develop new skills, knowledge, and insights that enhance your résumé as a more well-rounded candidate. For example, if you lack sales skills, look for internship opportunities that will help build such skills.

- Do not forget publications. If you are a good writer, there are often jobs that include a lot of writing responsibilities, especially with the Internet. You may want to consider starting a sports-related blog or writing for your school newspaper.

- If you have the financial flexibility and time to do so, seek out volunteer opportunities in the sports industry. It can often be easier to find these than you may think. For example, events such as golf tournaments, road races, and extreme sports events require a large number of volunteers. Take the initiative to seek out these opportunities and gain first-hand experience in the industry.

- In choosing your classes as an undergraduate, you should consider obtaining or improving your foreign language skills. With the trend of globalization of sports, this may be an important skill to have. At least one of my graduate students was allowed to audit a Spanish class at the University of Massachusetts while pursuing his graduate degree in sport management. Another student began Chinese classes in 2004 in hopes of increasing her chances of landing a job at the Beijing Olympics in 2008. (If you have access to *free* educational opportunities, *use them!*)

- It is becoming standard that most jobs in sport management require proficiency in most Microsoft Office products (Word, Excel, and often PowerPoint or Access). Brush up on these skills. Take a class if necessary.

  - More specialized: If you have Photoshop or other graphics/desktop publishing experience, this will open up additional opportunities in media relations and publications. The same goes for web design experience, HTML, and especially computer troubleshooting and information technology experience. Even if these skills are not required in the job description, they can be an asset to your bosses, especially older, more established ones who may not be highly computer literate.

  - Identify computer skills that are most helpful to your area(s) of interest. Professional sports player-personnel departments can always use employees with advanced database experience, such as proficiency in Microsoft Access. It is almost a necessity that those seeking business-related positions be very comfortable using spreadsheets.

To help illustrate the power of beefing up a résumé, consider the following example. **Figure 12-1** shows an actual résumé from a student (edited to protect his identity). All this résumé tells the employer is that the student has

---

First Name Last Name
Permanent Address
Cell Phone Number
Email

EDUCATION

University of Massachusetts: Amherst, MA

- 3.816 cumulative GPA
- Bachelor of Science in Sport Management

High School: City, State

- Class Valedictorian
- President of the National Honor Society

REFERENCES
Available upon request

Figure 12-1   Student Resume Without Experience

First Name Last Name
Permanent Address
Cell Phone Number
Email

EXPERIENCE

WMUA Sports Production Director: Amherst, MA
9/02–12/03

- Received award from the Associated Press (AP) for Best Collegiate Play-by-Play for coverage of the UMass Men's Basketball team
- Trained and maintained a staff of over twenty students
- Assigned game duties for broadcasters and engineers
- Produced spots using Samplitude, a digital audio editing program
- Broadcasted (play-by-play and color commentary) football, basketball, baseball, lacrosse, and hockey

New England PGA Media/Tournament Operations Intern: Boylston, MA
5/02–8/02 and 5/03–8/03

- Directed volunteers for the NEPGA Championship
- Managed and ran new junior golf program
- Helped to develop a system for live scoring updates at NEPGA Championship
- Wrote press releases that were used in a weekly article in *The Boston Globe*
- Researched information for NEPGA Championship Media Guide

Tournament Operations, SoccerFest: Amherst, MA
1/03–5/03

- Organized and developed new event with twenty classmates
- Responsible for tournament rules, schedule, scoring, and field set-up/breakdown
- Recruited, trained, and directed volunteers

EDUCATION

University of Massachusetts: Amherst, MA

- 3.816 cumulative GPA
- Bachelor of Science in Sport Management

High School: City, State

- Class Valedictorian
- President of the National Honor Society

REFERENCES
Available upon request

Figure 12-2   Student Resume With Experience

performed well in school. Although academic achievements are a very important consideration, they are not the only consideration. Now take a look at the résumé presented in **Figure 12-2**. This résumé belongs to the very same student as the résumé in Figure 12-1, but it highlights the many experiences he has had that set him apart from other candidates (only one aspect of which is an outstanding academic record).

The preceding student's résumé stood out enough that he was given an interview for an internship with the Pittsburgh Pirates, for which he subsequently received and accepted an offer. It should be noted that the student had very good grades; however, not everyone can be his high school valedictorian. More important than his grades (or at least *as* important) was what this student did outside of the classroom by becoming involved in student activities. As you can imagine, the student's résumé including the outside activities makes a much more powerful impression on employers.

COVER LETTERS

Similar to résumés, cover letters do not get you a job, but they can help get you an *opportunity to interview* for a job. Typically, employers view cover letters in one of two ways. First, hiring managers read the cover letter before reading a candidate's résumé, or they will initially skip over the cover letter and proceed directly to the résumé. If the hiring manager likes the résumé, she will then take a look at the cover letter to get a sense of the writing abilities of the candidate. Either way, the cover letter plays an important role because it is one of the few opportunities a job seeker has to introduce herself to an employer. Consequently, the cover letter is critical. It should *not* be more than one page. It must be well written, free of error, and individually tailored for the particular job.

INTERVIEWS

You should always be prepared for an interview, and you should realize that it may represent a good opportunity and you may not get a second chance for the job. Even if you are pessimistic about getting the job or not particularly excited about the job, you need to go into the interview with the frame of mind of wanting to have a great interview in order to get an offer. You never know. The job may be more interesting when you find out the details in the interview. Also, the employer may have some flexibility about the job responsibilities. There also may be some other jobs within the organization that could become available either during the interview or in the future. So for these various reasons, you should take the interview process seriously and be very well prepared for an interview.

Many, if not most, of the general principles of interviewing are the same in the sports industry as they are in any other sector of business. Therefore, you are encouraged to consult one or more books that deal exclusively with interviewing. For your convenience, a number of these books are listed at the end of this chapter. Also, if you are in a school setting, you should consult your campus career center and/or a professor who has interviewing expertise.

Some schools' career offices will help you with mock interviews. Go through the exercise of a mock interview. This process will help you to think about what types of questions you may be asked. If you can anticipate the questions ahead of time, you will be better prepared to provide solid answers. Although the goal is to put in enough preparation to provide answers that are succinct and articulate, make sure you do not memorize your answers. In answering questions, also make sure you actually provide an answer to the question at hand. It is easy to get off track and fail to provide a sufficient answer to the question that has been asked. Your answers should always provide insight into why you are the best person for the position. Include examples from your previous experiences that demonstrate your strong points.

Another good exercise is to conduct a mock interview from the employer's perspective. This can easily be accomplished by having friends or family members act as the interviewee while you act as the interviewer. Use a real job description as a guide, and think about what types of questions you would ask potential employees to find out whether they are a good fit for the position. The benefit of doing this is learning and understanding what employers are looking for in candidates. Such exercises are often an eye-opening experience for job seekers who have not had the luxury of being involved in the hiring process in the past.

> ### Box 12-1   Cover Letter Tip
> From conversations with many industry professionals, the worst thing you can do in a cover letter is to state something like, "I really love sports, and I want to work for you," or "Working for you would be a tremendous opportunity for me." If you are applying for a position in the sports industry, it is generally assumed you have a passion for sports, so this does not need to be stated in the cover letter. In fact, many cover letters that start off in this manner are discarded immediately. Additionally, employers are not interested in what the position will do for *you*; they are interested in what you can do for *them*. Therefore, you should explain in your cover letter why they should hire you. And be sure to highlight how your education, experience, and skills fit the job and its requirements. What do you bring to the table that other candidates do not? Your cover letter is a personal marketing statement, so use it to sell yourself to the employer.

You also want to make sure you have a good question or two ready to ask the interviewer about the job (perhaps more because the interviewer might answer your questions in the course of the interview, and you don't want to be caught speechless at the end when he asks if you have any questions). Make sure your questions are thoughtful and do not merely ask for information that can easily be found on the organization's website or press releases.

In closing out the interview, it is recommended that the job seeker make a final statement. During this time, it is important to reiterate your interest in the position. Make sure to give the employer a hook, a reason to hire you. It may seem rather obvious, but expressing a desire for the position can go a long way in the mind of the employer. Relate this desire for the job back to your skills and experiences. You can also use the final statement to cover anything you believe is important, but was not covered sufficiently during the interview. When finished with your closing remarks, thank the interviewer for his time.

An interview can vary a great deal in terms of its formality, length, and questions asked. Standard employment law has regulations for what types of questions can be asked of each candidate. Some employers may not choose to strictly adhere to employment law, or the standard questions may not cover all topics that a candidate wishes to talk about.

The best advice for candidates on how to handle poor interviews is to be prepared for anything that might arise. You may have to take the initiative and ask more questions. If you know what you want to say in the interview, make sure you have an opportunity to talk about these key points. The key to doing this is to take control of the interview without the interviewer knowing. The following are two examples on how you can accomplish this:

- A common issue is that the questions asked by the interviewer don't directly relate to the key points the candidate wishes to deliver. This situation can be remedied by expanding on the questions that are asked to include the desired information. The best way to do this is to incorporate the information into the answer of a related question. Be careful, though, not to expand too far beyond the scope of the original question—make sure there is a plausible relationship.

- Occasionally, an employer will finish asking questions and the candidate still has information and experiences they would like to share. In such cases, candidates should attempt to provide the additional information by asking a question, such as "There are a couple of other things I would like to add that we did not get a chance to cover, do you have a few extra minutes so that I can cover these?"

It can be difficult during an interview when you are thinking about what you are going to say, but try to listen to the interviewer. This allows you to specifically and directly answer the question(s), and sometimes you can pick up subtle questions, inferences, and/or likes and dislikes of the interviewer. Finally, be careful not to interrupt the interviewer. This can prove to be fatal to one's job or internship prospects.

Sometimes interviews are conducted by telephone. These can be a challenge and can be much different than in-person interviews. Here are a few things to consider. First, practice by having someone conduct a job interview by phone or practice on your own in front of a mirror. Second, make sure the connection is clear, so if possible, find a land line instead of a cell phone. Third, find a private room or office to make the call from, so you will not be distracted. Fourth, organize your notes in front of you (draft certain answers, a list of questions, and information about the interviewer and organization). You also have the advantage of taking notes, so if you think of a question during the interview, you can add it to your list of questions. Fifth, relax and smile. The interviewer will not see the smile, but he will hear it.

Interview Preparation

You should always prepare for an interview as much as you can. Obtain as much information as you can about the company, the organization, and the person who will interview you. For most companies in the sports industry, this information may be available on a website. Media guides and company promotional literature also may be available. Other sources of information, if you're involved with a sport management program, include your department's career services director or internship director. Many internship programs require that students submit student reports, and a lot of good information can be obtained in the reports of students who have previously worked in that organization. Also, reach out to your network to see if any of your contacts knows anything about or, better yet, anyone at the organization with whom you are interviewing. Through your network, you may be able to gain the inside scoop into what it's like to work at the organization and what the interview process is like.

Interview Follow-Up

After the interview, always follow up with a thank you note. A survey conducted by CareerBuilder.com found that nearly 15% of hiring managers would reject a job candidate who neglected to send a thank you note after the interview.[1] Additionally, 32% said they would still consider the thankless prospect, but their opinion of him would diminish.

Traditionally, thank you notes are expected to be handwritten. This may still be the best policy today; however, this is an area with differing opinions. E-mail certainly can arrive quicker than U.S. mail, but traditional mail often is considered more personal and thoughtful than e-mail, particularly if a note is handwritten. So the rule of thumb is likely to change over time. A CareerBuilder.com survey also provides insight into this topic. Respondents indicated 23% desire a handwritten thank you, 21% prefer a typed hard copy, and 19% favor an e-mailed followed up with a snail-mail letter.[1] As you can see, there is a wide range of opinions on this topic. It really depends on the person you are thanking, your relationship with that person, and what they have done for you. Even in the age of e-mail, a handwritten note is still appropriate, particularly for more important situations. The best advice is to use common sense and ask for guidance from trusted advisors when you are unsure. Remember, if you handwrite a note, obviously, use professional-looking thank you cards (no cartoons or jokes) and make sure the penmanship is legible.

Dress

If you are uncertain how you should dress for an interview, lean towards being overdressed. Go in expecting to wear a suit, rather than business casual. Even if the people interviewing you are dressed in business casual, wearing a suit states that you have respect for the organization and that you err on the side of caution. You do not need to overdo it. Do not wear a tuxedo. If your budget is limited, do not spend $1,000 on a new suit. If you are fortunate enough to get the job or internship, it is then perfectly acceptable to dress in accordance with office norms while at work; however, it does not hurt to ask, just to be sure.

Shoes should be polished. Jackets, pants, and skirts should be pressed and then kept as wrinkle free as possible. This can be difficult if, for example, you have a 3-hour flight or bus ride to your interview. But whatever you can do to project a great first impression, even something as subtle as proper and well-tailored apparel might make a difference for you.

This is another area where outside help and opinions can be very useful. There are books and/or sections in books on dress. Career advisors, internship directors, mentors, and faculty members may also be good resources.

REFERENCES

It is important to think about who you want to have as a reference ahead of time. This allows you time to develop a strong relationship with this person and to establish expectations for their role as a reference provider. Who are the best people to be references for you? As a starting point, the people who know you the best. Only pick people who you can rely on to give you a positive reference. This may seem obvious, but all too often people take for granted that someone they choose to be a reference will provide a good recommendation. Take the time to ensure this is the case by carefully selecting your references. For example, just because you received an A in a particular class does not mean that the

professor who taught the class will make a good reference choice, especially if you had little to no interaction with the professor outside of the classroom. Instead, it may be wiser for you to select a professor who taught a class in which you received only a B, but with whom you had numerous positive interactions. This person may be in a better position to talk about your interests, career goals, work ethic, and the like because they know you better as a person.

Regardless of who you choose, it is advisable that you take the time to make sure any person you ask to provide a reference knows what your career goals are and why you are a good fit for the type of career you are pursuing. This will put the reference giver in a position to talk about facts rather than assumptions.

You can often get more help from your references by doing a little bit of "coaching." If there are particular things that an organization is looking for, let your references know. This will allow your references to provide the best possible recommendation on your behalf. Note, you are not asking your references to lie or to make up stories, but you are guiding them as to the type of information the employer is most interested in learning about you.

Always provide your references with a current copy of your résumé and inform them of all employers to whom you have submitted their names. You may also want to provide your references with a college transcript, particularly if you are asking a faculty member to act as a reference. Finally, you may want to send the reference a copy of the job announcement. The reference can then gear his remarks to the particular position.

As a general rule, it is best that you include references with your résumé, even if they are not requested. The advantage of listing references is that the person reviewing the résumé might know one of the references. He might have been looking for a reason to call the person (perhaps on company time), and calling about you provides the perfect opportunity to make the call. In general, it is best to place the person who knows you the best at the top of your references list. Don't put the "biggest name" individual on the top of your list, unless he or she knows you well. Know how and when to use your references to get you looked at or to get an informational interview.

Good sources for references include professors (both undergraduate and graduate), supervisors at previous jobs, mentors, and advisors. Employers are looking for objective evaluations of your abilities, so you should not use family members as references, unless they have a significant tie to the particular industry or organization. You should also strive to have diversity among your references, so try to avoid having three professors or three former supervisors. Instead, find a mix among different types of references to provide the employer with some different perspectives on your abilities and skills. As you move into your career, you may make use of more former supervisors and fewer faculty members.

Often you will need to obtain a reference from someone you may have had little interaction with over a long period of time. A good tip for references is to make sure you periodically stay in contact with them. It can be rather difficult for a reference to provide a suitable referral if they have little knowledge about what you have been doing for the last 5 or 10 years. Make an effort to occasionally send an e-mail or make a phone call to potential references. Let them know what you have been doing and what your plans are for the future. This is also a good networking tip, and can be used to retain the network contacts you have worked so hard to obtain.

RESOURCES

The following list of books is included to guide you to additional resources in the areas of résumés, interviews, cover letters, and professional dress. Inclusion on this list is not meant to be used as a positive evaluation or endorsement of the book, nor is exclusion meant to be a negative evaluation. This list is merely presented for information purposes. Numerous books have been written on these topics, and new books are published on these subjects all the time, so be sure to consult your local bookstore and library for additional titles.

Résumé Construction

- *Resume Magic: Trade Secrets of a Professional Resume Writer*, by Susan Britton Whitcomb
- *The Elements of Resume Style: Essential Rules and Eye-Opening Advice for Writing Resumes and Cover Letters That Work*, by Scott Bennett
- *101 Best Resumes: Endorsed by the Professional Association of Resume Writers*, by Jay A. Block and Michael Betrus
- *The Resume Handbook: How to Write Outstanding Resumes & Cover Letters for Every Situation*, by Arthur D. Rosenberg and David H. Hizer
- *Resumes for Dummies*, by Joyce Lain Kennedy
- *Gallery of Best Resumes: A Collection of Quality Resumes by Professional Resume Writers*, by David F. Noble
- *Competency-Based Resumes: How to Bring Your Resume to the Top of the Pile*, by Robin Kessler and Linda A. Strasburg
- *Get the Interview Every Time:* Fortune *500 Hiring Professionals' Tips for Writing Winning Resumes and Cover Letters*, by Brenda Greene
- *Resumes That Knock 'em Dead*, by Martin Yate
- *The Resume.com Guide to Writing Unbeatable Resumes*, by Warren Simons and Rose Curtis

Cover Letter Construction

- *Dynamic Cover Letters Revised*, by Katherine Hansen and Randall Hansen, PhD
- *Cover Letter Magic: Trade Secrets of Professional Resume Writers*, by Wendy S. Enelow and Louise Kursmark
- *Cover Letters That Knock 'em Dead*, by Martin Yate
- *101 Best Cover Letters*, by Jay A. Block and Michael Betrus
- *Perfect Phrases for Cover Letters*, by Michael Betrus

Interview Preparation

- *Competency-Based Interviews: Master the Tough New Interview Style and Give Them the Answers That Will Win You the Job*, by Robin Kessler
- *301 Smart Answers to Tough Interview Questions*, by Vicky Oliver
- *Best Answers to the 201 Most Frequently Asked Interview Questions*, by Matthew DeLuca
- *How to Interview Like a Top MBA: Job-Winning Strategies from Headhunters,* Fortune *100 Recruiters, and Career Counselors*, by Dr. Shel Leanne
- *The Interview Rehearsal Book*, by Deb Gottesman and Buzz Mauro
- *Job Interviews for Dummies*, by Joyce Lain Kennedy
- *Winning Job Interviews: Reduce Interview Anxiety, Outprepare the Other Candidates, Land the Job You Love*, by Paul Powers
- *Sell Yourself!: Master the Job Interview Process*, by Jane Williams
- *Nail the Job Interview: 101 Dynamite Answers to Interview Questions,* 6th edition, by Caryl Krannich
- *You're Hired!: Interview Skills to Get the Job*, by Lorne Epstein

Advice on Professional Dress

- *The New Professional Image: Dress Your Best for Every Business Situation,* 2nd edition, by Susan Bixler and Nancy Nix-Rice
- *New Women's Dress for Success*, by John T. Molloy
- *John T. Molloy's New Dress for Success*, by John T. Molloy

Consulting Agencies

Another resource that is becoming more prevalent today is career-oriented consulting agencies. Some of these agencies provide counsel on a full range of services including professional dress, résumé/cover letter analysis, résumé construction, or general career path guidance. Other agencies focus on a few or one of these areas. Advice from these consulting agencies may be expensive for a recent graduate—they typically range from $75 to $300 depending on the level of service—but they can provide you with a more thorough and personalized analysis of the areas in which you need improvement.

Finally, another great resource is your college career center. Even if you are no longer a current student, your alma mater's career center is still a great place to turn. In addition to being free of charge, college career centers are highly motivated to find their recent graduates employment because it will improve the school's post-graduation employment statistics. These statistics are extremely important to colleges since they directly correlate to the number of applicants the school receives. An important advantage that college career centers have over private consulting firms is that they have detailed records of their alumni network. College career centers can put you in touch with alumni who often can be very willing to talk to recent graduates about career advice. Not only does this give you a good resource for career guidance, but it also is great way to make easy networking connections within an industry.

Endnotes

1. Barker, O. (2005, Dec. 27). Whatever Happened to Thank You Notes? *USA Today*. Retrieved July 20, 2008, from http://dictionary.reference.com/browse/mentor.

CHAPTER THIRTEEN

Mid-Career Moves

"Young people always ask me how they can have a career in sports. I always say, go to work in another business sector: telecom, banking, collective bargaining as an attorney. Stay out of sports until you acquire some skills. Acquire some perspective and experience and bring it to sports."

—Paul Tagliabue, former commissioner of the NFL

"Success isn't permanent, and failure isn't fatal."

—Mike Ditka, former head coach of the Chicago Bears and member of the NFL Hall of Fame

CAREER CHANGERS

Many prospective job seekers are looking to make a career move into the world of sports from the world of business. Such candidates often possess refined business skills that create value for sports entities. However, given the competitive challenges of finding gainful employment, a decision to make a career move into the sports industry should not be taken lightly. Consequently, in order to make the best decision possible, you should closely examine the motivating factors driving the desire to change careers. The following list of questions, based on a list published by *Newsweek*,[1] can be quite helpful in this regard. Although this list does not specifically target people looking to transition into the sports industry, the questions are relevant to such a decision. It is recommended that anyone looking to make a career change into sports take the time to answer these questions:

1. Are you thinking in terms of what you want to do in the sports industry and not simply what you want to leave in your current job?

2. Is your decision reversible? If your career move into the sports industry does not work out, could you return to a similar job if you leave for something new?

3. Have you thoroughly researched the field and know what type of role you are looking to transition into?

4. If you make a change, and for some reason a job in sports does not work out, would you think the risk of a new career had been worth it?

5. Do the most important people in your life agree with your contemplated change?

6. Are you prepared to work longer hours for a lower salary?

7. Are you ready to be the new kid on the block in a new job?

8. Are you ready to prove yourself all over again with a new employer in a new industry?

9. Are you ready to interact with younger people who may be your peers or even your managers?

10. Are you ready for the possibility that your new career will not meet your expectations or that you may not succeed in your new job?

It should be stressed that care and consideration must be given to the financial ramifications of making a career change into the sports industry. As discussed in Chapter 3, for the most part, jobs in the sports industry pay considerably less than comparable nonsports jobs. In addition to the lower pay, there may also be a reduced level of benefits such as insurance and retirement account options, such as 401(k)s. The financial impact may be greater than you initially realize. There may be the costs of additional education and the costs of moving to a new and possibly more expensive location, such as New York. It is not uncommon for people to believe that sacrificing a bit of income for the opportunity to work in the sports industry is quite doable. However, until they actually do so, it is difficult to gauge the likelihood of a happy outcome. Before making a move into the sports industry, pretend you are living on a reduced income for several months and see how it works for you. This will provide a great learning opportunity for you. If you can successfully make the change, then a transition into the sports industry may be a good move for you to make.

Often, the key to making a successful career transition into sports is to obtain that elusive first job, particularly for those looking to do a completely new type of work. This is easier said than done, though. If you are looking to move into an entirely new type of job within the sports industry, do not completely abandon your previous work experience—try to make it work for you. For example, say you have a legal background and you are looking to transition into college athletics administration. Because of similarities in the type of work, your legal skills may create opportunities to work in compliance. Even if compliance work does not seem highly desirable to you, taking such a position will allow you to get your foot in the door. Once you get started, you likely will have an opportunity to move around within college athletics to other departments and duties. You may need to pay your dues by working in a position that is not ideal, but suits the skill set you currently have. Use this opportunity to get started and then look for other positions in the industry.

As Tagliabue's statement at the beginning of this chapter indicates, you may want to consider working in the nonsports business first as a strategy/career path to get into sports. One can both build experience and gain responsibility in a job market that may be slightly less competitive. These people will probably receive better compensation. When they are ready to move into the sports industry, they may be able to move in at a mid-management level (thereby eliminating some of the "dues paying" internships and entry-level jobs). There are two helpful points to keep in mind with this strategy. First, make sure to maintain and build your sports industry network. Second, set your lifestyle at the sports industry compensation level and not the nonsports industry salary you are making.

SEEMINGLY OVERQUALIFIED CANDIDATES

Often, candidates looking to move into the sports industry seem overqualified for open positions. Such candidates can gain a false sense of confidence, assuming, "What employer wouldn't want an overqualified candidate?" Overqualification can create apprehension in the minds of employers for a variety of reasons. The employer may be worried that the candidate is simply looking for a point of entry into the sports world, and is not truly interested in the position. This can lead to a poorly motivated person, which can lead to poor work performance.

Employers also are often looking for continuity in employees. Rather than hire a new person every year, they want to hire employees who will remain in a position for a number of years. With overqualified candidates, there is a greater risk the new hire will become disenchanted with his position and look to improve the situation by either leaving the organization or moving into a different position. Such disenchantment may arise from the general low-paying nature of the industry (see "Show Me the Money" in Chapter 3). An employee paid at a level less than what he feels is commensurate with his or her skills generally does not maintain a good attitude. This, in turn, can harm the office morale of the entire organization. Additionally, some employers may just be intimidated by overqualified candidates, and choose not to hire them.

Consider the following example. A hiring manager for a professional sports team has an opening for an entry-level public relations position. He is down to two final candidates—a recent BA in journalism graduate and a recent joint MBA/law degree candidate. Which candidate do you think is a better fit to be doing entry-level work? From the employer's perspective, everything else being equal, the BA candidate is likely to be preferred. Why? This candidate is likely to stay in the position longer and won't feel as underpaid. This case study demonstrates how difficult it can be to place overqualified candidates.

From the job seeker's perspective, much of the same analysis applies. Employees should carefully consider jobs for which they are seemingly overqualified. Is the job just a means to break into the industry, or is the job truly going to help the job seeker achieve their ultimate career goals? If the job seeker does not have a genuine interest in the job (or if he feels grossly underpaid), work will quickly become routine and dull. Consequently, work performance may suffer.

Endnotes

1. McGinn, D. (2006, June 19). Second Time Around. *Newsweek*. Retrieved July 20, 2008, from http://www.newsweek.com/id/39541.

14

Final Tips

"I've always made a total effort, even when the odds seemed entirely against me. I never quit trying; I never felt that I didn't have a chance to win."

—Arnold Palmer, golfing great

"The difference between a successful person and others is not a lack of strength, not a lack of knowledge, but rather a lack of will."

—Vince Lombardi, former head coach of the Green Bay Packers and member of the NFL Hall of Fame

Thousands of people go to work each and every day for organizations in the sports industry. These people have found a way to combine their passion for sports with their need for a career. Although the sports industry can be very competitive, there's no reason to believe you can't be one of these chosen few. As this first section of the book comes to a close, here are a few tips:

- Network, network, network, and then network some more. It's not what you know, but *who* you know. And, more importantly, who knows you.

- Don't be afraid of rejection. This industry is competitive, and you will likely encounter rejection from time to time. It's how you deal with rejection that will determine the amount of success you have.

- Always maintain a positive attitude. *Always.*

- If you are given a chance, make the most of it. Strive to work harder and better than those around you. This will give your employer a reason to keep you.

The remaining four sections of this book have been designed to provide you with detailed information about careers and organizations found within the sports industry. This information should be quite helpful as you start to plan your career path and begin your job or internship search.

Section 2

The Sports Industry: Segment Descriptions

Introduction to the Sports Industry

In this section of the book, you will find a great deal of information about the major industry segments (such as basketball) and the organizations (such as the National Basketball Association [NBA]) found within the various segments of the sports industry. I have written about some of the more prominent organizations in more detail, providing greater depth of information such as an organizational timeline, an analysis of major sources of revenues and expenditures, and other information that can be used to gain an in-depth understanding of the organization. Smaller organizations, such the Continental Basketball Association (CBA), have been written about in less detail, providing some basic knowledge of the organization's operations.

This section of the book can be used in a number of different ways. You can use this section to research and learn about any industry segments and/or organizations that are of interest to you. You can also use this section to discover and learn about less-publicized industry segments that you may not know about, such as action sports or lacrosse. For readers with more defined interests, this section can be used to learn about lesser-known organizations within your area(s) of interest (such as the NBA Development League [D-League] in basketball or the independent leagues within baseball). Another way this section can be helpful is if you already have a firm grasp of the particular industry segment(s) or organization(s) you want to work for, you can use this section to refresh your knowledge of that area and possibly learn more. Finally, and also importantly, reviewing information contained within this section can be particularly helpful as you prepare for interviews and/or networking events. Use the information to generate thoughtful and meaningful questions to ask in these situations.

This section includes as wide a range of industry segments and organizations as possible; however, covering every industry segment and organization would greatly exceed the allowable length for this book. Therefore, an organization's exclusion from this section is not meant to be a poor reflection on the organization.

John Calipari, head basketball coach at Memphis University, speaks to his team during a time out. Memphis finished the 2007–2008 season with a record of 38-2, losing to Kansas in the finals of the NCAA tournament. Calipari became the head coach at Memphis in 2000, compiling a record of 219-65. Calipari previously was head coach of the NBA's New Jersey Nets and at the University of Massachusetts.

Information included in this section is based on the most recent news articles, press releases, media guides, financial reports, and other information as of the completion of the writing of this book. Therefore, important developments may have occurred after the book's publication. Despite this, the information contained within this section is still valuable because it lets you know where the organization and/or industry segment was at a specific point in time. This then provides a point of reference from which to examine what an organization has done since the publication of this book. To learn about an organization's activities that may have occurred since this book went to press, review an organization's website, press releases, and current news articles. Publications such as *Street & Smith's SportsBusiness Journal* will be particularly helpful in this regard.

CHAPTER SIXTEEN

Basketball

NATIONAL BASKETBALL ASSOCIATION[1]

The National Basketball Association (NBA) is the world's premier basketball league and considered one of the major sports leagues in North America. In many ways, the NBA views itself as an international steward of the game of basketball, working towards the global expansion of the game. The NBA broadcasts its games to 215 different countries in 41 different languages. In 2007–2008, the NBA had an average attendance of 17,311 per regular season game. Also in 2007–2008, the NBA had a Nielsen television rating of 2.2 on ABC, which means that approximately 3,175,000 viewers tuned in to each NBA basketball game aired on the ABC Network.[2]

The league was founded in New York City in 1946 as the Basketball Association of America (BAA), with 11 teams playing mostly in the Midwest and Northeast. A merger with the rival National Basketball League (NBL) occurred in 1949, and the newly formed 19-team league adopted the name National Basketball Association. Today, the NBA consists of 30 teams, all of which are based out of U.S. cities with the exception of a team based in Toronto, Canada.

Similar to other North American sports leagues, the NBA has increased its international exposure in recent years. The league forged a global presence through various marketing initiatives and overseas games[2] and with a significant increase in the number of international players. Continuing this trend, in May 2007 the league announced the creation of a new senior executive position responsible for the distribution of its international television and digital media assets. The league's move toward globalization has further extended the game's reach and enhanced its popularity with fans worldwide.

The NBA utilizes an annual draft process to add and distribute players to the teams. There are numerous paths that players take prior to the entering the draft. Most U.S. players play at the college level and leave at various times during their collegiate careers.[3] In more recent years, some of the more talented players eschewed college altogether and entered the draft straight out of high school; however, in 2006 a rule was instituted that prohibited players from entering the draft straight from high school. Currently, the NBA requires that players be at least 19 years of age during the calendar year in which the draft is held, and at least one NBA season to have elapsed since the player's graduation from high school.[4] As mentioned previously, the number and quality of overseas players has increased dramatically in recent years;[5] as a result, teams have increased their international scouting focus.

The NBA has one dedicated minor league, the National Basketball Association Development League (D-League), which is used as a player development platform for the teams. Most NBA players skip this level and go directly to the NBA. Thus, the development league is used primarily to augment teams with substitutes to fill in for injured players; however, it is also not uncommon for NBA teams to send rookies and second-year players to play a few games with an D-League affiliate in order to give these players more in-game experience. The D-League will be discussed in greater detail later in the chapter.

The league staff primarily operates from the headquarters in New York City, which also is the home of the Women's National Basketball Association (WNBA). With NBA owners serving as the original "operator investors" of the WNBA, the marketing goals of both leagues are closely aligned and aim to attract similar sponsors and partnerships. The league employs professionals in the following departments: administration, marketing, basketball operations, business development, creative services, events and attractions, finance and accounting, legal, public relations, information technology, TV production, retail, publishing, team business operations, and global merchandising. In addition, the league offers both an associates program and an internship program for individuals looking to break into professional basketball.

History of the National Basketball Association

1946

- The Basketball Association of America (BAA) started play with 11 teams: Boston Celtics, Chicago Stags, Cleveland Rebels, Detroit Falcons, New York Knickerbockers, Philadelphia Warriors, Pittsburgh Ironmen, Providence (RI) Steamrollers, St. Louis Bombers, Toronto Huskies, and Washington (DC) Capitols (11 teams).

1947

- The Baltimore Bullets joined the BAA and won the BAA title in their first year in the league (12 teams).
- The Cleveland Rebels, Detroit Falcons, Pittsburgh Ironmen, and Toronto Huskies left the BAA (8 teams).

1948

- Four teams from the National Basketball League (NBL) are added to the BAA: Fort Wayne (IN) Pistons, Indianapolis Jets, Minneapolis Lakers, and Rochester (NY) Royals (12 teams).

1949

- The remaining seven teams in the NBL joined the BAA: Anderson (IN) Packers, Denver Nuggets, Indianapolis Olympians, Sheboygan (WI) Redskins, Syracuse (NY) Nationals, Tri-Cities (IL) Blackhawks, and Waterloo (IA) Hawks (19 teams).
- The Providence Steamrollers and Indianapolis Jets folded (17 teams).
- The BAA was renamed the National Basketball Association (NBA).

1950

- The Anderson Packers, Chicago Stags, Denver Nuggets, Sheboygan Redskins, St. Louis Bombers, and Waterloo Hawks disbanded after the conclusion of the 1950 season (11 teams).
- Nat Clifton became the first African American to sign an NBA contract by signing with New York.

1941

- The Tri-Cities Blackhawks moved to Milwaukee and became the Milwaukee Hawks.
- The Washington Capitols disbanded before the end of the 1951 season (10 teams).
- The lane is widened from 6 feet to 12 feet.

1953

- The Indianapolis Olympians dropped out of the NBA (9 teams).

1954

- NBA players organized for the first time to form a player's union. Bob Cousy of the Boston Celtics was named as the first president of the new union, called the National Basketball Players Association (NBPA).
- The Baltimore Bullets dropped out of the NBA (8 teams).
- The 24-second shot clock was introduced.

1955

- The Milwaukee Hawks moved to St. Louis and became the St. Louis Hawks.

1957

- The Fort Wayne Pistons moved to Detroit and became the Detroit Pistons.
- The Rochester Royals moved to Cincinnati and became the Cincinnati Royals.

1960

- The Minneapolis Lakers moved to Los Angeles and became the Los Angeles Lakers.

1961

- The Chicago Packers joined the NBA as an expansion team (9 teams).

1962

- The Chicago Packers were renamed the Zephyrs.
- The Philadelphia Warriors moved to San Francisco and became the San Francisco Warriors.

1963

- The Chicago Zephyrs moved to Baltimore and became the Baltimore Bullets.
- The Syracuse Nationals moved to Philadelphia and became the Philadelphia 76ers.

1966

- The Chicago Bulls joined the NBA as an expansion team (10 teams).

1967

- The San Diego Rockets and Seattle SuperSonics joined the NBA as expansion teams (12 teams).

1968

- The Milwaukee Bucks and Phoenix Suns joined the NBA as expansion teams (14 teams).
- The St. Louis Hawks move to Atlanta and became the Atlanta Hawks.

1970

- A group of 14 NBA players challenged the legality of the NBA's "option" or "reserve" clause under federal antitrust laws. This clause bound a player to his team even after his contract had expired. The group of players, led by NBPA president Oscar Robertson, filed a class action lawsuit against the NBA, *Robertson v. National Basketball Association.*

- The Buffalo Braves, Cleveland Cavaliers, and Portland Trail Blazers joined the NBA as expansion teams (17 teams).

1971

- The San Diego Rockets moved to Houston and became the Houston Rockets.

- The San Francisco Warriors moved to Oakland and became the Golden State Warriors.

1972

- The Cincinnati Royals divided home games between Kansas City and Omaha (NE), and were renamed the Kansas City-Omaha Kings.

1973

- The Baltimore Bullets moved to Landover (MD) and became the Capitol Bullets.

1974

- The New Orleans Jazz joined the NBA as an expansion team (18 teams).

- The Capitol Bullets were renamed Washington Bullets.

1975

- The Kings dropped Omaha from their name and became the Kansas City Kings.

1976

- The court ruled in favor of the NBA players in *Robertson v. National Basketball Association* and ruled that the NBA's option or reserve clause violated antitrust laws by constraining competitions of labor. The option clause was thereby eliminated.

- Four teams from the ABA merged with the NBA: Denver Nuggets, Indiana Pacers, New York Nets, and San Antonio Spurs (22 teams).

1977

- The New York Nets moved to New Jersey and became the New Jersey Nets.

1978

- The Buffalo Braves moved to San Diego and became the San Diego Clippers.

1979

- The New Orleans Jazz moved to Salt Lake City and became the Utah Jazz.

- The three-point field goal was introduced and was set at 23 feet 9 inches away from the basket.

- Magic Johnson and Larry Bird entered the NBA. Johnson and Bird soon became the unofficial faces of the NBA, and many credit the popularity of these two superstars for the rejuvenation of the league during the 1980s. During the 1979–1980 season, Bird won the Rookie of the Year award and Magic led his team to an NBA championship and was named the NBA Finals MVP.

1980

- The Dallas Mavericks joined the NBA as an expansion team (23 teams).

1984

- The San Diego Clippers moved to Los Angeles and became the Los Angeles Clippers.

- Commissioner Larry O'Brien stepped down and named David Stern the new NBA Commissioner.

1985

- The Kansas City Kings moved to Sacramento and became the Sacramento Kings.

1988

- The NBPA settled another antitrust lawsuit brought against the owners by signing the Bridgeman Settlement Agreement. This agreement brought true, unrestricted free agency to the NBA, the first unrestricted free agency in any major professional sports league. The Bridgeman Agreement also loosened other restrictions, including reducing the college draft from seven rounds to two rounds. The terms of the Bridgeman Agreement became incorporated into a 6-year collective bargaining agreement.[6]

- The Miami Heat and Charlotte Hornets joined the NBA as expansion teams (25 teams).

1989

- The Minnesota Timberwolves and Orlando Magic joined the NBA as expansion teams (27 teams).

1993

- Michael Jordan, the reigning two-time MVP and arguably the best player in the world, abruptly announced his retirement from the NBA.

1995

- On March 18, Michael Jordan announced that he would come out of retirement and once again play for the Chicago Bulls, his former team. In his first game back from retirement, Jordan scored 19 points against the Indiana Pacers.

- The Toronto Raptors and Vancouver Grizzlies joined the NBA as expansion teams (29 teams).

- The Minnesota Timberwolves selected high school star Kevin Garnett with the fifth pick in the NBA draft. Garnett became the first player in over 20 years to make the jump straight to the NBA out of high school.

1997

- The Washington Bullets were renamed the Washington Wizards.

2001

- The Vancouver Grizzlies moved to Memphis and became the Memphis Grizzlies.

2002

- The Charlotte Hornets moved to New Orleans and became the New Orleans Hornets.

- The Houston Rockets selected Yao Ming with the first overall pick in the NBA draft. The 7'5" Chinese center was the first international player in NBA history to be selected with the first overall pick who did not play collegiate ball in the United States.

2004

- The Charlotte Bobcats joined the NBA as an expansion team (30 teams).

- With under a minute left to play in a game between the Indiana Pacers and the Detroit Pistons at the Palace at Auburn Hills (MI), the Pacers' Ron Artest charged into the stands and began to fight fans after being struck by a thrown cup of beer. The fight escalated into a full-scale brawl between Pistons fans and Pacers players. The final seconds of the game were never played and the Pacers, who were winning 97–82 at the time, were awarded the win. Artest was suspended for the remainder of the regular season and playoffs in what would be the longest suspension ever for on-court actions (86 games).

2005

- Due to the effects of Hurricane Katrina, the New Orleans Hornets played 35 of its 41 home games in Oklahoma City and became the New Orleans/Oklahoma City Hornets.

2006

- The NBA commissioner, David Stern, announced that the NBA would use a new composite game ball for the 2006–2007 season. This was the first time the ball was changed since 1970.

- The New Orleans/Oklahoma City Hornets played 35 home games in Oklahoma City and 6 home games in New Orleans.

2007

- The NBA announced that it would return to the old leather basketball midway through the 2006–2007 season. Commissioner Stern made this move after numerous high profile player complaints and the NBPA filed an unfair labor practice against the NBA with the National Labor Relations Board.

2008

- The NBA announced that the Seattle SuperSonics would relocate the franchise to Oklahoma City for the 2008–2009 season.

Structure of the National Basketball Association

League Alignment

- 30 total teams (**Table 16-1**)
- 2 conferences: Eastern Conference (15 teams) and Western Conference (15 teams)
  - Eastern Conference: 3 divisions (Atlantic, Central, Southeast); 5 teams per division
  - Western Conference: 3 divisions (Northwest, Pacific, Southwest); 5 teams per division

Competition Format

- Head-to-head contests between teams, unbalanced schedule[7]
- End-of-year playoffs

Schedule

- Game days
  - Games are played throughout the week, usually in the evenings on weekdays and during the day and evening on weekends.
  - Various games are televised throughout the week on a wide array of networks, which are outlined below in the television broadcast revenue section.
- Preseason (October): Training camps begin in September
  - 8 exhibition games per team (4 home, 4 away)
- Regular season (October–April): 82 total games (41 home, 41 away)
  - 52 games within conference (26 home games), 30 games out of conference (15 home games)
  - 16 games within division (8 home games)

Table 16-1 NBA Teams (2008–2009)

Eastern Conference		Western Conference	
Atlantic Division		**Northwest Division**	
Team	**Location**	**Team**	**Location**
Boston Celtics	Boston, MA	Denver Nuggets	Denver, CO
New Jersey Nets	East Rutherford, NJ	Minnesota Timberwolves	Minneapolis, MN
New York Knicks	New York, NY	Portland Trail Blazers	Portland, OR
Philadelphia 76ers	Philadelphia, PA	Oklahoma City Thunder	Oklahoma, OK
Toronto Raptors	Toronto, Ontario	Utah Jazz	Salt Lake City, UT
Central Division		**Pacific Division**	
Team	**Location**	**Team**	**Location**
Chicago Bulls	Chicago, IL	Golden State Warriors	Oakland, CA
Cleveland Cavaliers	Cleveland, OH	Los Angeles Clippers	Los Angeles, CA
Detroit Pistons	Auburn Hills, MI	Los Angeles Lakers	Los Angeles, CA
Indiana Pacers	Indianapolis, IN	Phoenix Suns	Phoenix, AZ
Milwaukee Bucks	Milwaukee, WI	Sacramento Kings	Sacramento, CA
Southeast Division		**Southwest Division**	
Team	**Location**	**Team**	**Location**
Atlanta Hawks	Atlanta, GA	Dallas Mavericks	Dallas, TX
Charlotte Bobcats	Charlotte, NC	Houston Rockets	Houston, TX
Miami Heat	Miami, FL	Memphis Grizzlies	Memphis, TN
Orlando Magic	Orlando, FL	New Orleans Hornets	New Orleans, LA
Washington Wizards	Washington, DC	San Antonio Spurs	San Antonio, TX

- Playoffs (April–June)
  - 4 rounds: First round, Conference Semi-Finals, Conference Finals, NBA Finals.
  - 16 teams: Top 8 teams from each conference.
  - The three division winners and the team with the third best regular season won-lost record are seeded 1–4, based on regular season won-lost records; the next four best teams based on their regular season won-lost records are seeded 5–8.
  - Playoff format
    - All series are best of seven games.
    - Home court advantage is based on regular season records throughout playoffs, not by seed; the format is 2 home, 3 away, then 2 home.
    - First round (Eastern and Western): Seed 1 vs. Seed 8; Seed 2 vs. Seed 7; Seed 3 vs. Seed 6; Seed 4 vs. Seed 5.
    - Conference Semi-Final round (Eastern and Western): Seed 1/Seed 8 winner vs. Seed 4/Seed 5 winner *and* Seed 2/Seed 7 winner vs. Seed 3/Seed 6 winner.
    - Conference Final round (Eastern and Western): Winners of semi-final rounds play one another.
    - NBA Finals: Eastern Conference Champion vs. Western Conference Champion.

- All-Star Game (February)
  - Mid-season game pits Eastern Conference All-Stars vs. Western Conference All-Stars.
  - All-Star weekend also includes the Rookie Challenge Game, Three-Point Shootout, Skills Challenge, Shooting Stars, and Slam Dunk Competition.
  - Site determined on a rotational basis:
    - 2007: Las Vegas, Nevada
    - 2008: New Orleans, Louisiana
    - 2009: Phoenix, Arizona

Money Matters for the National Basketball Association

Sources of Revenue

- Television broadcast revenues
  - The NBA negotiates its national television broadcast contracts on behalf of its teams, resulting in annual revenues of approximately $930 million.[8] After the NBA subtracts its expenses, the league distributes this money equally to the teams. In 2006–2007, each team received over $28 million from national deals.[9] In addition, the league developed the exclusive NBA TV station that broadcasts various games and NBA-

themed programming throughout the week. Each team may also negotiate a local television deal with its regional sports network. Their contracts may include many, if not all of the games that are not part of one of the national television broadcast contracts. The team keeps these revenues and does not have to share them with the NBA or other NBA teams.

- The league divides the national televised games into different packages and sells the packages to various networks.
  - TNT: Weeknight games (Tuesday and Thursday games)
  - ESPN/ESPN2: Night games (Wednesday, Friday, and Sunday games)
  - ABC: Sunday afternoon games
  - NBA TV: Various games throughout the week
- In conjunction with satellite and digital television, the league offers viewers the option to subscribe to the NBA League Pass for an annual subscription rate, which gives fans access to all games regardless of the region in which they live.
- Other media
  - Radio
    - National: The league has an agreement with Sirius Satellite Radio, which owns the rights to broadcast every NBA game, including playoffs and finals.
    - Local: All teams negotiate deals with local AM or FM stations to broadcast games of interest to fans in that region, and teams are able to keep the revenues generated from these agreements.
  - Internet
    - The NBA website (www.nba.com) is a platform for the league to showcase the game and inform fans of upcoming games, events, and online initiatives. The website overlaps with the Women's National Basketball Association (WNBA) and NBA Development League to some degree in theme, content, and accessibility, and each provides a website link to the others' sites. The sites are all formatted similarly for league consistency. Furthermore, the website is offered in various languages to accommodate for fans around the world.
  - Gate receipts
    - In the NBA, the home team keeps all the revenue from gate receipts. The home team does not share its receipts with the visiting team. Teams that own their own facility keep all gate receipt revenues whereas those teams that lease a facility typically are required to share a portion of the gate receipts with the arena owner or pay a flat fee.

- Sponsorship
  - There are typically 12–15 major sponsors of the NBA in varying product categories, such as airlines, beverages, and credit card companies. Sponsors pay an annual fee to the NBA to become a recognized partner and for other related services. Current sponsors include Gatorade, T-Mobile, Wrigley's Gum, and FedEx.
- Merchandise and licensing
  - Adidas is the official uniform and apparel supplier of the NBA. As the exclusive outfitter for all 30 NBA teams, Adidas provides a wide array of licensed apparel and footwear products to the retail marketplace. Under this agreement, the league and its members collect licensing fees from Adidas for this partnership.

WOMEN'S NATIONAL BASKETBALL ASSOCIATION

The Women's National Basketball Association (WNBA) is a league composed of teams competing at the highest level of women's basketball in the world. The WNBA season starts in May and ends in August. The WNBA was founded in 1997 as a competing league to the already established American Basketball League (ABL), which began play in 1996. Months into its third season, the ABL was forced to file for Chapter 11 bankruptcy protection due to the competition of the WNBA and the insurmountable financial strains and mounting debt issues. Today, the WNBA is the only professional women's basketball league in the United States. The WNBA's other competitor, the Women's National Basketball League (WNBL), which was composed of only four teams, was forced to shut down in 2007 due to financial troubles.

The first professional women's basketball league in the United States was the Women's Basketball League (WBL). Founded in 1978, the WBL lasted only 3 years due to overwhelming financial problems, which forced the league and teams to cease operations.

The WNBA was formed as a single entity league in which NBA owners were given the opportunity to be "operator-investors" of WNBA franchises. The NBA owners who chose to participate in the WNBA were those who also owned and/or operated the basketball arena. Most also chose to use some of their front office staff to run the WNBA team. This eliminated the need to add a significant amount of resources and infrastructure. The WNBA franchise therefore provided the owners with additional revenue streams and a greater return on their existing assets. At the time of its founding, the WNBA required all franchises to be located in NBA markets. In addition, the WNBA league office had a great amount of power and control in dealing with particular team issues such as signing players and selling sponsorships.

This was part of the single entity structure and was done for both legal and business reasons.

In 2002, the league loosened its restraints and control over the teams. Allowing individual team ownership by non-NBA team owners and allowing WNBA teams to be located in non-NBA markets were changes that were implemented to spur league-wide growth and prosperity. As of 2008, 7 of the league's 14 teams are owned by non-NBA team owners (Atlanta Dream, Chicago Sky, Connecticut Sun, Houston Comets, Los Angeles Sparks, Seattle Storm, and Washington Mystics). The league's president is Donna Orender.

However, the WNBA and NBA are still linked closely through numerous practices and relationships. The WNBA league offices are housed in the NBA building in New York City. WNBA teams typically play in the same arenas as their local NBA teams, with exceptions in the non-NBA markets. In addition, the marketing goals of both leagues are closely aligned and aim to attract similar sponsors and partnerships.

The majority of the WNBA players have played at U.S. colleges and are selected through an annual draft process. Most of the players were born in the United States, but the number of international players continues to grow on an annual basis. No minor league development system exists for the WNBA, so the league depends on the various college programs and international market for player talent.

The league's popularity in the United States and breadth of fan base has been and is a constant concern for the league. The average WNBA attendance dropped to 7,739 during the 2007 season, compared to 8,174 in 2005, and has been in a constant decline since the 2002 season. The average 2006 attendance (7,478) was the lowest in league history.[10] Nonetheless, the league expanded in 2008 with the addition of one new team in Atlanta.

History of the Women's National Basketball Association

1996

- The American Basketball League (ABL) began its inaugural season with seven teams: Atlanta Glory, Colorado Xplosion, Columbus (OH) Quest, New England Blizzard, Portland (OR) Power, San Jose (CA) Lasers, and Seattle Reign.

- The NBA Board of Governors announced that the Women's National Basketball Association (WNBA) would be a single entity league and begin play in 1997.

- Val Ackerman was named the WNBA president (1996–2004).

- Sheryl Swoopes became the first player signed to the WNBA.

- Eight teams were announced: Charlotte (NC) Sting, Cleveland Rockers, Houston Comets, New York Liberty, Los Angeles Sparks, Phoenix Mercury, Sacramento Monarchs, and Utah Starzz.

1997

- The inaugural season began.

- The Detroit Shock and Washington Mystics were added as expansion teams for 1998 (10 teams).

- The National Women's Basketball League (NWBL) was founded to govern a competitive league for women. The NWBL consisted of four teams: San Diego Waves, Columbus (OH) Lady Blazers, Washington DC Defenders, and Long Beach (CA) Lightning.

1998

- Two WNBA expansion teams were announced for the 1999 season: Minnesota Lynx and Orlando Miracle (12 teams).

- The ABL folded prior to its 1998–1999 season.

1999

- The WNBA and the Women's National Basketball Players Association (WNBPA) agreed to the first collective bargaining agreement, a 4-year agreement from 1999–2003.

- The Indiana Fever, Miami Sol, Portland (OR) Fire, and Seattle Storm were announced as expansion teams for the 2000 season (16 teams).

- The inaugural WNBA All-Star Game was held at Madison Square Garden.

2001

- The NWBL Pro League began. The original teams included the Atlanta Justice, Birmingham (AL) Power, Mobile (AL) Majesty, and Kansas City Legacy.

2002

- The NBA Board of Governors voted to restructure the WNBA to allow individual team ownership, non-NBA owners, and non-NBA market locations.

- The Utah Starzz relocated to San Antonio and became the San Antonio Silver Stars for the 2003 season.

- The Miami Sol and Portland Fire ceased operations (14 teams).

2003

- The Mohegan Sun Casino became the first non-NBA owner when it purchased the Orlando Miracle and moved them to Connecticut, renaming the team the Connecticut Sun. (Charlotte Sting, Detroit Shock, Houston Comets, Indiana Fever, Los Angeles Sparks, Minnesota Lynx, New York Liberty, Phoenix Mercury, Sacramento Monarchs, San Antonio Silver Stars, Seattle Storm, and Washington Mystics were owned by NBA owners.)

- The WNBA and the WNBPA signed the second collective bargaining agreement for 2003–2007, with an option for 2008. The Collective Bargaining Agreement

(CBA) provided the players with free agency rights for the first time in professional women's sports.

2004

- The Cleveland Rockers franchise disbanded and the WNBA held a dispersal draft for Cleveland's players (13 teams).

2005

- League president Val Ackerman resigned from her position.
- Donna Orender, former senior vice president of the PGA Tour, was appointed president of the WNBA by NBA Commissioner David Stern.

2006

- The Chicago Sky started their first season (14 teams).

2007

- The Charlotte Sting folded (13 teams).

2008

- The Atlanta Dream were added for the 2008–2009 season (14 teams).
- The WNBA and the WNBPA agreed on a new 6-year labor agreement that began with the 2008 season and lasts through 2013.

Structure of the Women's National Basketball Association

League Alignment

- 13 total teams (**Table 16-2**)
- 2 conferences: Eastern Conference (6 teams) and Western Conference (7 teams)

Competition Format

- Head-to-head contests between teams; unbalanced schedule
- End-of-year playoffs

Schedule

- Game days
  - Games are played throughout the week as well as on weekends. Weekend games are also played during the daytime and select day games are broadcasted nationally.
  - Nationally broadcast games: 1–2 weeknight games per week; 1 game on Saturday afternoon per week; 1 game on Sunday afternoon on the last day of the season.
- Preseason (May): Two to three exhibition games per team with each team hosting one to two games
- Regular season (May–August): 34 games (17 home, 17 away)
  - Each conference (Eastern and Western): 20 games within conference (10 home games), 14 games out of conference (7 home games)
- Playoffs (August–September)
  - 3 rounds: Conference Semi-Finals, Conference Finals, WNBA Finals
  - 8 teams: Top 4 teams from each conference
  - Teams seeded 1–4 in each conference based on regular season won-lost records
  - Conference Semi-Final round (Eastern and Western): Best of three games—Seed 1 vs. Seed 4; Seed 2 vs. Seed 3
  - Conference Final round (Eastern and Western): Best of three games; winners of Semi-Final rounds play one another
  - WNBA Finals: Best of five games—Eastern Conference Champion vs. Western Conference Champion
- All-Star Game (July)
  - Mid-season game pits Eastern Conference All-Stars vs. Western Conference All-Stars
  - 2009 All-Star game: Phoenix, AZ

Table 16-2   WNBA Teams (2008)

Eastern Conference		Western Conference	
Team	**Location**	**Team**	**Location**
Atlanta Dream	Atlanta, GA	Houston Comets	Houston, TX
Chicago Sky	Chicago, IL	Los Angeles Sparks	Los Angeles, CA
Connecticut Sun	Uncasville, CT	Minnesota Lynx	Minneapolis, MN
Detroit Shock	Auburn Hills, MI	Phoenix Mercury	Phoenix, AZ
Indiana Fever	Indianapolis, IN	Sacramento Monarchs	Sacramento, CA
New York Liberty	New York, NY	San Antonio Silver Stars	San Antonio, TX
Washington Mystics	Washington, DC	Seattle Storm	Seattle, WA

Money Matters for the Women's National Basketball Association

Sources of Revenue

- Television broadcast revenues
  - The WNBA negotiates the league's national television contracts on behalf of its teams. The league office coordinates the distribution of the national television revenues to each of the teams. There are no local television deals or regional sports networks.
  - The league divides national television programming into two distinct packages (weeknight games and weekend day games) and sells the packages to networks. In 2007, the league announced a new 8-year television broadcast deal with ESPN/ABC. The deal begins in 2009 and will go through the league's 20th season in 2016. Under the terms of the new deal, ESPN will pay an undisclosed broadcast rights fee. The deal calls for ABC, ESPN, and ESPN2 to televise a minimum of 18 regular season games, primarily on Mondays, Tuesdays, and weekend afternoons. ESPN also gains digital media rights.
- Other media
  - Radio
    - Local: All teams negotiate deals with local AM or FM stations to broadcast games of interest to fans in that region.
  - Internet
    - The WNBA website (www.wnba.com) is a platform for the league to showcase the game and provide some additional advertising revenues for the WNBA. The marketing goals of the WNBA and NBA are closely aligned; each league's website overlaps in some degree in theme, content, and accessibility, and each provides a website link to the other league.
  - Sponsorship
    - There are typically 12–15 major sponsors of the WNBA in varying product categories, such as airlines, beverages, and credit card companies. Sponsors pay an annual fee to the WNBA to become a recognized partner and for other related services. Some of the current WNBA sponsors include Discover Card, T-Mobile, and Toyota. Although many sponsors of the NBA often choose to sponsor the WNBA as well, they do not necessarily have sponsorship rights to the WNBA.
  - Merchandise and licensing
    - Adidas is the official uniform and apparel supplier of the WNBA. As the exclusive outfitter for all 14 WNBA teams, Adidas provides a wide array of licensed apparel and footwear products to the retail marketplace. Under this agreement, the league and its members receive an annual merchandise fee from Adidas for this partnership.

NATIONAL BASKETBALL DEVELOPMENT LEAGUE

The National Basketball Association Development League (D-League) is the official minor league of the NBA. It consists of 12 teams with a maximum of 10 players on each roster. Originally, teams were located solely in the southeastern states, but are now located throughout the country (**Table 16-3**). Since its inception in 2001, the D-League has gained exposure through its affiliation with the NBA. Each D-League team has between one and three NBA teams affiliated with it. All teams are privately owned except for Fayetteville and Roanoke, who are still owned by the NBA. The Los Angeles Lakers became the first NBA team to own a D-League team when the Los Angeles D-Fenders started play in the 2006 season. D-League teams play a 48-game schedule over 20 weeks from November through April. Tickets range anywhere from $8 to $80, and teams usually offer flexible season ticket plans. Average attendance for the D-League is roughly 2,000 fans per game, and can vary depending on where the game is played.

The league offers players the opportunity to improve their game and have a chance to be called up to the NBA. At the start of the 2008–2009 season, exactly 119 players in the history of the D-League have been called up to play in the NBA. Along with developing talent, the D-League also is designed to help grow the sport of basketball, while offering fans an affordable alternative to major league sports. NBA teams can send players down to their affiliated D-League teams up to three times in a given year provided that the player has been on an NBA roster for less than two seasons.

Along with player development, the D-League also is a training ground for coaches, trainers, referees, and front office executives. As of September 2005, 11 former D-League coaches, 5 athletic trainers, 11 referees, and 29 front office

Table 16-3   D-League Teams (2008–2009)

Team	Location
Albuquerque Thunderbirds	Albuquerque, NM
Anaheim Arsenal	Anaheim, CA
Austin Toros	Austin, TX
Bakersfield Jam	Bakersfield, CA
Colorado 14ers	Broomfield, CA
Dakota Wizards	Bismarck, ND
Erie BayHawks	Erie, PA
Fort Wayne Mad Ants	Fort Wayne, IN
Idaho Stampede	Boise, ID
Iowa Energy	Des, Moines, IA
Los Angeles D-Fenders	Los Angeles, CA
Reno Big Horns	Reno, NV
Rio Grande Valley Vipers	McAllen, TX
Sioux Falls Skyforce	Sioux Falls, SD
Tulsa 66ers	Tulsa, OK
Utah Flash	Provo, UT

executives have been called up to the NBA ranks since 2001, while 6 other front office executives earned positions in other major leagues. NBA commissioner David Stern continually discusses expansion plans for the D-League, in order to create a more integrated minor league structure similar to professional hockey (American Hockey League) and professional baseball (Minor League Baseball). In addition to the D-League, other minor league basketball organizations are the Continental Basketball Association (CBA), the International Basketball League (IBL), and the American Basketball Association (ABA); however, none of these other leagues has any affiliation with the NBA.

Each D-League team employs a staff comprising several departments, which include sales, marketing, accounting, player personnel, community relations, media relations, and sports medicine. In the summer of 2007, league headquarters moved from Greenville, South Carolina, to New York. There are currently 11 individuals employed at the league office.

CONTINENTAL BASKETBALL ASSOCIATION

Established in 1946, the Continental Basketball Association (CBA) is the oldest professional basketball league in the world. Headquartered in Boise, Idaho, the CBA is a professional minor league with no direct affiliation to the NBA, although it is affiliated with USA Basketball, the national governing body of basketball in the United States. The CBA is an active member of USA Basketball, which gives it representation on the board of directors and helps determine how USA Basketball is run. The CBA has been responsible for helping produce a number of players (e.g., Tim Legler, John Starks) and coaches (e.g., Phil Jackson, George Karl). For many years, the CBA acted as the unofficial development league for the NBA; however, when the D-League was formed in 2001 as the official development league of the NBA, the CBA lost some of its importance. Despite this, players can be and still are signed from the CBA to NBA rosters.

In 1999, Isiah Thomas purchased the CBA for $10 million and reorganized the league as a single entity. After a year as league owner, Thomas accepted an offer to become head coach of the Indiana Pacers of the NBA. Thomas abandoned the CBA in 2000, placing it in a blind trust, and within 4 months, in February 2001, the CBA suspended play and folded. The CBA was forced to declare bankruptcy in 2001. Two CBA teams joined the International Basketball League (IBL) to finish their season in 2001. The IBL then folded after the 2001 season, and the CBA reorganized with the remaining IBL teams and began play in November 2001. By 2008, the CBA had 10 teams that were located throughout the United States. However, on April 6, 2004, four teams (Dakota Wizards, Idaho Stampede, Sioux Falls Skyforce, and expansion team Colorado 14ers) left the CBA and

Table 16-4   CBA Teams (2007–2008)

American Conference	
Team	**Location**
Albany Patroons	Albany, NY
Atlanta Krunk	Atlanta, GA
East Kentucky Miners	Pikeville, KY
Minot Skyrockets	Minot, ND
Pittsburgh Xplosion	Pittsburgh, PA

National Conference	
Team	**Location**
Butte Daredevils	Butte, MT
Great Falls Explorers	Great Falls, MT
Oklahoma Cavalry	Lawton, OK
Rio Grande Valley Silverados	Edinburg, TX
Yakama Sun Kings	Yakima, WA

joined the NBA Development League. In 2007, the CBA was composed of 10 teams located throughout the United States (**Table 16-4**). Each CBA team plays a 48-game schedule from November through March. Tickets range anywhere from $5 to $50, and attendance at games averages over 2,400 fans per game.

Endnotes

1. Information obtained from the NBA league website (www.nba.com) unless otherwise noted.

2. Lombardo, J. (2008, Apr. 14–20). Attendance Down, TV Up for NBA. *Street and Smith's SportsBusiness Journal,* vol. 10, issue 50, pp. 1, 33.

2. As part of the McDonald's Open, in 1987 the Milwaukee Bucks defeated Tracer Milan of Italy to become the first NBA team to play an exhibition game against a European opponent. The following year the Atlanta Hawks traveled to the Soviet Union to play the Soviet National Team and became the first NBA team to compete in an official exhibition game outside of North America. In 1990, the Phoenix Suns and the Utah Jazz traveled to Tokyo, Japan, to play in the first regular season NBA game outside of North America. Starting in 1993 with the Orlando Magic and the Atlanta Hawks, the NBA has held preseason games outside of the United States and Canada. As of January 2008, NBA teams have played in a combined 101 exhibition, preseason, or regular season games outside of the United States or Canada.

3. International players and players that decide to forego their final year(s) of college eligibility must declare themselves eligible for the NBA 60 days prior to the NBA draft in which they wish to be selected.

4. Information obtained from National Basketball Players Association website (www.nbpa.com).

5. Between 1995 and 2007, 134 international players have been selected in the NBA draft. This includes two first overall selections: Yao Ming from China in 2002 and Andrea Bargnani from Italy in 2006.

6. National Basketball Players Association, op. cit.

7. Playing an unequal number of games against each team in a particular league is considered an unbalanced schedule. Typically, teams will play other teams in their own division with a greater frequency than other teams in the league. An unbalanced schedule works favorably for teams in a weaker division because teams within a division play one another more often in an unbalanced schedule. In contrast, this system works unfavorably for teams playing in a stronger division. Many leagues utilize an unbalanced schedule due to scheduling conflicts, travel issues, and to induce inter-division rivalries.

8. Associated Press. (2007, June 27). NBA Announces Extension of TV Deals with ESPN/ABC, TNT. *ESPN.com*. Retrieved January 18, 2008, from http://sports.espn.go.com/espn/wire?section=nba&id=2918075.

9. Information obtained from http://nbahoopsonline.com/Articles/2007-08/NBArevinuesharing.html.

10. England, N. (2006, June 27). Women's Sports Insider: Mercury Cruising While Rest of WNBA Falters. *San Antonio Express*. Retrieved January 18, 2008, from http://www.mysanantonio.com/sports/stories/MYSA082806.wnbainsider.en.3fc84d5b.html.

Hockey

NATIONAL HOCKEY LEAGUE

The National Hockey League (NHL) is the premier professional hockey league in the world. Composed of teams located throughout the United States and Canada, the NHL consists mostly of players from Canada, the United States, and Europe. Amateur players from high schools, junior leagues, colleges, and club teams are selected to play in the league during the annual NHL Entry Draft. NHL teams have affiliates in the American Hockey League (AHL) and the East Coast Hockey League (ECHL), which serve as the minor leagues for player development.

From 1967 to 1979, the NHL witnessed tremendous growth when 15 franchises were added to the "Original Six."[1] The NHL has not had competition from rival leagues, except for the World Hockey Association (WHA), which operated from 1972 to 1979. It differentiated itself from the NHL by not recognizing the reserve clause,[2] which resulted in multi-million-dollar salaries and unstable franchises. When the league folded for financial reasons, four WHA teams joined the NHL: Edmonton Oilers, New England (Hartford) Whalers, Quebec Nordiques, and Winnipeg Jets.

The late 1990s in the NHL were characterized by rapidly escalating player salaries and expansion into nontraditional hockey markets, particularly in the southeast United States. Revenues failed to keep up with the rising costs of operating an NHL franchise and many owners complained of significant financial losses. In the early 21st century, the NHL owners claimed to be faced with significant and escalating financial problems that eventually resulted in a lockout. The NHL, with support from the owners, decided to lock out the players before training camp in the fall of 2004. Negotiations for a new collective bargaining agreement

(CBA) failed, leading to the first cancellation of an entire season (2004–2005) in professional sports. The NHL and the NHL Players Association (NHLPA) subsequently reached a collective bargaining agreement on July 13, 2005, resulting in major changes, including the introduction of a hard salary cap, maximum player salaries, enhanced revenue sharing, drug testing, and new playing rules.

According to *Forbes*, 2004 team values ranged from $100 million (Carolina Hurricanes) to $282 million (New York Rangers). The goal of the owners in the new CBA was to minimize this gap and improve the overall health of the league. Citing feedback from its avid fan base, the NHL altered its playing rules in hopes of providing a more entertaining, offensive style of play. In reaction to the Congressional hearings on steroid use in professional sports, the NHL implemented its first drug-testing program in the 2005 CBA as well.

According to reports published in the *SportsBusiness Journal*, league-wide revenue grew by over 11% from 2007 to 2008 and reached approximately $2.56 billion for the 2007–2008 season. The league generates revenue through ticket sales, broadcast rights (both traditional and digital media), sponsorship, licensing, and international ventures. In 2007, *Forbes* reported that league franchise values had increased by an average of 23% after two seasons under the new CBA. Team values ranged from $143 million (Nashville Predators) to $413 million (Toronto Maple Leafs).

League headquarters are located in New York City and consist of several departments including administrative, communications, accounting, finance, hockey operations, legal counsel, retail/licensing, sales, marketing, and business development.

History of the National Hockey League[3]

1917

- The NHL began its first season of play with four teams: Ottawa Senators, Montreal Canadiens, Montreal Wanderers, and Toronto Arenas.
- Teacher and sports writer Frank Calder was elected as the first president of the NHL (1917–1943).

1918

- The Montreal Wanderers became the first team to fold from the NHL (3 teams).

1919

- The Toronto Arenas changed their name to the Toronto St. Patricks.
- The Quebec Bulldogs joined the NHL after suspending operations for two seasons (4 teams).

1920

- The Quebec Bulldogs moved to Hamilton, Ontario, and became the Hamilton Tigers.

1923

- Rules changed for the number of players on the ice at once from 7-on-7, to 6-on-6.
- The first hockey game (not an NHL game) was broadcast by Foster Hewitt.

1924

- The Boston Bruins and Montreal Maroons were granted expansion franchises in the NHL (6 teams).
- The Boston Bruins hosted the Montreal Maroons for the first NHL game ever played in the United States.

1925

- The Hamilton Tigers moved to New York and became the New York Americans; the Pittsburgh Pirates also joined the league (7 teams).

1926

- The New York Rangers, Chicago Blackhawks, and Detroit Cougars were added as expansion franchises in the NHL (10 teams).
- The Toronto St. Patricks changed their name to the Toronto Maple Leafs.

1931

- The Pittsburgh Pirates moved to Philadelphia and became the Quakers for the 1930–1931 season, but folded after the season (9 teams).

1932

- After two seasons as the Falcons, Detroit changed their nickname to Red Wings.

1934

- The first NHL All-Star game was held in Toronto.
- The Ottawa Senators moved to Missouri and were renamed the St. Louis Eagles.

1935

- The St. Louis Eagles franchise dissolved (8 teams).

1939

- The Montreal Maroons folded due to financial problems (7 teams).

1940

- The New York Rangers faced the Montreal Canadiens in the first televised hockey game in the United States.

1941

- The New York Americans changed their name to the Brooklyn Americans.

1942

- The Brooklyn Americans folded (6 teams).

1943

- Mervyn "Red" Dutton, former NHL player with the Montreal Maroons and New York Americans, was named NHL president (1943–1946).

1946

- Clarence Campbell, lawyer and former NHL referee, was named president of the NHL (1946–1977).

1952

- Hockey Night in Canada debuted on CBC Television.[4]

1957

- The first hockey players union was formed with Detroit Red Wing Ted Lindsay serving as president. The owners were able to soon dissolve the union and Lindsay was traded to the last place Chicago Blackhawks as retribution.[5]

1958

- The NHL color barrier was broken: Willie O'Ree of the Boston Bruins became the first African American to play in an NHL game.

1963

- Twenty-one players were selected in the NHL's first amateur draft.

1967

- The NHL added six expansion franchises: Pittsburgh Penguins, Minnesota North Stars, Philadelphia Flyers, Los Angeles Kings, Oakland (CA) Seals, and St. Louis Blues (12 teams).

- The NHLPA was formed by representatives from the original six NHL teams. Bob Pulford (Toronto) was elected the NHLPA's first president.[6]

1970

- The Vancouver Canucks and Buffalo Sabres were granted expansion franchises (14 teams).

- The Oakland Seals changed their name to the California Golden Seals.

1971

- The Atlanta Flames and New York Islanders were granted expansion franchises (16 teams).

1972

- The World Hockey Association (WHA) was started as a rival league to the NHL.

1974

- The Kansas City Scouts and Washington Capitals were granted expansion franchises (18 teams).

1976

- The Kansas City Scouts moved to Denver and became the Colorado Rockies.

- The California Golden Seals moved to Ohio and became the Cleveland Barons.

1977

- John Ziegler, a senior partner in a law firm in Detroit and an executive with the Detroit Red Wings, was named the president of the NHL (1977–1992).[7]

1978

- The Cleveland Barons dissolved in a merger with the Minnesota North Stars (17 teams).

1979

- Four WHA teams joined the NHL: Edmonton Oilers, Hartford Whalers, Quebec Nordiques, and Winnipeg Jets (21 teams).

- The All-Star game was replaced for one year with the Challenge Cup in which the NHL All-Stars faced off against the best Soviet Union players in a best of three series—the Soviet Union won the series 2–1.[8]

1980

- The Atlanta Flames relocated to Calgary, Alberta, and became the Calgary Flames.

1982

- The Colorado Rockies team was sold, relocated to New Jersey, and renamed the New Jersey Devils.

1990

- The San Jose Sharks were granted an expansion franchise in the NHL (22 teams).

1991

- The Tampa Bay Lighting and Ottawa Senators were granted expansion franchises (24 teams).

1992

- Gil Stein, an executive with the Philadelphia Flyers, was named president of the NHL (1992–1993).[9]

- Deputy executive of the NHLPA Bob Goodenow replaced Alan Eagleson as the head of the NHLPA (1992–2005). Under Goodenow's leadership, NHL players' salaries increased dramatically.[10]

1993

- Gary Bettman, lawyer and vice president of the NBA, was named the first commissioner of the NHL (1993–present).

- The Minnesota North Stars moved to Texas and became the Dallas Stars.

- The Florida Panthers and Mighty Ducks of Anaheim (CA) were granted expansion franchises (26 teams).

1995

- The Quebec Nordiques team was sold, relocated to Colorado, and renamed the Colorado Avalanche.

- The Winnipeg Jets team was sold and relocated to Phoenix, Arizona, where it was renamed the Phoenix Coyotes.

- The 1994–1995 season was shortened due to a 103-day lockout (October 1, 1994 to January 11, 1995), resulting in a 48-game regular season. The salary cap was the main point of contention during negotiations.[11]

1997

- The NHL announced that it would expand to 30 teams in the following cities: Atlanta, Columbus (OH), Nashville, and Minnesota.

- The Hartford Whalers relocated to Raleigh, North Carolina, and became the Carolina Hurricanes.

1998

- The Nashville Predators entered the NHL as an expansion franchise (27 teams).

1999

- The Atlanta Thrashers entered the NHL as an expansion franchise (28 teams).

2000

- The Minnesota Wild and Columbus Blue Jackets entered the NHL as expansion franchises (30 teams).

2003

- The first regular season outdoor game in NHL history took place in Edmonton, Alberta's Commonwealth Stadium. The game between the Montreal Canadiens and the Edmonton Oilers was billed as the Heritage Classic and shattered the NHL single-game attendance record with 57,167 fans in attendance.

2004

- The NHL lockout began on September 15, 2004, and the 2004–2005 season was cancelled on February 16, 2005.[12]

2005

- After 301 days, the NHL lockout ended on July 13, 2005, when the NHL and the NHLPA agreed to a new, 6-year CBA (2006–2011) with a salary cap and significant changes in the playing rules.[13]

2008

- The second regular season outdoor game, the Winter Classic, took place on New Year's Day at Ralph Wilson Stadium in Buffalo, New York. The heavily promoted matchup between the Pittsburgh Penguins and the Buffalo Sabres attracted a single-game record 71,217 fans. It was the first outdoor NHL game to be both played and nationally broadcasted in the United States. The overnight ratings were the highest for an NHL game in over 10 years.

Structure of the National Hockey League[14]

League Alignment

- 30 total teams (**Table 17-1**)
- 2 conferences: Eastern Conference (15 teams, 3 divisions) and Western Conference (15 teams, 3 divisions)

Competition Format

- Head-to-head contests between teams; unbalanced schedule[15]
  - Division winners and playoff schedule based on point system: Two points awarded for a win in regulation, overtime, or shootout; one point awarded for loss in overtime or shootout; no points awarded for loss in regulation.
  - End-of-year playoffs determine league champion, who is awarded the Stanley Cup.

Schedule

- Game days
  - Games are played throughout the week, usually during the evening. Weekend games are played in both the afternoon and the evening.
  - Preseason (September): 5–7 exhibition games per team with each team hosting 2–3 home games

- Regular season (October–April) format starting for 2008–2009 season[16]:
  - Each team plays 82 games (41 home, 41 away).
  - Split into 64 conference games (32 home), 24 games within division (12 home), and 18 out of conference games (9 home).
- Playoffs (April–June)
  - 4 rounds: Round 1, Conference Semi-Finals, Conference Finals, Stanley Cup Finals.
  - 8 top teams from each conference, based on points.
  - 3 division winners get top seeds for both conferences (based on points).
  - Remaining 5 spots from each conference are determined based on highest number of points.
  - Round 1: Eastern and Western Conference teams play only against teams in their own conference.
    - Seed 1 vs. Seed 8, Seed 2 vs. Seed 7, Seed 3 vs. Seed 6, Seed 4 vs. Seed 5
    - Best of 7 series
    - Higher seed hosts series
  - Round 2: Eastern and Western Conference teams play only against teams in their own conference
    - Highest seed remaining plays lowest seed remaining
    - Second highest seed remaining plays second lowest seed remaining
  - Round 3: Conference Finals
  - Round 4: Stanley Cup Finals
    - Conference champions play each other.
    - Home ice advantage is given to the team with the highest point total.
- All-Star Game (mid-season)
  - Mid-season exhibition game pits Eastern Conference All-Stars vs. Western Conference All-Stars.
  - Site is determined on a rotational basis.
    - 2008: Atlanta, January 16, 2008
    - 2009: Montreal, January 25, 2009
    - 2010: No game due to NHL player participation in the Winter Olympics

Money Matters for the National Hockey League

Sources of Revenue

- Television broadcasting revenues
  - National
    - The NHL televises many games nationally, mostly on an exclusive basis, meaning no other broadcaster can televise the same games. Regional sports networks sign agreements with their local team to broadcast many or all of the team's games, except for those broadcast nationally. In the United States,

Table 17-1   NHL Teams (2007–2008)

Eastern Conference		Western Conference	
Atlantic Division		**Central Division**	
Team	**Location**	**Team**	**Location**
New Jersey Devils	Newark, NJ	Chicago Blackhawks	Chicago, IL
New York Islanders	Uniondale, NY	Columbus Blue Jackets	Columbus, OH
New York Rangers	New York, NY	Detroit Red Wings	Detroit, MI
Philadelphia Flyers	Philadelphia, PA	Nashville Predators	Nashville, TN
Pittsburgh Penguins	Pittsburgh, PA	St. Louis Blues	St. Louis, MO
Northeast Division		**Northwest Division**	
Team	**Location**	**Team**	**Location**
Boston Bruins	Boston, MA	Calgary Flames	Calgary, Alberta
Buffalo Sabres	Buffalo, NY	Colorado Avalanche	Denver, CO
Montreal Canadiens	Montreal, Quebec	Edmonton Oilers	Edmonton, Alberta
Ottawa Senators	Ottawa, Ontario	Minnesota Wild	Minneapolis, MN
Toronto Maple Leafs	Toronto, Ontario	Vancouver Canucks	Vancouver, British Columbia
Southeast Division		**Pacific Division**	
Team	**Location**	**Team**	**Location**
Atlanta Thrashers	Atlanta, GA	Anaheim Ducks	Anaheim, CA
Carolina Hurricanes	Raleigh, NC	Dallas Stars	Dallas, TX
Florida Panthers	Miami, FL	Los Angeles Kings	Los Angeles, CA
Tampa Bay Lightning	Tampa Bay, FL	Phoenix Coyotes	Phoenix, AZ
Washington Capitals	Washington, DC	San Jose Sharks	San Jose, CA

the NHL televises games nationally on NBC on Sunday afternoon (starting in January), on Versus on Monday and Tuesday nights (starting at the beginning of the season), and on HDNet on Thursday and Saturday nights (starting at the beginning of the season). The NHL added a "flexible scheduling" option for the 2007–2008 season, allowing NBC to pick up to four games to broadcast with 13 days' notice. This allows NBC to broadcast marquee games that may not have already been on the broadcast schedule. HDNet also uses flexible scheduling and selects which games it will broadcast on a bi-monthly basis. NBC and Versus share coverage of the playoffs, with Versus covering the first two games of the finals and NBC covering the remaining games in prime time. In Canada, the NHL televises games nationally on Canadian Broadcasting Corporation (CBC) and The Sports Network (TSN) in English and on Resau Des Sports (RDS) in French. For the 2007–2008 season, CBC's 85-game schedule included 10 afternoon games, Saturday night doubleheaders all season long, 7 tripleheaders, and the All-Star Game. TSN broadcasted 70 national games during the 2007–2008 season. RDS carries all 82 Montreal Canadiens' games and additional contests featuring teams from around the NHL. All three Canadian networks feature extensive playoff coverage. The 2007–2008 schedule for the NHL Network (seen in the United States and Canada) included a 40-game live broadcast schedule and nightly live look-ins on various games around the NHL.[17]

- All national television revenues are shared equally among the 30 NHL teams. Teams earned approximately $2 million each, but television revenues accounted for only 3% of league revenues.[18]
- Versus: Two-year, $135 million contract, with a mutual option for a third year valued at $72.5 million that was picked up in 2007.[19] There are three additional option years with the compensation based on the number of Versus subscribers. The agreement began in October 2005 and has the potential to run through the 2010–2011 season. Versus will air 58–78 games each season, airing Monday–Thursday with some nights featuring doubleheaders. Only one NHL game will be shown on Mondays, with the rights to that granted exclusively to Versus. Versus also holds the rights to the NHL All-Star Game, NHL playoff games, and the first two games of the Stanley Cup. Comcast, the parent company of Versus, will also be allowed to provide streaming video of two NHL games per night and is

permitted to air other NHL games on its regional networks with consent from the organization and rights owner. Additionally, should Versus gain the rights to broadcast another major sports entity or fall short of targeted distribution quotas, Comcast will pay the NHL a $15 million fee.[20]

- NBC: A 2-year agreement was agreed upon prior to the cancelled 2004–2005 season. As a revenue-sharing agreement, the NHL receives no guaranteed revenues from the broadcasts of games on NBC. NBC has an option for the 2008–2009 season.[21]
- The NHL offers an NHL Center-Ice package that airs over 40 games a week to viewers with digital cable or satellite network at a cost of $149–$169.

- Local
  - Each NHL team has a local television territory where it may show telecasts of its games. A team will partner with a local television network, usually a regional sports network, to televise its games in its territory. Generally, each club and its local telecasters will decide which games will be televised locally and the financial terms of these partnerships.
- Other media
  - Radio
    - XM Radio has a 10-year, $100-million agreement with the NHL that began in October 2005. XM became the exclusive satellite broadcaster of the NHL at the start of the 2007–2008 season. XM holds the rights to broadcast every game for every team, including the NHL All-Star Game, Stanley Cup playoffs, and Stanley Cup finals.[22]
- Gate receipts
  - In 2007–2008, average gate revenues were about $37 million. The range was from $18.4 to $77.9 million.
- Sponsorship[23]
  - There are typically 12–15 major sponsors of the NHL in varying product categories, such as airlines, beverages, and credit card companies. Current sponsors of the NHL include Bud Light, Dodge, MasterCard, Bank of America, Best Buy, and McDonalds. Sponsors pay an annual fee to the NHL to become a recognized partner.[24]
- Merchandise and licensing
  - Reebok-CCM Hockey is the official uniform supplier of the NHL. As the exclusive outfitter for all 30 NHL teams, Reebok provides a wide array of licensed apparel and footwear products to the retail marketplace. Under this agreement, the league and its members receive an annual licensing fee from Reebok for this partnership.[25]

AMERICAN HOCKEY LEAGUE

The American Hockey League (AHL) is the class AAA[26]–level minor league in North America and serves as the most advanced affiliate league to the NHL. Teams are composed of NHL prospects and fringe NHL players looking to make an NHL roster. The AHL's roots go back to 1926 with the Canadian-American League, which had teams in Providence, Springfield, Quebec City, Boston, and New Haven. The Canadian-American (Can-Am) League merged with the International Hockey League (IHL) in 1936 to create the International-American League, and became the AHL when the remaining Canadian teams left the IHL in 1941. Another merger of the second International League and the AHL in the 2001–2002 season marked the beginning of a new era, as the AHL became the official minor league affiliate[27] of the NHL. As the official affiliate, NHL parent clubs will assign players under their control to their respective minor league club. AHL clubs serve as a way of both developing up-and-coming prospects and keeping a pool of veteran players for the parent club to call upon in case of injuries or poor performance.

The AHL is composed of 29 teams located in the United States and Canada, with the league headquarters located in Springfield, Massachusetts (**Table 17-2**). Teams play an 80-game schedule that begins in early October and ends in April. The league is divided into two conferences, the Eastern Conference and the Western Conference, with each having two divisions, the Atlantic and the East in the Eastern Conference, and the North and West in the Western Conference. Four teams from each division qualify for the playoffs; however, if the fifth place team in one division has more points than the fourth seed in the other division of the same conference, the fifth place team will be granted the playoff slot in the opposing division. Each division has a playoff to determine the division champion. The two division champions then face each other for the conference championship. The winners of each conference then play each other in the Calder Cup final.

During the 2006–2007 season, teams averaged 5,546 fans in attendance per game.[28] Ticket prices ranged from $9 to $50 depending on venue and seat location. Most arenas tend to have capacities between 6,000 and 12,000 persons. The majority of teams share arenas with other organizations and events. Games are broadcast via the Internet through the team's website; each game is a pay-per-view broadcast costing $6, and requires a high-speed Internet connection and Windows Media Player.

Affiliation deals between AHL teams and NHL teams are not permanent and usually last 2–3 years; however, the agreements can be extended. In addition to gate receipts, the AHL draws revenue from both corporate sponsorships, which topped $2 million for the 2005–2006 season, and television contracts. Corporate sponsors include Dodge, CCM, Reebok, Dodge, Comcast Sportsnet, and Fox Sports Net.[29]

Table 17-2   AHL Teams (2007–2008)

Eastern Conference		Western Conference	
Atlantic Division		**North Division**	
Team	**Location**	**Team**	**Location**
Hartford Wolfpack	Hartford, CT	Grand Rapids Griffins	Grand Rapids, MI
Lowell Devils	Lowell, MA	Hamilton Bulldogs	Hamilton, Ontario
Manchester Monarchs	Manchester, NH	Lake Erie Monsters	Cleveland, OH
Portland Pirates	Portland, ME	Manitoba Moose	Winnipeg, Manitoba
Providence Bruins	Providence, RI	Rochester Americans	Rochester, NY
Springfield Falcons	Springfield, MA	Syracuse Crunch	Syracuse, NY
Worcester Sharks	Worcester, MA	Toronto Marlies	Toronto, Ontario
East Division		**West Division**	
Team	**Location**	**Team**	**Location**
Albany River Rats	Albany, NY	Chicago Wolves	Chicago, IL
Binghamton Senators	Binghamton, NY	Houston Aeros	Houston, TX
Bridgeport Sound Tigers	Bridgeport, CT	Iowa Stars	Des Moines, IA
Hershey Bears	Hershey, PA	Milwaukee Admirals	Milwaukee, WI
Norfolk Admirals	Norfolk, VA	Peoria Rivermen	Peoria, IL
Philadelphia Phantoms	Philadelphia, PA	Quad City Flames	Moline, IL
Wilkes-Barre Scranton Penguins	Wilkes-Barre, PA	Rockford IceHogs	Rockford, IL
		San Antonio Rampage	San Antonio, TX

Additionally, individual teams can negotiate corporate sponsorship deals to help generate revenues. Although there are no league-wide broadcasting deals, teams do negotiate individual television contracts with local broadcasters. Although this does bring in revenue, it is usually a minimal amount.

Like Minor League Baseball, most AHL teams are independently owned and operated locally, and general managers and staff are responsible for running the business side of the organization. Departments within an AHL front office include public relations, community relations, facility management, business operations, new media, tickets, and marketing and sales.

ECHL

The ECHL (formerly known as the East Coast Hockey League, see below) is a class AA[30] minor league hockey organization that serves as a development league for AHL and NHL teams. The ECHL was founded in 1988 with the merger of five teams from the folding Atlantic Coast Hockey League and All-American Hockey League. In 2002, the league expanded by adding seven west coast teams from the defunct West Coast Hockey League. The league changed its official name to the acronym ECHL to reflect the fact that the league has teams throughout the country, not just on the east coast. The ECHL is composed of 25 teams (**Table 17-3**) and has continually searched for viable markets. Along with providing hockey fans with affordable family entertainment, the ECHL provides young, talented players the opportunity for professional development.

Teams are limited to four veteran players, which are players over the age of 24 or who have more than 260 games' experience in professional hockey. Most teams have an AHL and NHL affiliation; however, there are some franchises with either an NHL or AHL affiliation team and some are completely independent. At times, NHL affiliates send players to the ECHL; however, ECHL general managers cannot rely on their affiliate team or teams to provide them with enough players to fill their roster. Therefore, they must also sign players to be on the team.

A weekly team-wide salary cap is in place and is set at $11,550; the salary floor is $8,300. Affiliate teams are allowed to receive $525 per week from their AHL or NHL affiliate, but anything over that amount is considered a salary cap violation. The league minimum salary for rookies (players with less than 25 games of experience or who have not been on a playoff roster) is $350 per week; a "returning player" will receive a minimum of $395 per week.[31]

The 72-game regular season begins in late October and ends in early April. In 2006–2007, the ECHL drew an average of nearly 4,170 fans per game.[32] Tickets generally range from $11 to $29. Teams also generate revenue through corporate sponsorship. Typically, ECHL teams have roughly 40 corporate sponsorships supporting their franchise. Games are broadcast via the Internet through the team's website; each game is a pay-per-view broadcast costing $6, and requires a high-speed Internet connection and Windows Media Player.

Table 17-3   ECHL Teams (2007–2008)

National Conference		American Conference	
Pacific Division		**North Division**	
Team	**Location**	**Team**	**Location**
Bakersfield Condors	Bakersfield, CA	Cincinnati Cyclones	Cincinnati, OH
Fresno Falcons	Fresno, CA	Dayton Bombers	Dayton, OH
Las Vegas Wranglers	Las Vegas, NV	Elmira Jackals	Elmira, NY
Stockton Thunder	Stockton, CA	Johnston Chiefs	Johnston, PA
		Reading Royals	Reading, PA
West Division		Trenton Titans	Trenton, NJ
		Wheeling Nailers	Wheeling, WV
Team	**Location**		
Alaska Aces	Anchorage, AK	**South Division**	
Idaho Steelheads	Boise, ID		
Phoenix Road Runners	Phoenix, AZ	**Team**	**Location**
Utah Grizzlies	Salt Lake City, UT	Augusta Lynx	Augusta, GA
Victoria Salmon Kings	Victoria, British Columbia	Charlotte Checkers	Charlotte, NC
		Columbia Inferno	Columbia, SC
		Florida Everblades	Estero, FL
		Gwinnett Gladiators	Duluth, GA
		Mississippi Sea Wolves	Biloxi, MS
		Pensacola Ice Pilots	Pensacola, FL
		South Carolina Stingrays	North Charleston, SC
		Texas Wild Catters	Beaumont, TX

Departments within an ECHL front office include administrative, hockey operations, communications, marketing/sales, and community relations.

CENTRAL HOCKEY LEAGUE

The Central Hockey League (CHL) is an AA professional minor league that features lower-level AHL and NHL prospects, and has a lower quality of play than the ECHL. The CHL was established in the fall of 1992 as a single entity. By 1996, the CHL abandoned the single entity structure, and individual teams were operated independently. The CHL is operated by an independent firm, Global Entertainment Corporation. The CHL has 17 teams, mostly located in the Southwestern United States, with headquarters in Phoenix, Arizona (**Table 17-4**). The CHL merged with the Western Professional Hockey League in 2001 and added three teams to bring the league to 11 in total. From 2002 to 2005, the CHL expanded again and added four more teams (Laredo Bucks, Colorado Eagles, Rio Grande Valley Killer Bees, and Youngstown SteelHounds). In 2006–2007, the CHL added two new teams: the Rocky Mountain Rage and the Arizona Sun Dogs. The Rapid City (SD) Rush are scheduled to begin play during the 2008–2009 season, giving the CHL a total of 18 teams.[33]

Teams play a 64-game schedule, beginning at the end of October and finishing in the last week of March. There is a player salary cap of $8,500 a week, with players making an average of $500 per week. Coaches make anywhere from $30,000 to $80,000 per year. Teams also provide housing for the players.[34] Several teams have AHL and NHL affiliate agreements, but most teams are independent. CHL league officials are actively striving to make the CHL a development league for the NHL, with each team having an affiliation with an NHL parent club.

During the 2006–2007 season, CHL teams averaged 4,388 fans per game,[35] while ticket prices range from $8 to $35. Premium seats in most arenas cost between $16 and $22. Fans can also view games online via CHL TV. Additional team revenues come from corporate sponsorships.

INTERNATIONAL HOCKEY LEAGUE

The International Hockey League (IHL) is a class AA minor league hockey organization that serves as a secondary feeder system for AHL and NHL teams, roughly at the same level of play as the CHL. Originally known as the United Hockey League (UHL), the league renamed itself in June 2007 as the 10-team league lost five franchises to other leagues or financial difficulties.[36] The remaining five franchises (Bloomington Prairie Thunder, Flint Generals, Fort Wayne Komets, Kalamazoo Wings, and Muskegon Fury) were joined by the expansion Port Huron Icehawks to form the new six-team league (**Table 17-5**). The league was established in 1991 as the Colonial Hockey League with five franchises located in Michigan and Ontario. Over time, the league expanded and changed its name to the United Hockey League for the start of the 1997–1998 season.[37]

Table 17-4   CHL Teams (2007–2008)

Northeast Division	
Team	**Location**
Bossier-Shreveport Mudbugs	Bossier City, LA
Mississippi RiverKings	Southaven, MS
Texas Brahmas	North Richland Hills, TX
Youngstown SteelHounds	Youngstown, OH

Northwest Division	
Team	**Location**
Colorado Eagles	Loveland, CO
Oklahoma City Blazers	Oklahoma City, OK
Rocky Mountain Rage	Broomfield, CO
Tulsa Oilers	Tulsa, OK
Wichita Thunder	Wichita, KS

Southeast Division	
Team	**Location**
Austin Ice Bats	Austin, TX
Corpus Christi Rayz	Corpus Christi, TX
Laredo Bucks	Laredo, TX
Rio Grande Valley Killer Bees	Rio Grande Valley, TX

Southwest Division	
Team	**Location**
Amarillo Gorillas	Amarillo, TX
Arizona Sun Dogs	Prescott Valley, AZ
New Mexico Scorpions	Rio Rancho, NM
Odessa Jackalopes	Odessa, TX
Fresno Falcons	Fresno, CA

Table 17-5   IHL Teams (2007–2008)

Northeast Division	
Team	**Location**
Bloomington Prairie Thunder	Bloomington, IL
Flint Generals	Flint, MI
Fort Wayne Komets	Fort Wayne IN
Kalamazoo Wings	Kalamazoo, MI
Muskegon Fury	Muskegon, MI
Port Huron Flags	Port Huron, MI

Teams play a 76-game regular season, which begins in late October and concludes in mid-April. Teams may carry a maximum of seven veterans (players with 300 or more games of professional experience) and must carry a minimum of four rookies (players with less than 60 games of experience). A league-wide salary cap is set at $13,000 per week, with fines for owners found in violation of the cap. The IHL and NHL have a partnership in brand licensing, but no firm affiliation agreement for players.

In the 2006–2007 season, the league averaged just over 3,400 fans per contest.[38] Ticket prices range from $5 to $26, with the majority of tickets costing between $14 and $18. Fans also have the option of watching the games from their computer, and those webcasts cost approximately $6 per game. In addition to broadcasting and gate receipts, the league draws revenues from a number of corporate sponsorships including companies such as PepsiCo, OT Sports, and The Oryan Company.[39]

Teams offer job opportunities in hockey operations, administration, media relations, business operations, business services, sponsorship, and sales. The IHL operates like many other minor leagues. League headquarters are located in Rochester, Michigan.

SOUTHERN PROFESSIONAL HOCKEY LEAGUE

Established in 2004, the Southern Professional Hockey League (SPHL) was formed as a merger of teams from the World Hockey Association and South East Hockey League when both leagues collapsed. The SPHL is considered a lower-level minor league hockey league (below the ECHL, CHL, and IHL) with seven teams concentrated in southeastern states (**Table 17-6**). The league touts itself as "the leader in single A hockey."

The season begins in mid-October and finishes in mid-March, and each team plays a 56-game schedule. There is a $5,600 weekly salary cap for each SPHL team.[40] Ticket prices for games usually range from $10 to $25 and the league-wide average attendance for the 2006–2007 season was approximately 3,000 fans.[41]

League sponsors of the SPHL include Aflac, Bud Light, Miller Lite, Domino's Pizza, Sherwood, Pointstreak, and Our Sports Central. Most games are available on local radio broadcasts, while some teams offer streaming Internet feeds to the games.[42]

The league headquarters is based in Huntsville, Alabama, and the league staff includes a commissioner, director of hockey operations, and director of officials.

Table 17-6   SPHL Teams (2007–2008)

Northeast Division	
Team	**Location**
Columbus Cottonmouths	Columbus, GA
Fayetteville Fire Antz	Fayetteville, NC
Huntsville Havoc	Huntsville, AL
Jacksonville Barracudas	Jacksonville, FL
Knoxville IceBears	Knoxville, TN
Twin City Cyclones	Winston-Salem, NC
Richmond Renegades	Richmond, VA

JUNIOR HOCKEY: UNITED STATES HOCKEY LEAGUE

The junior leagues are amateur hockey leagues governed by USA Hockey and Hockey Canada, the official amateur hockey organizations for those countries. The junior leagues were created to act as a development organization for young amateur talent. Junior league hockey is considered the top level of youth hockey and it draws the best players from around North America. The goal of each junior league organization is not only to develop a player's skill set, but also to aid the athlete in maturing physically, mentally, and academically while providing him a chance to showcase his skills in front of collegiate and professional scouts.

American players are eligible to participate in junior hockey if they are 20 years of age or younger by December 31 of the given season. The top "Major A" Canadian Leagues (the Ontario Hockey League, the Quebec Major Junior Hockey League, and the Western Hockey League) are all professional leagues where players are paid. Any player who competes in these leagues loses his NCAA eligibility; therefore these leagues are used to focus on development for high levels of professional hockey. Players use these leagues as a transitional league to the professional ranks. Players there are usually between the ages of 16 and 21.

In the United States, junior hockey is divided into Tier I and Tier II. Tier I consists of the United States Hockey League (USHL), which is the top U.S. junior hockey league and is based out of Grand Forks, North Dakota. Originally formed as the Can-Am Junior Hockey League in 1972, it was renamed the USHL in 1977. The USHL consists of 11 teams based in Midwestern cities in the United States (**Table 17-7**). Teams typically play a 60-game regular season beginning in September and conclude at the end of March. Tier II consists of three subdivisions, A, B, and C, with teams and leagues across the United States and Canada.

Many junior players hope to go on to play in college, but in order to comply with NCAA rules, these players are not paid for playing. However, junior players have all housing and equipment expenses covered by their team. Teams charge admission to games with ticket prices ranging from $7 to $15. In addition, some games are broadcast through an online webcast for a fee of $6. During the 2006–2007 season, the USHL topped the 1-million-fan mark for the eighth consecutive year with an average crowd of over 2,900 per game.[43]

The USHL has potential job opportunities in the following departments: hockey operations, communications, sales, and marketing. Most teams are run by small staffs with people covering multiple areas managing the club.

Table 17-7   USHL Teams (2007–2008)

East Division	
Team	Location
Cedar Rapids Rough Riders	Cedar Rapids, IA
Chicago Steel	Bensenville, IL
Green Bay Gamblers	Green Bay, WI
Indiana Ice	Indianapolis, IN
Ohio Junior Blue Jackets	Columbus, OH
Waterloo Blackhawks	Waterloo, IA

West Division	
Team	Location
Des Moines Buccaneers	Des Moines, IA
Lincoln Stars	Lincoln, NE
Omaha Lancers	Omaha, NE
Sioux City Musketeers	Sioux City, IA
Sioux Falls Stampede	Sioux Falls, SD
Tri-City Storm	Tri-City, WA

Endnotes

1. The original six franchises in the NHL consisted of the Boston Bruins, Chicago Blackhawks, Detroit Red Wings, Montreal Canadiens, New York Rangers, and Toronto Maple Leafs.

2. The reserve clause bound players to their existing team, and thus did not allow for any type of free agency system.

3. Information obtained from the NHL website (www.nhl.com) unless otherwise noted.

4. Hockey Night in Canada: A History of Excellence. (n.d). *CBC Sports*. Retrieved July 21, 2008, from http://www.cbc.ca/sports/hockey/hnic/histrad.html.

5. Red Wings History: Ted Lindsay (n.d.) Detroit Red Wings Alumni Association. Retrieved July 27, 2008, from http://www.redwingalumni.com/legendLindsay.html.

6. Origins of the NHLPA (n.d.) National Hockey League Players Association. Retrieved July 27, 2008, from http://www.nhlpa.com/AboutTheNHLPA/WhatIs.asp.

7. The Legends: John A. Ziegler Jr. (2007). Hockey Hall of Fame. Retrieved July 27, 2008, from http://www.legendsofhockey.net:8080/LegendsOfHockey/jsp/LegendsMember.jsp?mem=b198701&type=Builder&page=bio&list=ByName#photo.

8. Hockey Hall of Fame Time Capsule: Challenge Cup 1979 (n.d.) Hockey Hall of Fame. Retrieved July 27, 2008, from http://www.hhof.com/HTML/GamesSummaryCHCUP1979.shtml.

9. Faculty Biographies: Gilbert Stein. (n.d.). Villanova University School of Law. Retrieved July 27, 2008, from http://www.law.vill.edu/academics/faculty/biographies/adjunct/stein.

10. Goodenow Steps Down as NHLPA Head. (2005, July 28). *Seattle Post-Intelligencer.* Retrieved February 27, 2007, from http://seattlepi.nwsource.com/scorecard/hockeynews.asp?articleID=135153.

11. Hochberg, L. (1995, Jan. 11). Last-Minute Deal Saves NHL Season; Owners, Player Representatives Agree to End 3 1/2-Month Lockout. *The Washington Post,* p. A1

12. O'Bannon, M. (2005, Feb. 16). NHL Lockout Timeline. *The Tampa Tribune.* Retrieved December 29, 2007, from http://bolts.tbo.com/lightning/MGB3ZYY1A5E.html.

13. Sides Will Have to Ratify New CBA. (2005, July 13). ESPN.com. Retrieved December 29, 2007, from http://sports.espn.go.com/nhl/news/story?id=2106776.

14. Classic Earns Higher Ratings Than Any Regular-Season Game in Decade. (2008, Jan. 2). Associated Press. Retrieved January 2, 2008, from http://sports.espn.go.com/nhl/news/story?id=3177745.

15. Playing an unequal number of games against each team in a particular league is considered an unbalanced schedule. Typically, teams will play other teams in their own division with a greater frequency than other teams in the league. An unbalanced schedule works favorably for teams in a weaker division because teams within a division play one another more often in an unbalanced schedule. In contrast, this system works unfavorably for teams playing in a stronger division. Many leagues utilize an unbalanced schedule due to scheduling conflicts and travel issues, and to induce interdivision rivalries.

16. NHL Owners Finally Approve Schedule Change; Nashville Sale Approved. (2007, Nov. 29). Canadian Press. Retrieved December 27, 2007, from http://www.nhl.com/nhl/app?articleid=344971&page=NewsPage&service=page.

17. NHL Releases 2007–08 National Television Schedule. (2007, Aug. 15). NHL. Retrieved December 26, 2007, from http://www.nhl.com/nhl/app?articleid=335977&page=NewsPage&service=page.

18. El Bashir, T., and Heath, T. (2006, June 5). NHL Strong Comeback Marred by Poor TV Ratings. *The Washington Post,* p. E01.

19. Consoli, J. (2005, Aug. 22). NHL Improves Standing with New OLN Deal. *Mediaweek.* Retrieved February 6, 2007, from http://www.mediaweek.com/mw/news/recent_display.jsp?vnu_content_id=1001016934.

20. Look Who's Talking: ESPN, NHL. (2007, July 30). *Street and Smith's SportsBusiness Journal.* Retrieved December 26, 2007, from http://www.sportsbusinessjournal.com/index.cfm?fuseaction=search.show_article&articleId=55770.

21. Ibid.

22. XM Satellite and NHL Announce Long-Term Agreement. (2005, Sep. 12). NHL. Retrieved October 2, 2007, from http://www.nhl.com/news/2005/09/234310.html.

23. A sponsor will pay for the right to be affiliated with a product or event. For example, for the 2008 Olympics, Visa paid the International Olympic Committee for the right to advertise as the "official card of the Olympic games." Sponsorships typically bring other benefits, such as tickets to the event, access to athletes, and exclusive supplying rights to event production staff.

24. NHL FAQ: NHL Corporate Marketing Partners (n.d.). NHL.com. Retrieved July 27, 2008, from http://www.nhl.com/nhlhq/corporate.html.

25. Abelson, J. (2007, June 6). NHL Suits Up Like Never Before. *Boston Globe.* Retrieved December 28, 2007, from http://www.boston.com/sports/hockey/articles/2007/06/21/nhl_suits_up_like_never_before/?page=full.

26. The AAA class league is the highest level of minor league sports, and thus serves as the highest development league for the professional league of its respective sport.

27. Each professional NHL team has an affiliation agreement with an AHL franchise. This partnership enables the NHL team (also known as the parent club) to use an AHL club as a breeding ground for development of its players as well as a source of replenishment to replace injured or underperforming players throughout the season.

28. 2006–2007 Minor-League Hockey Attendance by League. (n.d.). *Arena Digest.* Retrieved December 27, 2007, from http://www.arenadigest.com/ad_hockey/2006_2007_attendance_by_league.htm.

29. Corporate Partners (n.d.) TheAHL.com. Retrieved July 27, 2008, from http://www.theahl.com/theahl/partners.

30. The AA class league is the second highest level of minor league sports behind the AAA level.

31. ECHL: FAQ (n.d.). ECHL.com. Retrieved July 27, 2008, from http://www.echl.com/faq.shtml.

32. 2006–2007 Minor-League Hockey, op. cit.

33. CHL Announces 2008-09 Participating Teams (2008, June 2). Central Hockey League.com. Retrieved July 27, 2008 from http://www.centralhockeyleague.com/pressroom/index.html?article_id=2441.

34. Speer, A. (2004, Mar. 3) Perfect Timing. *The Tribune*. Retrieved December 29, 2007, from http://www.greeleytrib.com/apps/pbcs.dll/article?AID=/20040328/BUSINESS/103280047.

35. The CHL: About (n.d.) Central Hockey League.com. Retrieved July 27, 2008, from http://www.centralhockeyleague.com/thechl/about.

36. Hamm, D. (2007, June 6). UHL Becomes IHL, Adds Team. *Pantagraph*. Retrieved December 30, 2007, from http://www.pantagraph.com/articles/2007/06/21/sports/doc4679be978cd86274210399.txt.

37. Professional Hockey Coming Back to Fraser. (2004, June 25). *The Macomb Daily*. Retrieved July 28, 2008, from http://www.macombdaily.com/stories/062504/loc_hockey001.shtml.

38. 2006–2007 Minor-League Hockey, op. cit.

39. Partners. (2007, May 8). IHL-Hockey.com. Retrieved July 28, 2008, from http://www.ihl-hockey.com/index.php?option=com_content&task=view&id=21&Itemid=152.

40. Gates, N. (2007, Feb. 18). SPHL, Even Without a Leader, Has a Product That Attracts Fans. *Knoxville News Sentinel*. Retrieved December 31, 2007, from http://www.knoxnews.com/news/2007/feb/18/gates-sphl-even-without-a-leader-has-a-product.

41. 2006–2007 Minor-League Hockey, op. cit.

42. SPHL Partners (n.d.) TheSPHL.com. Retrieved July 28, 2008, from http://www.thesphl.com/partners.

43. USHL Surpasses One Million Mark in Attendance for 2006–2007. (2007, Apr. 10). USHL.com. Retrieved July 28, 2008, from http://www.ushl.com/news/story.cfm?id=266.

Football

NATIONAL FOOTBALL LEAGUE (NFL)

The National Football League (NFL) is composed of teams competing at the highest level of professional American football in the world. The game's popularity is greatest in the United States. The NFL utilizes many efforts to build a following in other countries, including Japan, China, Mexico, and those in Western Europe. The athletes come almost exclusively from U.S. colleges, where they typically have played 3 to 4 years of football with their collegiate program. Unlike the other three "Big Four" sports, the NFL does not have a formal minor league system for player development; however, accomplished athletes who play in the Canadian Football League and the Arena Football League can and have earned contracts with NFL teams.

Many consider the NFL to be the most popular of all American sports, as evidenced by the television ratings the games receive, the coverage given to the NFL by the national sports media, and its status among sports fans. Football has benefited from television exposure more than any other professional sport. Nielsen ratings for the NFL have routinely surpassed those of all other professional sports.[1] The NFL's championship game, the Super Bowl, consistently ranks as the most watched program by U.S. audiences with close to 100 million viewers annually. NFL television rights packages are the most lucrative deals in the professional sports segment due to the popularity of the sport. Major networks such ABC, CBS, ESPN, and Fox have long-term deals to broadcast NFL games, and these partnerships account for league-wide revenues of almost $4 billion.[2] These revenues are distributed equally among the NFL teams, providing teams with a substantial guaranteed revenue stream and further stabilizing the finances of the league and its member teams.

The NFL has made it a priority to achieve league parity, using measures such as a hard salary cap, a player draft, and

Mike Tannenbaum, executive vice president and general manager of the New York Jets, poses with Curtis Martin, former running back with the Jets. Tannenbaum was hired as GM in 2007 at the age of 37, making him one of the youngest GMs in the NFL. Martin last played with the Jets in 2005, retiring as the fourth leading rusher in NFL history.

an unbalanced schedule based on the previous year's record in order to enable win-loss balance among teams. Cost-certainty vehicles such as the salary cap and a substantial revenue sharing policy (television, licensing, and gate receipts), in particular, have provided the NFL with strong competitive balance and have contributed to the popularity of the sport.

The NFL headquarters are located in New York City, and the league employs staff in the following departments: administration, communication, community relations, finance, football operations, information systems, Internet/new media, legal, retail, and sales and marketing. In 2007–2008, the league office employed 792 people, and total compensation paid to these employees was $32.8 million.[3]

History of the National Football League

1920

- The American Professional Football Association (APFA) began in Canton, Ohio (14 teams).
- Jim Thorpe was elected president of the APFA (1920–1921).

1921

- The APFA named Joe Carr, of the Columbus Panhandles, president of the APFA (1921–1939).
- The APFA expanded to 22 teams, including the Green Bay Packers.
- Headquarters were located in Columbus, Ohio.

1922

- The APFA changed its name to the National Football League (18 teams).

1933

- The first NFL Championship game was played on December 17 at Wrigley Field, Chicago.

1936

- The NFL held its first player draft. The Philadelphia Eagles selected Heisman Trophy winner Jay Berwanger from the University of Chicago with the first selection.

1939

- APFA treasurer Carl Storck was named acting president when Joe Carr died.

1941

- Elmer Layden was named the first commissioner of the NFL (1941–1946).

  NFL headquarters were relocated to Chicago.

1946

- The All-America Football Conference (AAFC) was established as a rival league to the NFL.
- Bert Bell, co-owner of the Pittsburgh Steelers, replaced Commissioner Layden when Layden's contract was not renewed (1946–1959).
- Commissioner Bell moved the NFL headquarters to Philadelphia.

1941

- The All-America Football Conference disbanded due to financial problems. The Cleveland Browns, San Francisco 49ers, and Baltimore Colts merged with the NFL. The three teams started play in the 1950 NFL season.

1950

- The American and National Conferences were created to replace the Eastern and Western divisions.

- The Los Angeles Rams were the first team to have all of its games televised.

1951

- The first NFL Championship game was televised on the DuMont Network.

1956

- The NFL Players Association was founded.
- CBS began broadcasting games live.

1959

- Texas businessman Lamar Hunt announced his intention to establish a rival professional football league, the American Football League (AFL).
- Commissioner Bell died from a heart attack in Philadelphia at a game between the Philadelphia Eagles and Pittsburgh Steelers.

1960

- Pete Rozelle was elected NFL commissioner (1960–1989).
- Commissioner Rozelle moved the offices to New York City.
- Lamar Hunt was elected AFL president and established the league as a rival to the NFL. The original AFL included the Boston Patriots, Buffalo Bills, Houston Oilers, and New York Titans in the Eastern Division and the Dallas Texans, Denver Broncos, Los Angeles Chargers, and Oakland Raiders in the Western Division. The Miami Dolphins and Cincinnati Bengals were later added in 1966 and 1968, respectively.
- The AFL signed a 5-year television contract with ABC.

1961

- The Sports Broadcasting Act of 1961 was signed into law, allowing the NFL to pool the individual teams' television rights and show limited games without violating Sherman Antitrust laws.

1963

- NFL Properties, Inc., was founded as the first licensing arm of the NFL.

1964

- The AFL signed a 5-year, $36-million television contract with NBC.
- Commissioner Rozelle, on behalf of the NFL, purchased Ed Sabol's Blair Motion Pictures, which was renamed NFL Films.

1965

- According to a Harris survey, sports fans chose professional football (41%) as their favorite sport, for the first time overtaking baseball (38%).

1966

- Commissioner Rozelle announced plans of a merger between the NFL and AFL. All 24 franchises remained in their respective leagues. Commissioner Rozelle maintained his position as commissioner of the expanded league.

1967

- The first AFL–NFL World Championship Game (later known as the Super Bowl when the AFL–NFL merger was finalized in 1970) took place at the Los Angeles Coliseum as the Green Bay Packers (NFL) defeated the Kansas City Chiefs (AFL), 35–10.

1969

- Joe Namath made good on his guarantee that the 17-point underdog, the New York Jets, would win Super Bowl III over the powerhouse Baltimore Colts.

1970

- The NFL and AFL merged to stabilize both leagues and to eliminate the competition between the two leagues.
- Monday Night Football first aired with a game between the New York Jets and Cleveland Browns on ABC under the guidance of ABC producer, Roone Arlidge.
- The NFL Management Council and the NFL Players Association agreed to a 4-year collective bargaining agreement to include improvements to the players' pensions, insurance, and disability benefits.

1977

- The NFL Players Association and the NFL Management Council approved a 5-year collective bargaining agreement.
- Commissioner Rozelle negotiated a television contract with three networks that would air every regular and postseason game, along with select preseason games. Industry sources claimed it was the largest single television package ever negotiated.

1982

- The NFL Players Association (NFLPA) called a strike on September 20, 1982, that lasted 57 days. Due to the strike, the regular season was reduced from 16 games to 15 and the NFL adopted a 16-team tournament-style playoff for the Super Bowl.
- The NFLPA and the NFL Management Council ratified a new collective bargaining agreement to last through the 1986 season.
- The United States Football League (USFL) announced its formation and that it would begin its first season in the spring of 1983. The USFL was created to have a professional football league that played in the spring while the NFL was not playing.

1983

- The USFL began its first season of play with 12 teams. They had an average attendance of roughly 24,000 fans per game.

1986

- The USFL filed an antitrust lawsuit against the NFL charging that the league was a monopoly and used unfair labor practices to cause the USFL to fail.

1985

- The USFL announced that beginning in 1986 the league would change its schedule to play in the fall, competing directly with the NFL.
- Gene Upshaw, a former star offensive lineman, was named the executive director of the NFL Players' Association. Upshaw would go on to hold this position for 25 years and play a pivotal role in bringing free agency to the NFL.

1986

- Before beginning its fall season, the USFL disbanded.

1987

- The NFLPA went on strike during the third week of the season. Replacement players were hired to play during the strike. During the 24-day strike, 15% of NFLPA players crossed the picket lines to play.
- The NFLPA formally decertified as a union, a tactic used to sue the league on antitrust grounds.

1988

- In *USFL v. NFL*, the NFL was found to have a monopoly over football in the United States; however, it was not determined that the NFL used unfair labor practices to destroy the USFL. As a result, the USFL was awarded only $3, not nearly enough to restart the league.

1989

- Commissioner Rozelle announced his retirement and Paul Tagliabue was named his successor (1989–2006).

1991

- The World League of American Football's first game was played in Frankfurt, Germany, between the Frankfurt Galaxy and the London Monarchs.

1993

- The NFLPA and the NFL agreed to a 7-year collective bargaining agreement. This was the first CBA signed since the 1982 CBA, which had expired in 1987. The first hard salary cap in professional sports was introduced in this CBA.

1994

- The Dallas Cowboys defeated the Buffalo Bills for the second consecutive year in the Super Bowl by a score of 30–13. This was the Bills' fourth consecutive appearance in the Super Bowl and also their fourth consecutive loss.

1995

- The NFL became the first major professional sports league to establish a site on the Internet.
- In Super Bowl XXIX, Steve Young threw for 325 yards and a record 6 touchdowns, as the San Francisco 49ers beat the San Diego Chargers, 49–26.
- The Carolina Panthers and Jacksonville Jaguars started their first season in the NFL as expansion franchises. This was the first expansion since 1976.

1996

- Owner of the Cleveland Browns, Art Modell announced that he was moving the Browns to Baltimore. The NFL did not want him to move the franchise and came up with a compromise that he could move his team to Baltimore but all records and history would stay in Cleveland. In the compromise, the NFL said that the Cleveland Browns would restart in 1999 and have a new stadium. Art Modell's Baltimore team was named the Ravens.

1998

- The NFL and the NFLPA reached an agreement for a 6-year extension of the collective bargaining agreement through 2003.
- The World League of American Football name was changed to NFL Europe in hopes of leveraging the NFL brand in Europe.

1999

- After a 3-year absence, the Cleveland Browns returned to the NFL. During their first season, they ended with a record of 2–14.

2001

- NFL owners approved a realignment plan for the league beginning in 2002.

2002

- The Houston Texans began play as an expansion team and the 32 teams were divided into 8 four-team divisions. Seven teams changed divisions, and the Seattle Seahawks changed conferences, moving from the AFC to the NFC.
- The NFL and NFLPA agreed to a fourth extension of the 1993 CBA through 2007.
- The NFL held its first Thursday night opening kick-off game when the San Francisco 49ers played the New York Giants in a game that included special live entertainment to start the season.
- The NFL introduced the unbalanced schedule, which was based on the teams' previous year record.

2003

- The NFL Network, a television network devoted to professional football 24 hours a day, 7 days a week, was launched.

2005

- The NFL played its first regular season game outside the United States in Mexico City between the Arizona Cardinals and the San Francisco 49ers.[4]
- The NFL adopted the Olympic testosterone standards and strengthened its steroid testing program.

2006

- Commissioner Paul Tagliabue announced his retirement, and Roger Goodell was named as the commissioner of the NFL (2006–present).
- The NFL announced that in 2007, a preseason game between the New England Patriots and the Seattle Seahawks would be held in Beijing, China. The game was ultimately called off due to time and resource constraints.[5]
- NFL Europe changed its name to NFL Europa to create stronger ties with the German and Dutch markets, where all six of the teams were located.

2007

- A regular season game was played in Wembley Stadium in London, England, between the Miami Dolphins and the New York Giants. This was the first regular season game played on a different continent.
- NFL Europa folded due to financial trouble. Commissioner Roger Goodell says that the league will focus on regular season games being held outside of the United States as a new way to promote the NFL to international markets.

Structure of the National Football League

League Alignment

- 32 total teams (**Table 18-1**)
- 2 conferences: National Football Conference (NFC) and American Football Conference (AFC)
- 4 divisions in each conference: North, East, South, West
- 4 teams in each division

Competition Format

- Realignment in 2002 guarantees that all teams play each other on a rotating basis.

Table 18-1   NFL Teams (2008–2009)

American Football Conference		National Football Conference	
AFC East		**NFC East**	
Team	**Location**	**Team**	**Location**
Buffalo Bills	Orchard Park, NY	Dallas Cowboys	Irving, TX
Miami Dolphins	Miami Gardens, FL	New York Giants	East Rutherford, NJ
New England Patriots	Foxboro, MA	Philadelphia Eagles	Philadelphia, PA
New York Jets	East Rutherford, NJ	Washington Redskins	Landover, MD
AFC North		**NFC North**	
Team	**Location**	**Team**	**Location**
Baltimore Ravens	Baltimore, MD	Chicago Bears	Chicago, IL
Cincinnati Bengals	Cincinnati, OH	Detroit Lions	Detroit, MI
Cleveland Browns	Cleveland, OH	Green Bay Packers	Green Bay, WI
Pittsburgh Steelers	Pittsburgh, PA	Minnesota Vikings	Minneapolis, MN
AFC South		**NFC South**	
Team	**Location**	**Team**	**Location**
Houston Texans	Houston, TX	Atlanta Falcons	Atlanta, GA
Indianapolis Colts	Indianapolis, IN	Carolina Panthers	Charlotte, NC
Jacksonville Jaguars	Jacksonville, FL	New Orleans Saints	New Orleans, LA
Tennessee Titans	Nashville, TN	Tampa Bay Buccaneers	Tampa Bay, FL
AFC West		**NFC West**	
Team	**Location**	**Team**	**Location**
Denver Broncos	Denver, CO	Arizona Cardinals	Glendale, AZ
Kansas City Chiefs	Kansas City, MO	San Francisco 49ers	San Francisco, CA
Oakland Raiders	Oakland, CA	Seattle Seahawks	Seattle, WA
San Diego Chargers	San Diego, CA	St. Louis Rams	St. Louis, MO
		San Antonio Rampage	San Antonio, TX

- Every team within a division plays 16 games as follows:
  - Home and away against three division teams (6 games).
  - Four games against teams from a division in another conference on a rotating 4-year cycle (4 games).
  - Four intra-conference games against opponents that are selected based on a team's previous year's record (4 games).
  - Each team plays two games versus teams within its conference based on last year's standings (unbalanced schedule). Match-ups follow this guideline: first-place teams versus first-place teams in a different division, second-place teams versus second-place teams in a different division, third-place teams versus third-place teams in a different division, and fourth-place teams versus fourth-place teams in a different division (2 games).
- End-of-year playoffs to determine Super Bowl Champion.

Schedule

- Game days
  - Most games are played on Sunday afternoons at 1:00 PM and 4:15 PM EST and broadcasted regionally based on the teams playing in the games.
  - Nationally broadcast games: One on Sunday night; one on Monday night.
  - In December, some games occur on Saturday and Thursday nights after the end of the college football regular season (most games are on Saturdays); the Sports Broadcast Act prevents Saturday games earlier in the year.
- Preseason (late July and August): 4 exhibition games (2 at home) over 5 weeks, with one or two additional games for the Football Hall of Fame, and occasionally, an international game

- Regular season (first weekend after Labor Day through early January): 16 games (8 home, 8 away) over 17 weeks with one bye week for each team
- Playoffs (January through early February)
  - 12 teams: 8 division winners and 4 wild card teams (2 each from the AFC and NFC)
  - 4 rounds: First 3 rounds have inter-conference play to determine conference champions
  - Super Bowl
    - NFC champion against the AFC champion.
    - The Super Bowl site is determined years in advance and irrespective of the teams playing in the game.
    - The site is usually at a stadium of an existing NFL team and in a warm-weather climate (e.g., Florida, Arizona, California, Texas, Louisiana, Georgia). Northern cities occasionally host a Super Bowl; however, the warm weather locales are more appealing to fans and corporate sponsors traveling in February, and therefore more financially attractive to event organizers.
    - Super Bowl sites:
      - 2007: Dolphins Stadium: Miami, Florida
      - 2008: University of Phoenix Stadium: Glendale, Arizona
      - 2009: Raymond James Stadium: Tampa Bay, Florida
      - 2010: Dolphins Stadium: Miami, Florida
- All-Star game (mid-February): Called the "Pro Bowl"
  - Played one week after the Super Bowl in Honolulu, Hawaii

Money Matters for the National Football League

Sources of Revenue

- Television broadcast revenues
  - The NFL negotiates its television broadcast contracts on behalf of its teams, resulting in annual revenues of approximately $3.8 billion.[6] After expenses, the league distributes this money equally to the teams. There are no local regular season broadcast deals. The only local broadcast revenues are from preseason games.
  - The league divides the games into different packages and sells the packages to various networks.[7]
    - CBS: Primarily regular season AFC games (Sunday afternoons): $3.732 billion overall, $622 million annually (2006–2011)
    - Fox: Primarily regular season NFC games (Sunday afternoons): $4.275 billion overall, $712.5 million annually (2006–2011)
    - ESPN: Monday Night Football: $8.8 billion overall, $1.1 billion annually (2006–2013)
    - NBC: Sunday Night Football: $3.6 billion overall, $600 million annually (2006–2011)
    - The Super Bowl rotates among CBS, Fox, and NBC.
    - DirecTV: NFL Sunday Ticket is a package available for purchase by subscribers to the DirecTV satellite network. Through this medium, customers are able to receive the broadcast of every NFL regular season game, valuable for those who want to watch games that are not broadcast on their local CBS or Fox affiliates. Value of agreement: $3.5 billion overall, $700 million annually (2006–2010).
  - NFL Network
    - This is a round-the-clock cable/satellite network dedicated to NFL activities and is fully owned and operated by the NFL. It offers a variety of NFL programming, and reaches 35 million homes. Starting in 2006, the NFL Network broadcasted live games, five on Thursday nights and three on Saturday afternoons starting on Thanksgiving.
- Other media
  - Radio
    - Local: Radio stations (AM and FM) in each market broadcast games of interest to fans in that region. Individual teams negotiate deals with local or regional radio stations and keep all revenues generated from these agreements.
    - Sirius Satellite Radio: Sirius holds the rights to broadcast all games via its satellite radio network. It has a 7-year, $220-million contract with the NFL (2004–2010).
    - Westwood One: Westwood One broadcasts roughly 90 games a year and has a 3-year, $120-million contract with the NFL (2005–2008).
  - Mobile video (highlights)
    - Sprint, $600 million over 5 years (2005–2009)
    - Video games
      - Electronic Arts (EA): $300 million over 5 years (2005–2009)
    - Internet
      - The NFL creates and manages its site (NFL.com) in-house. It previously had a deal with CBS Sportsline to create and manage the website, but in 2006 decided to take it in-house in an attempt to increase the revenue generated from the website. The original deal with CBS Sportsline was worth $120 million over 5 years.[8]

- Gate receipts
  - Teams share ticket revenue with the visiting team, with 60% of receipts going to the home team and 40% for the visitors. Teams do *not* share revenue from the stadium, such as concessions, team sponsors, advertising, and luxury suites. Because this money is not shared, many owners seek to maximize these revenue streams.
- Sponsorship
  - There are typically 15–20 major sponsors of the NFL in varying product categories, such as fast food, cameras, computer hardware, medication, and airlines. Sponsors pay an annual fee to the NFL to become a recognized partner for other related services. Current NFL sponsors include Sprint, Burger King, and Pepsi.
- Merchandising and licensing
  - The NFL forged a 10-year deal worth $250 million for Reebok to be the official uniform supplier of the NFL.[9] As the exclusive outfitter for all 32 NFL teams, Reebok provides a wide array of licensed apparel products to the retail marketplace. All revenue generated from NFL licensing is shared equally among the 32 NFL teams.

ARENA FOOTBALL LEAGUE

The Arena Football League (AFL) is the premier indoor American football league in the world. In 2007, the AFL was composed of 17 teams located in cities across the United States. Founded in 1987 by Jim Foster, a former NFL and USFL executive, the AFL has created a new sport by moving the game of football to an indoor venue, providing a unique, high-scoring, fast-paced, high-impact style of play. The league also focuses on creating an entertaining, loud atmosphere for fans. The game is played indoors, on turf. The playing area is smaller than outdoor football (50 yards in length and 85 feet wide with 8-yard end zones). Eight players are on the field, some of whom play both offense and defense. The in-game experience is different from the NFL and average attendance has increased dramatically over the past few years, rising to over 12,400 people per game in 2007.[10]

The AFL schedule commences in late January, at the end of the NFL season, and finishes in early June with the annual ArenaBowl, which has been held in Las Vegas in recent years. AFL players are mostly former college football players from various programs throughout the United States. Unlike most professional leagues, there is no annual player draft, and players are signed as free agents. There has been some player movement from the AFL to the NFL; however, it is still rare for AFL players to earn starting roles in the NFL. One notable example is quarterback Kurt Warner, a two-time MVP and Super Bowl champion.

The AFL has not been fortunate enough to benefit from lucrative national television contracts like other major professional sports, and has continually tried negotiating deals with the major networks. In 2003, NBC reached an agreement with the AFL; however, it was a short-term deal that expired after the 2006 season. This is partially due to the fact that the AFL has struggled on television, as ratings on NBC were very low with an average of 0.9 in 2006.[11] The AFL has been considering putting games on the NFL Network, which could aid both the NFL and AFL, whose relationship continues to strengthen. A few AFL teams are owned by NFL owners and former players (John Elway and Pat Bowlen, Colorado Crush; Jerry Jones, Dallas Desperados; Arthur Blank, Georgia Force; Bud Adams, Nashville Kats; and Tom Benson, New Orleans VooDoo), who would like to develop and grow the AFL. In an attempt to expand its fan base and attract stronger customer loyalty, the AFL is targeting a younger crowd by licensing its brand with EA Sports and releasing the first AFL video game in 2006.

The league headquarters are located in New York City, and the AFL also operates a satellite office in Chicago. The AFL has various departments including community relations, human resources, facility operations, general management, legal, finance, and information and technology.

History of the Arena Football League

1981

- James F. Foster attended an indoor soccer game at Madison Square Garden and diagrammed a smaller size football field to be put over a hockey rink. From this diagram, the sport of arena football was conceived.

1986

- The first "test game" was played between the Rockford Metros and Chicago Politicians in Rockford, Illinois.

1987

- James Foster, the founder of the AFL, was named the league's first commissioner (1987–1992).
- A showcase game between the Chicago Bruisers and Miami Vise was staged at Rosemont Horizon, Illinois, before 8,257 spectators.
- An inaugural four-team league was created: Chicago Bruisers, Pittsburgh Gladiators, Denver Dynamite, and Washington Commandos (4 teams).
- The Dynamite defeated the Gladiators, 45–16, and won the first-ever ArenaBowl before 13,232 fans at Pittsburgh Civic Arena and a live ESPN audience.

1988

- The Detroit Drive, owned by Little Caesar's Pizza mogul and Detroit Tigers owner Mike Ilitch, started playing and claimed its first of four championships. The New England Steam Rollers, New York Knights, and Los Angeles Avengers began and disbanded in the same season (5 teams).

1989

- Detroit and Chicago competed in the league's first-ever European exhibition game, the Arenaball Transatlantic Challenge, in London, England.
- The Washington Commandos became the Maryland Commandos, and then disbanded in the same season. The Chicago Bruisers disbanded (3 teams).

1990

- The U.S. Patent Office issued a patent for the Arena Football Game System, making it the only sports league in history to play a patented, rival-free game.
- Foster and partners at Gridiron Enterprises sold licenses to investors in major markets, enabling privately owned teams.
- The Albany Firebirds and Dallas Texans began play as expansion franchises (5 teams).
- Following the 1990 season, the Detroit Drive and Dallas Texans competed in Paris, France, before 14,257 spectators.

1991

- AFL attendance reached an all-time high of 12,813 per game.
- The Orlando Predators, owned by Phoenix Suns owner Jerry Colangelo, joined the league as an expansion team. The Pittsburgh Gladiators became the Tampa Bay Storm, and set a then-all-time single-game attendance record against Denver (24,445). The Columbus Destroyers formed and disbanded in the same year after a 0–10 season. The New Orleans Night began play, and the Denver Dynamite disbanded (6 teams).

1992

- Before a sell-out crowd of 15,505, new expansion team the Arizona Rattlers defeated the Sacramento Attack, 51–36, in the first-ever sporting event in America West Arena in Phoenix.
- The Charlotte Rage, Cincinnati Rockers, Cleveland Thunderbolts, and Sacramento Attack began play. The San Antonio Force began play and disbanded in the same year. The New Orleans Night disbanded (10 teams).
- Joe O'Hara, former owner of the Albany Firebirds, was named the commissioner of the AFL (1992–1994).

1993

- Milwaukee was awarded an expansion team named the Milwaukee Mustangs. The Detroit Drive became the Massachusetts Marauders after the season. The Cincinnati Rockers and Dallas Texans disbanded (9 teams).

1994

- The Las Vegas Sting began play as an expansion franchise. The Sacramento Attack became the Miami Hooters. The Fort Worth Cavalry formed and disbanded in the same year. The Cleveland Thunderbolts and Massachusetts Marauders disbanded (8 teams).
- Jim Drucker, former commissioner of the Continental Basketball Association, was named the commissioner of the AFL (1994–1996).

1995

- Predators' Barry Wagner became the first player to claim both Ironman of the Year, which is awarded to the most outstanding two-way player, and Most Valuable Player awards.
- The Connecticut Coyotes, Iowa Barnstormers, St. Louis Stampede, San Jose SaberCats, and Memphis Pharos began play. The Minnesota Fighting Pike began and disbanded in the same season (13 teams).

1996

- The league attracted more than 1 million fans for the first time.
- ESPN's telecast of ArenaBowl X between Tampa Bay and Iowa was viewed in 1,037,582 households.
- The Texas Terror began the season. The Las Vegas Sting became the Anaheim Piranhas, and the Miami Hooters became the Florida Bobcats. The Charlotte Rage, St. Louis Stampede, and Connecticut Coyotes disbanded (11 teams).
- David Baker, former owner of the Anaheim Piranhas, was named commissioner of the AFL (1996–present).

1997

- The first class of the Arena Football Hall of Fame was inducted (Tim Marcum, Dwayne Dixon, Jim Foster, Craig Walls, Tate Randle, and Jerry Kurz).
- The Nashville Kats, New York City Hawks, and New Jersey Red Dogs began play. The Memphis Pharos moved to Portland and became the Portland Pharos. The Anaheim Piranhas disbanded (13 teams).

1998

- The AFL Board of Directors approved the application of New Orleans Saints owner Tom Benson to place a team in New Orleans. NFL bylaws previously prohibited NFL owners from investing in other football leagues or teams, but an amendment to NFL rules was adopted, allowing exception for AFL teams in the NFL club's own market.

- In ArenaBowl XII, Orlando claimed its first championship with a 62–31 win over Tampa Bay before 17,222 fans at Ice Palace in Tampa, Florida, with a national television audience watching on ABC, earning a 1.6 rating.
- The AFL completed purchase of worldwide patent, trademark, and copyrights from Gridiron Enterprises, Inc.
- Los Angeles was awarded a team for 2000 in the Staples Center.
- The Grand Rapids Rampage and Houston Thunderbears (formerly Texas Terror) began play (14 teams).

1999

- The NFL agreed to an exclusive option to purchase an equity interest in the AFL. The option could be exercised over the next 3 years and would give the NFL a minority ownership interest (up to 49.9%) in the AFL and voice in operation of the league. The NFL owners needed to approve the deal to exercise the option of the purchase of the AFL.
- The AFL board of directors approved the creation of Triple A Arena Football League 2 (AF2) for the 2000 season.
- Former Iowa Barnstormer (AFL) and current St. Louis Ram quarterback (QB) Kurt Warner became the first NFL QB in 50 years to throw three scoring passes in each of his first three starts. He earned Associated Press NFL most valuable player (MVP) honors and Super Bowl MVP accolades.
- The AFL announced multi-year television contracts with TNN, ESPN, ESPN2, and ABC.
- Detroit, under the ownership of Palace Sports & Entertainment and Detroit Lions chairman, William Clay Ford Jr., announced an AFL team to begin play in 2001.
- The AFL unveiled an expanded playoff format to 12 teams.
- The New York City Hawks became the New England Sea Wolves. The Buffalo Destroyers began play (15 teams).

2000

- A federal antitrust lawsuit was filed against the league by the AFL Players Association. The league's board of directors voted to cancel the 2000 season.
- The board of directors recognized the Arena Football League Players' Organizing Committee as collective bargaining representatives for all AFL players; the 2000 season started in April, without any games being canceled.

- AFL owners and players ratified a 6-year CBA.
- The NFL agreed to oversee and manage the game officials for both the AFL and AF2.
- The Portland Forest Dragons moved to Oklahoma City and became the Oklahoma Wranglers.
- The Los Angeles Avengers and Carolina Cobras began play as expansion franchises. The Avengers opened preseason before 15,928 fans, the largest opening night crowd for an indoor sport in Los Angeles history (17 teams).

2001

- Arena football debuted in Canada at Toronto's Air Canada Centre before a crowd of 10,023.
- Sporting News Radio broadcasted ArenaBowl XV.
- ABC televised the title game for the fourth consecutive season, featuring the broadcast talents of Brent Musberger, Gary Danielson, and Lynn Swann.
- The *Sporting News* listed AFL Commissioner David Baker among their "Power 100—Top 10 to Watch in 2002." The Power 100 is their list of the top 100 most powerful people in sports.
- The Chicago Rush and the Detroit Fury began play as expansion franchises.
- The Florida Bobcats became the Florida Firecats and the New Jersey Red Dogs became the New Jersey Gladiators. The Iowa Barnstormers moved to New York City and became the New York Dragons. The Albany Firebirds moved to Indianapolis and became the Indiana Firebirds. The New England Sea Wolves moved to Toronto and became the Toronto Phantoms.
- The Oklahoma Wranglers, Houston Thunderbears, and Milwaukee Mustangs disbanded (16 teams).

2002

- The Dallas Desperados began play as an expansion franchise.
- The Nashville Kats moved to Atlanta and became the Georgia Force.
- The Florida Firecats, New Jersey Gladiators, and Toronto Phantoms disbanded (14 teams).

2003

- NBC began broadcasting AFL games.
- The Colorado Crush and Las Vegas Gladiators began the season as expansion franchises.
- The Buffalo Destroyers disbanded (15 teams).

2004

- The Philadelphia Soul, Austin Wranglers, New Orleans Voodoo, and Columbus Destroyers began the season as expansion franchises.
- The Carolina Cobras, Indiana Firebirds, and Detroit Fury disbanded (16 teams).

2005

- The Nashville Kats re-emerged as an expansion franchise (17 teams).

2006

- The Kansas City Brigade and Utah Blaze began play as expansion franchises (19 teams).
- The New Orleans Voodoo did not compete in the 2006 season due to the damage of Hurricane Katrina.
- ESPN purchased a minority stake in the AFL and also agreed to a 5-year broadcasting rights deal.

2008

- All AFL players wore a small device on the back of their helmets that turns from green to red when a player experiences a significant impact to the head. The purpose of the device is to warn players, coaches, and trainers when a player has taken a dangerous hit to the head. The tentative name of the device is the "Shockometer."
- AFL Commissioner David Baker resigns after 12 years as commissioner.

Structure of the Arena Football League

League Alignment

- 19 teams (**Table 18-2**)
- 2 conferences: National and American

- 2 divisions in each conference: National: Eastern, Southern; American: Central, Western

Competition Format

- Head-to-head contests between AFL teams

Schedule

- Game days
  - Games are usually played over the weekend, with the first games being played Friday night and the last being Monday night.
  - No preseason games
- Regular season
  - 17 weeks (January–May)
  - Each team plays 16 games (8 home, 8 away)
- Playoffs
  - Divisional round: Top 4 teams from each conference make playoffs (8 teams total)
    - 2 division winners
    - 2 wild-card teams (teams with the remaining best records within conference)
  - Winners of the Divisional Playoff rounds within each conference advance to their respective Conference Championship games.
  - Winners of the Conference Championship games play in the ArenaBowl.

Money Matters for the Arena Football League

Sources of Revenue

- Television broadcast revenues

Table 18-2   AFL Teams (2008)

American Conference		National Conference	
Central Division		**Eastern Division**	
Team	**Location**	**Team**	**Location**
Colorado Crush	Denver, CO	Cleveland Gladiators	Cleveland, OH
Chicago Rush	Hoffman Estates, IL	Columbus Destroyers	Columbus, OH
Grand Rapids Rampage	Grand Rapids, MI	Dallas Desperados	Dallas, TX
Kansas City Brigade	Kansas City, MO	New York Dragons	Uniondale, NY
		Philadelphia Soul	Philadelphia, PA
Western Division		**Southern Division**	
Team	**Location**	**Team**	**Location**
Arizona Rattlers	Phoenix, AZ	Georgia Force	Atlanta, GA
Los Angeles Avengers	Los Angeles, CA	New Orleans Voodoo	New Orleans, LA
San Jose SaberCats	San Jose, CA	Orlando Predators	Orlando, FL
Utah Blaze	Salt Lake City, UT	Tampa Bay Storm	Tampa Bay, FL

- ESPN/ABC: As part of their agreement to purchase a minority stake in the league, ESPN became the lead broadcaster of the AFL for 5 years. ESPN will air 14 showcase games on Monday nights. A total of 26 regular season games and 9 postseason games will be broadcast on ESPN and ABC. ABC will televise the ArenaBowl.
- Fox Sports Net: Regional broadcasted games are shown on Fox Sports Net regional stations.
- Radio network
  - AP Network Sports
- Retail
  - Nike
- Trading cards
  - Upper Deck
- Video games
  - Electronic Arts (EA) Sports: Released the first AFL video game in February 2006
- Licensing/merchandising
  - Schutt: 4-year agreement (2005–2009) includes first-ever collectible helmet marketing plan for the league
  - Champs Sports
- Sponsors
  - There are roughly 10–12 major sponsors of the AFL in varying product categories; they include Champs Sports, EA Sports, Nike, Spalding, Schutt, and the U.S. Army. Sponsors pay an annual fee to the AFL to become a recognized partner.

CANADIAN FOOTBALL LEAGUE

The Canadian Football League (CFL) is the premier football league in Canada. Formally established in 1958, the CFL consists of nine teams (**Table 18-3**), with each team playing 18 games during the regular season, which spans from June through October. All teams vie for the ultimate prize of the CFL, the Grey Cup, which is Canada's largest annual professional sporting event. The location of the Grey Cup rotates on an annual basis.

CFL teams are individually owned, and the league headquarters are located in Toronto, Ontario. Teams operate under a salary cap, which was $3.8 million in 2006. The departments that comprise team operations include corporate sponsorship, football operations, external relations, communications, media relations, ticketing, sales, game day operations, accounting, technology, and customer services. League partners include Wendy's, Scotiabank, Sony, and Crown Royal. Canadian television affiliates include TSN and CBC, and various games are broadcast in Canada and in the United States through regional sports networks.

The popularity of the CFL continues to rise, as indicated by an increase in average attendance over the past 5 years. In 2007, the average attendance reached over 29,000 fans, an increase of nearly 17% over the 1999 benchmark.[12] Ticket prices vary by team and seating level, but the ranges for individual tickets are roughly $15 to $60 per game. The CFL is continually searching for viable markets to expand into, particularly in East Canada.

Many of the CFL players are brought into the league through an annual draft process, in which teams select players from both U.S. and Canadian colleges. Other players select to join the CFL and have previous playing experience in other professional football leagues such as the National Football League and the Arena Football League.

NFL EUROPA

Disbanded in 2007, NFL Europa (NFLE) was the designated development league of the NFL and consisted of five teams in Germany and one in the Netherlands (**Table 18-4**). The league was funded by the NFL and was the breeding ground for young, up-and-coming players who aspired to play in the NFL. The NFLE originated as the World League in 1991 but only lasted 2 years and ceased operations in 1993. In 1995, the NFL launched a development league in Europe named the World League, which then evolved into the NFLE throughout the years. The league served primarily as a way

Table 18-3   CFL Teams (2008)

East Division	
Team	**Location**
Ottawa Renegades	Ottawa, Ontario
Montreal Alouettes	Montreal, Quebec
Toronto Argonauts	Toronto, Ontario
Winnipeg Blue Bombers	Winnipeg, Manitoba
West Division	
Team	**Location**
British Columbia Lions	Surrey, British Columbia
Edmonton Eskimos	Edmonton, Alberta
Saskatchewan Rough Riders	Regina, Saskatchewan
Calgary Stampeders	Calgary, Alberta

Table 18-4   NFL Europa Teams (2006)

East Division	
Teams	**Country**
Amsterdam Admirals	The Netherlands
Berlin Thunder	Germany
Cologne Centurions	Germany
Frankfurt Galaxy	Germany
Hamburg Sea Devils	Germany
Rhein Fire	Germany

for the NFL to market the game of football in Europe and increase fan awareness of the NFL. One way they accomplished this task was through player exchange programs where marginal NFL players would play in NFLE, while the top European players were invited to NFL training camps. Each year NFL clubs assigned a minimum of six players from their rosters to participate in NFLE. In 2002, more than 250 NFL players participated in the league.

Games were played from April to June each year with each team participating in a total of 10 games. Ticket prices varied by team and seating location but were typically between $20 and $40.

Corporate sponsors of NFLE included Gatorade, Reebok, Riddell Sports, Wilson, and Skoda Auto. Various games were broadcasted in the United States through the NFL Network, DirecTV, and Fox. The World Bowl, the championship game of NFLE, culminated the season and was shown in the United States on the Fox network.

The NFLE was operated from the NFL's headquarters (based in New York City), with the exception of the human resources department, which was based in London. Most jobs in the league were filled by local professionals in the respective team markets.

In 2007, the NFL decided to cease operations of NFLE. Intent on refocusing the league's global initiatives, the NFL thought it would be more beneficial to stage international regular season games, and in 2007 the Miami Dolphins played the New York Giants in the first regular season game outside of North America. The league is currently considering holding contests in countries such as Great Britain, Germany, Mexico, and Canada. The league also plans to attract the widest global audience possible by expanding its media visibility. According to Mark Waller, senior vice president of NFL International, "We will continue to build our international fan base by taking advantage of technology and customized digital media that make the NFL more accessible on a global scale than ever before and through the regular-season game experience."[13]

UNITED INDOOR FOOTBALL

The United Indoor Football (UIF) league was founded in 2005 through the defection of nine teams from the National Indoor Football League (NIFL) and two teams from the Arena Football League 2 (AF2). The majority of the teams are located in the Midwest region of the United States (**Table 18-5**). Individual teams are run by operator-investors, with most of the teams having at least 4 years of indoor football league experience as of 2005.

The UIF season runs from March through June with each team playing 15 games. Postseason play consists of three rounds and culminates with a championship game to determine the league champion. League-wide average attendance numbers range from 3,000 to 4,000. Ticket prices vary by team and seat location, but typically cost $10 to $30 for each game.

The league headquarters are located in Omaha, Nebraska, and the league operates with a limited staff. Potential job opportunities may exist at the league or team level in operations, sales, or marketing.

WOMEN'S PROFESSIONAL FOOTBALL LEAGUE

Established in 1999, the Women's Professional Football League (WPFL) is the original and longest standing women's professional football league in the United States. The season begins in July and runs through October each year. As displayed in **Table 18-6**, the WPFL consists of 15 teams located throughout the United States. The 15 teams are owned and operated individually and play approximately 10

Table 18-5   UIF Teams (2008)

East Division	
Team	**Location**
Bloomington Extreme	Bloomington, IL
River City Rage	St. Charles, MI
Sioux City Bandits	Sioux City, IA
Wichita Wild	Wichita, KS
West Division	
Team	**Location**
Billings Outlaws	Billings, MT
Colorado Ice	Ft. Collins, CO
Omaha Beef	Omaha, NE
Sioux Falls Storm	Sioux Falls, SD

Table 18-6   WPFL Teams (2008)

American Conference	
Team	**Location**
Connecticut Cyclones	Norwalk, CT
Dallas Diamonds	Hurst, TX
Empire State Roar	Rochester, NY
Las Vegas Showgirlz	Las Vegas, NV
Los Angeles Amazons	Los Angeles, CA
New Jersey Titans	Clark, NJ
New Mexico Burn	Albuquerque, NM
So Cal Scorpions	San Diego, CA
National Conference	
Team	**Location**
Carolina Queens	Charlotte, NC
Houston Energy	Houston, TX
Indiana Speed	Indianapolis, IN
Minnesota Vixen	Eden Prairie, MN
New York Dazzles	Manhattan, NY
Toledo Reign	Toledo, OH
Wisconsin Wolves	Madison, WI

Table 18-7   IWFL Teams (2008)

Eastern Conference	
North Atlantic	
Team	**Location**
Baltimore Nighthawks	Baltimore, MD
Boston Militia	Somerville, MA
Central PA Vipers	Harrisburg, PA
DC Divas	Landover, MD
New York Sharks	Brooklyn/Staten Island, NY
Pittsburgh Passion	Pittsburgh, PA
Midwest	
Team	**Location**
Chicago Force	Chicago, IL
Columbus Phantoms	Grove City, OH
Detroit Demolition	Detroit, MI
Wisconsin Warriors	Kenosha, WI
Wisconsin Wolves	Middletown, WI
South Atlantic	
Team	**Location**
Atlanta Xplosion	Kennesaw, GA
Miami Fury	North Miami, FL
Orlando Mayhem	Orlando, FL
Palm Beach Punishers	West Palm Beach, FL
North Atlantic: Tier II	
Team	**Location**
Holyoke Hurricanes	Holyoke, MA
Montreal Blitz	Montreal, Quebec
Manchester Freedom	Manchester, NH
Southern Maine Rebels	Saco, ME
New England Intensity	East Providence, RI

South Atlantic: Tier II	
Team	**Location**
Cape Fear Thunder	Fayetteville, NC
Carolina Phoenix	Durham, NC
Carolina Queens	Charlotte, NC
Midsouth: Tier II	
Team	**Location**
Louisiana Fuel	Baton Rouge, LA
Shreveport Aftershock	Shreveport, LA
Clarksville Fox	Clarksville, TN
Western Conference	
Pacific Northwest	
Team	**Location**
Corvallis Pride	Corvallis, OR
Portland Shockwave	Portland, OR
Redding Rage	Redding, CA
Sacramento Sirens	Sacramento, CA
Santa Rosa Scorchers	Santa Rosa, CA
Seattle Majestics	Seattle, WA
Pacific Southwest	
Team	**Location**
California Quake	Long Beach, CA
Las Vegas Showgirlz	Las Vegas, NV
Southern California Breakers	Orange County, CA
Tucson Monsoon	Tucson, AZ
Midsouth	
Team	**Location**
Dallas Diamonds	Dallas, TX
Iowa Crush	Des Moines, IA
Kansas City Tribe	Kansas City, MO

regular games per season. A playoff system follows the regular season and culminates in a championship game that pits the National Conference Champion against the American Conference Champion.

Ticket prices vary by team but generally cost around $10 per game, with some teams offering discounts for students. League-wide attendances average between 850 and 1,000 fans per game. The league broadcasts typically one game per week during the season and the championship game via webcasts. Sponsors of the WPFL include various organizations such as the Arena Football League, DHL, O-Pro Mouthguards, Coca-Cola, Steak-n-Shake, and Panera.

The WPFL is headquartered in Hurst, Texas, but the league staff is small and is composed of executives from the teams.

INDEPENDENT WOMEN'S FOOTBALL LEAGUE

The Independent Women's Football League (IWFL) was founded in 2000 by a group of women dedicated to the sport of tackle football. The IWFL is a nonprofit organization with franchises located across the United States (**Table 18-7**). Many of the revenues are donated to local charities. Teams are owned and operated individually and play approximately eight games per season. The season begins in April and runs through June each year. The season culminates with a three-round playoff system and a championship game that matches up the Western Conference Champion against the Eastern Conference Champion. Ticket prices vary by team, but generally cost around $10 per game, with some teams offering free admission for children as well as other discounts. Nike is the official provider of footballs, and Athlete Web Services is the official web services provider for the IWFL.

Endnotes

1. According to *SportsBusiness Daily*, the 2006 Super Bowl had a 41.6 Nielsen rating, compared to an 8.5 rating for the NBA finals, an 11.1 average rating for the 2005 World Series, and a 2.6 rating for the 2006 Stanley Cup.

2. Shapiro, L. and Maske, M. (2005, Apr. 19). Monday Night Football Changes the Channel. *Washington Post*. Retrieved January 24, 2008, from http://www.washingtonpost.com/wp-dyn/articles/A63538-2005Apr18.html.

3. Kaplan, D. (2008). NFL Paying Goodell Like a Veteran. *Street and Smith's SportsBusiness Journal*, vol. 10, issue 43, pp. 1, 26.

4. NFL History: 2001 (n.d.) NFL.com. Retrieved July 21, 2008, from http://www.nfl.com/history/chronology/2001.

5. NFL Cancels China Bowl to Focus on London Game. (2007, Apr. 2). *ESPN.com*. Retrieved October 9, 2007, from http://sports.espn.go.com/nfl/news/story?id=2821706.

6. Simmons, R. (2007) Overpaid athletes? Comparing American and European Football. [Electronic version]. *Working USA: The Journal of Labor and Society,* vol. 10, issue 4, pp. 457–471.

7. Ibid.

8. Friske, B. (2006, Oct. 24). NFL Ready to Call Own Web Plays. *Variety*. Retrieved January 28, 2008, from http://www.variety.com/article/VR1117952550.html?categoryid=1011&cs=1&query=nfl+calls+its+own+plays.

9. Olson, E. (2003, Nov. 27). Small Business; Being Chased by the Big Boys. *New York Times*. Retrieved January 28, 2008, from http://query.nytimes.com/gst/fullpage.html?res=9D05E6DC143AF934A15752C1A9659C8B63.

10. Walker, J. (2008, Mar. 12). Kosar: Gladiators Will Fly in Cleveland. *Cleveland Dispatch,* p. 6C.

11. Ratings Down, NBC Drops Arena Football. (2008, July 1). *New York Times*. Retrieved January 24, 2008, from http://www.nytimes.com/2006/07/01/sports/football/01arena.html.

12. "Our League" to Kick Off 2008 Season. (2008, June 23). CFL.ca. Retrieved July 21, 2008, from http://www.cfl.ca/article/our-league-to-kick-off-2008-season.

13. NFL Europa Closes. (2007, Aug. 3). NFL.com. Retrieved August 15, 2007, from http://www.nfl.com/news/story?id=09000d5d801308ec&template=without-video&confirm=true.

Baseball

MAJOR LEAGUE BASEBALL

Major League Baseball (MLB) is the top professional baseball league in the world. MLB has long been considered one of the "Big 4" professional leagues in the United States along with the National Football League (NFL), National Basketball Association (NBA), and National Hockey League (NHL). Twenty-nine teams are located in major cities throughout the United States, and one team is based in Toronto, Canada. The teams, consisting of players from many foreign countries, compete in either the National or American League. Each organization is responsible for its affiliate teams that operate in the minor leagues at the AAA, AA, A, and Rookie levels throughout North America.

MLB was established as the first major professional league in the United States in 1903, and for many years it was recognized as America's most popular sport, often referred to as the national pastime. Over the years, however, many would say that the NFL surpassed MLB as the most popular professional sports league in America. MLB's long and storied past has helped it maintain the interest of a solid fan base that continues to flock to games throughout the spring, summer, and fall. MLB has yet to earn popularity around the globe; however, it is making great efforts and progress to be well known and supported internationally. Since the players' strike in 1994, MLB and the Major League Baseball Players Association (MLBPA) have avoided any work stoppages, which plagued MLB for the previous 20 years. This has helped the league to build and grow the popularity of the sport both in the United States and globally. Also, the MLB held the inaugural World Baseball Classic in 2006 in an attempt to promote the popularity of the game on a global scale.

Throughout MLB's history, a very contentious relationship between owners and the MLBPA has caused many disruptions that have altered the landscape of the game. The MLBPA, the first union for professional athletes in the United States, is known as one of the most powerful unions in sports. From MLB's inception through the 1970s, the commissioner and owners had the upper hand over the players. However, in the 1980s and 1990s, divergent interests among the owners contributed to the commissioner's lack of power during negotiations with players and the MLBPA.

The owners' diverse interests also have exacerbated the financial gap in team values, which in turn have strongly influenced a club's ability to field a competitive team. In 2007, *Forbes* magazine estimated that the Florida Marlins franchise was worth $244 million and the New York Yankees were worth $1.2 billion. This gap is, by far, the greatest financial disparity among the teams in any of the professional sports leagues in the United States.

Reports have indicated that MLB revenues overall are growing at a steady rate; it increased to $6 billion in 2007, up from $5.2 billion in 2006.[1] Nearly $1 billion of this revenue is generated through the league's various media rights deals with ESPN, Fox, TNT/TBS, DirecTV, XM Satellite Radio, ESPN Radio, and ESPN digital content. Key drivers of revenue growth include increasing rights fees, higher ticket prices, attendance increases, and anticipated future growth in online and international operations. In total, the league retains approximately $450 million as earnings before interest, taxes, depreciation, and amortization (EBITDA).[2]

Headquartered in New York City, the league office is responsible for the day-to-day operations of the league, as well as the league's advertising/marketing, broadcasting, public relations, corporate sales, labor relations, special events, league and teams' websites, and MLB Advanced Media (MLBAM). The international department, also located in the league headquarters, is striving to make MLB more popular in areas such as Europe, Asia, Latin America, Africa, and other parts of the world. Recognizing that a large proportion of its players come from outside the United States, MLB continually attempts to cultivate the game through initiatives such as developing academies, establishing offices in Europe and South America, and operating the World Baseball Classic.

Based on the league's tax filings, there are 236 employees at the league office. Total compensation paid to these employees for the 12-month period ending October 31, 2006, was $85.1 million. The league's commissioner, Bud Selig, was paid a reported $15.06 million. The total payroll figure of $85.1 million represents 69% of league office revenue, which is primarily funded through dues assessed to member teams.[3]

History of Major League Baseball[4-6]

1871

- A group of professional baseball teams formed the National Association of Professional Baseball Players.

1876

- The first professional game was played between the Boston Red Stockings and the Philadelphia Athletics in Philadelphia. The game drew 3,000 fans.
- The first major league, the National League (NL), was formed.

1877

- Morgan G. Buckley, who was the first elected president of the National Association, resigned and was replaced by William A. Hulbert, known as "the Czar of baseball." He reorganized the league, took power away from the teams, and consolidated it in the league office, which previously held little power.

1900

- The total of 12 teams was reduced to 8, eliminating Baltimore, Cleveland, Louisville, and Washington. The remaining 8 teams were the Brooklyn Superbas, New York Giants, St. Louis Cardinals, Cincinnati Reds, Chicago Orphans, Pittsburgh Pirates, Boston Beaneaters, and Philadelphia Phillies.
- Ban Johnson, a former sportswriter and entrepreneur, organized the American League (AL), which would compete with the NL. The AL consisted of the Baltimore Orioles, Philadelphia Athletics, Boston Americans, Washington Nationals, Cleveland Blues, Detroit Tigers, Milwaukee Brewers, and Chicago White Stockings. Three of the league's original clubs in Indianapolis, Minneapolis, and Buffalo were dropped (16 teams).

1902

- The Milwaukee Brewers became the St. Louis Browns, the Washington Nationals became the Washington Senators, and the Cleveland Blues became the Cleveland Bronchos.

1903

- The Baltimore Orioles became the New York Highlanders, the Boston Americans became the Boston Pilgrims, the Cleveland Bronchos became the Cleveland Naps, and the Chicago Orphans became the Chicago Cubs.
- On October 1, the first World Series began, to be decided in a best-of-nine-game series between the Boston Americans and the Pittsburgh Pirates.

1907

- The Boston Beaneaters became the Boston Doves.

1908

- The Boston Americans became the Boston Red Sox.

1909

- The Boston Doves became the Boston Rustlers.

1911

- The Boston Rustlers became the Boston Braves.

1913

- John K. Tener, former pitcher and governor of Pennsylvania, was elected president of the National League. He received a 4-year contract for $25,000 annually (1913–1918).
- The New York Highlanders became the New York Yankees.

1914

- The Brooklyn Superbas became the Brooklyn Robins.

1915

- The Cleveland Naps became the Cleveland Indians.

1918

- John Tener resigned as president, and John Heydler, who worked in the league office since 1902, replaced him.
- The first shortened MLB season took place due to World War I.

1919

- The 1919 World Series was marred by the infamous Black Sox scandal. Eight players from the Chicago White Sox were accused of throwing the series against the Cincinnati Reds and were subsequently banned from baseball for life.

1921

- Judge Kenesaw Mountain Landis was elected baseball's first commissioner. He exercised his authority frequently and to the fullest during his tenure (1921–1945).
- The first MLB game was aired on radio by KDKA in Pittsburgh, which broadcasted the World Series between the Giants and the Yankees.

1922

- In 1922, the U.S. Supreme Court ruled that Major League Baseball was exempt from the provisions of the Sherman Antitrust Act because baseball was not interstate commerce and was the states' affair (*Federal Baseball Club v. National League*, 1922).
- Willie Kamm became the first minor league player with a contract purchased for over $100,000.

1930

- NBC broadcasted the first MLB game between the Brooklyn Robins and the Cincinnati Reds from Ebbets field.

1932

- The Brooklyn Robins became the Brooklyn Dodgers.

1933

- The first Major League All-Star Game was played on July 6, 1933, at Comiskey Park in Chicago.

1934

- John Heydler resigned as president of the National League, and was replaced by Ford Christopher Frick, a former baseball writer and head of the league's publicity bureau (1934–1951).

1939

- The Baseball Hall of Fame officially opened in Cooperstown, New York.

1942

- President Roosevelt sent Commissioner Landis "the Green Letter" in which he voiced his desire to keep baseball going for the betterment of the United States during World War II.

1943

- The Philadelphia Phillies became the Philadelphia Blue Jays.

1945

- A. B. "Happy" Chandler was elected baseball's second commissioner on April 24 by a unanimous vote of the 16 club owners. Commissioner Chandler began negotiating both sponsorship and television deals for MLB (1945–1951).
- The Philadelphia Blue Jays became the Philadelphia Phillies again.

1947

- Jackie Robinson became the first African American to play Major League Baseball when Branch Rickey, general manager of the Brooklyn Dodgers, signed Robinson to a deal.

1949

- Commissioner Chandler negotiated a 7-year, $4,370,000 contract with the Gillette Safety Razor Company and the Mutual Broadcasting System for radio rights to the World Series, with the proceeds going directly into the pension fund.

1951

- Ford C. Frick, who had been serving as NL president, became the third commissioner of baseball when he was unanimously elected by the 16 club owners on September 20 (1951–1965).

1953

- The Boston Braves became the Milwaukee Braves, and Boston was left without a National League team.

1954

- The St. Louis Browns became the Baltimore Orioles.

1955

- The Philadelphia A's became the Kansas City A's.

1958

- The National League expanded west as the Brooklyn Dodgers became the Los Angeles Dodgers and the New York Giants became the San Francisco Giants.

1961

- The Washington (DC) Senators moved to Minnesota and became the Minnesota Twins.
- The Los Angeles Angels and a new Washington Senators were granted expansion franchises (18 teams).

1962

- The New York Mets and the Houston Colt .45s were granted expansion franchises (20 teams).

1965

- General William D. Eckert was elected baseball's fourth commissioner by a unanimous vote of the 20 major league club owners (1965–1968).
- According to a Harris survey, sports fans chose professional football (41%) as their favorite sport, for the first time overtaking baseball (38%).
- The first MLB First-Year Player Draft was held.

- The Houston Colt .45s became the Houston Astros and the Los Angeles Angels became the California Angels.

1966

- The MLBPA was created to represent MLB players in collective bargaining, as well as grievances and salary arbitration. Marvin Miller was elected as the first executive director of the MLBPA (1966–1983).
- The Los Angeles Dodgers played in the first international tour of baseball games in Japan.
- The Milwaukee Braves moved to Atlanta and became the Atlanta Braves.

1968

- The first collective bargaining agreement (CBA) was negotiated. The players won an increase in the minimum salary from $7,000 to $10,000, as well as larger expense allowances.
- The Kansas City A's became the Oakland Athletics.
- The National League completed its expansion to a 12-team league by granting expansion franchises to the Montreal Expos and San Diego Padres (22 teams).

1969

- Bowie K. Kuhn was elected baseball's fifth commissioner by a unanimous vote of the 24 club owners on February 4 (1969–1984).
- Each league, National and American, was separated into an East and West division.
- The Seattle Pilots and Kansas City Royals were granted expansion franchises (24 teams).

1970

- A 3-year CBA was negotiated, becoming the first time that owner-player disputes not involving the "integrity of baseball" could be arbitrated before an arbitration panel with a neutral chairman selected jointly by the players and owners.
- "Ten and 5" rights were agreed upon, which allowed a 10-year veteran who had been with the same team for at least 5 years to veto a trade.
- The Seattle Pilots moved to Milwaukee and became the Milwaukee Brewers.

1972

- The first player strike in baseball took place over the issue of increased player pensions, and lasted 13 days. One compromise was to raise the pension fund to $500,000 per season. The games missed because of the strike were not made up and as a result the Detroit Tigers played one more game than the Boston Red Sox, who finished only one-half game behind Detroit in the AL standings.

- *Flood v. Kuhn*, a landmark case in MLB history, was decided. Outfielder Curt Flood challenged the legality of the reserve clause and the right of clubs to trade players. Ultimately, the U.S. Supreme Court upheld the lower courts' decisions in favor of baseball, ruling that federal antitrust laws did not apply to baseball.
- The Washington Senators moved to Arlington, Texas, and became the Texas Rangers.

1973

- The designated hitter (DH) rule was introduced, allowing a player who is not playing in the field to bat instead of the pitcher. This rule applies only to the American League. National League pitchers still bat. During the World Series, the rules of the home team apply to the game.

1975

- In the landmark *Messersmith-McNally* arbitration decision, arbitrator Peter Seitz ruled that players were free to negotiate with any club after the option year of their contracts had been fulfilled. After several bargaining sessions, the players and owners agreed to the current system that allows players the right to free agency after 6 years in the majors. This marked the birth of free agency.

1977

- The Toronto Blue Jays and the Seattle Mariners were granted expansion franchises (26 teams).

1979

- Average player salaries exceeded $100,000 per year for the first time ($121,900).

1981

- A major strike took place, causing the cancellation of 712 games. The strike lasted from June 12 until July 31, 1981. The parties agreed on a form of indirect compensation: all clubs losing a Type A free agent could draft a replacement from the roster of any club eligible to sign Type A free agents, and such clubs were allowed to protect only about two dozen players in their entire organization. The parties also agreed to extend the CBA through 1984.
- Peter V. Ueberroth was elected baseball's sixth commissioner by a unanimous vote of the 26 club owners. During Ueberroth's tenure, MLB curbed costs and netted substantial profits from television and sponsorship deals (1984–1988).

1985

- Division playoffs went from best-of-five to best-of-seven.

1987

- Commissioner Ueberroth negotiated two landmark television deals—a 4-year, $1.1-billion contract with CBS, and a 4-year $400-million national cable deal with ESPN.

- Major League Baseball as an industry showed a net profit of $21.3 million, its first profitable year since 1973.

1988

- A. Bartlett Giamatti, former National League president, was elected to a 5-year term as baseball's seventh commissioner by a unanimous vote of the 26 club owners (1988–1989).

1989

- A. Bartlett Giamatti died of a heart attack. Deputy Commissioner Francis T. Vincent, Jr. was elected baseball's eighth commissioner in a unanimous vote of major league owners (1989–1992).

1990

- A lockout postponing the start of spring training was initiated by the owners. A settlement was reached on March 18, 32 days after the scheduled start of the spring training schedule. Due to the lockout, opening day was delayed 1 week to provide adequate time for spring training, but the settlement ensured that a full slate of 162 regular season games could be played.

1991

- Commissioner Vincent declared that the American League would receive $42 million of the National League's $190 million in expansion revenue and that the AL would provide players in the NL expansion draft. This marked the first time in expansion history that leagues were required to share revenue or provide players for the other league's expansion draft. Expansion franchises were granted to Colorado and Florida to begin play in 1993.

1992

- Commissioner Vincent resigned. Allan H. "Bud" Selig, owner of the Milwaukee Brewers, was named chairman of the Major League Executive Council, and acting commissioner (1992–1998).

- Oriole Park at Camden Yards opened in Baltimore, Maryland. Oriole Park was the first retro ballpark to be built, and the model that many teams used when they were designing their new stadiums, such as the Cleveland Indians' Jacobs Field.

1993

- The Colorado Rockies and Florida Marlins began play as expansion franchises, the first expansion in MLB since 1977 (28 teams).

1994

- A strike by the players beginning on July 28 wiped out the World Series and lasted for a total of 234 days.[7] A new CBA would not be agreed upon until 1996. The 1995 season was played under the terms of the old CBA.

- Both the American and National Leagues set up three divisions—East, Central, and West. The winners, plus a fourth team, called a wild card, qualified for the postseason playoffs.

1996

- The first MLB regular season game to take place outside of the United States and Canada is played in Monterrey, Mexico, between the New York Mets and the San Diego Padres.

1997

- For the first time in MLB history, teams from the American League and National League competed in regular season, head-to-head competition. The first interleague game was on June 12 as the Texas Rangers hosted the San Francisco Giants at The Ballpark in Arlington.

- The California Angels became the Anaheim Angels.

1998

- Bud Selig was elected the ninth commissioner of baseball by a vote of the 30 MLB club owners. Previously he had served as acting commissioner and was owner of the Milwaukee Brewers (1998–present).

- The Arizona Diamondbacks and Tampa Bay Devil Rays were granted expansion franchises (30 teams).

- The Milwaukee Brewers switched from AL Central to NL Central; the Detroit Tigers switched from AL East to AL Central.

1999

- Umpire Frank Pulli became the first to use a TV replay to reverse a call in a game, taking away a Marlins home run versus the Cardinals, although at the time there was no rule allowing the use of instant replay in Major League Baseball.

2000

- The first MLB regular season game in Asia took place on April 1, in Tokyo, Japan, in a game between the Chicago Cubs and the New York Mets. About 55,000 fans were in attendance at the game, which was held in the Tokyo Dome.

2001

- MLB and Fox agreed on a television deal worth $2.5 billion through the 2006 season.

2002

- A new 4-year CBA (2002–2006) was negotiated with provisions for a luxury tax to be placed on player payrolls exceeding prescribed thresholds, increased revenue sharing among the 30 teams, drug testing for illegal steroids, increased minimum player salaries, and new limitations on team debt. Drug testing for illegal steroids were included by having random testing in 2003, and if over 5% tested positive, drug testing would continue. Penalties for testing positive included mandatory treatment and ranged from a 30-day suspension to a 2-year suspension.

- MLB and XM Satellite Radio agreed to a deal worth approximately $650 million over the course of 11 years, allowing XM to broadcast games beginning with the 2005 season.

- MLB.com streamed the first Major League game between the Texas Rangers and the New York Yankees on the Internet via its Gameday Video service.

2004

- MLB and ESPN signed a 6-year, $66-million deal to broadcast Sunday Night Baseball games and various games throughout the season, as well as all of the postseason games through the 2010 season.

2005

- The U.S. Congress heard testimony about the use of performance-enhancing drugs in Major League Baseball, forcing MLB and the union to agree on a much stricter policy that permits off-season testing and a 10-day suspension for first-time abusers.[8]

- MLB and General Motors agreed on terms making Chevrolet the "Official Vehicle of Major League Baseball." As part of this agreement, Chevrolet was the presenting sponsor of two of the game's most prestigious awards, the Ted Williams All-Star Game Most Valuable Player Award and the World Series Most Valuable Player Award.

- MLB signed an 8-year, $2.37-billion agreement that granted ESPN the right to televise up to 80 MLB regular season games per season across the ESPN networks through 2013.

- The Montreal Expos moved to Washington, DC, and became the Washington Nationals. The Anaheim Angels became the Los Angeles Angels of Anaheim.

2006

- The inaugural World Baseball Classic was played in March and featured many of the best players in the world competing for their home countries. Japan won the inaugural World Baseball Classic. The championship game was played at PETCO Park in San Diego, California, in front of a sold-out crowd of 42,696. The total tournament attendance was 737,112.

- MLB and MLBPA announced a 5-year labor contract that will run through the 2011 season. Highlights of the contract included continued revenue sharing, competitive balance tax, and a continuation of the existing drug policy.

2007

- MLB signed 7-year television contracts with Fox and TNT/TBS for $1.8 billion and $1.05 billion, respectively.

- MLB set an all-time attendance record in 2007 with a season attendance totaling 79,502,524.

2008

- The Los Angeles Dodgers and the San Diego Padres played the first MLB-sanctioned game in China. The game was played in the 12,000-seat Wukesong Baseball Field in Beijing.

2009

- MLB launched the MLB Network, a specialty cable channel dedicated to MLB programming.

Structure of Major League Baseball

League Alignment

- 30 total teams (**Table 19-1**)
- 2 leagues: National League (16 teams) and American League (14 teams)
  - 3 divisions in each league: West, Central, and East

Competition Format

- Head-to-head contests between teams; unbalanced schedule
- End-of-year playoffs to determine World Series Champion

Schedule

- Game days
  - Games are played throughout the week. Most weekday games are played at night; however, there are exceptions. Weekend games are played either during the day or at night.
  - 3- to 4-game series are played each time teams face an opponent (e.g., games on Friday, Saturday, and Sunday all against the same opponent).
- Preseason (March–April): 30–32 exhibition games are played per team. Most teams play their preseason games at a spring training facility in one of two leagues: the Cactus League in Arizona or the Grapefruit League in Florida.

Table 19-1   MLB Teams (2008–2009)

American League	
East Division	
Team	**Location**
Baltimore Orioles	Baltimore, MD
Boston Red Sox	Boston, MA
New York Yankees	Bronx, NY
Tampa Bay Rays	St. Petersburg, FL
Toronto Blue Jays	Toronto, Ontario
Central Division	
Team	**Location**
Chicago White Sox	Chicago, IL
Cleveland Indians	Cleveland, OH
Detroit Tigers	Detroit, MI
Kansas City Royals	Kansas City, MO
Minnesota Twins	Minneapolis, MN
West Division	
Team	**Location**
Los Angeles Angels of Anaheim	Anaheim, CA
Oakland Athletics	Oakland, CA
Seattle Mariners	Seattle, WA
Texas Rangers	Arlington, TX

National League	
East Division	
Team	**Location**
Atlanta Braves	Atlanta, GA
Florida Marlins	Miami Gardens, FL
New York Mets	Flushing, NY
Philadelphia Phillies	Philadelphia, PA
Washington Nationals	Washington, DC
Central Division	
Team	**Location**
Chicago Cubs	Chicago, IL
Cincinnati Reds	Cincinnati, OH
Houston Astros	Houston, TX
Milwaukee Brewers	Milwaukee, WI
Pittsburgh Pirates	Pittsburgh, PA
St. Louis Cardinals	St. Louis, MO
West Division	
Team	**Location**
Arizona Diamondbacks	Phoenix, AZ
Colorado Rockies	Denver, CO
Los Angeles Dodgers	Los Angeles, CA
San Diego Padres	San Diego, CA
San Francisco Giants	San Francisco, CA

- Regular season (April–October): 162 games (81 home, 81 away)
  - National League: 70–80 divisional games, 15–18 against American League
  - American League: 57–72 divisional games, 15–18 against National League
- Playoffs (October)
  - 3 rounds: League Division Series, League Championship Series, World Series
  - 8 teams: 3 division winners and 1 wild card team from each league
  - Teams play each other according to best record (team with best record plays team with worst record); however, teams in the same division cannot play each other in the first round
  - League Division Series (American and National)
    - Best of 5 series.
    - The team with the better record receives home field advantage, unless it is a wild card team.
  - League Championship Series (American and National)
    - Winners of the League Division Series play each other to determine League Champion.
    - Best of 7 series.

- World Series (American vs. National)
  - The winners of each League Championship Series play each other to determine the World Series.
  - Best of 7 series.
  - The DH rule is in effect only for games are played in American League parks.
- All-Star Game (July)
  - This mid-season game pits the American League All-Stars against the National League All-Stars.
  - The league that wins the All-Star Game earns home field advantage for the World Series.
  - The site changes annually, as determined by the commissioner.
    - 2007: AT&T Park in San Francisco
    - 2008: Yankee Stadium in New York City
    - 2009: Busch Stadium in St. Louis

Money Matters for Major League Baseball

Sources of Revenue

- In 2007, overall revenues for MLB were a record $6.075 billion.[9]

- Television broadcast revenues
  - Fox and MLB have a 7-year, $2.1-billion television rights deal that started with the 2007 season.[9]
  - ESPN and MLB have an 8-year, $2.37-billion television rights deal that started during the 2006 season.
  - TBS and MLB have a 7-year, $490-million television rights deal that started in the 2008 season.
  - MLB TV broadcasts 2,300 games a season to subscribers. The subscription fee for a full season is $49.95.
  - MLB signed a 7-year, $175-million deal with DirecTV and a 7-year, $385-million deal with a group of cable companies to air out-of-market games on the dish company.
- Other media
  - ESPN Radio has a 5-year, $55-million deal through 2010 with MLB to broadcast games nationally.
  - XM Satellite Radio has an 11-year, $650-million deal through 2015 with MLB to broadcast games to subscribers of XM Satellite Radio.
  - MLB Advanced Media (MLBAM) runs the MLB website, and each individual team website. Through these websites viewers are able to read news, purchase tickets, watch live feeds, listen to radio broadcasts, and watch highlights from games. In 2007, MLBAM generated more than $450 million in revenue.[10]
- Gate receipts
  - The average attendance during the 2007 regular season was 32,785 fans with an average ticket cost of $22.69.
- Sponsorship
  - MLB has 18 official sponsors including mortgage companies, beverage distributors, hotel companies, and satellite radio. Sponsors pay MLB an annual fee to become a recognized partner and for other related services.
- Merchandising and licensing
  - Rawlings is the official supplier of baseballs and gloves for MLB.
  - New Era is the official supplier of hats for MLB.
  - Louisville Slugger is the official supplier of bats for MLB.
  - Majestic Athletics is the official jersey supplier of MLB.

MINOR LEAGUE BASEBALL[11]

Minor League Baseball (MiLB), formerly referred to as the National Association, is composed of 222 teams in 17 leagues located throughout North America. The umbrella organization, MiLB, consists of the teams that are affiliated with Major League Baseball organizations.

Professional teams that are not affiliated with MLB organizations are called Independent League teams, and are not considered members of Minor League Baseball. There are currently 10 Independent Leagues, the largest and most successful of these leagues are the Atlantic, Central, Frontier, Northeast, and Northern Leagues.

Minor League Baseball teams are, for the most part, independently owned and operated. However, the players are controlled and paid by their parent MLB organization. Minor League Baseball has been a central component to the development of young players throughout the history of baseball.

For many years, the term *farm system* characterized the minor leagues because players were grown or developed to become major leaguers. During the 1930s, Branch Rickey made the phrase famous when he took full advantage of the idea of affiliate teams. When Branch Rickey was general manager of the St. Louis Cardinals, they had over 30 affiliates across the nation in order to provide a supply of talent for the major league club. Today, major league organizations typically have six or seven minor league affiliates that are classified by the level of play. These categories are, from lowest to highest, Rookie, Short-Season A, Low A, A, High A, AA, and AAA. Major league clubs also send minor leaguers to off-season leagues like the Puerto Rican League, Mexican League, or Dominican League; however, these teams are not affiliated directly with MLB teams. Minor league affiliates all are governed under the National Association Agreement of Professional Baseball, which is a document that includes the by-laws between Minor League Baseball (National Association) and its member leagues.

Mike Tamburro, president of the Pawtucket Red Sox (a AAA team in the International League), catches a game from the stands. Tamburro was named International League Executive of the Year in 1984.

The president of Minor League Baseball works in conjunction with a 17-member board of directors (one club owner from each league).

Minor league teams are financially independent from their parent major league organizations; therefore, it is very important that minor league clubs generate enough revenue to cover expenses, and hopefully, make a profit. As player salaries are paid for by the MLB organization, teams have far fewer expenses than other sport teams. Depending on the level of play (A or AAA), teams are located in rural towns (Hickory, NC: Low A) or small to mid-size cities (Rochester, NY: AAA) with stadium capacity anywhere from 5,000 to 25,000. Community support and involvement with the team is critical to the team's health and longevity. Whether a team schedules "Rock and Roll Night" or "Bobblehead Day," minor league clubs have always relied on promotions and in-game entertainment to supplement the game and attract attendance to their ballparks.

Team values have increased significantly during the last 30 years, with AAA teams now worth in the $8 million range, and an AA team is worth over $7.2 million. Each team usually employs a general manager to oversee the entire operation, which is mainly business related, and includes community relations, marketing, facility management, ticketing, media relations, concessions, and merchandising. The higher level teams typically will employ more people so each person handles a specific task, while smaller, lower level teams may utilize fewer people to manage multiple tasks. Unlike the major leagues, minor league general managers (GMs) do not make personnel decisions, and therefore must rely on what the parent club provides for players. Minor league general managers are usually business oriented and entrepreneurial in nature and strive to create the most entertaining atmosphere possible, regardless of how well or badly the team performs.

History of Minor League Baseball

1901

- The National Association of Professional Baseball Leagues (NAPBL, or NA) was organized when presidents of seven minor leagues met in Chicago and established rules of operation that have generally remained through the history of minor league baseball.
- Patrick Powers was elected first president of the NA (1901–1909).

1902

- The NA, national in scope, began play with 14 leagues and 96 teams.

1910

- Michael Sexton was elected president of the NA after Powers resigned (1910–1932).

1914

- Membership in the NA grew to 41 leagues in a period of prosperity and stability.

1918

- Due to a loss of manpower caused by World War I and the rival Federal League, only nine leagues remained in the NA.

1921

- An agreement was signed that allowed a major league team to own minor league teams. Branch Rickey of the St. Louis Cardinals used this to establish the farm system, controlling players in the minor leagues and developing them for his MLB team.

1930

- The first night baseball game under permanent lights was played in Des Moines, Iowa, and attracted 12,000 fans for a team that averaged 600 at the time. The idea spread quickly through the minors and saved them during the Great Depression.

1931

- The NA established a promotional department to organize new leagues and aid the existing leagues and a press bureau to serve as a clearinghouse for information and player records.

1932

- Frank Shaughnessy, president of the International League, invented the playoff system to keep more teams in the race and sustain fan interest. This was done by having the first place team play the fourth place team, and the second and third place teams face each other. The two winners would play each other for the league championship.

1933

- William Bramham, who had practiced law and previously served as Chairman of the NA executive committee, was elected NA president during the Great Depression (1933–1946).

1944

- With players gone to serve in World War II and travel limitations in effect, only 10 minor leagues remained in operation.

1946

- Jackie Robinson made his debut in minor league baseball with Montreal of the International League. The next season, Branch Rickey made Robinson the first African American to play in the major leagues when he signed a contract with the Brooklyn Dodgers.

1947

- George Trautman, who had been executive vice president of the Detroit Tigers, was elected president of the NA (1947–1963).

1949

- A regular season attendance record of 39.7 million was set.

1951

- Emmett Ashford became the first African American umpire in the minor leagues, working in the Southwestern International League.

1964

- Phil Piton, who served as a top aide to Baseball Commissioner Kennesaw Mountain Landis, was elected president of the NA (1964–1971).

1972

- Hank Peters, who served with the St. Louis Browns (1946–1953) and later served as farm director for Kansas City, Cincinnati, and Cleveland, was elected president of the NA (1972–1975).

1976

- Bobby Bragan, who had been a player and manager at both the major league and minor league levels, a major league coach, a front office executive with two major league teams, and served 7 years as president of the Texas League, was elected president of the NA (1976–1978).

1979

- Johnny Johnson, who spent 24 years with the New York Yankees, was elected president of the NA (1979–1988).

1982

- The largest crowd in minor league history, 65,666, watched an American Association game at Denver's Mile High Stadium.

1987

- More than 20 million fans attended games, a figure not matched since 1953.

1988

- Sal Artiaga, who had been a manager at the NA level, was elected president of the NA (1988–1991).

1991

- The Buffalo Bisons of the American Association attracted 1,240,951 fans during the season to set the all-time record for minor league baseball.
- Baseball's Facilities Standards went into effect, setting minimum standards for minor league ballparks and touching off the biggest building boom in history. From 1991 to 2008, more than half the teams in the minors moved to stadiums built or completely renovated since these standards went into effect.

1992

- Mike Moore, previous co-owner and operator of an NA team and chief administrative officer of the NA, was elected president of the NA (1992–present).

1997

- All major league player development contracts became guaranteed for the 160 affiliated minor league teams through the life of the contract due to significant changes to the collective bargaining agreement between MLB and minor league baseball. The contract terms of this agreement were set to last 10 years.[12]

1998

- Triple-A baseball realigned from three leagues into two and established the Triple-A World Series, which was played in Las Vegas until 2000.
- The Professional Baseball Umpire Corporation was formed to operate and maintain the umpire program for the 16 domestic leagues, under terms of the historic 10-year Professional Baseball Agreement (PBA) that was negotiated with Major League Baseball.

1999

- The North American Professional Baseball League (NAPBL) formally changed its name to Minor League Baseball and started licensing itself with the Minor League Baseball brand, a name many both inside and outside the organization had been using for years.

2004

- The all-time season attendance record of 39,640,443, set in 1949, was broken when 39,887,755 fans attended regular season games.

2006

- The all-time season attendance record, which had been set 2 years before, was broken when 41,710,357 fans attended regular season games.
- The members of the National Association of Minor League umpires went on strike from April 6 until June 12. On June 12, the umpires settled for a $100 per month raise and an increase in per diem expenses totaling $90 per month.

2008

- MLB instituted a new rule that all first- and third-base coaches have to wear helmets. The rule came in the wake of the death of Mike Coolbaugh, a Rockies Double-A first-base coach, who was struck by a line drive and killed during a July 2007 game.

Structure of Minor League Baseball

- 17 leagues
- AAA (144-game schedule)
  - International League (**Table 19-2**)
  - Pacific League (**Table 19-3**)
- AA (142-game schedule)
  - Eastern League (**Table 19-4**)
  - Southern League (**Table 19-5**)
  - Texas League (**Table 19-6**)
- High A (140-game schedule)
  - California League (**Table 19-7**)
  - Carolina League (**Table 19-8**)
  - Florida State League (**Table 19-9**)
- A (140-game schedule)
  - Midwest League (**Table 19-10**)
  - South Atlantic League (**Table 19-11**)
- Low A (55–80-game schedule)
  - Short season
    - New York-Penn League (**Table 19-12**)
    - Northwest League (**Table 19-13**)
- Rookie
  - Appalachian League (**Table 19-14**)
  - Arizona League (**Table 19-15**)
  - Gulf Coast League (**Table 19-16**)
  - Pioneer League (**Table 19-17**)
  - Venezuela Summer League

Table 19-2   International League Teams (AAA Level)

North Division	
Team	**Location**
Buffalo Bisons	Buffalo, NY
Lehigh Valley IronPigs	Allentown, PA
Pawtucket Red Sox	Pawtucket, RI
Rochester Red Wings	Rochester, NY
Scranton/Wilkes-Barre Yankees	Scranton, PA
Syracuse Chiefs	Syracuse, NY
West Division	
Team	**Location**
Columbus Clippers	Columbus, OH
Indianapolis Indians	Indianapolis, IN
Louisville Bats	Louisville, KY
Toledo Mud Hens	Toledo, OH
South Division	
Team	**Location**
Charlotte Knights	Fort Mill, SC
Durham Bulls	Durham, NC
Norfolk Tides	Norfolk, VA
Richmond Braves	Richmond, VA

Money Matters for Minor League Baseball

Sources of Revenue range depending on level of play and size of stadium.

- Gate receipts
- Sponsorships/advertising
  - Corporate
  - Local
  - Licensing/merchandising: Revenues for 2005 reached an estimated $41.7 million.

Table 19-3   Pacific Coast League Teams (AAA Level)

American Conference		Pacific Conference	
North Division		**North Division**	
Team	**Location**	**Team**	**Location**
Iowa Cubs	Des Moines, IA	Colorado Springs Sky Sox	Colorado Springs, CO
Memphis Redbirds	Memphis, TN	Portland Beavers	Portland, OR
Nashville Sounds	Nashville, TN	Salt Lake Stingers	Salt Lake City, UT
Omaha Royals	Omaha, NE	Tacoma Rainiers	Tacoma, WA
South Division		**South Division**	
Team	**Location**	**Team**	**Location**
Albuquerque Isotopes	Albuquerque, NM	Fresno Grizzlies	Fresno, CA
New Orleans Zephyrs	Metairie, LA	Las Vegas 51s	Las Vegas, NV
Oklahoma Red Hawks	Oklahoma City, OK	Sacramento River Cats	West Sacramento, CA
Round Rock Express	Round Rock, TX	Tucson Sidewinders	Tucson, AZ

Table 19-4   Eastern League Teams (AA Level)

North Division	
Team	**Location**
Binghamton Mets	Binghamton, NY
Connecticut Defenders	Norwich, CT
New Britain Rock Cats	New Britain, CT
New Hampshire Fisher Cats	Manchester, NH
Portland Sea Dogs	Portland, ME
Trenton Thunder	Trenton, NJ

South Division	
Team	**Location**
Akron Aeros	Akron, OH
Altoona Curve	Altoona, PA
Bowie Baysox	Bowie, MD
Erie SeaWolves	Erie, PA
Harrisburg Senators	Harrisburg, PA
Reading Phillies	Reading, PA

Table 19-6   Texas League Teams (AA Level)

North Division	
Team	**Location**
Arkansas Travelers	Little Rock, AR
Northwest Arkansas Naturals	Springdale, AR
Springfield Cardinals	Springfield, MO
Tulsa Drillers	Tulsa, OK

South Division	
Team	**Location**
Corpus Christi Hooks	Corpus Christi, TX
Frisco RoughRiders	Frisco, TX
Midland RockHounds	Midland, TX
San Antonio Missions	San Antonio, TX

Table 19-8   Carolina League Teams (High A Level)

Northern Division	
Team	**Location**
Frederick Keys	Frederick, MD
Lynchburg Hillcats	Lynchburg, VA
Potomac Nationals	Woodbridge, VA
Wilmington Blue Rocks	Wilmington, DE

Southern Division	
Team	**Location**
Kinston Indians	Kinston, NC
Myrtle Beach Pelicans	Myrtle Beach, SC
Salem Avalanche	Salem, VA
Winston-Salem Warthogs	Winston-Salem, NC

Table 19-5   Southern League Teams (AA Level)

South Division	
Team	**Location**
Birmingham Barons	Birmingham, AL
Jacksonville Suns	Jacksonville, FL
Mississippi Braves	Pearl, MS
Mobile BayBears	Mobile, AL
Montgomery Biscuits	Montgomery, AL

North Division	
Team	**Location**
Carolina Mudcats	Zebulon, NC
Chattanooga Lookouts	Chattanooga, TN
Huntsville Stars	Huntsville, AL
Tennessee Smokies	Kodak, TN
West Tenn Diamond Jaxx	Jackson, TN

Table 19-7   California League Teams (High A Level)

North Division	
Team	**Location**
Bakersfield Blaze	Bakersfield, CA
Modesto Nuts	Modesto, CA
San Jose Giants	San Jose, CA
Stockton Ports	Stockton, CA
Visalia Oaks	Visalia, CA

South Division	
Team	**Location**
High Desert Mavericks	Adelanto, CA
Inland Empire 66ers	San Bernardino, CA
Lake Elsinore Storm	Lake Elsinore, CA
Lancaster JetHawks	Lancaster, CA
Rancho Cucamonga Quakes	Rancho Cucamonga, CA

Table 19-9   Florida State League Teams (High A Level)

East Division	
Team	**Location**
Brevard County Manatees	Melbourne, FL
Daytona Cubs	Daytona Beach, FL
Jupiter Hammerheads	Jupiter, FL
Palm Beach Cardinals	Jupiter, FL
St. Lucie Mets	Port St. Lucie, FL
Vero Beach Devil Rays	Vero Beach, FL

West Division	
Team	**Location**
Clearwater Threshers	Clearwater, FL
Dunedin Blue Jays	Dunedin, FL
Fort Myers Miracle	Fort Myers, FL
Lakeland Flying Tigers	Lakeland, FL
Sarasota Reds	Sarasota, FL
Tampa Yankees	Tampa, FL

Table 19-10   Midwest League Teams (High A Level)

Eastern Division

Team	Location
Dayton Dragons	Dayton, OH
Fort Wayne Wizards	Fort Wayne, IN
Lansing Lugnuts	Lansing, MI
South Bend Silver Hawks	South Bend, IN
Great Lakes Loons	Midland, MI
West Michigan Whitecaps	Comstock Park, MI

Western Division

Team	Location
Beloit Snappers	Beloit, WI
Burlington Bees	Burlington, IA
Cedar Rapids Kernels	Cedar Rapids, IA
Clinton LumberKings	Clinton, IA
Kane County Cougars	Geneva, IL
Peoria Chiefs	Peoria, IL
Quad Cities River Bandits	Davenport, IA
Wisconsin Timber Rattlers	Appleton, WI

Table 19-11   South Atlantic League Teams (High A Level)

Northern Division

Team	Location
Delmarva Shorebirds	Salisbury, MD
Greensboro Grasshoppers	Greensboro, NC
Hagerstown Suns	Hagerstown, MD
Hickory Crawdads	Hickory, NC
Lake County Captains	Eastlake, OH
Lakewood BlueClaws	Lakewood, NJ
Lexington Legends	Lexington, KY
West Virginia Power	Charleston, WV

Southern Division

Team	Location
Asheville Tourists	Asheville, NC
Augusta GreenJackets	Augusta, GA
Charleston RiverDogs	Charleston, SC
Columbus Catfish	Columbus, GA
Greenville Drive	Greenville, SC
Kannapolis Intimidators	Kannapolis, NC
Rome Braves	Rome, GA
Savannah Sand Gnats	Savannah, GA

Table 19-12   New York-Penn League Teams (Low A Level)

McNamara Division

Team	Location
Aberdeen IronBirds	Lutherville, MD
Brooklyn Cyclones	Brooklyn, NY
Hudson Valley Renegades	Wappinger Falls, NY
Staten Island Yankees	Staten Island, NY

Pickney Division

Team	Location
Auburn Doubledays	Auburn, NY
Batavia Muckdogs	Batavia, NY
Jamestown Jammers	Jamestown, NY
Mahoning Valley Scrappers	Niles, OH
State College Spikes	University Park, PA
Williamsport Cross Cutters	Williamsport, PA

Stedler Division

Team	Location
Lowell Spinners	Lowell, MA
Oneonta Tigers	Oneonta, NY
Tri-City ValleyCats	Troy, NY
Vermont Lake Monsters	Winooski, VT

Table 19-13   Northwest League Teams (Low A Level)

East Division

Team	Location
Boise Hawks	Boise, ID
Spokane Indians	Spokane, WA
Tri-City Dust Devils	Kennewick, WA
Yakima Bears	Yakima, WA

West Division

Team	Location
Eugene Emeralds	Eugene, OR
Everett AquaSox	Everett, WA
Salem-Keizer Volcanoes	Keizer, OR
Vancouver Canadians	Vancouver, British Columbia

Table 19-14   Appalachian League Teams (Rookie Level)

East Division

Team	Location
Bluefield Orioles	Bluefield, WV
Burlington Royals	Burlington, NC
Danville Braves	Danville, VA
Princeton Devil Rays	Princeton, WV

West Division

Team	Location
Bristol Sox	Bristol, VA
Elizabethton Twins	Elizabethton, TN
Johnson City Cardinals	Johnson City, TN
Kingsport Mets	Kingsport, TN
Pulaski Blue Jays	Pulaski, VA

Table 19-15   Arizona League Teams (Rookie Level)

Team	Location
Arizona League Angels	Tempe, AZ
Arizona League Athletics	Phoenix, AZ
Arizona League Cubs	Mesa, AZ
Arizona League Giants	Scottsdale, AZ
Arizona League Mariners	Peoria, AZ
Arizona League Padres	Peoria, AZ
Arizona League Royals	Surprise, AZ
Arizona League Rangers	Surprise, AZ

Table 19-17   Pioneer League Teams (Rookie Level)

Northern Division	
Team	Location
Billings Mustangs	Billings, MT
Great Falls Voyagers	Great Falls, MT
Helena Brewers	Helena, MT
Missoula Osprey	Missoula, MT
Southern Division	
Team	Location
Casper Ghosts	Casper, WY
Idaho Falls Chukars	Idaho Falls, ID
Ogden Raptors	Ogden, UT
Orem Owlz	Orem, UT

Table 19-16   Gulf Coast League Teams (Rookie Level)

East Division	
Team	Location
GCL Cardinals	Jupiter, FL
GCL Dodgers	Vero Beach, FL
GCL Marlins	Jupiter, FL
GCL Mets	Port St. Lucie, FL
GCL Nationals	Melbourne, FL
North Division	
Team	Location
GCL Braves	Kissimmee, FL
GCL Blue Jays	Dunedin, FL
GCL Indians	Winter Haven, FL
GCL Phillies	Clearwater, FL
GCL Tigers	Lakeland, FL
GCL Yankees	Tampa, FL
South Division	
Team	Location
GCL Orioles	Sarasota, FL
GCL Pirates	Bradenton, FL
GCL Reds	Sarasota, FL
GCL Red Sox	Fort Myers, FL
GCL Twins	Fort Myers, FL

Overview of the World Baseball Classic

The World Baseball Classic (WBC) is a World Cup–style competition between 16 countries. It started in 2006 and is scheduled to be held every 3 years. Established by MLB and the MLBPA, the WBC is designed to increase worldwide exposure of the game of baseball, increase global interest, and introduce new fans and players to the game. The tournament is sanctioned by the International Baseball Federation (IBAF) and is run in conjunction with Nippon Professional Baseball (NPB), the Korea Baseball Organization, their respective professional player associations, and other professional leagues from around the world. Each national federation is responsible for selecting the players that will represent their country. In 2006, nearly 60% of the players participating in the WBC played in Major League Baseball. The 16 teams compete in a bracket-style format in four groups, with the top two teams from each group moving on to the next round, similar to the World Cup soccer format. There are two rounds of pool competition and then a semifinal round and championship game between the remaining two teams. In 2006, WBC games were played in Japan, Puerto Rico, and the United States, with Japan defeating Cuba in the championship game 10–6 in San Diego.

The inaugural WBC was played in March 2006 and was a success at many levels. The total attendance was 737,112 with tournament profits estimated to be $10–$15 million. The profits were distributed to the participating countries with a stipulation that at least half of the money go towards the country's baseball federation. For the United States, MLB and the MLBPA split the other half of the profits. However, the tournament had several issues and concerns that will be addressed in the planning of the next WBC in 2009, such as the scheduling of the event during spring training; the tie breaker format, which could end the game with a tie; the questionable umpiring; and poor attendance in Japan.

Structure for the 2006 World Baseball Classic

Competition Format

- See **Table 19-18** for the 2009 roster.
- Round 1 features four pools of four teams each.
  - Every team will compete against each team in its assigned pool.
  - The top two teams by record will advance to the next round.

Table 19-18   WBC Teams (2009)

Pool A	Pool B	Pool C	Pool D
China	Australia	Canada	Dominican Republic
Chinese Taipei	Cuba	Italy	The Netherlands
Japan	Mexico	United States	Panama
Korea	South Africa	Venezuela	Puerto Rico

- Round 2 features two pools of four teams each.
  - Every team will compete against each team in its assigned pool.
  - The top two teams by record will advance to the semi-final round.
- Semi-final round
  - The winners of the semi-final games will compete in the final game.
- A total of 39 games were played.

Schedule

- Games were played at the following sites in 2006:
  - Round 1
    - Tokyo Dome: Tokyo, Japan
    - Hiram Bithorn Stadium: San Juan, Puerto Rico
    - The Ballpark at Disney's Wide World of Sports Complex: Orlando, Florida
    - Chase Field: Phoenix, Arizona
    - Scottsdale Stadium: Scottsdale, Arizona
  - Round 2
    - Hiram Bithorn Stadium: San Juan, Puerto Rico
    - Angel Stadium: Anaheim, California
  - Semi-finals and final round
    - PETCO Park: San Diego, California

Money Matters for the World Baseball Classic

Sources of Revenues

- Gate receipts
  - 737,112 fans attended WBC games, with prices ranging from $15 to $60 per ticket.
- Television broadcasting
  - ESPN, ESPN2, and ESPN Deportes aired all 39 games in 2006.
- Radio
  - XM had rights to all 39 games in 2006.

- Sponsorship
  - The WBC negotiated corporate sponsorship deals with a list of 26 global and regional companies. There were four U.S. companies: Anheuser-Busch, Gatorade, MasterCard, and MBNA. Some of the other participating sponsors included Konami, Asahi, Sun-Com, Banco Mercantil, and Presidente.
- Merchandise/licensing:
  - Rawlings was the official supplier of baseballs and gloves.
  - New Era was the official supplier of hats.
  - Louisville Slugger was the official supplier of bats.
  - Majestic Athletics was the official jersey supplier.

Expenses

- Operating costs were split by MLB and the MLBPA.

INDEPENDENT LEAGUES[13]

The Independent Leagues are the professional baseball teams and leagues that do not have an affiliation with Minor League Baseball or Major League Baseball. There are a total of 10 Independent Leagues (American Association, Atlantic, Canadian-American [Can-Am], Continental, Frontier, Golden Baseball, New York State, Northern, South Coast, and United)—see **Tables 19-19 through 19-28**. The level of play is comparable to the A to AA level for Minor League Baseball. Most teams are independently owned and operated and strive to provide fans affordable family entertainment in selected cities.

Many of the players are former minor leaguers trying to earn a spot with an MLB organization, and some players merely want to continue their careers part-time as a professional baseball player. Some players are still looking to earn a spot with an affiliated minor league team and are continuing to develop.

Job opportunities with Independent League teams are similar to those with affiliated minor leagues; however because most teams' budgets are much smaller than affiliated minor leagues there are fewer opportunities, on average. Job responsibilities include sales/marketing, promotions, game day operations, facility management, concessions, and administration.

Table 19-19   Atlantic League Teams

Liberty Division	
Team	Location
Bridgeport Bluefish	Bridgeport, CT
Camden Riversharks	Camden, NJ
Long Island Ducks	Central Islip, NY
Southern Maryland Blue Crabs	Waldorf, MD

American Division	
Team	Location
Lancaster Barnstormers	Lancaster, PA
Newark Bears	Newark, NJ
Somerset Patriots	Bridgewater, NJ
York Revolution	York, PA

Table 19-21   Canadian American League Teams

Team	Location
Atlantic City Surf	Atlantic City, NJ
Brockton Rox	Brockton, MA
Nashua Pride	Nashua, NH
New Jersey Jackals	Little Falls, NJ
Ottawa Rapids	Ottawa, Ontario
Quebec Les Capitales	Quebec City, Quebec
Sussex Skyhawks	Augusta, NJ
Worcester Tornadoes	Worcester, MA

Table 19-23   Frontier League Teams

East Division	
Team	Location
Chillicothe Paints	Chillicothe, OH
Florence Freedom	Florence, KY
Kalamazoo Kings	Kalamazoo, MI
Midwest Sliders	Waterford, MI
Traverse City Beach Bums	Traverse City, MI
Washington Wild Things	Washington, PA

West Division	
Team	Location
Evansville Otters	Evansville, IN
Gateway Grizzlies	Sauget, IL
River City Rascals	O'Fallon, MO
Rockford RiverHawks	Rockford, IL
Southern Illinois Miners	Marion, IL
Windy City ThunderBolts	Crestwood, IL

Table 19-25   New York State League Teams

Team	Location
Herkimer Trailbusters	Herkimer, NY
Oneida Barge Bucs	Oneida, NY
Rome Coppers	Rome, NY
Utica Brewmasters	Utica, NY

Table 19-20   American Association Teams

North Division	
Team	Location
Lincoln Saltdogs	Lincoln, NE
Sioux City Explorers	Sioux City, IA
Sioux Falls Canaries	Sioux Falls, SD
St. Paul Saints	St. Paul, MN
Wichita Wingnuts	Wichita, KS

South Division	
Team	Location
El Paso Diablos	El Paso, TX
Fort Worth Cats	Fort Worth, TX
Grand Prairie AirHogs	Grand Prairie, TX
Pensacola Pelicans	Gulf Breeze, FL
Shreveport Sports	Shreveport, LA

Table 19-22   Continental Baseball League Teams

Team	Location
Bay Area Torros	League City, TX
Corpus Christi Beach Dogs	Corpus Christi, TX
Tarrant County Blue Thunder	Tarrant County, TX
Texarkana Gunslingers	Texarkana, TX

Table 19-24   Golden Baseball League Teams

North Division	
Team	Location
Calgary Vipers	Calgary, Alberta
Chico Outlaws	Chico, CA
Edmonton Cracker Cats	Edmonton, Alberta
Reno SilverSox	Reno, NV

South Division	
Team	Location
Long Beach Armada	Long Beach, CA
Orange County Flyers	Fullerton, CA
St. George Roadrunners	St. George, UT
Yuma Scorpions	Yuma, AZ

Table 19-26   Northern League Teams

Team	Location
Fargo-Moorehead Redhawks	Fargo, ND
Gary Southshore Railcats	Gary, IN
Joliet Jackhammers	Joliet, IL
Kansas City T-Bones	Kansas City, KS
Schaumberg Flyers	Schaumberg, IL
Winnipeg Goldeyes	Winnipeg, Manitoba

Table 19-27   South Coast League Teams

Team	Location
Aiken Foxhounds	Aiken, SC
Anderson Joes	Anderson, SC
Bradenton Juice	Bradenton, FL
Charlotte County Red Fish	Port Charlotte, FL
Macon Music	Macon GA
South Georgia Peanuts	Albany, GA

Table 19-28   United League Teams

Team	Location
Alexandria Aces	Alexandria, LA
Amarillo Dillas	Amarillo, TX
Edinburg Coyotes	Edinburg, TX
Laredo Broncos	Laredo, TX
Harlingen WhiteWings	Harlingen, TX
San Angelo Colts	San Angelo, TX

Endnotes

1. Isodore, C. (2007, Oct. 25). Baseball Close to Catching NFL as Top $ Sport. CNNMoney.com. Retrieved February 25, 2007, from http://money.cnn.com/2007/10/25/commentary/sportsbiz/index.htm.

2. FSG Targets Major Acquisitions. (2007, Oct. 29). *Street and Smith's SportsBusiness Journal*. Retrieved February 27, 2008, from http://www.sportsbusinessjournal.com/index.cfm?fuseaction=search.show_article&articleId=56863&keyword=MLB%20earnings%20before%20interest.

3. Fisher, E., and Kaplan, D. (2008, Mar. 10). Selig's Pay Climbs 4 Percent to $15.06 Million. *Street and Smith's SportsBusiness Daily*. Retrieved April 1, 2008, from http://www.sportsbusinessjournal.com/article/58312.

4. Pappas, D. (2002, Sep. 5). A Contentious History: Baseball's Labor Fights. *ESPN.com*. Retrieved October 10, 2007, from http://espn.go.com/mlb/columns/bp/1427632.html.

5. Barry, H., and Cook, B. (1976). *A Baseball Century: The First 100 Years of the National League*. New York: Macmillan.

6. History of the Game: From Doubleday to Present Day. (n.d.). MLB.com. Retrieved July 27, 2008, from http://mlb.mlb.com/mlb/history/index.jsp.

7. Lopresti, M. (2004, Aug. 12). Baseball Strike of 1994–95 Timeline. *The Cincinnati Enquirer*. Retrieved October 10, 2007, from http://reds.enquirer.com/2004/08/12/STRIKEBOX12-LOPRESTI.html.

8. Bodley, H. (2005, Jan. 12). Baseball Officials Announce Tougher Steroids Policy. *USA Today*. Retrieved October 10, 2007, from http://www.usatoday.com/sports/baseball/2005-01-12-steroid-policy_x.htm.

9. Hiestand, M. (2006, July 11). TBS Drops Braves Games, Join Fox in Rich TV Deal. *USA Today*. Retrieved October 10, 2007, from http://www.usatoday.com/sports/columnist/hiestand-tv/2006-07-11-hiestand-mlb_x.htm.

10. MLB Advanced Media. (2008, May 26). *Street and Smiths Sports-Business Journal*. Retrieved July 21, 2008, from http://www.sportsbusinessjournal.com/article/59101.

11. Information obtained at http://web.minorleaguebaseball.com/index.jsp.

12. History: Minor League Baseball Timeline. (n.d.). MiLB.com. Retrieved July 27, 2008, from http://web.minorleaguebaseball.com/milb/history/timeline.jsp.

13. Information obtained at http://www.baseball-links.com.

CHAPTER TWENTY 20

Soccer

MAJOR LEAGUE SOCCER

Major League Soccer (MLS), founded December 13, 1993, is the top professional soccer league in the United States. A member of Fédération Internationale de Football Association (FIFA), MLS is the only Division I league sanctioned by soccer's governing body in the United States, the U.S. Soccer Federation. Major League Soccer is the result of a promise from U.S. Soccer to FIFA in exchange for the right for the United States to host the 1994 World Cup. FIFA wanted to, and continues to try to, grow the game in the United States. MLS is the first soccer league established in the United States since the North American Soccer League (1967–1984), which failed due to overexpansion and exorbitant spending on player procurement.

The MLS was the first professional sports league to operate under the single entity structure. The MLS teams are controlled by "operator-investors" who do not sign players for their individual teams. Instead, all players sign contracts to play for the league, which then assigns the players to their respective teams. This allows the league to have control over where the athletes will play, choosing to place players where they will be the most valuable to the league, such as in their hometowns. The single entity strategy also allows operator-investors to have control of more than one team. In 2000, the players challenged the single entity structure in an antitrust theory case, *Fraser v. MLS*. The MLS prevailed in *Fraser* and continues to operate under the single entity structure.

Since its inception in 1996, the MLS has experienced expansion, contraction, reorganization, and expansion again. Originally, the league contained 10 teams divided into two conferences, but in 1998, two teams, the Chicago Fire and Miami Fusion, were added and the league reorganized into an East, West, and new Central Division. However, this structure lasted for only three seasons and the MLS returned to the two-conference structure. In 2002, the

league contracted two teams, Miami and Tampa Bay, and then expanded in 2005 with Real Salt Lake and Chivas USA. The league expanded again in 2007 and 2008, with new franchises in Toronto and San Jose, bringing the number of teams in the MLS to 14. The MLS plans to continue the expansion movement with a team based out of Seattle in 2009, and a team in Philadelphia in 2010 (bringing the league total to 16 teams).

In regards to player salaries, MLS has less money to attract the best players than other professional soccer leagues, especially those in Europe. In part due to a salary cap of $2 million per team, the average player salary in the MLS is approximately $115,000 and the median salary of players in the league is $52,965.[1] In comparison, the average player salary in the English Premier League is expected to be approximately £1.1 million, which is equivalent to $1.93 million U.S. dollars.[2] Because of this extreme disparity, due in large part to smaller revenue streams in the United States, the most talented soccer players in the world (including U.S. citizens) tend to migrate towards the international markets for more lucrative contracts and the chance to compete against the best players in the world.

In hopes of attracting some of the world's best players, MLS instituted the designated player rule in 2006. Under the new system, each team is granted a one-player exemption from the salary cap. The rule was unofficially dubbed the "Beckham Rule," because the league hoped to use the rule to attract top-level European talent such as David Beckham. This goal came to fruition in 2007, when David Beckham signed a 5-year contract with the L.A. Galaxy. The terms of the deal call for Beckham to receive an annual salary of $5.5 million, plus a $1 million marketing and promotional bonus. Beckham also gets a share of all revenue he helps generate, including TV rights, merchandise, jersey deals, and sponsorships. It has been estimated that Beckham's total compensation over the course of the 5 years could exceed $250 million.

The high salaries given under the "Beckham Rule" also required a significant change in how these high-paid MLS players are paid. Historically, all player salaries were paid with MLS central funds; however, for players falling under the new Beckham Rule, the league will pay only $400,000 of the player's salary and the player's team is obligated to pay the remaining amount. Ultimately, it is the goal of MLS to provide players with greater financial incentives to play in the MLS. "The leagues growth and development is going to [depend on] the kind of player we're able to develop domestically. That's an absolute priority for us. It's also a priority for us that we continue to make the level of play better every year, and there is no other way to do that other than to dip into the international markets," said MLS Deputy Commissioner Ivan Gazidis in an interview with the *Los Angeles Times*.[3]

As a means of generating more revenue and improving the overall fan experience, the league plans to construct soccer-specific stadiums for each team. The typical soccer-specific stadium will have a capacity of just over 20,000. Soccer-specific stadiums have already been built in Bridgeview, Illinois; Carson, California; Columbus, Ohio; Commerce City, Colorado; Toronto, Ontario; and Frisco, Texas. These state-of-the-art facilities offer fans and players a more intimate setting for soccer than the traditional, massive American football stadiums in which most original teams played. This will also improve the MLS brand and enhance other revenue streams because the venues are being set up to host concerts as well.

MLS executives are also hoping to benefit from the growing Latin American population throughout the United States by increasing the league's cultural diversity marketing platform. Although the MLS is experiencing strong growth, MLS superstar David Beckham said in a *60 Minutes* interview, "Things aren't going to turn around and get bigger in the next six months or a year. It's going to take five, ten years to obviously grow the game."[4]

The league headquarters are located in New York City and the MLS employs staff in various departments such as marketing, sponsorships, legal, and finance.

History of Major League Soccer

1967

- The United Soccer Association and National Professional Soccer League merged and created the North American Soccer League (NASL).

1974

- League owners were desperate for expansion revenue, so the NASL added eight teams prior to the 1974 season.

1975

- The New York Cosmos of the NASL signed Brazilian star Pelé for a reported $4.5 million. The Cosmos

became the league's most popular franchise, drawing an average of 40,000 fans.

1977

- The NASL and ABC signed a seven-game national television contract.

1981

- The NASL lost 17 of its 24 franchises as owners ceased operations.

1985

- The NASL folded due to financial reasons.

1993

- Major League Soccer (MLS) was formed in fulfillment of U.S. Soccer's promise to FIFA and was established as the first single entity league in exchange for the World Cup being held in the United States.
- FIFA selected Major League Professional Soccer (MLPS), the precursor to MLS, to develop a Division I professional soccer league in the United States. The MLPS was headed by U.S. Soccer President Alan Rothenberg.

1994

- The United States hosts the World Cup in nine different U.S. cities: Boston, Chicago, Dallas, Detroit, Los Angeles, New York, Orlando, San Francisco, and Washington, DC.
- The U.S. Men's National team did better than expected, advancing to the second round before being eliminated by Brazil, the eventual champions.
- The average attendance was 69,000 fans, which was a World Cup record, although this was made possible by the higher capacities of the stadiums in the United States.
- The two highest U.S. television rankings for a soccer match were recorded during the 1994 World Cup for the second round game between the United States and Brazil (9.3) and the championship game between Brazil and Italy (9.5).[5]

1996

- MLS began its first season with 10 teams: Columbus Crew, DC United, New England Revolution, NY/NJ MetroStars, Tampa Bay Mutiny, Colorado Rapids, Dallas Burn, Kansas City Wiz, Los Angeles Galaxy, and San Jose Clash.
- Douglas Logan was named the first MLS commissioner (1996–1999).
- The Kansas City Wiz changed their name to the Wizards on November 18, 1996.

1997

- MLS players filed a lawsuit challenging MLS's single entity structure by accusing the league of violating antitrust laws (*Fraser v. MLS*).

1998

- The Chicago Fire and Miami Fusion were added to the MLS (12 teams).

1999

- Don Garber was named the commissioner of the MLS after spending 16 years in a variety of positions with the NFL, including head of NFL International (1999–present).
- Columbus Crew Stadium, located in Columbus, Ohio, opened as the first soccer-specific stadium. The success of this venue reaffirmed for the MLS operator-investors that soccer-specific stadiums would be crucial to the success of MLS.

2000

- *Fraser v. MLS* was decided. The U.S. Supreme Court found that MLS and its teams were not in violation of the Sherman Antitrust Act. This decision made it possible for MLS to continue operating under its single entity structure.
- MLS reorganized to create three divisions: Eastern, Central, and Western.

2002

- The Miami Fusion and Tampa Bay Mutiny disbanded (10 teams).
- The league returned to the original conference structure: Eastern and Western.

2003

- The Home Depot Center, located in Carson, California, on the campus of California State University Dominguez Hills, became MLS's second soccer-specific stadium and is home to the Los Angeles Galaxy and, beginning in 2004, C.D. Chivas USA.

2004

- Real Salt Lake (Utah) and C.D. Chivas USA (Los Angeles) were granted expansion franchises (12 teams).
- The two teams were added to the Western Conference and Kansas City moved to the Eastern Conference.

2005

- The San Jose Earthquakes franchise was relocated to Houston, Texas, and was renamed the Houston Dynamo.

2006

- The Red Bull GmbH Company purchased the Metro-Stars and renamed the team Red Bull New York.

- The league instituted a new designated player rule. Under this rule, each team is allowed a one-player exemption from the league's $2 million salary cap. The league is obligated to pay only $400,000 of the player's salary, with the player's club picking up any remaining salary obligation.

2007

- Toronto FC began play as an expansion franchise, playing in its own soccer-specific stadium and becoming the first MLS franchise located outside of the United States.
- The Los Angeles Galaxy signed David Beckham to a 5-year deal. Beckham, one of the most famous players in the world, became the first player signed under the league's designated player rule.
- MLS announced that it plans to expand the league to 16 teams and granted Seattle a team to begin play in 2009.

2008

- MLS granted Philadelphia a team to begin play in 2010.

Structure of Major League Soccer[6]

League Alignment

- 12 total teams (**Table 20-1**)
- 2 conferences: Eastern Conference (6 teams) and Western Conference (6 teams)

Competition Format

- Head-to-head contests between teams; unbalanced schedule
- End of year playoffs

Schedule

- Game days
  - Games are played throughout the week but primarily on Wednesday, Saturday, and Sunday. Weekday games are played in the evening; weekend games are played during the day and at night. Select games are broadcast nationally.
- Regular season (April–October): 32 games (16 home, 16 away)
  - Eastern Conference: 20 games within conference (10 home games), 12 out of conference (6 home games)
  - Western Conference: 20 games within conference (10 home games), 12 out of conference (6 home games)
- Playoffs (October–November)
  - The top four teams in each conference make the playoffs and are seeded based on their regular season record.

Table 20-1   MLS Teams (2008)

Eastern Conference	
Team	**Location**
Chicago Fire	Bridgeview, IL
Columbus Crew	Columbus, OH
DC United	Washington, DC
Kansas City Wizards	Kansas City, MO
New England Revolution	Foxboro, MA
Red Bull New York	East Rutherford, NJ
Toronto FC	Toronto, Ontario

Western Conference	
Team	**Location**
C.D. Chivas USA	Carson, CA
Colorado Rapids	Denver, CO
FC Dallas	Frisco, TX
Houston Dynamo	Houston, TX
Los Angeles Galaxy	Carson, CA
Real Salt Lake	Salt Lake City, UT
San Jose Earthquakes	San Jose, CA

- 3 rounds: Conference Semi-Finals, Conference Finals, and MLS Cup Finals
- Conference Semi-Finals round (Eastern and Western)
  - 1 seed vs. 4 seed, 2 seed vs. 3 seed
  - Format: 2-match series, aggregate goals, similar to what is used throughout the world
- Conference Finals round (Eastern and Western) The winners of the Conference Semi-Finals play one game to determine conference champion.
- MLS Cup Finals
  - The winner of each conference plays one game to determine the winner of the MLS Cup, which is awarded the Alan I. Rothenberg Trophy.
- All-Star Game (July)
  - Mid-season game pits MLS All-Stars against a football club of the English Premier League
  - Site determined on a rotational basis
    - The 2008 All-Star Game was played at BMO Field in Toronto with MLS All-Stars playing against West Ham United.

Money Matters for Major League Soccer

Sources of Revenue

- Television broadcasting revenues[7]
  - National broadcasting is done by ESPN and ABC, who broadcast one game during the weekend. The agreement, signed in 2006, runs through 2014 and pays MLS between $7 and $8 million per season. In the past, MLS has paid Disney (the owner of both ESPN and ABC) several million dollars to buy broadcast time in order to have its games shown on national television.[8] Under the previous deal, MLS kept the advertising revenues.
    - ABC: Broadcasts the All-Star Game and MLS Cup
    - ESPN/ESPN2: Broadcast games on Thursday night, Saturday, and Sunday, as well as the playoff games leading up to the MLS Cup
  - Teams are responsible for working out local television deals with regional sports networks.
  - MLS offers an MLS Direct Kick package that broadcasts 115 games a season to viewers with DirecTV, Dish Network, or digital cable at an extra charge of $67 a season.
  - MLS also has an 8-year agreement, starting in 2006, with Univision. In 2008, it broadcasted 24 regular season games, the MLS All-Star game, two playoff matches, and the MLS Cup, as well as MLS highlights on two sports programs. In addition, it broadcast five international games held in the United States. All Univision broadcasts are in Spanish. The deal is reportedly worth $9 to $10 million per season through 2014.
  - MLS also has a 4-year agreement, starting in 2006, with Fox Soccer Channel/Fox Sports en Espanol. The deal is reportedly worth $2.2 million per year and allows Fox Soccer Channel to broadcast 32 MLS Games of the Week on Saturday nights, up to three playoff games, two men's and two women's national team games a year through 2010, and three international friendly matches.
  - MLS also has a 3-year agreement, starting in 2005, with HDNet. The deal is reportedly worth $1.08 million and allows HDNet to broadcast 30 regular season games, including 12 exclusively. In addition, HDNet has the rights to broadcast up to three playoff games.
- Other media
  - Radio
    - Teams are responsible for negotiating local radio deals.
  - New media
    - League website: The site is run by MLB Advanced Media.
    - YouTube Dedicated Channel: In 2007, the league struck a revenue-sharing partnership deal with YouTube, through which YouTube will host a dedicated MLS channel. Although the YouTube partnership is not expected to generate significant new revenue, it should provide additional exposure for the league.
- Gate receipts
  - Gate receipts are a large percentage of the MLS teams' revenues because MLS does not yet have the significant media revenues that the other major professional sports leagues have.

- Sponsorship
  - MLS has official sponsors in varying product categories such as beverage distributors, snack foods, and car companies. Sponsors pay an annual fee to become a recognized partner of the league and for other related services. Adidas, Aquafina, Visa, Kraft, NAPA, and American Airlines are a few of the league's current official sponsors.
- Merchandise and licensing
  - Adidas is the official uniform supplier of MLS. Adidas paid the league approximately $150 million to outfit all MLS teams, fund an Adidas Development Program, and invest in league properties.[9]

FÉDÉRATION INTERNATIONALE DE FOOTBALL ASSOCIATION

The Fédération Internationale de Football Association (FIFA) is the international governing body of football (soccer) for both men and women. Headquartered in Zurich, Switzerland, FIFA organizes a variety of worldwide tournaments, most notably the World Cup, the preeminent international soccer tournament in which national teams from 32 countries compete for the prestigious trophy. The World Cup is held every 4 years in a different country. The competition to be one of the 32 teams in the World Cup begins 3 years before the next World Cup, and is fierce and competitive. The previous champion and host country receive automatic bids while the other 30 slots are determined by qualifying tournaments in various pre-established regions throughout the world. The World Cup is the most watched sporting event in the world. In 2006, more than 30 billion viewers in 214 countries watched the World Cup on television and more than 3.3 million spectators attended the 64 matches of the tournament.[10]

FIFA recognizes 208 national soccer federations and their associated national teams. An example of one of these federations is the United States Soccer Federation (USSF), which is the governing body of soccer in the United States. The overall mission of the USSF is to develop the game of soccer at all recreational and competitive levels in the United States. As the governing body of the national team, the USSF orchestrates and organizes the participation in FIFA-sponsored tournaments, including the World Cup.

In addition to the World Cup, FIFA organizes World Championships for the U-17 (under-17) level and other youth levels. Furthermore, it has developed the Confederations Cup (originally the King Fahd Cup), a tournament held every 2 years that features the winning teams from each of the six continental confederations, the host of the next World Cup, and the past World Cup Champion. The tournament is held in an upcoming World Cup host city and serves as a platform to test the facilities prior to the World Cup.

FIFA also is responsible for the organization of the Women's World Cup and the U-19 (under-19) Women's World Championships. The Women's World Cup is equivalent in prestige to the men's version and is also held every 4 years in a different country, through a selection process. The tournament consists of 16 national teams, which are determined through qualifying tournaments held prior to the World Cup.

Establishing and enforcing the rules and regulations that govern the game of soccer is an important aspect of FIFA's responsibility. The International Football Association Board (IFAB) was enacted in the 19th century to serve as the guardian of the Laws of the Game and is responsible for studying, modifying, and overseeing any changes to it.[11] Moreover, FIFA is responsible for the regulation of the player registration process as well as the international transfer of players from one club to another.[12]

FIFA receives significant revenues through a variety of initiatives; however, the majority of its revenues (90%) are realized from producing and running the World Cup. Revenue streams include broadcasting rights, sponsorship fees, gate receipts, licensing, and merchandising. *Street & Smith's SportsBusiness Journal* estimates the 2006 World Cup earned FIFA $2.36 billion in revenue, resulting in $1.6 billion in profit. A majority of this revenue was generated by television and marketing rights.[13]

FIFA's administration is carried out by the General Secretariat, which employs some 280 staff members. At its head is the FIFA general secretary, who is responsible for implementing the decisions of the executive committee. The general secretary is also responsible for FIFA's finances, international relations, the organization of the FIFA World Cup, and other FIFA football competitions.[14]

Various divisions exist in the structure of FIFA including development, competitions, football administration, finance, business, personnel, services, and communications.[15]

History of FIFA

1904

- The Fédération Internationale de Football Association (FIFA) was founded as the premier professional European football league, uniting the Football Associations of France, Denmark, Netherlands, Belgium, Spain, Sweden, and Switzerland.

- Robert Guérin is elected president at the first FIFA Congress (1904–1906).

- The oldest organized union of professional athletes, the English Professional Footballers Association (PFA), is formed to defend the interests and rights of the players.

1905

- The Executive Committee of the Football Association Limited recognized the national associations affiliated to FIFA and joined the league.

- The Associations from Germany, Austria, Italy, and Hungary joined FIFA; Scotland, Wales, and Ireland decided not to join FIFA at this time.

1906

- Englishman Daniel Burley Woolfall, who previously served on the administrative board of the Football Association, was elected the new FIFA president (1906–1918).

1908

- The first major international competition was held at the Olympics; the football (soccer) tournament was won by England in London.

1913

- FIFA became a member of the International Football Association Board (IFAB), a regulatory body of the *Laws of the Game*, which was responsible for studying, modifying, and overseeing any changes to the sport.

1921

- Frenchman Jules Rimet, former representative of the French Football Association, was elected president of FIFA (1921–1954). The World Cup trophy would later be named after Rimet.

1927

- The first live broadcast of a FIFA game was on BBC radio.

1930

- The first FIFA World Cup was played at the Centenary Stadium in Montevideo, Uruguay. The 1930 World Cup had 13 participating countries. The United States advanced to the semi-finals. The World Cup Championship began its cycle of being held every 4 years.

1934

- The United States lost in the preliminary round of the World Cup.

1936

- The first soccer match was televised in England.

1938

- The United States withdrew from World Cup qualification due to World War II (WWII).

1942

- The World Cup was not held due to WWII.

1946

- The World Cup was again not held due to WWII.

1948

- Construction began on the biggest and most expensive stadium in the world in Rio de Janiero, Brazil; the Maracana, officially known as the Mario Filho Stadium, has a capacity of over 200,000.

1950

- The United States qualifies for the World Cup, but loses in the group stage. During the tournament, the U.S.

upsets England 1–0 in what is called the Greatest Upset Ever. This will be the last time the United States competes in the World Cup until 1990.

1954

- Belgian Rodolphe William Seeldrayers was elected as president of FIFA. He had assisted Jules Rimet for 25 years as vice president, but served as president for only a year before passing away from a heart attack (1954–1955).
- The 50th anniversary of FIFA takes place. FIFA has 85 members.

1955

- Englishman Arthur Drewry, who had served as interim president after the death of Seeldrayers, was elected president (1955–1961).

1961

- Englishman Sir Stanley Rous was elected president (1961–1974).

1962

- FIFA's membership reached 100.

1974

- Brazilian Dr. João Havelange was elected president (1974–1998).

1982

- President Havelange increased the number of World Cup competitors to 24 teams.

1990

- The United States competed in its first World Cup since 1950, but was eliminated in the group stage.

1994

- The United States hosted the World Cup for the first time and advanced to the round of 16.

1998

- The number of teams competing in the World Cup increased to 32, making it the largest field in the history of the event.
- Switzerland-born Joseph Blatter, who had served as general secretary and technical director of FIFA, was elected as the successor to João Havelange as the eighth FIFA president (1998–present).
- The United States lost in the group stage of the World Cup in France.

2000

- During the Olympic Games in Sydney, Australia, the United States soccer team finished in fourth place. The team advanced to the bronze medal match against Chile but lost 2–0.

2002

- 28.8 billion viewers in 213 countries watched the 2002 FIFA World Cup held in Korea and Japan on television. The official website of the league, www.fifaworldcup.com, set a new milestone in the history of sports websites on the Internet by registering over 2 billion page views for tournament coverage.

- The United States advanced to the quarterfinals at the World Cup.

2006

- Twelve of the 15 Official Partners of the 2002 FIFA World Cup re-signed deals for the 2006 FIFA World Cup.

- The United States lost in the group stage at the World Cup in Germany.

- South Africa will host the 2010 World Cup and will be the first African country to host the tournament.

Structure of FIFA[16]

Events

- FIFA World Cup
  - Competition between 32 national teams for the most prestigious title worldwide
- FIFA Confederations Cup
  - Competition between 8 national teams; serves as a precursor to the World Cup
- Olympic soccer tournaments
  - Competition between countries held during the summer Olympics; competitors are restricted to the age of 23 or younger (three average players are allowed per team)
- FIFA World Youth Championship (U-20)
  - Competition between 24 national teams, held every 2 years to determine the best U-20 (under-20) national team in the world
- FIFA U-17 World Championships
  - Competition between 16 national teams, held every 2 years to determine the best U-17 national team in the world
- FIFA Women's World Cup
  - Competition between 32 national teams for the most prestigious women's title worldwide
- FIFA U-19 Women's World Championship
  - Competition between 12 national teams, held every 2 years to determine the best U-19 national team in the world
- FIFA Futsal World Championship
  - Indoor competition between 16 national teams, held every 2 years to determine the best indoor national team worldwide

Money Matters for FIFA

Sources of Revenue

- Television broadcast revenues
  - The global sales of all broadcast rights for the 2006 FIFA World Cup worldwide and host broadcast are handled by Infront Sports & Media.[17]
  - FIFA receives significant revenues from a plethora of television outlets for the rights to broadcast the World Cup. FIFA, ABC/ESPN, and Univision have a comprehensive agreement that calls for the networks to carry all FIFA events in both English and Spanish from 2007 to 2014 in the United States for $425 million. This includes the 2010 and 2014 Men's World Cups, the 2007 and 2011 Women's World Cups, and the 2013 Confederations Cup.

- Other media
  - FIFA manages the delivery of content of its organization and the World Cup over two websites, www.fifa.com and www.fifaworldcup.com. Each of these sites serves as a platform to inform soccer enthusiasts about the FIFA organization and the events surrounding the World Cup.

- Gate receipts
  - FIFA receives the gate revenues from the fans attending the matches in the host country.

- Sponsorship
  - FIFA divides its sponsorship affiliates into three categories: Official Partners, Official Suppliers, and Licensees. FIFA's aim is to enable the Official Partners to fully leverage the advantages that come from being an official sponsor and to develop innovative and attractive marketing solutions to promote the FIFA World Cup.[18] For the 2006 World Cup, 15 Official Partners existed in various product categories such as beverages, airlines, and film products. Sponsors pay a fee to FIFA to become a recognized partner and for other related services.

- Merchandising
  - FIFA signs partnership agreements with several merchandising and marketing companies, granting them geographic exclusivity to sell FIFA merchandise. FIFA receives a fee from these partnerships; in exchange the companies are allowed to use the FIFA logo and mark on merchandise sold to the public.

- Licensing
  - FIFA has licensed its name and copyrighted content to computer game maker EA Sports to provide a number of soccer simulation games for computers and various game consoles. A new installment of FIFA series games is launched annually and versions of a World Cup game are introduced to coincide with the tournament. For this agreement, FIFA receives fees for allowing EA Sports to use its name and copyrighted information.

The FIFA World Cup[19]

The FIFA World Cup is the most important competition in international football (soccer), and the world's most popular team sport event. Organized by FIFA, the sport's governing body, the World Cup is contested by the men's national football teams of FIFA member nations. Although the championship is awarded every 4 years, it is more of an ongoing event as the qualifying rounds of the competition (which narrow the field down to the final 32 teams) take place over the 3 years leading up to the final rounds and the year of the event. The only times the World Cup was not played was in 1942 and 1946 due to World War II. The first World Cup tournament occurred in 1930 in Uruguay, with the host country, Uruguay, defeating Argentina 4–2.

The final tournament phase involves 32 national teams competing over a 4-week period in a previously determined host nation. The World Cup games are the most widely viewed sporting event in the world. Historically, Brazil has been the most successful team in World Cup history, having won a total of five times ('58, '62, '70, '94, '02), followed by Italy ('34, '38, '82, '06), and Germany ('54, '74, '90) with four and three titles each, respectively. Future World Cup sites are determined years in advance (**Table 20-2**). The 2010 World Cup will be played in South Africa. The winning team will earn 24.5 million Swiss Francs, which is roughly $19 million U.S.[20] Tickets for the World Cup cost roughly $40 to $120 for the Group Stage and roughly $145 to $725 for the Finals.

Companies are eager to become part of the World Cup experience, either through a sponsorship agreement or by supplying equipment for the event. The 15 2006 FIFA World Cup Official Partners were Adidas, Anheuser-Busch, Avaya, Coca-Cola, Continental AG, Deutsche Telekom AG, Emirates Airline, Fujifilm, Gillette, Hyundai, MasterCard, McDonalds, Philips, Toshiba, and Yahoo!. The six Official Suppliers of the 2006 World Cup were Energie Baden-Württemberg AG (EnBW), OBI AG, Hamburg-Mannheimer Versicherungs-AG, Postbank, Oddset, and Deutsche Bahn AG. These partnerships last just one tournament and thus are renegotiated prior to the next tournament. The World Cup relies on more than 15,000 volunteers for planning and operating the World Cup every 4 years. It is estimated by some sources that the 2006 World Cup generated $1 billion in advertising revenue.[21]

MAJOR INDOOR SOCCER LEAGUE[22]

Established in 2001, Major Indoor Soccer League (MISL) is the only national professional indoor soccer league in the United States. MISL is the sixth professional indoor soccer league established in North America. The previous professional indoor soccer leagues were the World Indoor Soccer League (1998–2001), National Professional Soccer League (1984–2001), Continental Indoor Soccer League (1993–1997), Major Indoor Soccer League (1978–1992), and North American Soccer League Indoor Season (1979–1984).

Formed from six former National Professional Soccer League (NPSL) teams, MISL is a member of U.S. Soccer and FIFA. Like MLS, MISL operates under a single entity structure. MISL expanded in 2002 by adding two teams from the World Indoor Soccer League (Dallas Sidekicks and San Diego Sockers). MISL added four more teams from 2003–2005, but also had five teams cease operations during this time period. In 2007, MISL was composed of nine teams located throughout the United States (**Table 20-3**). Expansion teams have been awarded to Detroit, MI (2006); Newark, NJ (2007); Monterrey, Mexico (2007); and Orlando, FL (2007).

In 2008, MISL announced that it would temporarily cease operations while the league was restructured to help lower costs and attract new owners.

Tickets for MISL games range from $8 to $24 and attendance figures have slowly declined from an average of 6,000 fans per game in 1999 to 4,737 in 2006. MISL teams play 30 games from November to April. Corporate sponsors of the MISL include Midwest Airlines, MBNA, Spalding, Aircast, and New Haven Travel Service.

The league headquarters are located in Westport, Connecticut, and all teams operate in the United States or Canada. Potential job opportunities exist in the following departments at the league headquarters: executive, finance, operations, sales, and marketing and communications.

UNITED SOCCER LEAGUE (USL)

The United Soccer League (USL) is the parent organization for the men's lower division professional soccer leagues in the United States and Canada. The USL oversees the operations of the following leagues: First Division, Second Division, Premier Developmental League (PDL), W-League, and Super Y League. They are dedicated professional soccer

Table 20-2   Future World Cup Sites

Year	Host County
2010	South Africa
2014	Brazil
2018	TBD

Table 20-3   MISL Teams (2007–2008)

Team	Location
Baltimore Blast	Baltimore, MD
California Cougars	Stockton, CA
Chicago Storm	Chicago, IL
Detroit Ignition	Plymouth Township, MI
Milwaukee Wave	Milwaukee, WI
Monterrey LaRaZa	Monterrey, Mexico
Orlando Sharks	Orlando, FL
Philadelphia KiXX	Philadelphia, PA
St. Louis Steamers	St. Louis, MO

leagues that rank just below Major League Soccer (MLS) in terms of competitiveness. The First Division would be equivalent to baseball's AAA and the Second Division would be closest to AA. MLS is considered the premier league and highest level of soccer in North America.

The USL was originally formed as the Southwest Indoor Soccer League (SISL) in 1986; the league expanded to outdoor soccer in 1999 and changed its name to the Southwest Outdoor Soccer League (SOSL). In 1999, the league changed its name to the USL.

Corporate sponsors play a large role in the success of the USL and they have formed the following partnerships:

- Official Sponsors/Suppliers: Umbro, Sprinturf

- Corporate Partners: HOK, Superkick

- Media Partners: 90 Minutes, Fox Soccer Channel

- Strategic Partners: Coast Soccer League, Constant Contact, NSCAA, The Patchworks.com

- Affiliate Partners: Canada Soccer Association, Puerto Rico Soccer Association, U.S. Club Soccer, USASA Adult Soccer, U.S. Soccer

The league headquarters are located in Tampa, Florida, and potential job opportunities exist in the following departments: business development, communications, public relations, and operations.

United Soccer League First Division[23]

The First Division is the USL's highest level of professional soccer in the United States, Canada, and the Caribbean. In 2008, 11 teams played 30 regular season matches, in a season that goes from April through September (**Table 20-4**). First Division matches average approximately 4,500 fans. Ticket prices vary from team to team but generally cost between $12 and $35 depending on seat location. Fox Soccer Channel and Fox Sports World Canada broadcast 20 regular season games as well as the annual championship game.

Although the revenue generated from the television broadcasts is helpful to the league, the primary benefit to the league is the exposure of being on television. The USL First Division schedule is augmented by participation in the Lamar Hunt U.S. Open Cup, a tournament open to the best professional and amateur soccer teams, and various exhibitions.

United Soccer League Second Division[23]

One level below the USL First Division is the USL Second Division. The 2008 campaign features 10 teams playing a regional schedule consisting of 20 regular season matches, in a season that goes from April through August (see **Table 20-4**). Second Division games average approximately 1,600 fans and ticket prices vary by team but typically cost around $10 for adults and $7 for children. Fox Soccer Channel and Fox Sports World Canada broadcast the annual championship game. Although the revenue generated from the broadcast is helpful to the league, the primary benefit to the league is the exposure of being on television. The USL Second Division is in the Lamar Hunt U.S. Open Cup.

United Soccer League Premier Development League (PDL)[25]

The top U-23 (under-23) men's amateur league in North America is the USL Premier Development League (PDL), the development league for elite amateur players. The 2008 season featured 67 teams in four conferences, with each team playing 16 regular season matches, from April through July (**Table 20-5**). PDL games average approximately 470 fans per contest and ticket prices are approximately $6 for adults, with most teams offering free admission to children. Fox Soccer Channel and Fox Sports World Canada broadcast the annual championship game. The primary benefit to the league is the exposure of being on television, rather than to make a profit. The schedule is augmented by participation in the Lamar Hunt U.S. Open Cup, a tournament open to the best professional and amateur soccer teams, and various exhibitions. Players have the ability to compete in the PDL

Table 20-4   USL First and Second Division Teams (2008)

USL First Division		USL Second Division	
Team	**Location**	**Team**	**Location**
Atlanta Silverbacks	Chamblee, GA	Bermuda Hogges	Hamilton, Bermuda
Carolina RailHawks	Cary, NC	Charlotte Eagles	Matthews, NC
Charleston Battery	Charleston, SC	Cleveland City Stars	Twinsburg, OH
Miami FC	Miami, FL	Crystal Palace Baltimore	White Marsh, MD
Minnesota Thunder	Saint Paul, MN	Harrisburg City Islanders	Harrisburg, PA
Montreal Impact	Montreal, Quebec	Pittsburgh Riverhounds	Washington, PA
Portland Timbers	Portland, OR	Real Maryland Monarchs	Silver Spring, MD
Puerto Rico Islanders	Bayamon, Puerto Rico	Richmond Kickers	Richmond, VA
Rochester Raging Rhinos	Rochester, NY	Western Mass Pioneers	Ludlow, MA
Seattle Sounders	Seattle, WA	Wilmington Hammerheads	Wilmington, NC
Vancouver Whitecaps	Burnaby, British Columbia		

throughout the summer months in a professionalized setting while maintaining their collegiate eligibility.

United Soccer League W-League[26]

The USL W-League is recognized as North America's best women's soccer development organization. The W-League also gives the nation's best college players the opportunity to play alongside established international players while maintaining their collegiate eligibility. The 2008 season featured 41 teams in three conferences playing 12 or 14 regular season matches from May through July (**Table 20-6**). W-League games average roughly 630 fans per contest and ticket prices typically are around $8 for adults and $5 for children. Fox Soccer Channel and Fox Sports World Canada broadcast the

Table 20-5   USL PDL Teams (2008)

Central Conference		Southern Conference	
Great Lakes Division		**Mid-South Division**	
Team	**Location**	**Team**	**Location**
Chicago Fire Premier	Chicago, IL	Austin Lightning	Cedar Park, TX
Cleveland Internationals	North Royalton, OH	Baton Rouge Capitals	Baton Rouge, LA
Fort Wayne Fever	Fort Wayne, IN	DFW Tornados	Euless, TX
Indiana Invaders	South Bend, IN	El Paso Patriots	El Paso, TX
Kalamazoo Kingdom	Portage, MI	Laredo Heat	Laredo, TX
Michigan Bucks	Berkley, MI	Mississippi Brilla	Clinton, MS
Toronto Lynx	Toronto, Ontario	New Orleans Shell Shockers	Metairie, LA
West Michigan Edge	Kentwood, MI		
Heartland Division		**Southeast Division**	
		Team	**Location**
Team	**Location**	Atlanta Silverbacks U23's	Atlanta, GA
Colorado Springs Blizzard	Colorado Springs, CO	Bradenton Academics	Bradenton, FL
Des Moines Menace	West Des Moines, IA	Carolina Dynamo	Greensboro, NC
Kansas City Brass	Overland Park, KS	Cary RailHawks U23's	Morrisville, NC
Sioux Falls SpitFire	Sioux Falls, SD	Central Florida Kraze	Oviedo, FL
Springfield Demize	Ozark, MO	Cocoa Expos	Cocoa, FL
St. Louis Lions	Cottleville, MO	Nashville Metros	Nashville, TN
Thunder Bay Chill	Thunder Bay, Ontario	Palm Beach Pumas	Lake Worth, FL
Eastern Conference		Western Conference	
Mid-Atlantic Division		**Northwest Division**	
Team	**Location**	**Team**	**Location**
Delaware Dynasty	Wilmington, DE	Abbotsford Rangers	Abbotsford, British Columbia
Fredericksburg Gunners	Fredericksburg, VA	BYU Cougars	Provo, UT
Hampton Roads Piranhas	Chesapeake, VA	Cascade Surge	Salem, OR
Northern Virginia Royals	Woodbridge, VA	Ogden Outlaws	Ogden, UT
Reading Rage	Reading, PA	Spokane Spiders	Spokane, WA
Richmond Kickers Future	Richmond, VA	Tacoma Tide	Fircrest, WA
Virginia Legacy	Williamsburg, VA	Yakima Reds	Yakima, WA
West Virginia Chaos	Charleston, WV		
Northeast Division		**Southwest Division**	
		Team	**Location**
Team	**Location**	Bakersfield Brigade	Bakersfield, CA
Albany Admirals	Albany, NY	Fresno Fuego	Fresno, CA
Brooklyn Knights	Brooklyn, NY	Lancaster Rattlers	Lancaster, CA
Cape Cod Crusaders	Sagamore Beach, MA	Los Angeles Storm	Glendora, CA
Long Island Rough Riders	Plainview, NY	Orange County Blue Star	Costa Mesa, CA
Ottawa Fury	Ottawa, Ontario	San Fernando Valley	Calabasas, CA
Rhode Island Stingrays	East Providence, RI	San Francisco Seals	San Francisco, CA
Vermont Voltage	Enosburg Falls, VT	San Jose Frogs	Los Gatos, CA
Westchester Flames	New Rochelle, NY	Southern California Seahorses	La Mirada, CA
		Ventura County Fusion	Ventura, CA

Table 20-6   USL W-League Teams (2008)

Central Conference	
Atlantic Division	
Team	**Location**
Atlanta Silverbacks Women	Atlanta, GA
Bradenton Athletics	Bradenton, FL
Carolina Dynamo	Greensboro, NC
Carolina RailHawks	Cary, NC
Charlotte Lady Eagles	Matthews, NC
Cocoa Expos Women	Cocoa, FL
Fredericksburg Lady Gunners	Fredericksburg, VA
Hampton Roads Piranhas	Chesapeake, VA
Richmond Kickers Destiny	Richmond, VA
Tampa Bay Hellenic	Tampa Bay, FL
West Virginia Illusion	Morgantown, WV

Midwest Division	
Team	**Location**
Chicago Gaels	Chicago, IL
Cleveland Internationals Women	Cleveland, OH
FC Indiana Lionesses	Indianapolis, IN
Fort Wayne Fever Women	Fort Wayne, IN
Kalamazoo Outrage	Kalamazoo, MI
Michigan Hawks	Livonia, MI
Minnesota Lightning	St Paul, MN
West Michigan Firewomen	Holland, MI

Eastern Conference	
Northeast Division	
Team	**Location**
Boston Renegades	Waltham, MA
Connecticut Passion	Southington, CT
Fredericksburg Lady Gunners	Fredericksburg, VA
Jersey Sky Blue	Bedminster, NJ
Long Island Lady Riders	Long Island, NY
New Jersey Wildcats	Princeton, NJ
New York Magic	New York, NY
Northern Virginia Majestics	Dumfries, VA
Washington Freedom	Germantown, MD

Northern Division	
Team	**Location**
Hamilton Avalanche	Hamilton, Ontario
Laval Comets	Laval, Quebec
London, Gryphons	London, Ontario
Ottawa Fury Women	Ottawa, Ontario
Rochester Rhinos Women	Rochester, NY
Toronto Lady Lynx	Toronto, Ontario
Vermont Lady Voltage	Enosburg Falls, VT
Western Mass Lady Pioneers	Ludlow, MA

Western Conference	
Team	**Location**
Fort Collins Force	Fort Collins, CO
Pali Blues	Santa Monica, CA
Real Colorado Cougars	Lone Tree, CO
San Diego Gauchos Women	National City, CA
Seattle Sounders	Tukwila, WA
Vancouver Whitecaps Women	Vancouver, British Columbia
Ventura County Fusion	Ventura, CA

annual championship game. Like the other USL leagues, the primary benefit of the broadcast is to gain exposure rather than make money.

United Soccer League Super Y-League[27]

The Super Y-League is a platform for developing elite youth soccer players in North America. Affiliated with U.S. Soccer and partnered with U.S. Club Soccer, the amateur league is designed for the most talented youth players who aspire for professional or international careers. The league contains the youth academies of USL First Division, USL Second Division, Premier Development League, W-League, and Major League Soccer clubs, as well as many of the established premier youth clubs. Through Olympic Development Program status events such as the North American Finals and National ODP Camps, the nation's top players are identified for selection to U.S. National Team Programs. The 2006 season featured over 800 teams within the U13–U17 boys and girls age groups competing within 10 geographic divisions of the United States and Canada. The season runs from April through August with matches played all over the United States and Canada.

WOMEN'S PREMIER SOCCER LEAGUE

The Women's Premier Soccer League (WPSL) is an independent national league focused on the development of highly competitive, amateur women's soccer teams. Formed in 1998, the WPSL is sanctioned by the United States Adult Soccer Association (USASA). USASA is an affiliate of the United States Soccer Federation (USSF), the governing body of U.S. Soccer, and FIFA, the world's governing body for soccer. A comparable league to the WPSL is the USL W-League.

The WPSL is unique in that it operates as an open league and is run by the member teams. An open league allows each team owner to be involved in the league expansion committee. More specifically, each team gets one vote on league-wide issues, with the majority deciding the outcome for these issues.

The WPSL season runs from May 1 to August 1 with each team playing between 14 and 18 games during the season. The league is composed of six conferences that are based on geographic location and have between 5 and 11 teams (**Table 20-7**). A league championship tournament is held the last weekend of July. Average attendance for games is approximately 400 fans per match and ticket prices range from no cost to $5 to $12. The league does not have national sponsors, but on a local level teams are able to negotiate various types of sponsorships.

Typical jobs with the WPSL are available in operations, public relations, finance, general management, sales, and marketing. League headquarters are located in San Francisco, California, with regional offices in San Diego, South Florida, and Springfield, Massachusetts.

WOMEN'S UNITED SOCCER ASSOCIATION

The Women's United Soccer Association (WUSA) was the world's premier women's professional soccer league. In its 2001 inaugural season, the eight-team league featured the best players from the 1999 U.S. World Cup Championship Team and top-flight international players. The league was founded by the 20 United States National Team players, and each of these players held an equity stake in the WUSA along with a number of outside investors.

The league operated its season during the summer and average attendance levels declined from a high of 8,103 in 2001 to 6,667 in 2003.[28]

Unfortunately, the financial backing did not continue to support the league after its third season and the announcement was made on September 15, 2003, that the league was suspending its operations.

Table 20-7   WPSL Teams (2008)

East-North Conference	
Team	**Location**
Adirondack Lynx	Gansevoort, NY
Boston Aztecs	Salem, MA
Maine Tide	Easton, MA
Massachusetts Stingers	Fall River, MA
New England Mutiny	Agawam/Longmeadow, MA
New York Athletic Club	Pelham Manor, NY
SoccerPlus Connecticut	Farmington, CT

East-Mid-Atlantic	
Team	**Location**
Atlantic City Diablos	Richland, NJ
Central Delaware SA Future	Dover, DE
Lancaster Infernos	Lancaster, PA
Long Island Fury	Long Island, NY
Milburn Magic	Milburn, NJ
Northampton Laurels FC	Allentown, PA
Philadelphia Liberty	Westtown, PA

Midwest Conference	
Team	**Location**
Chicago United Breeze	Algonquin, IL
FC St. Louis	St. Peters, MO
FC Twente3 IL	Chicago, IL
MYSC Lady Blues	Madison, WI
Ohio Premier Women's SC	Dublin, OH

Sunshine Conference	
Team	**Location**
Brevard County Cocoa Expos	Cocoa, FL
FC Thomasville Dragons	Thomasville, GA
Florida Surge	Orlando, FL
Miami Kickers FC	Plantation, FL
Orlando Falcons	Orlando, FL
Palm Beach United	West Palm Beach, FL
Puerto Rico Capitals FC	Ponce, PR

Big Sky-North	
Team	**Location**
Albuquerque Lady Asylum	Albuquerque, NM
Colorado Springs United	Colorado Springs, CO
Denver Diamonds	Denver, CO
Northern Arizona Cheetahs	Prescott, AZ
Salt Lake City Sparta	Salt Lake City, UT
Utah Spiders	Draper, UT

Big Sky South Conference	
Team	**Location**
Fort Worth FC	Forth Worth, TX
Oklahoma Alliance FC	Oklahoma City, OK
South Select	Houston, TX
Tulsa Spirit	Tulsa, OK
Vitesse Dallas	Dallas, TX

Pacific North Conference	
Team	**Location**
California Storm	Folsom, CA
FC Sacramento Pride	Sacramento, CA
Monterey Blues	Aptos, CA
San Francisco Nighthawks	San Francisco, CA
Sonoma County FC SOL	Santa Rosa, CA
Walnut Creek Power	Pleasant Hill, CA

Pacific South Conference	
Team	**Location**
Ajax America Women	Rolling Hills Estate, CA
Claremont Stars	Claremont, CA
Los Angles Rampage	Lafayette, CA
San Diego WFC SeaLions	San Diego, CA
SD United	El Cajon, CA
West Coast FC	Yorba Linda, CA

Table 20-8   WPSL Teams (2009)

Location
Boston, MA
Chicago, IL
Dallas, TX
Los Angeles, CA
New York/New Jersey
St. Louis, MO
Washington, DC
TBA

In April 2007, Women's Soccer Initiative, Inc. announced the rebirth of the league under the new name of Women's Professional Soccer (WPS). Originally planned to relaunch in 2008, the start of WPS play was pushed back until 2009 to allow for more preparation time for the teams and to properly promote the league in marketing campaigns. Seven teams are expected to play a 20-game schedule from April to October, beginning in 2009 (**Table 20-8**), and the league is looking actively to expand with additional teams located throughout the United States.

Endnotes

1. Beckham's Salary Revealed; Reyna Top U.S. Earner (2007, May 4). *ESPN.com.* Retrieved February 27, 2008, from http://soccernet.espn.go.com/columns/story?id=427678&cc=5901.

2. Annual Review of Football Finance. (2007). Deloitte.com. Retrieved February 27, 2008, from http://www.deloitte.com/dtt/article/0,2297,sid%253D2855%2526cid%253D56148,00.html.

3. New Owners Spark High Hopes as MLS Season Kicks Off. (2008, Mar. 28). *SportsBusinessDaily.com.* Retrieved April 11, 2008, from http://www.sportsbusinessdaily.com/article/119567.

4. Beckham "Passionate" About Move to MLS, Believes Sport Can Grow. (2008, Mar. 25). *SportsBusinessDaily.com.* Retrieved April 11, 2008, from http://www.sportsbusinessdaily.com/article/119484.

5. World Cup Final Receives Its Highest Rating Since 1994 (2006, July 11). *The Washington Post.* Retrieved February 27, 2008, from http://www.washingtonpost.com/wp-dyn/content/article/2006/07/10/AR2006071001163.html.

6. Halpin, J. (2004, Nov. 14). Gazidis Discusses Expansion, Future. MLSnet.com. Retrieved October 7, 2007, from http://web.mlsnet.com/news/mls_events_news.jsp?ymd=20041114&content_id=19050&vkey=mlscup2004&fext=.jsp.

7. MLS Media Rights Deal for '08 Season. (2008, Mar. 27). *Sports Business Daily.* Retrieved April 11, 2008, from http://www.sportsbusinessdaily.com/article/119563.

8. MLS: TV Deal Shapes Future. (2006, Apr. 2). *Soccer America.* Retrieved July 25, 2008, from http://www.socceramerica.com/index.cfm?fuseaction=Articles.showArticle&art_aid=20657&passFuseAction=PublicationsSearch.showSearchReslts&art_searched=&page_number=0.

9. Trusdell, B. (2004, Nov. 10). Adidas Deal with MLS Contains Plans for Reserve League. *USA Today.* Retrieved July 28, 2008, from http://www.usatoday.com/sports/soccer/mls/2004-11-10-adidas-development_x.htm.

10. Facts and Figures. (n.d.). *FIFA.com.* Retrieved July 28, 2008, from http://www.fifa.com/aboutfifa/marketingtv/factsfigures/index.html.

11. The History of the Laws of the Game. (n.d.). FIFA.com. Retrieved July 28, 2008, from http://www.fifa.com/classicfootball/history/law/ifab.html.

12. FIFA Statutes. (n.d.). FIFA.com. Retrieved July 28, 2008, from http://www.fifa.com/aboutfifa/federation/statutes.html.

13. Kaplan, D. (2007, Aug. 27–Sep. 2). How U.S. Open Profits Hit a Whopping $110M. *Street & Smith's SportsBusiness Journal*, p. 20.

14. About FIFA: Who We Are—Administration. (n.d.). FIFA.com. Retrieved July 28, 2008, from http://www.fifa.com/aboutfifa/federation/administration/index.html.

15. Ibid.

16. Tournaments. (n.d.). FIFA.com. Retrieved July 28, 2008, from http://www.fifa.com/tournaments/index.html.

17. TV Data. (n.d.). FIFA.com. Retrieved July 28, 2008, from http://www.fifa.com/aboutfifa/marketingtv/factsfigures/tvdata.html.

18. About FIFA: Marketing. (n.d.). FIFA.com. Retrieved July 28, 2008, from http://www.fifa.com/aboutfifa/marketingtv/marketing/index.html.

19. FIFA World Cup. (n.d.). FIFA.com. Retrieved July 28, 2008, from http://www.fifa.com/worldcup/index.html.

20. FIFA. (2006). *FIFA Financial Report 2006.* Retrieved February 27, 2008, from http://www.fifa.com/mm/document/affederation/administration/2006_fifa_ar_en_1766.pdf.

21. Holmes, S. (2006, May 21). Advertisers Kick Up for the World Cup. *Business Week.* Retrieved February 27, 2008, from http://www.businessweek.com/globalbiz/content/may2006/gb20060521_080724.htm.

22. Information obtained at http://www.misl.net.

23. Information obtained at http://www.uslsoccer.com/aboutusl/index_E.html.

24. Ibid.

25. Ibid.

26. Ibid.

27. Ibid.

28. Smith, M. (2006, Sep. 16). U.S Women's Soccer League Closes. *San Francisco Chronicle.* Retrieved July 21, 2008, from http://www.sfgate.com/cgi-bin/article.cgi%3Ffile=/c/a/2003/09/16/MN149199.DTL.

Lacrosse

MAJOR LEAGUE LACROSSE

Major League Lacrosse (MLL) is the premier outdoor lacrosse league based in the United States. In 1999, the MLL was formed by Jake Steinfeld, Dave Morrow, and Tim Robertson as a single-entity league. The league was founded as an alternative to the National Lacrosse League (NLL), a professional indoor lacrosse league, which has been in existence since 1987.

Lacrosse is an emerging, fast growing "niche" sport that was once primarily played at the youth level in the Northeast region. The popularity of the sport has widened and the game is now played at the youth, high school, and collegiate levels all over the country. Although the breadth and size of the MLL pales in comparison to the major North American professional sports leagues, the MLL started in large part because of the rapid growth and interest in lacrosse.

The MLL's inaugural season was in 2001 with six teams located in Boston; Bridgeport, CT; Baltimore; Long Island, NY; Montclair, NJ; and Rochester, NY. With the success of the original Northeast-based franchises and the growth of the sport across the country, the MLL strategically implemented expansion plans for the 2006 season. The formation of a Western Conference with expansion franchises in San Francisco, Los Angeles, Denver, and Chicago complemented the existing and newly named Eastern Conference.

An annual draft of college players is used to distribute talent to the various teams. In addition, the league utilizes an annual supplemental draft to allow teams to select unprotected, underutilized players from other teams. An expansion draft was held in 2006 to provide the Western Conference franchises the opportunity to select players from existing teams to form an initial roster of players that could be competitive with the existing teams.

MLL franchises hold games at various types of venues. Some teams utilize local high school or collegiate fields whereas others use shared multipurpose facilities such as the Home Depot Center in Los Angeles, home to Major League Soccer's Los Angeles Galaxy. The league averaged 4,889 fans per game in 2007, which was a slight increase from 4,295 fans per game in 2006.[1,2] The attendance has been increasing since the 2003 season, which provided validation for the league expansion in 2006. Ticket prices for regular season games vary from team to team but typically are between $15 and $30. Special events, such as the mid-season All-Star Game and league playoffs, carry higher ticket prices, usually starting at $20.

League-wide salaries are minimal compared to the compensation for other professional athletes. Most players earn less than $18,000 per season, and thus most professional lacrosse players have full-time positions in other industries. This may hinder the development of the league talent level due to limited training opportunities.

Headquartered in Brighton, Massachusetts (a suburb of Boston), the MLL employs six full-time professionals who oversee such functions as operations, corporate sponsorships, public relations, finance, and corporate operations. New Balance, the athletic footwear company, owns 41% of the league. David Gross is the league's commissioner.

History of Major League Lacrosse
1999

- Major League Lacrosse (MLL) was founded by Jake Steinfeld, Dave Morrow, and Tim Robertson.

- Steinfeld was a professional fitness instructor and founded Body by Jake Global.

- Morrow owned Warrior Lacrosse, a lacrosse equipment and apparel company.

- Robertson served as president and CEO of International Family Entertainment, a television production company.

2000

- Yahoo! became an official sponsor of MLL.

- MLL conducted a summer showcase tour featuring two All-Star teams. Tour games were played to test potential markets in Ohio, Philadelphia, Baltimore, Long Island, Buffalo, and Rochester, NY.

2001

- MLL began its first season with six teams: Boston Cannons, Long Island Lizards, Bridgeport (CT) Barrage, Baltimore Bayhawks, New Jersey Pride, and Rochester (NY) Rattlers.

- MLL conducted its first draft, although each team was assigned three players prior to the draft.

- MLL held a supplemental and a collegiate draft.

- Bridgeport and Long Island completed the first MLL trade: Bridgeport goalie Sal LoCascio was traded to Long Island for a first round pick.

- Anheuser-Busch and SoBe were introduced as league sponsors.

- The first LacrosseStar, MLL's All-Star Game, was held at the Ballpark at Harbor Yard in Bridgeport, Connecticut.

- Long Island won the first MLL title, 15–11 over Baltimore.

2002

- MLL introduced a new orange "grippy" ball that was more easily followed by fans.

2004

- David Gross was named first commissioner of the MLL. Gross previously headed the Boston franchise and served as the league's chief operating officer.

- The Bridgeport team moved to Philadelphia and became the Philadelphia Barrage.

2005

- MLL signed a TV contract with ESPN to broadcast weekly regular season games, the MLL All-Star Game, and the championship games during primetime television hours.

2006

- The league expanded west by adding the Los Angeles Riptide, Denver Outlaws, Chicago Machine, and San Francisco Dragons as expansion franchises (10 teams). The Baltimore Bayhawks moved, becoming the Washington Bayhawks.

- Due to the addition of four more teams, the MLL split into two conferences: Eastern and Western. The original six teams comprised the Eastern Conference and the expansion teams made up the new Western Conference.

2007

- MLL signed a 10-year deal with ESPN2. The agreement runs through the 2016 campaign and is the longest commitment given by any television outlet to a lacrosse entity. As part of the agreement, 11 games per season will be shown in high definition (HD), with six of these games being televised live or in primetime. Also, the league will use goalie cameras (Goalie Cam), telestrators, and microphones on players to give fans the feeling of being on the field in the action.

- MLL signed a 2-year deal with Bud Light. The agreement extended Bud Light's position as the "Official and Exclusive Malt Beverage and Alcohol Sponsor" of MLL, its 10 teams, its All-Star Game, and its postseason.

2008

- Dick's Sporting Goods became an official partner of the MLL by agreeing to a multi-year sponsorship agreement. As part of the agreement, Dick's became the official presenter of the in-game Goalie Cam.

Structure of Major League Lacrosse[3]

League Alignment

- 10 total teams (**Table 21-1**)

- 2 conferences: Eastern Conference (6 teams) and Western Conference (4 teams)

Competition Format

- Head-to-head contests between teams; unbalanced schedule

- End-of-year playoffs

Schedule

- Game days

  - Games are played throughout the 12-week regular season. The majority of the games are played on Saturdays and a few games are scheduled for Thursday and Friday.

Table 21-1   MLL Teams (2008)

Eastern Conference	
Team	**Location**
Boston Cannons	Boston, MA
Long Island Lizards	Uniondale, NY
New Jersey Pride	Piscataway, NJ
Philadelphia Barrage	Radnor Township, PA
Rochester Rattlers	Rochester, NY
Washington Bayhawks	Washington, DC

Western Conference	
Team	**Location**
Chicago Machine	Lisle, IL
Denver Outlaws	Denver, CO
Los Angeles Riptide	Carson, CA
San Francisco Dragons	San Francisco, CA

- Nationally broadcast games: Approximately 12 regular season games, the mid-season All-Star Game, and the MLL Championship Game are televised on ESPN2.[4]
- Regular season (May–August): 12 games (6 home, 6 away)
  - Eastern Conference: 8 games within conference (4 home games), 4 games out of conference (2 home games)
  - Western Conference: 9 games within conference (4–5 home games), 3 games out of conference (1–2 home games)
- Playoffs (August)
  - 4 teams: Conference winners (Eastern and Western) and two wildcard entries (based on best regular season records irrespective of conference)
  - MLL Championship Weekend (held at predetermined site)
    - Semi-final games (Friday; Seed 1 vs. Seed 4, Seed 2 vs. Seed 3): Conference winners are seeded 1 and 2 automatically, with the number 1 seed given to the team with the superior regular season record. Wildcard entries are seeded 3 and 4, with the number 3 seed given to the team with the superior regular season record.
    - Championship game (Sunday): Winners of semi-final games
- All-Star Game (early July)
  - Mid-season game pits MLL All-Stars vs. U.S. National Team.
  - Location changes on a year-to-year basis. Previous All-Star games were held in Baltimore, Long Island, Denver, and Boston.

Money Matters for Major League Lacrosse

Sources of Revenue

- Television broadcast revenues
  - The MLL negotiates the league's national television contracts on behalf of its teams. The league office coordinates the distribution of the national television revenues to each of the teams. Each individual team negotiates agreements with regional or local television networks to broadcast games locally. Local networks concede broadcasting rights when the game is selected to be broadcast nationally.[5]
  - The current deal with ESPN2 is considered a "joint venture," which does not consist of a time-buy on the part of MLL or a rights fee provided by ESPN. Instead, the agreement provides for potential league equity for ESPN and ad inventory sales for MLL. This agreement is an exposure vehicle for MLL aimed at increasing the fan base and popularity of lacrosse and the league.
  - ESPN2: Weekly regular season games, MLL All-Star Game, and MLL Championship Game

Other Media

- Radio
  - Local: Teams negotiate deals with local AM or FM stations to broadcast games of interest to fans in that region and keep any revenues from these agreements.
- Internet
  - The MLL website is a platform for the league to showcase the game and provide some additional advertising revenues for the MLL. The website provides information on the league initiatives and links to the individual team websites.
- Gate receipts
  - Teams keep 40% of gate revenues. The remaining 60% is sent to the league offices to cover salaries and other expenses. In total, gate revenues make up approximately 50% of revenues of MLL teams.[6]
- Sponsorship
  - There are typically five or six major sponsors of the MLL in varying product categories, such as footwear, beverages, and apparel. Sponsors pay an annual fee to the MLL to become a recognized partner and for other related services.
- Merchandise and licensing
  - New Balance athletic shoes is the official footwear supplier of the MLL; it signed a 6-year agreement in 2003 that runs through the 2009 season. As the exclusive footwear provider for all 10 MLL teams, New Balance provides a wide array of licensed apparel and footwear products to the retail marketplace. Under this agreement, the MLL receives an annual licensing fee from New Balance for this partnership.[3,7]

NATIONAL LEAGUE LACROSSE[8]

National League Lacrosse (NLL) is the premier professional indoor lacrosse league in North America. Established in 1987 as the Eagle Pro Box Lacrosse League, the NLL has 13 teams that compete in major league cities throughout the United States and Canada (**Table 21-2**). In 2009, the league will expand to 13 teams, by adding a team in Boston. The NLL schedule runs from December through April. All games are played on the weekend and ticket prices for NLL games range from $22 to $45. Average attendance for the NLL in 2008 regular season was 10,475 fans per game, with some teams averaging as high as 17,464 (Toronto and Colorado) whereas others averaged under 5,000 (San Jose, Chicago).[9] It has been reported that 80% of the league's fans had their first experience with the sport of lacrosse through the NLL. The rules for indoor lacrosse vary from traditional, outdoor lacrosse in that there are only five runners and a goalie, with players rotating in shifts with teammates, similar to ice hockey. NLL strives to offer fans an exciting, fast-paced version of lacrosse.

Table 21-2　NLL Teams (2008)

East Division	
Team	**Location**
Buffalo Bandits	Buffalo, NY
Chicago Shamrox	Chicago, IL
Minnesota Swarm	St. Paul, MN
New York Titans	New York, NY
Philadelphia Wings	Philadelphia, PA
Rochester Knighthawks	Rochester, NY
Toronto Rock	Toronto, Ontario

West Division	
Team	**Location**
Calgary Roughnecks	Calgary, Alberta
Colorado Mammoth	Denver, CO
Edmonton Rush	Edmonton, Alberta
Portland Lumberjacks	Portland, OR
San Jose Stealth	San Jose, CA

The league headquarters are located in New York City. NLL teams typically are composed of several departments including general management, media relations, marketing, sales, business operations, and game day operations. Some of the major corporate sponsors associated with the NLL are Reebok, Vonage America, Dodge Motor Company, and U.S. Lacrosse.

Endnotes

1. Malloy, D. (2007, July 7). The Small-Stars Game. *Boston Globe*. Retrieved July 31, 2008 from http:// www.boston.com/sports/articles/2007/07/07/ the_small_stars_game.

2. Major League Lacrosse Attendance up 3.1% from Last Season. (2007, Apr. 14). *SportsBusinessDaily.com*. Retrieved April 24, 2008, from http://www.sportsbusinessdaily.com/article/114196.

3. Major League Lacrosse Completes 2006 Expansion. (2005, Aug. 21). Major League Lacrosse. Retrieved October 17, 2007, from http://www .majorleaguelacrosse.com/news/pressreleases/ index.html?article_id=155.

4. Lefton, T. (2003, May 13). Major League Lacrosse Moves to ESPN2. *Street & Smith's SportsBusiness Journal*. Retrieved October 17, 2007, from http:// www.sportsbusinessjournal.com/index.cfm? fuseaction=search.show_article&articleId= 30439&keyword=Major%20League%20Lacrosse%20 Moves%20to%20ESPN2.

5. Information obtained from an interview with MLL official Shaun May.

6. Ibid.

7. New Balance Announces Corporate Sponsorship of Major League Lacrosse. (2003, May 14). New Balance. Retrieved October 17, 2007, from http:// www.newbalance.com/corporate/pressroom/2003/05/ sponsorship_2003_05_13_92.php.

8. National Lacrosse League. (n.d.). NLL.com. Retrieved July 31, 2008, from http://www.nll.com.

9. League Attendance. (n.d.). Pointstreak.com.Retrieved July 31, 2008, from http://www.pointstreak.com/ prostats/attendance.html?leagueid=230&seasonid= 1995.

CHAPTER TWENTY-TWO

Golf

PROFESSIONAL GOLF ASSOCIATION TOUR

The The Professional Golf Association (PGA) Tour is the membership organization of professional golfers who compete for prize money at over 100 events on three different tours: the PGA Tour, the Champions Tour, and the Nationwide Tour. It is important to differentiate between the PGA Tour and the PGA. The PGA Tour is a membership group for Tiger Woods, Ernie Els, Phil Mickelson, and many others. The PGA (also referred to as the PGA of America) is the Professional Golfers' Association of America, which is a membership organization for all of the nation's club professionals. The PGA members are instructors, businesspersons, and community leaders who are charged with teaching the game and conducting the business of golf. The PGA and its leaders also oversee the business responsibilities in the $195 billion golf industry.[1]

The PGA Tour was established in 1968, when a group of golfers broke away from the PGA to form the Tournament Players Division to gain more control of their finances and tournament schedule. Joseph C. Dey acted as the first commissioner of the Tournament Players Division. In 1974 Deane R. Beman took over for Dey as commissioner, and in 1975 the Tournament Players Division was renamed the PGA Tour. During Beman's tenure the PGA Tour's assets increased from $500,000–$700,000 in 1974 to between $500 and $800 million in 1994.[2]

The PGA Tour has 48 official events offering more than $250 million in prize money. Players on the PGA Tour need to qualify to play on the tour in one of five different ways:[3]

1. Finish in the top 25 and tie at the annual qualifying tournament.

2. Win a cosponsored or approved Tour event.

3. Finish among the top 150 players on the official money list in the previous year. (Players can qualify for individual tournaments through a variety of means, such as sponsor exemptions, foreign exemptions, and qualifying tournaments, and have their winnings count on the money list.)

4. Win during the course of a Tour season as much as or more than last year's 150th-place finisher on the official money list.

5. Finish in the top 20 on the official Nationwide Tour money list.

The PGA requires all members to be 18 years old or older.

The Nationwide Tour consists of players who have failed to qualify for the PGA Tour. There are over 30 annual events on the Nationwide Tour with nearly $18 million in total prize money. The Champions Tour, for players 50 years of age or older, consists of nearly 35 events annually with almost $53 million in total prize money. The Champions Tour events are mostly 3-day events, as opposed to the normal 4-day events on the PGA Tour and Nationwide Tour. Professional golfers also can compete on the European Tour, which has over 40 events.

The PGA Tour strives to increase the financial benefits and provide better opportunities for its members while it protects the integrity of the game. Although it is not publicized much, the PGA Tour also is very involved with fundraising initiatives for various charitable causes in their local communities. The PGA Tour is estimated to have donated more than $1 billion to charities since 1938.[4]

Headquartered in Ponte Vedra Beach, Florida, the PGA Tour employs roughly 3,000 professionals in a wide range of roles in various departments, including marketing, championship management, human resources, legal, communications, business development, retail licensing, information systems, and broadcasting.

History of the PGA Tour[3,5]

1930

- Bob Harlow, manager of the PGA Tournament Bureau, introduced the idea of year-round tournament circuits.

1932

- The Playing Pros organization was formed. The Playing Pros was the first organization that organized a year-round tour circuit for professional golfers.

1933

- Hershey Chocolate Company unofficially became the first corporate sponsor of the Playing Pros' Tour when it held the Hershey Open in Hershey, Pennsylvania.

1938

- Babe Didrikson, one of the founders of the LPGA, became the first woman to play in a men's tour event when she played in the Los Angeles Open. She was granted a sponsor exemption into the tournament.

1954

- The U.S. Open, played at Baltusrol Golf Club in New Jersey, was nationally televised for the first time.

1955

- The World Championship of Golf offered a purse of $100,000, which at the time was the largest in tour history.

1961

- The Caucasians-only clause was taken out of the PGA of America constitution.

1968

- A group of professional golfers broke away from the PGA and started the Tournament Players Division in order to have more control over the tour schedule.

1969

- Former USGA executive director, Joe Dey, became the first commissioner of the Tournament Players Division (1969–1974).

1974

- Former U.S. Amateur golf champion, Deane Beman, became the commissioner of the Tournament Players Division (1974–1994).

1975

- The Tournament Players Division was renamed the PGA Tour. The PGA Tour and PGA of America maintain a close working relationship, with most professional golfers having dual membership.

- An agreement was signed between the PGA Tour and the PGA of America, creating a joint property called the World Series of Golf. This pitted the winners of the previous year's four major tournaments around the world against each other. Later, the tournament would expand the field to include the winners of the other tournaments as well.

1977

- The first sub-60 round of golf in a PGA Tour event was recorded by Al Geiberger when he shot a 59 in the Danny Thomas Memphis Classic at Colonial Country Club.

1979

- PGA Tour Headquarters were moved from Washington, DC, to Ponte Vedra Beach, Florida.

1980

- The PGA Tour opened the Tournament Players Club at Sawgrass. The course introduced the era of stadium golf, a fan-friendly course designed for spectators, which helped popularize golf as a spectator sport. It is owned and operated by the PGA Tour.

- The Senior PGA Tour was created, which allowed for players 50 or older to compete. There were two tournaments played in its first year.

1985

- PGA Tour Productions was created. PGA Tour Productions creates network specials, made-for-TV events, commercials and sales/marketing videos for the PGA Tour.

1987

- The PGA Tour prize money reached $30 million.

1990

- The PGA Tour created the Ben Hogan Tour. In its first year, 30 tournaments were played and there was $3 million in prize money. The tour was designed for up-and-coming young players.

1992

- The PGA Tour prize money reached $50 million.

1993

- Nike Inc. bought the naming rights for the Ben Hogan Tour and renamed it the Nike Tour.

1994

- Former deputy commissioner and chief operating officer of the PGA Tour, Timothy Finchem, was named as the commissioner of the PGA Tour (1994–present). Finchem concentrated on developing the Tour's international scope by forming the International Federation of PGA Tours, which included golf's five world-governing bodies.

1996

- The International Federation of PGA Tours was created by including the European Tour, Japan Golf Tour, PGA Tour, PGA Tour of Australasia, and Southern African Tour. The International Federation of PGA Tours created a worldwide player ranking system.

1999

- Buy.com bought the naming rights to the Nike Tour and renamed it the Buy.com Tour.

2002

- The Senior PGA Tour changed its name to the Champions Tour.

2003

- Annika Sorenstam became the first women since Babe Didrikson in 1938 to play in a PGA Tour event when she participated in the Colonial Tournament on a sponsor exemption.
- Nationwide Mutual Insurance Company bought the naming rights of the Buy.com Tour and renamed it the Nationwide Tour.

2005

- The PGA Tour reached $250 million in prize money over 48 events.

2007

- The Tour announced long-term television broadcast agreements with NBC, CBS, and The Golf Channel.
- A new point system was established for the FedEx Cup competition. Points are earned from the season-opening Mercedes Championships in January through the Carolina Classic in August; the top 144 players will be eligible for the four tournament-long playoffs.

Structure of the PGA Tour

2008 Schedule

- 48 official events (see **Table 22-1**)
- 1 unofficial money event
- 49 total events
- The 2008 Tour played in 17 states as well as Canada, Mexico, and the United Kingdom.
- 4 major championships
  - Masters Tournament
  - U.S. Open
  - British Open
  - PGA Championship

See **Tables 22-2** through **22-4** for schedules of future U.S. Open, British Open, and PGA Championship tournaments.

Competition Format

- Four 18-hole rounds: After the first two rounds there is a cut in the field, where a certain percentage of players move on to the final two rounds.
- Players' aggregate scores over the 4-day tournament decide the winners.
- Usually takes place Thursday–Sunday, depending on the weather.
- Total prize money in 2006: More than $250 million.

Money Matters for the PGA Tour

Sources of Revenue

- Television broadcast revenues
  - The PGA Tour reaches 400 million households in 160 nations worldwide.
  - Networks, NBC, CBS: A 6-year agreement (2007–2012) with CBS and NBC gives each network rights to broadcast various events. CBS will broadcast 19 tournaments, primarily early in the season. NBC will air 10 tournaments, including the final three FedEx Cup events. NBC also gains rights to two World Golf Championship events and maintains rights to air the Presidents Cup, a series of matches between a team of U.S. golfers and a team of golfers from around the world (excluding Europe).
  - Cable, The Golf Channel: A 15-year agreement (2007–2021) ensures The Golf Channel exclusive cable rights to broadcast PGA tour events. The Golf Channel will provide early-round coverage of all tour events, and all fall series events following the FedEx Cup. Terms of the deal were not disclosed.
- Radio
  - XM Satellite Radio: The PGA announced a 4-year broadcasting and marketing agreement with XM Radio in 2005. Both sides reached a multi-year extension early in 2008, but terms were not disclosed.[6] Includes exclusive XM broadcasts of PGA Tour events, as well as sales and rentals of portable XM2go radios at PGA Tour tournament courses.
- Sponsorship
  - The PGA has over 45 corporate sponsors including Anheuser-Busch, FedEx, MasterCard, Nature Valley, Starwood Hotels & Resorts, *Forbes*, and Delta.
- Merchandising and licensing
  - The PGA Tour has close to 70 domestic retail and consumer marketing licensees and 20 international licensees.

Table 22-1   PGA Tour Schedule (2008)

Date	Event	Course(s)	Location
Jan. 3–6	Mercedes Championships	Plantation Course at Kapalua	Kapalua, Maui, HI
Jan. 10–13	Sony Open in Hawaii	Waialae Country Club	Honolulu, HI
Jan. 16–20	Bob Hope Chrysler Classic	The Classic Club PGA West (Palmer Course) La Quinta Country Club Bermuda Dunes Country Club	Palm Desert, CA La Quinta, CA La Quinta, CA Bermuda Dunes, CA
Jan. 24–27	Buick Invitational	Torrey Pines (South Course) Torrey Pines (North Course)	La Jolla, CA San Diego, CA
Jan. 31–Feb. 3	FBR Open	TPC Scottsdale	Scottsdale, AZ
Feb. 7–10	AT&T Pebble Beach National Pro-Am	Pebble Beach Golf Links Poppy Hills Spyglass Hill Golf Course	Pebble Beach, CA
Feb. 14–17	Northern Trust Open	Riviera Country Club	Pacific Palisades, CA
Feb. 20–24	WGolf Course-Accenture Match Play Championship	La Costa Resort and Spa	Carlsbad, CA
Feb. 21–24	Mayakoba Classic	El Camaleon	Riviera Maya, Mexico
Feb. 28–Mar. 2	The Honda Classic	PGA National Champion Course	Palm Beach Gardens, FL
Mar. 6–9	PODS Championship	Innisbrook Resort	Palm Harbor, FL
Mar. 13–16	Arnold Palmer Invitational	Bay Hill Club & Lodge	Orlando, FL
Mar. 20–23	Puerto Rico Open	Trump International Golf Course	Rio Grande, PR
Mar. 20–23	WGolf Course-CA Championship	Doral Golf Resort & Spa	Miami, FL
Mar. 27–30	Zurich Classic	TPC Louisiana	Avondale, LA
Apr. 3–6	Shell Houston Open	Redstone Golf Course Tournament Course	Humble, TX
Apr. 10–13	The Masters	Augusta National Golf Course	Augusta, GA
Apr. 17–20	Verizon Heritage	Harbour Town Golf Links	Hilton Head, SC
Apr. 24–27	EDS Byron Nelson Championship	TPC Four Seasons Resort	Irving, TX
May 1–4	Wachovia Championship	Quail Hollow Country Club	Charlotte, NC
May 8–11	Players Championship	TPC Sawgrass	Ponte Verda, FL
May 15–18	AT&T Classic	TPC Sugarloaf	Duluth, GA
May 22–25	Crowne Plaza Invitational	Colonial Country Club	Ft. Worth, TX
May 29–June 1	Memorial Tournament	Muirfield Village Golf Course	Dublin, OH
June 5–8	Stanford St. Jude Championship	TPC Southwind	Memphis, TN
June 12–15	U.S. Open	Torey Pines (South Course)	San Diego, CA
June 19–22	Travelers Championship	TPC River Highlands	Cromwell, CT
June 26–29	Buick Open	Warick Hills Golf & Country Club	Grand Blanc, MI
July 3–6	AT&T National	Congressional Country Club	Bethesda, MD
July 10–13	John Deere Classic	TPC Deere Run	Silvis, IL
July 17–20	U.S. Bank Championship	Brown Deer Park Golf Course	Milwaukee, WI
July 17–20	British Open	Royal Birkdale Golf Course	Lancashire, UK
July 24–27	Bell Canadian Open	Glen Abbey Golf Course	Oakville, Ontario
July 31–Aug. 3	Legends Reno-Tahoe Open	Montreux Golf & Country Club	Reno, NV
July 31–Aug. 3	WGolf Course-Bridgestone Invitational	Firestone Country Club (South Course)	Akron, OH
Aug. 7–10	PGA Championship	Oakland Hills Country Club	Bloomfield Township, MI
Aug. 14–17	Wyndham Championship	Sedgefield Country Club	Greensboro, NC
Aug. 21–24	Barclays Classic*	Ridgewood Country Club	Paramus, NJ
Aug. 29–Sep. 1	Deutsche Bank Championship*	TPC Boston	Norton, MA
Sep. 4–7	BMW Championship*	Bellerive Country Club	St. Louis, MO
Sep. 25–28	Tour Championship*	East Lake Golf Course	Atlanta, GA
Dec. 3–8	PGA Tour Qualifying Tournament	PGA West Stadium Course Jack Nicklaus Course	La Quinta, CA

Note: Events listed in order of occurrence. *Denotes playoffs.

LADIES PROFESSIONAL GOLF ASSOCIATION

Founded in 1950, the Ladies Professional Golf Association (LPGA) is the longest-running women's sports association in the world. The organization began as a playing tour but grew into a nonprofit organization involved in most facets of women's golf. Today, the LPGA consists of two major entities: the LPGA Tour and the LPGA Teaching & Club Professional (T&CP). These two entities comprise the backbone of the LPGA and serve to promote the game though various tournaments as well as grassroots initiatives such as junior and women's programs. Clinics and workshops, as well as professional leadership, and business and personal development training sessions, are some of the women's programs offered to LPGA members. Since 2000, the LPGA has spent a considerable amount of time developing strategies to further the brand and market the game in a positive manner.[7]

The LPGA Tour is a series of weekly golf tournaments for elite female golfers. In 2008, the LPGA Tour consisted of 35 events with total prize money reaching over $62 million, the highest total ever in LPGA history. Over 400 golfers participate on the tour, with many of the golfers coming from overseas to participate. The four annual major tournaments are the Kraft Nabisco Championship, the McDonald's U.S. LPGA Championship, the U.S. Women's Open, and the Weetabix Women's British Open.

The Teaching & Club Professional Division was established in 1959 to serve as a platform to produce and educate teaching professionals. It has almost 1,200 members worldwide. As the largest organization of its kind, the T&CP membership is dedicated to the advancement and promotion of golf through teaching, coaching, and managing golf facilities. A staff of full-time professionals oversees the day-to-day operations and sets guidelines for the T&CP program.[8]

The LPGA seeks to promote the game of golf through partnerships, charitable causes, and the development of tournaments. Through its partnership with the Susan G. Komen Breast Cancer Foundation and the creation of the LPGA foundation, the LPGA made it a priority to increase its involvement in charitable causes.

The LPGA has developed tournaments to further the growth and participation of the game, including the Futures Tour, a developmental tour, and the Women's Senior Golf Tour, a tour designed for women age 45 years old or older that also is referred to as the Legends Tour. Furthermore, the LPGA administers an annual Qualifying School, which is similar to the one used on the PGA tour, to determine whether a player receives a playing card on either the LPGA Tour or the Futures Tour.

According to the LPGA's 2006 tax return, the organization had total revenues of $69.7 million that year. This only accounts for money that flows through the organization and does not account for money that flows through affiliated tournaments not under the ownership of the LPGA. Revenues were derived from tournament sanction fees ($50 million), television rights ($9.5 million), sponsorships ($4.8 million), and other sources. The LPGA disbursed this revenue by distributing nearly $45 million in prize money. Sponsorship and membership expenses accounted for a significant portion of funds, using approximately $26 million, while television expenses accounted for $5.7 million. The

Table 22-2   Men's U.S. Open Tournament Schedule

Year	Course	Location
2006	Winged Foot Golf Course	Mamaroneck, NY
2007	Oakmont Country Club	Oakmont, PA
2008	Torrey Pines Golf Course (South Course)	La Jolla, CA
2009	Bethpage State Park (Black Course)	Farmingdale, NY
2010	Pebble Beach Golf Links	Pebble Beach, CA
2011	Congressional Country Club	Bethesda, MD
2012	Olympic Club	San Francisco, CA
2013	Merion Golf Club	Ardmore, PA

Table 22-3   Men's British Open Tournament Schedule

Year	Course	Location
2006	Royal Liverpool Golf Club	Hoylake, England
2007	Carnoustie Golf Club	Carnoustie, Scotland
2008	The Royal Birkdale Golf Club	Southport, England
2009	The Westin Turnberry Resort	Ayrshire, Scotland
2010	St. Andrew's Links	St. Andrew's, Scotland
2011	Royal St. George's Golf Club	Sandwich, England
2012	Royal Lytham & St. Anne's Golf Club	Lytham St. Anne's, Lancashire, England

Table 22-4   PGA Championship Tournament Schedule

Year	Course	Location
2006	Winged Foot Golf Course	Mamaroneck, NY
2006	Medinah Country Club	Medinah, IL
2007	Southern Hills Country Club	Tulsa, OK
2008	Oakland Hills Country Club	Bloomfield Township, MI
2009	Hazeltine National Golf Club	Chaska, MN
2010	French Lick Resort Casino	French Lick, IN
2011	Atlanta Athletic Club	Atlanta, GA
2012	The Ocean Course at Kiawah Island Resort	Kiawah Island, SC

LPGA has created sponsorship partnerships with many companies, some of which include Titleist, Michelob, MasterCard, Rolex, Bear Com Wireless, Choice Hotels International, Schick, and ADT.

The LPGA's headquarters in Daytona, Florida, has departments that are responsible for the organization's communications, marketing, network administration, creative services, finance, legal, national partnerships, new media, teaching and club professional membership, television and broadcast affairs, and tournament business affairs. Carolyn Bivens, LPGA commissioner since late 2005, receives annual compensation approximately $700,000.

History of the LPGA[9-13]

1950

- The LPGA Tour was founded by 13 members, which included female golfing legends Babe Didrikson Zaharias, Louise Suggs, and Patty Berg.

1952

- Patty Berg received the first Vare Trophy, given to the player with the lowest scoring average at the end of the season.

1959

- LPGA Tour prize money reached $200,000.
- The Teaching & Club Professional Division was founded.

1963

- The LPGA aired its first television coverage at the final round of the U.S. Women's Open Championship.

1969

- LPGA Tour prize money reached $600,000 with 34 scheduled events.

1975

- Ray Volpe became the first LPGA commissioner. During his tenure, he helped to increase purses from $600,000 to $6.4 million (1975–1982).
- The LPGA offices moved from Atlanta to New York City.

1979

- LPGA Tour prize money reached $4.4 million.

1982

- John D. Laupheimer, a former executive director for the LPGA, became the commissioner of the LPGA. Under his direction purses increased from $6.4 million to $14 million (1982–1988).
- Commissioner Laupheimer relocated LPGA headquarters to Sugar Land, Texas.
- The Nabisco Dinah Shore tournament became the first LPGA event to receive national television coverage for all four rounds.

1988

- William A. Blue, a former director of international marketing for the Kahlua Group, became the commissioner of the LPGA. The LPGA Urban Youth Golf Program and LPGA Girls Golf Club were established while he was commissioner (1988–1990).
- Commissioner Blue relocated LPGA headquarters to Daytona Beach, Florida.

1989

- LPGA Tour prize money reached $14 million.

1990

- Charles S. Mechem Jr., former chairman of Great American Broadcasting Company, became the commissioner of the LPGA. During his time with the LPGA, he was able to substantially increase television coverage of LPGA events (1990–1996).
- The Solheim Cup was developed; this is a biennial team event where the best female players from the United States play against the best female players from Europe, much like the men's Ryder Cup.

1996

- Jim Ritts, former CEO of Channel One News, became the commissioner of the LPGA. He is credited with adding tour events during his time with the LPGA (1996–1999).

1999

- Ty Votaw, the general counsel for the LPGA, became the commissioner of the LPGA. During his tenure, he focused on gaining fan support for the tour (1999–2005).
- LPGA Tour prize money reached $36.2 million.

2001

- Annika Sorenstam recorded the first-ever 59 (13 under par) in an LPGA event. She went on to win $2 million in prize money in 2001.
- Twelve-year-old Morgan Pressel qualified for the U.S. Open with a 2-under par 70 at the 6,300-yard Bear Lakes Country Club in Palm Beach, Florida.

2002

- Twelve-year-old Michelle Wie played in her first LPGA tour event but failed to make the cut at the Takefuji Classic in Hawaii.

2003

- Annika Sorenstam became the first women in 58 years to compete in a PGA Tour event when she was granted a sponsors exemption to compete in the Bank of America Colonial in Fort Worth, Texas.

2004

- At age 14, Michelle Wie became the youngest person and fourth female to play in a PGA tour event when she played in the Sony Open.

2005

- Carolyn Vesper Bivens, former president and chief operating officer of Initiative Media North America, the largest media services company in the United States, became the first female commissioner of the LPGA (2005–present).
- Michelle Wie turned pro, earning close to $20 million in endorsements and appearance money overseas.

2006

- The LPGA instituted its first-ever playoff system with the winner taking home a $1 million prize.

2007

- The LPGA began development of a drug testing policy to be implemented in 2008.

Structure of the LPGA

Events

- LPGA Tour: There are 36 tournaments each year with total purse money reaching over $62 million (2008).[14] (See **Table 22-5**.)
- Futures Tour: There are 18 tournaments during the year with total purse money of approximately $1.75 million.[15]
- The Legends Tour: Anywhere from four to seven tournaments are held annually with tournament purse money ranging from $500,000 to $0, as some of the tournaments are played entirely for charity and worth approximately $750,000.[16]

Money Matters for the LPGA

Sources of Revenue

- Television broadcast revenues
  - ESPN and ESPN2 will televise 10 to 12 LPGA Tour events each year through 2009.[17] The Golf Channel has television rights through 2009 to broadcast a minimum of 10 regular season tournaments, the 2007 and 2009 Solheim Cup, the Women's World Cup of Golf, the first two rounds of the McDonald's LPGA Championship, and the first three rounds of the limited-field season-ending ADT Championship.[18]
- Other media
  - LPGA Advanced Media Group runs the LPGA website (www.lpga.com), which sells tickets, memberships, and advertisements for the LPGA.
- Sponsorship
  - There are typically 12–15 major sponsors of the LPGA in varying product categories, such as airlines, beverages, and credit card companies. Sponsors pay an annual fee to the LPGA to become a recognized partner and for other related services. Sponsors include State Farm, Rolex, and Choice Hotels International.
- Merchandising
  - The LPGA has signed deals with several companies to produce LPGA licensed apparel and golf equipment, both in the United States and internationally. Some of the companies include One World Golf, Total Kids Wear, and Benchmark.

UNITED STATES GOLF ASSOCIATION[19]

The United States Golf Association (USGA) is the national golf governing body for the United States, its territories, and Mexico. Its three main responsibilities include conducting championships, establishing and enforcing rules, and promoting the game of golf. The USGA is a collective group of golfers, professionals, and regional volunteers. It is composed of 1,300 volunteers on the standing committees and 12,000 volunteers nationwide.

Administering championships is the most visible component to the USGA. A nonprofit organization, the USGA runs 13 national championships annually, three of which are professional championships: the U.S. Open, the U.S. Women's Open, and the U.S. Senior's Open. The U.S. Open, one of the four major championships in golf, maintains and fuels the growth of the USGA and generates the bulk of USGA revenues. *Street & Smith's SportsBusiness Journal* estimates the USGA can generate upwards of $30 million in profit from the 4-day U.S. Open event.

The USGA runs 10 amateur national championships and conducts 3 biennial championships: the Walker Cup, the Curtis Cup, and the Men's and Women's World Amateur Team Championships.

The USGA, in conjunction with the Royal and Ancient Golf Club (R&A) in St. Andrews, Scotland, writes and interprets the *Rules of Golf* and *Decisions on the Rules of Golf*, including the USGA Handicap System. Rules established by the USGA involve not only playing rules, but also equipment standards for balls, clubs, shafts, gloves, tees, and other devices. The USGA attempts to maintain the integrity of the game when determining rules and regulations on equipment. Technological advances in the golf industry have caused challenges and some difficult decisions for the USGA. These rules are accepted and followed by the many local golf courses across the United States. The USGA Handicap System allows players of varying abilities to enjoy competing against each other on different courses throughout the country. Proper golf etiquette is enforced by courses and clubs

Table 22-5   Women's U.S. Open Tournament Schedule

Date	Event	Course(s)	Location
Jan. 18–20	Women'sWorld Cup of Golf	Gary Player Country Club	Sun City, South Africa
Feb. 14–16	SBS Open at Turtle Bay	Turtle Bay Resort (Palmer Course)	Oahu, HI
Feb. 21–23	Fields Open in Hawaii	Ko Olina Golf Club	Kapolei, HI
Feb. 28–Mar. 2	HSBC Women's Champions	Tenah Mera CC	Oahu, HI
Mar. 14–16	MasterCard Classic	Bosque Real Country Club	Mexico City, Mexico
Mar. 27–30	Safeway International presented by Coca-Cola	Superstition Mountain Golf and Country Club (Prospector Course)	Gold Canyon, AZ
Apr. 3–6	Kraft Nabisco Championship	Mission Hills Country Club (Dinah Shore Tournament Course)	Rancho Mirage, CA
Apr. 10–13	Corona Championship	Tres Marias Golf Club	Morellia, Mexico
Apr. 17–20	Ginn Open	Reunion Resort & Club	Reunion, FL
Apr. 24–27	Stanford International	Fairmont Turnberry Isle Resort & Club	Aventura, FL
May 1–4	SemGroup Championship	Cedar Ridge Country Club	Broken Arrow, OK
May 8–11	Michelob ULTRA Open at Kingsmill	Kingsmill Resort & Spa	Williamsburg, VA
May 15–18	Sybase Classic	Upper Montclair Country Club	Clifton, NJ
May 22–25	LPGA Corning Classic	Corning Country Club	Corning, NY
May 29–June 1	Ginn Tribute Hosted by Annika	RiverTowne Country Club	Mt. Pleasant, SC
June 5–8	McDonald's LPGA Championship presented by Coca-Cola	Bulle Rock Golf Course	Havre de Grace, MD
June 19–22	Wegmans LPGA	Locust Hill Country Club	Pittsford, NY
June 26–29	U.S. Women's Open Championship	Interlachen Country Club	Edina, MN
July 4–6	P&G Beauty NW Arkansas Championship	Pinnacle Country Club	Rogers, AR
July 10–13	Jamie Farr Owens Corning Classic	Highland Meadows Golf Club	Sylvania, OH
July 17–20	LPGA State Farm Classic	Panther Creek Country Club	Springfield, IL
July 24–27	Evian Masters	Evian Masters Golf Club	Evian-les-Bains, France
July 31–Aug. 3	RICHO Women's British Open	Sunningdale Golf Club	Berkshire, England
Aug. 14–17	CN Canadian Women's Open	Ottawa Hunt and Golf Club	Ottawa, Ontario
Aug. 22–24	Safeway Classic Presented by Pepsi	Columbia Edgewater Country Club	Portland, OR
Sept. 11–14	Bell Micro LPGA Tournament of Champions	Robert Trent Jones Golf Trail (Magnolia Grove Crossings Course)	Mobile, AL
Sept. 25–28	Navistar LPGA Classic	RTJ Golf Trail, Capitol Hill, The Senator	Prattville, AL
Oct. 2–5	Samsung World Championship	Half Moon Bay Golf Links (Ocean Course)	Half Moon Bay, CA
Oct. 9–12	Longs Drugs Challenge	Blackhawk Country Club	Danville, CA
Oct. 16–19	Kapalua LPGA Classic	Bay Course, Kapalua Resort	Maui, HI
Oct. 24–26	Grand China Air LPGA	Haikou West Golf Club	Haikou, Hainana Island, China PRC
Oct. 31–Nov. 2	Korea Championship Presented by SEMA Sports	TBA	South Korea
Nov. 7–9	Mizuno Classic	Kinetsu Kashikojima Country Club	Shima-shi Mie, Japan
Nov. 13–16	Lorena Ochoa Invitational	Guadalajara Country Club	Guadalajara, Mexico
Nov. 20–23	ADT Championship	Trump International Golf Club	West Palm Beach, FL
Nov. 28–30	Lexus Cup	Singapore Island Country Club	Singapore
Nov. 28–30	Wendy's 3-Tour Challenge	Reflection Bay Golf Club, Lake Las Vegas Resort	Henderson, NV

that adhere to USGA standards, which helps provide golfers with a safe, enjoyable, and consistent experience while playing golf. Since its inception in 1894, the USGA preserves and promotes the best interests and spirit of the game of golf throughout the United States. In order to cultivate the game, the USGA works along with its members, some of which include the PGA of America, Golf Course Superintendents Association of America, and American Junior Golf Association (AJGA) on various initiatives, including education, leadership, and environmental initiatives.

The USGA has 900,000 members and is directed by a 15-member volunteer group, referred to as the Executive Committee. A Women's Committee includes 16 volunteers who oversee the USGA Women's championships. Nine regional offices located throughout the United States make up the Regional Affairs Directors Committee, which acts as a liaison between the USGA and state and regional golf associations.

Headquartered in Far Hills, New Jersey, the USGA employs professionals in a wide variety of departments. Some of the departments include handicap manager, assistant tournament director, and manager of web operations. The USGA also offers internships in golf administration, turf management, and museum archive administration.

History of the USGA[20]

1894

- The Amateur Golf Association of the United States, soon to be called the United States Golf Association (USGA), was formed with charter members: Newport Golf Club (RI), Shinnecock Hills Golf Club (NY), The Country Club (MA), St. Andrews Golf Club (Yonkers, NY), and Chicago Golf Club.

1895

- The first U.S. Open was held at Newport Golf Club. Horace Rawlings won the $150 first place prize over a field of 11 competitors.
- The first official U.S. Amateur Championship was held at Newport Golf Club. Charles Macdonald won the event.
- The USGA took over the running of the U.S. Open.

1898

- The U.S. Open expanded from 36 holes to 72 holes.
- Coburn Haskell and Bertram Work designed and patented a wound-rubber golf ball that flew further than existing balls.

1913

- Amateur and former caddie Francis Ouimet, 20 years old at the time, won the U.S. Open at The Country Club in Brookline, Massachusetts, and sparked a huge interest in the game of golf for Americans.

1917

- The USGA Championships were suspended because of World War I. The Championships began again in 1919.

1920

- The USGA standardized golf balls: 1.62 inches in diameter and 1.62 ounces.

1922

- An admission fee of $1 was charged at the U.S. Open for the first time.
- The first Walker Cup match between the amateurs from the United States and Great Britain was held at National Golf Links of America in Southampton, New York. The United States won the event. The Walker Cup is a team event held every 2 years and has a combination of individual, best ball, alternate shot, and doubles competition.
- The USGA held its first Amateur Public Links Championship at Ottawa Park Course in Ohio. The Amateur Public Links Championship is for public course golfers.

1923

- The second Texas Open had the largest purse to date ($6,000). The event was won by Walter Hagen.

1924

- Steel-shafted clubs were permitted in the United States by the USGA, replacing hickory shafts.
- The USGA introduced sectional qualifying rounds for the U.S. Open.

1927

- The first Ryder Cup match was played. The United States defeated Great Britain at Worcester Country Club in Massachusetts. The Ryder Cup is an international competition between selected (based on accumulated points) golf professionals from the United States and Europe. The U.S. and European teams compete against one another in various forms of match play.

1930

- Bobby Jones became the first player to win golf's Grand Slam. He won all four majors (the U.S. Open, U.S. Amateur, British Open, and British Amateur) in 1930 and then retired at the age of 28.

1932

- The first Curtis Cup Match was played between U.S. women amateurs and Great Britain. The United States won the match. The Curtis Cup has a similar playing format to the Walker Cup.

1934

- Horton Smith won the first Augusta National Invitational, at Augusta National Golf Club in Georgia. The tournament name was changed to The Masters in 1939.

1938

- A new rule was made by the USGA that limited players to carrying only 14 clubs.

1939

- The Ryder Cup was canceled because of World War II.

1940

- The Walker Cup, British Open, and British Amateur were canceled due to World War II.

1942

- The USGA canceled all its championships for the duration of World War II. The championships resumed in 1946.

1944

- A record purse of $42,000 was offered at the Tam O'Shanter Open in Chicago. Byron Nelson won the event.

1946

- The USGA held its first U.S. Women's Open at Spokane Country Club. Patty Berg, one of the founders of the LPGA, won the event.

1947

- The U.S. Open was televised for the first time on a local station, KSD-TV St. Louis. The Championship was played at the St. Louis Country Club.

1948

- The USGA held its first U.S. Junior Amateur, for boys under the age of 18, at the University of Michigan Golf Course. Dean Lind won the event.

1949

- The USGA held its first U.S. Girls Junior Championship, for girls under the age of 18, at Philadelphia Country Club. It was won by 15-year-old Marlene Bauer.

1951

- The USGA and the Royal and Ancient Golf Club (R&A), golf's world rules and development body, had a joint conference and agreed on uniform rules of golf worldwide.

1953

- The World Championship became the first nationally televised golf tournament.

1954

- The World Championship had the first $100,000 purse, with $50,000 for first place, which was won by Bob Toski.

1955

- The USGA held its first U.S. Senior Amateur Championship, for men 55 and older, at Belle Meade Country Club in Tennessee.

1957

- Great Britain won the Ryder Cup for the first time since 1933 at Lindrick Golf Club in England.

1958

- The USGA and the R&A organized the World Amateur Golf Council and held the first World Amateur Team Championship at the Old Course in St. Andrews, Scotland.

1962

- The USGA held its first U.S. Senior Women's Amateur, for women 50 and older, at Manufacturers' Golf and Country Club in Pennsylvania.

1963

- Arnold Palmer became the first golfer to surpass $100,000 in earnings for a single year.

1968

- Arnold Palmer became the first golfer to top $1 million in career earnings.

1972

- Spalding introduced the two-piece golf ball, which was constructed of a solid core inside a durable synthetic cover.

1973

- The graphite shaft was introduced to golfers.

1977

- The USGA held its first U.S. Women's Amateur Public Links Championship at Yahara Hills Golf Club in Wisconsin. The Championship is for public course golfers.

1979

- TaylorMade introduced its first metal wood golf club.
- Great Britain's Ryder Cup team was expanded to include players from all of Europe.

1980

- The USGA added the U.S. Senior Open to its championships; the championship was for players 55 and older. Roberto De Vicenzo won the first event at Winged Foot Golf Club in New York.

1981

- The USGA held its first U.S. Mid-Amateur Championship for players 25 and older. The event was played at Bellerive Golf Club in Missouri.

1985

- The USGA introduced the Slope System to adjust handicaps according to the difficulty of the courses being played.

1987

- The USGA held its first U.S. Women's Mid-Amateur at Southern Hills Country Club in Oklahoma. The Championship was for women 25 and older.

1999

- The USGA implemented testing protocol for "spring-like" effect in metal woods.

2002

- The U.S. Open was held for the first time at a publicly owned course, Bethpage State Park's Black Course in New York. Tiger Woods won the event.

2006

- The USGA and R&A made 111 changes and clarifications to the rules of golf in the book *Decisions on the Rules of Golf*. The book is published every 2 years.
- Walter Driver Jr. was elected president of the USGA after previously serving as vice president.
- The Royal & Ancient Golf Club, which sets the rules for everywhere in the world except the United States and Mexico, began drug testing at the World Amateur Team Championships in South Africa.

2007

- The USGA and Lexus agree to a multi-year partnership.

Structure of the USGA

Departments

- *The Rules of Golf*: Book written with the R&A, outlines the rules of play.
- Amateur Status and Conduct: Balances modernization of the game with preserving the traditions of amateurism.
- Championships: 19 events
  - Amateur events
    - U.S. Amateur
    - U.S. Women's Amateur
    - USGA Senior Amateur
    - USGA Men's State Team Championship
    - USGA Women's State Team Championship
    - U.S. Amateur Public Links
    - U.S. Women's Amateur Public Links
    - U.S. Junior Amateur
    - U.S. Girl's Junior Amateur
    - U.S. Mid-Amateur
    - U.S. Women's Mid-Amateur
    - Men's World Amateur Team
    - Women's World Amateur Team
  - Professional events
    - U.S. Open
    - U.S. Women's Open
    - U.S. Senior Open
  - International competitions
    - Walker Cup
    - Curtis Cup
    - Men's and Women's World Amateur Team Championships
- The USGA Grants Initiative: provides golf opportunities for personal development in disadvantaged communities. It includes instruction, caddy- and work-based curriculum, facility construction, and educational programs.
- Communications: Responsibilities include informing USGA members and serving and managing media at USGA championships via their website, publications, and DVDs.
- USGA Members Program and Club Membership: Assists and educates member clubs, courses, and training facilities with information and materials on new rules, regulations, and strategies on improvements to the game.
- Museum and Archives: Arnold Palmer Center for Golf History, Far Hills, New Jersey.
- Handicap: Combines the USGA Handicap System and Course Rating System to establish a player's handicap. The purpose of the system is to allow golfers of differing abilities to compete equally.
- Golf Handicap and Information Network (GHIN): Handicapping service provided by the USGA to participating associations and clubs that allows members to post scores, calculate handicaps, and retrieve handicap information online.
- Equipment Standards: Ensures that all equipment used in sanctioned competition adheres to standard guidelines in order to protect the integrity of the game and keep it a game of skill rather than technology.
- Regional and Sectional Affairs: Volunteer committee formed to promote USGA programs and to serve as a link among the USGA; its member clubs; the golfing public; and state, regional, and district men's and women's golf associations.
- Intercollegiate Relations: Maintains the lines of communication between the USGA and college golf.
- Regional Associations: Disseminate information from the USGA for regional, district, and junior amateur golf associations.

- Green Section: Involved with many activities and programs designed to educate and help course superintendents with turfgrass science and culture.

- USGA Course Rating System: Provides a course rating and slope rating for every rated course in the United States.

Money Matters for the USGA[21]

Sources of Revenues for 2007

- For the year ending November 30, 2007, the USGA realized a total of $136.77 million in revenues, broken down as follows:
  - Championships: $100.9 million
  - USGA membership fees and contributions: $19.2 million
  - GHIN services: $4.5 million
  - Corporate sponsorships and royalty fees: $3.2 million
  - Green section services: $2.8 million
  - Publications and merchandising: $2.2 million
  - Member club and course dues: $940,000
  - Other: $3 million

Expenses for 2007

- For the year ending November 30, 2007, the USGA had approximately $135.50 million in expenses, broken down as follows:
  - Championships: $72.9 million
  - Members programs: $15.7 million
  - Green section services: $6.9 million
  - GHIN services: $4.6 million
  - Other program services: $30.2 million
  - Administrative: $3.9 million
  - Other expenses: $1.3 million

Marketing/Sponsorships

- The USGA has no corporate sponsors, but has developed corporate partnerships in recent years. Current partners include Rolex, American Express, and Lexus.

- Most partnerships are used to promote the sport of golf to the youth population and are not actual revenue generators for the USGA. Some of the organizations that the USGA partners with include American Junior Golf Association, the LPGA and Girl Scouts of America, World Golf Foundation, and Special Olympics International.

PROFESSIONAL GOLFERS' ASSOCIATION OF AMERICA[23]

The Professional Golfers' Association of America (PGA of America) is a nonprofit organization devoted both to the promotion of the game of golf and to providing standards for the profession. These goals have been the foundation for the PGA since its establishment in 1916. Today, it is the largest working sports organization in the world with more than 28,000 professionals working across the United States. The PGA of America was once in charge of organizing the professional tour events, but in 1968 the PGA Tour separated from PGA of America and assumed the responsibility for organizing weekly professional tour events. However, the PGA of America is still responsible for organizing several elite tournaments such as the PGA Championship, the Senior PGA Championship, the PGA Grand Slam of Golf, and the Ryder Cup Tournament.

The PGA of America has also developed numerous education programs that help to promote the game of golf. For instance, the PGA operates a Professional Golf Management University Program, a 4.5-year college curriculum designed for aspiring PGA professionals. Offered at 18 PGA-accredited colleges and universities nationwide, the program trains students to work in the golf industry.

Endnotes

1. PGA Welcome Eight New Members to Association's Board of Directors. (2008, Jan. 18) PGA.com. Retrieved August 3, 2008, from http://www.pga.com/2008/news/pga/01/18/board011808/index.html.

2. Member Bio: Deane Beaman (n.d.). World Golf Village. Retrieved August 3, 2008 from http://www.wgv.com/hof/member.php?member=1023.

3. About Us: FAQ. (n.d.). PGATour.com. Retrieved November 14, 2007, from http://www.pgatour.com/company/faq.html.

4. Stricklin, A. (2007, May 22). Texas Mess. Golf.com. Retrieved February 20, 2008, from http://www.golf.com/golf/tours_news/article/0,28136,1623890,00.html.

5. About Us: PGA Tour History. (n.d.). PGATour.com. Retrieved November 14, 2007, from http://www.pgatour.com/company/pgatour-history.html.

6. Show, J. (2008, Feb. 11). XM Renews Deal with PGA Tour; Dedicated Network Averaging about 1M Listeners Weekly. Retrieved February 21, 2008, from http://www.sportsbusinessjournal.com/article/58086.

7. About the LPGA. (n.d.). LPGA.com. Retrieved November 14, 2007, from http://www.lpga.com/content_1.aspx?mid=0&pid=52.

8. Teaching and Club Professionals. (n.d.). LPGA.com. Retrieved November 14, 2007, from http://www.lpga.com/teaching_club_index.aspx.

9. Shaw, J. (2007, Dec. 10). Bivens Gets 45% Pay Increase in First Full Year. *SportsBusinessJournal.com*. Retrieved September 21, 2008, from http://www.sportsbusinessjournal.com/article/57357.

10. The LPGA: A Timeline. (n.d.). LPGA.com. Retrieved November 14, 2007, from http://www.lpga.com/content/Timeline100305.pdf.

11. Ferguson, Doug. (2005, Nov. 17). LPGA Tweaks Play-off System During Season of Record Prize Money. *USA Today*. Retrieved October 17, 2007, from http://www.usatoday.com/sports/golf/lpga/2005-11-17-lpga-schedule_x.htm.

12. LPGA. (2007, Nov. 14). 2008 LPGA Tour Schedule Announced. Retrieved February 28, 2008, from http://www.lpga.com/content_1.aspx?pid=13362&mid=1.

13. Associated Press. (2006, Nov. 19). LPGA to Implement Drug-Testing Program in '08. Retrieved February 29, 2008, from http://sports.espn.go.com/golf/news/story?id=2662865.

14. LPGA: Schedule, op cit.

15. Duramed Futures Tour Press Release (2007, Dec. 19). Duramed Futures Tour Announces 2008 Schedule. Retrieved August 3, 2008, from http://www.duramedfuturestour.com/News/DuramedFUTURESTour2008Schedule.pdf.

16. The Legends Tour: Home (n.d.). TheLegendsTour.com. Retrieved August 3, 2008, from http://www.thelegendstour.com.

17. In Their Words: Ty Votaw. (n.d.). Golf Press Association. Retrieved November 14, 2007, from http://www.golftransactions.com/20050325_votaw.php.

18. Ibid.

19. History: USGA. (n.d.). USGA.org. Retrieved August 3, 2008, from http://www.usga.org/aboutus.index.html.

20. Ibid.

21. Ibid.

22. History of the PGA of America. (n.d.). PGA.com. Retrieved August 3, 2008, from http://pgajobfinder.pgalinks.com/helpwanted/empcenter/pgaandyou/pro.cfm?ctc=1669.

23

Tennis

UNITED STATES TENNIS ASSOCIATION

The United States Tennis Association (USTA) is the national governing body for the sport of tennis and the recognized leader in promoting and developing the sport's growth on every level in the United States, from local communities to the crown jewel of the professional game, the U.S. Open. The USTA is the largest tennis organization in the world, with 17 geographic sections, more than 700,000 individual members and 7,000 organizational members, thousands of volunteers, and a professional staff of approximately 55 professionals dedicated to running the USTA and growing the game.

Founded in 1881, the USTA is a diverse non-profit organization whose volunteers, professional staff, and financial resources support a single mission: to promote and develop the growth of tennis. The USTA accomplishes its mission through two distinct business entities: Professional Tennis and Community Tennis.

Professional Tennis manages all aspects of the USTA's involvement in the professional sport, including the U.S. Open. The U.S. Open is the USTA's most visible activity and is one of four Grand Slam tennis events, collectively considered the most prominent tournaments in the sport. The U.S. Open, held every summer in Flushing Meadows, New York, is the backbone of the organization from both a financial and a visibility standpoint. Reports estimate that the USTA's total 2007 revenue from the U.S. Open was $220 million, and resulted in an estimated $110 million in profit. Profits are used to fund the overall mission of the USTA, including using approximately 60% on community tennis initiatives. The money is used to provide grants, direct aid, and to build tennis courts. The profits are also used to renovate and upgrade the Billie Jean King National Tennis Center. With an estimated 2007 total attendance of 700,000, the U.S. Open is the world's highest attended annual sporting event.[1]

Professional Tennis also manages the USTA's involvement in the U.S. Open Series. Created in 2004 as a means to build awareness and drive attendance, the U.S. Open Series links six men's and five women's tournaments leading up to the U.S. Open (**Table 23-1**). Players receive points based on how they finish in U.S. Open Series events, and a Series winner is crowned. Bonus money is then awarded to players at the U.S. Open based on both the player's final position in the U.S. Open Series and the player's play in the U.S. Open. For example, a player winning both the U.S. Open Series and the U.S. Open stands to receive $1 million in bonus prize money. Since the Series' creation, TV viewership, live television coverage, and attendance at U.S. Open Series events have all increased.

Table 23-1 U.S. Open Series Schedule (2008)

Tournament	Location	Event(s)
Indianapolis Championships	Indianapolis, IN	Men
Bank of West Classic	Stanford, CA	Women
Rogers Masters	Toronto, Ontario	Men
East West Bank Classic	Carson, CA	Women
Western & Southern Financial Group Masters	Cincinnati, OH	Men
Rogers Cup	Montreal, Canada	Women
Countrywide Classic	Los Angeles, CA	Men
Legg Mason Tennis Classic	Washington, DC	Men
Pilot Pen Tennis	New Haven, CT	Men & Women
U.S. Open	Flushing Meadows, NY	Men & Women

Note: Events are listed in order of occurrence.

In addition, Professional Tennis also oversees three professional tour events, 94 Pro Circuit events nationwide, and all operations of the USTA National Tennis Center—the world's largest public tennis facility and home of the U.S. Open—and it manages and selects the U.S. teams for the Davis Cup, the Fed Cup, the Olympics, and the Paralympic Games. The Davis Cup is an annual tournament where nations send teams consisting of the top male players compete against other countries. The Fed Cup is the women's version. The Pro Circuit events are held for both men and women, and are generally the proving ground for top-ranked juniors, college players, and pros at the beginning of their careers.

Designed to operate as a true sports marketing, entertainment, and media group, the Professional Tennis business unit generates the revenue (through television, sponsorship, ticket sales, merchandising, membership, and advanced media) for funding the USTA mission, and works to increase the popularity of the pro game.

Community Tennis strives to grow tennis at every level, with a goal of making the game accessible to everyone. It supports a wide range of programs designed to help people learn the game, play the game, and benefit from its many health/fitness and social benefits. Tennis, which has experienced a 10% growth in its participation rate in the United States since the turn of the century, is the only traditional sport to experience such growth.[2] Some of the grassroots initiatives include the USA School Tennis, National Junior Tennis League (NJTL), and USA Tennis Wheelchair programs. All of these programs include clinics and provide unique educational vehicles that are geared towards growing the game of tennis.

The USTA is a volunteer-based organization led by a board of directors headed by a volunteer chair and president. The policies and priorities are established by the board of directors. Dozens of volunteer committees, which represent the USTA membership and serve the tennis public, assist in this process. The USTA board employs an executive director, who is also chief operating officer, to manage the day-to-day operations of the organization, its offices, and its national staff.

Various positions are available at both the National Tennis Center and the USTA headquarters in White Plains, New York, to help run and organize the U.S. Open as well as other USTA-sponsored tournaments and initiatives. Departments in the Professional Tennis business unit include tournament operations, business operations and sales, marketing and communications, and National Tennis Center facility operations. On the Community Tennis side, opportunities are available in the player and network services, recreational tennis, and marketing departments.

History of the USTA

1881
- The United States National Lawn Tennis Association (USNLTA) was founded to establish uniform rules and grow participation in the sport.
- The first tennis national championship was held at the Newport Casino in Newport, Rhode Island.

1886
- Canadian and other foreign players sent entries to the USNLTA National Championship for the first time.

1889
- Women players were made official members of the USTA.

1892
- Mixed Doubles Championships were added to the USNLTA National Tournament.

1900
- The first Davis Cup match was played between the United States and England at the Longwood Cricket Club in Boston.

1910
- The inaugural National Clay Court Championships were played at Field Club of Omaha in Omaha, Nebraska.

1913
- Women players were ranked for the first time.

1915
- The National Championships were moved from Newport, Rhode Island, to New York.

1916
- National Junior and National Boys Championships were added to the National Tennis Championships.

1917
- National Girls Championships were added to the National Tennis Championships.

1918
- National Juniors, Boys, and Girls were ranked for the first time.

1920
- "National" was dropped from the official name, so the name became the United States Lawn Tennis Association (USLTA).

1922
- Seeding was established in sanctioned tournaments.
- The USLTA joined the International Lawn Tennis Federation (ILTF), the worldwide governing body for tennis.

1928

- The Junior Development Program was instituted to promote the growth of tennis among America's youth.

1931

- The ranking system was expanded to improve the results of matches involving Americans in foreign-sanctioned tournaments in other countries.

1958

- The USLTA began registering all tournament players, thus creating a "membership."

1968

- The International Lawn Tennis Federation unanimously passed a motion allowing "open tennis," which permitted participation by professionals in all major tournaments.[3]

- The USLTA began its open tennis format as all five U.S. tennis championships (men's singles, women's singles, men's doubles, women's doubles, and mixed doubles) were all played during a single event. It also marked the first time professionals were allowed to enter the tournament.[4]

1969

- The National Junior Tennis League (NJTL) was founded by Arthur Ashe, Charlie Pasarell, and Sheridan Snyder.

1970

- The rules of tennis changed significantly with the introduction of the nine-point tiebreaker at the U.S. Open.

1971

- The USLTA established the National Teachers Conference in cooperation with the American Association for Health Physical Education, Recreation, and Dance (AAHPERD) as a means of training tennis teachers how best to coach and manage young players and professional prospects in order to better the sport of tennis.

- The Virginia Slims Circuit (women's) commenced its inaugural season with 19 tournaments, and purses totaling over $300,000.

1973

- The Women's Tennis Association (WTA) was formed by Billie Jean King, bringing together all professional women's tennis players under a single organization.

- This was the first year that men and women received equal prize money at the U.S. Open.

- The Association of Tennis Professionals (ATP) began ranking players based on a computerized system.[5] (The ATP will be discussed in greater detail later in this chapter.)

- Billie Jean King defeated Bobby Riggs 6–4, 6–3, 6–3 in tennis's famed "Battle of the Sexes" played in Houston's Astrodome.

1975

- The USLTA's name was shortened to the current United States Tennis Association (USTA).

- The 9-point tiebreaker was changed to a 12-point tiebreaker.

1977

- The U.S. Open was played at Forest Hills for the last time; it was moved to Flushing Meadows, New York, for the 1978 tournament.

1978

- The USTA National Tennis Center in Flushing Meadows, New York, which hosts the U.S. Open, was dedicated.

- The USTA's involvement with the Olympics began with the USTA being recognized as the official national governing body for tennis through the Amateur Sports Act and the U.S. Olympic Committee.

1979

- The USTA created one national circuit for the next tier of professional players by converging three smaller regional circuits, also known as satellite tours.

1980

- Under USTA guidance, tennis was included in the International Special Olympics for the first time.

1984

- Membership reached a milestone of 250,000 members.

1988

- Adult membership age was lowered from 21 to 19.

- Tennis made its Olympic debut in Seoul, South Korea.

1990

- USTA Junior Team Tennis programs began at local levels to promote the game of tennis and physical fitness to the youth of America.

1991

- The national Senior League Tennis was added for USTA members over the age of 50 looking to play recreationally.

1993

- Membership increased to 500,000 for the first time.

1995

- Significant renovations began on the USTA National Tennis Center; existing stadiums and courts were redone and facilities were upgraded. Additionally, the USTA built a brand-new, 22,000-seat stadium as part of the project.

1997

- The new main stadium at the USTA National Tennis Center was named for Arthur Ashe and opened with great fanfare. The entire project is completed at a final cost $285 million, paid for entirely by the USTA.

1998

- The Wheelchair Tennis Players Association came under the auspices of the USTA.

2000

- ATP began the ATP Champions Race. Under this new system, each player starts the year with zero points and the player who accumulates the most points by season's end is ranked the #1 player in the world.[6]

2004

- The new U.S. Open Series was launched, combining six men's and five women's summer tournaments under one series, with bonus money for the winners at the final Grand Slam of the year, the U.S. Open.

2005

- Sony-Ericsson signed a 6-year, $88-million agreement to become the global title sponsor for the WTA.[7]

2006

- USTA membership exceeded 670,000 members.
- The USTA renamed the National Tennis Center, the largest public tennis facility worldwide, in honor of women's tennis pioneer Billie Jean King.

2007

- U.S. Open attendance reached 700,000 for the first time in U.S. Open history.

Structure of the USTA

Events

- USTA Pro Circuit
  - USTA Men
    - Futures Circuit: Professional tournaments typically for top-ranked juniors (age groups include U-12, U-14, U-16, and U-18), college players, and pros at the beginning of their career. Players who compete in this circuit usually have an ATP Entry System ranking between 150 and 900. There are 30 tournaments a year and purses range from $10,000 to $15,000 per tournament.
    - Challengers Circuit: Professional tournaments that act as a bridge for players between the Futures Circuit and the ATP Tour, which is for the world's premier tennis players. There are 25 tournaments a year and purses range from $35,000 to $100,000 per tournament.
  - USTA Women
    - $10,000 Tournaments: Tournaments for entry-level players who are usually top-ranked juniors (age groups include U-12, U-14, U-16, and U-18), college players, or players who are ranked as high as 250 on the WTA Tour rankings. There are 10 tournaments a year.
    - $25,000 Tournaments: Tournaments for players who are determining whether they are able to have a career as a touring pro. Often other countries' top players will start on this level. There are 12 tournaments a year.
    - $50,000 and $75,000 Tournaments: For top players, ranked as high as 40 on the WTA Tour rankings, who aspire to be on the WTA Tour. The WTA Tour consists of the premier women's tennis players. There are 20 tournaments a year.
  - U.S. Open Series: A 6-week-long summer tennis season, for men and women, that typically consists of 9 or 10 tournaments in North America and leads up to the U.S. Open. Players collect points each tournament based on how they finished, and a total from all tournaments is added up to determine the series winner.
  - U.S. Open: A 2-week-long Grand Slam event beginning in late August, in which the top men's and women's tennis players compete. The Grand Slam is held at the USTA National Tennis Center in Flushing Meadows, New York. It is the highest attended annual sporting event in the world.[8] The U.S. Open has five championships: men's singles, women's singles, men's doubles, women's doubles, and mixed doubles.

Management and Selection

- Davis Cup: The USTA is responsible for selecting and managing the Davis Cup team. The Davis Cup is an annual men's tennis event that involves over 100 nations that compete against each other in singles and doubles matches.
- Fed Cup: The USTA is responsible for selecting and managing the Fed Cup team. The Fed Cup is an annual women's event that has a similar structure to the Davis Cup.
- Olympics: The USTA is responsible for selecting and managing the U.S. Olympic team. The team participates in the Summer Olympics, which are held every 4 years.

Money Matters for the USTA

Sources of Revenue

- Television broadcast revenues
  - CBS has a 6-year, $145-million deal with the USTA to broadcast the U.S. Open through 2011.[9]
  - CBS holds rights to men's and women's third- and fourth-round action. Additionally, CBS owns the network broadcast rights to the men's semifinals, final, and doubles final competitions along with the women's semifinals and final.
  - ESPN and the Tennis Channel signed a 6-year agreement with the USTA that gives them the rights to broadcast the U.S. Open and the Olympus U.S. Open Series beginning in 2009.
- Other media
  - USTA Advanced Media Group runs the USTA website (www.USTA.com), which sells tickets, memberships, and advertisements for the USTA.
- Sponsorship
  - There are typically 15–20 major sponsors of the U.S. Open in varying product categories, such as airlines, financial services, beverages, and credit card companies. Sponsors pay an annual fee to the USTA to become a recognized partner and for other related services. Current sponsors include Lexus, American Express, Canon, and Heineken.

ASSOCIATION OF TENNIS PROFESSIONALS

The governing body of the men's premier professional tennis circuit, the Association of Tennis Professionals (ATP), runs 64 professional tennis tournaments in over 30 countries around the globe (**Table 23-2**). The ATP negotiates television/media rights and sponsorships, and handles player-tournament relations. Formed in 1972, the ATP's main responsibility is to enhance and protect the interests of men's professional tennis. The ATP Tour was established in 1990, and is a worldwide tour consisting of five categories: Grand Slam events (not sponsored by the ATP), ATP tournaments, Challenger tournaments, Satellite Series circuits, and Futures tournaments. Professional players compete for the Tennis Masters Cup by earning points throughout the year during tournaments.

Additionally, the ATP issues weekly computerized rankings for both the ATP Champions Race and the ATP Entry System. Both are based on the player's top 18 performances including any Grand Slam event for which they qualify. The two rankings differ in that the Champions Race is based on the calendar year whereas the Entry System is based on performance over the last 52 weeks. The Women's Tennis Association serves the same purpose as the ATP for professional women tennis players (see the following section).

Much like in golf, tournaments seek sanctioning from the ATP to be included on the official ATP tour schedule. ATP tournaments are granted to organizations for a fee based on the level of the tournament. Each tournament is able to select its own director who is in charge of handling the event portion of the tournament. The ATP sends both a tour manager and an ATP supervisor to ensure the tournament is conducted in accordance with ATP regulations.

ATP's headquarters are located in Ponte Vedra Beach, Florida, with satellite offices located in Sydney, Australia; London, England; and Monte Carlo, Monaco. The ATP's departments include web editing, accounting/finance, media relations, and event management.

WOMEN'S TENNIS ASSOCIATION

The Women's Tennis Association (WTA) is the governing body for the top professional women's tennis tournaments and is comparable to the men's ATP. Originally known as the Virginia Slims Circuit in 1970, the WTA conducts 62 events in 35 countries worldwide (**Table 23-3**). Players compete to earn portions of the $60 million in total prize money. In 2005, the WTA Tour was renamed the Sony Ericsson WTA Tour and includes all Tier Tournaments, the Grand Slam events, and the Season-Ending Championships (SEC). There are 45 Tier Tournaments in total along with four Grand Slam events (Australian Open, French Open, U.S. Open, and Wimbledon). These Tier Tournaments are divided into four tiers, each signifying the minimum amount of prize money awarded to the tennis players, with Tier I signifying the most lucrative purses and Tier IV signifying the least. These tiers then factor into the yearly WTA player rankings because points are awarded based on the player's success in a tournament and the tier of the event.

WTA headquarters are located in St. Petersburg, Florida. The WTA offers jobs in such areas as tour operations, media relations, web editing, professional development, marketing, and sponsorships.

WORLD TEAM TENNIS

World Team Tennis (WTT) is a unique professional tennis league where professional players compete on a team basis. In 2008, the league consisted of 11 teams based in various cities throughout the country (**Table 23-4**). Each team is composed of two men, two women, and a coach. Team matches are five sets, with one set each of men's singles, women's singles, men's doubles, women's doubles, and mixed doubles. Teams participate in a 14-game regular season played entirely in July. The top two teams in both the Eastern Division and Western Division advance to the

Table 23-2   ATP Tour Schedule (2008)

Location	Tournament
Adelaide, Australia	Next Generation Adelaide International
Doha, Qatar	Qatar ExxonMobil Open
Chennai, India	Chennai Open
Auckland, New Zealand	Heineken Open
Sydney, Australia	Medibank International
Melbourne, Victoria	Australian Open*
Viña del Mar, Chile	Movistar Open
Marseille, France	Open 13
Delray Beach, FL	Delray Beach International Tennis Championships
Costa do Sauipe, Brazil	Brasil Open
Rotterdam, Netherlands	ABN AMRO World Tennis Tournament
San Jose, CA	SAP Open
Buenos Aires, Argentina	Copa Telmex
Memphis, TN	Regions Morgan Keegan Championships
Acapulco, Mexico	Abierto Mexicano Telcel
Zagreb, Croatia	PBZ Zagreb Indoors
Dubai, United Arab Emirates	The Dubai Tennis Championships
Las Vegas, NV	Tennis Channel Open
Indian Wells, CA	Pacific Life Open
Miami, FL	Sony Ericsson Open
Estoril, Portugal	Estoril Open
Valencia, Spain	Open de Tenis Comunidad Valenciana
Houston, TX	U.S. Men's Clay Court Championships
Monte Carlo, Monaco	Masters Series Monte-Carlo
Barcelona, Spain	Open Sabadell Atlantico 2008
Munich, Germany	BMW Open
Rome, Italy	Internazionali BNL d'Italia
Hamburg, Germany	Masters Series Hamburg
Poertschach, Austria	The Hypo Group Tennis International 2008
Casablanca, Morocco	Grand Prix Hassan II
Germany	ARAG ATP World Team Championship
Paris, France	Roland Garros*
London, Great Britain	The Stella Artois Championships

Location	Tournament
Sopot, Poland	Orange Prokom Open
Halle, Germany	Gerry Weber Open
's-Hertogenbosch, Netherlands	Ordina Open
Nottingham, Great Britain	Nottingham Open
Wimbledon, Great Britain	Wimbledon*
Stuttgart, Germany	Mercedes Cup
Gstaad, Switzerland	Allianz Suisse Open Gstaad
Newport, RI	Campbell's Hall of Fame
Båstad, Sweden	Catella Swedish Open
Kitzbühel, Austria	Austrian Open
Amersfoort, Netherlands	Dutch Open Tennis
Indianapolis, IN	RCA Championships
Umag, Croatia	ATP Studena Croatia Open
Montreal, Canada	Rogers Cup
Cincinnati, OH	Western & Southern Financial
Los Angeles, CA	Countrywide Classic
Beijing, China	2008 Olympics
Washington, DC	Legg Mason Tennis Classic
New Haven, CT	Pilot Pen Tennis
New York, NY	U.S. Open*
Bucharest, Romania	BCR Open Romania
Beijing, China	China Open
Bangkok, Thailand	Thailand Open
Tokyo, Japan	AIG Japan Open Tennis Championships
Metz, France	Open de Moselle
Mumbai, India	Mumbai Open
Vienna, Austria	BA-CA Tennis Trophy
Stockholm, Sweden	If Stockholm Open
Moscow, Russia	ATP Kremlin Cup
Madrid, Spain	Mutua Madrilena Masters Madrid
Basel, Switzerland	Davidoff Swiss Indoors Basel
Lyon, France	Grand Prix de Tennis de Lyon
St. Petersburg, Russia	St. Petersburg Open
Paris, France	BNP Paribas Masters
Shanghai, China	Tennis Masters Cup Shanghai

Note: Tournaments are listed in order of occurrence. *Grand Slam events and the Davis Cup are not ATP-sponsored events.

Championship Weekend. Teams are then seeded by their regular season records to compete for the King Cup.

Co-founded by Billie Jean King in 1974, WTT offers an entertaining alternative to traditional professional tennis found on the ATP and WTA tours. WTT strives to create a unique, fun atmosphere for its fans and communities. Each year, the teams' rosters are reshuffled through a reverse order draft. Teams are allowed to protect players from the previous year's roster. Many famous professional tennis players have participated in the WTT including Bjorn Borg, Maria Sharapova, Andre Agassi, Chris Evert, Pete Sampras, Billie Jean King, Serena and Venus Williams, and Andy Roddick. WTT rosters offer the flexibility to allow players to compete in a few events each season, so they are not obligated to commit themselves for an extended period of time. This strategy helps attract some of the best players who have busy schedules with their tour events. The WTT offers multiple ticket packages with an average of $20 per ticket.

Table 23-3 WTA Tour Schedule (2008)

Name	Location	Name	Location
Mondial Australian Women's Hardcourts	Gold Coast, Australia	Internazionali femminili di tennis di Palermo	Palermo, Italy
ASB Classic	Auckland, New Zealand	Bank of the West Classic	Stanford, CA
Medibank International	Sydney, Australia	Gastein Ladies	Bad Gastein, Austria
Moorilla Hobart International	Hobart, Australia	Western & Southern Financial	Cincinnati, OH
Australian Open*	Melbourne, Australia	East West Bank Classic	Los Angeles, CA
FedEx Cup First Round	Tokyo, Japan	Banka Koper Slovenia Open	Portoroz, Slovenia
Open Gaz de France	Paris, France	Rogers Cup	Montreal, Canada
Pattaya Open	Pattaya City, Thailand	Kitzbühel Cup	Kitzbühel, Austria
Proximus Diamond Games	Antwerp, Belgium	Acura Classic	San Diego, CA
Cacchantun Cup	Vina Del Mar, Chile	Nordea Nordic Light Open	Stockholm, Sweden
Qatar Total Open	Doha, Qatar	2008 Olympics	Beijing, China
Copa Colsanitas	Bogota, Colombia	Western & Southern Financial Group Women's Open	Cincinnati, OH
Dubai Tennis Championships	Dubai, United Arab Emirates	Pilot Pen Tennis presented by Schick	New Haven, CT
Abierto Mexicano TELCEL presented by HSBC	Acapulco, Mexico	Forest Hills Classic	Forest Hills, NY
Regions Morgan Championships & the Cellular South Cup	Memphis, TN	U.S. Open*	Flushing Meadows, NY
		Commonwealth Bank Tennis Classic	Bali, India
Canara Bank Bangalore Open	Bangalore, India	Torray Pan Pacific Open	Tokyo, Japan
Pacific Life Open	Indian Wells, CA	Guangzhou International Women's Open	Guangzhou, China
Sony Ericsson Open	Miami, FL	China Open	Beijing, China
Bausch & Lomb Championships	Amelia Island, FL	Hansol Korea Open	Seoul, South Korea
Family Circle Cup	Charleston, SC	Porsche Tennis Grand Prix	Stuttgart, Germany
Estoril Open	Estoril, Portugal	AIG Japan Open Tennis Championships	Tokyo, Japan
Grand Prix de SAR La Princesse Lalla Meryem	Fes, Morocco	Kremlin Cup	Moscow, Russia
Qatar Telecom German Open	Berlin, Germany	Sunfeast Open	Kolkata, India
Internazionali BNL d'Italia	Rome, Italy	Zürich Open	Zürich, Switzerland
Istanbul Cup	Istanbul, Turkey	Generali Ladies Linz presented by Raiffeisenlandesbank Oberösterreich	Linz, Austria
Internationaux de Strasbourg	Strasbourg, France		
Roland Garros*	Paris, France		
DFS Classic	Birmingham, Great Britain		
Barcelona KIA	Barcelona, Spain	FORTIS Championships Luxembourg	Luxembourg, Luxembourg
International Women's Open	Eastbourne, Great Britain	Bell Challenge	Québec City, Canada
Ordina Open	's-Hertogenbosch, Netherlands	Sony Ericsson Championships	Madrid, Spain
Wimbledon*	Wimbledon, Great Britain		
Budapest Grand Prix	Budapest, Hungary		

Note: Tournaments are listed in order of occurrence. *Grand Slam events are not WTA sponsored.

Headquartered in New York City, the WTT is composed of the following departments: new franchise, professional league, recreational league, national qualifiers and championships, and sponsorship opportunities. The WTT also runs recreational leagues in more than 1,000 communities throughout the United States. Community involvement and charities are an integral part of the foundation of WTT. Under the guidance of Billie Jean King, the WTT Charities, Inc. was established in 1987 to promote health, fitness, education, and social change. A list of the WTT corporate and event sponsorship deals includes Advanta, USTA, Equinox,

Wilson, Gatorade, Comcast, Bristol-Myers Squibb, Wal-Mart, and Geico. The WTT is broadcast on several networks such as Charter Communications, Comcast Sports Net, Cox Communications, ESPN2, Fox Sports Net, In Demand, Madison Square Garden Network, Mediacom, and The Tennis Channel.

Endnotes

1. Kaplan, D. (2007, Aug. 27–Sep. 2). How U.S. Open Profits Hit a Whopping $110M. *Street & Smith's SportsBusiness Journal*, pp. 1, 19–20, 24.

Table 23-4   WTT Teams (2008)

East Division	
Team	**Location**
Boston Lobsters	Boston, MA
Delaware Smash	Wilmington, DE
New York Buzz	Schenectady, NY
New York Sportimes	Park Mamaroneck, NY
Philadelphia Freedoms	Radnor, PA
Washington Kastles	Washington, DC

Western Conference	
Team	**Location**
Kansas City Explorers	Kansas City, MO
Newport Beach Breakers	Newport Beach, CA
Sacramento Capitals	Citrus Heights, CA
Springfield Lasers	Springfield, MO
St. Louis Aces	St. Louis, MO

2. ATP, WTA Chiefs Discuss Pros, Cons of Merging into One Tour. (2008, Mar. 28). *Sports Business Daily.* Retrieved August 3, 2008, from http://www.sportsbusinessdaily.com/article/119531.

3. Off with the Shackles. (1968, Apr. 12). *Time.* Retrieved October 3, 2007, from http://www.time.com/time/magazine/article/0,9171,838160,00.html.

4. History and Records. (n.d.). *U.S. Open.* Retrieved October 3, 2007, from http://www.usopen.org/en_US/about/history/index.html.

5. Clarey, C. W. (2000, Dec. 2). But New Ranking System Deserves a Chance: The Confusing Race to Find World No. 1. *The International Tribune.* Retrieved October 1, 2007, from http://www.iht.com/articles/2000/12/02/a20_0.php.

6. Sandomir, R. (1999, Dec. 10). ATP Tour: New Ranking System Is Introduced. *The New York Times.* Retrieved October 1, 2007, from http://query.nytimes.com/gst/fullpage.html?res=9A02E2D81431F933A25751C1A96F958260.

7. Sony Ericsson Signs $88 Million Title Sponsorship Deal. (2005, Jan. 6). *Promo.* Retrieved October 9, 2007, from http://promomagazine.com/news/ericcson_sponsorship_010605/.

8. U.S. Open: News. (2008, Mar. 5). US Open Sets All-Time Tournament Records. USOpen.com. Retrieved August 4, 2008, from http://www.usopen.org/news/fullstory.sps?iNewsid=538370&itype=12162.

9. CBS Secures U.S. Open for Six Years at Cost of $145M. (2007, May 7). Cbssportsline.com. Retrieved February 28, 2008, from http://cbs.sportsline.com/tennis/story/10170852.

CHAPTER TWENTY-FOUR

Volleyball

ASSOCIATION OF VOLLEYBALL PROFESSIONALS

The Association of Volleyball Professionals (AVP), established in 1983, organizes and promotes the only professional beach volleyball competition in the United States. The AVP works in conjunction with USA Volleyball and the Federation of International Volleyball (FIVB). The AVP is responsible for conducting the AVP Crocs Tour, which includes 16 tournaments running from March through September (**Table 24-1**). The AVP Crocs Tour consists of two-on-two beach volleyball for both men and women. Initially, events were played mostly in California; however, beginning in 2006, the AVP hosted events in cities such as Atlanta; Chicago; Brooklyn; Las Vegas; Lake Tahoe, California; and Birmingham, Alabama.

Tickets for the all-day events range from $35 courtside to $15 for general admission. In 2006, total revenues increased to $17.4 million (up from $12.7 million in 2005).[1] Corporate sponsorships comprise the majority of revenues for the AVP and include McDonald's, Nautica, Anheuser-Busch, Nature Valley Granola Bars, and Microsoft's Xbox video game system as key partners. In 2006, the AVP signed a contract with Crocs Inc. as the title sponsor of the tour; however, financial terms of the agreement were not disclosed. Fox and NBC have also signed up for broadcasting deals, primarily for championship round coverage.

The AVP awarded $4 million in prize money in 2007. This represented a $500,000 increase over the $3.5 million awarded in 2006, and a considerable improvement over the $900,000 awarded in 2001.[2]

The AVP also relies on minimizing operational costs by hiring volunteers to reduce expenses. When the AVP Tour travels to each location, the AVP relies on hundreds of volunteers to help run their events. Volunteers typically work as ball boys/girls, hospitality personnel, and scorekeepers. During the off-season between the 2005 and 2006 AVP Tour, management decided to convert to a business model where local promoters run each tournament. For instance, a local management company, Ratner Cos., which owns the New Jersey Nets, ran the 2006 AVP Brooklyn Open. AVP Tour officials are hoping to extend the AVP brand and fan base by having a third party run the events. AVP has not been profitable since 2001.[3]

Endnotes

1. AVP. (2007, Mar. 28). AVP Reports Record 2006 Revenue Up 38%; 2006 Gross Profit up 8% Year-Over-Year. Information obtained from APV press release.

2. AVP: News and Features. (2007, July 12). AVP Announces Tour Debut on NBC. AVP.com. Retrieved August 4, 2008, from http://web.avp.com/news/article.jsp?ymd=20070717&contentid=29850.

3. Reed, K. (2007, June 13). Henry to Test Water for Volleyball. *Boston Globe*, p. C1.

Table 24-1 AVP Crocs Tour Schedule (2008)

Date	Event	Site
Apr. 11–13	AVP Crocs Tour Cuervo Gold Crown Miami Open	Miami, FL
Apr. 18–20	AVP Crocs Tour Cuervo Gold Crown Dallas Open	Arlington, TX
May 2–4	AVP Crocs Tour Cuervo Gold Crown Huntington Beach Open	Huntington Beach, CA
May 8–10	AVP Crocs Tour Charleston	Charleston, SC
May 24–27	AVP Crocs Tour Louisville Presented by Kentucky Unbridled Spirit	Louisville, KY
May 30–June 1	AVP Crocs Tour Atlanta	Atlanta, GA
June 5–8	AVP Crocs Tour Hermosa Beach Open Presented by Bud Light	Hermosa Beach, CA
June 20–22	AVP Crocs Tour Belmar Presented by Bud Light	Belmar, NJ
July 4–6	AVP Crocs Tour Slam Boulder	Boulder, CO
July 1–13	McDonald's AVP Crocs Tour Chicago Open Presented by Nautica	Chicago, IL
July 18–20	AVP Crocs Slam Brooklyn Presented by Cushman and Wakefield	Brooklyn, NY
July 25–27	AVP Crocs Slam Bud Light Long Beach Open	Long Beach, CA
Aug. 1–3	AVP Crocs Slam San Diego	San Diego, CA
Aug. 29–31	AVP Crocs Cup Shootout-Mason Presented by Budlight	Mason, OH
Sept. 6–7	AVP Crocs Cup Shootout-Santa Barbara Presented by Bud Light	Santa Barbara, CA
Sept. 12–14	AVP Crocs Cup Shootout-San Francisco Presented by Bud Light	San Francisco, CA
Sept. 19–21	AVP Crocs Cup Shootout-Manhattan Beach Presented by Bud Light	Manhattan Beach, CA
Sept. 25–27	AVP Crocs Tour Sanderson Ford Glendale Best of the Beach	Glendale, AZ

CHAPTER TWENTY-FIVE

Auto Racing

NASCAR

The National Association for Stock Car Auto Racing (NASCAR) is one of most popular sports in the United States. The largest sanctioning body of the motor sports industry in the United States, NASCAR is responsible for the operations of three racing series: the Sprint Cup Series, the Busch Series, and the Craftsman Truck Series. NASCAR sanctions approximately 1,800 races at 120 tracks in 38 states. As a sanctioning body, NASCAR is responsible for enforcing the rules and regulations of the race cars, scheduling races and events, organizing championships, enforcing ownership rules, handing out disciplinary measures, ensuring safety, and licensing.

Stock cars are automobiles that have not been modified from their original factory configuration. Over time, NASCAR has required certain safety regulations and modifications for all of the stock cars racing in each series. However, modern racing stock cars use a body template modeled from automobiles that are currently available to the public. Dodge, Chevrolet, Toyota, and Ford manufacture all of the stock cars in the Sprint Cup. Along with these four manufacturers, Pontiac manufactures stock cars for the Busch Series. The Craftsman Series trucks are manufactured by Dodge, Chevrolet, Ford, and Toyota.

Originally, NASCAR's popularity was primarily in the southeastern United States; however, during the 1980s and 1990s, NASCAR gained recognition and strong support from fans throughout the rest of the country. Headquartered in Daytona Beach, Florida, NASCAR has four additional offices in North Carolina: Charlotte (licensing), Concord (research and development), Conover (transportation), and Mooresville (technical). NASCAR also has satellite offices in New York, Los Angeles, and Arkansas, and international offices in Mexico City, Mexico, and Toronto, Canada. When expanding throughout the country, NASCAR focused

on building race tracks that varied in size and speeds. Some racetracks are ovals, many are tri-ovals, and others have unique configurations to add to the track's character. Racetracks also have various degrees of banking on the curves in order to control for speed. By designing and tailoring each racetrack differently, NASCAR has provided its fans with an assortment of distinct races throughout the season.

NASCAR is also responsible for negotiating sponsorship deals with companies and broadcast deals with television and radio networks. Corporate sponsorships have provided NASCAR with a significant financial base, allowing it to expand across the country while improving the standards and benefits for its racers. As NASCAR developed over the years, sponsorship fees have increased and more sponsors have been added, both from the organization side and the individual team side. Sponsors include Budweiser, Minute Maid, Visa, Coca-Cola, and Sprint among many others.

In addition, over 100 *Fortune* 500 companies sponsor NASCAR drivers, spending approximately $2.9 billion in 2006.[1] In return for their investment, corporate sponsors generally get their company's logo placed somewhere on the hood of the car, and on the team's hats and coats. Sponsors gain significant national television exposure without having to pay the network for an advertisement. In addition, drivers may be required to make appearances with the corporate sponsor employees and clients before races. NASCAR's success can be at least partially attributed to the development of its strong brand association with well-known corporate sponsors.

Prior to 2001, each track was allowed to negotiate its own television rights deal, which led to a great deal of inconsistency in the contracts. A race may have been on ABC one week and CBS the next. Plus, there was no guarantee as to what time a race would be on, and some races were shown on a delayed basis. In 2001, NASCAR began to negotiate deals with television networks, packaging the rights to several races instead of having each track individually negotiate television rights. This was a tremendous move forward for the sport. By consolidating multiple races into packages, NASCAR was able both to generate higher broadcasting rights deals (i.e., more revenue) and to give viewers more consistent viewing output. The first package deal was split among Fox, NBC, FX, and TNT. By airing races on broadcast television and major cable channels, NASCAR also was able to reach a much broader audience.

In 2005, NASCAR negotiated its largest television rights deal, worth up to $4.48 billion over 8 years (2007–2014). NASCAR also has benefited immensely from its licensing agreements. NASCAR products generate an estimated $2 billion annually in licensing fees.[2] With television ratings exceeding all major sports except for the NFL, NASCAR is one of the most popular sports in the United States.

One of the contributing factors of NASCAR's recent success has been its innovative measures in enhancing fan experience. NASCAR brings the race to the fan digitally through its Trackpass to enhance the experience of fans who cannot attend a race. Launched in 2002, Trackpass provides numerous features to fans via their home computer or Sprint cellular phone. One feature is PitCommand, a GPS-based technology that lets fans see the positioning of the cars as the race unfolds. Additionally, the program provides in-car audio of what drivers say during the race as well as rapidly updated statistics for both the race and season. A 1-year subscription to PitCommand costs $64.95 for the basic application and $10.99–$15.99 for the cell phone features.[3]

The auto racing industry as a whole is quite large, and therefore provides various job opportunities with NASCAR and with the individual racing teams. Some departments in NASCAR include brand and consumer marketing, competition, human resources, information technology, licensing, member services, digital entertainment, community relations, and finance. There are also jobs within individual racing teams. Additionally, each race track has its own staff where positions include, but are not limited to, business, marketing, communications, operations, security, logistics, accounting, special events, ticketing, emergency services, and guest relations. At the corporate level, some areas of NASCAR employment are marketing, licensing, sales, finance, and public relations. In addition, NASCAR has a Diversity Internship Program that has hired 170 students as interns since its inception.

There are racing organizations that govern other types of racecars. Championship Auto Racing Teams (CART) and Indy Racing League (IRL) sanction Indy car racing. (See more on these organizations later in this chapter.) The National Hot Rod Association (NHRA) is the largest governing body of drag racing (and also discussed later in this chapter). There are other forms of racing as well, including rally, off-road, and dirt track racing, which are all separately governed.

History of NASCAR[4,5]

1949

- The NASCAR Strictly Stock Series was established with Bill France as president.

1950

- The first NASCAR Grand National (now known as Sprint Cup Series) championship race took place.
- The country's first asphalt superspeedway, the Darlington Raceway in South Carolina, opened for racing.

1954

- Lee Petty, a NASCAR pioneer, won his first of three NASCAR Grand National championships.

1959

- The first running of the Daytona 500 was won by Lee Petty in a photo finish. NASCAR officials took 3 days to determine the winner.

1964

- Racing legend Richard Petty, son of Lee Petty, won the first of his seven Winston Cup Championships.[6]

1969

- NASCAR's largest track, the Talladega Superspeedway, was built.

1972

- NASCAR President Bill France stepped down and appointed his son, Bill France Jr., president.
- R.J. Reynolds Tobacco Company became the title sponsor of the NASCAR Grand National championship, which was renamed the NASCAR Winston Cup Series.

1975

- A new point system was established, which is still used today. Drivers earn 185 points for winning a race while the runner-up receives 170. Points decrease by increments of five until sixth place. All subsequent finishes decrease by four points per slot (e.g., 1st = 185, 2nd = 170, 3rd = 165 . . . 6th = 150, 7th = 146, 8th = 142, etc.). Five bonus points are added for any driver who leads for an entire lap and an additional five points are given to the driver who leads the most laps during the race.

1976

- NASCAR attracted 1.4 million fans, becoming the world leader in attendance in an auto racing organization.[7]

1979

- The Daytona 500 was broadcast in its entirety, thereby becoming the first live television auto racing event.

1980

- Dale Earnhardt Sr. won his first NASCAR Winston Cup Series.

1982

- NASCAR consolidated the Late Model Sportsman (LMS) Division into a new series with title sponsorship from Anheuser-Busch. The Busch Series, as it is known today, serves as the minor league, driver development program of NASCAR.

1984

- The LMS Division became known as the NASCAR Busch Series, Grand National Division.

1989

- First year in which every NASCAR race was televised, with most events broadcast live.[8]

1993

- NASCAR expanded its racing territory to the Northeast when it scheduled its first event at the New Hampshire International Speedway.[9]

1994

- NASCAR introduced the NASCAR Craftsman Truck Series. Full-bodied American-made pickup trucks compete on the NASCAR Winston Cup frames.
- NASCAR entered into the home of open wheel racing, holding its first event at the Indianapolis Motor Speedway.[10]

1995

- Jeff Gordon, at age 24, became the second youngest driver to win the NASCAR Winston Cup Series when he edged out legend Dale Earnhardt Sr. for the title.
- TV ratings broke all-time NASCAR records with the entire NASCAR Winston Cup, NASCAR Busch Series, and NASCAR Craftsman Truck Series schedules aired on television.
- NASCAR online began: www.nascar.com.

1997

- The NASCAR Winston Cup Series expanded to the California Speedway and the Texas Motor Speedway, in Dallas/Ft. Worth, as well as a second date at the New Hampshire International Speedway.
- The NASCAR Busch series expanded to St. Louis, Los Angeles, Dallas/Ft. Worth, and Las Vegas.

- The NASCAR Craftsman Truck Series expanded to Orlando, Los Angeles, and Dallas/Ft. Worth.

1999

- The NASCAR Winston Cup Series expanded to Miami-Dade Homestead Motorsports Complex.

2000

- The New Hampshire International Speedway became the first NASCAR track to host more than 100,000 fans for a single race when it hosted the thatlook.com 300.

2001

- NASCAR legend Dale Earnhardt Sr. died in a fatal car crash during the final lap of the Daytona 500.
- NASCAR negotiated its first packaged broadcasting rights deal, awarding races to Fox, NBC, and TNT.

2003

- Nextel Communications signed on as title sponsor for NASCAR's top series, formerly known as the NASCAR Winston Cup Series. The change ended NASCAR's 33-year partnership with R.J. Reynolds Tobacco Company. RJR declined to extend the deal due in large part to 1998 lawsuit settlements barring it from advertising its flagship brand Winston Cigarettes on television or radio and explicitly prohibiting it from marketing to minors.

2004

- NASCAR Winston Cup officially became the NASCAR Nextel Cup.
- NASCAR announced a 10-race playoff system called the "Chase for the Cup."

2005

- NASCAR signed a $4.48-billion deal with Fox, Fox-owned Speed Channel, TNT, Disney-owned ABC, ESPN, and ESPN2 beginning in 2007.

2006

- NASCAR and Toyota Motorsports announced the arrival of Toyota cars to be used by drivers in Sprint Cup Races and Busch Series events.

2007

- NASCAR announced that it will expand the Chase for the Cup from 10 drivers to 12 drivers.
- Toyota became the first foreign-manufactured car to compete in a NASCAR event.

2008

- Sprint replaced Nextel as the title sponsor of NASCAR's premium racing series.

Structure of NASCAR

Sprint Cup

- Formerly known as the Nextel (2004–2007), Winston Cup Series (1972–2003), and Grand National Series (1950–1971).

- Most profitable and popular series operated by NASCAR. The most popular race is the Daytona 500.

- 36 races per race season starting with the Daytona 500 on the third Sunday in February (**Table 25-1**).[11]

- All races are held on weekends from February through November.

- 43 race cars per race.

- Points are given based on performance in the race, and standings are recorded for the entire season.

- After 26 races, the Chase for the Cup is implemented. The Chase for the Cup is a playoff system that selects the top 10 drivers based on point totals from the previous 26 races.

- Sprint Cup points are readjusted and the driver with the highest regular season point total is given 5050 points. The point readjustment declines by increments of five, so the driver that qualifies with the lowest point total starts the Chase for the Cup with 5005 points.

- The top 10 racers and any other driver within 400 points of the point leader qualify for the Chase. Drivers seeded 10 and below are all granted 5005 points.

- After the final 10 races, the driver with the most points (gained only during the Chase for the Cup races) is awarded the Spring Cup.

Busch Series

- Formed as a short track racing circuit, and eventually evolved into normal length races.

- Became more of a minor league circuit in the mid-1980s.[12]

- 35 races per season starting with a race at the Daytona International Speedway.

- All races are held on Fridays and Saturdays from February to November.

- Most of the races are held on the same weekend and at the same tracks used by NASCAR for their Sprint Cup events, with several races held at smaller venues.

- 43 cars per race.

- Standings are recorded for the entire season, and the winner at the end is awarded the championship.

Craftsman Truck Series

- Created after off-road racers produced a prototype of a racing truck.

- Established in 1995 as the Super Truck Series.

- 23 races per season starting with a race at the Daytona International Speedway.

- 43 race trucks per race.

Money Matters for NASCAR

Sources of Revenues

- Television broadcast revenues
  - Eight-year deal with Fox, Fox-owned Speed Channel, TNT, Disney-owned ABC, ESPN, and ESPN2 from 2007–2014, worth $4.48 billion.
  - Rights holders: Fox (13 races: $205 million per year); TNT (6 races: $80–$85 million per year); and ABC/ESPN (17 races: $270 million per year). All agreements are good for the 2007–2014 seasons.[13]
  - Daytona 500: Exclusive deal with Fox.
  - Busch Series: At least four races on ABC with the rest on ESPN2.
  - Chase for the Cup: ABC.
  - Broadcast revenues are split as follows: tracks receive 65% of revenue, teams and drivers receive 25%, and NASCAR receives the remaining 10%.

- Other media
  - Sirius satellite radio: 5 years for a total of $107.5 million starting in 2007.[14]
  - Internet deal with Turner Interactive: 6 years for $100 million through 2008. In 2008, NASCAR extended its Internet contract with Turner Sports Interactive through 2014.

- Sponsorships
  - NASCAR is one of the strongest brands in sports and has over 55 official sponsors.
  - 106 companies in the *Fortune* 500, including 31 of the top 50, sponsor NASCAR or NASCAR teams.

- Licensing
  - $2.1 billion in annual licensed product sales
  - Works with more than 200 licensees nationwide
  - Based in Charlotte, North Carolina

OPEN WHEEL RACING

Open wheel racing is characterized by specifically designed racecars whose wheels are located outside the main body or frame of the car. Open wheel racing includes Formula One, American Championship Car Racing, sprint cars, and midget cars. The largest open wheeled racing bodies in the United States are the Indy Racing League (IRL); Championship Auto Racing Teams, also known as CART racing; and the National Hot Rod Association. IRL and CART were

Table 25-1   Sprint Cup Schedule (2008)

Race	Track	Date
Budweiser Shootout	Daytona International Speedway—Daytona Beach, FL	Feb. 9
Gatorade Duel	Daytona International Speedway—Daytona Beach, FL	Feb. 14
Daytona 500	Dayton International Speedway—Daytona Beach, FL	Feb. 17
Auto Club 500	California Speedway—Fontana, CA	Feb. 24
UAW-DaimlerChrysler 400	Las Vegas Motor Speedway—Las Vegas, NV	Mar. 2
Kobalt Tools 500	Atlanta Motor Speedway—Atlanta, GA	Mar. 9
Food City 500	Bristol Motor Speedway—Bristol, TN	Mar. 16
Goody's Cool Orange 500	Martinsville Speedway—Martinsville, VA	Mar. 30
Samsung 500	Texas Motor Speedway—Fort Worth, TX	Apr. 6
Subway Fresh Fit 500	Phoenix International Speedway—Phoenix, AZ	Apr. 12
Aaron's 499	Talladega Superspeedway—Talladega, AL	Apr. 27
Crown Royal Presents the Your Name Here 400	Richmond International Raceway—Richmond, VA	May 3
Dodge Challenger 500	Darlington Raceway—Darlington, SC	May 10
NASCAR Sprint All Star Challenge	Lowe's Motor Speedway—Concord, NC	May 17
Coca-Cola 600	Lowe's Motor Speedway—Concord, NC	May 25
Dover 400	Dover International Speedway—Dover, DE	June 1
Pocono 500	Pocono Raceway—Long Pond, PA	June 8
Michigan 400	Michigan International Speedway—Brooklyn, MI	June 15
Toyota/SaveMart 350	Infineon Raceway—Sonoma, CA	June 22
Lenox Industrial Tools 300	New Hampshire International Speedway—Loudon, NH	June 29
Coke Zero 400 Powered by Coca-Cola	Daytona International Speedway—Daytona Beach FL	July 5
Chicagoland 400	Chicagoland Speedway—Joliet, IL	July 12
Allstate 400 at the Brickyard	Indianapolis Motor Speedway—Indianapolis, IN	July 27
Pennsylvania 500	Pocono Raceway—Long Pond, PA	Aug. 3
Centurion Boats at The Glen	Watkins Glen International—Watkins Glen, NY	Aug. 10
3M Performance 400	Michigan International Speedway—Brooklyn, MI	Aug. 17
Sharpie 500	Bristol Motor Speedway—Bristol, TN	Aug. 23
NASCAR Sprint Cup Series 500	California Speedway—Fontana, CA	Aug. 31
Chevy Rock & Roll 400	Richmond International Raceway—Richmond, VA	Aug. 6
Sylvania 300	New Hampshire International Speedway—Loudon, NH	Aug. 14
Dover 400	Dover International Speedway—Dover, DE	Aug. 21
Kansas 400	Kansas Speedway—Kansas City, KS	Aug. 28
Amp Energy 500	Talladega Superspeedway—Talladega, AL	Oct. 5
Bank of America 500	Lowe's Motor Speedway—Concord, NC	Oct. 11
NASCAR Sprint Cup Series 500	Martinsville Speedway—Martinsville, VA	Oct. 19
Pep Boys Auto 500	Atlanta Motor Speedway—Atlanta, GA	Oct. 26
Dickies 500	Texas Motor Speedway—Fort Worth, TX	Nov. 2
Checker Auto Parts 500 presented by Pennzoil	Phoenix International Speedway—Phoenix, AZ	Nov. 9
Ford 400	Homestead-Miami Speedway—Homestead, FL	Nov. 16

Table 25-2   Indy Race League Schedule (2008)

Race	Track	Date
GAINSCO Auto Insurance 300	Homestead-Miami Speedway—Homestead, FL	Mar. 29
Grand Prix of St. Petersburg	Streets of St. Petersburg, FL	Apr. 6
Indy Japan 300	Twin Ring Motegi—Motegi, Japan	Apr. 19
RoadRunner Turbo 300	Kansas Speedway— Kansas City, KS	Apr. 27
Indianapolis 500	Indianapolis Motor Speedway—Indianapolis, IN	May 25
AJ Foyt Indy 225	Milwaukee Mile—Milwaukee, WI	June 1
Bombardier Learjet 550	Texas Motor Speedway—Fort Worth, TX	June 7
Iowa Corn Indy 250	Iowa Speedway—Newton, IA	June 22
Suntrust Indy Challenge	Richmond International Raceway—Richmond, VA	June 28
Camping World Grand Prix	Watkins Glen International—Watkins Glen, NY	July 6
Firestone Indy 200	Nashville Superspeedway—Nashville, TN	July 12
The Honda 200 at Mid-Ohio	Mid-Ohio Sports Car Course—Lexington, OH	July 20
Meijer 300	Kentucky Speedway—Sparta, KY	Aug. 19
Indy Grand Prix of Sonoma	Infineon Raceway—Sonoma, CA	Aug. 24
Detroit Belle Isle Grand Prix	The Raceway at Belle Isle—Detroit, MI	Aug. 31
Chicagoland Indy 300	Chicagoland Speedway—Joliet, IL	Sept. 7

once the same league but split in 1996. In February 2008, IRL and CART reunited once again as a single open wheel racing league.[15]

Indy Racing League

The Indy Racing League (IRL) is the sanctioning body for oval-based, open wheel racing series in the United States and Japan. Headquartered in Indianapolis, Indiana, the IRL's main event is the Indianapolis 500. This event is an annual race, held over Memorial Day weekend. The first Indianapolis 500 occurred in 1911.

Originally, the IRL only raced on oval tracks; however, in 2004, 3 of the 14 scheduled races were on nonoval tracks at Watkins Glen International (Watkins Glen, New York), Infineon Raceway (Sonoma, California), and in the streets of St. Petersburg, Florida. All but one race takes place in the United States, with the lone international event being the Indy Japan 300, which was held in Motegi, Japan (**Table 25-2**). As many as 27 drivers compete each week to earn points for the overall IRL standings from March to September. Cars have sponsors similar to NASCAR, with XM Satellite Radio, Marlboro, and Target as some of the 16 individual car sponsors. League sponsors include Sunoco and Firestone Tires. The IRL merged with the Champ Car Series in 2008 (**Table 25-3**).

The IRL has departments in production, retail, concessions, media relations, web design, sales, and marketing.

National Hot Rod Association

The world's largest auto racing organization, the National Hot Rod Association (NHRA) has over 35,000 licensed competitors and 80,000 members. Established in 1951 and located in Glendora, California, the NHRA promotes and conducts more than 20 categories of professional drag racing competition. There are over 140 member tracks located throughout North America with competitions running all year long. Tickets to the events range anywhere from $10 to $60. The NHRA's key business partners are Coca-Cola, Lucas Oil, and Summit Racing Equipment. Along with these key partners, the NHRA is officially sponsored by more than 25 companies that help fuel the growth of the association. ESPN is the NHRA's exclusive multimedia partner.

With over 300 employees, the NHRA is composed of nine departments: sales and marketing, national ticket office, membership services, NHRA field marketing, NHRA field office, technical department, junior drag racing league, youth and education services, and online national event registration.

Endnotes

1. Peltz, J. (2006, July 28). Stars and Cars Align. *Los Angeles Times*. Retrieved October 22, 2007, from http://articles.latimes.com/2006/jul/28/sports/sp-nascar28.

2. Lemasters, R. (2007, Sept. 20). Already Ahead of Curve with Junior Merchandise. NASCAR.com. Retrieved August 4, 2008 from http://www.nascar.com/2007/news/business/09/20/dearnhardtjr.merchandise/index.html

3. Trackpass. (n.d.). NASCAR. Retrieved October 22, 2007, from http://www.nascar.com/trackpass.

Table 25-3   Champ Car World Series Schedule (2008)

Race	Circuit	Date
Toyota Grand Prix of Long Beach	Streets of Long Beach, CA	Apr. 20
Champ Car Grand Prix of Houston at JAGFlo Speedway	JAGFlo Speedway at Reliant Park—Houston, TX	Apr. 27
Champ Car Grand Prix at Mazda Raceway Laguna Seca	Mazda Raceway—Monterey, CA	May 18
Champ Car Grand Prix of Belgium at Circuit Zolder	Circuit Zolder-Heusden—Zolder, Belgium	June 1
Gran Premio Champ Car de Espana	Circuitio De Jere—Jerez, Spain	June 8
Grand Prix of Cleveland	Burke Lakefront Airport—Cleveland, OH	June 22
Champ Car Mont-Tremblant	Circuit Mont Tremblant—St. Jovite, Canada	June 29
Steekback Grand Prix of Toronto	Exhibition Place—Toronto, Canada	July 6
Rexall Grand Prix of Edmonton	Rexall Speedway—Edmonton, Canada	July 20
Champ Car Grand Prix of Portland	Portland International Speedway—Portland, OR	July 27
Road America Grand Prix	Road America—Elkhart Lake, WI	Aug. 10
Champ Car Grand Prix of Holland at the TT Circuit Assen	TT Circuit Assen—Assen, Holland	Sept. 14
Gold Cost Indy 300	Gold Coast—Surfers Paradise, Queensland Australia	Oct. 27
Gran Primo Tecate Presentado por Banamex	Autodromo Hermanos Rodriguez—Mexico City, Mexico	Nov. 19

4. History of NASCAR. (n.d.). Racehippie.com. Retrieved October 22, 2007, from http://www .racehippie.com/nascar-history/history-of-nascar.php.

5. History. (n.d.). NASCAR. Retrieved October 22, 2007, from http://www.nascar.com/kyn/history.

6. History of NASCAR. (n.d.). California Motor Speedway. Retrieved October 22, 2007, from http://www .californiaspeedway.com/fan_info/nascar_101_/ history_of_nascar.

7. Ibid.

8. Ibid.

9. Ibid.

10. Ibid.

11. Daytona USA to Celebrate 10th Anniversary with Special Giveaway. (2006, Jan. 24). Race2Win. Retrieved October 22, 2007, from http://www. race2win.net/wc/06/dusac10anni.html.

12. McCullough, B. (2002, Mar. 4). Minor League Status Major League Cost. *The Sporting News.* Retrieved October 22, 2007, from http://findarticles.com/p/ articles/mi_m1208/is_9_226/ai_83667199.

13. Bernstein, A. (2005, Dec. 12). NASCAR Deals: It's All in There. *SportsBusiness Journal.* Retrieved October 22, 2007, from http://www.sportsbusinessjournal .com/index.cfm?fuseaction=search.show_article& articleId=48248&keyword=NASCAR%20deals: %20It%E2%80%99s%20all%20there.

14. NASCAR Dumps XM for Lucrative Five-Year Deal with Sirius. (2005, Feb. 23). *Street and Smith's SportsBusiness Daily*. Retrieved February 18, 2008, from http://www.sportsbusinessdaily.com/index .cfm?fuseaction=sbd.main&storyID=SBD2005022307.

15. After 12 Years of Conflict, IRL and Champ Car Merge. (2008, Feb. 22). *ESPN.com.* Retrieved October 7, 2008, from http://sports.espn.com/rpm/ news/story?id=3259364.

Horse Racing

NATIONAL THOROUGHBRED RACING ASSOCIATION[1,2]

The National Thoroughbred Racing Association (NTRA) is the primary governing body for horse racing in the United States, and also runs the World Thoroughbred Racing Championship, known as the Breeders' Cup. Other major thoroughbred horse races include the Kentucky Derby, Preakness Stakes, and Belmont Stakes, which make up the Triple Crown of horse racing. Thoroughbred racing started in the United States in 1863 when the first major races took place at Saratoga Springs in New York. The NTRA was established in 1998 and has offices located in New York City and Lexington, Kentucky. The NTRA responsibilities include the following:

- Setting rules for thoroughbred racing and racing venues

- Monitoring memberships within the NTRA

- Organizing races throughout the United States

- Promoting thoroughbred racing and selling merchandise

- Lobbying on behalf of the pari-mutuel wagering (handi-capping)

- Licensing breeders

The NTRA is composed of these subsidiaries: NTRA Charities; NTRA Purchasing; NTRA Investments, LLC; and NTRA Productions, LLC. Within these subsidiaries, the NTRA strives to address the economic issues that impact horse racing. Sponsorships and membership dues generate around half of the revenue for the NTRA, while Breeders' Cup Championships and nominations, which are fees paid by the horse's owner in order for them to be eligible to race, generate the other half of the revenues.

The NTRA has several departments, some of which include television and sponsorship, media, sales, communications, and marketing.

THE UNITED STATES TROTTING ASSOCIATION[3]

The United States Trotting Association (USTA) is the official governing body for harness racing in the United States. Harness racing is an equine sport, run with standard-bred horses on tracks of 1/2, 5/8, 7/8, or 1 mile. The drivers are seated behind the horse in a racing bike, also known as a sulky, which the horse pulls around the racetrack. These horses, on average, usually race up to once a week.

Racing occurs year round at some racetracks whereas other tracks operate only during certain months. There are a total of 45 tracks located throughout the United States. Wagering on the races exists at the tracks and at off-track locations. Each track relies heavily on wagering to finance their day-to-day operations.

Created in 1939, the USTA is responsible for setting and enforcing rules in order to promote safe, entertaining competition for the racers and fans. The USTA board of directors consists of 60 members and is headed by a president and an executive vice president. The USTA also is responsible for licensing officials and participants, and registering the horses for racing and breeding purposes.

With headquarters in Columbus, Ohio, the USTA has nearly 80 employees who are divided into districts covering the United States. The USTA has the following administration departments: customer service/human resources, information technology, finance/administrative, public relations, regulations, and strategic planning.

Endnotes

1. NRTA: Industry (n.d.). NRTA.com. Retrieved August 4, 2008, from http://www.ntra.com/industry.aspx.

2. NTRA Annual Reports. (n.d.). *NTRA*. Retrieved October 24, 2007, from http://www.ntra.com/content.aspx?type=other&style=red&id=4396.

3. About the USTA (2008). USTrotting.com. Retrieved August 4, 2008, from http://www.ustrotting.com/usta/ustahome.cfm.

Action Sports

X GAMES

The novel idea of the Extreme Games (X Games) was developed by ESPN management in 1993 to serve as a platform for international action sport athletes to showcase their skills and talents. Designed initially as a summer event, the X Games have evolved into annual summer and winter multi-sport events. The Summer X Games are typically held in August and the Winter X Games are usually held in January and February.

Although the structure has changed over time, currently the Summer Games consist of events in four different sport categories: BMX, moto X, skateboarding, and rally car racing. The Winter Games entail events in the following three sport categories: skiing, snowboarding, and snowmobiling. More information on the various events are outlined in the "Structure" section later in this chapter.

Rhode Island hosted the inaugural Summer X Games in 1995 and Big Bear Lake, California, was the site of the first Winter X Games in 1997. Both the Summer X Games and Winter X Games are held in a different city every few years and the events are subject to change from year to year. The Summer X Games for 2006–2009 are scheduled to be held in Los Angeles, California; the Winter X Games for 2007–2010 are earmarked for Buttermilk Mountain in Aspen, Colorado. The X Games are aired on ESPN and ESPN2 with occasional supplemental coverage on ABC. All of these television outlets are owned and operated by ESPN's parent company, the Walt Disney Company.

ESPN owns and operates the X Games series, and thus reaps all the revenue derived from the production of both events. The company has formed a specific division to run the operations of the X Games. The following departments make up the X Games division: operations, marketing, sponsorship, legal, communications, and network administration. Employees both work at the ESPN offices and are deployed to the various venues for on-site work. The staff relies heavily on local and regional volunteers to assist in spectator management, distributing credentials to guests, and other responsibilities during the event.

History of the X Games[1]

1993

- ESPN management assembled a team to create an event that gathered international action sports athletes to display their skills.

1994

- ESPN announced the first ever Extreme Games to be held in Rhode Island in June 1995.

1995

- The Extreme Games were held in Rhode Island and Vermont from June 24 to July 1.

- Athletes competed in 27 events in nine different sport categories: bungee jumping, eco-challenge, in-line skating, skateboarding, sky surfing, sport climbing, street luge, biking, and water sports.

- For the 1995 games, 198,000 fans turned out.

- Advil, Mountain Dew, Taco Bell, Chevy Trucks, AT&T, Nike, and Miller Lite Ice signed on as sponsors of the first Extreme Games.

- ESPN announced the Extreme Games would be held annually. Rhode Island was selected as the site for the 1996 games.

1996

- The name Extreme Games was changed to X Games, mainly for the sake of brevity and for better branding opportunities.

- The first ever Winter X Games were introduced to begin in 1997. California's Big Bear Lake was chosen as the site for the inaugural games.

1997

- Winter X Games and ABC Sports teamed up, and the events were televised in 198 countries and territories in 21 different languages.
- 38,000 fans turned out for first Winter X Games.
- Athletes in Winter X Games competed in snowboarding, ice climbing, snow mountain bike racing, super-modified shovel racing, and a crossover multi-sport event.
- XTrials was introduced as a way for athletes to qualify for upcoming X Games.

1998

- The Asian X Games, the first ever international qualifying event, was held in Phuket, Thailand.[2]
- Pacific Rim athletes began competing for a limited number of spots for X Games IV.

1999

- Winter X III introduced new disciplines, including women's free skiing.
- Nearly 275,000 fans attended Summer X Games V.

2000

- Winter X IV was held on the East Coast (Mount Snow, Vermont) for the first time, and set attendance records for the Winter Games, drawing 83,500 fans.

2001

- Los Angeles hosted the inaugural Action Sports and Music Awards. The awards event combined action sports athletes, sports legends, musicians, and Hollywood celebrities.

2002

- ESPN announced a new event, X Games Global Championship, to begin in 2003. This event consisted of athletes being grouped by their region of origin to compete in Winter and Summer X Games events. Each region's winter and summer scores were combined to determine a winner.
- Summer X Games VIII was broadcast on ABC, ESPN, and ESPN2 to a record 63 million viewers.

2003

- The Inaugural X Games Global Championship was held in San Antonio, Texas, for the summer events and Whistler Blackcomb Resort in British Columbia for the winter events.
- Team USA accumulated 196 points to win the event, narrowly defeating second place Team Europe who finished second with 176 points. South America, Australia, Asia, and Canada also participated in the event.

2004

- During the Summer X Games IX in Los Angeles, ESPN recognized the Women's Street and Vert contest as an official X Games event.
- Tony Hawk retired after he became the first skateboarder to hit 900 (a trick in which the skater spins 2 1/2 times in the air).[3]

2005

- Inline skating was dropped from the X Games lineup.
- ESPN signed a contract to keep the X Games in Los Angeles through 2009.

2006

- August television viewership across the three networks that carried coverage (ABC Sports, ESPN, and ESPN2) set an all-time record of 747,130 households, a 45% increase from 2004.[4]
- The downhill derby (combining elements of freestyle snowboarding, alpine racing, and high-flying motocross with four racers snowboarding down the track at once), a Winter X Games staple, made its first Olympic debut in Turin, Italy.
- New Balance became a gold-level sponsor of the Winter X Games, valued at $2 million.

2007

- The events Mono-Skier X, Snowmobile Freestyle, and Snowboarding Best Trick Showdown were all added to the competition schedule. However, the Moto X event was removed from the Winter X games competition.
- $11 billion was spent in the United States on skateboarding, snowboarding, and surfing gear. This number was up from $5 billion in 1995, the year of the first X Games.[5]

Structure of X Games

Events

- Summer Games
  - Held annually (typically in August)
  - Site determined through partnerships forged by ESPN with various host cities
    - 2006–2009: Los Angeles, California
  - Sport categories
    - BMX
    - Moto X
    - Skateboarding
    - Rally car racing

- Winter Games
  - Held annually (typically January or February)
  - Site determined through partnerships forged by ESPN with various host cities
    - 2007–2010: Buttermilk Mountain, Aspen/Snowmass, Colorado
  - Sport categories
    - Skiing
    - Snowboarding
    - Snowmobiling

Money Matters for the X Games

Sources of Revenue

- Television broadcast revenues
  - The Summer and Winter X Games events are televised on ESPN and ABC; both stations are owned by Walt Disney, so ESPN receives advertisement revenues for commercials aired during the games. Therefore, ESPN does not receive rights fees for the broadcasting rights.
- Other media
  - EXPN Radio programming is available through 79 affiliates across the country. The program features X Games events, a calendar of recent action sports events, and interviews with action sports athletes.[6] ESPN receives the advertising revenues.

Sponsorship

- The X Games have different sponsors for the Summer and Winter Games and divides the sponsors into three categories: Gold, Associate, and Sponsor. Both games attract sponsors from varying product categories such as beverages, food, and consumer products. Sponsors pay an annual fee to ESPN to become a recognized partner and for other related services. Sponsors include Taco Bell, Schick, and Oakley.

Merchandise and Licensing

- Ultimate Athletic Sportswear is the exclusive supplier of ESPN X Games merchandise. Under this agreement, ESPN allows Ultimate Athletic Sportswear the right to use the X Games logo to create merchandise to be sold to fans. In return, ESPN receives a merchandise fee from Ultimate Athletic Sportswear for this partnership.

AST Dew Tour[7]

The AST Dew Tour, or Action Sports Tour, was founded in 2005. The tour, owned by NBC Universal and recently MTV (replacing Live Nation), is composed of five events in different cities throughout the United States. Each tour stop hosts multiple action sports competitions. The winner of

Shaun White, nicknamed the "Flying Tomato," participates in the Skateboard VERT during a recent AST Dew Tour event. In the 2007 tour, White had three first-place finishes and two third-place finishes in the VERT. White also is a 2006 Olympic Gold medalist in the halfpipe.

each event wins prize money in addition to accumulating points towards the $1 million bonus pool that is distributed based on year-end standings. Total event coverage of the tour consists of 22 hours of live action on NBC and 10 hours on USA, and a 1-hour highlight on NBC.

The Tour is composed of primary sports such as skateboarding, BMX, and freestyle motocross. In addition, each tour stop features a unique event such as snowboarding or BMX Supercross. At the end of the season, the Tour awards champions in each sport category the Dew Cup. The AST Dew Tour runs from June until October. There is one Tour stop per month and each event last 4 days: Thursday–Sunday. In 2008, the Tour stops were the following:

- Panasonic Open: Baltimore, Maryland
- Right Guard Open: Cleveland, Ohio
- Wendy's Invitational: Portland, Oregon
- Toyota Challenge: Salt Lake City, Utah
- PlayStation Pro: Orlando, Florida

Beginning in December 2008, the AST launched the AST Winter Dew Tour. The Winter Dew Tour shares a similar structure to the summer competition and is based on a cumulative points system that decides the champion of each sport at the final winter event. However there also is a $15,000 first-place purse at each stop. In 2008–2009, the AST Winter Dew Tour stops were the following:

- Breckenridge, Colorado
- Mount Snow, Vermont
- Lake Tahoe, California

The AST Dew Tour also incorporates entertainment festivals within each Tour venue and includes live music, video gaming, and interactive events. Tickets to tour events cost

$12 for both adults and children. The Tour has formed broadcasting partnerships with NBC Sports, USA Network, Fuel TV, Fox Sports Radio, and Universal HD to broadcast the Tour events on television and over the radio.

Mountain Dew is the title sponsor of the Tour. Event title sponsors include Panasonic, Right Guard Xtreme, Toyota, Vans, and Sony PlayStation. Associate sponsors include MasterCard, Mongoose bikes, Oxy, Peanut Chews, Slim Jims, Verizon, and most recently Ball Park Franks. The AST Dew Tour is headquartered in Aurora, Illinois. Departments at the APST Dew Tour include administration, event marketing and promotions, public relations, and partner relations.

LG Action Sports World Tour[8]

The LG Action Sports World Tour was created in 2003 to take advantage of the exploding growth and popularity of action sports. The tour is designed to showcase action sports athletes to new audiences and to expand the footprint of action sports worldwide.

In 2007, the LG Action Sports program comprised seven events in the following locations worldwide: Amsterdam, Netherlands; Birmingham, England; Berlin, Germany; Paris, France; Richmond, Virginia; Los Angeles, California; and Dallas, Texas, with expanded worldwide television. The season culminated with the LG Action Sports Championships, which were held in October at the Manchester Evening News Arena in Manchester, England. Events included BMX, freelance motocross, skateboarding, and inline skating. The tour is televised internationally to more than 180 countries globally via 19 different networks. In the United States, tour events are broadcast on Versus and CBS.

The LG Action Sports World Tour is produced by ASA Events and is sponsored by LG Electronics, Inc., a major electronics and telecommunication company based in Seoul, South Korea. ASA Events is the largest action sports event and television production company in the United States. The company develops, manages, and executes over 200 action sports events annually. ASA Events is headquartered in Marina del Rey, California, and consists of several departments including sponsor services, sales, event production, accounting, and public relations.

Endnotes

1. The History of X. (n.d.). ESPN.com. Retrieved November 14, 2007, from http://www.espneventmedia.com/files/HistoryofX-XG13.pdf?eventmedia_session=b5e3ba113.

2. About International X Games. (n.d.). EXPN.com. Retrieved October 30, 2007, from http://expn.go.com/intl/s/about.html.

3. Tony Hawk. (n.d.). SkaterLegends.com. Retrieved October 30, 2007, from http://www.skaterlegends.com/skaters/tony_hawk.htm.

4. The History of Winter X. (2007). *ESPNEventMedia.com*. Retrieved August 4, 2008, from http://www.espneventmedia.com/pdf/BriefHistoryofWinterX.pdf?eventmedia_session=b5e3ba113.

5. Iwata, E. (2008, Mar. 10). Tony Hawk Leaps to Top of Financial Empire. *USA Today*, p. 1B.

6. EXPN Radio. (n.d.). *ESPNRadio.com*. Retrieved August 4, 2008, from http://espnradio.espn.go.com/espnradio/story?storyId=1757562.

7. AST Dew Tour: Home. (n.d.). Retrieved August 4, 2008, from http://www.ast.com.

8. LG Action Sports: Home. (n.d.). Retrieved August 4, 2008, from http://www.lgactionsports.com.

Olympic Sports

THE OLYMPIC GAMES

The Olympic Games have been a part of sports history since ancient Greece; however, although the underlying concept of the games may still be intact, the modern games have changed significantly. The first documented occurrence of the Olympic Games was in 776 B.C. In their original form, Olympic competitions were held in conjunction with religious ceremonies. As the Romans gained power in Greece, the Olympic Games slowly dissipated and eventually ceased to exist.

The Olympic Games were revived in 1896 by a newly created International Olympic Committee (IOC). The first modern games were held in Athens, Greece, and, with that, the Olympics as we know them today was born. In the early years, competitions such as figure skating and ice hockey were included in the Olympic program alongside track and other summer-based sports. However, starting in 1924, two separate competitions were created, called the Winter Olympics and the Summer Olympics. The Olympics were held every 4 years, with the Summer and Winter Games taking place in the same year; however, this changed following the 1992 Games. Under a revised schedule, the Winter Games were held in Lillehammer, Norway, in 1994 and the Summer Games were held in Atlanta, Georgia, in 1996. This schedule of alternating the Summer and Winter Games every 2 years has been followed ever since. In 2008, the Summer Olympics were held in Beijing, China. The next games will be the Winter Olympics in Vancouver, Canada, in 2010, followed by the Summer Olympics in London, England, in 2012 and the 2014 Winter Olympics in Sochi, Russia.

The Olympic Games are a large operation that takes a great deal of work, time, planning, and money to operate successfully. In the 2008 Beijing Games (Summer Olympics), a record 205 countries were represented at the Olympic Games. In total, there were 302 events and over 11,000 participating athletes. The 2006 Torino Games (Winter Olympics) witnessed 81 countries competing with 2,987 athletes participating in 15 sports and a total of 84 events.

The planning process for the Olympic Games includes overall planning and program management services. The venue's responsibilities for the Games range from structuring and managing systems to developing plans, budgets, schedules, and performance protocols necessary to ensure the successful delivery of the Games. The main areas of focus when planning are program integration, master scheduling, and operations management.

The host city for an Olympic Games is chosen 7 years prior to the Games' beginning; however, the Organizing Committee of the Olympic Games (OCOG) begins its preparation to bid years ahead of the final vote.

Prior to the 1984 Summer Olympics in Los Angeles, funding for the Olympics mostly came from governments; however, starting with the 1984 Olympic Games, there has been a significantly increased reliance on private funding from television rights, sponsorships, and corporations to generate revenues to cover the cost of hosting the Olympics.

OCOGs typically have 25,000 volunteers for the Winter Games and 100,000 volunteers for the Summer Games to help with planning and execution. The Olympic Games headquarters are located in Lausanne, Switzerland, and the IOC consists of over 100 active members. The active members come from International Federations, National Olympic Committees, Olympic Organizing Committees, administrators in the sports world, and Olympic athletes.

Structure of the Olympics

The Olympics have become more businesslike, much like other sporting events. To manage successfully the complicated nature of the Games, a formal organizational structure has been put in place. The significant entities involved with the Games include the International Olympic Committee (IOC), International Federations (IFs), National Governing Bodies (NGBs), National Olympic Committees (NOCs), and Organizing Committees of the Olympic Games (OCOGs). **Figure 28-1** illustrates how these parties relate to one another.

International Olympic Committee

At the top of Figure 28-1 is the International Olympic Committee (IOC). Created in 1894 to revive the ancient Greek games, the IOC is an international, nongovernmental, not-for-profit organization located in Switzerland. Its main duty is to oversee all aspects of the Olympic movement, and its most visible role is that of supervisor for the Summer and Winter Olympic Games. The IOC is also responsible for selecting host cities for the Games. As the governing body of the Olympics, the IOC owns all rights to the Olympic symbol, anthem, flag, and motto.

International Federations

International Federations (IFs) are the next level of the Olympic structure. The IFs are nongovernmental bodies given the authority by the IOC to administer specific sports on the international level. Among other things, it is the role of the IFs to determine who is eligible to compete in that sport, including whether to allow professional athletes to compete in the Olympic Games in that sport. A turning point occurred in 1992, when NBA players were first allowed to compete in Olympic basketball competition, resulting in the United States fielding a Dream Team of future NBA Hall of Famers. The decision to allow NBA players to compete at the Olympics was made by Federation Internationale de Basketball, or FIBA, the IF for basketball. Other prominent IFs, including the IIHF (hockey) and ITF (tennis), have

allowed professional athletes to compete in the Olympic Games. In general, it is the responsibility of the IF to safeguard its particular game against corruption, to grow the game worldwide, and to foster competition among member nations. One particular International Federation, FIFA, is discussed in Chapter 20, *Soccer*.

National Governing Bodies

While the IFs govern a particular sport on the international level, National Governing Bodies (NGBs) govern the sport on a national level. For example, USA Basketball is the NGB for international basketball in the United States. As an NGB, USA Basketball is subject to the rules and regulations set forth by FIBA, the designated IF for basketball; however, within this framework, USA Basketball governs all basketball-related activities undertaken by the United States as they pertain to FIBA-sanctioned international competition. USA Basketball counts among its members a number of prominent sports organizations, including the NCAA, the Amateur Athletic Union (AAU), and the NBA—entities operating nationally active basketball programs.

USA Basketball is discussed later in this chapter. It provides greater detail on the specific operations and activities of a prominent NGB. For additional information about the structure of NGBs, see the organizational chart for USA Swimming found in Chapter 68.

National Olympic Committees

Under the supervision of the IOC, National Olympic Committees (NOCs) administer Olympic programs for a particular nation. For example, the United States Olympic Committee (USOC) is the NOC for all activities related to the Olympics in the United States. The NOCs ensure all Olympic activities throughout the country comply with IOC standards. This helps to create a uniform playing field from country to country. It is also the responsibility of the NOC to provide its athletes with a competitive opportunity to earn a spot on the Olympic roster. This is primarily accomplished through the development of training programs and fundraising. In addition, the NOCs supervise any attempt by a city in their country to host an Olympic Games. If more than one city from a country is vying to host the Games, then that country's NOC will select the city for consideration in the IOC's selection process. More information about the USOC can be found in the section "United States Olympic Committee" later in this chapter.

Organizing Committees of the Olympic Games

When a city decides to submit a bid to host the Olympic Games, a governing body from that city is formed. These bodies are known as Organizing Committees of the Olympic Games (OCOGs), or Local Organizing Committees (LOCs). If the city is chosen by the IOC to host an Olympic Games, the OCOG is responsible for coordinating all the operations

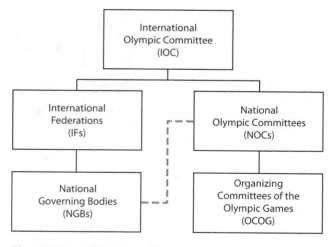

Figure 28-1   Olympic Structure

undertaken to stage the Games. For example, the Salt Lake Organizing Committee was the governing body for Salt Lake City, Utah, when it hosted the 2002 Winter Olympics. Once a city is named as the host city, the OCOG works in collaboration with the IOC, the host country's NOC, and the host city itself. The OCOG acts as a legal and administrative entity employing hundreds of workers and thousands of volunteers in the organizing, planning, implementation, and operational phases of preparing for and running the Olympic Games. The OCOGs are responsible for developing infrastructure, facilities, transportation, athlete housing, and any other elements deemed necessary by the IOC to ensure a successful Olympiad. Most countries' OCOGs receive funding from their national government to stage the Games; the United States is one of the only countries that does not grant any federal government subsidies to a city hosting the Olympic Games. Therefore, a U.S. host city has the additional responsibility of providing additional revenue from the Games in order to offset the expenditures undertaken in hosting the games.

Timeline of Recent Olympic Games

1980

- The highlight of the Winter Olympic Games at Lake Placid, New York, was an unexpected gold medal victory by the U.S. men's hockey team. The United States' victory over the Soviet Union in the semi-finals was nicknamed "The Miracle on Ice."

- The largest boycott of an Olympics in history took place at the Summer Olympic Games in Moscow following the Soviet invasion of Afghanistan in December 1979. The United States and 61 other countries decided to boycott the Olympics. Approximately 5,000 athletes participated, representing 81 countries.

1984

- Corporate sponsors emerged for the first time in the Summer Games held in Los Angeles, California. The Games had 43 companies who were licensed to sell official Olympic products. The Olympic Games generated a profit of $225 million, the first Olympic profit since 1932.[1]

- Fourteen Eastern Bloc countries and allies including the Soviet Union, Cuba, and East Germany (but not Romania) boycotted the Los Angeles Games. The USSR announced its intention not to participate on May 8, 1984, citing security concerns, but some believed that it was revenge for the boycott of the 1980 Moscow Games by the United States.

1985

- The Olympic Program (TOP) was established by the IOC. TOP is used to establish a diversified revenue base for the Olympic Games and Olympic Movement. TOP

Sponsors, who are multinational corporations, receive exclusive marketing rights and use of all Olympic symbols. TOP Partners are also official sponsors of the Olympic Games, the IOC, the Organizing Committees, and the 199 National Olympic Committees and Olympic teams.

1988

- Because they were not chosen as the site of the Games, North Korea boycotted the Seoul Olympic Games.

- Drug tests resulted in the disqualification of several athletes from the Seoul Olympic Games, including 100-meter champion and "The World's Fastest Man," Canadian Ben Johnson. Testing was first introduced at the 1968 Olympic Winter Games in Grenoble, France, and at the Summer Olympic Games in Mexico City in 1968.

1992

- For the first time in 20 years, every nation with a National Olympic Committee (NOC) was represented at the Summer Olympic Games in Barcelona, Spain.

- The amateur rule was revised, allowing men's basketball to be open to all players, including professionals. The United States sent the Dream Team, which featured NBA stars such as Magic Johnson, Michael Jordan, and Larry Bird.

- The 1992 Olympic Games in Albertville, France, were the last Winter Games to be staged in the same year as the Summer Games.

1994

- In 1986, the IOC voted to change the schedule of the Olympic Games so that the Summer and Winter Games would be held in different years. To adjust to this new schedule, the Winter Games in Lillehammer, Norway, were held in 1994, the only time that two Games have been staged two years apart.

1996

- U.S. government support of the Olympic Games ceased with the Atlanta Games, leading to further commercialization of the Games for financial support. The U.S. Olympic Committee was one of only a few of the 198 NOCs that did not receive a government subsidy.

- On July 27, during a concert held in the Centennial Olympic Park in Atlanta, a terrorist bomb killed one person and injured another 110 people.

1998

- The Winter Olympic Games in Nagano returned to Japan after 26 years.

- Snowboarding debuted as an official Olympic sport.

2000

- The Summer Olympic Games in Sydney were the largest to date, with 10,651 athletes from 199 nations competing in 300 events.
- 16,033 media individuals were present, consisting of 5,298 written press and 10,735 broadcasters.[2]

2002

- The Salt Lake City Winter Olympic Games saw the expansion of the Olympic program to 78 events, more than any previously held Winter Olympic Games.

2004

- The Summer Olympic Games in Athens returned to Greece, the home of both the ancient Olympics and the first modern Olympics.
- A record 201 countries participated in the Olympic Games.
- The Athens Games reached a larger audience than ever before, as 3.9 billion people had access to the television coverage compared to 3.6 billion for Sydney in 2000.[3]

2006

- The Winter Olympic Games in Torino returned to Italy for the first time since 1956.
- A record 2,508 athletes competed, and a record 26 countries took home medals.

2008

- The summer Olympics were held in Beijing, People's Republic of China, with over 11,000 athletes and approximately 20,000 accredited media.
- A new service was developed where the media could connect to the IOC NewsRoom, a multimedia platform where broadcast-quality videos of the latest IOC activities and events, audio files, photographs, press releases, and background information could be downloaded free of charge.

Money Matters for the Olympic Games

Revenue

- Television contracts
  - Sales of television rights for the 2010 Winter Games in Vancouver and the 2012 London Olympics will bring the International Olympic Committee $3.8 billion, a 40% increase on the $2.6 billion they received for the 2006 and 2008 games in Turin and Beijing.[4]
- Sponsorship revenue
  - From 2001–2004, sponsorship revenues generated more than $1.45 billion. Along with TV rights, they are the most important revenue streams for the Olympics. Approximately 35% of the operating budget is expected to be raised through commercial sponsors.[5]
- TOP program (2001–2004 numbers)[6]
  - Multinational corporations pay for exclusive marketing and sponsorship rights for the Olympic Games and Olympic Movement.
  - Some of the TOP partners include Coca-Cola, IBM, John Hancock, Kodak, Matsushita/Panasonic, McDonald's, Samsung, *Sports Illustrated/Time*, UPS, Atos Origin, Swatch, Visa, and Xerox.
  - Ticket sales: $441 million (11% of total revenues)
  - Licensing: $86.5 million (2% of total revenues)[7]
  - Other: National funding and local sponsorships
- Distribution of revenues
- The IOC distributes 92% of its revenues to organizations throughout the Olympic Movement to support the staging of the Olympic Games and to promote the worldwide development of Olympic sport. The IOC retains approximately 8% of the revenue for its operational and administrative expenses. Each country's Olympic committee also generates revenues from its own sponsorship deals and national funding.
- National Organizing Committees receive the majority of the other revenues because they are responsible for the athletes and teams that compete in the Games.

Expenses (vary by location)

- Facilities
  - Rental
  - Construction
  - Security
    - China spent $6.5 billion on security for the 2008 Summer Olympics.[8]
  - Media
  - Marketing
  - Technology

UNITED STATES OLYMPIC COMMITTEE

The United States Olympic Committee (USOC) is the National Olympic Committee (NOC) for the United States. A nonprofit organization, it was created by Congress through the Amateur Sports Act of 1978, which was later amended by the Ted Stevens Olympic and Amateur Sports Act (1998) to give the USOC the structure it still uses today.

The USOC is designed to support U.S. Olympic and Paralympic athletes in achieving athletic competitive excellence. Located in Colorado Springs, Colorado, the USOC is composed of 72 member organizations. The USOC is also responsible for all activities in the United States related to the Olympics, Paralympics, and Pan American Games. As an NOC, it establishes training programs and funds so athletes have an opportunity to develop and compete for a spot on the Olympic team, and then compete on an international basis. The USOC's Games Preparation Committee and the USOC Board of Directors approve the selection procedures and/or Olympic Trial dates to determine who will represent the United States at the Olympics. Each athlete must meet the requirements of his or her respective sport's International Federation and National Governing Body (NGB) to be eligible. It is also the responsibility of the USOC to manage the overall performance of the U.S. team.

Along with funding responsibilities, the USOC oversees, selects, and supervises any bid by a U.S. city to host an Olympic Games. During the bidding process, applicant cities submit a questionnaire that includes summaries of the bid book and an outline of how the city plans to stage the Games broken down into 18 topics, including venues, budgets, marketing, finance, security, accommodation, past experience, and transportation. Once the bid book is reviewed, a short-list is created from the pool of applicant cities based on the questionnaires. If requirements are met based on the questionnaires, the applicant cities will become candidate cities. The five highest-rated candidates proceed to the evaluation stage. After the evaluations, USOC board members vote to determine which host city to support and recommend to the IOC.

The USOC also must implement any rule changes passed by the IOC in its national Olympic programs. This helps maintain uniform rules from country to country. Thus, the USOC must conform to the policies and regulations set forth by the IOC. Generally, an NOC is responsible for representing the interests of its country with respect to the Olympic Games, and is obligated to follow the rules and regulations as defined by the IOC. When disputes arise, NOCs have extensive arbitration procedures to address the issues.

The USOC is led by an administrator and a 12-member and leadership staff along with an 11-member board of directors who are responsible for establishing policies to be followed by the USOC staff when carrying out the business and activities of the committee. The staff is responsible for providing the vision for the USOC, as well as deciding on various issues, including budgeting and educating athletes on rules and regulations.

The USOC places considerable emphasis on how U.S. athletes and teams perform at the Games. The emphasis is reflected in how the NGB and Paralympic Sports Organization (PSO) are funded through USOC resources. The NGB is authorized to govern each specific amateur sport through establishing the rules of the sport, choosing teams for international competitions, certifying officials, and running national championships.

The Paralympic games are held in the Olympic host city 10 days after the Olympic Games and are the responsibility of the Olympic Games Organizing Committee. Olympic-style games for athletes with disabilities were organized for the first time in Rome in 1960. Since then, the number of athletes participating in the Summer Paralympic Games has increased from 400 athletes and 23 countries in 1960 to more than 4,200 athletes and 148 countries in 2008.

The USOC relies heavily on interns to help with its operations. Interns have been used in the past in areas such as broadcasting, journalism, marketing, sports administration, and sport sciences. Immediate news and updates involving the USOC and any one of the 48 summer and winter sports can be accessed at www.usocpressbox.org.

Structure of the USOC

Organization

- The USOC has a volunteer leadership group consisting of a board of directors and four committees. There is also a chief executive officer who heads a paid administrative staff.
- Administrators and leadership staff: 13 administrators including a CEO, CCO (chief communications officer), COO, CFO, chief of sport performance, general counsel, and others
- Board of directors: 11-member board
- National Governing Bodies: 39
- Pan American Sports Organizations: 6 (bowling, karate, racquetball, roller sports, squash, and water skiing)
- Affiliated sport organizations: 3 (dancesport, orienteering, and underwater swimming)
- Community-based multi-sport councils: 15
- Education-based multi-sport councils: 4 (National Association of Intercollegiate Athletics [NAIA], National Collegiate Athletic Association [NCAA], National Federation of State High School Associations [NFSHSA], National Junior College Athletic Association [NJCAA])

Facilities

- Olympic training complexes
  - Olympic Training Center: Colorado Springs, Colorado
  - Olympic Training Center: Lake Placid, New York
  - Arco Olympic Training Center: Chula Vista, California
  - Home Depot Center: Carson, California
  - Olympic Education Center: Marquette, Michigan
  - Olympic and Paralympic Training Center: Lakeshore Foundation, Birmingham, Alabama

Money Matters for the USOC[9]

Revenues

- In 2006, the USOC reported revenues of approximately $221 million.

Sponsorship

- Worldwide sponsors are the highest level of international sponsors. These TOP (The Olympic Program) sponsors can exercise marketing rights across NOC borders (i.e., across multiple countries). Some of these TOP sponsors include Coca-Cola, Atos Origin, General Electric, McDonald's, Omega, Panasonic, Visa, Samsung, Lenovo, John Hancock, and Eastman Kodak.

- Partner sponsorships are the domestic-level sponsorships that support U.S. Olympic teams. Anheuser-Busch, AT&T, Bank of America, General Motors, The Home Depot, and Johnson & Johnson are partner sponsors of the USOC.

- Other sponsors contribute enough money to be official sponsors of the Olympic Games and the USOC. These include Hilton Hotels, Jet Set Sports, Kellogg's, Nike, and 24-Hour Fitness.

- There is also a list of suppliers who contribute private funds to the Olympics and USOC.

- There is no continuous government subsidy. The USOC is one of the few NOCs without such a subsidy.

Licensing

- For the 2008 U.S. Olympic & Paralympic Teams, there are 33 license agreements, which allow the licensee to use the USOC logo on various products.

- Some licensees include Nike, Roots, XP Apparel, Omega, and Dale of Norway.

- The licensed merchandise represents over 85% of revenue for the USOC's 2005 budget.

Expenses

- In 2006, the USOC reported $149.2 million in total expenses.
- Program services: $108.4 million
  - $52.5 million for direct NGB and athlete support
  - $7.2 million for paralympic sports
  - $48.71 million for member services, including:
    - $23.6 million to operate the U.S. Olympic Training Centers in Colorado Springs, Colorado; Chula Vista, California; and Lake Placid, New York
    - $7.8 million for international competitions
    - $3.4 million for sports science
    - $4.06 million for drug control
  - Support services: $40.37 million for support services such as sales and marketing and general and administrative activities

USA BASKETBALL

USA Basketball is the National Governing Body (NGB) for basketball in the United States. Based in Colorado Springs, Colorado, USA Basketball is a nonprofit organization, and is recognized by the International Basketball Federation (FIBA), which is the International Federation for basketball, and the U.S. Olympic Committee. Governed by a 10-member executive committee and 25-member board of directors, USA Basketball is run by representatives from both the professional and amateur ranks. Val Ackerman, founding president of the WNBA; James Delany, commissioner of the Big Ten Conference; and Stu Jackson, NBA senior vice president, are some of the board members of USA Basketball.

Along with several administrative responsibilities, USA Basketball is responsible for organizational work, which includes developing athletes, organizing teams, instructing coaches and officials, and scheduling events. USA Basketball is responsible for selection, training, and fielding of all U.S. teams that compete in FIBA-sponsored international basketball competitions, as well as for some national competitions. These teams compete internationally, and must abide by the rules established and administered by FIBA, which differ slightly from traditional NCAA or NBA rules. Some of the international basketball competitions sponsored by FIBA include the FIBA World Championship, Pan American Games, U21 FIBA World Championships, World University Games, U19 World Championships/Junior National Teams, and Hoop Summit.

Prior to October 1989, FIBA prohibited professional basketball players from participating in international competition; however, once FIBA modified its rules, USA Basketball admitted the NBA as an active member of USA Basketball. This led to the creation of the original Dream Team that competed in the Olympic Games held in Barcelona, Spain, in 1992. The Dream Team defeated its opponents by an average of 44 points, won the gold medal, and provided the world with an opportunity to witness the greatest NBA players compete together for the first time internationally.

USA Basketball is sponsored by Nike, McDonald's, State Farm Insurance, and Gatorade. As marketing partner and exclusive apparel outfitter, Nike provides uniforms, warm-ups, and practice gear for all USA Basketball events and teams including the 2008 Beijing Olympics and the 2010 FIBA World Championships in Istanbul, Turkey. The deal with all four sponsors is estimated at $16 million, with each sponsor contributing close to $4 million.

Headquartered in Colorado Springs, Colorado, USA Basketball employs professionals in departments such as communications, finance and administration, and competitive programs.

History of USA Basketball

1932

- The International Basketball Federation (FIBA) was formed by Argentina, Czechoslovakia, Greece, Italy, Latvia, Portugal, Romania, and Switzerland. FIBA is the world governing body for basketball.

1934

- The United States, Austria, Belgium, Egypt, Estonia, France, Germany, Poland, and Spain joined FIBA. At this time, 17 nations were members of FIBA.

1936

- The first Olympic basketball competition was played in Berlin. Twenty-three of the 32 teams in FIBA played in the games.

1937

- The National Basketball League (NBL) started its first season of play in the United States.

1946

- The Basketball Association of America (BAA), a rival league of the NBL, was established.

1949

- The NBL joined the BAA and they created the National Basketball Association (NBA). At the time, there were 17 teams.

1972

- The United States suffered its first loss in international competition by losing to the Soviet Union in the gold-medal game of the Munich Olympics.

1974

- The Amateur Basketball Federation of the United States of America (ABAUSA) was formed and officially recognized by FIBA and the U.S. Olympic Committee. ABAUSA became the national governing body of basketball in the United States.

1976

- For the first time, women's basketball was recognized as a medal sport at the Olympics in Montreal, Canada.
- The ABA merged four teams with the NBA, with the remaining three ABA teams dissolving.

1978

- The Amateur Sports Act of 1978 was enacted by Congress. This act created the United States Olympic Committee to promote and support physical fitness and public participation in athletic activities by encouraging development programs in its member organizations.

1979

- ABAUSA Basketball relocated from Jacksonville, Illinois, to the U.S. Olympic Training Center in Colorado Springs, Colorado, as a result of the Amateur Sports Act of 1978.

1980

- For the first time, ABAUSA handled the selection of the men's and women's Olympic basketball teams.

1989

- The FIBA world congress voted to eliminate the distinction between professional and amateur basketball players in FIBA events. This made professional basketball players eligible to play in the Olympics.
- ABAUSA changed its name to USA Basketball.

1992

- Professional players participated for the first time at the Summer Olympics in Barcelona, Spain. The U.S. team was known as the Dream Team and went on to win the gold medal at the games.

1996

- The U.S. Olympic Team dominated competition as the second Dream Team defeated Yugoslavia to win the gold medal in the Atlanta Olympics.

2000

- The U.S. men's basketball team defeated France for the gold medal in the 2000 Sydney Games. The U.S. played in several tight games during the 2000 Olympics en route to their third consecutive Olympic gold medal.

2002

- FIBA membership reached 211 nations.

2004

- For the first time since NBA players were allowed to participate in the Olympics (1992), the U.S. men's basketball team failed to win the gold medal in the Olympic Games in Athens, Greece. The U.S. team finished in third place and received the bronze medal.

2006

- The U.S. men's basketball team received the bronze medal in the 2006 FIBA World Championships in Japan. Spain won gold and Greece received silver.

2008

- Nicknamed the "Redeem Team," the U.S. Men's basketball team won the gold medal in the 2008 Summer Games in Beijing.

Structure of USA Basketball

Member Associations

- Amateur Athletic Union (AAU)
- Continental Basketball Association (CBA)
- National Association of Basketball Coaches (NABC)
- National Association of Intercollegiate Athletics (NAIA)
- National Basketball Association (NBA)
- National Basketball Association Developmental League (D-League)
- National Collegiate Athletic Association (NCAA)
- National Federation of State High School Associations (NFSHSA)
- National Junior College Athletic Association (NJCAA)
- National Pro-Am City League Association (NPACLA)
- National Wheelchair Basketball Association (NWBA)
- United States Armed Forces
- USA Deaf Sports Federation (USADSF)
- Women's Basketball Association (WNBA)
- Women's Basketball Coaches Association (WBCA)

Organization

- Executive committee: 10-member committee headed by Val Ackerman
- Board of directors: 25 members, appointed and elected by active members

Money Matters for USA Basketball

Sources of Revenue

- Television broadcast revenues
  - USA Basketball receives revenue from selling rights fees to its exhibition games to different countries. Countries such as France, Germany, Italy, and Spain pay fees of over $100,000 while smaller countries like Lithuania pay significantly less, generally around $15,000.
- Other media
  - Radio
  - Internet
  - Sponsorship
    - USA Basketball has sponsorship agreements with Nike, State Farm Insurance, Gatorade, and McDonald's. These sponsors pay an annual fee to USA Basketball to become a recognized partner and for other related services. USA Basketball realizes $16 million in revenues from these partnerships, with each agreement totaling roughly $4 million.
- Merchandise and licensing
  - Nike is the Official Uniform and Footwear supplier of USA Basketball and provides uniforms, warm-ups, and practice gear for all USA Basketball events. Under this agreement, USA Basketball garners an annual merchandise fee from Nike.

PAN AMERICAN GAMES

The Pan American Games are an international multi-sport competition between the countries of the Americas every 4 years in the year preceding the Olympic Games. Modeled after the International Olympic Committee, the Pan American Sports Organization (PASO) was created in 1955 as the organizer of the games, and includes members from 42 countries from North America, Central America, South America, and the Caribbean. The Pan American Games consist of all Summer Olympic sports as well as some non-Olympic sports, and serves as an Olympic qualifying event for the athletes in many of the sports. Some of the sports that are played at the games include baseball, basketball, field hockey, sailing, soccer, and squash.

The first Pan American Games took place in 1951 in Buenos Aires, Argentina; however, the origin of the games dates back to 1932 when several Latin American representatives of the International Olympic Committee proposed the creation of a competition that would include all the countries in the Americas. The 2007 Pan American Games were held in Rio de Janeiro, Brazil, and in 2011 they will be held in Guadalajara, Mexico. Typically, the Pan American Games are held in the summer, from June to August.

The PASO works in collaboration with the host city, and it relies on 5,000–10,000 volunteers to help run the games.

Official sponsors, partners, and suppliers of the Pan American Games vary depending on the site of the host city.

SPECIAL OLYMPICS[10]

Founded in 1968 by Eunice Kennedy Shriver, younger sister of former President John F. Kennedy, the Special Olympics is an international, nonprofit organization that provides opportunities for individuals with intellectual and physical disabilities to develop physically and socially through athletic training and competition. Nearly 2.2 million adults and children participate in the Special Olympics in more than 200 programs in 150 countries. The Special Olympics offers year-round training and competition in 26 Olympic-type summer and winter sports.

Since 2000 and the inception of the Campaign for Growth campaign, the Special Olympics experienced tremendous growth and has become a worldwide organization. The Special Olympic Games are held every 4 years, like the Olympics, with summer and winter games alternating every 2 years. Ireland hosted the Summer Games in

2003; Japan hosted the Winter Games in 2005; and China hosted the Summer Games in 2007. There is no cost for individuals to compete in the Special Olympics. The Special Olympics provides athletes with a chance to compete at various levels ranging from local and state/provincial competitions to the national and global games.

The headquarters of the Special Olympics are located in Washington, DC. The types of jobs available at the Special Olympics include visual media manager, global event marketing manager, media and public relations manager, online fundraising director, corporate sponsorships director, and health programs manager.

Endnotes

1. Burbank, M. J., Andranovich, G., and Heying, C. H. (2002). Mega-Events, Urban Development, and Public Policy. *Review of Policy Research,* vol. 19, issue 3, pp. 179–202.

2. Lyles, C. (2008, Feb. 12). Countdown to the Beijing Olympics. *British Daily Telegraph.* Retrieved August 4, 2008, from http://www.telegraph.co.uk/sport/othersports/2432940/Countdown-to-the-Beijing-Olympics.html.

3. 2004 Olympic Section. (n.d.). Olympic Movement. Retrieved August 4, 2008, from http://www.olympic.org/uk/games/past/index_uk.asp?OLGT=1&OLGY=2004.

4. Olympic TV Revenue to Increase. (2008, May 8). *Sportsbusiness.com.* Retrieved August 13, 2008, from http://www.sportbusiness.com/news/167610/olympic-tv-revenue-to-increase.

5. Downes, S. (2006, Feb. 1). Charities and Others Fear Olympics Cash Drought. *The Times* (London). Retrieved August 4, 2008, from http://business.timesonline.co.uk/tol/business/industry_sectors/media/article723708.ece.

6. Introduction to Olympic Marketing: Revenue Sources 2001–2004. (2008). Olympics.org. Retrieved August 14, 2008, from http://www.olympic.org/uk/organisation/facts/introduction/index_uk.asp.

7. Ibid.

8. Roberts, D. (2008, Aug. 7). Olympic Security Is No Game. *BusinessWeek.* Retrieved September 20, 2008 from http://www.businessweek.com/magazine/content/08_33b4096046844911.htm.

9. USOC Annual Report (2006). USOC.org. Retrieved August 12, 2008, from http://teamusa.org/content/index/1537.

10. Special Olympics: About Us. (2008). SpecialOlympics.org. Retrieved August 18, 2008, from http://www.specialolympics.org/Special+Olympics+Public+Website/English/About_Us/default.htm.

CHAPTER TWENTY-NINE

Amateur Sports

NATIONAL COLLEGIATE ATHLETIC ASSOCIATION

The National Collegiate Athletic Association (NCAA) is a nonprofit organization responsible for governing athletic programs in colleges and universities across the United States. The NCAA is the largest collegiate athletic organization in the world and is made up of 1,044 institutions. These institutions range from large, public universities with up to 40,000 students to small, private schools with fewer than 1,000 students. In order to properly advise and compete with these diverse institutions, the NCAA is divided into three divisions: Division I, Division II, and Division III. Division I institutions tend to be the largest schools, offer athletic scholarships, and compete at the highest level. Within Division I are the subcategories of Football Bowl Subdivision (formerly Division I-A), Football Championship Subdivision (formerly Division I-AA), and I-AAA, schools that do not field a football team, which signify different levels of competition and some differences in rules and regulations. Division II schools offer scholarships and are mostly small to mid-sized institutions. Division III schools are mostly smaller institutions that do not offer athletic scholarships (**Table 29-1**).

The NCAA was originally known as the Intercollegiate Athletic Association of the United States (from 1906 to 1910), and it was formed by 13 institutions in response to concerns over the violence associated with collegiate football games. In the early years, the NCAA's primary role was devising rules and regulations to govern the athletic programs of its member institutions. With an increasing membership, championships offered in many sports, and business developments, the NCAA developed into a large organization with numerous and various responsibilities.

The NCAA serves as a governance and administrative entity for its member schools and conferences. Some of the primary duties for the NCAA include the following:

- Enacting legislation to deal with issues that arise with its member institutions
- Interpreting legislation adopted by membership
- Promoting and sanctioning NCAA postseason and championship events
- Negotiating sponsorship and television deals for NCAA postseason events
- Compiling and distributing the statistics in each sport.
- Maintaining committees to write and interpret playing rules in the sports
- Maintaining compliance services programs to assist member institutions with interpretations of the rules
- Enforcing NCAA rules and regulations
- Administering insurance programs
- Supporting participation in international events through the U.S. Olympic Committee and National Governing Bodies
- Encouraging participation in community service programs located at many NCAA championship locations

The national office, located in Indianapolis, Indiana, consists of 350 staff members who work in several departments that are responsible for servicing its members, such as eligibility, recruiting, rules and bylaws, and compliance, in addition to various oversight committees. Also, the NCAA has a comprehensive list of association-wide committees that specialize in certain areas, such as the Minority Opportunities and Interests Committee, Athlete Advisory Committee, and the Committee on Sportsmanship and Ethical

Table 29-1 NCAA Divisions

Division	Number of Member Institutions	Number of Sports Sponsored	Sponsors Football	Minimum Attendance Requirements for Football	Minimum Scheduling Sponsors	Minimum Grant-in-Aid
I: Football Bowl Subdivision	119	16 total; minimum 6 male/mixed, minimum 8 all female	Yes	Yes	Yes	$4,000,000
I: Football Championship Subdivision	119	7 for men/mixed, 7 for women (or 6 and 8)	Yes	No	Yes	$964,700
I-AAA	93	7 for men, 7 for women (or 6 and 8)	No	No	Yes	$877,000
II	291	5 for men, 5 for women (or 4 and 6)	Maybe	No	No	$250,000
III	429	5 for men, 5 for women	Maybe	No	No	No athletic-based scholarships permitted

Conduct. The NCAA staff does not serve on these committees, but does provide administrative support.

From a financial standpoint, the NCAA's most significant annual event is the NCAA Division I Men's Basketball Tournament. In 2007, the NCAA anticipated this event generating $564 million in revenue, mostly from TV, gate receipts, and marketing rights.[1]

History of the NCAA[2–4]

1905

- U.S. President Theodore Roosevelt summoned college athletics leaders to two White House conferences to encourage reforms for football due to its violent nature that had recently caused 18 deaths and 149 serious injuries.

- In early December, Chancellor Henry M. MacCracken of New York University convened a meeting of 13 institutions to initiate changes in football playing rules.

1906

- The Intercollegiate Athletic Association of the United States (IAAUS) was founded by 62 members to formulate rules making football safer and more exciting to play at 35 institutions.

1910

- The IAAUS changed its name to the National Collegiate Athletic Association and became the primary rule-making body for college athletics in the United States.

1917

- Many schools, citing decreased enrollment, suspended varsity athletics after Congress declared war on Germany.

1921

- The first NCAA national championship was held: the National Collegiate Track and Field Championships.

- After the track and field championship in 1921, the NCAA added championships in swimming, wrestling, boxing, gymnastics, cross country, and golf—all for men because the Association dealt exclusively in men's athletics.

Rich Ensor, commissioner of the Metro Atlantic Athletic Conference (MAAC), speaks at an NCAA meeting. Ensor, an attorney, has been commissioner of MAAC since 1990. He also has served on the NCAA Management Council, the NCAA Strategic Planning Committee, and the women's basketball selection committee.

1927

- The Rose Bowl was broadcast across the country on NBC Radio, becoming the first transcontinental radio broadcast of a sporting event.

1939

- The NCAA added men's basketball, giving the NCAA a total of eight championships. The men's basketball championships debuted at Philadelphia's Palestra Center, where the eastern half of the tournament was played. Three days later, the western half of the tournament began in the San Francisco Coliseum. On March 28, the University of Oregon became the first NCAA basketball champion.
- The first televised intercollegiate contest was aired on NBC. It was a baseball game between Princeton and Columbia.

1940

- In response to complaints of violations of the amateurism regulations, the NCAA Convention authorized the executive committee to investigate the allegations as well as to interpret the NCAA Constitution.

1946

- The inaugural Conference of Conferences, a meeting of all NCAA member conferences, took place in July, which produced the "Principles for the Conduct of Intercollegiate Athletics."

1947

- The NCAA developed policies in five crucial areas: amateurism, institutional control and responsibility, sound academic standards, financial aid, and recruiting as a result of the Conference of Conferences.
- The National Collegiate Athletic Bureau's football statistics service was granted funding by the NCAA Executive Committee.

1950

- The NCAA passed the Byrd Resolution, mandating that colleges and universities of comparable size enact and maintain similar standards.
- The NCAA Executive Committee approved a proposal to grant $5,000 to investigate the impact of television broadcasting on attendance at collegiate football contests.

1951

- Walter Byers was promoted from part-time director to the executive director of the NCAA (1951–1987).
- The NCAA banned live television broadcasts of college football for the 1951 season because it believed that live broadcasts led to decreased game attendance.

- NBC paid $1.14 million for the rights to broadcast 12 weeks of college football, including one national broadcast a week, with the opportunity to add games of regional interest to be broadcast within regions.

1952

- The NCAA national headquarters were established in Kansas City, Missouri.
- The NCAA allowed live broadcasts of college football games for 1952, on the condition that the NCAA controlled the broadcasts. The NCAA wanted to ensure that as many colleges as possible would appear on television.
- The NCAA and NBC reach a $1.4 million agreement for the limited live television rights of collegiate football games.

1953

- A Conference of Conferences was held in Chicago to solidify plans to improve relations and collaboration between conferences and the NCAA.
- The NCAA Intercollegiate Athletic Group Insurance program was established to provide health coverage to student-athletes suffering severe injuries. More than 100 NCAA schools joined the program.

1954

- The Certification of Compliance program was initiated by the NCAA Council. The program called for a school's administrative office to earn a certificate of compliance from the NCAA.

1955

- The first punishments were levied by the NCAA Council to the coaching staff of an NCAA institution as a result of a case heard by the committee on ethics.

1956

- The NCAA announced that the Association had become fiscally secure for the first time in the history of the NCAA.

1959

- The NCAA created a new policy prohibiting athletic department employees from working for professional sports teams in the following capacities: scouting, evaluating talent, or negotiating professional sports contracts.

1960

- In response to competition from the NIT, the executive committee declared that NCAA teams should decline any other invitation to postseason play if selected for the University Division tournament (currently known as the NCAA Tournament).

1961

- The 5-year rule was established, allowing student-athletes a 5-year time period to complete their 4 years of athletic eligibility.

1962

- A special committee on basketball television announced that the televising of NCAA basketball contests had no negative effect on fan attendance.

1966

- ABC gained the rights to broadcast NCAA football for $7.8 million for the first year of that agreement; by the 16th year of the agreement ABC paid $31 million in rights fees to the NCAA. This exclusive agreement between the NCAA and ABC ended NBC's 14-year run as the television home of collegiate football.

- Texas Western College defeated the University of Kentucky in basketball to become the first team to win an NCAA national championship with a starting lineup entirely made up of African American student-athletes.

1967

- A committee was appointed to explore the feasibility for providing governance and structure for women's athletics.

1968

- The NCAA divided its members into two divisions: University and College. A total of 223 members selected University Division; 386 selected College Division. The University Division consisted of teams that would later become Division I teams and the College Division contained future Division II and Division III schools.

1970

- The number of allowed regular-season football games increased from 10 to 11.

1971

- A new group, the Association for Intercollegiate Athletics for Women (AIAW) was formed as a means of providing national championships for women's athletics. The AIAW coordinated 41 national championships in 19 different sports.

- Freshmen were allowed to participate in all NCAA championships except for football and basketball.

1972

- Congress passed the Educational Amendment Act, which included Title IX, which states: "No person in the United States shall, on the basis of sex, be excluded from participation in, be denied the benefits of or be subjected to any education program or activity receiving Federal financial assistance." Originally, it was unclear whether this legislation applied to athletic departments, setting the stage for many years of litigation.

- Freshmen were declared eligible for all varsity sports, including basketball and football.

1973

- The NCAA ended its partnership with the U.S. Olympic Committee.

- At the NCAA Convention, the schools voted to increase the minimum GPA from 1.6 to 2.0.

- The NCAA called a special convention to plan and establish the current three-division system made up of Division I, Division II, and Division III. The change was made to create flexibility and parity among schools of varying sizes.

1974

- The Department of Health, Education, and Welfare interpreted Title IX to apply to athletic departments.

1975

- The NCAA Convention mandated the need for a plan to incorporate women's athletics into the NCAA. Previously, women's athletics was administered by the AIAW.

- A NCAA-convened special convention passed regulations regarding recruiting activities, the number and amount of financial awards, and squad and coaching staff sizes for football and basketball.

1976

- The convention voted down initiatives to provide a need-based financial aid plan and a plan calling for the equal distribution of football television revenue to participating schools.

1977

- The NCAA and HBO agreed to a cable television rights deal for the 1977 College World Series Championship game.

- The NCAA reached its first 4-year agreement for the television rights to football games by signing a deal with ABC.

1978

- Division I created two subdivisions, I-A and I-AA, for members with football programs.

- The NCAA and USOC partnership was re-established.

1979

- The NCAA and ESPN agreed to a 2-year agreement for the rights to several NCAA championship events.

- The NCAA Division I Basketball Championship featuring Indiana State University (Larry Bird) against Michigan State University (Magic Johnson) drew a record television rating of 24.1. (One rating point is the equivalent of 1% of American homes with a television.)
- The Executive Committee voted to expand the Division I Basketball Championship to 48 teams, while abolishing the rule limiting a conference to two representatives in the tournament.

1980

- The NCAA passed legislation to allow championships in women's athletics.

1981

- The NCAA created a comprehensive plan to regulate women's athletics, allowing championship participation for women at Division I schools. The plan also called for 19 new championships in addition to those added in 1980, spreading them out across Divisions I, II, and III.
- The national field hockey championship was held, marking the first women's NCAA championship.

1982

- The AIAW sued the NCAA on antitrust claims. The AIAW lost in the case of *AIAW v. NCAA* and subsequently folded.

1983

- Proposition 48 was enacted in an attempt to establish initial academic eligibility standards in order to compete for Division I colleges. Requirements included a 700 SAT or 17 ACT score in addition to a 2.0 GPA in 11 core classes. Student-athletes not meeting those standards were not eligible to play or practice in their first year.

1984

- The U.S. Supreme Court weakened Title IX in the case of *Grove City College v. Bell*. The court ruled that Title IX only pertains to programs that directly receive federal funds, thereby eliminating Title IX coverage of most athletic programs.
- The U.S. Supreme Court ruled that the NCAA's regulations limiting a university's ability to negotiate its own television rights violated the Sherman Antitrust Act in *NCAA v. The Board of Regents of the University of Oklahoma*.

1986

- The NCAA began a drug testing program after several U.S. student-athletes failed drug tests at the 1983 Pan American Games.

1987

- Walter Byers retired as the Association's executive director after 36 years in office. Richard D. Schultz, former athletic director at the University of Virginia, was named his successor (1987–1993).

- Southern Methodist University's football team was suspended for one year for repeated and flagrant NCAA rules violations. This penalty is known as the "Death Penalty" because of the severity of the punishment, and this was the first time it was used.

1988

- Congress passed the Civil Rights Restoration Act, extending the coverage of Title IX to collegiate athletics, effectively overturning the *Grove City v. Bell* decision.

1989

- CBS signed a 7-year, $1-billion contract to air the NCAA Men's Basketball Tournament.
- In response to a public opinion poll indicating that 78% of Americans felt that intercollegiate athletics were out of control, a group of university presidents and athletic directors formed the Knight Foundation Commission.

1990

- NCAA headquarters moved to Overland Park, Kansas.
- The NCAA mandated that Division I institutions publish graduation rates by 1991.
- Reports from the special committee on cost reduction and the special committee to review the NCAA membership structure were released. Proposals included creation of a "restricted-earnings" coaching position.
- The University of Notre Dame and NBC signed a 5-year, $37.5-million deal for the rights for its regular-season home football games. The move separated Notre Dame from the College Football Association, which had previously negotiated television rights for college after 1984.
- Sara Lee Corporation made a $6-million pledge to the NCAA to help promote the growth of women's collegiate athletics. One initiative included creating the Woman of the Year award, which still exists.
- The Student Right-to-Know Act was passed by Congress, mandating public disclosure of graduation rates of both students and student-athletes.
- A disability coverage insurance program was developed by the NCAA as a means of protection for student-athletes expecting to be chosen in the first several rounds of the NFL or NBA drafts.
- The Executive Committee adopted a new revenue distribution plan for television revenue. The distribution to Division I schools was based on three pools: basketball performance, academic enhancement, and broad-based (the number of varsity sports sponsored).

1991

- The President's Commission announced new reforms for the NCAA. Legislation was created to reduce costs and limit the time demands for student-athletes. Other new regulations strengthened membership criteria and created restricted-earnings coaching positions.

- The Knight Foundation Commission issued a 47-page report recommending changes to college athletics. Reduction in the time athletes spent on their sport (the 20-hour rule), cost-containment measures (reduction in scholarships and recruiting time), and institutional restructuring (college presidents were placed in charge of all policy and budgeting decisions) were all changes that the NCAA adopted as a result of the Knight Commission Report.

- Canisius College's Mary Beth Riley became the first recipient of the NCAA Woman of the Year award.

1992

- Five Division I-A conferences and the University of Notre Dame came to terms with representatives of several major postseason football bowl games to form the Bowl Coalition.

- The U.S. Supreme Court ruled in *Franklin v. Gwinnet County Public Schools* that successful Title IX claims can result in the award of monetary damages for actions deemed intentional violations.

- The first NCAA gender-equity report highlighted major disparities between the treatment of males and females in intercollegiate athletics. As a result, the NCAA created the Gender-Equity Task Force.

1993

- Schultz announced his resignation as NCAA executive in light of an independent investigation that found that he was aware of loans to student-athletes that were in violation of NCAA regulations while director of athletics at the University of Virginia.

- Dr. Cedric W. Dempsey, director of athletics at the University of Arizona, became executive director of the NCAA (1993–2003).

- The NCAA Council agreed with the report from the Gender-Equity Task Force, which recommended that gender equity should be met on an "institution by institution basis."

- A special committee headed by UCLA Chancellor Charles E. Young was created to explore the impact and effects of implementing a Division I-A football playoff system.

1994

- The NCAA drug-testing program was upheld by the California Supreme Court in the case of *Hill v. NCAA*. Hill and others sued in state court, claiming that the drug tests were an invasion of privacy.

- A special committee to study a Division I-A Football Championship reported that there was justification to enact a playoff system; however, it could not suggest specific legislation to move the process forward.

1995

- A federal circuit court of appeals determined that Brown University was in violation of Title IX in the case of *Cohen v. Brown University*. Brown University had discontinued two men's and two women's sports in an attempt to comply with Title IX. Instead, the judge determined that in order to comply with Title IX, opportunities in athletics for men and women must be substantially equal in proportion to the male-to-female student body ratio at the school.

- The NCAA opened a federal relations office in Washington, DC.

- The NCAA eliminated the restricted-earnings coaches positions after a federal judge ruled in favor of the plaintiffs in the case *Law v. NCAA*. Previously, the NCAA had put in place a salary limit of $16,000 for all entry-level coaching positions. Assistant basketball coaches filed the suit claiming a violation of the Sherman Antitrust Act. (See the settlement under 1999.)

1996

- A tiebreaker plan was developed and approved by the football rules committee for use in all regular-season football games.

- Proposition 16 was enacted by the NCAA, replacing proposition 48. Proposition 16 called for an increase from 11 core courses to 13 to achieve initial eligibility and mandated a high school student complete 4 years of English classes. Additionally, a sliding scale was implemented where SAT scores and grade point average (GPA) were used. For example, an 800 SAT score would require a minimum 2.5 GPA, whereas a 1,000 SAT score would require a GPA of 2.025.

1997

- NCAA Division I schools approved legislation that would allow a student-athlete to work during the school year to cover the costs of attendance not covered by scholarships.

1998

- The NCAA settled a lawsuit with former University of Nevada, Las Vegas, men's basketball coach Jerry Tarkanian for $2.5 million. Tarkanian had alleged that the NCAA violated his Fourteenth Amendment right to due process when it imposed sanctions on UNLV and threatened additional sanctions if Tarkanian was not suspended. In *Tarkanian v. NCAA*, the U.S. Supreme Court ruled that the NCAA's role in the suspension did not qualify as a "state action," thus the Fourteenth Amendment was not applicable to the NCAA.

- The inaugural Bowl Championship Series (BCS) took place, with the champions of the Southeastern Conference (SEC), Big Ten, Atlantic Coast Conference (ACC), Pac-10, Big East, Big 12, and two at-large teams playing in the Sugar Bowl, Fiesta Bowl, Orange Bowl, and Rose Bowl. Based on a newly established rankings system, the Fiesta Bowl hosted the two top-ranked teams, Tennessee and Florida State, to determine the national champion. Tennessee, ranked #1, defeated the #2-ranked Florida State 23–16.

1999

- The NCAA national office moved to Indianapolis, Indiana.

- The NCAA and CBS reached an 11-year, $6-billion agreement for television, radio, Internet, corporate marketing, licensing, and publishing for the Division I Men's Basketball Championship.

- The U.S. Supreme Court ruled in *NCAA v. Smith* that Title IX cannot be applied to the NCAA itself, because it was not considered a direct recipient of federal funds.

- The NCAA and plaintiffs in the restricted-earnings coaches case announced a $54-million settlement in the case of *Law v. NCAA*.

2000

- The basketball rules committee approved the use of replay on last-second shots.

- The NCAA Hall of Champions exhibit opened at NCAA Headquarters in Indianapolis.

2001

- The NCAA and ESPN announced an 11-year agreement beginning September 2002 for the right to broadcast 21 championships, including the Division I Women's Basketball Championship.

- The U.S. Supreme Court ruled in *Cureton v. NCAA* that the NCAA was not a direct recipient of federal funds and thus not held to the standards of Title VII, which prohibits discrimination based on race, among other criteria. The plaintiffs had claimed that the NCAA's initial-eligibility legislation (Proposition 16) had an unequal and illegal impact upon African Americans.

2003

- Myles Brand became the fourth executive director of the NCAA after serving as president of both University of Oregon and Indiana University (2003–present).

2004

- The NCAA passed legislation to permit student-athletes who declare for the professional draft in their respective sport to return to intercollegiate athletics if they have not hired an agent or otherwise compromised their eligibility.

2005

- The NCAA purchased the rights to operate the preseason and postseason National Invitation Tournaments (NIT) from the Metropolitan Intercollegiate Basketball Association (MIBA) for $40.5 million. An additional $16 million was paid as a settlement to the five schools that composed the MIBA (Fordham, Manhattan College, St. John's, Wagner, and NYU) to end 4 years of antitrust litigation (*MIBA v. NCAA*).

- The Division I board of directors passed an Academic Progress Rate (APR), which will penalize schools when its student-athletes are not making satisfactory progress towards graduation.

2006

- The NCAA and Fox Sports agreed to a 4-year, $320-million contract for the rights to broadcast the Fiesta, Sugar, and Orange Bowls beginning in 2007 as well as the rights to the BCS National Championship Game from 2007 to 2009.[5]

- The NCAA added an additional bowl game to the BCS to be played on a rotating basis at one of the current four bowl locations (Fiesta Bowl, Sugar Bowl, Orange Bowl, and Rose Bowl). This championship game will be played a week after the other four BCS Bowl games and feature the top two teams according to the BCS rankings.

2008

- The NCAA and CBS signed a deal with IMG to sell marketing packages for the NCAA's 88 championships.

Structure of the NCAA[6]

Members

- 1,027 active members composed of Division I, II, and III schools
  - Approximately 360,000 student-athletes participate in athletics at these schools, but student-athletes are not actual members of the NCAA.
  - 135 conferences

NCAA Executive Committee

- Highest governing body in the NCAA. It consists of institutional chief executive officers (presidents and chancellors) who oversee all issues pertaining to the NCAA. The committee supervises each division and makes sure that each operates within the policies and principles of the NCAA.

Championships

- The NCAA sponsors and operates 88 championships each year.
  - 41 men's championships
  - 44 women's championships
  - 3 co-ed championships (skiing, fencing, rifle)
- Approximately 49,000 student-athletes compete in NCAA championships each year.

NCAA National Office Departments

- Executive
- Championships
- Services, Research, and Education Services
- Branding and Communications
- Administrative Services
- Enforcement
- Office for Diversity and Inclusion
- Eligibility Center, LLC
- NIT, LLC

Association-Wide Committees

- Executive Committee Subcommittee on Gender and Diversity Issues
- Committee on Competitive Safeguards and Medical Aspects of Sports
- Honors Committee
- Minority Opportunities and Interests Committee
- Olympic Sports Liaison Committee
- Playing Rules Oversight Panel
- Postgraduate Scholarship Committee
- Research Committee
- Committee on Sportsmanship and Ethical Conduct
- Walter Byers Scholarship Committee
- Committee on Women's Athletics
- Athlete Advisory Committee

Money Matters for the NCAA[7]

Revenues for 2005–2006

- Total revenues: $558.2 million

- $470.8 million in television and marketing rights fees: 84.3% of revenues
- Television contracts
  - CBS has an 11-year, $6-billion deal with the NCAA to broadcast the Men's Basketball Tournament through 2013.
- Radio
  - Sirius Radio has exclusive rights to broadcast the Men's Basketball Tournament games to subscribers.[8]
- Sponsorships
  - Cingular Wireless, Coca-Cola, and Pontiac serve as the primary sponsors, also called Corporate Champions. The firms spend an average of $35 million annually in sponsorship fees.
  - DiGiorno, Kraft, The Hartford, Lowe's, and State Farm Insurance make up the next level of corporate sponsors. They contribute between $10 and $12 million annually.
- Merchandising and licensing
  - The NCAA has over 35 licensees who pay royalties to the NCAA.
  - The NCAA has 19 Official Championship Suppliers who provide products such as gymnastic mats, golf equipment, supplies for track and field, and bowling equipment.
  - $57.2 million from championship events—10.2% of revenues
  - $19.3 million earned from investments—3.5% of revenues
  - $10.9 million from sales, services, and contributions—2% of revenues

Expenses for 2005–2006

- Total expenses: $526.8 million
  - $307.6 million redistributed to Division I schools: 58.4% of total expenses
  - $56.3 million spent on Division I championships and other programs (other than basketball): 10.7% of total expenses
  - $24.3 million allotted to Division II schools, championships, and programs: 4.6% of total expenses
  - $15.6 million spent on Division III championship events and programs: 3% of total expenses
  - $96.5 million disbursed association-wide: 18.3% of total expenses
  - $26.5 million in managerial and other expenses: 5% of total expenses

Distribution of Revenues

- The NCAA redistributed over 55% of its revenues to Division I institutions. The formula that it followed to determine the amount that is redistributed is based on three pools of money:
  - Basketball
  - Academic enhancement
  - Broad-based

Division I

Division I schools are required to have at least seven men's and seven women's varsity sports or eight women's sports and six men's sports. As of February 2008 there were 327 Division I schools. According to the NCAA philosophy statement, a Division I school "sponsors at the highest feasible level of intercollegiate competition or one of the traditional spectator oriented, income producing sports of football and basketball," while striving for "regional and national excellence and prominence" in all of its sports.[9] In 2006, the NCAA reclassified its Division I schools with football programs into two subdivisions, the Football Bowl Subdivision and the Football Championship Subdivision. Member schools formerly in Division I-A make up the Football Bowl Subdivision. The requirements to be a member of the Football Bowl Subdivision are the same as they were to be in Division I-A. The Football Championship Subdivision (formerly Division I-AA) consists of primarily smaller schools who put slightly less emphasis on football. In 2003, Division I schools in the Football Bowl Subdivision averaged $29 million in revenues with $2.8 million provided by the school. Division I Football Championship Subdivision schools had revenues of $7.2 million including $3.4 million in institutional support. Schools without football programs (Division I-AAA) averaged $6.2 million in revenues, of which $3.2 million came from the college or university.

Scholarships are available for Division I athletes with maximums for each sport set by the NCAA. The number of scholarships vary by sport, and it is up to each institution to determine the number of scholarships it offers for each particular sport. Coaches are allowed to divide scholarships and distribute partial scholarships to several athletes in all sports except for football, men's and women's basketball, women's tennis, women's gymnastics, and women's volleyball. These sports are often referred to as "head count" sports. Each person who receives a scholarship, regardless of whether they receive a full or partial scholarship, is counted as a full scholarship toward the maximum scholarship allotment. Therefore, for the most part, student-athletes in these sports receive full scholarships. There is also a maximum and minimum amount of financial aid that can be given to student-athletes who are not on scholarship or do not receive a full scholarship.

Freshman eligibility is determined on a sliding scale based on GPA and SAT scores. For example, a student with a 2.0 grade point average (GPA) would need to score a 1,010 on the SAT to be eligible whereas a student with a 3.55 GPA would require an SAT score of 400. Retention of eligibility is based on the institution's minimum GPA for graduation, with mandates that student-athletes meet 90% of the minimum GPA beginning their second year, 95% when beginning their third, and 100% when entering their fourth or fifth year.[10]

Division II

Division II schools are required to have at least four sports for men and four for women. In September 2006, there were 281 Division II schools. Division II teams in the sports of football and men's and women's basketball must have schedules consisting of at least 50% Division I or II schools. In other sports, teams do not have this scheduling requirement. In 2003, Division II schools with football averaged $2.6 million in revenues with $1.5 million coming from institutional funding; schools without football averaged $1.7 million with $1.1 million coming from the institution. Fewer scholarships are offered in Division II schools when compared to Division I. There is a cap of 60 scholarships, excluding those awarded to basketball and football participants, that can be distributed to male student-athletes. Similar to Division I athletics, Division II also has limits on scholarships depending on the sport. Student-athletes in Division II schools often need to finance college tuition with a combination of scholarship, financial aid grants and loans, and employment.

The Division II mission statement states that "Members of Division II believe that a well-conducted intercollegiate athletics program, based on sound educational principles and practices, is a proper part of the educational mission of a university or college and that the educational welfare of the participating student-athlete is of primary concern."[11]

Division III

Division III schools must offer a minimum of five sports for men and five sports for women. Division III institutions must also offer sports for both genders in every season. As of September 2006, there were 437 Division III schools. These institutions can only offer financial aid based on need, and do not allow athletic scholarships. In the 2003 NCAA Division III revenue report, the average cost to operate an athletic department with a football program was $1,570,000; it cost $900,000 for those institutions without football. The primary focus of Division III athletics is to ensure the best possible experience for the student-athlete; the spectators' experience is secondary. Schedules consist mainly of local rivals and conference foes.

The mission statement of Division III states that:

Colleges and universities in Division III place highest priority on the overall quality of the educational experience and on the successful completion of all students' academic programs. They seek to establish and maintain an environment in which a student-athlete's athletics activities are conducted as an integral part of the student-athlete's educational experience, and in which coaches play a significant role as educators. They also seek to establish and maintain an environment that values cultural diversity and gender equity among their student-athletes and athletics staff.[12]

NATIONAL ASSOCIATION OF INTERCOLLEGIATE ATHLETICS

The National Association of Intercollegiate Athletics was founded in 1952 as the expansion of the National Association of Intercollegiate Basketball. The NAIA, based out of Olathe, Kansas, is the governing body for 360 small colleges and universities across the United States. It holds 23 national championship events in 13 sports for men and 10 sports for women. In 1948, the NAIA became the first governing body to allow black student-athletes to participate in postseason sporting events as well as, in 1953, becoming the first to accept historically black colleges into the association. The NAIA organizes schools into one of 25 conferences in 14 regions, along with 31 independent schools that do not belong to a conference. NAIA schools are located in both the United States and Canada. In 2005, the NAIA held approximately $2.4 million in net assets.

In order to be eligible for NAIA play as a freshman, student-athletes must have achieved two of the following three criteria: a combined 860 on the math and critical reading portion of their SAT, a 2.0 GPA out of 4.0, or having finished in the top half of their graduating high school class. NAIA schools do provide athletic scholarships to some student-athletes.

NATIONAL JUNIOR COLLEGE ATHLETIC ASSOCIATION[13]

The National Junior College Athletic Association (NJCAA) was founded in 1937 in Fresno, California, by seven California junior colleges. The NJCAA is the governing body for approximately 510 schools grouped into 24 regions with 15 men's sports and 13 women's sports. In some sports such as baseball, basketball, soccer, track and field, tennis, and golf, there are separate divisions (I, II, or III). The other sports have only one central division with all NJCAA schools competing together. Incoming freshman students are eligible to play if they have earned a high school diploma or a general equivalency diploma (GED). Student-athletes without a diploma or GED can earn their eligibility by taking 12 credits

at the college and obtaining at least a 1.75 GPA. Student-athletes can be awarded financial aid and athletic scholarships. Scholarship amounts depend on the division. Division I NJCAA schools can offer full athletic scholarships whereas Division II schools can offer a scholarship for only the cost of tuition, fees, and books. Division III schools cannot offer any form of scholarship. NJCAA schools also can choose to participate at Division I or II level, and not award athletics scholarships. The NJCAA headquarters are located in Colorado Springs, Colorado.

NATIONAL CHRISTIAN COLLEGE ATHLETIC ASSOCIATION[14]

The National Christian College Athletic Association (NCCAA) is an association of approximately 100 institutions that was founded in 1968. The NCCAA is a Christian-based organization that functions for the promotion of athletics as an opportunity for Christian fellowship and ministry, rather than training for future professional athletes or an opportunity to make a profit for its member institutions. Its purpose is to give 4-year Christian institutions a chance to compete in an atmosphere of shared values. Two divisions comprise the NCCAA: Division I (student athletes are eligible for athletic financial aid) and Division II (schools that do not provide athletic scholarship and have a graduation requirement of 20 semester hours or 30 quarter hours of Biblical study).[15] The NCCAA has corporate partnerships with Brine Inc., Choice Hotels International, Wilson Sports, and Spalding.

NORTHWEST ATHLETIC ASSOCIATION OF COMMUNITY COLLEGES

The Northwest Athletic Association of Community Colleges is an organization responsible for 36 community colleges located in the states of Washington and Oregon. The NWAACC acts as a governing body for these community colleges by providing administrative support in areas such as eligibility, publications, rules enforcement, sports information, marketing, and conference tournaments. The NWAACC is the largest single community college conference in the United States. An executive board provides the NWAACC with direction and leads it towards the association's goals. The board is composed of an executive director as well as athletic directors, presidents, and commissioners of member schools. NWAACC headquarters are located in Vancouver, Washington. Some other community college athletic associations include Community College League of California, Scenic West Athletic Conference, and Arizona Community Colleges.

Endnotes

1. Budget and Finances. (n.d.). NCAA.org. Retrieved August 5, 2008, from http://www.ncaa.org/wps/ncaa?ContentID=4.

2. The History of the NCAA: The NCAA Century Series. (n.d.). NCAA.org. Retrieved November 14, 2007, from http://www.ncaa.org/about/ncaacenturyseries.html.

3. King, B. (2006, Jan. 9–15). At 100, NCAA Still Defining Its Role. *Street & Smith's SportsBusiness Journal.* Retrieved October 10, 2007, from http://www.sportsbusinessjournal.com/index.cfm?fuseaction=search.show_article&articleId=48768&keyword=At%20100%20NCAA%20still%20defining%20its%20role.

4. Masteralexis, L., Barr, C., and Hums, M. (2005). *Principles and Practices of Sport Management.* Sudbury, MA: Jones and Bartlett.

5. Buckeyes and Gators Want Some BCS Money. (2007, Jan. 5). CSTV.com. Retrieved October 26, 2007, from http://www.cstv.com/sports/m-footbl/stories/010507abn.html.

6. NCAA, op cit.

7. Ibid.

8. Sirius Satellite Radio Brings NCAA March Madness to College Hoops Fans Nationwide. (2004, Nov. 29). Sirius Satellite Radio. Retrieved October 26, 2007, from http://investor.sirius.com/ReleaseDetail.cfm?ReleaseID=152850&cat=&newsroom.

9. Mission, Goals, and Strategies. (n.d.). California State University, Fullerton Athletics. Retrieved August 4, 2008, from http://webcert.fullerton.edu/athleticspolicy/mission.htm#DIVISION.

10. NCAA. (2005). Article 14.3 Freshman Eligibility. *2005–06 NCAA Manual.* Indianapolis, IN: Author.

11. Division II Philosophy Statement. (n.d.). NCAA.org. Retrieved August 5, 2008, from http://www1.ncaa.org/membership/governance/division_II/index.html.

12. Division III Philosophy Statement. (n.d.). Retrieved August 5, 2008, from http://www1.ncaa.org/membership/governance/division_III/d3_philosophy_stmt.

13. NJCAA: Home. (n.d.). NJCAA.org. Retrieved August 5, 2008, from http://www.njcaa.org.

14. National Christian College Athletic Association: Home. (n.d.). NJCAA.org. Retrieved August 5, 2008, from http://www.njcaa.org.

15. NCAA. (1968). Article 3.6 Participation in the NCCAA. NCCAA Constitution. Detroit, MI: Author.

Event Management

Event management is the planning, organization, and execution of athletic contests or events. This chapter examines three of the largest annual sporting events in the United States to show the work that goes into managing a major sporting event. Event management opportunities also exist in areas that are not primarily involved in running an event, such as community relations or charity events.

NCAA COLLEGE FOOTBALL BOWL GAMES[1]

After the conclusion of the regular season, NCAA college football teams can be selected to compete in one of 32 individual bowl games by having at least six qualifying wins (**Table 30-1**). College bowl games have been played for over 90 years; however, the Bowl Championship Series (BCS), which crowns the national champion, was not formed until 1998. Each bowl game is planned, organized, and run by a year-round paid staff, along with a host. These local host committees are composed of government officers, community leaders, volunteers, employees, and businespeople. Almost all bowl games and organizing committees are nonprofit entities. The bowl-organizing committees are typically located in cities close to the stadiums where the bowl games will be held. For instance, the headquarters for the Orange Bowl Committee are located in Miami-Dade County near the Miami International Airport. The Orange Bowl Committee is composed of nearly 30 full-time staff members, 12 part-time assistantship workers, and close to 310 volunteers. There is also an assistantship program that offers opportunities in business operations, youth sports, media relations, events, sponsorship sales, ticket operations, executive administration, marketing and promotions, and new business development.[2]

Total revenues for the four 2006 BCS games were over $96 million. Revenues are generated from ticket sales, corporate sponsorships, and broadcast rights. The payouts distributed to bowl teams and conferences were nearly $225 million in 2007.[3] Bowl games help generate exposure for schools, increase donations, and can lead to lucrative licensing, broadcasting, and endorsement deals. Attendance at bowl games was close to 1.7 million fans in 2007, and television ratings were as high as 14.4 (Sugar Bowl: LSU v. Ohio State).[3,4]

NCAA FINAL FOUR BASKETBALL TOURNAMENTS

The NCAA Men's and Women's Final Four Basketball Tournaments are two of the largest annual events held in the United States. During the end of the second week of March, 65 Division I teams compete in 13 sites located throughout the country. The first NCAA Tournament was held in 1939 when Oregon defeated Ohio State, 46–33.

Teams can gain entry to the tournament in two ways: they can win their conference championship or they can receive an at-large bid. The first two rounds of the NCAA basketball tournament are held in eight locations while the third and fourth rounds (the regionals) are held in four locations. In order to satisfy demand and maximize revenues, the NCAA has determined that the last three tournament games, called the Final Four, should be played in large dome stadiums, which usually accommodate 50,000 or more fans.

Managing the Final Four Tournament is a challenging endeavor that requires a full-time paid staff, as well as collaborative efforts from several organizations. The Final Four host also plans, organizes, and runs a number of events during the championship weekend. The following list of events is from the 2008 schedule in San Antonio, Texas:

• NCAA Hoop City refreshed by Coca Cola

• Final Four Teams Gathering

Table 30-1   College Football Bowl Schedule (2007–2008)

Bowl Game	Date/Time	Site	Match-Up	Network
San Diego Co. Credit Union Poinsettia	Dec. 20, 9 PM	San Diego, CA	Mountain West vs. At-Large	ESPN
R+L Carriers New Orleans	Dec. 21, 8 PM	New Orleans, LA	Sun Belt Champ vs. C-USA	ESPN2
New Mexico	Dec. 22, 4:30 PM	Albuquerque, NM	Mountain West vs. WAC	ESPN
PapaJohn's.com	Dec. 22, 1 PM	Birmingham, AL	Big East vs. C-USA	ESPN2
Pioneer PureVision Las Vegas	Dec. 22, 8 PM	Las Vegas, NV	Mountain West vs. Pac-10	ESPN
Sheraton Hawaii	Dec. 23, 8 PM	Honolulu, HI	C-USA vs. WAC	ESPN
Motor City	Dec. 26, 7:30 PM	Detroit, MI	Big Ten vs. MAC	ESPN
Pacific Life Holiday	Dec. 27, 8 PM	San Diego, CA	Big 12 vs. Pac-10	ESPN
Champs Sports	Dec. 28, 8 PM	Orlando, FL	ACC vs. Big Ten	ESPN
Emerald	Dec. 28, 8:30 PM	San Francisco, CA	ACC vs. Pac-10	ESPN
Texas	Dec. 28 8:00 PM	Houston, TX	Big 12 vs. C-USA	NFL
Alamo	Dec. 29, 8 PM	San Antonio, TX	Big Ten vs. Big 12	ESPN
Meineke Car Care	Dec. 29, 1 PM	Charlotte, NC	ACC vs. Big East	ESPN
AutoZone Liberty	Dec. 29, 4:30 PM	Memphis, TN	C-USA vs. SEC	ESPN
Petro Sun Independence	Dec. 30, 8 PM	Shreveport, LA	SEC vs. Big 12	ESPN
Bell Helicopter Armed Forces	Dec. 31, 8 PM	Fort Worth, TX	Pac-10 vs. Mountain West	ESPN
Chick-fil-A	Dec. 31, 7:30 PM	Atlanta, GA	ACC vs. SEC	ESPN
Gaylord Hotels Music City	Dec. 31, 4 PM	Nashville, TN	ACC vs. SEC	ESPN
Humanitarian	Dec. 31, 2 PM	Boise, ID	ACC vs. WAC	ESPN2
Insight	Dec. 31, 7:30 PM	Tempe, AZ	Big Ten vs. Big 12	NFL
Sun	Dec. 29, 2 PM	El Paso, TX	Big 12/Big East vs. Pac-10	CBS
Allstate Sugar	Jan. 3, 8:30 PM	New Orleans, LA	BCS vs. BCS	FOX
AT&T Cotton	Jan. 1, 11:30 AM	Dallas, TX	Big 12 vs. SEC	FOX
Capital One	Jan. 1, 1 PM	Orlando, FL	Big Ten vs. SEC	ABC
Gator	Jan. 1, 1 PM	Jacksonville, FL	ACC vs. Big 12/Big East	CBS
Outback	Jan. 1, 11 AM	Tampa, FL	Big Ten vs. SEC	ESPN
Rose presented by Citi	Jan. 1, 5 PM	Pasadena, CA	BCS vs. BCS	ABC
Tostitos Fiesta	Jan. 2, 8 PM	Glendale, AZ	BCS vs. BCS	FOX
FedEx Orange	Jan. 3, 8 PM	Miami, FL	BCS vs. BCS	FOX
International	Jan. 5, 12 PM	Toronto, Canada	Big East vs. MAC	ESPN2
GMAC	Jan. 6, 8 PM	Mobile, AL	C-USA vs. MAC	ESPN
BCS National Championship	Jan. 7, 8 PM	Glendale, AZ	BCS #1 vs. BCS #2	FOX

- DiGiorno College All-Star Game
- YES (Youth Education through Sports Program) Clinic fueled by PowerAde
- The Big Dance (Pep Rally)
- Official NCAA Elite Experience Hospitality
- Dome Dribble to Hoop City
- My Coke Fest

These events require much advanced preparation and hundreds of volunteers. Therefore, future sites of the Final Four are selected years in advance (**Table 30-2**). The Final Four Local Organizing Committee staff members are hired over a year in advance of the tournament. The Local Organizing Committee is responsible for attracting and training volunteers to help with event management, organization, and most importantly, hospitality for guests, fans, coaches, players, and attendees. The entire 2008 men's event was a collaborative operation involving the NCAA, the State of Texas, the City of San Antonio, the San Antonio Convention and Visitors Bureau, the San Antonio Sports Foundation, the University of Texas at San Antonio, and the Alamo Dome.

Table 30-2   Final Four Locations

Year	Men's	Women's
2007	Atlanta, GA	Cleveland, OH
2008	San Antonio, TX	Tampa, FL
2009	Detroit, MI	St. Louis, MO
2010	Indianapolis, IN	San Antonio, TX
2011	Houston, TX	Indianapolis, IN

The NCAA Final Four is a very attractive event to host. Because there are a large number of out-of-town visitors, it generates significant revenues for the host city. Studies have estimated that the 2008 NCAA Final Four generated $47 million in economic impact for the city of San Antonio, Texas.

The NCAA receives significant financial benefits from its $6 billion deal with CBS in which CBS receives the right to broadcast 66 NCAA championships, including men's basketball, through 2013. The revenue from the NCAA tournament is the primary funding source to run the NCAA's national office, the operations of the NCAA, and the non-revenue-generating sports championships.

PROFESSIONAL GOLF AND TENNIS EVENTS

Every year there are dozens of professional sporting events at various venues throughout the world that require event management. For instance, in professional golf, the U.S. Open takes place in a different location each year. Because the location changes each year, preparation and event management are critical to the event's success. The golf course's management, the club members, and the employees must cooperate with town, county, state, and U.S. Golf Association (USGA) officials over an extended period of time—normally up to 2 years for major events. Although the USGA is responsible for the planning and coordination of the event, course officials are responsible for staffing and executing operations for a number of committees. Events on tours such as the World Tennis Association (WTA), Association of Tennis Professionals (ATP), Professional Golfers' Association (PGA), and Ladies Professional Golf Association (LPGA) have become very large events with many operational issues to handle. These events often have between 200,000 and 300,000 spectators during the week of a golf

tournament. At the 2006 U.S. Open at Winged Foot Golf Club, there were more than 70 corporate tents with a 36,000-square-foot pavilion for merchandise sales. As the host, most courses are rewarded financially by the organization or association overseeing the event. The compensation varies depending on the scope of the event. (Reports have indicated that Winged Foot Golf Club received upwards of seven figures.) In addition to monetary benefits, the host club gains much prestige by hosting a U.S. Open and is perceived as one of the top courses in the nation.

Volunteers are necessary and vital for the operation to run efficiently. Major events can involve up to 5,000 volunteers working on a number of committees prior to and during the event. Volunteers are responsible for a myriad of activities, some of which involve merchandise, medical, grounds keeping, hole marshalling, and player hospitality. Aside from the volunteer positions, there are often jobs available in operations, administration, media relations, and player services.

Endnotes

1. Bowl Championship Series. (n.d.). BCSFootball.org. Retrieved August 5, 2008, from http://www.bcsfootball.org/bcsfootball.

2. Orange Bowl Employment. (n.d.). OrangeBowl.org. Retrieved August 5, 2008, from http://www.orangebowl.org/ViewArticle.dbml?DB_OEM_ID=11800&KEY=&ATCLID=695651&SPID=7637&SPSID=69636.

3. NCAA Football. (2008, Jan. 24). TV Ratings and Bowl Games Highlight America's Passion for College Football in 2007. NCAAfootball.com. Retrieved April 17, 2008, from http://www.ncaafootball.com/index.php?s=&url_channel_id=34&url_article_id=11994&change_well_id=2.

4. Hiestand, M. (2008, Jan. 8). Bowl Season Finishes with a Decline in Viewership. Retrieved February 11, 2008, from http://www.usatoday.com/sports/columnist/hiestand-tv/2008-01-08-bcs-television-ratings_N.htm.

5. NCAA News Release. (2008, Aug. 28). 2008 Men's Final Four Generates 47 Million in Economic Impact. NCAA.org. Retrieved September 20, 2008, from http://www.ncaa.org/wps/ncaa?ContentID=36144.

CHAPTER THIRTY-ONE

Facility Management

Facility management is a broadly defined industry segment that includes several areas of business such as event management, consulting, construction, risk management/security operations, operations management, customer service, marketing, budgeting, and concessions. Facility management covers a wide range of activities, some of which are related to sports. The core function of a facility is to bring shows, concerts, and games, and therefore spectators, to the facility. To book a show, concert, or game, promoters and the general manager of the facility negotiate a deal. Once the event is booked, the facility will work to market the event and sell tickets to it.

Depending on the capacity and scale of the operation, facility management can be a very diverse business with many different events (such as at the Wachovia Center in Philadelphia or TD Banknorth Garden in Boston) or it can be specifically designed for a narrow purpose (a football stadium or hockey arena). Some facility operations can involve one sport (football) for six games a year, whereas other operations are as complex as running an arena where events are booked over 300 days a year. Therefore, the amount of time spent on the different functions will vary with the size and the event mix of the facility.

Facilities are generally built to accommodate large groups of people and include arenas, stadiums, convention centers, and theaters. Arenas are indoor facilities that host sports and other entertainment. "Permanent" tenants with multiple dates (40 to 55 games), such as basketball and hockey, often coexist in the same arena. These permanent tenants usually have first priority in terms of scheduling. In addition, many arenas also host indoor soccer, arena football, concerts, ice shows, family shows, graduations, and conventions. Venues such as the FedEx Forum in Memphis, Tennessee, and the Nationwide Arena in Columbus, Ohio, have attached additional practice facilities to their arenas to increase flexibility and be able to host more events, thus increasing revenues.

John Wentzell, president of the TD Banknorth Garden, accepts a distinguished alumnus award at the University of Massachusetts. The Garden is home to the Boston Celtics and Boston Bruins as well as host to a number of family events, shows, concerts, and other sporting events.

Stadiums are outdoor or domed facilities where baseball, football, and outdoor soccer games are typically played. In terms of generating revenue, stadiums face different challenges than arenas. There are different challenges to managing stadiums because they are significantly larger than arenas, making it difficult to host nonsport events, primarily because of their inability to attract stadium-sized crowds. However, the large parking areas of some facilities of the stadiums are utilized for fairs, carnivals, outdoor marketplaces, car shows, and circuses.

Other types of facilities are convention centers and theaters. These are generally less sport oriented. Convention centers are usually built, owned, and funded by a public entity. They are generally built in the downtown districts of large cities and are publicly owned because the fees and rents charged are not substantial enough to cover the overall expenses of an event. Although states and municipalities lose money on the actual convention center, the hope is to increase tax revenue and other economic benefits through hotels, restaurants, shopping, and other entertainment options. The Allen County War Memorial Coliseum outside of Fort Wayne, Indiana, is a complex that includes both an athletic arena and an exposition center, and it is estimated that the coliseum complex contributes approximately $100 million to the Fort Wayne economy.[1] The variety of events that a convention center may host can include trade shows, home shows, corporate meetings, and banquets.

Theaters are usually constructed by universities, public entities, and private groups and are used for popular and classical concerts, Broadway-style musicals, plays, dance troupes, lectures, and children and family shows. Similar to convention centers, revenues earned through the events do not cover all the costs. Theaters can be publicly or privately owned and are usually subsidized by government and corporate entities.[2]

Some facilities are private (e.g., FedEx Field, home of the Washington Redskins); some are public (e.g., Lambeau Field) and controlled by the city, county, or state. Some facilities are owned by the same entity that runs the sports team (e.g., TD Banknorth Garden is owned by the Delaware North Companies, which also owns the Boston Bruins). Also, some facilities are run by the same entity that owns the facility (e.g., TD Banknorth Garden) and some are run by facility management companies such as Global Spectrum (e.g., MassMutual Center and the University of Massachusetts' Mullins Center).

The management of the building and services is the primary responsibility of facility management; however, within the operation of each event are a multitude of tasks that make facility management different each day. MassMutual Center, a publicly owned facility in Springfield, Massachusetts, runs approximately 100 events a year. Events include the Springfield Falcons hockey games, concerts, conventions, meetings, and trade shows in their exhibition halls. There are 35 full-time employees at the MassMutual Center with positions ranging from marketing and sales for the events to operations, which sets up and takes down the events. The event staff typically ranges between 250 and 300 employees, depending on the size of the show.

In comparison, a much larger, 18,000+ capacity venue may run more than 270 events per year, including:[3]

- 41 professional basketball games (NBA)
- 41 professional hockey games (NHL)
- 25 concerts
- 65 family shows
- 98 other events, such as conventions, meetings, and trade shows

To manage such extensive operations, a larger facility will employ more people than a smaller venue. For example, a venue such as the one described above may have 150 full-time employees in areas such as management, operations, finance, information technology, human resources, legal, sales, customer service, and food and beverage. Furthermore, the arena is likely to hire a large number of event-day, part-time employees, such as ushers, ticket takers, and concession workers. In total, a large arena may need upwards of 500 part-time employees to meet the operational needs of a sold-out event.

Structure of Facility Management

Departments

- Event management
- Operations management
- Convention center services
- Consulting
- Construction
- Marketing/advertising/sales
- Event booking
- Risk management/security
- Ticketing

Types of Facilities

- Arenas
- Amphitheaters
- Auditoriums
- Convention centers/exhibit halls
- Performing arts centers
- Stadiums
- University complexes

Money Matters in Facility Management

Sources of Revenues
These vary depending on ownership, size, and scope:

- Gate receipts
- Personal seat licenses

- Luxury suites
- Club seating
- Rent or lease
- Sponsorship (naming rights, signage, etc.)
- Concessions
- Parking

Expenses

These depend on the size of the event and the facility:

- Marketing and advertising costs
- Food and beverage
- Maintenance
- Payroll
- Operations
- Security
- Debt

Although some facilities are independently operated, several companies specialize in operating facilities as an outside management company. Two such companies are Global Spectrum and JRV Management.

GLOBAL SPECTRUM[4]

Created in January 2000 when Comcast-Spectacor joined with Globe Facility Services of Tampa, Global Spectrum is a management, consulting, and event development company for public assembly facilities. The company provides full-service management for arenas, stadiums, convention centers, ice rinks, exposition centers, auditoriums, and theaters. Global Spectrum manages more than 70 facilities (31 arenas, 22 convention/exposition centers, 10 stadiums, and 5 ice rinks); and 5 performing arts centers, including the Miami Convention Center, University of Phoenix Stadium (Glendale, AZ), and the Comcast Community Ice Rink (Everett, WA). In addition to operating facilities, the company provides management and consulting services for the design, construction, and pre-opening phases of a new facility.

In addition, Global Spectrum operates other businesses, including:

- Front Row Marketing Services: Provides clients with assistance with the sale of commercial rights, such as naming and pouring rights, advertising signage, premium seating, sponsorships, branding, and memorial gifts.
- Global Spectrum Asia, Ltd.: Produces and promotes international trade shows and conventions.

Global Spectrum is a subsidiary of Comcast-Spectacor, a sports and entertainment firm. Both Global Spectrum and Comcast-Spectacor are located at the Wachovia Center in Philadelphia. Some departments within Global Spectrum include the following: operations managers, event managers, operations supervisors, concessions managers, and director of event services.

JRV MANAGEMENT[5]

Established in 1986, JRV Management provides services to clients in the development, planning, and management of facilities, projects, and programs. The company works with individuals, communities, municipalities, colleges, and professional organizations in planning, constructing, or renovating a facility. In addition, JRV provides facility management for existing buildings.

The company is involved in approximately 200 projects worldwide. Examples of JRV's projects include the following facilities: The Palace of Auburn Hills (Auburn Hills, Mich.), Reunion Arena (Dallas, Texas), Taylor Sportsplex (Taylor, Mich.), Viking Arena (Hazel Park, Mich.), and the Daniel L. Ritchie Wellness & Fitness Center (University of Denver).

JRV's headquarters are located in Taylor, Michigan, and it has the following positions in Michigan and Ohio: general managers, assistant general managers, marketing managers, and business/scheduling managers.

Endnotes

1. Copeland, K. and Joyner, C. (2008, Mar. 28). Lights Out for Some Aging Arenas. *USA Today*, p. 3A.

2. Masteralexis, L., Barr, C., and Hums, M. (2005). *Principles and Practice of Sport Management*. Sudbury, MA: Jones and Bartlett.

3. These numbers are an approximation based on the number of events held at the TD Banknorth Garden in Boston. These numbers will differ from one venue to another, but are meant to give the reader a general idea of the busy schedule of a large-scale arena.

4. Welcome to Global Spectrum. (2008). Global-Spectrum.com. Retrieved August 5, 2008, from http://www.global-spectrum.com/default.asp?lnopt=-1&sn1opt=1&sn2opt=1&month=8&year=2008&newsID=0.

5. JRV: Home. (2008). JRVManagement.com. Retrieved August 5, 2008. from http://www.jrvmanagement.com/home.html.

Ticketing

Ticketing is the buying and reselling of tickets for athletic and other entertainment events. The ticketing business is becoming an increasingly important area in the sports industry as ticketing companies are using the Internet to find new ways in which to sell tickets. The ticketing industry, which once primarily consisted of traditional ticketing agencies that held agreements with arenas and stadiums to sell their tickets at face value, now boasts many new forms of ticketing such as online auction sales, and re-selling. These companies may also package the tickets along with hotel rooms, transportation, and other entertainment. This chapter discusses a few of the leading companies in the ticketing industry in order to provide a general idea of the business.

TICKETMASTER[1]

Established in 1976, Ticketmaster is one of the world's largest ticketing companies. It provides ticket sales and distribution through its website, approximately 6,500 retail outlets, and 20 telephone call centers.

Ticketmaster serves more than 9,000 clients worldwide in countries such as the United States, Canada, Ireland, United Kingdom, Norway, Australia, Finland, Denmark, Mexico, Brazil, Sweden, Chile, Argentina, and the Netherlands. Tickets are available for all different types of events. The company provides exclusive ticketing services, such as ticket sales and distribution, for arenas, stadiums, performing arts venues, museums, and theaters. In 2007, Ticketmaster sold 128 million tickets worth over $7 billion.

Ticketmaster is owned and operated by IAC/InterActiveCorp (IACI), a publicly traded company on the NASDAQ Stock Exchange (ticker symbol IACI). IACI generated overall revenues of $6.37 billion in 2006, and Ticketmaster contributed $1 billion to the company's overall revenues.[2]

Ticketmaster is headquartered in West Hollywood, California, and has departments in retailing, services, and marketing. Specific job titles at the company include client service representatives, who launch new Ticketmaster products and develop special products; marketing associates, who develop and implement marketing plans; and retail area managers, who are responsible for analyzing and evaluating business needs. These jobs are located throughout the United States and Canada.

STUBHUB[3]

Created in March 2000, StubHub is an open marketplace where fans can buy and sell tickets to sporting, concert, theater, and other live entertainment events. The company provides a platform via the Internet or by telephone that gives fans the opportunity to purchase tickets at fair market value, even for events that are sold out.

Founded as a class project by Stanford MBA students Jeff Fluhr and Eric Baker, StubHub brings together sellers and buyers through its ticket service. The company's partners include 15 colleges, 8 NFL teams, 4 NBA teams, and 2 NHL teams. In addition, StubHub partners with artists such as Britney Spears, Coldplay, and Alanis Morissette to offer tickets to exclusive events, often in support of the performers' favorite charities. StubHub works with partners to market their available tickets, but does not directly acquire the tickets from the teams or events. Instead, they serve as a way to connect buyers and sellers.

In 2005, the company sold $200 million worth of tickets, which was triple the amount sold in 2004. As a result, StubHub generated approximately $50 million in commissions. StubHub charges the seller 15% commission of the ticket price and the buyer 10% of the ticket price. In 2007, eBay purchased StubHub for $310 million.

The company employs nearly 200 professionals in departments such as business operations, inside sales, accounting, marketing, and technical operations. Examples of jobs within the company include corporate account sales manager and director of sports business development. StubHub is headquartered in San Francisco, California, and operates an east coast office in East Granby, Connecticut.

FIRSTDIBZ[4]

Founded in 2001 as the Ticket Reserve and renamed First-DIBZ in 2008, this company provides a marketplace for fans to purchase and sell tickets to popular sporting events. Modeled after financial futures, a "DIBZ" is traded through an online marketplace that allows individuals to purchase and sell tickets based on potential contingent events. For example, a fan can buy a "DIBZ" that represents an ability to buy a ticket at face value for a playoff or championship game for their favorite team, if that team reaches that game. The fan has the choice to hold onto the "DIBZ" or sell the "DIBZ" up until the team is eliminated or the market is closed.

"DIBZ" are available for such events as the Super Bowl, NBA Finals, Stanley Cup, BCS Championship Series, and the Final Four. The price of each "DIBZ" is initially set by FirstDIBZ, but after that it depends on how much another fan is willing to pay for it. FirstDIBZ charges a transaction fee of 7% for the seller and 10% for the buyer. FirstDIBZ headquarters are located in Chicago, Illinois, and the company employs professionals in departments such as customer service, sales, human resources, and marketing.

Endnotes

1. IAC: Home. (n.d.). IAC.com. Retrieved August 5, 2008, from http://www.iac.com.

2. Smith, E. and Vascellaro, J. (2007, Aug. 23). Ticketmaster Halts Live Nation Talks. *The Wall Street Journal*, p. B3.

3. StubHub: Home. (n.d.). StubHub.com. Retrieved August 5, 2008, from http://www.stubhub.com.

4. FirstDIBZ: Home. (n.d.). FirstDIBZ.com. Retrieved August 5, 2008, from http://www.firstdibz.com/home.html.

Concessions

Concessions is a large segment of the sports industry, specializing in providing food service to fans at sporting events. Concessions is not limited to the typical "ball game fare"; it also provides food service to luxury suites, high end club seats that have personal service, and the newest trend in the concession segment, in-stadium restaurants. Two of the companies in the concessions industry are Aramark and Centerplate, which are discussed in this chapter.

ARAMARK[1,2]

Aramark Corporation is a publicly traded company specializing in food services for sports arenas and stadiums, facilities management, and uniform and career apparel to healthcare institutions, universities and school districts, and businesses around the world. Aramark provides food service to all areas of stadiums and arenas including general foods, luxury suites, and in-stadium restaurants. Established in 1936 by Dave Davidson, Aramark began as a vending business. In December 2001, Aramark went public and currently is traded on the New York Stock Exchange under the ticker symbol RMK. Headquartered in Philadelphia, Aramark has approximately 250,000 employees serving clients in 19 countries.[3] Aramark has over 75 clients including professional sports teams, colleges and universities, and convention centers, and has serviced 13 Olympic Games. In 2007, Aramark had total sales of $12.4 billion and earned $30.9 million in net income. Aramark has the following departments: culinary, finance/accounting, human resources, information technology, marketing, operations, sales, and supply chain management. Departments in Aramark include marketing, operations, and sales located in sports and entertainment venues such as Shea Stadium, Coors Field, and Fenway Park.

CENTERPLATE[4,5]

Centerplate is a catering, concessions, management, and merchandise service provider for sports facilities, convention centers, and other entertainment venues across North America. Established in 1973 with headquarters in Spartanburg, South Carolina, Centerplate has over 30,000 full-time and part-time employees and generates over $600 million in revenues annually. Since December 2003, Centerplate has been a publicly traded company on the American Stock Exchange under the ticker symbol CVP.[5] Centerplate's client list includes 11 NFL teams, 6 MLB teams, 4 MLB spring training facilities, 25 minor league baseball teams, 2 NBA teams, 2 NHL teams, 30 convention centers, 27 arenas, 9 amphitheaters, 15 raceways, 17 college athletic facilities, 3 facility management centers, 7 parks and recreation areas, and 8 miscellaneous areas in Hawaii. Management services include construction and opening services, sales and marketing, management, security, retail food and merchandise, suite and club catering, ticketing and box office services, financial management, and staffing/labor negotiations. Internship opportunities are available in marketing, operations, and sales located in sports and entertainment venues such as Yankee Stadium, the Superdome, the Rose Bowl, and the Palace at Auburn Hills.

Endnotes

1. About Aramark. (n.d.). Aramark.com. Retrieved August 5, 2008, from http://www.aramark.com/MainLanding.aspx?PostingID=336&ChannelID=187.

2. Bramhall, J. (n.d.). ARAMARK Corporation. *Hoovers*. Retrieved November 15, 2007, from http://www.hoovers.com/aramark/--ID__40038--/free-co-factsheet.xhtml.

3. ARAMARK Ranks First in Its Industry on FORTUNE'S List of America's Most Admired Companies. (2006, Feb. 21). Aramark Press Release. Retrieved November 15, 2007, from http://www.aramark.com/PressReleaseDetailTemplate.aspx?PostingID=680&ChannelID=321.

4. Centerplate: Home. (n.d.). Centerplate.com. Retrieved August 5, 2008, from http://www.centerplate.com.

5. Centerplate Profile. (n.d.). Yahoo! Finance. Retrieved November 15, 2007, from http://finance.yahoo.com/q/pr?s=CVP.

34

Multimedia

Multimedia is content that is distributed in a variety of forms, such as via print, radio, television, online, and digitally. Some of these individual areas are discussed in Chapters 35–37. This chapter examines ESPN, the leading distributor of multimedia sports news. ESPN is a leader in the sports media industry, along with such companies as CBS Sports and *Sports Illustrated*.

ESPN

Founder Bill Rasmussen created Entertainment and Sports Programming Network (now just ESPN) in 1978 to deliver sports-related content via television to viewers throughout the nation via satellite. As originally intended, the television network continues to be the main driver of ESPN's business. However, ESPN now has a total of seven domestic networks devoted to sports entertainment that reach more than 89 million homes across the United States and another 190 countries through ESPN International. (See information later in this chapter on all the networks.) Famous for its daily sports news show, *SportsCenter*, ESPN has diversified its content and has produced nearly 40 different programs and movies. ESPN negotiates television deals with many different leagues and entities, including the NFL, NCAA, Little League Baseball, and the Masters Gold Tournament (**Table 34-1**). ESPN has used its strong brand, accessibility, and customer loyalty to gain its top spot among sports networks.

In 1992, ESPN first began to expand from the television business and established ESPN Radio. From 1992 to 2000, ESPN experienced tremendous growth as it added two more television networks (ESPN2 and ESPN Classic), its highly visited website (ESPN.com), its first restaurant (ESPN Zone in Baltimore), and its magazine publication (*ESPN: The Magazine*).

Today, ESPN is the world's leading multimedia sports entertainment company. With over 50 business entities, ESPN has the most diverse portfolio of multimedia sports assets in the world. A conglomerate of television networks, radio stations, websites, magazine publications, and restaurants, ESPN has leveraged its world-renowned brand into several distinct areas of business.

- ESPN's ownership structure is divided between Walt Disney, which owns 80%, and Hearst, which owns 20%. Walt Disney owns an array of media networks including ABC, Touchstone Television, ABC Radio, and Disney Channel.

- Headquartered in Bristol, Connecticut, ESPN employs professionals in a multitude of departments in Bristol as well as in regional offices throughout the United States. The various departments include accounting, finance, marketing, promotions, new media, publishing, on-air talent, research, sales, and production (both remote and onsite). ESPN also operates an internship program for both undergraduate and graduate students, with most positions located at the company headquarters.

History of ESPN[1,2]

1978

- Founded as the Entertainment and Sports Programming Network (ESPN) by former Hartford Whalers play-by-play man Bill Rasmussen and his son Scott Rasmussen, by putting $9,000 on several credit cards.

1979

- Bill Rasmussen sold 85% of the company to Getty Oil to gain funding for the project, including the cost of building the Bristol, Connecticut, operations base and the satellites.

Table 34-1   ESPN Major Sports Rights

Property	Years	Value	Final Season
NFL: Monday Night Football	8	$8.8 billion	2013
NASCAR (shared with ABC)	8	$4.48 billion	2014
NBA (shared with ABC/TNT)	8	$7.6 billion	2016
MLB	8	$2.4 billion	2013
NCAA Championships (multiple sports)	11	$200 million	2013
Men's & Women's World Cup	8	$100 million	2014
MLS (shared with ABC)	8	$7–8 million	2014

- ESPN signed its first major sports television contract on March 1, gaining exclusive rights to broadcast many NCAA sporting events.

- Anheuser-Busch signed the then-largest advertising contract in the history of cable television with ESPN.

- ESPN debuted with its signature telecast *SportsCenter* on September 7.

- One week after its debut, prominent sports announcer Jim Simpson left NBC and joined ESPN.

1983

- ESPN was distributed internationally for the first time.

- The network became the largest cable network in terms of accessibility.

1984

- Bill Rasmussen sold his remaining 15% share in ESPN to Getty Oil for $20 million.

- ABC acquired ESPN from Getty Oil, which was then owned by Texaco Inc, for $237 million. ABC later sold a 20% stake to Nabisco for $60 million.[3]

1985

- The name of the company was officially changed to ESPN.

1987

- ESPN signed the NFL to the first cable contract to broadcast games in primetime on Sunday evenings, an event that marked a turning point for the company as a cable TV network because it could then compete with the networks (ABC, NBC, and CBS).

1988

- ESPN International was launched, airing much material similar to that on ESPN but in 12 different languages. It also added such sports as International Cricket, Formula One auto racing, Indy Racing League, English Premier League soccer, and UEFA Champions League soccer.

- Hearst Corporation bought a 20% position that was held at the time by RJR Nabisco.

1992

- ESPN Radio network was introduced.

- The retail sector, ESPN Enterprises, was created in November.

1993

- ESPN2, a new cable channel, was launched in over 10 million homes.

- The ESPY awards were started to honor both professional and amateur athletes. Proceeds from the event went to the V Foundation, a cancer-fighting nonprofit group founded in honor of former North Carolina State basketball coach Jim Valvano, who died of cancer.

1995

- Disney purchased the ABC Media Network (including ESPN) for $19 billion.

- The Internet site ESPNET SportsZone was launched, starting with coverage of the NCAA Final Four basketball tournament. The website's name later changed to ESPN SportsZone and eventually to ESPN.com.

- ESPN developed, produced, and broadcasted the first ever Extreme Games in Rhode Island in June. The event became an annual competition referred to as the X Games. (See Chapter 27 for more on the X Games.)

1996

- ESPNEWS cable channel was launched with over 1.5 million subscribers, providing 24-hours-a-day sports highlights, scores, and news.

1997

- ABC Radio purchased WMVP-AM in Chicago and named it ESPN Radio 1000, the network's flagship station.

1998

- ESPN purchased the Classic Sports Network (CSN) and renamed it ESPN Classic. CSN was established in 1994 by Stephen Greenberg, and the network aired documentaries and replays of some of the greatest games in sports history.

- ESPN Zone opened in Baltimore, Maryland, becoming the first in a franchise of ESPN-themed restaurant and entertainment complexes. ESPN Zones feature hundreds of televisions with sports programming, live radio and television broadcasts, and an ESPN Arena where customers can play sport arcade games.

- *ESPN: The Magazine*, an all-sports magazine appealing to the younger generation of sports fans, was launched in March.

2003

- The first Major League Baseball game of the season aired as the first telecast of ESPN HD (high definition). This high-definition simulcast was available to 1.1 million subscribers.

- ESPN.com received the General Excellence in Online Journalism award.

- *ESPN: The Magazine* was awarded the Circulation Excellence Award and the National Magazine Award for General Excellence.

2004

- ESPN Deportes, a 24-hour Spanish-language sports network, was launched. Live broadcasts included games from the Dominican Baseball League and Pacific Baseball League, many professional American sports, and a Spanish *SportsCenter.*

- ESPN and MLB agreed on a $2.4-billion 8-year deal in September, which represented a 50% increase in annual rights fees.

- ESPN and the NFL agreed to a rights fee of $8.8 billion for a new 8-year Monday Night Football deal.

2005

- ESPNU was launched covering solely college sports with many live college games.

- Electronic Arts (EA) acquired the ESPN license to use for 15 years on its video games such as All-Pro Football 2K8, NHL 2K8, and NBA 2K9.

- ESPN added a new section to its website, ESPN Cars, a joint venture with Autobytel.

- The ESPN 360 website was launched through 14 different broadband providers, offering short video clips of game highlights.

- ESPN2 HD was launched in the same fashion as ESPN HD with over 100 live telecasts in high definition in its first year.

2006

- ESPN Mobile, a wireless service marketed to its fan base, was launched; the service included sports data and video feeds delivered to the handset.

- ESPN Mobile shut down effective December 31, 2006. ESPN Mobile agreed to refund the price of all handsets that were sold.

- Monday Night Football moved to ESPN after being broadcast for 36 years on the ABC Network.

2008

- ESPN launched a live "morning" *SportsCenter.* Traditionally in the morning, ESPN would run replays of the previous night's *SportsCenter.*

Structure of ESPN

Television Networks

- ESPN: Original, primary television network dedicated to games, highlights, news, commentary, and scheduled daily shows.

- ESPN2: Secondary television network that airs games, highlights, news, and scheduled daily shows.

- ESPN Classic: Network devoted to classic historic footage including games, documentaries, and highlights; also airs an occasional live game.

- ESPNEWS: Network showing 24 hours of current news, information, and highlights.

- ESPN HD: Network airing the same content as ESPN, but in a high-definition format.

- ESPN2 HD: Network airing the same contents as ESPN2, but in a high-definition format.

- ESPNU: Network covering and televising solely collegiate sports.

- ESPN International: Syndicates programming of 25 networks (e.g., ESPN Latin America, ESPN Brazil, ESPN+, NHL Network, etc.) in over 190 countries. *SportsCenter* is locally produced in five languages: Spanish, Portuguese, Hindi, English, and Mandarin.

- ESPN Deportes: 24-hour Spanish language sports network.

- ESPN Regional TV: Syndicated sports television broadcasted in certain areas.

- ESPN Now: A station featuring live sports news, headlines, and scores from ESPN.com and updated sports television listings.

- ESPN Today: The first interactive sports channel that uses "on demand" features to provide viewers with text and graphics of sports-related information including top news stories, scores, statistics, standings, and schedules, plus links that directly tune to the ESPN Networks.

- ESPN Pay-Per-View: A service that includes television packages such as certain NCAA Baseball Championship games, martial arts programs, fantasy league specials, ESPN Full Court, ESPN Original Entertainment (EOE), ESPN Game Plan, and various movies.

Radio

- ESPN Radio: 24-hour syndicated nationwide radio with game broadcasts and daily shows, including Mike and Mike in the morning (Greenberg and Golic), The Fantasy Focus, GameDay, and GameNight.

Website

- ESPN.com: One of the most viewed sports sites on the World Wide Web; includes scores, highlights, stories, articles, and information on teams and leagues.
- ESPN 360: Delivers live Internet viewing of games and events for college football and basketball, UEFA, U.S. Open Golf, French Open, NASCAR Busch Series, AFL, and MLS.

Publications

- *ESPN: The Magazine:* Bi-weekly publication

Restaurants

- ESPN Zone: Locations in Anaheim, Atlanta, Baltimore, Chicago, Denver, Las Vegas, New York, and Washington, DC

Ownership of ESPN

- Walt Disney: 80%
- Hearst Company: 20%

Endnotes

1. ESPN. (n.d.). Funding Universe. Retrieved November 15, 2007, from http://www.fundinguniverse.com/company-histories/ESPN-Inc-Company-History.html.

2. Lowry, T. (2005, Oct. 17). ESPN: The Empire. *Business Week.* Retrieved November 15, 2007, from http://www.businessweek.com/magazine/content/05_42/b3955001.htm.

3. Eskenazi, G. (1989, Sep. 18). The Media Business; ESPN's 10-Year Journey to the Top. *The New York Times.* Retrieved August 5, 2008, from http://query.nytimes.com/gst/fullpage.html?res=950DE5DA1338F93BA2575AC0A96F948260&sec=&spon=&pagewanted=all.

CHAPTER THIRTY-FIVE

Television

Television has played a major role in the development and growth of the sports world as we know it today. Every year hundreds of millions of fans tune in to watch sports broadcasts. In 2008, the NFL's Super Bowl alone is estimated to have been seen by nearly 100 million people worldwide. Due to the large number of people who watch sports, sports broadcasts are prime advertising platforms and have been a driving forcing in turning sports broadcasting into a billion-dollar industry. This chapter examines five of the leading television networks and their presentation of sporting events.

ABC SPORTS

ABC Sports was founded in 1960 under the leadership of Roone Arledge. ABC Sports was the pioneer in bringing sports to primetime television, most notably in the development of Monday Night Football, which debuted in the fall of 1970. The sports department continued to grow in the 1980s with the purchase of ESPN in 1984. (For more on ESPN, another leading television network, see Chapter 34.) ABC and ESPN were eventually purchased in 1995 by the Disney Company for $19 billion.[1] In addition to its television broadcasts, the network has a radio division called ABC Sports, which provides play-by-play coverage of ABC events. ESPN Radio also falls under the ABC Sports umbrella and provides 24-hour sports programming. As of 2007, ABC Television was the home to NBA Basketball, including the NBA Finals; PGA Tour events; Indy Car Racing; The Belmont Stakes; and U.S. Figure Skating Championships (**Table 35-1**). In November 2005, ABC acquired the rights to the Men's and Women's World Cup from 2007 to 2014. ABC Sports has various departments including communications, distribution, sales, programming and talent, and advertising/sponsorships. ABC Sports headquarters are located in New York City.

CBS SPORTS[2]

CBS Sports is a division of the Columbia Broadcasting System (CBS). CBS is a mass media company with more than 14 divisions, and is one of the largest television networks in the United States. CBS has had a long tradition of sports broadcasting dating back to the 1940s and 1950s in both radio and television transmissions. In 1946, CBS became the first station to broadcast NFL games, and CBS later broadcast the first baseball game in color in 1951. Currently, CBS holds the rights to AFC football games of the NFL, the NCAA Men's Basketball Tournament, the PGA Championship, and The Masters (**Table 35-2**). In 2007, approximately two thirds of CBS's programming budget was spent on sports.[3] CBS Sports also delivers its content via the Internet. In 2004, CBS's parent company, Viacom, purchased Sportsline.com and later renamed the site CBS Sportsline.com.

Table 35-1   ABC Major Sports Rights

League	Years	Value	Final Season
NBA	8	$7.4 billion	2015–2016
MLS	8	$64 million	2014
Rose Bowl	8	$300 million	2014
ACC Football	7	$258 million	2010
Pac 10 Football	5	$229 million	2011
Big East Football	6	$200 million	2012
Big Ten Football/ Basketball	10	$1 billion	2017
Big Twelve Football	8	$480 million	2016
NASCAR	8	$4.8 billion	2013

Table 35-2   CBS Major Sports Rights

Property	Years	Value	Final Season
NFL	6 Years	$3.7 billion	2011
PGA	6 Years	Unavailable	2012
NCAA Men's Basketball Tournament	11 Years	$6 billion	2013
ACC Basketball	10 Years	$300 million	2011
SEC Basketball and Football	4 Years	$52 million	2009
Big Ten Basketball	5 Years	Unavailable	2010
U.S. Open (Tennis)	6 Years	$228 million	2008
The Masters (Golf)	1 Year	$3 million/year	Year to year

Table 35-3   NBC Major Sports Rights

League	Years	Value	Final Season
Summer/ Winter Olympics	3 Summer and 3 Winter Games	$4.3 billion	2012
NFL	6 Years	$3.6 billion	2011
PGA	6 Years	Unavailable	2012
NHL	2 Years	Revenue sharing agreement	2007
Wimbledon	4 Years	$52 million	2006
Notre Dame Football	5 Years	$45 million	2010
U.S. Open (Golf)	9 Years	Unavailable	2014

CBS also acquired College Sports Television (CSTV) for $325 million in November 2005.[4] CSTV, which has since been renamed CBS College Sports Network (CSN), is a multimedia company that broadcasts college events. CSN also provides content via the Internet for over 175 Division I schools' athletic programs and 12 athletic associations including USA Baseball, National Association of College Directors of Athletics (NACDA), and National Association of Intercollegiate Athletics (NAIA). CSN has a cable channel that is available nationally to digital cable and satellite subscribers. CSN also produces the broadcast of some games and sells these games to stations and networks that are interested in broadcasting them. CBS Sports is involved with several CBS networks and stations, including CBS Corporation, CBSTV, UPN, CBS TV stations, CBS Radio, CSTV networks, and CBS Outdoor. CBS Sports is divided into several departments including operations and engineering, marketing, law, and sports. CBS headquarters are located in New York City.

NBC SPORTS

NBC Sports is a subsidiary of the National Broadcasting Company, which is owned by General Electric. NBC Sports has a long history of sports television, dating back to the late 1940s, when its broadcasts sparked the sale of televisions. As of 2007, NBC had rights agreements with the NFL for the Sunday night game, PGA Tour, U.S. Open (golf), NASCAR, Wimbledon, the Kentucky Derby, Arena League Football, and the NHL, including the rights to the Stanley Cup Playoffs and Finals (**Table 35-3**). NBC is also home to the Olympics through the 2012 games, providing 24-hour coverage of the games since the Athens games in 2004.

The network has an Internet presence on the MSNBC website with sports news and features from NBC Sports personalities. Departments in NBC Sports include production,

development, marketing, web programming, new media, finance, communications, and project management. NBC Sports main headquarters are located in New York City.

NBC Universal Olympic Games rights:[5]

- 2006 Winter Games—Torino: $614 million
- 2008 Summer Games—Beijing: $894 million
- 2010 Winter Games—Vancouver, BC: $820 million
- 2012 Summer Games—London: $1.181 billion

FOX SPORTS[6]

Fox Sports encompasses both national programming that is seen on the Fox Network and regional programming that can be seen on 19 cable regional sports channels. Fox Sports, a subsidiary of the Fox Entertainment Group, was created in 1994 with the acquisition of the broadcasting rights to the National Football Conference games of the NFL for $1.58 billion. The Fox Entertainment Group is a film and television production and distribution entity with the following divisions: broadcast television, cable and satellite television, film, television production, sports, and corporate. In 1996, Fox acquired the rights to Major League Baseball games, including all postseason games. Fox also has the rights to several NASCAR events, including the Daytona 500, as well as select NFL games (**Table 35-4**). Fox Sports is divided into several departments that include Fox Sports; foxsports.com (in conjunction with MSN); Fox Sports Net; Fox Sports en Espanol; Fox Sports Enterprises; Fox Sports Pacific, Central, and Atlantic; Fox Sports World; Fox Sports Interactive Media; Fox Soccer Channel; Fuel TV; and the Speed Channel.

In order to deliver regional coverage, Fox created Fox Sports Net (FSN). As of 2007, there were 16 FSN regional sports networks that delivered local broadcasts of games, talk

Table 35-4   Fox Major Sports Rights

League	Years	Value	Final Season
NFL (NFC)	6	$4.3 billion	2011
MLB	6	$2.5 billion	2006
NASCAR*	8	$2.4 billion	2008
Bowl Championship Series (Orange, Sugar, Fiesta, BCS Championship Game)	4	$340 million	2010

*Shared with other networks.

shows, and other local programming. Many of these stations have local broadcast rights agreements with MLB, NBA, and NHL teams. National programs on FSN include *Best Damn Sports Show Period*, *The Sports List*, *Beyond the Glory*, and poker. In addition, Fox has a nationally syndicated radio station, which provides 24-hour sports talk radio where fan participation is strongly encouraged. Some of Fox Sports' departments include production, sports advertising sales, research and programming, business and legal affairs, and communications. Fox Sports headquarters are located in Los Angeles, California.

COMCAST SPORTSNET

Comcast SportsNet (or CSN) is a group of regional sports networks (RSN). The group is primarily owned by the Comcast cable television company, but some RSNs are co-owned with local sports teams. The channel lineup includes CSN Chicago, CSN Philadelphia, CSN Mid-Atlantic (serving Baltimore/Washington), CSN West (serving northern and central California), CSN Northwest (serving Portland, Oregon), and SportsNet New York. In 2007, Comcast also acquired 100% control of FSN New England (serving Boston) and a 60% stake in FSN Bay Area (serving the San Francisco/Oakland area).[7] In addition, Comcast would also like to expand the channel's programming with new shows, such as a newscast and talk shows. This would require the channel to hire additional employees in the areas of production and on-air talent. The *Boston Globe* reported Comcast would need to hire between 8 and 10 anchors and reporters and a host of producers and other staff to pull off its strategy for FSN New England.[8]

The RSNs typically have rights to carry some or all of the local professional teams in baseball, basketball, hockey, and soccer. They also air nightly sports-news and talk shows, postgame shows, and other shoulder programming related to local NFL teams, as well as a variety of college sports programming.

Comcast SportsNet typically hires professionals in the following areas: production, sports advertising sales, research and programming, business and legal affairs, on-air talent, and communications.

Endnotes

1. Einstein, D. and Pelline, J. (1995, Aug. 1). Disney's Stunning Deal to Buy ABC. *The San Francisco Chronicle*, p. A1. Retrieved April 17, 2008, from http://www.sfgate.com/cgi-bin/article.cgi?f=/c/a/1995/08/01/MN58745.DTL&hw=Disney&sn=008&sc=797.

2. Our Company. (n.d.). CBSCorporation.com. Retrieved August 5, 2008, from http://www.cbscorporation.com/our_company/index.php.

3. Boughton, D. (2008, Mar. 26). Eye Drops: CBS Sports Programming Costs Down Again. *Street and Smith's Sports Business Daily*. Retrieved April 11, 2008, from http://www.sportsbusinessdaily.com/article/119527.

4. Hiestand, M. (2005, Nov. 3). CBS Paying 325 Million for Purchase of CSTV. *USA Today*, p. C3.

5. Isadore, C. (2004, Aug. 17). Covering the Business Side of the Olympics. Donald W. Reynolds National Center for Business Journalism. Retrieved February 6, 2007, from http://www.businessjournalism.org/pages/biz/2004/08/covering_the_business_side_of.

6. Fox Careers: TV and Sports. (n.d.). FoxCareers.com. Retrieved August 5, 2008, from http://www.foxcareers.com/tv_sports.

7. Reidy, C. (2007, Apr. 30). Comcast to Buy Rest of FSN New England. *Boston Globe*. Retrieved April 17, 2008, from http://www.boston.com/business/ticker/2007/04/comcast_to_buy.html.

8. Reed, K. (2007, June 6). Comcast Plans to Beef Up Fox Sports New England. *Boston Globe*, p. C1.

CHAPTER THIRTY-SIX

Radio

Since the 1920s, radio has played a major role in the growth of the sports industry. With the invention of the radio, fans for the first time were able to experience a live sporting event without actually being in attendance. Very few people could attend every sporting event they wished to see, so radio presented an easy way for fans to stay connected to the game. Today, there are radio networks dedicated entirely to broadcasting sporting events, sports news, and sports-related talk shows. This chapter examines a few of the leading sports radio networks in the United States today.

WFAN 660 AM

WFAN 660 AM, commonly referred to as "The Fan," was the first 24-hour sports radio network in the United States. WFAN, which is owned by Viacom and based out of Astoria, New York, started broadcasting on July 1, 1987. WFAN features primarily sports talk radio that encourages fans to participate by voicing their opinions on air. WFAN's signature sports program was Mike and the Mad Dog, featuring Mike Francesa and Christopher "Mad Dog" Russo. It was also broadcast on the YES network. WFAN was the first radio network to be syndicated, and can now be heard on over 90 sports radio stations (and markets) across the United States. In 2008, Mad Dog left for Sirius Satellite Radio.

In addition to sports talk programming, WFAN also holds the radio broadcasting rights to several New York and New Jersey franchises including the New York Giants, New York Mets, New Jersey Devils, and New Jersey Nets. WFAN also holds the New York–area game rights to Notre Dame Football. WFAN grossed the highest revenue among radio stations in 2005, totaling $54 million.[1] According to Arbitron ratings for fall 2006, WFAN posted a 2.2 average rating, which was tops for sports networks in New York and the 14th most listened to radio station in New York. Some other leading radio networks are WEEI (Boston), WWLS (Oklahoma City), and KFAN (Minneapolis/St. Paul).

SATELLITE RADIO

Satellite radio is a radio service that is sent via satellite to cars, homes, and public locations for subscribers who have special radios that can receive the signal. There are two satellite radio providers in the United States, XM and SIRIUS. Each transmits more than 100 channels of radio, most of which are commercial free. Subscribers pay a monthly fee to receive the service. In 2008, XM and Sirius merged to form a single company.

XM Satellite Radio

XM Satellite Radio (XM) has forged partnerships with a host of sports leagues and entities to provide fans with live game broadcast and other sports news and features through satellite radio. Included in the sports portfolio are Major League Baseball, NASCAR, PGA Tour, college sports, ESPN Radio, Sporting News Radio, Fox Sports Radio, Indy Car Series Racing, and other sports talk shows and news programs. XM offers over 160 digital channels, including 36 sports channels.

Founded in 1997, XM is considered the leading provider of satellite radio, producing revenues of $240 million in the third quarter of 2006. However, as of 2006, it had yet to have a profitable year (losing $666 million in 2005).[2] XM's corporate headquarters and broadcast facilities are located in Washington, DC, but it also operates broadcast facilities in New York and Nashville, and additional offices in Boca Raton, Florida; Southfield, Michigan; and Yokohama, Japan. XM is publicly traded on the NASDAQ stock exchange under the symbol XMSR. The company has departments and internships in a wide variety of areas including sales, marketing, and programming.

SIRIUS Satellite Radio

SIRIUS Satellite Radio has forged partnerships with a host of sports leagues to provide fans with live game action through satellite radio. Included in the sports portfolio are the National Football League, National Basketball Association, National Hockey League, NCAA sports, English Premier Soccer, and various sports talk shows and news programs. SIRIUS offers over 125 channels of satellite radio including 9 sports channels.

Founded in 1998, SIRIUS is considered the #2 satellite radio provider behind XM, and produced revenues of $922 million in 2007. Like XM, SIRIUS has yet to post a profitable year and lost $565.25 million in 2007.[3] The company is headquartered at Rockefeller Center in New York City and also has offices in New Jersey and Michigan. SIRIUS is publicly traded on the NASDAQ stock exchange under the symbol SIRI. SIRIUS offers full-time and internship opportunities in the following departments: music/talk programming, marketing, retail, public relations, information and technology, engineering, human resources, and finance.

Endnotes

1. The Continued Rise of Sports Radio. (2006, Apr. 24). *Street and Smith's SportsBusiness Journal*, p. 17.

2. XM Satellite Radio Holdings Inc. (n.d.). *Yahoo! Finance*. Retrieved November 15, 2007, from http://finance.yahoo.com/q/pr?s=XMSR.

3. SIRIUS Satellite Radio 2007 Annual Report. (2008, Feb. 29). SIRIUS.com. Retrieved August 5, 2008, from http://investor.sirius.com/edgar.cfm?DocType=Annual&Year.

Print

Print is another form of media, but unlike television and radio its content is delivered on paper in newspapers, magazines, and trade journals. This chapter examines *Sports Illustrated*, one of the leading sports magazines in the United States, and *Street and Smith's SportsBusiness Journal*, the leading trade journal for the sports industry. However, there are many other popular magazines, newspapers, and trade journals that cover the topic of sports.

SPORTS ILLUSTRATED

Sports Illustrated is the premier sports magazine publication, with an average of over 20 million readers per week. *Sports Illustrated* was launched in 1954 and was the first magazine with a million-plus circulation to win the National Magazine Award for General Excellence twice, earning the award in both 1986 and 1989. Published weekly, *Sports Illustrated* provides in depth coverage of all major sports with features on professional, collegiate, and amateur athletes and opinion pieces from several outstanding writers. *Sports Illustrated* has made several attempts to branch out to other markets including the creation of *Sports Illustrated for Kids* in 1989 and *SI on Campus*, which was launched in 2003. In 2007, *SI* subscriptions were over 3.1 million; its main competitor, *ESPN: The Magazine,* had approximately 2 million subscribers.[1]

In 1996, Turner Broadcasting System merged with Time-Warner, *Sports Illustrated*'s parent company. The merger led to the creation of CNN and *Sports Illustrated*'s joint online news venture, CNNSI.com, which was launched on July 17, 1997. In 2003, the website's title was changed to SI.com, hoping to drive brand awareness to its online content. From the website *SI Digital* was born, which consists of all nonprint media, the majority of which is SI.com but

Jeff Price, president of *Sports Illustrated Digital* (SI.com), speaks at a professional conference. As president, Price is responsible for all digital properties belonging to *SI*: SI.com, SIKids.com, FanNation.com, Golf.com, and DanPatrick.com. In addition, he oversees *SI*'s digital products such as video on demand, broadband television, and satellite radio.

which also includes streaming video features, photos, and fantasy football leagues.

In 2007, SI.com launched FanNation.com, a social networking website that provides users with up-to-the-minute scores, popular blogs, and a forum where users can debate current sports topics. In addition to FanNation, SI also launched Golf.com, a golf-oriented website that has many interactive features including a place to officially track one's golf handicap with the USGA.

Departments in *Sports Illustrated* include photography, advertising sales, subscriptions sales, writing/reporting, editing, copy editing, photography editing, technology, marketing, brand marketing, legal operations, and athlete and team relations. *Sports Illustrated* headquarters are located in New York City.

STREET AND SMITH'S SPORTSBUSINESS JOURNAL[2]

Street and Smith's SportsBusiness Journal (SBJ) is a weekly publication that provides news, analysis, and commentary about the business side of the sports industry. It is the largest trade journal for the sports industry. Launched in April 1998, *SBJ* has an average readership of 54,400, with 17,000 subscriptions as of August 2008. The cost of the journal is $249 for 49 issues. *SBJ* targets many different markets including people who work in the sports industry, people who work with the industry, people who want to get into the industry, and college sport management programs. *SBJ* focuses on the major areas of the sports industry, specifically with features in marketing, media, facilities, the law, and human resources. Articles consist of trends within the sport marketplace, emerging companies and leagues, inter-

views with industry leaders, and commentary on the issues surrounding the business aspects of sport. *SBJ* is based in Charlotte, North Carolina, and has 67 reporters and editors in 44 offices around the country. In addition to its circulation, *SBJ* has a website, sportsbusinessjournal.com, which provides archived stories for its subscribers. Also, a subsidiary to *SBJ*, *Sports Business Daily (SBD)* provides subscribers with daily sports business content, delivered by e-mail, and geared towards the same issues reported in *SBJ*. *SBD* draws information from over 400 news sources and provides up-to-date reporting. The various departments at *SBJ* include writing/reporting, editing, graphic design, research, advertising, production, and administration. *SBJ* also regularly holds conferences pertaining to issues such as marketing, sponsorship, intercollegiate athletics, facilities, and franchises.

Endnotes

1. Average Paid & Verified Subscription Circulation for Top 100 ABC Magazines. (2007). Magazine Publishers of America. Retrieved August 5, 2008, from http://www.magazine.org/CONSUMER_ MARKETING/CIRC_TRENDS/26645.aspx.

2. About Us. (n.d.). *Street and Smith's Sports Business Journal*. Retrieved August 5, 2008, from http://www .sportsbusinessjournal.com/index.cfm?fuseaction= page.static&staticId=2.

Manufacturers

Manufacturers in the sports industry produce a wide range of sports equipment, apparel, and accessories. The majority of these manufacturers' products are sold to department stores and other retail outlets for resale. In addition, many manufacturers also operate their own retail stores where they can better display their products without the competition that would be found in department stores. This chapter discusses some of the leading sports manufacturers, but there are many others from within the sports industry.

NIKE, INC.

Nike, Inc. and its subsidiaries form the largest and most widely known footwear, sports apparel, equipment, and accessory products company worldwide. The company is highly regarded for its innovative product designs as well as its creative and cutting edge marketing and growth strategies. The company sells its products to retail accounts, through its own retail stores, and through a mix of independent distributors and licensees.

University of Oregon track and field coach Bill Bowerman and Phil Knight, a former runner at Oregon and then a Stanford MBA student, developed a shoe to aid runners' performances. Bowerman and Knight each agreed to contribute $500 to create Blue Ribbon Sports in 1964. In the early stages, Blue Ribbon operated out of the basement of Knight's house and the back of his car, but the first 300 pairs of shoes sold in 3 weeks. Ten years later, they changed the name of their company to Nike, which signifies the Greek winged goddess of victory, and simultaneously unveiled the now iconic "swoosh" logo.

Over the last 40 years, Nike has grown from a small business to an international leader in athletic footwear and apparel. In 2008, Nike earned revenues of $18.62 billion and currently employs more than 32,000 workers across six continents. Nearly 60% of its annual sales occur outside of the United States; international sales have exceeded domestic earnings since 2003. In 2008, the Beaverton, Oregon, company operated 297 retail stores in the United States and 260 retail stores internationally.[1]

The company has been considered the innovative leader in the sports retail sector through unique strategic and marketing initiatives. Nike was the first company to utilize top tier athletes to advertise its products. Chicago Bulls rookie Michael Jordan signed on with the company in 1985 and soon after his Air Jordans revolutionized the basketball shoe industry. Many attribute the significant growth of Nike to the alliance with Jordan and his legendary status on and off the court. As of 2008, the company uses premier athletes such as Tiger Woods (golf), Lebron James (basketball), Ladainian Tomlinson (football), Freddy Adu (soccer), and Maria Sharapova (tennis) to promote and market its apparel and equipment. In addition to using star athletes to advertise its products, Nike also sponsors teams and leagues on both the professional and the collegiate levels. According to Nike's quarterly report released February 29, 2008, the company has contract agreements with teams and athletes for $3.37 billion.[2] Using the aforementioned superstars to showcase products has enabled the company to broaden and diversify its portfolio of merchandise and allowed Nike to extend its reach to a wide variety of sports.

When diversifying into more product lines, the company has utilized creative marketing and advertising platforms to build brand awareness and equity. For example, Nike has used Tiger Woods and his immense popularity to build its line of golf products. The theme "Just Do It" has been synonymous with Nike products and has been incorporated into advertising campaigns and television commercials, which include athletes such as Michael Jordan. In 2006, Nike and Apple joined forces to create Nike+iPod Sport Kit, which allows users to install a small device in their shoe that will wirelessly send workout information such as speed and distance to the iPod. The information can then be uploaded onto a PC to track progress over a period of time.

Nike employs professionals in a wide variety of departments including distribution, finance, marketing, product management, research, design and development, and information technology. Nike also operates an internship program every summer that gives students insight on a variety of Nike's business units including sports marketing, logistics, product development, and information technology. The program runs for 10 weeks from June to August; although some of the positions are regionally based, most are located at Nike World Headquarters in Beaverton, Oregon.

Fortune magazine named Nike one of the "100 Best Companies to Work For" in 2008. It recognized the company for employee benefits such as campus fitness centers and a 50% discount on company products, as well as for the company's corporate responsibility efforts in addressing conditions in overseas contract factories.

History of Nike[3]

1962

- Phil Knight, former runner at the University of Oregon, graduated with his MBA from Stanford University.
- Knight's company, Blue Ribbon Sports (BRS), became the distributor of Onitsuka Tiger brand (Japan) footwear in the western United States.

1964

- Phil Knight and his former track coach at University of Oregon, Bill Bowerman, joined together and contributed $500 each to the partnership. Working full time as an accountant, Knight spent his spare time distributing shoes from his father's basement and out of the back seat of his car at track meets.

1965

- Jeff Johnson, an intramural track teammate of Knight's at Stanford, became BRS's first full-time employee.

1966

- Johnson opened the first BRS store in Santa Monica, California.

1967

- Knight and Bill Bowerman incorporated BRS, Inc. The company still operated under the name Blue Ribbon Sports.

1968

- The first BRS West store opened in Eugene, Oregon.

1969

- Knight resigned from teaching at Portland State University to devote himself full time to the company.

1971

- Carolyn Davidson, a graphic design student, designed the famous swoosh trademark, for a $35 fee.
- Johnson gave the business its new name, Nike, the Greek goddess of victory, which was chosen over Knight's idea of calling the company "Dimension 6."
- Bowerman created the "waffle" sole by pouring a liquid rubber compound into his wife's waffle iron.

1972

- BRS and Onitsuka Tiger ended their relationship over a distribution dispute.
- BRS launched the Nike shoe with the waffle sole for athletes competing at the U.S. Olympic Track and Field Trials in Oregon.
- BRS signed its first professional endorser: Romanian tennis star Ilie Nastase.

1973

- American record-holder Steve Prefontaine signed an endorsement to wear Nike brand shoes.

1974

- Shortly after being introduced, the Waffle Trainer featuring Bowerman's famous Waffle outsole became the country's best-selling training shoe.

1977

- BRS started Athletics West, the first U.S. track and field training club for elite athletes.

1978

- BRS officially changed its name to Nike.
- Nike signed tennis great John McEnroe to an endorsement contract.

1979

- Nike and Frank Rudy, a former NASA employee, engineered Nike Air cushioning, the first Air-Sole cushioning system.
- Nike introduced Tailwind, the first running shoe with Nike Air.

1980

- Nike issued an initial public offering of 2,377,000 shares of stock. The original price was $22 per share.
- British runner Steve Ovett became the first athlete to win an Olympic medal wearing Nike shoes.
- Nike overtook Adidas as the top selling shoe in America.

1982

- Nike expanded east by opening a footwear distribution center in Memphis, Tennessee.

- Nike aired its first national television advertisement during the New York Marathon.
- The Air Force 1 basketball shoe became the first Nike basketball shoe to feature the use of the Nike Air technology.

1983

- Joan Benoit, wearing Nike shoes, shattered the women's world marathon record.
- Twenty-three Nike-supported athletes captured medals in the inaugural World Track and Field Championships in Helsinki, Finland.

1984

- Fifty-eight Nike-supported athletes from around the world took home 65 medals at the Olympics in Los Angeles.

1985

- Chicago Bulls basketball rookie, Michael Jordan, endorsed a newly created Nike line of Air Jordan shoes and apparel.

1986

- Corporate revenues surpassed $1 billion.
- Nike began producing apparel collections, first with John McEnroe's tennis line, then a basketball line endorsed by Michael Jordan.

1987

- Nike introduced the Air Max shoe with a controversial "Revolution" ad campaign that used the Beatles' hit song "Revolution" in the background. This was the first time a Beatles song was used by a company for a television advertisement.

1988

- Nike introduced the "Just Do It" marketing campaign slogan.
- Nike acquired the American luxury brand Cole Haan.

1990

- Doors opened to the Nike World Campus located in Beaverton, Oregon. The Nike headquarters included 16 buildings named after athletes who helped grow the company.
- The first Niketown store opened in downtown Portland, Oregon. Niketown is a store featuring only Nike products.

1992

- Nike signed an exclusive agreement with the governing body of U.S. Track & Field to outfit the entire U.S. Olympic Track & Field team with Nike apparel.

1993

- Nike introduced Reuse-A-Shoe, a program that collected athletic shoes and ground them up into Nike Grind, which was used to make new athletic courts, tracks, and fields.

1995

- Nike diversified into hockey by acquiring Canstar Sports Inc., which included the Bauer line of hockey equipment.
- Nike introduced the first Nike skate: Air Excell Elite.
- Nike and the Brazilian National Soccer team came to terms on a $200-million, 10-year sponsorship agreement.

1996

- Niketown New York opened in November.
- Tiger Woods signed with Nike to coincide with Nike's diversification into golf.
- The controversial slogan, "You Don't Win Silver—You Lose Gold," was advertised during the Summer Olympics in Atlanta.

1998

- Nike came under fire from worldwide labor groups such as Global Exchange Organization, the Campaign for Labor Rights, and the National Organization for Women for labor practices. Nike was alleged to have been paying workers $1.60 an hour and maintaining hazardous working conditions in violation of the labor laws overseas. Knight pledged to improve the standards of its manufacturing facilities.[4]

1999

- Nike athlete and cancer survivor Lance Armstrong won his first of seven consecutive Tour de France cycling titles.
- Bill Bowerman, co-founder of Nike, died at age 88.

2000

- Tiger Woods switched to Nike Precision Tour Accuracy golf balls and won the U.S. Open, the British Open, and the PGA Championship during the year.

2002

- Nike acquired Hurley International. Hurley clothing is marketed primarily to surfing, skateboarding, and snowboarding athletes.
- Nike launched NikeGo, a nationwide community program to increase physical activity in American youth.

2003

- For the first time in company history, international sales exceeded U.S. sales with approximately $4.7 billion domestically and approximately $5.1 billion internationally.[5]

- Nike acquired once-bankrupt rival Converse for $305 million. Converse was the pioneer in the athletic footwear market with its Chuck Taylor All-Star model. Converse began manufacturing shoes in 1908, but filed for bankruptcy in 2001.

2004

- Nike created the Exeter Brands Group, a wholly owned subsidiary for athletic footwear and apparel brands at lower prices; brands included Starter, Team Starter, Asphalt, Shaq, and Dunkman.

- William D. Perez, former president and chief executive officer of S.C. Johnson and Son, Inc., became Nike's new president and chief executive officer, after Phil Knight stepped down. Knight remained involved with Nike, serving as the chairman of the board of directors.

2006

- Mark Parker became president and CEO of Nike in January, replacing William Perez. Parker had been a Nike employee since 1979 and is credited by Nike to be the driving force behind the Nike Air franchise.

2008

- Nike, who purchased the Bauer hockey line in 1995 for $395 million, sold its branch of hockey operations, Nike Bauer Inc., and the rights to the Bauer name to Canadian businessman Graeme Roustan for $200 million.

Structure of Nike[6]

Locations

- Nike headquarters are located on 176 acres in Beaverton, Oregon. They currently feature 17 separate buildings, each named after an athlete whose performance and endorsement has made a contribution to the development of the company. In addition to offices, the operations center also has several gyms, athletic fields, and trails for employee use.

- Other offices are located in Tennessee, North Carolina, and the Netherlands.

- There are over 100 sales and administrative offices.

Subsidiaries

- Cole Haan Holdings, Inc.: Based out of Yarmouth, Maine, produces dress and causal attire, footwear, and accessories for both men and women. Produces the Cole Haan G Series, and Bragano clothing lines.

- Converse, Inc.: The North Andover, Massachusetts–based company and former athletic footwear giant now produces both athletic and casual shoes with a lesser focus on apparel and accessories. Its featured line is the Chuck Taylor All-Star, which was once used for athletic competition but now is more commonly associated with casual footwear.

- Exeter Brands Group LLC: Designs and markets shoes and clothing with a headquarters located in New York. Owns the rights to Starter, Team Starter, and Asphalt as well as being the primary licensee of Shaq and Dunkman brands.

- Hurley International LLC: A Costa Mesa, California–based company that focuses on design and sale of clothing appealing to snowboarders, surfers, and skateboarders. Also produces footwear.

- Nike IHM, Inc.: Located in Oregon, Nike IHM designs and manufactures the air soles used in Nike products.

Employees

- Approximately 30,000 people worldwide

- Approximately 650,000 workers are employed in Nike-contracted factories throughout the world

Retail

- Niketown
  - The first Niketown opened in Portland, Oregon, in 1990.
  - Stores average over 30,000 square feet of selling space.
  - They employ more than 4,000 Nike retail associates in the United States.
  - There are more than 10 U.S. Niketown stores.

- Nike factory stores
  - The first factory store opened in 1984. Nike uses factory stores to help sell overstocked inventory or discontinued models.
  - There are more than 80 factory stores in the United States.

NikeWomen

- The first store opened in 2001, catering to women athletes.

- In 2008, there were 14 stores in the United States, Canada, and Europe.

Manufacturing

- Nike does not manufacture any of its own shoes. Instead, it contracts with over 700 factories throughout the world to make the shoes. Nike is the first company in its industry to publish the names and addresses of all factories making Nike branded products.

Money Matters for Nike[7]

- Approximately $18.6 billion in net revenues for the 2008 fiscal year

- U.S. revenues:
  - $6.38 billion in total revenue, up from $5.1 billion in 2005
- Main revenues sources:
  - Footwear: $4.3 billion
  - Apparel: $1.7 billion
  - Equipment: $306.1 million
- Europe, Middle East, and Africa revenues:
  - $5.62 billion in total revenue, up from $4.2 billion in 2005
  - Footwear: $3.11 billion
  - Apparel: $2.08 billion
  - Equipment: $424.3 million
- Asian Pacific market:
  - $2.88 billion in total revenue, up from $1.9 billion in 2005
  - Footwear: $1.5 billion
  - Apparel: $1.14 billion
  - Equipment: $242.2 million
- The Americas (excluding the United States):
  - $1.15 billion in total revenue, up from $695.8 million in 2005
  - Footwear: $792.7 million
  - Apparel: $265.4 million
  - Equipment: $96.0 million

ADIDAS AG[8]

Adidas AG is a global sporting goods company that designs and produces a wide variety of sports footwear and apparel. Adidas was founded as a company in 1948 by Adolf (Adi) Dassler, after Dassler had been making high performance footwear for 28 years. In 2005, Adidas purchased Reebok International in its attempt to challenge Nike for the top sporting goods brand in the world. The merger enabled Adidas to increase its presence in North America and gave the Reebok brand a greater reach on the global stage. Combined, the company realized revenues of $15.8 billion in 2007, second only to Nike, which generated revenues of $16.3 billion over the same time period. The Adidas Group's common shares are listed on the German stock exchange and as over the counter securities as American Depository Receipts (ADRs) in the United States.

Adidas is the official partner with many of the world's biggest sports organizations, including the 2006 FIFA World Cup.

At the end of the year in 2007, Adidas had 31,344 employees in various offices worldwide; its headquarters are located in Herzogenaurach, Germany. Full-time opportunities exist in the following departments: production, retail marketing, sales, accounting/finance, information technology, market research, and design. An internship program exists at the company's headquarters with approximately 340 interns accepted on an annual basis.

History of Adidas[9]

1920

- Adolf Dassler began making athletic shoes at the age of 20.

1925

- By adding spikes and cleats to shoes, Dassler created the first soccer– and track and field–specific shoes.

1949

- After World War II, Dassler founded Adidas as a company.
- Dassler trademarked the now-famous three-stripe trademark for his company.

1963

- Adidas began to manufacture soccer balls.

1967

- Adidas began to produce sports apparel.

1974

- Adidas produced its first tennis raquets.

1976

- Adidas entered the winter sports marketplace by developing cross-country ski bindings.

1978

- Dassler died at the age of 78. His son, Horst, took over running Adidas.

1987

- Horst Dassler died at the age of 51.

1991

- Adidas launched Adidas EQUIPMENT for performance-oriented footwear and apparel.

1993

- Robert Louis-Dreyfus was named president of Adidas AG.

1995

- Adidas went public on the Deutsche Börse stock exchange.

1997

- Adidas acquired the Salomon group, which is composed of the Salomon, TaylorMade, Mavic, and Bonfire brands. With the acquisition, Adidas changed its name to Adidas-Salomon AG.

2001

- Herbet Hainer succeeded Louis-Dreyfus as CEO of Adidas-Salomon AG.

- The "Customization Experience" was launched, allowing each customer to create their own shoes in terms of function, fit, and looks.

- Adidas Originals stores opened in Berlin and Tokyo. They were followed by Adidas megastores in Paris and Amsterdam.

2002

- Adidas opened new North American headquarters outside Portland, Oregon.

2004

- Adidas introduced the "Adidas 1," a shoe that electronically senses the level of cushioning provided and adjusts it to the optimal level.

2005

- Adidas-Salomon AG sold off the Salomon segment of the company.

- Adidas announced that it had agreed to purchase rival footwear and apparel manufacturer Reebok for $3.8 billion.

2006

- After selling off its Salomon brand, the company was renamed Adidas AG.

2007

- European soccer star David Beckham, the top Adidas-sponsored athlete, signed a 5-year $250-million deal with the Los Angeles Galaxy.

2008

- Adidas opened a flagship retail store in Beijing, China, and announced its official sponsorship of the 2008 Summer Olympics in Beijing.

- Adidas sold more than 300,000 Beckham replica jerseys since he signed with the Galaxy in January 2007.

Structure of Adidas

- Adidas: This brand creates footwear, apparel, and equipment such as golf bags and golf balls. It accounted for 69% of sales in 2007.[10] Adidas is divided into three divisions: Adidas Sport Performance, Adidas Sport Heritage, and Adidas Sport Style. Adidas Sport Performance

is focused on performance over style and focuses on running, football, basketball, and training apparel. Adidas Sport Heritage focuses on products that are geared more towards style than performance, with an emphasis on retro. Adidas Sport Style is focused solely on style, but with designs that are more contemporary.

- Reebok: Reebok also produces footwear, apparel, and equipment. It accounted for 23% of sales in 2007. The Reebok division encompasses three business units: Reebok, Reebok-CCM Hockey, and Rockport. Reebok creates sports and lifestyle products, focusing on creativity and innovation. Reebok-CCM Hockey produces hockey equipment and apparel under the brands Rbk Hockey and CCM. Rockport produces dress and casual footwear, apparel, and accessories.

- TaylorMade Adidas-Golf: This division produces golf equipment, golf apparel, and golf shoes. It accounted for 8% of sales in 2007. This division is also made up of three business units: TaylorMade, Adidas Golf, and Maxfli. TaylorMade creates golf clubs and balls. Adidas Golf creates golf apparel and footwear. Maxfli creates a large variety of golf balls with different playing attributes.

Money Matters for Adidas[11]

- For the fiscal year 2007, Adidas AG realized an operating profit of $1.45 billion from approximately $15.8 billion in sales.

- The Adidas division recognized a gross profit of $5.1 billion from approximately $10.9 billion of sales.

- The Reebok division recognized a gross profit of approximately $1.4 billion from approximately $3.6 billion in sales.

- The TaylorMade-Adidas Golf division realized a gross profit of $552 million from approximately $1.2 billion in sales.

AND 1

And 1 develops and markets specialty footwear for the sport of basketball. The company utilizes ideas and suggestions from professional basketball players to design and develop specialized shoe designs. And 1 uses both professional and street players to market and promote its products and enhance its overall brand image.

In addition, And 1 has expanded its vision and uses creative platforms to build its brand. The company has partnered with Ubisoft Software to create a video game called "And 1 Streetball," which was released in June 2006 and is available for all major gaming consoles.[12]

And 1 is considered a boutique shoe company, and generated revenues of over $150 million in 2005. Although it is much smaller than Nike and the Adidas Group, its basketball shoes compete directly with those from the larger companies.

The company was established in 1993 and is headquartered in Paoli, Pennsylvania. Irvine, California–based American Sporting Goods Inc. (ASG) purchased the company in July 2005. And 1 operates domestic and international offices and distribution facilities, as well as a factory in Switzerland.

PUMA[13,14]

Founded in 1948, PUMA is engaged in the development and marketing of a broad range of sport and lifestyle items including footwear, apparel, and accessories. The company uses its resources and experiences to provide consumers with products that fuse aspects from the world of sport, lifestyle, and fashion. These products are developed under two global brands: PUMA and Tretorn.

In 2007, PUMA generated revenues of approximately $3.7 billion, with 54% of the company's sales derived from footwear products. PUMA operates production facilities in over 40 countries and distributes its products to over 80 countries worldwide. The company is considered a mid-tier sporting goods firm behind industry leaders such as Nike and the Adidas Group.

PUMA is a publicly traded company and its common shares are traded at XETRA on the Frankfurt and Munich stock exchanges as well as an American Depository Receipt (ADR) in the United States. As of December 2007, the company employed over 9,200 professionals in various offices worldwide; its headquarters are located in Herzogenaurach, Germany. Potential job opportunities exist across the United States, particularly in Westford and Boston, Massachusetts, in the following departments: sales, marketing, finance, and design.

SPALDING[15]

Established by Boston Red Stockings pitcher A.G. Spalding in 1876, Spalding was one of the first sporting goods manufacturers in the United States. A.G. Spalding drove brand recognition by making the Spalding baseball the first official ball of professional baseball.

The company manufactures equipment for basketball, football, baseball, soccer, volleyball, and softball. Spalding is also well known for its relationship with the National Basketball Association (NBA), and it has been the league's official supplier of basketballs since 1983.

In 2006, Spalding changed the design of the official NBA Game Ball, replacing the original leather version with a ball composed of synthetic material. The synthetic material was designed to increase the ability to grip the ball and remove excess moisture from sweat. The new design also featured "two interlocking cross-shaped panels" in place of the eight-paneled ball used previously. The ball was not received well by the players, who complained that the ball was slippery and bounced differently and more inconsis-

tently than the leather version. After the union filed a labor grievance with the National Labor Relations Board, the NBA settled the grievance and reverted back to the traditional leather basketball.

Spalding basketball equipment is sold in over 18,000 retail locations in over 70 countries worldwide. In addition to the NBA and MLB, Spalding supplies official balls for the Women's National Basketball Association (WNBA), the D-League, Arena Football League (AFL), Pop Warner Football, and Major Indoor Soccer League (MISL).

Spalding is privately held by Russell Corporation, Spalding is headquartered in Springfield, Massachusetts. Potential job opportunities exist in the following departments at the company headquarters: sales, marketing, accounting, finance, and administration.

TITLEIST[16,17]

Founded in 1932, Titleist is a global sporting goods company that designs and produces golf-related equipment including golf clubs, golf balls, and golf accessories. The company uses a vast number of professional golfers as endorsers to market and promote its wide array of products. In 2007, Titleist sales numbers reached approximately $800 million.

Titleist is a subsidiary of Fortune Brands, Inc., a worldwide consumer brand conglomerate. Under the umbrella of Fortune Brands are three main business categories: home and hardware, spirits and wine, and golf. Fortune Brands is a publicly traded company on the New York Stock Exchange under the ticker symbol FO.

The various departments at Titleist include production, engineering, marketing, and sales. The company's headquarters are located in Fairhaven, Massachusetts, with regional offices in various parts of the United States, Europe, Asia, and Australia. Competitors of Titleist include Nike and Callaway.

CALLAWAY GOLF COMPANY[18]

Established in 1982, Callaway Golf Company is a global sporting goods company that designs and produces golf-related equipment including golf clubs, golf balls, golf apparel, and golf accessories. The company sells golf equipment under the Callaway Golf, Odyssey, Ben Hogan, and Top-Flite brands. Callaway Golf was the pioneer of the revolutionizary driver technology with the original Big Bertha Driver, which helped lead the way in converting golfers from using wood drivers to metal ones. The company has a number of endorsement agreements with professional golfers on the PGA, LPGA, and other tours to market and promote its wide array of products.

Callaway Golf is a publicly traded company on the New York Stock Exchange under the ticker symbol ELY. In 2007, the company realized sales of $1.1 billion, a 10.5%

increase from its 2006 sales numbers. Competitors of Callaway include Titleist, Adams Golf, TaylorMade (Adidas Group), and Ping.

The company's headquarters are located in Carlsbad, California, with regional offices in Canada, Europe, Asia, and Australia. Callaway employs roughly 3,000 professionals in various departments such as production, finance, marketing, and sales.

HILLERICH AND BRADSBY COMPANY[19]

Hillerich and Bradsby Company (H&B) is a privately owned manufacturing company famous for making Louisville Slugger baseball and softball equipment. In addition, H&B manufactures hockey and golf equipment (PowerBilt golf clubs), licenses soft drinks, and operates the Louisville Slugger Museum (opened in 1996).

In 1884 in Louisville, Kentucky, H&B produced its first baseball bat. By the 21st century, the Louisville Sluggers brand had become recognized worldwide and is the official bat of Major League Baseball. In 2008, H&B serviced over 60% of the major league market with bats and earned roughly $110 million in sales worldwide. Over 75% of H&B's annual revenue comes from the sale of baseball and softball bats.

H&B employs nearly 470 people throughout nine locations across North America. Some of the job opportunities at H&B include supply chain management, product design, manufacturing, information technology, marketing, sales, merchandising, research, and professional baseball operations. Wilson, Rawlings, and Easton are some of Hillerich and Bradsby's main competitors.

Endnotes

1. Nike Annual Report. (2008). Nikebiz.com. Retrieved August 5, 2008, from http://phx.corporate-ir.net/phoenix.zhtml?c=100529&p=irol-sec.

2. Kaplan, D. (2008, Apr. 14–20). Nike's Tab for Endorsements Spikes to $3.4 Billion. *Street and Smith's SportsBusiness Journal*, vol. 10, issue 50, pp. 1, 33.

3. Nike Timeline. (2008). Nikebiz.com. Retrieved September 21, 2008, from http://www.nikebiz.com_overview/timeline.

4. Knight, D. (1998, May 12). Labor: Nike's Initiative to Improve Factory Conditions. *Inter Press Service*. Retrieved October 23, 2007, from the LexisNexis online database.

5. Nike annual report. (2003). Nike.com. Retrieved November 15, 2007, from http://www.nike.com/nikebiz/nikebiz.jhtml?page-18.

6. Nike Annual Report 2008, op. cit.

7. Ibid.

8. Adidas Group: Home. (n.d.). Adidas-Group.com. Retrieved August 5, 2008, from http://www.adidas-group.com/en/home/welcome.asp.

9. At a Glance: The Story of Adidas Group. (n.d.). Adidas.com. Retrieved November 15, 2007, from http://www.adidas-group.com/en/overview/history/Historye.pdf.

10. Annual Report 2007. (2008, Nov. 5). Adidas.com. Retrieved April 10, 2008, from http://www.adidasgroup.com/en/investor/_downloads/pdf/annual_reports/2007/GB_2007_En.pdf.

11. Ibid.

12. Surette, T. (2006, May 25). And 1 Streetball Has Mad Hops. Gamespot.com. Retrieved October 23, 2007, from http://www.gamespot.com/ps2/sports/and1/news.html?sid=6151862.

13. About Puma. (n.d.). Puma.com. Retrieved August 5, 2008, from http://about.puma.com/EN/1.

14. Puma Annual Report. (2007). Puma.com. Retrieved April 10, 2008, from http://about.puma.com/downloads/150677656.pdf.

15. Spalding: Heritage. (n.d.). Spalding.com. Retrieved August 5, 2008, from http://www.spalding.com.

16. Titleist: Home. (n.d.). Titleist.com. Retrieved August 5, 2008, from http://www.titleist.com.

17. Fortune Brands Annual Report. (2007). Retrieved May 13, 2008, from http://www.fortunebrands.com/downloads/2007_annual.pdf.

18. Callaway: Corporate Overview. (n.d.). CallawayGolf.com. Retrieved August 5, 2008, from http://ir.callawaygolf.com/phoenix.zhtml?c=68083&p=irol-IRHome.

19. H&B Slugs Away in Battle to Be Baseball's Biggest Batmaker. (2003, Apr. 11). *Street and Smith's SportsBusiness Daily*. Retrieved November 7, 2007, from http://www.sportsbusinessdaily.com/index.cfm?fuseaction=article.main&articleId=74871&keyword=H&B%20Slugs%20Away.

Retail is the buying of large quantities of product from manufacturers or importers and the subsequent selling of those products to the general public. Retailers come in many different forms, such as large department stores, small individually owned shops, and online stores. This chapter examines Dick's Sporting Goods and REI, two of the leading sports retailers, to give a general idea of the retail industry and the career opportunities that it presents.

DICK'S SPORTING GOODS[1]

Dick's Sporting Goods is a sports and fitness specialty retailer with locations in over 250 stores in 34 states across the United States. Dick's Sporting Goods started as a small bait and tackle shop in 1948 in Binghamton, New York. Today, Dick's offers a vast range of products from sporting goods and apparel to footwear, hunting and fishing gear, exercise equipment, golf equipment, bicycles, and camping gear. Items can be purchased in stores, online, and by phone.

Dick's Sporting Goods is a publicly traded company listed on the New York Stock Exchange under the ticker symbol DKS. In 2007, Dick's Sporting Goods finished first in sales among national sporting goods retailers with $3.8 billion in sales. Corporate headquarters are located in Pittsburgh, Pennsylvania, and are composed of several divisions, some of which include product development, merchandising, information technology, and human resources. Dick's operates three separate distribution centers located in Smithtown, Pennsylvania, one near Pittsburgh, Pennsylvania, and one near Indianapolis, Indiana. Some competitor retail chains include Foot Locker, REI, Modell's, and the Sports Authority.

Jobs at the corporate offices include positions in the following areas: customer services, human resources, legal service, merchandising, marketing, information technology, and recruiting. Positions within distribution centers include loss prevention and supply chain managers. Within each Dick's store, there are opportunities in several areas including project management, general management, retail, and sales.

RECREATIONAL EQUIPMENT, INC.

In 1938, mountain climbers Lloyd and Mary Anderson collaborated with 21 fellow Northwest climbers and founded Recreational Equipment, Inc. (REI). During the past six decades, REI has grown into a renowned supplier of specialty outdoor gear and clothing. REI serves the needs of outdoor enthusiasts through 78 retail stores in the United States and by direct sales via the Internet, telephone, and mail.

REI is one of the leading recreational equipment suppliers along with Hudson Trail Outfitters. In 2005, the company achieved sales numbers of over $1 billion. REI is the nation's largest consumer cooperative with more than 2 million members.[3]

REI headquarters are located in Kent, Washington, 18 miles south of Seattle, and its distribution and contact center is located in Sumner, Washington, approximately 37 miles southeast of Seattle.

Career opportunities exist in REI's four divisions: headquarters, distribution center, contact center, and retail management. Almost 80% of REI's 6,500 employees work in the retail management division in stores that are located nationwide.

Endnotes

1. About Us. (n.d.). DicksSportingGoods.com. Retrieved August 5, 2008, from http://www.dickssportinggoods.com/corp/index.jsp?page=aboutUs.

2. Dick's 2007 Annual Report. (2008). DicksSportingGoods.com. Retrieved September 28, 2008 from http://thomson.mobular.net/thomson/7/2712/3257.

3. Street & Smith's Sports Group. (2007). *2006 Sports Business Resource Guide & Fact Book*. Charlotte, NC: Author, p. J-42.

CHAPTER FORTY

Licensees

In the sports industry, licensees are companies that pay a fee for the right to sell products containing league-owned content, such as league and team names and logos. Examples of licensees in the sports industry include producers of replica apparel, video games, and trading cards. This chapter examines Twins Enterprises, Inc., a leading producer of apparel and souvenirs, to help you gain a better understanding of the licensee industry.

TWINS ENTERPRISES, INC.[1]

Twins Enterprise, Inc. is a wholesale and merchandise operation established in 1967 by twin brothers Arthur and Henry D'Angelo. Twins Enterprise, Inc.'s operation consists of both a wholesale business and a retail business. The retail business consists of the Souvenir Store (the world's largest souvenir store), which is located across from Fenway Park in Boston. The wholesale department distributes hats to MLB teams and over 160 minor league clubs' concession vendors throughout those leagues while also supplying hats to over 250 college bookstores. Twins also sells hats to national retailers such as Lids, Olympia Sports, and Foot Locker. Twins has a manufacturing facility in Massachusetts that is used to produce "hot market" items, such as professional or collegiate championship hats, but most of its items are produced overseas.

Twins also is a licensee of MLB, NCAA, NBA, and the NHL, and is the official retail store of Boston Red Sox apparel, selling its own brand along with Nike, Majestic, New Balance, Russell, Lee Sports, Gear, College Concepts, Adidas, Antigua, Fifth and Ocean, and Mitchell and Ness. The Boston-based company has recently launched a company named Banner, which will produce high-end college and MLB apparel.

Twins is headquartered in Boston and has offices in New York and England. Twins has both a full in-house and national sales force, a customer service department, and an in-house art department. The family-owned company employs 150 people in the following areas: accounting, customer service, electronic ordering systems, graphic design, licensing, sales, and warehouse staffing.

Endnotes

1. Twins Enterprise: Home. (n.d.). TwinsEnterprise.com. Retrieved August 5, 2008, from http://www.twinsenterprise.com/default.asp.

CHAPTER FORTY-ONE

Sports Agencies

Sports agencies are firms that represent athletes, teams, or organizations in such matters as contract negotiations, sponsorship and endorsement deals, public relations, and marketing. These agencies may represent players, coaches, teams, colleges, organizations, events, networks, and/or corporate entities. Sports agencies vary greatly both in size and in the services they offer. Some agencies, like IMG, have over 1,000 employees and provide multiple services, whereas other agencies consist of a single agent who might focus on one area, such as contract negotiation. This chapter examines some of the leading sports agencies in the industry, but many career opportunities exist outside of the firms discussed in this chapter.

IMG[1,2]

IMG is the largest and leading sports agency in the world. Founded by Mark McCormack in 1960 when Arnold Palmer signed on as the first client, IMG began the representation business specializing in professional golfers. Today, IMG has expanded into a conglomerate with 2,500 employees worldwide and business properties in many different areas that are dedicated to the marketing and management of sport and nonsport areas, such as leisure and lifestyle. IMG has a global presence with 60 offices located in 30 countries. The sports marketing division includes several subdivisions such as sponsorship, television, endorsements, promotions, licensing, hospitality, and the Internet.

IMG boasts a diverse portfolio of clients including artists, writers, models, broadcasters, world-class events, cultural institutions, recreational resorts, and top professional athletes. Trans World International (TWI), IMG's television, radio, and new media arm, is the world's largest independent distributor and producer of televised sports. Famous for its made-for-TV sporting events, such as the

Hockey agent Matt Keator (center) attends a promotional event with two of his clients, Blake Wheeler (left) and Zdeno Chara (right) of the Boston Bruins. Keator runs a small boutique-style agency, Olympic Sports Management, which caters only to professional hockey players. Keator's agency represents roughly 15 NHL players, including 8 NHL players who are projected to compete in the 2010 Winter Olympics. Keator's responsibilities as an agent include providing support for his clients at promotional events and charitable functions, finding/securing endorsement deals, and negotiating contracts.

Skins Game and *Superstars*, the company produces and distributes 10,000 hours of live sports programming a year to about 200 countries covering over 240 sports. TWI has played a major part in IMG, accounting for more than half the company's revenue, which was $1.3 billion in 2005. There are a total of 26 separate divisions within IMG, which are divided by either sport (golf, tennis, football) or service (licensing, television and media, fashion).

IMG's corporate consulting business provides clients with innovative strategies for areas such as marketing, event management, and technology. With staff located around the globe, IMG Consulting's diverse portfolio ranges from grassroots marketing, to tour operations, to property management, to marketing the Olympic Games. By having a stake in both media and consulting of events around the world, IMG has achieved economies of scale and gained control of certain areas of business. However, IMG's vertically integrated structure also leads to a potential conflict of interest, both within IMG and with outside entities. For example, IMG owns and operates the Sony Ericsson Open on the WTA Tennis Tour. As an event owner, IMG needs to find sponsors to support the event. At the same time, IMG advises corporations on which events to sponsor. This leads to a natural conflict of interest—IMG represents both an event looking for sponsors and sponsors looking for an event.

IMG represents arguably some of the best athletes in the world including Tiger Woods, Arnold Palmer, Maria Sharapova, and Wayne Gretzky. Athletes also have taken advantage of IMG's expertise in Bradenton, Florida, home of the IMG Academy. The academy first started as solely a tennis school. Acquired in 1987, Nick Bollettieri's Tennis Academy has been responsible for developing and nurturing some of the best tennis players in the world including Andre Agassi, Anna Kournikova, Serena and Venus Williams, and Roger Federer. IMG Academy, which expanded its breadth of sports from solely tennis, develops and prepares young athletes in several sports including golf, tennis, soccer, basketball, and baseball. The Academy also has a year-round boarding school for student athletes.

IMG continues to focus on maintaining and expanding its global presence in each business property. Shortly after McCormack's death in 2003, IMG had to trim a reported $200-million debt by cutting jobs and selling real estate before it was purchased by Ted Forstmann in 2004. Forstmann, senior partner of Forstmann Little & Company, purchased IMG for $750 million and named himself IMG's new chief executive officer. George Pyne, the former NASCAR chief operating officer, was recruited by Forstmann to serve as president of sports and entertainment. Under the new management, IMG has focused on expansions in the fashion world, and placing an increasing emphasis on its media business. In 2006, IMG acquired two London-based independent nonsports television companies, Darlow Smithson and Tiger Aspect. Also in 2006, IMG strategically eliminated its baseball, football, and hockey divisions to focus more on global divisions such as golf and fashion, where the company is more dominant.

IMG made an entrance into the world of collegiate licensing in May 2007, with its acquisition of Collegiate Licensing Co. (CLC). The purchase price reportedly was between $130 million and $140 million. At the time of acquisition, CLC held the licensing rights to 155 colleges and universities and nine conferences, as well as the Bowl Championship Series and the Heisman Trophy. It is believed IMG will expand its collegiate portfolio beyond licensing to include marketing, promotions, and multimedia rights.

In 2007, *Street & Smith's SportsBusiness Journal* reported Goldman Sachs performed a valuation of IMG, estimating the agency's value at more than $1.5 billion.[3]

IMG offers a formalized 2-month internship lasting from the beginning of June to the end of July, with most of the opportunities in its Cleveland and New York offices. Internships also are available during the school year. Job opportunities exist in a wide variety of areas including sales, marketing, client and event management, licensing, television production, law, promotions, and account management.

History of IMG[4]

1960

- Mark McCormack, a young lawyer, signed golfer Arnold Palmer, then 31 years old, as a client.
- Prominent golfer Gary Player signed as a client at the age of 25.

1961

- Young golfer Jack Nicklaus signed as a client at the age of 21.

1964

- The first IMG office opened in Asia, known then as International Management Group.

1966

- TWI was founded and a Los Angeles office was opened. TWI is a branch of IMG that deals with television, radio, and media coverage of sports.

1968

- IMG Broadcasting was founded when radio and television commentator Chris Schenkel was signed as a client.
- Premier tennis player Rod Laver was signed as IMG's first tennis client.
- A contract between TWI and Wimbledon Tennis was negotiated to sell broadcast rights of the Wimbledon Tournament to overseas television programs.

1969

- IMG Football was founded when Fran Tarkenton, quarterback of the New York Giants, signed as the first IMG football client.
- IMG Motorsports was founded when racecar driver Jackie Stewart signed as a client.
- Brooks Robinson, third baseman for the Baltimore Orioles, signed as IMG's first baseball client.

1970

- John Havlicek, guard for the Boston Celtics, signed as IMG's first basketball client.

1971

- IMG Consulting was founded. IMG Consulting assists corporations in the development and management of world-class sports, events, and entertainment marketing strategies.
- Legendary soccer star Pelé was signed as a client.

1973

- The TV show *Superstars* aired for the first time. *Superstars* was a group of premier athletes from all different sports who competed in various events, such as kayaking, obstacle course, and bicycling.

1977

- Female golfer Nancy Lopez signed as the first female golf client.

1983

- TWI produced the first golf Skins Game, in which Jack Nicklaus, Arnold Palmer, Gary Player, and Tom Watson all competed. Gary Player won the event.

1984

- IMG Artists was founded when IMG acquired Hamden/Landau Management. IMG Artists provides business management for artists such as conductors, singers, painters, and dancers.

1986

- IMG created the World Golf Rankings that are still used today by the PGA Tour as a means to rank professional golfers.

1990

- Superstar hockey player Wayne Gretzky, center for the Los Angeles Kings, and Joe Montana, quarterback for the San Francisco, signed as clients.

1996

- Golfer Tiger Woods signed as a client at the age of 21.

1999

- Peyton Manning, quarterback of the Indianapolis Colts, signed as a client.

2003

- Founder Mark McCormack died at the age of 72. Bob Kain, creator and director of IMG Tennis, and Alastair Johnston, former IMG Director of Golf, take over as co-CEOs.
- IMG formed a corporate alliance with Creative Artists Agency (CAA) to help each agency's clients with speaker representation, licensing, and corporate consulting.

2004

- Ted Forstmann, senior partner at Forstmann Little & Co. purchased IMG and became the CEO.

2005

- IMG sold off its baseball, football, and hockey divisions to eliminate conflicts of interest and to focus on endeavors that were more profitable.
- Roger Federer, the number one tennis player in the world, signed as a client.

2006

- George Pyne, former chief operating officer of NASCAR, was named president.
- IMG signed a 3-year agreement to be the title sponsor of the annual World Congress of Sports Conference, the first IMG-sponsored event.

2007

- IMG acquired Collegiate Licensing Co. for a reported $130–$140 million.
- IMG was reported to be valued at more than $1.5 billion by *Street and Smith's SportsBusiness Journal*.

2008

- IMG signed a deal with CBS and the NCAA in which it will sell marketing packages for the NCAA's 88 athletic championships.

Structure of IMG

Sports Marketing

- Sponsorship: Activating sponsors at events by creating a platform for sponsors to gain visibility with fans. This includes coordinating giveaways, games for fans, fan experience stations, etc. This division is broken down into two different groups—a Strategic Partnership Group, which is responsible for securing sponsors for IMG-run events, and a Sponsorship Consulting Division, which advises clients on how to maximize sponsorship rights to non-IMG run events.
- Television: TWI (see the following section).
- Endorsements: Clients endorse various products (e.g., Tiger Woods: TAG Heuer, Buick; Arnold Palmer: Rolex).
- Promotions: Coupons, sweepstakes to win packages, prizes, tickets, etc.
- Licensing: Extend brand awareness by associating products with famous athletes, events, or organizations (i.e., Arnold Palmer, Wimbledon, and Major League Baseball).

- Hospitality: A place for clients to be at an event, usually involves a place to sit and talk and also provides food and beverages (e.g., IMG Corporate Golf).

- Internet: E-commerce and the delivery of web-based content to fans, clients, and athletes.

TWI

- The media/content arm of IMG (television/broadcasting and new media).

- The world's largest distributor and producer of televised sports.

IMG Consulting

- Establishes relationships with some of the world's largest corporations.

- Designs and implements marketing and sponsorship programs for its clients.

IMG Academies

- Develops and trains young athletes.

Money Matters for IMG

Sources of Revenue

- IMG realizes roughly $1.083 billion in annual operating revenues, which equates to about $433,200 in sales revenue generated per employee.

- Marketing and sponsorship partnerships
  - Oversees a wide range of marketing and sponsorship agreements on behalf of its numerous professional athletes, including Tiger Woods and Arnold Palmer. As a result, IMG takes a portion of the contract for its services, which is usually 20% and can be up to 40%.

- Licensing
  - Manages licensing and retail partnerships for a wide variety of sports leagues and organizations, companies, and athletes including Major League Baseball, ESPN, USGA, WTA, U.S. Olympic Committee, Fodor's Travel Publications, Tiger Woods, Derek Jeter, and Peyton Manning.

IMG COLLEGE[5]

In 2007, IMG Worldwide acquired Host Communications, Inc., and combined it with the Collegiate Licensing Company to form its branch known as IMG College. Focusing almost exclusively on college athletics, IMG College is a leader in sports marketing and media services. IMG College provides a variety of services to clients in the areas of collegiate marketing, radio and television, association management, national sales, and publishing and design.

The company has collegiate multimedia rights deals with many universities, some of which are: University of Arizona, Furman University, University of Kansas, University of Kentucky, University of Michigan, University of Nebraska, Oklahoma State University, Rice University, University of Tennessee, University of Texas, and Western Kentucky University. IMG also represents several conferences, including the Southeastern Conference (SEC). Although not all agreements are the same, each rights agreement includes some, or all, of the following elements: radio and television programs; publishing; printing; creative design; marketing; licensing; Internet; national advertising and signage sales; and numerous lifestyle and event marketing platforms. Under a typical agreement, IMG College is responsible for such activities as selling, producing, and distributing radio broadcasts, coaches' television shows, and television broadcasts of any games not picked up as part of a school's conference package. Additionally, IMG College will commonly print and sell advertising for game-day programs; administer a school's athletic website; and handle hospitality, corporate sponsorships, and signage for its clients.[6]

In addition to its collegiate sports division, IMG College also manages five associations and more than 30 websites, and has a printing and publishing division that produces more than 700 publications annually. The company has long-standing relationships with the College Football Hall of Fame, American Football Coaches Association, National Association of Basketball Coaches, Naismith Memorial Basketball Hall of Fame, and the National Association of Collegiate Directors of Athletics.

Originally founded in 1972, Host was acquired by publicly traded Triple Crown Media in 2005 and then was sold to IMG Worldwide in 2007. The company is headquartered in Lexington, Kentucky, and has collegiate offices at universities located throughout the country.

OCTAGON[6]

Founded in 1997 by Frank Lowe, Octagon Worldwide Inc. is a global sports management and marketing company composed of Octagon Marketing, Octagon Athlete Representation, Octagon CSI, and Octagon Motorsports. The company, a subsidiary of the publicly traded Interpublic Group, manages sports and entertainment content with a focus on several different areas.

The marketing arm of Octagon has eight sectors focusing on different aspects of marketing: consulting, games marketing, marketing solutions, public/private partnerships, property representation, event management, talent procurement, and global game. The Octagon Consulting group helps companies develop and implement strategic, targeted, and measurable marketing programs. The other marketing services Octagon provides range from serving corporate sponsors worldwide and domestically for the Olympics to delivering cost-effective marketing programs. In the global sector of marketing, Octagon works with international companies to build portfolio sponsorship programs to generate revenue.

In television and new media, Octagon assists clients in negotiation, distribution, and production of sports and entertainment programming. Octagon Television focuses on creating and acquiring new property rights and producing events for global broadcasters worldwide. Octagon CSI negotiates, produces, packages, and markets international sports for television, producing roughly 300 hours of original programming and 200 live events a year. These programs are distributed to about 200 countries.[7] Some of the global programming includes work for the English Football Association, live matches for the three divisions of the Coca-Cola Football League and Carling Cup, and the England and Wales Cricket Board.

Octagon also represents athletes and entertainers across all disciplines of sports and entertainment. The services provided for its clients include contract negotiations, endorsements, financial planning, public relations, television opportunities, and event management. In addition, Octagon has an athlete and entertainment procurement program.

Octagon serves a wide range of clients, including individual athletes, coaches, *Fortune* 500 companies, and corporate clients who want to get involved with sporting events. The company owns and manages more events around the world.

Headquartered in New York City, the company employs over 1,000 professionals in 45 offices across 24 countries. The company also has other prominent U.S.-based offices in Norwalk, Connecticut (marketing and consulting) and McLean, Virginia (athlete representation). Potential job opportunities exist in the following departments: consulting, game marketing, event management, talent production, representation, public relations, and television.

WASSERMAN MEDIA GROUP

Wasserman Media Group (WMG) is one of the largest player representation practices in the United States and Europe, representing over 200 players and coaches. Casey Wasserman, owner of the Arena Football League's Los Angeles Avengers, founded Wasserman Media Group in 1998. Since then, WMG has expanded its offices to Los Angeles; New York; London; Carlsbad, California; Charlotte, North Carolina; and Raleigh, North Carolina. WMG handles top basketball, baseball, and action sports clients through its entertainment management, marketing, and content divisions. The strategy of WMG is to focus on representing high-quality sports and media properties on a global basis. In January 2006, WMG Management added Arn Tellem's athlete management business to its portfolio of

sports and media properties. Tellem, recognized as one of the most successful player agents, brought with him a client base of about 50 NBA and 50 MLB athletes including Jason Giambi, Hideki Matsui, and Tracy McGrady.[9]

WMG continued to expand by acquiring SportsNet in 2006, the largest U.S.-based soccer player representation practice consisting of 60 clients including MLS soccer players Freddy Adu and Landon Donovan. As a strategy to expand globally, WMG purchased SFX Sports Group, Europe in November 2006 from Live Nation. SFX Europe's client list includes European soccer players Michael Owen and Steven Gerrard, and rugby players Jonny Wilkinson and Lawrence Dallagio. Wasserman Media Group also has a content division; WMG Content has launched Studio411, the largest action sports studio, and produces action sports videos.

In June 2007, WMG announced the acquisition of OnSport consultancy. The acquisition adds corporate sponsorship, media, and property expertise to WMG's existing portfolio, placing the agency in a position to compete with the likes of IMG and Octagon in the sports marketing consultancy field. OnSport's corporate clients at the time of acquisition included American Express, Nationwide Insurance, Nokia, and Wachovia. Following the acquisition of OnSport, WMG's employee count is approximately 300 individuals.

WMG Management consists of a marketing division specializing in corporate consulting and naming rights, an investment division that identifies investment opportunities in media and sports, and a content division that includes a production studio. WMG also expects an expansion into individual sports such as golf and tennis.

WMG is privately owned and is headquartered in Los Angeles. Job opportunities exist in sales, marketing, video production, event management, athlete representation, and promotions.

VELOCITY SPORTS AND ENTERTAINMENT

Velocity Sports and Entertainment is a sponsorship, lifestyle, and event marketing agency. The company works with clients to develop strategic plans and creative experiential programs for its customers. Velocity's capabilities include the following services: strategic consulting, promotions development and execution, retail marketing, event management, customer entertainment, meeting planning, municipal marketing, property alliances, and research and evaluation. Its clients include a large number of *Fortune* 500 companies such as IBM, Toyota, AT&T, and FedEx. *Promo* magazine ranked Velocity the No. 2 promotion agency in 2005.

Founded in 1999, Velocity has realized significant growth and currently employs over 125 professionals. The company's headquarters are located in Norwalk, Connecticut, and it has offices in Atlanta; Chicago; San Francisco;

Washington, DC; and London. David Grant is one of the co-founders of the company. He helps manage overall agency operations and oversees the agency's work for clients. Mike Reisman, also a founding partner, is involved with the company's sponsorship marketing business. The company is currently a subsidiary of publicly traded Aegis Group.

Job opportunities at Velocity include corporate sponsor consulting, events management, research, and client servicing. In addition, Velocity offers one of the only management training programs in the sponsorship industry. This program trains college students for 6 months in the five core areas of the company, which are consulting, alliance marketing, research, municipal marketing, and event planning/hospitality.

MILLSPORT[10]

Founded in 1975, Millsport is a sports sponsorship and marketing agency and is a subsidiary of the Omnicom Group. The Omnicom Group is a global network of advertising agencies, marketing and specialty communications, interactive/digital, and media buying companies. Millsport is publicly owned and has about 500 employees nationally.

Millsport helps its clients gain awareness among their consumers and helps create emotional connections with sports entities. It works to achieve these objectives through consulting with clients on sports sponsorship and sports marketing strategy, property and media acquisition and management, creative and conceptual development, and hospitality. Some of Millsport's clients include Frito-Lay, XM Satellite Radio, Wells Fargo, NASDAQ, AT&T, Sunoco, Taco Bell, Wal-Mart, Tylenol, and Yahoo!

Millsport is headquartered in Stamford, Connecticut, and operates satellite offices in Charlotte, San Francisco, Dallas, and Athens, Georgia. Potential job opportunities exist in departments such as marketing, account services, motorsports, and hospitality.

CREATIVE ARTISTS AGENCY

Creative Artists Agency (CAA) is one of the most powerful talent agencies in the entertainment business. CAA represents clients working in music, TV, film, art, and literature, including Julia Roberts, Angelina Jolie, Tom Hanks, and Bruce Springsteen, and corporate entities such as Coca-Cola and Procter & Gamble. Since its creation in 1975, CAA has been known as a Hollywood agency; however, following a recent trend blurring the division between sports and entertainment, CAA entered the sport industry in June 2006 when it bought IMG's football, baseball, and hockey practices as well as SFX's football portfolio.

With representation of over 380 athletes, CAA is currently (2008) representing the highest-paid players at eight NFL positions, the five consecutive NFL MVPs (2002–2008), the 2006 National League baseball MVP, the

No. 1 selection in the last two NHL drafts, and a former NBA MVP. Some clients include Peyton and Eli Manning, Derek Jeter, Sergei Fedorov, Sidney Crosby, Ryan Howard, and, most recently, Tony Hawk. The agency also played a lead role in negotiating the $250-million deal that brought David Beckham to MLS for 5 years.

CAA is a private company that generates revenues between $250 million and $300 million.[11] Like other more-traditional sports agencies, CAA provides clients with services such as contract negotiation, marketing representation, strategic counseling, and financial management. CAA sets itself apart through its Hollywood connections, though. Calling upon previous experience in the entertainment industry, CAA works to secure endorsement deals and guest spots on popular television shows for its athletes. This creates some opportunities for its athletes to cross over into the world of entertainment, if they so choose. Headquartered in Beverly Hills, California, CAA has job opportunities in representation and marketing.

SFX SPORTS GROUP[12]

Founded in 1977, SFX Sports Group is one of the largest sports marketing and management agencies in the world, representing athletes, corporations, teams, leagues, universities, events, and properties. The company represents over 500 athletes in baseball, basketball, football, golf, tennis, soccer, and the Olympics. Some of SFX's clients include David Ortiz, Andre Agassi, and Andy Roddick. *Street and Smith's SportsBusiness Journal* named SFX Baseball and SFX Basketball as the No. 1 representation business in their respective sports in terms of player contracts and number of clients.

SFX Sports Group provides full-service representation to its athlete clients with both contract negotiations and marketing opportunities. In addition, the company develops and produces sporting events and offers a wide range of corporate hospitality services.

The SFX Sports Group is headquartered in Washington, DC, and maintains numerous offices in the United States as well as branches in Europe and Australia. Potential job opportunities exist at the headquarters and the branch offices in representation, marketing, and event management.

CINDRICH AND COMPANY[13–15]

Founded in 1977, Cindrich and Company is a mid-sized agency headquartered in Pittsburgh, Pennsylvania, that specializes mostly in the representation of NFL players. Headed by veteran NFL agent Ralph Cindrich, the company is seeking to diversify and hire agents to focus on other sports and areas of entertainment such as the Professional Bull Riders (PBR) Tour. As of 2006, Cindrich represented over 35 active football players; three active baseball players; Kurt

Angle of World Wrestling Entertainment (WWE); Jenna Morasca, winner of *Survivor: The Amazon*; and several other sports broadcasters, celebrities, and entertainers.

Composed of eight members, Cindrich acts as a one-stop shop for its athletes with the following services: preparation for the draft, preparation for training camps, player development training, endorsements, sport-related services (grievances, medical assistance, career counseling), media relations, legal advice and assistance, taxes, television and radio, and financial planning.

INTERSPORT, INC.[16]

Intersport, Inc. is an agency specializing in media, event management, and hospitality. The media division creates, produces, and distributes a variety of live, taped, and studio television programming around the world. Some of Intersport's production projects include The College Slam Dunk and Three Point Competition, the Masters Special 2006, and Hispanic Athletes of the Year. Intersport strives to integrate sponsors' brands and messages into program content. The events division works with its clients to implement sports marketing programs, promotions, brand awareness initiatives, lead generation events, mobile marketing events and displays, and made-for-television sporting events. One of Intersport's popular events is the Cadillac Championship Clinic, a private golf clinic for over 1,000 targeted consumers in 12 markets. The hospitality division focuses on delivering premium, customized corporate hospitality to its clients at major events such as the Super Bowl, Pro Bowl, Final Four, and the Masters. Intersport was the NFL's first official corporate hospitality provider.

Established in 1985, Intersport is headquartered in Chicago, Illinois. The privately held company may have job opportunities in the following divisions: sales, marketing, media, production, finance, strategic partnership, business development.

THE BONHAM GROUP[17]

The Bonham Group is a privately owned sports and entertainment marketing and consulting firm with about 25 employees. Founded in 1988, the Bonham Group offers its clients a wide range of services including sponsorship evaluation, strategic consulting, market research, sponsorship sales, and negotiation.

The Bonham Group's core competency is sponsorship evaluation. The company interprets data to give corporate and property clients valuable strategic insight and direction. The Bonham Group consults with sports facilities, convention centers, universities, and entertainment properties. Some clients include Texas Tech, the Cleveland Indians, the Atlantic Coast Conference, ECHL, Adidas Group, Delta, Citgo, Qwest, and FedEx.

As of 2007, the Bonham Group has helped negotiate over $2.5 billion in sponsorship contracts, and the total sponsorship value of its sports and entertainment properties is upwards of $9.68 billion.[18] The Bonham Group is headquartered in Greenwood Village, Colorado, a suburb of Denver. Job opportunities may exist in a wide variety of areas including sales, marketing, research, and account management.

FENWAY SPORTS GROUP

Fenway Sports Group (FSG) is a strategic sports marketing agency with experience in both professional sports and college athletics. The agency is owned by New England Sport Ventures (NESV), which also owns the Boston Red Sox, Fenway Park, and 80% of the New England Sports Network (NESN). FSG's core strengths include property representation and acquisitions, entertainment marketing, sponsorships, and consulting services.

FSG was formed in 2004 with the directive of generating new revenue for NESV, and some consider it a blueprint for how an MLB team can increase club revenue outside the limitations of the league's revenue-sharing provisions.[19]

Shortly after forming, FSG entered into an exclusive sponsorship sales agreement with Boston College. The agency also created Fanfoto, a fan-centric sports photography business focusing on helping spectators commemorate their experience at sports venues throughout the country. In 2006, the Boston Red Sox and FSG collaborated to create Red Sox Destinations, providing travel services for Red Sox fans wanting to attend select Red Sox away games. (See Chapter 46 for more on sport-specific travel.) The agency's client roster includes the PGA's Deutsche Bank Championship, mlb.com, Dunkin' Donuts, EMC, Verizon Wireless, and Lumber Liquidators.

The agency's most significant venture, though, was its purchase of a 50% ownership stake in NASCAR's Roush Racing in 2007. (The team name was subsequently renamed Roush Fenway Racing.) The deal reportedly cost FSG $60 million. In making such a significant investment, FSG hopes to expose Red Sox fans to NASCAR, creating new sponsorship and cross-marketing opportunities.

FSG's headquarters are located in Boston, Massachusetts, directly across the street from Fenway Park. The agency employs approximately 20 full-time dedicated employees and relies on the shared services of seven Red Sox executives. FSG also utilizes the services of about a dozen contract workers and part-timers. Job opportunities may exist in a wide variety of areas including sales, marketing, research, and account management. For more information about FSG, see the organizational structure for New England Sports Ventures in Chapter 71.

Endnotes

1. Revamped IMG Targets Key Growth Areas. (2006, Oct. 16). *Street & Smith's SportsBusiness Journal.* Retrieved October 24, 2007, from http://www .sportsbusinessjournal.com/index.cfm?fuseaction= article.main&articleId=52272.

2. About IMG. (n.d.). IMG. Retrieved October 24, 2007, from http://www.imgworld.com/about/default.sps.

3. Kaplan, D. (2007, Aug. 6–12). IMG Valued at $1.5 Billion, Sources Say. *Street & Smith's SportsBusiness Journal*, pp. 1, 34.

4. About IMG. (2008). IMGWorld.com. Retrieved August 5, 2008, from http://www.imgworld.com/ about/default.sps.

5. IMG College: About Us. (2008). IMGCollege.com. Retrieved August 12, 2008, from http://www .imgcollege.com/index.php/story/Corporate_Overview.

6. Smith, M. (2007, Apr. 16). Host Paying $65M for 10-Year KU Deal. *Street & Smith's SportsBusiness Journal*, p. 3.

7. Octagon: Home. (n.d.). Octagon.com. Retrieved August 5, 2008, from http://www.octagon.com/ home_view.

8. Octagon CSI Overview. (n.d.). Octagon CSI. Retrieved October 24, 2007, from http://enjoy.underwired.com/ portfolio/sites/octagonCSI/overview.html.

9. Mullen, L. (2006, Jan. 27). Wasserman Acquires Tellem Business; SFX Promotes Pelinka. *Sports Business Daily.* Retrieved October 24, 2007, from http://www.sportsbusinessdaily.com/article/100061.

10. Information obtained from the Millsport website.

11. Flemming, M. (2006). CAA: Super-Size Me. *Variety.* Retrieved February 8, 2008, from http://www .variety.com/article/VR1117948712.html? categoryid=13&cs=1&s=h&p=0.

12. Information obtained from the SFX Sports website.

13. Information obtained from the Cindrich website.

14. Marano, R. (2002, July). Ralph Cindrich: This Sports Agent Swings Hard and Often. Smart Business Pittsburgh. Retrieved November 9, 2007, from http:// www.sbnonline.com/National/Article/127/1182/ Ralph_Cindrich.aspx.

15. Rovell, D. (2005, Aug. 8). Riding Tall in the Saddle. Cindrich & Company. Retrieved November 9, 2007, from http://www.cindrich.com/bullRiding.htm.

16. About Us. (n.d.). InterSportnet.com. Retrieved August 5, 2008, from http://www.intersport.com/company.

17. The Bonham Group: Home. (2007). Bonham.com. Retrieved August 5, 2008, from http://www.bonham .com/default.aspx.

18. About. (2007). Bonham.com. Retrieved August 5, 2008, from http://www.bonham.com/content .aspx?CID=1.

19. Fisher, E. (2007, July 9–15). Fenway Sports Picks Up Speed in 4th Year. *Street & Smith's SportsBusiness Journal*, pp. 3, 30.

Corporate Sponsorship

Corporate sponsorship has become an increasingly important component of the sports and entertainment industry during the past 10 to 15 years. In 2007, almost $10 billion was spent on global sponsorship of major sports organizations.[1] Sports entities use the money they receive from corporate sponsorship to pay for top athletes, facilities, and coaches. It can also significantly enhance the bottom line for the owners of a team or property.

During the period from 2004 to 2008, sports sponsorships increased approximately 51%.[2] This increase coincided with a growing viewpoint that a sports sponsorship can help a corporation increase product awareness, media exposure, and/or brand loyalty, all of which ultimately lead to increased revenues. Some of the usual sponsorship categories are payment services, carbonated beverages, wireless providers, and financial services. This should not be a surprise because it is common to find companies like Master-Card, Coca-Cola, Sprint, and Bank of America attaching their names and brands to prominent sporting events. These companies are continually searching for ways to reach fans, ages 18 to 45, who happen to be the primary audience for most sporting events. In the end, corporations spend money to gain access to this targeted group of consumers.

As technology and its capabilities have increased in the 21st century, the new media wave has made a meaningful impact on how corporations utilize their sponsorships within the sports world. It is no longer commonplace for a company to just put an advertisement on television or to place a sign at the stadium of a team it is sponsoring. Instead, companies are looking to leverage their sponsorships in a multi-platform fashion. For example, in addition to traditional approaches like television and radio, sponsors are looking to create web- or mobile-specific content. This includes having interactive content such as polls and sweepstakes to attract consumers and establishing web-based loyalty programs. A good example of an interactive sports sponsorship is Diet

Pepsi's efforts involving Reggie Bush. Pepsi created an interactive web-page called "The Reggie Bush Project" that synched its brand with that of the athlete.

Increasingly, as corporations are being asked by teams and leagues to spend more money to become sponsors, sponsors are, in return, asking for a clear, measured return on their investment (ROI). The measurement of sponsorships has become somewhat controversial

Barney Hinkle is the manager of Entertainment Marketing at Anheuser-Busch, the largest sponsor in the sports industry. Hinkle has worked with Anheuser-Busch since 1988 in various sports marketing and entertainment positions.

because no one standard measurement method is accepted in the industry. Should a company measure publicity gained from a sponsorship, eyeballs viewing a sponsor's sign or commercial, sponsor satisfaction, or incremental profit? The key to proper measurement is to establish the company's objectives. That way, success can be measured by determining whether the objectives were met. The measurement of sports sponsorship has grown so complex, specialized companies such as International Event Group (IEG) have been created with the sole purpose of measuring sponsorship value.

Another relevant sponsorship issue deals with the purity of the sport. Corporate sponsors want to get their names closely associated with the teams and leagues they are sponsoring, yet there is a fine line between what is acceptable and what is not. For example, should sponsor logos be allowed on uniforms or on the playing surface? In 2004, MLB attempted to place *Spider Man 2* logos on the

Case Study   *Coca-Cola, Sports Sponsorship, and the NCAA Basketball Tournament*

It has been reported that Coca-Cola spends between $800 million and $1 billion globally on sports sponsorship.[3] This includes approximately $111 million in sports advertising spending alone. The company holds sponsorship deals with NASCAR, the NCAA, the National Horse Racing Association, the PGA, and the U.S. Olympic Committee (among others). In 2007, Coke secured the sponsorship rights to the NCAA basketball tournament, which had previously been held by rival Mountain Dew. In order to activate the sponsorship, the company staged My Coke Fest during the NCAA finals. This mini-festival included live music hosted by *American Idol*'s Ryan Seacrest. Coke used the event to leverage its NCAA relationship into a proprietary Coke-owned event. In order to generate awareness of the company's sponsorship, Coke also aired more than 100 TV spots in the 6 weeks leading up to the NCAA Tournament and created numerous store-level promotions (typically called point of purchase displays). Using NCAA-themed contests and prizes (such as a visit from a major college basketball coach and tickets to the Final Four), Coke was able to drive college basketball fans to its new online loyalty program, My Coke Rewards.

This case study demonstrates the level of complexity sports sponsorship entails. Coke could have simply been satisfied with being named a sponsor of the NCAA Tournament, but instead the company chose to activate its sponsorships on various levels—on television, in stores, on the web, and outside the arena at the actual event. A successful activation such as this requires a great deal of planning and effort by several employees in the sponsorship field.

bases, but was met with considerable opposition by the general public. In the end, MLB withdrew its plans to add the logos, primarily to appease its fans. Sponsors, teams, and leagues wrestle with sport integrity issues on a daily basis. The ultimate goal is to make sure the integrity and purity of the sport are maintained in the minds of the fans.

Corporate sponsors have an ever-increasing place in the sports industry. The competition from teams and leagues to attract sponsors, in addition to the competition among corporations to become affiliated with certain sports properties, makes this component of the industry one to watch closely. Positions exist in the corporate sponsorship area at the team, league, corporation, and agency levels. At a team or league level, sponsorship jobs primarily focus on sales and service. Such positions may also entail research and measurement responsibilities. Working in sponsorship on the corporate side requires management of the company's sports properties, as well as working with league/team representatives and agency professionals. It is the responsibility of corporate representatives to make sure the company gets the most out of its sponsorship opportunities. Therefore, corporate employees typically consult with agency professionals to maximize the value obtained from the company's sponsorships. Sponsorship work for an agency may involve marketing, research, valuation, or measurement-driven responsibilities.

Endnotes

1. Chipps, W. (2008, Jan. 18). Sponsorship Spending to Total 16.78 Billion in 2008. IEG. Retrieved February 8, 2008, from http://www.sponsorship.com/About-IEG/Press-Room/Sponsorship-Spending-To-Total-$16.78-Billion-In-20.aspx.

2. 2007 IEG Sponsorship Report (2007). Sponsorship.com. Retrieved August 12, 2008, from http://www.sponsorship.com/documents/SR_Promo_Issue_01-07.pdf.

3. Stanley, T. L. (2007, May 14–20). Seeking More Pop from Sponsorship. *Street & Smith's SportsBusiness Journal*, pp. 17–23.

Unions

In the sports industry, unions are organizations that hire an executive staff to represent the players in that league in the negotiation and administration of labor agreements, commonly knows as collective bargaining agreements. Each of the four major U.S. sports has a players' union that negotiates with the league and team owners on such issues as player wages, working conditions, retirement benefits, contractual regulations, and other issues such as drug testing. This chapter examines the history and operation of the four major player unions, as well as those for WNBA and MLS players unions.

MAJOR LEAGUE BASEBALL PLAYERS ASSOCIATION

Established in 1965, the Major League Baseball Players Association (MLBPA) is the bargaining unit for all major league players, managers, coaches, and trainers. The MLBPA was the fifth attempt by professional baseball players to unionize. In 1966, Marvin Miller, an economist with the United Steelworkers of America union, was chosen to lead the MLBPA as executive director. During his tenure, Miller helped develop and establish group licensing, player pensions, benefits, and rights while substantially increasing salaries by providing salary arbitration and free agency for eligible players. In 1968, the MLBPA and Major League Baseball signed the first collective bargaining agreement in professional sports. The MLBPA was the first union to provide professional athletes with employment rights similar to other unionized nonsport employees.. The MLBPA is the most powerful union in sports and one of the most powerful unions in the United States.

The MLBPA's primary responsibility is to represent players in matters concerning wages, hours, and working conditions and to protect their rights. The most important

way to achieve this is by negotiating the collective bargaining agreement (CBA) with Major League Baseball. In addition to negotiating the CBA, the MLBPA administers the CBA insurance, and ensures the terms and conditions of the CBA are adhered to by management. This may include the playing conditions for all major league games, testifying about drug testing, or participating in international competition. The MLBPA also works with the players on salary arbitration and contracts, grievance arbitration, and negotiating of licensing deals. The MLBPA also is responsible for certifying and regulating player agents. There are over 300 certified agents approved by the MLBPA. Headquartered in New York City, the MLBPA is a relatively small operation with approximately 35 employees. The central office is divided into many departments including legal, communications, licensing, finance, and administration.

History of the MLBPA[1,2]

1966

- The Major League Baseball Players Association (MLBPA) was created and recognized to represent MLB players in collective bargaining, as well as grievance, career, and salary arbitration matters.

- Marvin Miller, a former economist for first the U.S. government and then the United Steelworkers of America, was elected as executive director of the MLBPA (1966–1983).

1968

- Miller led a committee of players that negotiated the first collective bargaining agreement in the history of professional sports. The agreement raised the minimum salary in baseball from $6,000 (the level at which it had been for two decades) to $10,000, and set the tone for future advances.

1970

- *Flood v. Kuhn*, a landmark case in MLB history, was decided by the U.S. Supreme Court. Outfielder Curt Flood challenged the legality of the reserve clause and the right of clubs to trade players at will. Ultimately, the U.S. Supreme Court upheld the lower courts' decisions in favor of MLB and Kuhn, ruling that federal antitrust laws did not apply to the game of baseball.

1972

- Player representatives of the MLBPA, in a 47–0 vote, authorized a strike to begin April 1. The first general strike in baseball took place over the issue of player pension amounts, and lasted 13 days (canceling 86 regular-season games). A compromise increase of a $500,000 management contribution to the pension fund was agreed upon.[3]

- Miller helped players negotiate the right to arbitration to resolve grievances, which was a major improvement for the union.

1973

- Owners announced that spring training would not begin as scheduled without a new CBA. Players and owners soon reached a 3-year agreement that included establishing salary arbitration for players with 2 or more years of major league service.

1975

- Marking the birth of free agency and the end of the reserve clause, the landmark *Messersmith v. McNally* case was decided. Arbitrator Peter Seitz ruled that players were free to negotiate with any club after the option year of their contracts had been fulfilled. After several bargaining sessions, the players and owners agreed to a modification that granted players the right to free agency after 6 years of major league service.

1976

- MLB owners announced spring training would not begin as scheduled until a new agreement was reached. Shortly thereafter, players shut down informal training camps, but MLB Commissioner Bowie Kuhn ordered training camps open.

- In July, players and owners agreed on a 4-year agreement that established procedures for free agency: players with at least 6 years' service could become free agents but players then must wait 5 years before becoming a free agent a second time. Players with 2 years of major league service were eligible for salary arbitration.

1977

- Don Fehr, who assisted the MLBPA's defense in the *Messersmith* case as a Kansas City–based attorney, was hired by Miller to join the MLBPA as general counsel.

1980

- In March, the players, in a 967–1 vote, authorized a strike. One month later the strike was staged on the final 8 days of spring training, forcing cancellation of 92 exhibition games.

- Players and owners reached a 4-year agreement but agreed to allow the issue of free agency to be reopened the following season.

1981

- In February, the executive board of the MLBPA approved a May 29 strike date.

- In June, after a 2-week extension of the original strike deadline caused by a National Labor Relations Board action, players staged the first midseason strike in baseball history.

- One month later, players and owners reached an agreement, ending the strike after 50 days resulting in 712 canceled games. The agreement extended the contract 1 year through December 31, 1984, and the season restarted.

1985

- On the day before the All-Star game in Minneapolis, the MLBPA set an August strike date, and players later staged a strike in midseason for the second time. After 2 days, the union and the league signed a 5-year agreement, ending the strike. No games were lost due to the strike.

1986

- Miller retired and Don Fehr, former MLBPA general legal counsel, was elected as MLBPA executive director (1986–present).

1990

- In March, the MLBPA agreed on a 4-year contract after a 32-day lockout. The season started on April 9, a week behind schedule, and the 78 games postponed by the lockout were rescheduled.

1994

- In July, the executive board of the MLBPA set an August 12 strike date.

- On September 14, the World Series was canceled for the first time since 1904, and 669 games of the regular season were lost.

1995

- After a U.S. district judge issued an injunction restoring terms and conditions of the expired agreement, the owners accepted the MLBPA's offer to return to work (March 31).

- Opening day was pushed back from April 2 to April 25. The first 23 days and 252 games of the season were canceled and teams played 144-game schedules.

1996

- The Players Trust was established. It was funded through player and public donations and gives a percentage of licensing revenue and revenue produced from MLBPA special events to various charities. It is the first charitable foundation in sports to be administrated and established by the players.

1997

- A new CBA was signed for 1997–2000, with an MLBPA option to extend it through 2001.

1998

- The Curt Flood Act was signed by President Clinton. The act gives Major League Baseball players the right to sue the league under U.S. antitrust laws.

1999

- The Baseball Tomorrow Fund (BTF) was established through a $10-million commitment from MLB and the MLBPA. The goal of the BTF was to promote and enhance the growth of youth participation in baseball and softball throughout the world by funding programs, fields, coaches' training, and the purchase of uniforms and equipment.

2002

- MLB and MLBPA agreed on a new CBA including increased revenue sharing, a luxury tax above defined payroll thresholds, a 50% increase in the minimum salary, and the elimination of contraction talks during the life of the deal, which ended in 2006.

2005

- The U.S. Congress heard testimony about the use of performance-enhancing drugs in Major League Baseball from MLB and MLBPA representatives.
- The MLBplayers.com website was launched, becoming the official website for the MLBPA.

2006

- The MLBPA and MLB agreed to a new 5-year CBA.

2007

- CDM Fantasy Sports successfully sued the MLBPA and MLB Advanced Media for the right to use player names and statistics without need of a license.

Structure of the MLBP

- Executive board: Meets twice a year and is responsible for directing the affairs of the association
  - Two MLBPA representatives
  - Two alternate MLBPA representatives
  - Club player representatives
  - Pension committee representatives

- Legal: A group of lawyers who provide legal guidance during salary arbitration, grievance arbitration, collective bargaining, and other legal matters
- Licensing: Handles products that use the names or likenesses of more than two players (baseball cards, video games, etc.)
- Finance
- Communications
- Community relations
- Players Trust: A not-for-profit foundation created by the players in 1996 to assist charities around the world. Programs include:
  - Buses for Baseball, Inspiration Fields, Medicines for Humanity, Players Choice Awards, Volunteers for America, and Matching Grant Program
- Media/public relations

Money Matters for the MLBPA[4]

Sources of Revenue for 2007

- Licensing fees
  - Baseball card licensing
    - $10.41 million from Upper Deck
    - $10.57 million from Topps
    - Major League Baseball Advanced Media (MLBAM), licensee of players' digital and interactive rights: $7.7 million
    - Majestic Athletic, producer of replica baseball apparel: $3.95 million[5]
    - Take-Two, developer of popular video games such as MLB 2K: $13.6 million

In 2007, total licensing revenue generated up to $32,437 each for players who spent the entire season in the major leagues. As of 2008, the union held a total of $113.7 million in investments (primarily Treasury securities) as a safety net to guard against future work stoppages from a strike or a lockout.

Players pay dues in the amount of $50 per day for each of the 183 days of the major league season (total annual dues of $9,150). The union's executive director, Donald Fehr, earns an annual salary of $1 million. In 2007, chief operating officer Gene Orza was paid $676,250 while general counsel Michael Weiner earned $746,250.

NATIONAL FOOTBALL LEAGUE PLAYERS ASSOCIATION[6]

The National Football League Players Association (NFLPA) is the officially recognized union for NFL players. The NFLPA represents players in matters concerning wages, hours, and working conditions and protects their rights. It assures that the terms of the collective bargaining agreement, a legally binding relationship between the players and owners, are carried out by both parties.

The NFLPA also negotiates and monitors retirement and insurance benefits. In addition, it provides other membership services and activities, provides assistance to charitable and community organizations, and enhances and defends the image of players and their profession on and off the playing field. The NFLPA assists players with financial management along with setting agent rules and regulations to ensure proper representation for the players. The NFLPA is also a member of the AFL-CIO.

The union is the first line of defense for professional football players. Established in 1956, the NFLPA has a long history of assuring proper recognition and representation of players' interests. The NFLPA has shown that it will do whatever is necessary to assure that the rights of players are protected—including ceasing to be a union, if necessary, as it did in 1989.

The NFLPA also has the rights to use player names and likenesses collectively, which is called group licensing. When a company wants to use more than six players in a campaign, it must go through the NFLPA to gain those rights; otherwise, all deals are negotiated individually between the players and companies.

For the fiscal year ending February 28, 2007, Players, Inc. (the licensing arm of the NFLPA) generated $115 million in licensing and sponsorship revenue, up 6.5% from the previous year. Significant portions of the revenue came from Electronic Arts ($28 million for video game rights) and trading cards ($24.6 million). In the same time frame, the NFLPA collected $19 million in dues from its players. The union typically rebates dues back to the players, but elected not to do so in 2007. Instead, the union leaders decided to build a reserve fund to be used to fund operations during future work stoppages (strikes or lockouts). As of February 28, 2007, the NLPA controlled $264 million in assets, of which $167 million is in cash and investments.

Headquartered in Washington, DC, the NFLPA employs over 40 professionals in 12 departments including legal, communications, finance and asset management, and salary cap and agent administration. The NFLPA also operates a western office located in San Francisco, California. The union's annual report (called an LM-2) is considered public information and can be obtained through the U.S. Department of Labor. Gene Upshaw was the executive director of the NFLPA through September 2008. According to the LM-2, he earned $6.7 million in annual compensation for the year ended February 28, 2007.[7]

NATIONAL BASKETBALL PLAYERS ASSOCIATION[8]

The National Basketball Players Association (NBPA) is the officially recognized union for NBA players. The NBPA's main duty is to represent players in matters concerning

wages, hours, and working conditions and to protect their rights. Similar to the other player associations, the NBPA assures that the terms of the CBA with the National Basketball Association are carried out by both parties.

The NBPA also negotiates and monitors retirement and insurance benefits. In addition, it provides other membership services and activities, provides assistance to charitable and community organizations, and enhances and defends the image of players and their profession on and off the court. In addition, the NBPA certifies and regulates player agents.

Unlike the MLBPA and the NFLPA, the NBPA sold the player licensing rights to the National Basketball Association for a fixed $25-million annual fee. The league, in turn, sells the rights to various companies and keeps all proceeds. The arrangement guarantees the NBPA revenues every year, and it does not have to be involved in the licensing business. In addition to the player rights, the NBPA receives $8 million per year from the NBA to use the NBPA logo. Each player receives the same distribution of approximately $50,000 after their $10,000 annual dues.

The NBPA was founded in 1958, and its headquarters are located in New York City. Billy Hunter is the executive director for the NBPA. He earns a reported $2.1 million in annual compensation.[9] The union's annual report (called an LM-2) is considered public information and can be obtained through the U.S. Department of Labor. The NBPA employs over 30 professionals in various departments such as agent regulation, finance, legal, and operations.

NATIONAL HOCKEY LEAGUE PLAYERS ASSOCIATION[10]

The National Hockey League Players Association (NHLPA) is the officially recognized union for NHL players. Like the other player associations, the NHLPA represents players in matters concerning wages, hours, and working conditions and protects their rights. It also assures that the terms of the CBA with the National Hockey League are carried out by both parties.

The NHLPA also negotiates and monitors retirement and insurance benefits. In addition, it provides other membership services and activities, provides assistance to charitable and community organizations, and enhances and defends the image of players and their profession on and off the ice.

Like the MLBPA and the NFLPA, the NHLPA sells group player licensing rights to companies. Any companies that would like to use three or more player likenesses must obtain those rights from the NHLPA. Some deals in this area include a 6-year, $44.2-million deal with EA Sports for use of player names and likenesses in video games and a 5-year, $25-million deal with Upper Deck for use on trading cards.

Established in 1967, the NHLPA has defended the best interests of the players on and off the ice for almost 40 years. The union's executive director position was filled in 2007 with the hiring of Paul Kelly. The previous executive director, Ted Saskin, earned a reported $2.1 million in annual compensation.[11] The NHLPA is not required to file an annual report with the U.S. Department of Labor because the union is a Canadian entity. Headquartered in Toronto, Ontario, the NHLPA has a staff of approximately 50 employees who work in departments such as labor law, product licensing, and community relations.

WOMEN'S NATIONAL BASKETBALL PLAYERS ASSOCIATION

The Women's National Basketball Players Association (WNBPA) is the union for professional basketball players of the WNBA. The WNBPA is overseen by the NBPA and represents the WNBA players in matters concerning wages, hours, and terms and conditions of employment. The WNBPA is responsible for interpreting and enforcing the rules outlined in the CBA with the WNBA. Other responsibilities include negotiating the CBA, pursuing grievances on a player's behalf, and counseling a player on educational opportunities.

The overall mission of the WNBPA is to ensure that the rights of its constituents are protected, and that players maximize their opportunities and achieve their goals on and off the court. NBPA Executive Director Billy Hunter and WNBPA Director Pam Wheeler lead the WNBPA in negotiations, management, and other initiatives with respect to the WNBPA. The WNBPA employs over 30 professionals in various departments such as agent regulation, finance, legal, and operations; its headquarters are located in New York City.

MAJOR LEAGUE SOCCER PLAYERS UNION[12,13]

The Major League Soccer Players Union (MLSPU) is headquartered in New York City and is the officially recognized union for MLS players. The MLSPU represents players in matters concerning wages, hours, and working conditions and protects their rights. It assures that the terms of the CBA with Major League Soccer are carried out by both parties.

The MLSPU also negotiates and monitors retirement and insurance benefits. In addition, it provides other membership services and activities, provides assistance to charitable and community organizations, and enhances and defends the image of players and their profession on and off the playing field.

After the MLS players lost an antitrust lawsuit, *Fraser v. Major League Soccer*, claiming that the MLS was acting as a monopolistic entity in 2000, the players decided to unionize. In 2005, the MLSPU and MLS negotiated its first CBA, a 4-year agreement between the MLS and its players.

Like the NBPA, the MLSPU sells its licensing rights to the league. In 2005, the MLSPU received $425,000 for

those rights. In addition, the MLSPU generates revenue through player dues. The amount of the dues varies depending on a player's salary (from $20 to $70 a month), with the average player paying $210 annually.

Endnotes

1. Major League Baseball Players Association: Home. (2008). MLBPlayers.com. Retrieved August 12, 2008, from http://mlbplayers.mlb.com/pa/index.jsp.

2. History of the Major League Baseball Players Association. (n.d.). MLBPA. Retrieved November 15, 2007, from http://mlbplayers.mlb.com/pa/info/history.jsp.

3. Baseball Stoppages Date Back to 1972. (2002, Aug. 29). *ESPN.com*. Retrieved October 24, 2007, from http://espn.go.com/mlb/news/2002/0829/1424697.html.

4. Fischer, E. and Mullen, L. (2008, May 5). MLB Players Receive Labor Peace Dividend. *Street and Smith's SportsBusiness Journal*. Retrieved May 13, 2008, from http://www.sportsbusinessjournal.com/article/58875.

5. Information obtained from the MLBPA's 2007 LM-2 form in its 2007 filing with the U.S. Department of Labor.

6. NFL Players Association: Home. (2008). NFLPlayers.com. Retrieved August 12, 2008, from http://www.nflplayers.com/user/index.aspx?fmid= 378&lmid=378&pid=0&type=l.

7. Kaplan, D. (2007, July 9–15). Upshaw's Compensation At Least $6.7M. *Street & Smith's SportsBusiness Journal*, vol. 10, issue 11, pp. 1, 32.

8. National Basketball Players Association: Home. (n.d.). NBPA.com. Retrieved August 12, 2008, from http://www.nbpa.com.

9. Kaplan, op.cit.

10. National Hockey League Players' Association: Home. (2008). *NHLPA.com*. Retrieved August 12, 2008, from http://www.nhlpa.com.

11. Kaplan, op. cit.

12. Major League Soccer Players Union. (2007). MLSPlayers.org. Retrieved August 12, 2008, from http://www.mlsplayers.org.

13. Mickle, T. (2006, Nov. 6). Soccer Players Bank Licensing Checks for Later. *Street and Smith's SportsBusiness Journal*. Retrieved May 13, 2008, from http://www.sportsbusinessjournal.com/article/52620.

CHAPTER FORTY-FOUR

Professional Associations and Organizations

This chapter examines a number of associations and organizations within the sports world that have been formed with the purpose of improving and monitoring either individual sports or sports as a whole. The organizations discussed in this chapter provide their members with an outlet where they can voice their concerns, learn from other members in their field, and discuss other matters such as rules, trends, and awards.

NATIONAL ASSOCIATION OF COLLEGIATE DIRECTORS OF ATHLETICS[1]

The National Association of Collegiate Directors of Athletics (NACDA) was founded in 1965 and held its inaugural convention in 1966. Headquartered in Cleveland, Ohio, NACDA serves as the professional association for intercollegiate athletics administrators. The organization provides educational opportunities for its members and provides advocacy on behalf of the profession and networking opportunities.

NACDA features a membership body of over 6,100 individuals and an additional 1,600 institutions, making it the largest collegiate athletic administration association. Members range from athletic administrators (directors, associates, and assistants) to conference commissioners to institutions or corporations affiliated with collegiate athletics. In addition to the United States, NACDA also has a presence in both Canada and Mexico.

NACDA sponsors an annual convention in June, which serves as a platform to discuss the contemporary and important issues facing college athletics. The annual convention caters to all intercollegiate athletics administrators with breakout sessions on topics such as compliance, event management, alumni development, and business management.[2]

NACDA is governed by a group of officers and executive committee members. The officers consist of a president, three vice presidents, and a secretary. NACDA has committees such as Finance-Management, Continuing Education, Investment, and Honors and Awards. The Executive Committee includes representatives from NCAA Division I, II, and III schools; National Association of Intercollegiate Athletics (NAIA) Division I and II schools; junior colleges, community colleges, and at-large members from several different colleges and collegiate athletic organizations.

NACDA has a staff of 10 with jobs such as exhibits manager, membership coordinator, and director of communications. In addition, an internship program was started in 1984 and has provided opportunities for more than 150 college students and graduates from 26 states and 71 NACDA-member institutions. NACDA selects four interns each year who are young, aspiring collegiate athletics administrators to participate in the year-long program.

History of the NACDA

1959

- The first national conference on Athletic Administration in Colleges and Universities was held in Louisville, Kentucky.

1965

- At the third conference on Athletic Administration in Colleges and Universities, the National Association of Collegiate Directors of Athletics (NACDA) was founded.

1966

- The NACDA national office opened in Minneapolis, Minnesota.
- NACDA held its first convention, in Chicago, Illinois; 307 members attended.
- The first issue of its magazine, *NACDA Quarterly*, was published.

1968

- NACDA published the *National Directory of College Athletics* (men's edition), a directory of colleges and universities that compete in intercollegiate athletics, for the first time.

1969

- NACDA relocated its headquarters to Cleveland, Ohio.

1973

- Individual membership reached 1,000.
- NACDA published the *National Directory of College Athletics* (women's edition) for the first time.

1977

- Institutional membership reached 1,000.

1980

- Individual membership reached 2,000.

1985

- NACDA opened new headquarters in suburban Cleveland, Ohio.

1990

- Individual membership reached 3,000.

1991

- Institutional membership reached 1,500.

1992

- NACDA adopted the administrative duties for the National Association of Collegiate Marketing Administrators (NACMA). NACMA serves as the professional association for people working in collegiate marketing, communications, and revenue generation.

1993

- NACDA established the National Association of Athletic Development Directors (NAADD), a committee that promotes and creates strategies to improve the development of athletes under the guidance of athletic departments.
- The Sears Directors' Cup Program for Division I was established, which honors excellence in men's and

women's collegiate sports. Member institutions accumulate points based on their teams' success in national competition. Each team's points are then totaled for a score for the university.

- Individual membership reached 4,000.

1994

- Individual membership reached 5,000.

1995

- The Sears Directors' Cup was expanded to include all divisions of the NCAA and the NAIA.

1996

- The NACDA website was launched (www.nacda.com).

1997

- NCAA Football and NAIA Football are formed with the cooperation of NACDA with the American Football Coaches Association, NCAA, NAIA, and the Collegiate Commissioners Association. The alliance between these bodies was forged in order to promote and market collegiate football at the national level.[3]

1998

- NACDA adopted the administrative duties for the National Association of Athletics Compliance Coordinators (NAACC). NAACC develops and promotes ethical standards of compliance while providing opportunities for those involved in collegiate athletics to gain a better understanding of the compliance regulations of the governing body.
- NACDA adopted the administrative duties for the Division I-AA Athletics Directors Association, which provides a forum for discussion and improvement of the issues and concerns facing Division I-AA athletic directors.
- NACDA adopted the administrative duties for the Division II Athletics Directors Association, which provides surveys and newsletters, and holds meetings for Division II athletic directors.

1999

- NACDA established the National Collegiate Licensing Association (NCLA). The NCLA is concerned with the development of collegiate licensing and trademark opportunities in an ethical manner.
- NACDA adopted the administrative duties for the National Alliance of Two-Year Collegiate Athletics Administrators (NATYCAA). NATYCAA is an organization that represents all 2-year institutions in the United States and promotes academic excellence and increases communication between those colleges.

2000

- NACDA adopted the administrative duties for the College Athletic Business Management Association (CABMA). CABMA is an organization that establishes and maintains the highest standards of integrity and efficiency in the management and administration of business in athletic departments and associations of colleges and universities.

2001

- NACDA established the Division I-AAA Athletic Directors Association (D I-AAA ADA). The D I-AAA ADA helps D I-AAA athletic programs expand and improve through sharing viewpoints and ideas.

2002

- NCLA merged with the Association of Collegiate Licensing Administrators (ACLA) to form the International Collegiate Licensing Association (ICLA). NACDA assumed responsibility to administer the ICLA.

2003

- The United States Sports Academy became the title sponsor of NACDA's Director's Cup, formerly called the Sears Director's Cup.[4]

2005

- Individual membership reached 6,100.
- Institutional membership reached 1,600.

2007

- The NACDA announced its inaugural Mentoring Institute, a program that aims to prepare athletic administrators for careers as athletic directors. The program covers such topics as how to fire your coaches, dealing with the media, financial planning, and crisis management.

Structure of the NACDA

Programs

- NACDA Foundation
  - The association's educational arm and backbone of the organization
  - Sponsors clinics, workshops, and seminars
  - Manages the postgraduate scholarship and intern programs
  - Administers scholarship programs
    - Directors' Cup and John McLendon Memorial Minority Programs.
    - The NACDA Foundation has awarded more than 1,100 scholarships totaling more than $2.7 million.

- Directors' Cup Program
  - Developed as a joint venture with *USA Today*, the Directors' Cup program is the only all-sports competition that recognizes the institutions in NCAA Divisions I, II, and III, and the NAIA with the best overall athletics program.
  - Each institution is awarded points in a predetermined number of sports for men and women.
  - Overall winners in the four categories are recognized as the top athletics program and are the recipient of the coveted Directors' Cup Crystal Trophy along with $5,000 worth of postgraduate scholarships.
- John McLendon Memorial Minority Program
  - Presented to minority students who intend to pursue a graduate degree in athletics administration.
  - Five recipients receive a $10,000 grant towards postgraduate work in the field of sports administration.
- Coca-Cola Community All-American Awards
  - Recognizes community service in intercollegiate athletics at NCAA, NAIA, and junior/community college member institutions.
  - The program is designed to help institutions recognize, celebrate, and applaud student athletes who are making a difference in their communities.
  - Each national winner receives an award, and Coca-Cola donates $5,000 to the philanthropic/community organization of the student's choice.
- NACDA Awards
  - NACDA awards and recognizes outstanding work and contributions made by collegiate athletics administrators. The following are the awards presented by NACDA:
    - James J. Corbett Memorial Award: Presented to an administrator who demonstrates outstanding dedication to the betterment of collegiate athletics
    - NACDA/NIT Athletics Directors Award
    - Awards for Administrative Excellence
    - NACDA/USOC Collegiate Olympic Coaches
    - NACDA/Sports Management Institute (SMI) Honorary Degree
    - NACDA Merit of Honor Award
    - General Sports TURF Systems AD of the Year Award
    - Special Recognition of Service to NACDA

Money Matters for the NACDA

Sources of Revenue

- Membership dues
  - NACDA receives membership dues on an annual basis. Two categories of memberships exist (institutional and individual), and all memberships run concurrently with the academic year.
    - Institutional: Major sustaining (up to 15 members) and sustaining (up to 7 members) memberships are paid for by an institution, conference association, or bowl. For institutions only, the primary member (director of athletics) has voting privileges.
    - Individual: Individual memberships are available to commercial firms and to administrators from institutions that do not have enough people for a sustaining membership.
- Sponsorship
  - At the end of 2008, NACDA had 18 sponsors and partners. Some of the companies aligned with NACDA include Coca-Cola, Delta Airlines, Adidas, and *USA Today*. Sponsors pay an annual fee to NACDA to become a recognized partner and for other related services.
- Licensing
  - NACDA formed the International Collegiate Licensing Association (ICLA) through a merger of the National Collegiate Licensing Association (NCLA) and the Association of Collegiate Licensing Administrators (ACLA) in 2002 to hold schools to high ethical standards while promoting the growth and development of member licensing agreements.

AMERICAN HOCKEY COACHES ASSOCIATION[5]

The American Hockey Coaches Association (AHCA) is a professional association that strives to publicize and enhance exposure for hockey. In addition, the AHCA works with the NCAA rules committee to improve collegiate hockey. Another primary goal of the AHCA is to maintain high educational standards when coaching the game of hockey.

Founded in 1947 in Boston, Massachusetts, by a group of college hockey coaches, the AHCA is governed and run by members of the association, rather than having a full-time staff. The only staff to speak of is a part-time executive director and part-time treasurer who oversee the operation of the association. Additionally, members of the ACHA elect a group of officers and a group of governors. The officers consist of a president, vice president of membership, vice president of convention planning, vice president of sponsorships, and the past-president. The 2006–2007 officers also had a position of a senior advisor to the president. The board of governors consists of at least a five-member panel representing six schools. ACHA directors are made up of representatives from around the nation, and from all levels of men's and women's hockey.

In order to reach its goals and objectives, the AHCA has established the following committees: awards, convention planning, ethics, legislative, rules, high school, sponsorship, and women's hockey. The AHCA's website (www.ahca-hockey.com) provides its members with news and updates and serves as a forum for coaches to voice opinions and concerns for the benefit of amateur hockey and, in particular, hockey coaches. The association is also responsible for naming several postseason awards in addition to selecting the Jofa-AHCA All-American team. Over the years, the association has expanded its membership to include professional, junior, high school, and youth coaches in addition to referees, hockey administrators, journalists, and even fans. The AHCA has over 1,300 members and is headquartered in Gloucester, Massachusetts.

NATIONAL ASSOCIATION OF BASKETBALL COACHES[6]

The National Association of Basketball Coaches was founded in 1927 by University of Kansas Coach Forrest C. "Phog" Allen. The association began as a result of a series of rule changes implemented by the Joint Basketball Rules Committee that would, in essence, eliminate dribbling from the game of basketball. Allen rallied the coaches to protest the changes and the proposed rules were never implemented. Since the protest, the NABC has been one of the most influential groups in the history of basketball, as it has initiated several long-lasting activities, including the Naismith Memorial Basketball Hall of Fame, the NCAA Basketball Championship, and the Coaches vs. Cancer fund. The NABC strives to improve and promote the game of basketball while working with the NCAA to maintain the integrity of the game. In addition, the association's responsibilities include the Coaches vs. Cancer Classic, the *USA Today*–NABC Top 25 Coaches Poll, and the NABC Championship trophy, a Waterford crystal trophy presented to the national champion the morning after the NCAA championship.

The association is composed of 5,000 coaches at the NCAA, NIAA, junior college, and high school levels. The governing structure is composed of 18 board members, 7 of whom are executives. All members of the board of directors are college coaches. The NABC also has an executive staff made up of noncoaches who handle administrative duties. The NABC offices are located in Kansas City, Missouri.

The NABC is composed of several divisions including business operations, association affairs, membership services, convention management, internal operations, and general management. Some comparable associations include the Black Coaches Association, the Women's Basketball Coaches Association, and the European Association of Basketball Coaches. However, the NABC is the largest and most influential of all the coaches associations.

BLACK COACHES AND ADMINISTRATORS[7]

The Black Coaches and Administrators (BCA) was founded in 1988 as a cooperative effort of African American assistant basketball and football coaches. The goal of the BCA is to improve employment opportunities within athletics for minorities. The nonprofit organization is based out of Indianapolis, Indiana, and has members representing 44 states. The BCA is run by a board of directors composed of current and former head and assistant coaches, members of various athletic departments, and college professors. Membership is not limited to coaches or African Americans, but is open to anyone involved with basketball including any and all races. The BCA plans conventions and sends newsletters to members to inform them of developments and concerns regarding issues facing minorities. The BCA has a staff of four that handles marketing and communications, membership, and administration. There are internship positions that last 6–7 months in areas such as marketing, information services, media, information technology, and administration.

KNIGHT FOUNDATION COMMISSION[8]

The Knight Foundation Commission is an organization formed by John S. and James L. Knight in 1989 with William C. Friday and Rev. Theodore M. Hesburgh serving as the founding co-chairs. The commission's purpose is to report and recommend agenda and ideas geared towards achieving the underlying goals of higher education. It was created in response to the growing number of visible scandals and the commercialization of college athletics. The commission strives to develop stronger institutional control by focusing on the academic and financial integrity of athletic programs across the nation.

Headed by a chairman, two vice chairmen, and 17 members, the commission is made up of college presidents, businesspeople, and former student athletes. The day-to-day staff is composed of an executive director and an associate director. Since its inception, the commission has presented a series of recommendations, including *Keeping the Faith with the Student-Athlete* (1991) and *A Call to Action* (2001). Major reforms enacted by the NCAA in response to commission recommendations have included raising academic standards for student athletes, providing increased control to college and university presidents over NCAA decisions, and setting standards in graduation rates. The commission held its inaugural Summit on the Collegiate Athlete experience on January 30, 2006. The summit concentrated primarily on the impact of academic reform from the vantage point of the student athlete.

Endnotes

1. National Association of Colligate Directors of Athletics: Home. (2008). NACDA.com. Retrieved August 10, 2008, from http://nacda.cstv.com.

2. National Association of Colligate Directors of Athletics: 2008 Convention Week. (2008). NACDA.com. Retrieved August 10, 2008, from http://nacda .cstv.com/convention/nacda-convention.html.

3. NCAA Fast Facts. (2002, Sep. 8). *AFCA*. Retrieved October 24, 2007, from http://www.afca.com/ ViewArticle.dbml?SPSID=61517&SPID=6697&DB_ OEM_ID=9300&ATCLID=289540.

4. NACDA Announces United States Sports Academy as Directors' Cup Sponsor. (2003, Sep. 22). United States Sports Academy. Retrieved October 24, 2007, from http://www.ussa.edu/news/2003/09/22/01nacdadirec-torscupsponsor.asp.

5. American Hockey Coaches Association: Home. (2008). AHCAHockey.com. Retrieved August 10, 2008 from http://www.ahcahockey.com.

6. NABC: Home. (2008). Retrieved August 11, 2008, from http://nabc.cstv.com.

7. BCA: Home. (2008). Retrieved September 21, 2008, from http://bcasports.cstv.com/about/bca_about.html.

8. Knight Commission: Home. (2008). Retrieved September 21, 2008, from http://knightscommission.org.

CHAPTER FORTY-FIVE

Sports Marketing Research

As previously discussed in Chapter 42, corporate sponsorship in the sports industry has experienced tremendous growth in recent years, and in 2007 over $10 billion was spent on global sponsorship of major sports organizations.[1] With so much money being spent on sponsorship and marketing in sports, it is not surprising that firms dedicated to the study of sports marketing are beginning to emerge. This chapter examines IEG, Inc., one of the firms specializing in sports marketing and research.

IEG, INC.[2]

Established in the late 1980s by Lesa Ukman, IEG, Inc. is a private, for-profit company dedicated to measuring and evaluating sponsorships through a host of practices and tools. IEG advises sponsors, properties, and agencies by providing sponsorship research and analysis for marketing issues. IEG works with clients in a wide variety of areas including sports, arts, entertainment, events, and non-profit organizations. Through its products and services, IEG analyzes and predicts trends, forecasts revenues, tracks financing, and prepares valuations of sponsorships and sponsor programs.

This Chicago-based company was purchased by GroupM, a WPP-owned firm, in April 2006. IEG employs more than 50 professionals in five business units: learning, measurement, consulting, training, and research and databases. These units provide IEG with vast resources to provide comprehensive sponsorship research and analysis to its clients.

Some of the other firms providing sports marketing research include Turnkey Sports, Shugoll Research, Sponsorship Research International (SRI), the Bonham Group, and Knowledge Networks.

Endnotes

1. Chipps, W. (2008, Jan. 18). Sponsorship Spending to Total $16.78 Billion in 2008. IEG. Retrieved February 8, 2008, from http://www.sponsorship.com/About-IEG/Press-Room/Sponsorship-Spending-To-Total-$16.78-Billion-In-20.aspx.

2. WPP's GroupM Announces Acquisition of IEG, Inc. (2006, Apr. 27). Sponsorship.com. Retrieved November 15, 2007, from http://www.sponsorship.com/About-IEG/Press-Room/WPP-s-GroupM-Announces-Acquisition-of-IEG-Inc.aspx.

CHAPTER FORTY-SEVEN

Corporate Law

The sports industry presents a number of unique legal issues and has led a number of legal firms to create specific divisions that concentrate solely on sports law. These firms often practice within specific areas of sports law in which they can use their expertise. They may represent teams, players, coaches, universities, leagues, associations, and/or owners. This chapter discusses three law firms with a sports law division and their specific areas of practice.

PROSKAUER ROSE, LLP[1]

Proskauer Rose, LLP, is an international law firm that provides clients with a wide variety of legal services. Founded in 1875 in New York City, Proskauer Rose is one of the nation's largest law firms. The firm has seven domestic offices (New York, Los Angeles, Washington, DC, Boston, Boca Raton, Newark, and New Orleans) and one overseas office in Paris. The company's expertise spreads across many industries as the firm services clients in 45 different practice areas.

The Sports Law Group, a division of Proskauer Rose, mainly consists of numerous litigation, tax, labor, new media, transactional, antitrust, bankruptcy, intellectual property, and real estate lawyers with extensive experience in sports matters. Proskauer Rose's Sports Law Group has been in existence for over 35 years and has represented sports leagues and sports teams in all aspects of their operations. They currently serve as counsel to leagues such as the NBA, MLB, NHL, and MLS. They also have represented prospective franchise buyers for sports teams such as the Philadelphia Eagles, New York Jets, and Montreal Expos. In addition, they have advised such entities as the U.S. Olympic Committee, World Cup USA 1994, the LPGA, the New York Yankees, the Kansas City Royals, and the Anaheim Angels.

Former members of the firm hold senior business and legal positions throughout the sport industry and include NBA Commissioner David Stern and NHL Commissioner Gary Bettman. Almost all potential job opportunities that exist at Proskauer Rose are lawyer positions and require a JD degree.

ROPES & GRAY[2]

Ropes & Gray is a national law firm with offices in Boston, New York, Palo Alto, San Francisco, and Washington, DC, and a conference center in London. The company has been in existence for over 140 years. Ropes & Gray employs approximately 850 lawyers providing legal representation and advice in 28 different sectors.

The Sports Law Practice has a client list that includes coaches, colleges and universities, sporting goods manufacturers, and professional sports franchises. Ropes & Gray advises clients on issues involving contract negotiations and dispute resolution, commercial transactions, licensing, intellectual property rights, privacy regulations, and NCAA investigations and compliance.

Ropes & Gray employs nine attorneys in its sports practice. Like the other law firms, almost all potential job opportunities that exist at Ropes & Gray are lawyer positions and require a JD degree.

MCKENNA, LONG, & ALDRIDGE, LLP[3]

McKenna, Long, & Aldridge, LLP (MLA) is an international law firm composed of approximately 400 lawyers and public policy advisors with offices in Atlanta, Brussels, Denver, Los Angeles, Philadelphia, San Diego, San Francisco, and Washington, DC. MLA's clients include *Fortune* 500 and mid-size companies, government contractors, real estate developers, and nonprofit organizations. The firm was developed through a merger of McKenna & Cuneo (formed in 1939) and Long Aldridge & Norman (formed in 1974).

MLA's Sports and Entertainment practice focuses on the legal and business issues in the sports and entertainment industry. Over the past 25 years, MLA has advised clients on a wide variety of legal and business issues including stadium and arena matters, sponsorship and licensing transactions, and athlete-agent issues. The Sports and Entertainment practice is one of 19 sectors within MLA and has seven dedicated lawyers that serve clients in the sports and entertainment industry.

Endnotes

1. Proskauer Rose: Home. (2008). Proskauer.com. Retrieved August 12, 2008, from http://www .proskauer.com/index.html.

2. Ropes & Gray: Home. (2008). RopesGray.com. Retrieved August 12, 2008, from http://www .ropesgray.com.

3. McKenna, Long, and Aldridge: Home. (2008). McKennaLong.com. Retrieved August 12, 2008, from http://www.mckennalong.com.

48

Cottage Industries

Cottage industries are usually small companies that offer a particular service and/or area of expertise to a client in some aspect of the sports industry. This chapter examines three companies who have found a niche in the sports industry.

BASEBALL INFO SOLUTIONS[1]

Baseball Info Solutions (BIS) specializes in collecting, packaging, and delivering baseball data to a host of clients including major league teams, agents, fantasy services, baseball card publishers, and computer game developers. Established in 2002, BIS customizes data reports and provides personalized customer service to its clients. BIS employees gather data (such as pitch charts, fielding charts, and spray charts that reflect the areas of the field where a player hit the ball) from professional baseball games and package them into reports on hard copy, CDs, disk, e-mails, and books, such as *The Fielding Bible*.

BIS headquarters are located in Bethlehem, Pennsylvania, and the company has 10 employees and several interns. BIS employees have previously worked with statistical companies, scouting companies, fantasy websites, and information technology companies. Sabermetrician Bill James, who is well-known for his groundbreaking statistical analysis, is a consultant at BIS. BIS offers internship opportunities during the season to assist with data collection.

HCC SPECIALTY UNDERWRITERS[2]

HCC Specialty Underwriters, a subsidiary of HCC Insurance Holdings, Inc., is an insurance firm that provides specialty insurance and underwriting services to the promotion, marketing, sports, and entertainment industries. Established in 1982 as ASU International, HCC Specialty Underwriters offers nontraditional disability insurance products and contingency insurance products for professional athletes, teams, leagues, entertainers, and high profile individuals in the business world. Also, HCC provides disability insurance for the NCAA. It also has event cancellation policies for the Olympics, and NCAA and World Cup events. In addition,

HCC offers event cancellation policies to protect an event in case it must be cancelled or postponed due to inclement weather and other unforeseen circumstances. HCC also offers prize insurance to the promotion industry for such programs as the "$1-million field goal kick."

HCC Insurance Holdings, Inc., purchased the rights to ASU in 2001 and changed the name to HCC Specialty Underwriters in 2005. HCC Insurance Holdings is publicly traded on the New York Stock Exchange under the ticker symbol HCC. Headquartered in Houston, Texas, HCC has assets exceeding $6.6 billion. In 2005, HCC Specialty earned a net income of nearly $200 million. Divisions within the headquarters include finances, marketing, promotions, events, high limit disability, legal affairs, and cinefinance insurance services. Other insurance companies that compete with HCC are Team Scotti, Hartford Financial Services, and AIG.

NACDA CONSULTING

As the amount of revenue generated by the college athletics industry has grown, so too has the need for proper decision making within athletic departments. NACDA Consulting provides advice in variety of areas concerning the administration of college athletics with numerous services such as business operations review, compliance assessment, facility development, Title IX reporting, emergency/disaster planning, executive recruitment, and creative marketing. The company was established in 2005 when the NACDA joined with Strategic Marketing Associates and Collegiate Licensing Co. The company currently has 11 clients including University of Georgia, Florida Atlantic University, and Miami University.

Endnotes

1. Baseball Info Solutions: Home. (2008). BaseballInfoSolutions.com. Retrieved August 10, 2008, from http://www.baseballinfosolutions.com.
2. HCC Specialty Underwriters, Inc: Home. (2008). HCCSU.com. Retrieved August 10, 2008, from http://www.hccsu.com/default.htm.

Section 3

Career Tracks of Executives in the Sports Industry

CHAPTER FORTY-NINE

Introduction to Career Tracks

If you have a goal of becoming an executive in the sports industry, it can be very helpful in planning your career path to look at the career paths of executives who currently hold the position you want to obtain. For example, if it is your goal to become a general manager of a major league baseball team, examining how current general managers such as Theo Epstein, Brian Cashman, and Billy Beane obtained their positions can be helpful.

This section of the book presents career track analysis for a number of prominent positions in the sports industry, including baseball general managers, college athletic directors, conference commissioners, and marketing professionals at both the college and professional level. In reading this analysis, you will learn about common trends and patterns found in the educational backgrounds and work experiences of current sports executives. This information can help you form a foundation from which to build your own career plan.

The ultimate goal is to devise a career plan that will enable you to "create" a résumé that is similar to the profile of what a "typical" person in a particular position might be. In creating such a plan, it is important to analyze what you need to accomplish in the next 2 years, 5 years, 10 years, and so on. Consider the type of education you need to obtain, the types of skills and abilities you need to develop and/or demonstrate, and the types of people with whom you need to build network connections. All of these elements are likely to play a crucial role in your career development.

To demonstrate how the analysis of this section can aid in developing a career plan, consider the following example. In reading this section, you will learn it is common for high-ranking executives in college athletics administration to possess a graduate-level education. For someone interested in obtaining a position such as athletic director or conference commissioner, this is valuable information to know. Earning a graduate degree may improve this person's

chances of obtaining his or her desired position, and that person can create a career plan with this in mind.

The information provided in this section will help you to create a career plan of your own; however, this information should not be used in isolation. The organizational charts in Section 4 and the job descriptions in Section 5 also can be used to aid in the process.

NOT ALL CAREER TRACKS CAN BE FOLLOWED

It should be evident that some career tracks can be followed, whereas others cannot. For example, some executives played their sport professionally or had a significant coaching career. This type of experience often plays a vital role in the person's development and can be helpful in the pursuit of certain positions within the sports industry. If you have no such playing or coaching experience, it may not be possible for you to follow this career path. In such cases, it is helpful to look at the career tracks of other executives (i.e., nonathletes and noncoaches) who are in that position and see how they came to obtain their position. This will provide you with ideas on how to create your own career path despite not having playing or coaching experience.

THERE ARE OTHER WAYS

Utilizing the information provided in this section to create a career plan may make it more likely for you to ultimately reach your career goals. This does not mean there are not other ways, though. The sports industry is constantly changing, which often results in corresponding changes to the make-up of its most prominent executives. Twenty years ago, it would have been unheard of to hire a baseball general manager with little baseball experience. Yet, as baseball transitioned into big business, the prevailing mindset has

Table 50-1 Career Tracks: Major League Baseball General Managers (As of April 2008)

Team: Arizona Diamondbacks

GM: Josh Byrnes[1]

Education: Undergraduate: Haverford College (PA)

Professional Playing Experience: None

Career Path

Baseball Playing Career:

Standout Division III player in college (first baseman).

Health Care Industry:

Began professional career as a health care consultant.

Cleveland Indians:

Hired by the Indians as an intern in 1994. Worked various jobs for the Indians before being promoted to director of scouting in 1998.

Colorado Rockies:

In 1999, followed Dan O'Dowd to the Rockies and was named assistant GM.

Boston Red Sox:

In 2002, accepted the position of assistant GM at the Red Sox, working under Theo Epstein.

Arizona Diamondbacks:

Hired by the Diamondbacks in 2005 as the senior vice president/GM.

Notes: Was only 35 years old when hired as GM by the Diamondbacks.

Team: Atlanta Braves

GM: Frank Wren[2]

Education: Undergraduate: St. Petersburg Junior College

Professional Playing Experience: None

Career Path

Montreal Expos:

Joined the Expos front office in 1987 as the assistant director of scouting.

Florida Marlins:

Hired as the assistant GM in 1993.

Promoted to a vice president's role in 1996.

Baltimore Orioles:

Named GM of the Orioles in 1998, lasting one season.

Atlanta Braves:

Hired by the Braves as VP and assistant GM in 2000.

Promoted to GM in September 2007.

Team: Baltimore Orioles

GM: Mike Flanagan[2,4*]

Education: Undergraduate: Attended the University of Massachusetts

Professional Playing Experience: MLB

Career Path

Baseball Playing Career:

18-year Major League career as a pitcher.

Baltimore Orioles:

Served as Orioles pitching coach in 1995 and 1998.

Worked as Orioles broadcaster from 1996 to 1997 and again from 1999 to 2002.

In 2002, was hired as VP of baseball operations and co-GM (working in tandem with Jim Beattie).

Jim Beattie was let go in 2005, giving Flanagan GM duties. Jim Duquette was hired to assist Flanagan.

Notes: Most successful playing career of any current GM. Won the American League Cy Young Award in 1979.

Team: Boston Red Sox

GM: Theo Epstein[2,5]

Education: Undergraduate: Yale University (American Studies). Law School: University of San Diego

Professional Playing Experience: None

Career Path

Baltimore Orioles:

During the summers of 1992–1994, interned with the Orioles in public relations.

San Diego Padres:

Moved to the Padres with Larry Lucchino, starting in public relations.

Worked as assistant in baseball operations in 1998 and 1999.

Promoted to director of baseball operations in 2000.

Boston Red Sox:

Brought to the Red Sox by Lucchino; hired as Red Sox GM in 2002.

Resigned as Red Sox GM in 2005.

Returned to the Red Sox in 2006 as the team's GM and added the title of executive vice president.

Notes: Named GM of the Red Sox at only 28 years of age. Earned his law degree while working full time for the Padres.

Team: Chicago Cubs

GM: Jim Hendry[2,6]

Education: Undergraduate: Spring Hill College (Communications & Journalism). Graduate: St. Thomas University (MS Athletic Administration)

Professional Playing Experience: None

Career Path

High School Teacher and Coach:

Worked as a high school teacher and baseball coach while obtaining a master's degree (1978–1983).

Creighton University:

Named head baseball coach at Creighton University in 1983, where he coached until 1991.

Florida Marlins:

Became special assistant to the Marlins' GM in 1991.

Coached minor league teams in 1993 and 1994.

Chicago Cubs:

Hired by the Cubs as the director of player development in 1994.

Named scouting director in 1995.

Took on combined director of player development and scouting in 1999 and 2000.

Title changed to assistant general manager/player personnel.

Promoted to vice president/GM in 2002.

Team: Chicago White Sox

GM: Kenny Williams[2,7]

Education: Undergraduate: Stanford

Professional Playing Experience: MLB

Career Path

Baseball and Football Playing Career:

Played baseball and football at Stanford.

Played for the White Sox, Tigers, Blue Jays, and Expos from 1986 to 1991, with marginal success.

Chicago White Sox:

Retained by the White Sox as a scout in 1992.

Named special assistant to Chairman Jerry Reinsdorf in 1994.

Served as director of minor league operations in 1995–1996.

Promoted to vice president of player development in 1997.

Promoted to senior VP and GM in 2000.

---

*In addition to Flanagan, Andy McPhail, the Orioles' president of baseball operations, also is involved with player personnel decisions and may fulfill some tasks typically associated with the position of GM.

1. Arizona Diamondbacks Media Guide (2008). Arizonadiamonbacks.com. Retrieved August 12, 2008, from http://arizona.diamondbacks.mlb.com/ari/fan_forum/media_guide.jsp.

2. Baseball America Executive Database. Retrieved August 10, 2007, from http://www.baseballamerica.com/today/execdb.

3. Atlanta Braves Media Guide (2000).

4. Baltimore Orioles Media Guide (2000).

5. Meet Boston GM Theo Epstein. (2002, Nov. 30). *USA Today*. Retrieved August 10, 2007, from http://asp

.usatoday.com/sports/baseball/al/redsox/2002-11-30-epstein-feature_x.htm.

6. Chicago Cubs Media Guide. (2000).

7. Front Office Directory. (n.d.). Chicago White Sox. Retrieved August 10, 2007, from http://chicago.whitesox.mlb.com/team/front_office.jsp?c_id=cws.

Table 50-1   Continued

Team: Cincinnati Reds
GM: Walt Jocketty[2]
Education: Undergraduate: University of Minnesota (Business)
Professional Playing Experience: None
Career Path
Iowa Oaks:
"Jack-of-all-trades" for AAA Iowa Oaks (Astros/White Sox) from 1974 to 1978.
Oakland A's:
Worked as A's director of minor league operations from 1979 to 1983.
Transitioned to director of baseball administration in 1984. Held the position until 1993.
Colorado Rockies:
Hired by the Rockies as an assistant GM in 1993.
St. Louis Cardinals:
Hired by the Cardinals as vice president and GM in 1994.
Cincinnati Reds:
Hired by the Reds in January 2008 as a special advisor.
Promoted to GM in May 2008.

Team: Cleveland Indians
GM: Mark Shapiro[2,9]
Education: Undergraduate: Princeton University (History)
Professional Playing Experience: None
Career Path
College Football Playing Career:
Played 4 years of football in college.
Real Estate Industry:
First worked as a real estate developer out of school.
Cleveland Indians:
Hired by the Indians in 1992 as an assistant in player development.
Promoted to manager of minor league operations in 1993.
Named director of minor league operations in 1994. Worked in this capacity until 1998.
Worked as the VP of baseball operations and assistant GM from 1999 to 2001.
Promoted to executive VP and GM in 2001.

Team: Colorado Rockies
GM: Dan O'Dowd[2,10]
Education: Undergraduate: Rollins College (Business)
Professional Playing Experience: None
Career Path
Balitmore Orioles:
Started baseball career with the Orioles, working in a variety of marketing roles, including major accounts coordinator, sales manager, and director of corporate marketing. Also worked in the Orioles broadcast department.
Last 2 years with Orioles spent as assistant director of player development and scouting.
Cleveland Indians:
Joined the Indians front office in 1988 as the senior VP of baseball administration and player development.
Promoted to director of player development and scouting in 1989.
Named director of baseball operations and assistant GM in 1993.
Fired from the Indians in 1998 for interviewing for the Orioles GM job.
Colorado Rockies:
Hired by the Rockies in 1999 as executive vice president and GM.

Team: Detroit Tigers
GM: Dave Dombrowski[2,11,12]
Education: Undergraduate: Western Michigan University (Business Administration). Also attended Cornell University for one year.
Professional Playing Experience: None
Career Path
Chicago White Sox:
Interviewed White Sox GM for college thesis; hired by White Sox in 1978 as administrative assistant.
Promoted to assistant director of player development in 1979.
Named director of player development in 1981.
Promoted to assistant GM in late 1981.
Named vice president of baseball operations in 1985.
Fired from the White Sox in 1986.
Montreal Expos:
Hired by the Expos in 1986 as director of minor league clubs.
Promoted to assistant GM in 1987.
Named vice president player personnel in 1988 and added the title of GM prior to the 1990 season.
Florida Marlins:
Hired by the expansion Marlins as the team's first executive VP and GM in 1991.
Added the duties of president in 2000.
Detroit Tigers:
Hired by the Tigers as president in 2001. Added the duties of GM in 2002.
Notes: Played college football at Cornell University.

Team: Florida Marlins
GM: Mike Hill[2,33]
Education: Undergraduate: Harvard University (1993)
Professional Playing Experience: Minors
Career Path
Tampa Bay Rays:
Worked as an assistant director of scouting in 1998.
Colorado Rockies:
Hired by the Rockies in 2000 to be the director of player development.
Florida Marlins:
Hired as VP and assistant GM for the Marlins in 2003.
Promoted to general manager in 2007
Notes: Captain of Harvard Baseball team. Led the football team in rushing his senior year. Named to *Black Enterprise* magazine's 2003 Hot List of African American executives under age 40.

Team: Houston Astros
GM: Tim Purpura[2,13]
Education: Undergraduate: Loyola University-Chicago. Law degree: Thomas Jefferson School of Law
Professional Playing Experience: None
Career Path
California Angels:
Worked for the California Angels as assistant in player development during spring training from 1990 to 1992.
San Diego Padres:
Headed special projects for the San Diego minor league department in 1991.
Houston Astros:
Joined the Astros in 1994 as the assistant director of minor leagues and scouting.
Served as director of major league and minor league player relations in 1995 and 1996.
Promoted to assistant GM/director of player development in 1997.
Promoted to GM in 2005.
Notes: Founding member of the Arizona Fall League.

8. Executive Office: Wayne A. Krivsky. (n.d.). Cincinnati Reds. Retrieved August 10, 2007, from http://cincinnati.reds.mlb.com/team/front_office.jsp?c_id=cin.
9. Cleveland Indians Media Guide. (2000).
10. Front Office Directory. (n.d.). Colorado Rockies. Retrieved August 10, 2007, from http://colorado.rockies.mlb.com/team/front_office.jsp?c_id=col.
11. 1998 Distinguished Alumni Award Recipient: David Dombrowski. (n.d.). Western Michigan University.

Retrieved November 13, 2007, from http://www.wmich.edu/alumni/awards/distinguished-alumni/recipients/1990-1999/dombrowski.html.
12. Front Office Directory. (n.d.). Detroit Tigers. Retrieved August 10, 2007, from http://detroit.tigers.mlb.com/team/front_office.jsp?c_id=det.
13. Front Office Directory. (n.d.). Houston Astros. Retrieved August 10, 2007, from http://houston.astros.mlb.com/team/front_office.jsp?c_id=hou.

Table 50-1   Continued

Team: Kansas City Royals **GM:** Dayton Moore[14] **Education:** Undergraduate: George Mason University (Physical Education and Health). Graduate: George Mason University (Athletic Administration) **Professional Playing Experience:** None **Career Path** *Coaching Career:* Served as an assistant baseball coach at George Mason University from 1990 to 1994, while working on a graduate degree at GMU. Also managed the Winchester Royals of the Shenandoah Valley League from 1991 to 1993. *Atlanta Braves:* Joined the Braves as an area scouting supervisor and was promoted to the front office in 1996 as an assistant in the Baseball Operations department. Named assistant director of scouting in 1996. Added the title of assistant director of player development in 1999. In 2000, promoted to director of international scouting. Became director of player personnel in 2002. Promoted to assistant GM baseball operations in 2005. *Kansas City Royals:* Hired by the Royals as senior VP baseball operations and GM in 2006. **Notes:** Was named one of the top 10 up and coming power brokers in MLB.	**Team:** Los Angeles Angels of Anaheim **GM:** Tony Reagins[15] **Education:** Associates Degree: College of the Desert (Business Administration). Undergraduate: California State University, Fullerton (Marketing) **Professional Playing Experience:** None **Career Path** *Los Angeles Angels of Anaheim:* Hired as a marketing intern in 1992. Promoted to marketing assistant in 1994. Promoted to sponsorship services representative in 1996. In 1998, promoted to manager of baseball operations. Served as the director of player development beginning in 2002. Promoted to GM in 2007.	**Team:** Los Angeles Dodgers **GM:** Ned Colletti[16] **Education:** Undergraduate: Northern Illinois University **Professional Playing Experience:** None **Career Path** *Chicago Cubs:* A former sportswriter, began his professional baseball career with the Chicago Cubs in 1982. Worked for the Cubs in media relations and baseball operations until 1994. *San Francisco Giants:* In 1994, hired by the Giants to work in the team's public relations department. Named assistant GM in 1996. Worked in this role for nine seasons. *Los Angeles Dodgers:* Hired by the Dodgers as GM in 2005. **Notes:** Author of four books and has been a guest speaker at many law firms and law schools. Honored with the Robert O. Fishel Award for Public Relations Excellence in 1990.
Team: Milwaukee Brewers **GM:** Doug Melvin[2,17] **Education:** No record of college attendance, unclear if he graduated from high school **Professional Playing Experience:** Minors **Career Path** *Baseball Playing Career:* Pitched in the minor leagues for six seasons. *New York Yankees:* Joined the Yankees baseball operations as assistant scouting director in 1983. Promoted to director of scouting in 1985. *Baltimore Orioles:* Moved to the Orioles in 1986 as a special assistant to the GM. Promoted to assistant GM/director of player personnel in 1987. Title changed from director of player personnel to director of player development in 1994. *Texas Rangers:* Hired by Rangers as vice president/GM in 1994. Title changed to executive vice president/GM in 1997. Fired by Rangers in 2001. *Boston Red Sox:* Worked as a consultant in minor league operations for the Red Sox in 2002. *Milwaukee Brewers:* Hired as Brewers' senior vice president/GM in 2002. **Notes:** Only Canadian-born GM.	**Team:** Minnesota Twins **GM:** Bill Smith[2] **Education:** Undergraduate: Hamilton College (French) **Professional Playing Experience:** None **Career Path** *MLB:* In 1980, one of the initial participants in Major League Baseball's Executive Development Program. *Chicago White Sox:* Named the assistant director of minor leagues and scouting. Spent three seasons as the GM of the White Sox' "A" affiliate in Appleton, WI. *Minnesota Twins:* Moved to the Twins organization in 1986 as the assistant director of minor leagues and scouting. Promoted to director of baseball administration in 1989. Named assistant GM in 1992 and added the title of vice president in 1995. Promoted to GM in September 2007.	**Team:** New York Mets **GM:** Omar Minaya[18] **Education:** No record of college attendance, but did complete high school **Professional Playing Experience:** Minors and 2 seasons in Italy **Career Path** *Baseball Playing Career:* Minor League player in the A's system and played some pro ball in Italy and the Dominican Republic. *Texas Rangers:* Joined the Texas Rangers scouting team in 1985. Named the Latin American scouting coordinator in 1989. Promoted to director of professional and international scouting in 1994. *New York Mets:* Left the Rangers to join the staff of the New York Mets, working his way up to assistant GM in 1997. Also in charge of international scouting for the Mets. *Montreal Expos:* Hired in 2002 by the Expos as the vice president/GM. *New York Mets:* Hired in 2004 by the Mets as the executive vice president/GM. **Notes:** Renowned as a scout, signing Sammy Sosa at 16 for $3,500. First person of Hispanic descent to hold the position of GM.

14. Front Office: Baseball Operations. (n.d.). Kansas City Royals. Retrieved August 10, 2007, from http://kansascity.royals.mlb.com/team/front_office.jsp?c_id=kc.
15. Tony Reagins Promoted to Angels GM. (2007, Oct. 16). MLB.com. Retrieved April 29, 2008, from

http://losangeles.angels.mlb.com/content/printer_friendly/ana/y2007/m10/d16/c2268962.jsp.
16. Front Office Directory. (n.d.). Los Angeles Dodgers. Retrieved August 10, 2007, from http://losangeles.dodgers.mlb.com/team/front_office.jsp?c_id=la.

17. McCalvy, A. (2002, Sep. 26). Melvin Grateful for Second Chance. MLB.com. Retrieved August 10, 2007, from http://www.mlb.com/news/article.jsp?ymd=20020926&content_id=137885&vkey=news_mil&fext=.jsp&c_id=mil.

Table 50-1   Continued

Team: New York Yankees
GM: Brian Cashman[2,19]
Education: Undergraduate: The Catholic University of America (History)
Professional Playing Experience: None
Career path

New York Yankees:

Started with the Yankees as an intern in 1986.

Worked his way up to baseball operations assistant by 1989.

Promoted to assistant farm director in 1990.

Named assistant GM in 1992.

Became Yankees GM in 1998.

Named Yankees GM at the age of 30.

Winningest GM in MLB history.

Aspires to be commissioner of MLB.

Team: Pittsburgh Pirates
GM: Neal Huntington[2,23]
Education: Undergraduate: Amherst College. Graduate: University of Massachusetts (MS Sport Management)
Professional Playing Experience: None
Career path

Montreal Expos:

Joined the Expos in 1995 as the assistant director of player development.

Role expanded to oversee scouting in 1996.

Cleveland Indians:

In 1998, moved to the Indians organization and was named assistant director of minor league operations.

Promoted to director of player development in 1999.

Named assistant GM in 2002.

Became the special assistant to the GM in 2005.

Pittsburgh Pirates:

Hired by the Pirates as the team's general manager in September 2007.

Division III All-American infielder at Amherst College; played football at UMass.

Team: Oakland Athletics
GM: Billy Beane[2,20,21]
Education: Undergraduate: Attended the University of San Diego
Professional Playing Experience: MLB
Career path

Baseball Playing Career:

Brief MLB playing time throughout six seasons.

Oakland A's:

Hired as an advance scout for the A's in 1990.

Promoted to assistant GM in 1993.

Promoted to GM in 1997.

Previous two Oakland assistant GMs were Harvard graduates with no pro ball experience.

Prominently featured in the book *Moneyball.*

Team: St. Louis Cardinals
GM: John Mozeliak[25]
Education: Undergraduate: University of Colorado (Business)
Professional Playing Experience: None
Career path

Colorado Rockies:

Hired in 1993 and held a variety of positions in the baseball operations department.

In 1995, his duties were changed to increase focus on the Major League club and professional scouting.

St. Louis Cardinals:

Hired in 1996 as assistant in scouting operations.

Became the assistant scouting director in 1998.

Named scouting director in 1999.

Promoted to director of baseball operations in 2001.

Named assistant GM in 2003 with responsibilities as Cardinal scouting director in 2003 and 2004.

Promoted to GM in 2007.

Team: Philadelphia Phillies
GM: Pat Gillick[2,22]
Education: Undergraduate: University of Southern California (Business)
Professional Playing Experience: Minors
Career path

Baseball Playing Career:

Won a national championship at USC as a pitcher. Pitched five years in the Orioles' minor league system, venturing as high as Triple-A.

Houston Astros:

Began front office career with the Houston Astros in 1963, starting out as the assistant farm director. By 1973, worked his way up to director of scouting.

New York Yankees:

In 1974, hired by the Yankees as a coordinator of player development and scouting.

Toronto Blue Jays:

Moved to the expansion Blue Jays in 1976, hired as the vice president of player personnel.

Promoted to vice president of baseball operations and GM in 1977.

Promoted to executive vice president of baseball operations and GM in 1984.

Retired as Blue Jays GM after the 1994 season.

Baltimore Orioles:

Hired by the Orioles as GM in 1995. Resigned in October 1998.

Seattle Mariners:

Hired by the Mariners as executive VP baseball operations and GM in 2000; served in this role until 2003.

Worked as a special consultant to the GM in 2004 and 2005.

Philadelphia Phillies:

Hired by the Phillies as GM following the 2005 season.

Notes: Inducted into the Blue Jays Level of Excellence in 2002.

Team: San Diego Padres
GM: Kevin Towers[2,26]
Education: Undergraduate: Attended Brigham Young University
Professional Playing Experience: Minors
Career path

Baseball Playing Career:

First round draft choice of the Padres in 1982. Pitched seven seasons in the minors, ending his career at Triple-A.

San Diego Padres:

Worked as an area scout and single-A pitching coach for the Padres from 1989 to 1991.

Pittsburgh Pirates:

In 1992 and 1993, worked as a crosschecker for the Pirates.

San Diego Padres:

Returned to the Padres in 1993 as the team's director of scouting.

Promoted to VP baseball operations and GM in 1995.

Title changed to executive VP and GM in 2003.

Notes: Teammates in the minor leagues with former Padres manager (and current Giants manager), Bruce Bochy.

18. Anderson, J. (2003, Apr.). Managing the Impossible. Inc.com. Retrieved August 10, 2007, from http://www.inc.com/magazine/20030401/25319.html.
19. King, B. (2000, Nov. 13–19). Brian Cashman. *Street & Smith's SportsBusiness Journal*, p. 29.
20. Chat Wrap: A's GM Billy Beane. (2000, Apr. 19). *ESPN.com*. Retrieved August 10, 2007, from http://espn.go.com/community/s/2000/0417/487251.html.
21. Bush, D. (1998, Feb. 18). A's Beane Is a Born GM. *San Francisco Chronicle*. Retrieved August 10, 2007, from http://www.sfgate.com/cgi-bin/article.cgi?file=/chronicle/archive/1998/02/18/SP104662.DTL.
22. Pat Gillick Named General Manager of Philadelphia Phillies. (n.d.). *About.com*. Retrieved August 10, 2007, from http://philadelphia.about.com/library/weekly/blpat_gillick.htm.
23. Executive Bios. (n.d.). Pittsburgh Pirates. Retrieved April 28, 2008, from http://pittsburgh.pirates.mlb.com/pit/team/exec_bios/huntington_neal.jsp.
24. St. Louis Cardinals Promote John Mozeliak as Team General Manager. (2007, Oct. 31). MLB.com. Retrieved April 29, 2008, from http://tampabay.rays.mlb.com/news/press_releases/press_release.jsp?ymd=20071031&content_id=2289806&vkey=pr_stl&fext=.jsp&c_id=stl.
25. Kevin Towers. (n.d.). BaseballLibrary.com. Retrieved August 10, 2007, from http://www.baseballlibrary.com/ballplayers/player.php?name=Kevin_Towers_1961.
26. Brian R. Sabean. (n.d.). *San Francisco Giants*. Retrieved August 10, 2007, from http://sanfrancisco.giants.mlb.com/sf/team/frontoffice_bios/sabean_brian.jsp.

Table 50-1   Continued

Team: San Francisco Giants
GM: Brian Sabean[2,27]
Education: Undergraduate: Eckerd College (FL)
Professional Playing Experience: None
Career Path
Coaching Career:
Began career in coaching as an assistant coach at St. Leo College, Fla. (1979), assistant coach at the University of Tampa (1980–1982), and head coach at the University of Tampa (1983–1984).
New York Yankees:
Worked for the Yankees as a scout from 1984 to 1986.
Promoted to director of scouting in 1986. Worked in this capacity until 1990.
Promoted to VP player development and scouting in 1991.
San Francisco Giants:
Hired by the Giants in 1993 as the assistant to the GM and VP of scouting and player personnel.
Named senior VP player personnel in 1995.
Promoted to senior VP and GM in 1996.

Team: Seattle Mariners
GM: Bill Bavasi[2,28]
Education: Undergraduate: University of San Diego
Professional Playing Experience: None
Career Path
San Diego Padres:
Worked in the baseball operations department of the Padres while still in high school.
California Angels:
Hired by the California Angels in 1981 as an assistant to the minor league department.
Named minor league administrator in 1982.
Promoted to director of minor league operations in 1983.
Named vice president and GM of the Angels in 1994. Resigned under pressure in 1999.
Los Angeles Dodgers:
Worked for the Dodgers as director of player development in 2001 and 2002.
Seattle Mariners:
Hired as the executive VP and GM of the Mariners in 2003.
Notes: Father, "Buzzie," served as general manager of the Brooklyn and Los Angeles Dodgers, founding president and part-owner of the San Diego Padres, and general manager of the California Angels.
Brother, Peter, was general manager of the San Diego Padres, founding president of the Toronto Blue Jays, and president of the Cleveland Indians, where he served on Major League Baseball's Executive Council.

Team: Tampa Bay Rays
GM: Andrew Friedman[29]
Education: Undergraduate: Tulane University (Management, Concentration in Finance)
Professional Playing Experience: None
Career Path
Baseball Playing Career:
Played college baseball at Tulane.
MidMark Capital:
Worked 3 years as an associate at MidMark Capital (private equity firm).
Bear, Stern, & Co.
Worked 2 years as an analyst at Bear, Sterns, & Co.
Tampa Bay Rays:
Hired as the director of baseball development for the Rays from 2004 to 2005.
Promoted to executive vice president of baseball operations for the Rays after the 2005 season.
Notes: Took over control of the Rays' baseball operations at the age of 28.

Team: Texas Rangers
GM: Jon Daniels[30]
Education: Undergraduate: Cornell University (Economics)
Professional Playing Experience: None
Career Path
Business Development:
Spent 2 years doing business development work in Boston.
Colorado Rockies:
Hired by the Rockies as an intern in 2001.
Texas Rangers:
Following internship with Rockies, hired by the Rangers as assistant director of baseball operations.
Promoted to assistant GM in 2004.
In 2005, named general manager.
Notes: At the age of 28 years and 41 days, Jon Daniels became the youngest GM in baseball history.

Team: Toronto Blue Jays
GM: J.P. Ricciardi[2,31]
Education: Undergraduate: Attended University of Florida
Professional Playing Experience: Minors
Career Path
New York Yankees:
At 23, became a coach in the Yankees farm system.
Oakland A's:
Joined the Oakland organization in 1986 as a minor league instructor and New England area scout.
Promoted to East Coast scouting supervisor in 1991.
Promoted to national crosschecker in 1993.
Promoted to special assistant to the GM in 1996.
Title changed to director player personnel in 1999; worked in this role until 2001.
Toronto Blue Jays:
Hired by the Blue Jays in 2001 as GM and vice president.
Title changed from VP to senior VP baseball operations in 2003, retained GM role.
Notes: Coached high school basketball for 11 years.

Team: Washington Nationals
GM: Jim Bowden[2,32]
Education: Undergraduate: Attended Rollins College (FL)
Professional Playing Experience: None
Career Path
Pittsburgh Pirates:
Started baseball career in 1985 as a media relations assistant for the Pirates.
Transferred into the Pirates' baseball operations department where he worked as the assistant director of minor leagues and scouting from 1987 to 1989.
Cincinnati Reds:
Moved to the Reds in 1990 as an administrative assistant in player development and scouting.
Promoted to director of player development in 1991.
Promoted to GM in 1992. Served as GM until 2003.
ESPN:
Worked as an analyst for ESPN in 2003–2005.
Washington Nationals:
Hired by the Nationals as the team's interim GM in 2005. Named full-time GM in 2006.
Notes: In 1992, at the age of 31, was the youngest GM in MLB history. His college roommate's father and grandfather were principal owners of the Pirates.

27. Hickey, J. (2003, Nov. 7). Bill Bavasi Named Mariners GM. *Seattle Post-Intelligencer*. Retrieved August 10, 2007, from http://seattlepi .nwsource.com/baseball/147344_mari07.html.
28. Front Office Directory. (n.d.). Tampa Bay Rays. Retrieved August 10, 2007, from http://tampabay .devilrays.mlb.com/team/front_office.jsp?c_id=tb.
29. Texas Rangers Media Guide. (2007).
30. Batter's Box: An Interview with J.P. Ricciardi. (n.d.). *Batter's Box*. Retrieved August 10, 2007, from

http://www.battersbox.ca/article. php?story=20030826091305999.
31. Nationals Extend GM Bowden's Contract Through April. (2005, Oct. 27). *USA Today*. Retrieved August 10, 2007, from http://www.usatoday.com/sports/base-ball/nl/nationals/2005-10-27-bowden-extension_x.htm.
32. Snow, C. (2005, Nov. 19). Sox Search Relaunched. *Boston Globe*. Retrieved April 28, 2008, from http://www.boston.com/sports/baseball/redsox/ articles/2005/11/19/sox_search_relaunched.

What type of education do MLB general managers have

- It appears that 28 of the 30 MLB GMs attended some sort of 4-year, undergraduate college. It is difficult to ascertain whether all of these individuals actually graduated from their respective institutions, but there is at least a record of college attendance.

- Three GMs attended Ivy League schools, while another went to Stanford.

- Six of the 30 GMs have an advanced degree (two law degrees and four master's degrees, including three Sport Management/Athletic Administration degrees).

How many MLB general managers have family connections to the sports industry?

- Only two current MLB GMs (Bavasi and Shapiro) have strong family connections in the industry:

  - Bavasi's father, Buzzie Bavasi, served as general manager of the Brooklyn and Los Angeles Dodgers, founding president and part-owner of the San Diego Padres, and general manager of the California Angels. In addition, Bill's brother, Peter Bavasi, also worked in baseball, as general manager of the San Diego Padres, founding president of the Toronto Blue Jays, and president of the Cleveland Indians. During his time with the Indians, Peter also served on Major League Baseball's Executive Council.

  - Shapiro's father, Ron Shapiro, is a prominent sports player agent. His list of past clients includes Hall of Famers Cal Ripken, Jr., Jim Palmer, Brooks Robinson, Kirby Puckett, and Eddie Murray. Ron has also been included on *The Sporting News'* list of "100 Most Powerful People in Sports."

  - The degree to which Bavasi and Shapiro benefited from their family connections is difficult to determine, and it should not be suggested that these individuals failed to "earn" their roles as GM. It should merely be pointed out that these individuals started with a larger network of contacts than the average reader of this book, and this likely aided them in their pursuit of obtaining a GM position.

How did MLB general managers begin their nonplaying baseball careers?

- For their first nonplaying baseball job, MLB GMs started in a variety of positions, as follows:

  - Five GMs (Beane, Wren, Melvin, Minaya, and Williams) started in a scouting position.

  - Fourteen GMs (Purpura, Hill, Byrnes, Friedman, Huntington, Mozeliak, Shapiro, Bavasi, Smith, Gillick, Daniels, Dombrowski, Jocketty, and Cashman) started in nonscouting positions within baseball operations (such as player development).

- Five GMs (Colletti, Bowden, Reagins, Epstein, and O'Dowd) started in nonbaseball operations positions within baseball (such as public relations, marketing, etc.).

- Six GMs (Ricciardi, Hendry, Sabean, Flanagan, Towers, and Moore) started as coaches.

Do all MLB general managers have experience in talent evaluation?

- With the possible exception of Friedman and Flanagan, all of the GMs appear to have had some experience in talent evaluation before being given their current job. In most cases, the individuals spent time in a scouting department and/or a player development ("farm") department of an MLB team. In some cases, this talent evaluation may have come purely via coaching. Note that some GMs started in other departments such as public relations or marketing; however, nearly all of these GMs worked their way into scouting or player development at some point. The exceptions should be pointed out:

  - Friedman came from a business background (outside of baseball) and worked only one year as director of baseball development prior to becoming GM for the Tampa Bay Rays.

  - Flanagan had the most extensive Major League career of all current GMs and made a quick transition from player to GM. In between, Flanagan served as a broadcaster and briefly as a pitching coach.

Do MLB general managers have extensive nonbaseball, business experience?

- At least four MLB GMs started their professional careers working outside of baseball in the business world, and then made a mid-career move into the baseball industry.

  - Byrnes worked as a health care consultant.

  - Freidman worked for a private equity firm and as an analyst for Bear, Sterns, & Co.

  - Shapiro worked as a real estate developer.

  - Daniels worked in business development.

  - The remaining 26 MLB GMs all appear to have worked almost exclusively within the baseball world.

How many different teams have MLB GMs generally worked for during their career?

- On average, each MLB GM has worked for 2.7 different teams during his career. (This does not take into account a GM who may have worked for a team on more than one occasion—each team has been counted only once.)

- On the high end of the scale, Gillick has worked for six teams and Melvin has worked for five teams.

- Seven GMs (Beane, Friedman, Shapiro, Flanagan, Reagins, Williams, and Cashman) have worked exclusively for only one team.

How long did it take for current MLB GMs to become a general manager?

- Current MLB GMs worked in baseball an average of 11.7 years prior to obtaining a GM position. Friedman, with only one year of prior baseball experience, represents the low end of the range, while Krivsky, with 29 years of prior baseball experience, represents the high end.

Do MLB general managers get more than one opportunity to be a GM?

- Eight GMs (Melvin, Minaya, Bavasi, Bowden, Wren, Jocketty, Gillick, and Dombrowski) have held more than one general manager position during their career.

- Interestingly, two of the eight (Minaya and Dombrowski) held the GM position for the Montreal Expos at one point in time.

- Gillick has held four GM positions (Blue Jays, Orioles, Mariners, and Phillies) and Dombrowski has held three (Expos, Marlins, and Tigers).

Have any MLB general managers worked their way up through the minors?

- Of the 30 current MLB GMs, only one got his start in the minors—Jocketty worked 5 years in the minors before he began working with MLB clubs. He then worked another 15 years in the majors before becoming the GM for the Cardinals. Based on his lengthy tenure in MLB, it is difficult to determine to what extent Jocketty's minor league experience may have played in his development. Nonetheless, because there is only one current GM with any real minor league (nonplaying) experience, a common path to MLB general manager does not appear to travel through the minor leagues.

- Although there are some prominent historical examples of minor league GMs ascending to major league GMs (e.g., Bob Howsam, who started out as a minor league GM and became the GM behind the "Big Red Machine" Cincinnati Reds of the 1970s), there are *zero* current general managers who took this career path. As noted previously, *MLB* GMs are a distinct entity from *minor league* GMs. The jobs have vastly different duties and responsibilities, and require different skills and abilities. Consequently, it is not surprising that the career tracks of MLB GMs and minor league GMs rarely cross.

- Nevertheless, there are many more minor league baseball teams, all with GMs or similar executive roles, and only 30 GMs in the major leagues. Thus, there are many more job opportunities in the minors. For more information on minor league GM career tracks, turn to Chapter 52.

IS THERE A PATTERN IN THE CAREER TRACKS?

There is not *one* prototypical career path, but the GMs can be divided into a few distinct groups. Each person in these groups rose to the GM level in a similar way. The tracks are best summarized as the "player" track, the "coach" track, and the "apprentice" track.

The Player Track

A number of teams have turned to former MLB and minor league players to fill their GM positions. Frequently, these players were not "star" players, but nevertheless, impressed the organization with their knowledge of other teams' players and tendencies. To demonstrate how the player path might progress, a player may be hired immediately upon retirement to scout for the organization for which he last played. The individual can then progress through the baseball operations department by receiving promotions to positions such as regional scout, minor league director, or scouting director. The amount of turnover in an organization may dictate how quickly a player ascends to higher-level positions such as director of player personnel, assistant GM, and eventually GM. The career paths of Beane, Melvin, Hill, Minaya, Towers, Gillick, and Williams demonstrate the many variations to be found within the player track.

It should be noted that Flanagan, who experienced the most playing success of all current GMs, followed a less "traditional" player path. Upon retiring as a player, Flanagan bypassed spending any significant amount of time in a baseball operations position prior to becoming a GM—he moved from player to pitching coach to broadcaster to co-GM. Despite the nontraditional nature of his ascent to the GM position, Flanagan is an ex-player and his career path should be considered a variation of the player track.

The Coaching Track

Some who reached the level of GM through the coaching track were also once minor league players. However, it maybe the individual's ability to motivate and succeed as a coach, or to recognize baseball talent, that is attractive to major league organizations. For example, a successful high school or college coach may be approached by a big league organization and asked to become a minor league instructor, scout, or both. This gives the individual a start within the organization's baseball operations department. The person then may move up to become director of player development or scouting director and eventually assistant GM. Unlike other major sports where prominent top-level coaches have become GMs (e.g., Bill Parcells and Bill Walsh in the NFL), Major League Baseball is currently devoid of a correlating ex-star manager-turned-GM. Ricciardi, Hendry, Sabean, and Moore all began as coaches. Their career tracks provide examples of different variations of the coaching track.

The Apprentice Track

The current GMs who neither played professional ball nor achieved prominence as coaches commonly entered an organization as an intern or assistant. Although their entry-level jobs were not always in the area of scouting or player development, these individuals eventually moved to such departments. Lacking extensive playing or coaching experience may result in a longer trek to becoming a GM, but this is not always the case (see the career path of Friedman). Ultimately, the time interval between obtaining a first job in baseball operations and being named GM varies greatly from organization to organization, and is dependent on organizational turnover. The career paths of Purpura, Wren, Smith, Reagins, Jocketty, Byrnes, Colletti, Huntington, Mozeliak, Friedman, Shapiro, Bavasi, Bowden, Daniels, Epstein, O'Dowd, Dombrowski, and Cashman provide examples of how one can become a GM without extensive playing and/or coaching experience.

CREATING YOUR OWN TRACK

This chapter provides insight into how current MLB general managers came to obtain their position. There are good examples of career tracks for former players and coaches, as well for people without either of these experiences. If it is your goal to obtain a GM position with an MLB team, study the career tracks and GMs that most closely match your specific situation (that is, if you are a former player, review the career tracks of GMs who are also former players, etc.). This should give you ideas about how you might want to plan your own career path.

THINGS TO KEEP IN MIND

Although the analysis of this chapter provides a great deal of valuable information, there a number of things to keep in mind. The analysis represents a very small and elite sample group, and the information presented here demonstrates only how GMs (as of April 2008) came to obtain their general manager positions. This may not necessarily correlate to the experiences and educational backgrounds of *future* GMs. Due to rapidly evolving scouting technologies and economic factors, the skill set possessed by most current GMs will not necessarily be the same set that will be required for GMs in 10 or 20 years. For example, only 20% of current GMs have attended graduate school, but will this be the case going forward?

Had this study focused on assistant GMs, or perhaps on personnel executives under the age of 30, the results might have been different. Consider that the Oakland A's Billy Beane is a highly respected GM and former major league player who did not finish college; however, Beane has hired Harvard graduates in their 20s and 30s as his last two assistant GMs. As stated by Masteralexis, Barr, and Hums:

> As the position has become more complex, individuals with sport management degrees, MBAs, and/or law degrees have become more desirable employees. . . . Some teams will continue to have a general manager who has risen from the playing and/or coaching ranks, but will hire one or more assistant general managers.[1(p. 294)]

Often, an organization will hire assistant GMs with different skills that compliment the GM's skills. Then, as these individuals advance through the organization, they will likely work their way up to become the next generation of GMs. If you are interested in becoming a GM, be aware that changing industry trends could potentially alter the make-up of future GMs. Therefore, it is recommended that you stay as up-to-date as possible on developments within baseball.

Finally, it is important to remeber that this chapter provides an analysis of only MLB GMs and that an analysis of GMs in other sports would likely look much different. For example, in 2008 there were over a dozen NBA GMs who were former professional players. Hopefully this analysis of MLB GMs has provided you with the framework for how to undertake your own analysis.

Endnotes

1. Masteralexis, L., Barr, C., and Hums, M. (2005). *Principles and Practice of Sport Management*. Sudbury, MA: Jones and Bartlett.

CHAPTER FIFTY-ONE

Major League Baseball Executives

WHO'S IN CHARGE OF MAJOR LEAGUE BASEBALL?

Major League Baseball lists seven of the league's most prominent executives on its website:[1]

- Bud Selig: Commissioner

- Bob DuPuy: President and chief operating officer

- Jimmie Lee Solomon: Executive vice president, baseball operations

- Tim Brosnan: Vice president, business

- Rob Manfred: Executive vice president, labor relations and human resources

- Jonathan Mariner: Executive vice president, finance

- John McHale, Jr.: Executive vice president, administration

As of 2008, these individuals were the top in Major League Baseball, responsible for managing the league's day-to-day operations.

Table 51-1 illustrates the career tracks for these seven MLB executives, including their educational backgrounds and work experiences. Table 51-1 also includes a summary of the duties each executive performs. This provides insight into the type of work conducted at a major professional sport's league office. Each of the seven executives plays a significantly different role in the organization, so it is reasonable to expect the executives to possess different educational backgrounds and work experiences. For example, Jonathan Mariner, who oversees the league's finances, is likely to have a different educational background and previous work experience than Rob Manfred, who oversees the league's labor relations and human resources. The jobs require different skills, educational backgrounds, abilities, and decision making.

Due to the diversity of job functions, summarizing the career tracks of the seven executives may not be very helpful. A career track leading to one position is likely to be significantly different from a career track leading to another position. Nonetheless, the following trends are important to note:

- Five of the seven executives hold law degrees, although only one position (executive VP of labor relations and human resources) is primarily a legal position. This provides an indication of the complex legal environment within which MLB operates. It also indicates a law degree may be helpful in pursuing job opportunities at the league office. The high volume of law degrees is consistent with the analysis of NBA executives found in Chapter 54.

- None of the seven executives has a significant baseball playing background. Instead, each executive possesses certain business and/or legal expertise. This is not unexpected because positions at the league level are largely business-oriented. The absence of playing experience in this group of executives supports the notion that Major League Baseball is truly a business, run by businesspeople.

- It is important to point out the caliber of schools from which the executives received their education. Prestigious schools such as Dartmouth, Cornell, Harvard, Georgetown, Notre Dame, and Boston College are all represented in the educational backgrounds of the executives. This demonstrates a growing trend in professional sports leagues—leagues are looking for the best and brightest when it comes to hiring employees. This is consistent with the analysis of NBA executives found Chapter 54.

Endnotes

1. MLB Executives. (n.d.). Retrieved September 12, 2008, from http://mlb.mlb.com/mlb/official_info/about_mlb/executives.jsp.

Table 51-1   Career Tracks: Major League Baseball Executives (As of August 2007)

Name: Alan H. (Bud) Selig
Title: Commissioner
Education: Undergraduate: University of Wisconsin-Madison (American History and Political Science)
Career Path
Armed Forces:
Served 2 years in the armed forces.
Auto Industry:
Began his professional career working in the auto industry with his father.
Milwaukee Braves:
Became the largest public stockholder of the Milwaukee Braves.
Sold his stock in the Braves when they decided to move from Milwaukee to Atlanta.
Teams, Inc./Milwaukee Brewers:
Upon the Braves' move to Atlanta, formed Teams, Inc., an organization dedicated to returning MLB to Milwaukee.
Teams, Inc., changed its name to The Brewers and successfully arranged for nine Chicago White Sox games to be played in Milwaukee in 1968. The Sox also played 11 games in Milwaukee in 1969.
In 1969, attempted to purchase the White Sox, but those efforts failed.
Was awarded the Seattle Pilots franchise by a Seattle bankruptcy court in 1970. Moved the team to Milwaukee and changed its name to the Brewers.
Major League Executive Council:
Named chairman of the Major League Executive Council following the resignation of Commissioner Fay Vincent on September 7, 1992.
Served a dual role as president of the Milwaukee Brewers and chairman of the Executive Council from 1992 to 1998.
Major League Baseball:
Elected as commissioner of MLB on July 9, 1998, by a unanimous vote of 30 MLB team owners. At that time, his financial interest in the Brewers was placed in trust and he relinquished involvement in all matters dealing with the operation of the Brewers.
In January 2005, the Brewers were sold to Mark Attanasio, thus ending Selig's 35-year relationship with the club.
Notes:
- Helped introduce significant changes to the game of baseball, such as:
  - Interleague play
  - Current three-division format found in the American and National Leagues
  - Expanded playoff system with wild card participants
  - Unbalanced schedule
  - Significant revenue sharing among clubs
  - Awarding home field advantage in the World Series to the league that wins the All Star Game
  - Performance-enhancing drug testing policy
  - World Baseball Classic
- Member of the board of directors of the Green Bay Packers.

Name: Bob DuPuy
Title: President and chief operating officer
Education: Undergraduate: Dartmouth College
Law School: Cornell University
Career Path
Armed Forces:
Served in the U.S. Army from 1968 to 1970.
Served a year in Vietnam in the 504th Military Police Battalion.
Foley and Lardner:
Joined Foley and Lardner, one of the nation's largest law firms, in 1973. Became a partner in 1980.
Involved in most of MLB's legal issues since 1989, when he was brought in as outside legal counsel.
Negotiated the settlement of the collusion grievance in 1990, and served as the principal outside counsel to the commissioner and the Executive Council from 1992 until 1998.
Major League Baseball:
Hired by Selig as the MLB executive vice president of administration and chief legal officer in 1998.
Served as initial CEO of Major League Baseball Advanced Media (MLBAM) after its formation in 2000.
Named president and chief operating officer of Major League Baseball in March 2002.
Notes: As president and chief operating officer of Major League Baseball, he is responsible for all phases of baseball's central offices, including licensing, sponsorship, international, broadcasting, publishing, marketing, public relations, government relations, baseball operations, legal affairs, finance, baseball's Internet operations, and the labor relations committee.
Oversaw the consolidation of the American and National Leagues into one central office; the consolidation of MLB's office in Washington, DC; and the formation MLBAM.

Name: Jimmie Lee Solomon
Title: Executive vice president, baseball operations
Education: Undergraduate: Dartmouth College
Law School: Harvard University
Career Path
Baker & Hostetler:
Spent 10 years at the law firm of Baker & Hostetler, working his way up to partner. During his time at Baker & Hostetler, he represented and provided counsel to corporate and sports industry clients.
Major League Baseball:
Joined MLB in 1991 as director of minor league operations. Subsequently promoted to executive director minor league operations.
Promoted to senior VP of baseball operations, and worked in this capacity for 5 years.
Named executive VP baseball operations in 2005.
Notes: While serving as senior VP of baseball operations, oversaw major league, minor league, and international baseball operations, the Major League Scouting Bureau, the Arizona Fall League, and numerous special projects, including the launching of the Major League Baseball Youth Academy at Compton College in Compton, California. During this time, he also generated the idea that became the All Star Futures game.
As executive VP baseball operations, he is responsible for such areas as on-field discipline, security, and facility management. He reports to MLB president and chief operating officer Bob DuPuy.

Table 51-1   Continued

Name: Tim Brosnan
Title: Vice president, business
Education: Undergraduate: Georgetown University
Law School: Fordham University School of Law
Career Path
Kelley, Drye, & Warren:
Began his career practicing law at the Park Avenue offices of Kelley, Drye, & Warren.
New York State Commission on Government Integrity:
Appointed to the New York State Commission on Government Integrity by Governor Mario Cuomo in 1987, and 2 years later was appointed counsel to the chairman for that commission.
Major League Baseball:
Joined the office of the commissioner in 1991 as vice president of international business affairs.
Promoted to chief operating officer of Major League Baseball International in 1994.
In 1998 was promoted once again, this time to the position of senior vice president, domestic and international properties.
Named executive vice president, business in February 2000, reporting directly to MLB president and COO, Bob DuPuy.
Notes: In his role as VP of business, he oversees all domestic and international business functions of Major League Baseball's office of the commissioner, including licensing, sponsorship, domestic and international broadcasting, special events, and MLB Productions.

Name: Jonathan Mariner
Title: Executive vice president, finance
Education: Undergraduate: University of Virginia (Accounting)
Graduate: Harvard Business School (MBA)
Career Path
MCI Communications:
Began his professional career with MCI Communications, Inc, serving as a senior financial analyst, and later, senior manager of corporate planning and budgets.
Ryder Truck Rental:
Moved to Ryder Truck Rental in 1985, serving as senior manager of mergers and acquisitions. He also worked for Ryder as senior manager of strategic planning and budgets and controller of insurance operations.
Greater Miami Convention and Visitors Bureau:
Appointed vice president of finance and administration for the Greater Miami Convention and Visitors Bureau.
Florida Marlins (MLB) and Florida Panthers (NHL):
Served as executive vice president and chief financial officer for the Florida Marlins Baseball Club from 1992 to 2000. Also worked as president of Marlins Ballpark Development Corp.
Held other positions for Wayne Huizenga, owner of the Marlins, including vice president and chief financial officer for the Florida Panthers Hockey Club (during their initial start-up and 1993–1994 inaugural season) and chief financial officer for Pro Player Stadium.
Charter Schools USA:
From 2000 to 2002, served as COO and CFO of Charter Schools USA (CSUSA), one of the nation's leading and fastest growing charter school development and management companies.
Major League Baseball:
Returned to baseball in 2002, hired as executive vice president and chief financial officer of Major League Baseball in the office of the commissioner.
Notes: Oversees MLB's central office budgeting, financial reporting, and risk management activities. Also responsible for administering MLB's $1.5-billion league-wide credit facility, providing updates at owners' meetings on the industry's financial health, overseeing all team-level financial reporting through the team CFOs, and providing financial reviews on potential ownership applications.
Serves on several commissioner-appointed, league-wide committees including the Finance and Compensation, Revenue Sharing, Long-Range Planning, Franchise Relocation, and Debt Service Rule Committees.
Licensed as a CPA.

Name: Rob Manfred
Title: Executive vice president, labor relations and human resources
Education: Undergraduate: Cornell University
Law School: Harvard Law School
Career Path
U.S. District Court:
Following law school, served as a clerk to U.S. District Court Judge Joseph L. Tauro in the District of Massachusetts.
Morgan, Lewis, & Bockius, LLP:
Prior to joining MLB, worked as a partner in the Labor and Employment Law section of Morgan, Lewis, & Bockius, LLP in their Washington, DC office.
Major League Baseball:
Appointed executive vice president of labor relations and human resources in 1998.
Notes: Responsible for managing the relationship between the clubs and the MLB Players Association. Also oversees human resource functions of the commissioner's office.
Reports directly to the president of MLB, Bob DuPuy, and the commissioner, Bud Selig.
While working at Morgan, Lewis, & Bockius, participated directly in the formulation and negotiation of economic and noneconomic proposals for MLB in collective bargaining negotiations. Also represented individual teams in salary arbitrations and in grievance arbitrations and provided advice to teams on their individual salary negotiations with players.

Name: John McHale, Jr.
Title: Executive vice president, administration
Education: Undergraduate: University of Notre Dame
Law School: Boston College and Georgetown University
Career Path
Colorado Rockies (MLB):
Worked as executive vice president of baseball operations for the Colorado Rockies for more than 3 years.
Detroit Tigers (MLB):
Served as chief executive officer of the Detroit Tigers from 1995 to 2001.
Tampa Bay Rays (MLB):
Hired by the Rays as the club's first chief operating officer in 2002.
Major League Baseball:
Named vice president of administration for MLB in 2002.
Notes: Father, John McHale, once served as general manager and president of the Milwaukee Braves, leading to a close friendship with Selig. He also held GM positions with the Detroit Tigers and Montreal Expos.
In his capacity as executive VP of administration, has done a variety of tasks including leading negotiations between the Expos and Puerto Rico for the Expos to play home games in San Juan, and meeting with suspended players/coaches in regards to suspension appeals.
Member of the Official Playing Rules Committee and the Relocation Committee (which ultimately resulted in the Expos' relocation to Washington, DC).

Endnote: MLB Executives. (n.d.). MLB.com. Retrieved November 12, 2007, from http://mlb.mlb.com/mlb/official_info/about_mlb/executives.jsp.

CHAPTER FIFTY-TWO

Minor League Baseball General Managers

If a person has an interest in becoming a minor league general manager, a lot can be learned from examining current general managers employed in the minor leagues. To conduct this analysis, information was gathered on seven AAA GMs as of July 2007. (Four GMs represent the Pacific Coast League and three GMs represent the International League.) In total, there are 30 general managers at the AAA level. The selection of the seven GMs was based on the availability of information, and should not be considered a scientific study. However, the sample of seven GMs does account for 23% of all current AAA GMs, providing an indication of the general make-up of GMs at the AAA level.

Table 52-1 lists the educational background and work experiences of the seven AAA general managers. As you read through the career paths, it is important to keep one thing in mind—the position of *minor league* general manager is very different from the position of *major league* general manager. General managers for major league teams are primarily focused on player personnel matters, such as making trades, signing free agents, and scouting and drafting players. Minor league general managers typically do not get involved in such matters, relying on the major league club to manage player personnel matters for the minor league roster. Instead, a minor league GM is typically responsible for such things as marketing, public relations, game management, sponsorship sales, and ticket sales (i.e., the business aspects of a minor league team).

Minor league GM positions are very much business positions, not player personnel positions, which requires a successful minor league GM to possess different skills and abilities than a successful major league GM. This fact is reflected in the backgrounds of the seven GMs analyzed in this chapter. Noticeably absent is any significant playing or coaching experience. Such experiences are not needed to successfully fulfill the duties of a minor league GM. Instead,

business skills (and business education) are likely to play a larger role in determining one's success.

To better understand the organizational context of the minor league general manager position, Section 4 provides an example organizational chart for a minor league baseball team (see Chapter 62). Although the team represented in the chart is an independent league team, reviewing the chart does provide insight into how a minor league baseball team structures its operations. A team at the AAA level is likely to utilize a similar structure, but may employ a larger number of people in more specialized roles. In addition, Section 5 provides information on the common job requirements, duties, and responsibilities for minor league general managers. An actual job announcement for a dual president/general manager position for a Triple-A team can be found in Chapter 81, and a minor league general manager "Position Spotlight" can be found in Chapter 81. Reviewing this information will help explain what it means to be a minor league general manager.

It is important to note that AAA baseball is only one level of the current minor league baseball system. General manager positions can also be found at the A, AA, and independent levels as well. More information about the minor league system can be found in Chapter 19.

BACKGROUNDS OF MINOR LEAGUE BASEBALL GENERAL MANAGERS

What is the current make-up of AAA general managers? The following analysis provides some insight into answering this question.

Table 52-1   Career Tracks: Minor League Baseball General Managers (AAA) (As of July 2007)

Team (League): Albuquerque Isotopes (PCL)
Name: John Traub[1]
Title: General manager
Education: Undergraduate: UCLA (Psychology)
Career Path
Los Angeles Angels of Anaheim (MLB):
Began career as a public relations assistant for the Angels.
Calgary Cannons (Class AAA):
Hired by the Cannons as director of public and media relations.
Served as vice president of business operations from 1997 to 1999.
Promoted to vice president and general manager in 2000.
Albuquerque Isotopes (Class AAA):
Hired by the Isotopes as director of baseball and business operations in 2003, the team's inaugural season.
Promoted to general manager after the 2003 season.
Notes: Appointed to the New Mexico Sports Authority. Serves on the Pacific Coast League's Scheduling Committee. Chairman of the PCL Travel Committee. Helped form the PCL Public Relations Committee.

Team (League): Buffalo Bisons (IL)
Name: Michael Buczkowski[2]
Title: Vice president and general manager
Education: Undergraduate: Canisius College (Communications)
Career Path
Buffalo Bisons (Class AAA):
Began career with the Bisons in 1987 as a public relations assistant.
Promoted to public relations coordinator in 1988 and public relations manager in 1989.
During the 1992 season, promoted to assistant general manager.
Appointed general manager in December 1993.
Notes: Played hockey while attending Canisius College and was named team captain.
Has served on various local committees and boards, including Western New York United Against Drug & Alcohol Abuse Foundation, Greater Buffalo Sports Hall of Fame, Western New York Special Olympics Advisory Committee, and the organizing committee for the 2003 Frozen Four NCAA Hockey Tournament. Grandfather played for the Bisons from 1935 to 1937.

Team (League): Colorado Springs Sky Sox (PCL)
Name: Tony Ensor[3]
Title: President and general manager
Education: Undergraduate: University of Tennessee-Chattanooga (Marketing)
Career Path
Chattanooga Lookouts (Class AA):
Worked as a groundskeeper for five seasons from 1985 to 1989.
Birmingham Barons (Class AA):
Hired as director of stadium operations in 1990.
Became an assistant GM in the mid-1990s.
Promoted to president and general manager in 1998.
Colorado Springs Sky Sox (AAA):
Hired by the Sky Sox in August 2004 as president and general manager.
Notes: Serves on the Pacific Coast League Board of Directors. While at Birmingham, served on the Southern League's Board of Directors and Rules and Competition Committee.

Team (League): Durham Bulls (IL)
Name: Mike Birling[4]
Title: General manager
Education: Information not available
Career Path
LaCrosse Catbirds (CBA—Basketball):
Began career in 1993 as an account executive for the LaCrosse Catbirds of the Continental Basketball Association.
Wisconsin Timber Rattlers (Class A):
Worked for the Timber Rattlers of the Midwest League from 1994 to 1998.
Spent the last three seasons as the organization's GM.
Durham Bulls (Class AAA):
Hired as assistant GM in 1998. Served as assistant GM for four seasons.
Promoted to GM in 2002.
Notes: Named Midwest League Executive of the Year in 1998.

Team (League): Indianapolis Indians (IL)
Name: Carl Burleson[5]
Title: Vice president and general manager
Education: Undergraduate: Ohio University (Business Administration)
Graduate: Ohio University (MS Sports Administration)
Career Path
Indianapolis Indians (Class AAA):
Hired in 1975 as ticket manager.
Assumed the role of business manager from 1977 to 1980.
Took on responsibilities of publicity director in 1981.
Promoted to assistant GM in 1987.
Named general manager in 1998.
Notes: Named International League's Executive of the Year in 2000. Serves as vice chairman on the American Red Cross of Greater Indianapolis' board of directors.

Team (League): Nashville Sounds (PCL)
Name: Glenn Yaeger[6]
Title: General manager and chief operating officer
Education: Undergraduate: University of Illinois (Accounting)
Graduate: University of Chicago (MBA)
Career Path
Nonsports Work Experience:
Worked in public accounting for Price Waterhouse, served as senior vice president of finance for Heitman Office Properties, and founded a consulting practice specializing in providing assistance to national retail organizations.
AmeriSports Companies, LLC (Owner of Sounds-AAA):
Joined AmeriSports in 1997 as chief financial officer.
Promoted to general manager of the Sounds and chief operating officer of AmeriSports in 2001.
Notes: Works for both the Sounds (as GM) and the team's ownership group, AmeriSports (as COO). Lives and works in the Chicago area, where AmeriSports is based. Licensed as a certified public accountant (CPA).

Team (League): Sacramento River Cats (PCL)
Name: Alan Ledford[7]
Title: President, general manager, and chief operating officer
Education: Undergraduate: University of California, Berkeley
Career Path
Oakland Athletics (MLB):
Worked 15 years for the Oakland A's, and was eventually promoted to the position of vice president of business operations.
Sports Consulting Firm:
Opened a sports consulting firm in the Bay Area, which created strategic business plans for sports franchises and organizations (including the Sacramento River Cats).
Sacramento River Cats (Class AAA):
Named president and chief operating officer of the River Cats in 2002.
Assumed general manager duties in 2004.
Notes: Named Minor League Baseball Executive of the Year by Baseball America in 2006. Worked with the River Cats as a consultant, playing an instrumental role in successfully launching the franchise.

1. Albuquerque Isotopes Media Guide. (2007.) p. 3.
2. Buffalo Bisons Media Guide. (2007).
3. Colorado Springs Sky Sox Media Guide. (2007). p. 4.
4. Durham Bulls Media Guide.
5. Indianapolis Indians Media Guide. (2007). p. 3.
6. Nashville Sounds Media Guide. (2007).
7. Sacramento River Cats Media Guide. (2007).

How many AAA general managers played professional baseball?

- Of the seven GMs examined, none appears to have a significant professional playing background. In fact, only one GM, Buczkowski (Bisons), appears to have even a significant collegiate athletic career, and he played hockey. Having an athletic playing career does not seem to be a precursor to becoming a minor league GM. This is consistent with the business-like nature of minor league GM positions.

How many AAA general managers have coached or managed?

- Similar to baseball playing experience, of the seven GMs examined, none appears to have any coaching or managerial experience.

What type of education do AAA GMs have?

- The educational backgrounds of the seven AAA GMs include earning an undergraduate degree to a graduate degree.
  - It appears that at least six of the seven GMs completed a 4-year, undergraduate college education. Majors include psychology, marketing, communications, accounting, and business administration (all very much business in focus).
  - Two GMs—Burleson (Indians) and Yaeger (Sounds)—attended graduate school. Burleson also is the only GM with a Sport Management degree, having obtained an MS in Sports Administration.

How did AAA general managers begin their careers?

- Two GMs began their careers working for MLB teams:
  - Traub began with the Angels in public relations.
  - Ledford began with the Athletics, working 15 years for the team.
- Three GMs began their careers working in minor league baseball:
  - Buczkowski began with the Buffalo Bisons in public relations.
  - Ensor began with the Chattanooga Lookouts as a groundskeeper.
  - Burleson began with the Indianapolis Indians as a ticket manager.
- One GM began his career working in minor league basketball:
  - Birling began with the LaCrosse Catbirds as an account executive.
- One GM began his career working outside of the sports industry:

- Yaeger began his career in public accounting and held multiple accounting/finance positions before transitioning into professional sports.

Do AAA general managers have extensive nonsports, business experience?

- Only one of the seven GMs appears to have significant experience outside of professional sports:
  - As noted above, Yaeger's career path started outside of professional sports, in the accounting/finance industry. He arguably holds the most nontraditional career path of the seven AAA GMs, having gained a great deal of business experience prior to starting his career in professional sports.
  - The remaining six GMs appear to have worked almost exclusively within the professional sports industry.

How many different teams have GMs generally worked for during their baseball career?

- On average, each GM has worked for 1.57 different minor league teams during his career. Two GMs have also worked for an MLB team.
  - Traub: 1 MLB team, 2 AAA teams
  - Buczkowski: 1 AAA team
  - Ensor: 2 AA teams, 1 AAA team
  - Birling:1 A team, 1 AAA team
  - Burleson: 1 AAA team
  - Yaeger: 1 AAA team
  - Ledford: 1 MLB team, 1 AAA team

Do general managers get more than one opportunity to be a GM?

- On average, each AAA GM has held 1.43 minor league general manager positions in his career.
  - Traub: GM of two AAA teams
  - Buczkowski: GM of one AAA team
  - Ensor: GM of one AA team and one AAA team
  - Birling: GM of one A team and one AAA team
  - Burleson: GM of one AAA team
  - Yaeger: GM of one AAA team
  - Ledford: GM of one AAA team
  - In addition, at least four of the GMs held an assistant general manager position at one point during his career.

Do minor league GMs hold other positions?

- Two GMs, Ensor (Sky Sox) and Ledford (River Cats), hold the title of team president in conjunction with their GM duties. Ledford is also the River Cats' chief operating officer.

- In addition to his GM duties, Yaeger (Sounds) is also the chief operating officer for the team's ownership group, AmeriSports.

IS THERE A PATTERN IN THE CAREER TRACKS?

From the analysis of AAA general managers, two career track patterns stand out—the "learn-on-the-job" track and the "outside experience" track.

The Learn-on-the-Job-Track

One common path towards a minor league general manager position is to find an entry-level position in minor league baseball, gain work experience, and advance through the ranks to higher-level positions. A person following such a path typically finds they enjoy the work involved in minor league baseball, and they decide to make a career out of it. Over time, such a person receives more responsibility and authority, and eventually works his or her way up through the organization into a general manager position.

Given the small office size of minor league teams, as a person moves up through an organization, he or she will have an opportunity to wear multiple hats and to work in many different areas of the team's business operations. Such multitasking results in a great deal of learning on the job and can adequately prepare a candidate to handle the multiple duties and responsibilities of a minor league general manager position. For example, if someone starts out in marketing, over time he or she will develop a level of expertise in this area; however, due to the small office/multitasking nature of minor league baseball, it is likely this person will be asked to contribute to other aspects of the team's operations, such as sponsorship sales, public relations, or game management. This allows the person to learn other parts of the job outside of his or her area of expertise, creating a better-rounded general manager candidate. In addition, when the person is promoted to a GM position, it is likely he or she will hire people with expertise in areas outside of marketing (such as operations or public relations). Such a system results in the expertise of the other employees complementing the general manager's marketing expertise. The GM is likely to continue to play a significant role in the team's marketing efforts, and will rely on the expertise of other employees to manage nonmarketing operations.

There is not one ideal way to follow the learn-on-the-job path. For example, someone could start out in marketing, accounting, public relations, or game management for a minor league team and still follow this path. The key to success is one's ability to learn on the job and to gain a better understanding of a team's operations. This, in turn, should place the person in a better position to manage those operations.

Although each GM took a slightly different path, five of the seven GMs (Traub, Buczkowski, Ensor, Birling, and Burleson) followed some variation of the learn-on-the-job track. They started in a variety of positions such as public relations, stadium operations, tickets, and marketing, but all five worked their way up through the ranks and eventually earned the position of minor league GM. Many of the five also worked for more than one level of minor league organization (i.e., A, AA, AAA) during his career. Reviewing the career tracks of Traub, Buczkowski, Ensor, Birling, and Burleson can help you to plan your own learn-on-the-job minor league general manager career track.

The Outside Experience Track

Although previous experience working in minor league baseball can be helpful in obtaining a minor league general manager position, the career tracks of Ledford and Yaeger demonstrate it is not absolutely necessary. Their career tracks provide examples of how one can obtain a minor league GM position with little to no minor league baseball experience.

The key to successfully following the outside experience track is to first develop the skills and abilities required of a minor league GM, before attempting to make the transition into minor league baseball. This development process can take place either within the sports industry or outside of it. For instance, Ledford developed his skill set in sports-related positions, working for a major league baseball team and a sports consulting agency. In contrast, Yaeger developed his skill set working primarily in businesses outside of the sports industry. Despite their differences, both Ledford and Yaeger were able to use their outside business skills and abilities to obtain minor league general manager positions.

If you have previous work experience outside of minor league baseball, review the career tracks of Ledford and Yaeger for insight on how to make the transition into a minor league general manager position. Keep in mind, following such a path likely requires strong networking connections. In order to make the move, you will need to network your way into minor league baseball. (See Chapter 6 for more information on networking.)

CREATING YOUR OWN TRACK

The GMs presented in this chapter help to demonstrate there are a number of paths you can take to arrive at a minor league GM position. If you are interested in becoming a minor league general manager, obtaining a position with a minor league team is a good way to start. If you are early in your career, consider taking an internship with a local minor league team. This will give you an idea of what minor league baseball is all about. If you find that you like it, stick with it and work your way up through the organization. If you are later in your career, business skills developed outside of minor league baseball can be transferable, but networking your way into a minor league organization will be important to your success.

NBA Marketing Professionals

The professional sports industry is significantly marketing driven, which creates many opportunities for people looking for marketing positions. This chapter takes a look at marketers for NBA teams, examining their educational backgrounds and previous work experience. This information can be very valuable as one considers a career in this area and develops a career plan.

The career tracks of 22 prominent NBA marketing professionals are presented in **Table 53-1**. The NBA has 30 teams in total, so this group represents 80% of the league's teams. The 22 individuals were selected based on the availability of information, and each person is the highest-ranking marketing executive for his or her team as of August 2007.

It is important to note, the highest-ranking marketing executive for an NBA team may be a chief marketing officer or a senior VP of marketing, or may only be a director of marketing; it all depends on the organization's structure. In cases where a director is the highest-ranking employee designated to work in marketing, it is likely the organization also has a more senior executive (such as a VP of business operations) who oversees the work of the marketing department. The breakdown of titles among the 23 marketing professionals presented in Table 53-1 is as follows:

- Four executive vice presidents/chief marketing officers
- Two executive vice presidents
- One senior vice president/chief marketing officer
- Seven senior vice presidents
- Six vice presidents
- Three marketing directors

Each team also uses slightly different language when referring to the head of its marketing department. For example, the Pistons have an executive VP of corporate marketing, whereas the Warriors have an executive VP of team market-

ing. Even though these individuals may have slightly different duties and responsibilities, for the purpose of this book, they are grouped together as the team's head of marketing.

It should be pointed out that a growing number of NBA team owners also own non-NBA sports properties and arenas as part of their sports portfolios. Kroenke Sports provides a good example. Kroenke Sports owns the Denver Nuggets, and it also has ownership stakes in the Colorado Avalanche (NHL), Colorado Mammoth (NLL), Colorado Crush (AFL), Colorado Rapids (MLS), and the Pepsi Center (the arena). Often, such situations create opportunities for employees to work with more than one professional sports team. This is the case for Paul Andrews, CMO for Kroenke Sports, who oversees the marketing for all of Kroenke Sports' teams. A challenging work environment, more diversity in daily duties, and more opportunities for career advancement are all benefits of working for more than one sports team simultaneously. In total, 9 of the 22 marketing professionals analyzed in this chapter work with more than one entity. The additional entities include NHL teams, WNBA teams, a Triple-A Minor League Baseball team, large indoor arenas, and the list of Kroenke properties.

The high percentage of marketing professionals working with multiple sports properties reflects a growing trend in professional sports—team owners are continuing to expand their sports businesses to include more than one sports franchise. It also indicates a level of transferability of marketing skills from one professional sports organization to another. This transferability takes place because the foundation skills and abilities needed to successfully operate as a sports marketer in a professional team environment does not change significantly from one sports property to the next. No matter what team you work for, you will draw upon similar selling, branding, and promotional skills. If you are looking to start a career in sports marketing, take note of this important trend, and find a way to develop these skills.

Table 53-1   Career Tracks: NBA Marketing Professionals (As of August 2007)

Team: Atlanta Hawks
Name: Lou DePaoli[1]
Title: Executive VP and chief marketing officer
Works with: Atlanta Hawks, Atlanta Thrashers (NHL), Philips Arena
Education: Undergraduate: University of Massachusetts (Sports Management)
Career Path
Insurance Industry:
Prior to getting his start in professional sports, worked 5 years with Prudential Insurance and owned his own insurance agency.
Worcester IceCats:
VP of sales for the Worcester IceCats of the American Hockey League (AHL) from 1994 to 1996.
Florida Marlins:
Worked for the Florida Marlins from 1996 through 2000, working his way up to VP of sales and marketing.
NBA League Office:
Worked at the league office from 2000 to 2005 as the NBA's VP of team marketing and business operations.
Atlanta Hawks (owned by the Atlanta Spirit):
Joined the Atlanta Spirit as its executive VP and chief marketing officer in 2005.
In addition to his duties with the Hawks, also oversees marketing for the Atlanta Thrashers (NHL) and Philips Arena.

Team: Charlotte Bobcats
Name: Greg Economou[2]
Title: Executive vice president and chief marketing officer
Education: Undergraduate: University of Connecticut (Communications and History)
Career Path
Basketball Playing Career:
Member of the 1988 NIT Championship basketball team at UConn. Also played professionally in Europe.
SME Branding:
Worked as a partner and CMO, where he developed branding programs for sports properties and leagues.
SFX Sports Group:
Operated as senior vice president, brand consulting, where his clients included major corporate sponsors and sports properties.
BRANDTHINK:
Was managing director and CEO of BRAND-THINK, a management consulting firm specializing in sports marketing and management strategy development.
Responsible for helping sports properties develop their brand positioning, sponsorship marketing, and consumer segmentation programs.
NBA League Office:
Appointed as NBA senior vice president of marketing and communications in April 2006.
Charlotte Bobcats (Bobcats Sports & Entertainment):
Named executive vice president and chief marketing officer in September 2006.

Team: Denver Nuggets
Name: Paul Andrews[3]
Title: Executive vice president and chief marketing officer
Works with: Denver Nuggets, Colorado Avalanche (NHL), Colorado Mammoth (NLL), Colorado Crush (AFL), Colorado Rapids (MLS), Pepsi Center
Education: Undergraduate: University of Wyoming (Marketing)
Career Path
Denver Nuggets (Kroenke Sports Enterprises):
Began career with Nuggets in 1990 as an account executive.
Duties expanded in 1991 to include directing in-game entertainment for Nuggets games.
Promoted to ticket sales manager in 1994.
With the Quebec Nordiques' (NHL) move to Denver for the 1995–1996 season, took on ticket sales duties for the team. (The team was subsequently renamed the Colorado Avalanche.)
Worked his way up through the Nuggets organization; named executive vice president and chief marketing officer in April 2005.
Oversees marketing for other Kroenke Sports Enterprises, including the Colorado Avalanche (NHL) and the Pepsi Center.

Team: Detroit Pistons
Name: Dan Hauser[4]
Title: Executive vice president, corporate marketing
Works with: Detroit Pistons, Detroit Shock (WNBA), The Palace of Auburn Hills
Education: Undergraduate: University of Wisconsin, Stevens Point (Education)
Graduate: Ohio University (Sport Management)
Career Path
Detroit Pistons (Palace Sports & Entertainment):
Started as an intern with the Pistons and then moved to group sales.
Quickly followed by a move to the promotions department.
Spent 6 years as ticket sales manager.
Moved into the corporate marketing area and worked his way into a leadership position in the department.
Since being named executive vice president, corporate marketing in 1991, the team has added a WNBA team (Detroit Shock) and now owns its arena. This has added to Hauser's responsibilities.

Team: Golden State Warriors
Name: Travis Stanley[5]
Title: Executive vice president, team marketing
Education: Undergraduate: Florida Southern College (Journalism)
Career Path
Basketball Playing Career:
Played 2 years of NCAA Division II basketball at Florida Southern.
Orlando Magic:
Career began as the assistant director of publicity/media relations for the Magic (1988–1992).
Sacramento Kings:
Moved to the Kings as director of media relations (1992–1998).
Golden State Warriors:
Spent four seasons as the Warriors' VP of public relations before being promoted to his current position as executive VP of team marketing in 2002.

Team: Houston Rockets
Name: Ken Sheirr[6]
Title: Director of marketing
Education: Undergraduate: Cornell University
Career Path
NBA City:
Worked for 3 years as a business analyst/project manager for NBA City in Orlando (1999–2002).
Houston Rockets:
Spent 4 years working for the Rockets as manager/director of business development (2002–2005).
Promoted to current role as director of marketing in 2005.

---

1. Lou DePaoli. (n.d.). NBA.com. Retrieved November 12, 2007, from http://www.nba.com/hawks/news/ Lou_DePaoli_Bio.

2. Bobcats 2007–2008 Executive Staff Bios: Greg Economou. (n.d.). NBA.com. Retrieved November 12, 2007, from http://www.nba.com/bobcats/ 0607_executive_bios.

3. Denver Nuggets Media Guide. (2006–2007).p. 71.
4. Information obtained via phone conversation with Dan Hauser.

Table 53-1   Continued

Team: Indiana Pacers
Name: Larry Mago[7]
Title: Senior vice president of marketing
Works with: Indiana Pacers, Indiana Fever (WNBA), Conseco Fieldhouse
Education: Undergraduate: Butler University
Career Path
Radio:
Started his career as on-air broadcaster for several radio stations, including the Pacers' flagship station, WIBC AM-1070.
At WIBC, served as program manager and helped establish the first Indianapolis Colts (NFL) network.
Indiana Pacers (Pacers Sports & Entertainment):
Joined the Pacers in 1985 as general manager of the Pacers' Network Indiana.
In 1988, assumed the title of broadcast production director.
Served as Pacers Sports and Entertainment's vice president of entertainment for 3 years.
Promoted to senior vice president of marketing.

Team: Los Angeles Clippers
Name: Carl Lahr[8]
Title: Senior vice president of marketing and sales
Education: Undergraduate: Penn State University
Career Path
Los Angeles Clippers (formerly of San Diego): Started with San Diego Clippers in 1981; has been with the team ever since.
Has held positions in ticket sales, promotions, operations, and marketing.
Named senior vice president of marketing and sales in 1997.

Team: Memphis Grizzlies
Name: John Pugliese[9]
Title: Senior director, marketing communications
Education: Undergraduate: University of British Columbia
Career Path
Memphis Grizzlies (formerly of Vancouver): Started with the Vancouver Grizzlies and Canucks (NHL) right out of college in 1998.
Worked as assistant coordinator of game presentation from 1998 to 2000.
Moved with the team to Memphis.
Served as manager of game presentations from 2000 to 2003.
Promoted to director of promotions and event presentations from 2003 to 2005.
Worked his way up to senior director of marketing and communications.

Team: Miami Heat
Name: Michael McCullough[10]
Title: Executive vice president and chief marketing officer
Education: Undergraduate: Utah State University (Political Science)
Career Path
Basketball Playing Career:
Was a 3-year starter for the Utah State Aggies basketball team.
Sacramento Kings:
Worked for the Kings from 1988 to 1990 as the team's director of broadcasting.
NBA League Office:
Assisted teams in the production of game telecasts, playing an integral role in national NBA broadcasts.
Sacramento Kings:
Returned to the Kings, overseeing the team's business development endeavors.
Promoted to vice president of marketing and broadcasting in 1993.
Miami Heat (The HEAT Group Enterprises):
Joined the Miami Heat and is now the team's executive VP and CMO.

Team: Minnesota Timberwolves
Name: Liz Hogenson[11]
Title: Director of marketing
Works with: Minnesota Timberwolves, Minnesota Lynx (WNBA)
Education: Undergraduate: Drake University (Journalism and Mass Communication)
Career Path
Advertising/Public Relations:
Before working in professional sports, worked for several different advertising/public relations agencies.
Minnesota Timberwolves:
Has been with the Timberwolves and Lynx (WNBA) for six seasons, first as an advertising and promotions manager and then as a senior advertising manager.
In 2005 was promoted to her current role as director of marketing.

Team: New Jersey Nets
Name: Tom Glick[12]
Title: Senior vice president and chief marketing officer
Works with: New Jersey Nets. Proposed new Nets arena in Brooklyn, N.Y.
Education: Undergraduate: Cornell University (Government)
Career Path
Minor League Baseball:
Served as general manager for two minor league baseball teams, including the Lansing Lugnuts.
Served as senior vice president of sales and marketing of the Sacramento River Cats (AAA) for five seasons.
NBA League Office:
From 2004 to 2006 was VP of marketing and team business operations for the NBA.
New Jersey Nets (Nets Sports & Entertainment):
Named senior VP and CMO of the Nets in February 2006.

5. Golden State Warriors Media Guide. (2006–2007). p. 26.
6. Information obtained via e-mail from Ken Sheirr.
7. Information obtained via e-mail from Wendy Rosner, Larry Mago's secretary.

8. Los Angeles Clippers Media Guide. (2006–2007). p. 6.
9. Memphis Grizzlies Media Guide. (2006–2007).

10. Michael McCullough. (n.d.). NBA.com. Retrieved November 12, 2007, from http://www.nba.com/heat/contact/directory_mccullough.
11. Information obtained via e-mail from Liz Hogenson.
12. New Jersey Nets Media Guide. (2006–2007). p. 12.

Table 53-1   Continued

Team: New York Knicks
Name: Hunter Lochmann[13]
Title: Vice president, marketing
Education: Undergraduate: University of Kansas (Sport Management)
Graduate: University of Massachusetts (Sport Management)
Career Path
Harvard University:
Got his start as an athletics department intern at Harvard.
MAI Sports:
Had an internship at MAI Sports in Kansas City, which turned into a full-time job.
Spent 4 years at MAI where he managed Sprint's relationship with the NFL and NASCAR.
NBA League Office:
Moved to the NBA league office where he worked on team marketing and business operations for 4 years.
New York Knicks (Madison Square Garden, LP):
Transferred to the team side as director of marketing for the Knicks.
Promoted to his current role of vice president of marketing for the Knicks.

Team: Oklahoma City Thunder
Name: Brian Byrnes[14]
Title: Senior vice president of sales and marketing
Education: Undergraduate: St. Mary's University-San Antonio (Marketing)
Southwest Sports Group:
Started with the NHL's Dallas Stars in 1993.
Promoted to director of ticket sales.
After 4 years, promoted again to vice president of sales for the Stars.
Two years later, promoted to vice president of sales for all of Southwest Sports Group, which owns and/operates the NHL Stars, MLB Texas Rangers, and other sports properties.
Phoenix Coyotes (NHL):
Served as the team's CMO and executive vice president of business operations.
Seattle Sonics:
Joined the Sonics and Storm (WNBA) organization in April 2005 as vice president of sales and marketing.
Promoted to senior vice president in June 2006; the promotion expanded his responsibilities to include facilities and telecommunications, suite and club services, and guest relations.

Team: Orlando Magic
Name: Chris D'Orso[15]
Title: Vice president of marketing and ticket sales
Education: Undergraduate: Fairfield University (Communications)
Career Path
Orlando Magic:
Joined the Magic in 1989 when the team was founded; started as a promotions/publicity coordinator.
After two seasons became a corporate account manager.
In 1994, was promoted to assistant director of marketing.
In 1998, was promoted to director of marketing.
Appointed to his current position of VP marketing and ticket sales in 2002.

Team: Phoenix Suns
Name: Lynn Agnello[16]
Title: Senior vice president, marketing partnerships
Education: Undergraduate: Indiana University (Telecommunications and Business)
Career Path
Radio Stations and Cable Networks:
Prior to working in professional sports, spent 10 years in Miami as the national sales manager for various top radio stations and cable networks.
Phoenix Suns:
Hired by the Phoenix Suns in 2001
Currently holds the title of senior vice president, marketing partnerships.

Team: Portland Trail Blazers
Name: Sarah Mensah[17]
Title: Senior vice president, marketing and sales
Education: Undergraduate: University of Oregon (Journalism and Telecommunications)
Career Path
Radio and Television:
Before working in professional sports, got her start working in television production for a local Portland station.
Also worked in radio sales for local Portland stations.
Portland Trailblazers:
Started as a corporate sales manager for the team, working in this capacity from 1993 to 1997.
Promoted to director of corporate sales.
Assumed responsibilities for ticket sales and service.
Promoted to senior VP, marketing and sales in May 2006.

Team: Sacramento Kings
Name: Danette Leighton[18]
Title: Vice president, marketing and brand development and Monarchs business operations (WNBA)
Works with: Sacramento Kings, Sacramento Monarchs (WNBA), ARCO Arena
Education: Undergraduate: University of Arizona (Political Science)
Career Path
Fiesta Bowl:
Served as assistant public relations director.
Pacific-10 Conference:
Worked as the conference's manager of information services, overseeing public relations and marketing for Pac-10 women's basketball, as well as both men's and women's golf and soccer.
NCAA Women's Final Four:
Served as executive director of the 1999 NCAA Women's Final Four.
Sony:
Worked for Sony Sports Marketing as marketing director.
Sacramento Kings and Monarchs (Maloof Sports & Entertainment):
Hired as director of Monarchs business operations.
After one year with the Monarchs, took on the added responsibility of senior director of marketing for the Kings, Monarchs, and ARCO Arena (all owned by Maloof Sports and Entertainment).
In 2004, promoted to vice president, marketing and brand development and Monarchs business operations.

Team: San Antonio Spurs
Name: Bruce Guthrie[19]
Title: Vice president of marketing
Education: Undergraduate: Western Illinois University
Career Path
San Antonio Spurs (Spurs Sports & Entertainment):
Came to the Spurs in 1982 as an account executive.
Worked as director of marketing for six seasons before being promoted to VP of marketing in 1992.

Team: Utah Jazz
Name: Jim Olson[21]
Title: Senior vice president of sales and marketing
Works with: Utah Jazz, EnergySolutions Arena, Salt Lake Bees (AAA Baseball)
Education: Undergraduate: University of Utah (Communications)
Graduate: Boston University (Sports and Recreation Management)
Career Path
Utah Jazz (Larry H. Miller Sports & Entertainment):
Hired by the Jazz in 1994 as the phone center ticket manager.
Promoted to director of tickets and the arena ticket manager in 1996.
In June 2003, promoted to vice president of ticket sales.
In 2005, responsibilities expanded to include ticket and suite sales for the Salt Lake Bees minor league baseball team (AAA).
Promoted in 2007 to current position as senior vice president of sales and marketing.

Table 53-1   Continued

Team: Toronto Raptors

Name: Beth Robertson[20]

Title: Vice president of marketing

Education: Undergraduate: University of Western Ontario (History)

Career Path

Revlon Canada:

Started her career in packaged goods at Revlon Canada, first in public relations then in marketing, eventually working her way up to a brand management position.

Bell Canada:

Joined Bell Canada as an advertising manager, which was her entrance into the sports industry.

Worked at Bell for 2 years.

Orca Bay Sports and Entertainment (owner of the Vancouver Canucks-NHL):

Joined Orca Bay Sports and Entertainment in Vancouver as manager, corporate partnership service.

MacLaren Momentum:

Returned to Toronto as an account director with MacLaren Momentum in the firm's events and sponsorship division.

Impact/FCB:

Worked in promotional marketing as account director with Impact/FCB.

Toronto Raptors (Maple Leafs Sports & Entertainment):

In 2000, joined Maple Leaf Sports and Entertainment (owner of the Raptors) as director of corporate partnership service.

In 2001, was named director of marketing.

In 2004, was promoted to her current position, vice president of marketing.

Team: Washington Wizards

Name: Rick Moreland[22]

Title: Senior vice president, corporate marketing/executive seating

Works with: Washington Wizards, Verizon Center, George Mason University Patriot Center (NCAA basketball)

Education: Undergraduate: University of Maryland-Baltimore County (Broadcasting/Media)

Graduate: University of Maryland (Public Relations)

Career Path

Basketball Playing Career:

Played basketball at UMBC and was drafted by the Washington Bullets in 1983.

University of Maryland-Baltimore County:

Worked as an associate athletic director (sports information) at his alma mater, UMBC.

Washington Wizards (Washington Sports & Entertainment):

From 1988 to 1991, was the team's director of public relations.

In 1991, was named VP of communications.

In 1993, assumed management of the entire sales business of the organization.

13. Information obtained via e-mail from Hunter Lochmann.
14. Oklahoma City Thunder Media Guide (2007–2008).
15. Orlando Magic Media Guide. (2006–2007). p. 18.
16. Phoenix Suns Media Guide. (2006–2007). p. 14.
17. Portland Trailblazers Media Guide. (2006–2007). p. 29.
18. Sacramento Kings Media Guide. (2008). NBA.com, p. 25. Retrieved November 12, 2007, from http://www.nba.com/media/kings/02-staff-08.

19. Sacramento Kings Media Guide. (2008). NBA.com, p. 25. Retrieved November 12, 2007, from http://www.nba.com/media/kings/02-staff-08.
20. San Antonio Spurs Media Guide. (2006–2007). p. 19.
21. Seattle Sonics Media Guide. (2006–2007). p. 22.
22. Information obtained via e-mail from Deirdre Molloy, Beth Robertson's secretary.
23. Jim Olson. (n.d.). *Salt Lake Bees.* Retrieved November 12, 2007, from http://www.slbees.com/staffProfile.cfm?StaffID=32.
24. Washington Wizards Media Guide. (2006–2007). p. 23.

BACKGROUNDS OF NBA MARKETING PROFESSIONALS

What is the current make-up of marketing professionals in the NBA? The following analysis provides some insight into answering this question.

How many NBA marketers had a significant athletic career?

- At least 4 of the 22 NBA marketers played collegiate basketball (Economou, Stanley, McCullough, and Moreland); however, it appears that only Economou played professionally, and that was in Europe. Therefore, being a star athlete does not seem to be a prerequisite to obtaining an NBA marketing position.

- Also important, none of the 23 marketers has any strong ties to basketball from the coaching or personnnel side. There do not appear to be any former coaches or player personnel in the group. This is to be expected, because marketing for an NBA team is a business position, not a player personnel position.

What type of education do NBA marketers have?

- The educational backgrounds of the 22 NBA marketers include both undergraduate degrees and graduate degrees.

- It appears that all 22 NBA marketers completed an undergraduate program. Although specific information was available for only 17 of the marketers, undergraduate majors included communications, history, political science, marketing, education, journalism, government, telecommunications, broadcasting/media, and sport management.

- Four NBA marketers completed a graduate program. Three of the four (Hauser, Lochmann, and Olson) received a graduate degree in sport management, while the fourth (Moreland) received a graduate degree in public relations.

- Detailed education information (such as undergraduate major) could be found on only 17 of the 22 NBA marketers. Of these 17 NBA marketers, 12 received either an undergraduate or graduate degree that directly relates to their current job (i.e., marketing, communications, business, or sport management). This represents 71%, indicating that although an education in marketing or business may not be required, it can be useful and a number of current NBA marketers do have such an educational background.

How did NBA marketers begin their careers?

The NBA marketers had a wide variety of starting points, which can be summarized as:

- Seven of the 22 NBA marketers (Andrews, Hauser, Lahr, Pugliese, D'Orso, Guthrie, and Olson) started their career with the same team for which they currently work. They started at the entry levels of the organization in positions such as interns, account executives, coordinators, and phone ticket managers.
- Of the remaining 15 NBA marketers (not accounted for above):
  - Five got their start working for a professional sports team or entity.
    - Stanley started in public relations with the Orlando Magic.
    - Sheirr started as a business analyst with NBA City (a league-owned entity).
    - McCullough started in broadcasting with the Sacramento Kings.
    - Glick started in minor league baseball working in business operations.
    - Byrnes started with Southwest Sports Group working for the Dallas Stars (NHL) in a marketing capacity.
  - Two got their start working in public relations/sports information at the collegiate level.
    - Leighton started in public relations with the Fiesta Bowl.
    - Moreland started in sports information with the University of Maryland-Baltimore County.
  - Two got their start working for a sports marketing agency (Economou and Lochmann).
  - Three got their start working in radio and television.
    - Mago started in broadcasting in a sports capacity.
    - Agnello started in radio/cable network sales in a nonsports capacity.
    - Mensah started in radio sales and television production in a nonsports capacity.
  - Two got their start in nonsports, marketing-related work (Hogenson and Robertson).
  - One got his start in a nonsports, nonmarketing position (DePaoli in the insurance industry).

The above information indicates there are a variety of positions from which one can start his or her career and still obtain an NBA marketing position. The analysis includes people who started their careers in the sports industry and some who did not, as well as people who started their careers in marketing and some who did not.

Do NBA marketers have extensive nonsports, business experience?

- Four of the 22 NBA marketers (Hogenson, Agnello, Mensah, and Robertson) developed their marketing skills in a nonsports environment prior to transitioning into the sports industry.
- Of the 22 NBA marketers, only one appears to have significant nonsports experience that is neither marketing nor broadcasting in nature:
  - DePaoli worked five years with Prudential Insurance and owned his own insurance agency.

Do NBA marketers have extensive sports experience outside the NBA?

- As noted earlier, a number of NBA marketers are also given the marketing responsibilities for the team owner's other sports entities (such as a WNBA team or the team's arena). This results in the marketers gaining non-NBA sports experience in conjunction with their current positions.
- Excluding their current positions (and thereby any situations covered in the first bullet point), 9 of the 22 NBA marketers have gained sports industry experience working outside of the NBA:
  - DePaoli worked for a minor league hockey team and an MLB team (Marlins).
  - Economou worked with multiple sports marketing agencies.
  - Mago worked in radio sports broadcasting.
  - Glick worked as the general manager for two minor league baseball teams and was the senior VP of sales and marketing for a Triple-A team (River Cats).
  - Lochmann worked as an intern in college athletics (Harvard) and for a sports marketing agency.
  - Leighton worked for the Fiesta Bowl, the Pac-10 Conference, the NCAA Women's Final Four, and Sony Sports Marketing (corporate sponsorship).
  - Byrnes worked for Southwest Sports Group (which owns the NHL's Dallas Stars and MLB's Texas Rangers) and the Phoenix Coyotes (NHL).
  - Robertson worked in a corporate sports sponsorship department, for Orca Bay Sports and Entertainment (which owned the NHL's Vancouver Canucks), and at a sports marketing agency.
  - Moreland worked as an associate athletic director at the University of Maryland, Baltimore county.

How many different NBA teams have NBA marketers generally worked for during their career?

- All but 2 of the 23 (Stanley and McCullough) have worked for only one NBA team.
  - Stanley has worked for three NBA teams.
  - McCullough has worked for two different NBA teams (and the Sacramento Kings twice).
- Six of the 22 have worked for the NBA league office or a league-owned entity:
  - DePaoli, Economou, Glick, and Lochmann worked in a marketing capacity for the league office, while McCullough worked in broadcasting.
  - Sheirr worked for NBA City, a league-owned entity, as a business analyst.
  - Although there does not appear to be a great deal of movement by NBA marketers from one NBA team to another, working in marketing at the league office appears to be a good training ground for a marketing position at the team level.

IS THERE A PATTERN IN THE CAREER TRACKS?

From the 22 NBA marketers analyzed in this chapter, three career tracks can be found—the "learn-on-the-job" track, the "league office" track, and the "lateral move" track.

The Learn-on-the-Job Track

Eight of the 22 NBA marketers started their career with a particular team and remain with that team today. This represents one third of the marketers analyzed in this chapter. For these individuals, the career track started at the lowest levels of the organization, in positions such as internships, account executives, and coordinators. They have worked their way up through the ranks of that organization, essentially learning on the job, and they now hold prominent positions atop their marketing departments.

Given the high percentage of marketers who have followed this path, this appears to be a viable option for someone looking to obtain a prominent marketing position with an NBA team. If you plan to follow a similar path, examine the career tracks of Andrews, Hauser, Lahr, Pugliese, D'Orso, Guthrie, and Olson to see how they successfully followed the learn-on-the-job track.

A variation of the learn-on-the-job track can also be followed by taking an entry-level position with one NBA team and then changing teams to acquire a higher-level position. Such flexibility and a willingness to move may be necessary due to the limited number of positions and low turnover of higher-level positions in professional sports. As an example, a senior account executive may be ready for a promotion to a marketing director position, but his or her current team may not be in need of a marketing director. As a result, rather than waiting for a marketing director position to open up at his or her current team, this person may consider working for another NBA team that is looking to hire a new marketing director. By making such a move, the person is able to advance his or her career more quickly. The career track of Stanley provides an example of working for multiple teams on the learn-on-the-job track.

The League Office Track

Another popular career track travels through the NBA's league office. Six of the 22 NBA marketers, or 27%, spent time working directly for the league. Working in the league office provided an opportunity for these individuals to hone their marketing skills at the league level and make contacts with various teams before moving to a team. Obtaining a marketing position at the league level appears to be a strong stepping stone toward a marketing position at the team level. For more information on the league office track, review the career tracks of DePaoli, Economou, Shirr, McCullough, Glick, and Lochmann.

The Lateral Move

The remaining eight NBA marketers who did not follow the learn-on-the-job track or the league office track followed a wide variety of career paths. Some started in the sports industry in fields such as broadcasting, public relations, and marketing. Others started outside of the sports industry all together. Nonetheless, they all have one thing in common: They all developed their marketing skills in one manner or another, and then transferred this skill set to an NBA team.

The lateral move from a non-NBA marketing position to an NBA marketing position is exemplified by the career tracks of Mago, Hogenson, Agnello, Mensah, Leighton, Byrnes, Robertson, and Moreland. It is important to note that Mago, Leighton, Byrnes, and Moreland all made a lateral move within the sports industry (from another sports-related entity to the NBA). In contrast, Hogenson, Agnello, Mensah, and Robertson all started in nonsports positions and then made lateral moves into the sports industry (either directly to an NBA team or first to a non-NBA entity and then to an NBA team).

CREATING YOUR OWN TRACK

The NBA marketing professionals presented in this chapter help to demonstrate there are a number of paths you can take to arrive at an NBA marketing position. If you are interested in becoming a marketing professional for an NBA team, you must develop solid skills in marketing, selling, branding, and promotions. This development process can take place at an NBA team, the NBA league office, a non-NBA professional sports team, a sports marketing agency, or even a nonsports marketing environment. If you obtain your marketing skills outside of the NBA, you will likely need strong network connections to make the transition to the NBA.

different educational backgrounds and work experiences. Nonetheless, the following items are important to note:

- Three of the five executives, including the commissioner and deputy commissioner, hold law degrees. This provides an indication of the type of complex legal environment within which the NBA operates.

- Stu Jackson, who manages the league's basketball operations, is the only executive of the five with a significant basketball background. He played basketball at the college level, and has coached at both the pro and college level. He is responsible for overseeing the on-court operations of the NBA, so it seems only natural that he would have an extensive background in the sport as a player and a coach.

- Heidi Ueberroth is the highest-ranking female executive in any of the four major professional sports leagues. She also has significant family connections to the sports industry that the average reader of this book is not likely to have (her father, Peter Ueberroth, is the former commissioner of MLB and current chairman of the USOC). Although such connections do not automatically get one a job, they often result in a larger network of sports contacts that can lead to more opportunities.

- It is important to point out the caliber of schools from which the executives received their education. Prestigious schools such as Columbia, Duke, the University of Chicago, the Wharton School of Business (Penn), New York University, and Vanderbilt are all represented in the educational backgrounds of the executives. This demonstrates a growing trend in professional sport leagues—leagues are looking for the best and brightest when it comes to hiring its employees.

Endnotes

1. NBA 101. (n.d.). NBA.com. Retrieved November 19, 2007, from http://www.nba.com/nba101/index.html.

2. Information on additional NBA executives can be found at http://icq.nba.com/careers/management_team.html.

NCAA Football Bowl Subdivision Athletic Directors

If a person has an interest in working as an athletic director for an NCAA Football Bowl Subdivision (FBS) school (formerly Division I-A), a lot can be learned from examining the educational backgrounds and previous work experiences of current athletic directors. To conduct this analysis, information was gathered on every athletic director from schools in the Pac-10 and Big Ten conferences as of April 2008. The Pac-10 and the Big Ten represent 2 of the 11 college athletic conferences that compete at the NCAA Football Bowl Subdivision level. In total, 21 athletic directors are analyzed in this chapter, providing an indication of the general make-up of current athletic directors working at NCAA Football Bowl Subdivision schools.

Tables **55-1** and **55-2** list the educational background and work experience of the 10 Pac-10 and 11 Big Ten athletic directors, respectively. These individuals represent the highest leadership position in each school's athletic department.

To better understand the organizational context of the athletic director position, Chapter 61 provides example organizational charts for college athletic departments. Reviewing these charts provides insight into how schools structure their athletic departments, including what positions report directly to the athletic director and how the athletic director reports to the school's administrative offices (such as a university's president or chancellor). In addition, Section 5 provides information on the common job requirements, duties, and responsibilities for athletic directors. An actual job announcement for an athletic director position at a Football Bowl Subdivision school can be found in Chapter 73, and an Athletic Director "Position Spotlight" also can be found in Chapter 73. Reviewing this information will help you to understand the job of an athletic director at the FBS level.

Athletic directors at the Division III level have been analyzed in a separate career section. This information can be found in Chapter 56.

BACKGROUNDS OF NCAA FOOTBALL BOWL SUBDIVISION ATHLETIC DIRECTORS

What is the current make-up of athletic directors in the Pac-10 and Big Ten? The following analysis provides some insight into answering this question.

How many FBS athletic directors had a significant athletic career?

- 13 of the 21 FBS athletic directors played sports at the collegiate level. This represents almost 62% of the group.

- Of the 13 FBS athletic directors who participated in college athletics, two went on to play professional football in the NFL (Murphy and Garrett).

- Although it is not a job *requirement* to have previous playing experience at the college level, such playing experience does seem to provide some benefit to people looking to work in college athletics. This benefit may come from firsthand knowledge gained during the person's athletic playing career, or it may come from networking opportunities with coaches, college administrators, and alumni.

Table 55-1   Career Tracks: Pac-10 Conference Athletic Directors (As of April 2008)

School: University of Arizona

Athletic Director: Jim Livengood[1]

Education: Undergraduate: Washington State, Everett Community College and Brigham Young University (Physical Education)
Graduate: Central Washington University

Career Path

High School Teaching and Coaching Career: Was a teacher and coach at Moses Lake High School (WA) in 1968–1969; assistant football coach and head track coach.

Was a teacher, head football coach, and head basketball coach at Oroville High (WA) from 1969 to 1972.

Was athletics director, head football and basketball coach, and counselor at Ephrata High (WA) from 1972 to 1980.

Washington State University: Washington State hired Livengood as its Cage Camp director in 1980–1981, and promoted him to assistant athletics director in charge of Cage Camp and high school relations in 1981–1982.

Was associate athletics director responsible for development and public relations from 1982 to 1985.

Southern Illinois University: Became director of athletics at Southern Illinois University from 1985 to 1987.

Also served as president of the Gateway Conference in 1986–1987.

Washington State University: Rehired by Washington State as athletics director in September 1987.

University of Arizona: Named athletic director at Arizona in 1994.

Notes: Earned honorable mention all-state honors in basketball at Quincy High School. Served as of National Association of Collegiate Directors of Athletics (NACDA) president in 1998–1999.

School: Arizona State University

Athletic Director: Lisa Love[2]

Education: Undergraduate: Texas Tech University (Physical Education)
Graduate: University of North Texas (Education Administration)

Career Path

High School Volleyball Coach: Compiled a 79–40 record as head coach at Bowie High School in Arlington, Texas (1978–1982).

University of Texas at Arlington: Head women's volleyball coach from 1982 to 1988 at Texas Arlington.

University of Southern California: Served as head women's volleyball coach (1989–1998) and administrator (1991–2005).

After leaving the coaching ranks following the 1998 season, devoted herself full time to administration, eventually ascending to the position of senior associate athletic director in 2002.

Arizona State University: Named Arizona State's vice president for university athletics (athletic director) in April 2005.

Four-year volleyball starter and an all-region performer at Texas Tech.

Notes: Member of the Texas Tech University and Texas Arlington athletic Halls of Fame as a volleyball player.

School: California University

Athletic Director: Sandy Barbour[3]

Education: Undergraduate: Wake Forest University (Physical Education)
Graduate: University of Massachusetts (Sport Management); Northwestern University (MBA)

Career Path

University of Massachusetts: Began as a field hockey assistant coach and lacrosse administrative assistant at UMass in 1981.

Northwestern University: Between master's degree programs, Barbour served as assistant field hockey and lacrosse coach at Northwestern from 1982 to 1984. She also held the position of director of recruiting services during that period.

Promoted to assistant athletic director for intercollegiate programs in 1984, a position she held until 1989.

FOX Sports Net: Worked in programming and production for FOX Sports Net in Chicago during the summer of 1990.

Tulane University: In 1991, was recruited to Tulane as an associate athletic director.

Appointed Tulane's athletic director in 1996; served in this capacity for 3 years.

University of Notre Dame: Hired as associate athletic director in 2000.

Served as deputy director of athletics at Notre Dame from 2003 to 2004.

California University: Named Cal's athletic director in September 2004.

Notes: While attending Wake Forest, was a 4-year letterwinner and served as captain of the field hockey team. She also played two varsity seasons of women's basketball.

School: University of Oregon

Athletic Director: Pat Kilkenny[4,5]

Education: Attended the University of Oregon as an undergraduate, but did not receive a degree.

Career Path

Central West/Puritan Insurance Company: Initiated his career in business as western regional manager of Central West/Puritan Insurance Company (a subsidiary of General Electric Credit Corp.) from 1974 to 1979.

The Managing General Agency: Became president of The Managing General Agency in Seattle in 1980; sold the insurance business 4 years later to purchase Arrowhead.

Arrowhead General Insurance: Served as chairman and chief executive officer of the San Diego–based Arrowhead General Insurance Agency (1984–2006); sold the company in 2006.

University of Oregon: Hired as the school's athletic director in February 2007, despite possessing no college athletics administration experience.

Notes: Served on the University of Oregon's athletic department advisory board and the board of trustees for the University of Oregon Foundation.

Served on the University of California San Diego's athletic advisory board and the San Diego State University athletic director's cabinet.

Currently serves on the board of directors of the San Diego International Sports Council.

---

1. Mr. Jim Livengood. (n.d.). Retrieved November 9, 2007, from http://www.arizonaathletics.com/sport/page.aspx?id=1272.

2. Lisa Love Profile. (n.d.). Retrieved November 9, 2007, from http://thesundevils.cstv.com/genrel/love_lisa00.html.

3. Sandy Barbour Profile. (n.d.). Retrieved November 9, 2007, from http://calbears.cstv.com/genrel/barbour_sandy00.html.

4. Athletic Director Pat Kilkenny. (n.d.). Retrieved November 9, 2007 from http://www.goducks.com/ViewArticle.dbml?DB_OEM_ID=500&KEY=&ATCLID=885642.

5. Andrews, L. (2007, Mar. 14). The New Face of Oregon Athletics. *Oregon Daily Emerald.* Retrieved November 9, 2007, from http://media.www.dailyemerald.com/media/storage/paper859/news/2007/03/14/News/The-New.Face.Of.Oregon.Athletics-2775266.shtml.

Table 55-1   Continued

School: Oregon State University
Athletic Director: Bob De Carolis[6]
Education: Undergraduate: Bloomsburg State College (Business Education)
Graduate: University of Massachusetts (Sport Management)
Career Path
Bloomsburg State College: Served as an assistant coach in baseball and football from 1976 to 1978.
University of Michigan: Started his Michigan career in 1979 as an administrative assistant.
Promoted to assistant business manager in 1980.
In addition to his assistant business manager duties, was also named the head softball coach; he held this position until 1984.
Promoted to business manager in 1983.
In 1987, promoted to assistant athletic director for business.
Named associate athletic director for internal operations in 1990.
His title and duties were expanded again in 1994, when he was named senior director for financial operations.
In 1996, was named senior associate athletic director and became responsible for all athletic facilities and venues.
Oregon State University: Joined the OSU staff in 1998 as associate athletic director of internal operations
Promoted to senior associate athletic director in 1999.
Appointed to the position of athletic director in 1999.
Notes: During his undergraduate days at Bloomsburg, De Carolis was a 2-year letterwinner in football and baseball from 1973 to 1975.

School: Stanford University
Athletic Director: Bobby Bowlsby[7,8]
Education: Undergraduate: Moorhead State University
Graduate: University of Iowa
Career Path
University of Northern Iowa: Served as assistant athletic director for facilities.
Worked his way up to the athletic director position; served in this capacity from 1984 to 1991.
University of Iowa: Hired as the school's athletic director in 1991; spent nearly 15 years in this role at Iowa.
Stanford University: Named the Jaquish & Kenninger director of athletics at Stanford University in April 2006.
Notes: Wrestled at Moorhead State University.

School: UCLA
Athletic Director: Daniel Guerrero[9,10]
Education: Undergraduate: UCLA
Graduate: Cal State Dominguez Hills (Public Administration)
Career Path
Cal State Dominguez Hills: Took an unpaid position as Cal State Dominguez Hills' associate athletic director in 1982.
Led the program to national prominence while serving as athletic director from 1988 to 1992.
University of California-Irvine: Served as athletic director from 1992 to 2002.
UCLA: Appointed athletic director at UCLA in 2002.
Played second base in the Bruin baseball program for 4 years.
Notes: Inducted into the UCLA Baseball Hall of Fame in 1996.

School: University of Southern California
Athletic Director: Michael Garrett[11,12]
Education: Undergraduate: University of Southern California (Sociology). Law School: Western State University College of Law
Career Path
NFL Playing Career: Played 8 seasons (1966–1973) in the NFL with the Kansas City Chiefs and San Diego Chargers.
Post-Playing Career: Following his NFL career, had a variety of experiences, including working for the San Diego district attorney's office; holding management positions in the retail, construction, and real estate industries; and doing color commentary on USC football telecasts.
Great Western Forum: Worked as director of business development.
University of Southern California: Returned to USC as associate athletic director in December 1990.
Named USC's athletic director in 1993.
Notes: A football star as a student, was a two-time All-American and set 14 NCAA, conference, and USC records.
In 1965, became USC's first Heisman Trophy winner.
In 1985, was inducted into the National Football Foundation's College Football Hall of Fame.
Ran for Congress (1982) and San Diego City Council.

6. Bob De Carolis. (n.d.). Retrieved November 9, 2007, from http://www.nmnathletics.com/ViewArticle.dbml?&SPSID=25034&SPID=1968&DB_OEM_ID=4700&ATCLID=130561.
7. Bob Bowlsby, the Jaquish and Kenninger Director of Athletics. (n.d.). Retrieved November 9, 2007, from http://gostanford.cstv.com/school-bio/stan-athdir.html.
8. Smith, M. (2006, Apr. 26). Cardinals Hire Iowa AD Bowlsby. *San Francisco Chronicle.* Retrieved November 9, 2007, from http://www.sfgate.com/cgi-bin/article.cgi?f=/c/a/2006/04/26/SPGCRIFFVJ1.DTL.
9. Daniel G. Guerrero Profile. (n.d.). Retrieved November 9, 2007, from http://uclabruins.cstv.com/genrel/guerrero_danielg00.html.
10. King, D. (2002, May 20). Courting Success: Incoming UCLA Athletic Director Dan Guerrero Returns to His Alma Mater Intent on Maintaining Its Level of Excellence While Defending Its Graduation Rate. *Los Angeles Business Journal.* Retrieved November 9, 2007, from http://findarticles.com/p/articles/mi_m5072/is_20_24/ai_91092124.
11. Michael Garrett Athletic Director. (n.d.). Retrieved November 9, 2007, from http://www.usc.edu/about/administration/senior/garrett.html.
12. Berkowitz, K. (2003, Mar. 20). Winning Ways: USC A.D. Mike Garrett Talks with Athletic Management Magazine about His Strategies for Success. *Athletic Management.* Retrieved November 9, 2007, from http://usctrojans.cstv.com/genrel/032003aaa.html.

Table 55-1   Continued

School: University of Washington
Athletic Director: Todd Turner[13,14]
Education: Undergraduate: University of North Carolina (Religion)
Graduate: Ohio University (Sports Administration)
Career Path
University of Virginia:
Began his career at Virginia, holding positions such as athletic ticket manager, sports information director, director of sports promotions, and associate athletic director.
Spent 11 years at UVA.
University of Connecticut:
Hired by UConn as the school's athletic director; served in this capacity from 1987 to 1990.
North Carolina State University:
Hired by NC State in 1990; served as the school's athletic director until 1996.
Vanderbilt University:
In 1996, accepted Vanderbilt's athletic director position, a job he held until 2003.
University of Washington:
Hired as Washington's athletic director in June 2004.

---

13. Todd Turner Profile. (n.d.). Retrieved November 9, 2007, from http://gohuskies.cstv
.com/genrel/turner_todd00.html.
14. Turner resigned from his position at the University of Washington in January 2008, but was included in this study because no full-time replacement has been found prior to this study.
15. James (Jim) Sterk Profile. (n.d.). Retrieved November 9, 2007, from http://
wsucougars.cstv.com/genrel/sterk_jamesjim00.html.

School: Washington State University
Athletic Director: Jim Sterk[15]
Education: Undergraduate: Western Washington University (Physical Education and Business Education)
Graduate: Ohio University (Sports Administration)
Career Path
University of North Carolina:
In 1986, held an internship, working as the assistant to the director of ticket operations.
University of Maine:
Started as assistant business manager and ticket manager in 1987–1988.
Promoted to director of athletic services in 1988–1989.
From 1989 to 1990, worked as the assistant athletic director for finance.
Seattle Pacific University:
From 1990 to 1991, served as associate athletic director.
Tulane University:
Hired as associate athletic director for administration and external affairs in 1991.
In 1992, promoted to senior associate athletic director and executive director of the Green Wave Club (the school's fundraising organization).
Portland State University:
From 1995 to 2000, served as the school's athletic director.
Washington State University:
Hired as WSU's athletic director in 2000.
Notes: In high school, earned varsity letters in football, basketball, baseball, and track. At Western Washington University, earned four varsity letters in football and one in basketball; was the football team captain, team MVP, and all-district first team as a senior in 1977.

How many FBS athletic directors have coaching experience?

- 10 of the 21 FBS athletic directors (47%) have coaching experience:
  - Five ADs (Barbour, DeCarolis, Phillips, Smith, and Curley) have college coaching experience.
  - Two ADs (Maturi and Livengood) have high school coaching experience.
- Three ADs (Guenther, Alvarez, and Love) have both high school and college coaching experience.
- At least 7 of the 10 former coaches were also collegiate athletes (included above).

What type of education do FBS athletic directors have?

- Twenty of the 21 FBS athletic directors completed a 4-year, undergraduate program. Majors included physical education, business education, sociology, religion, behavioral science, mass communication, government, business administration, and industrial management. The diversity in degrees indicates athletic directors can come from a variety of educational backgrounds.

- None of the 21 FBS athletic directors completed a sport management undergraduate program; however, at least 6 ADs received a degree in physical education.

- Seventeen of the 21 FBS athletic directors completed at least one graduate program, while three ADs (Barbour, Hollis, and Martin) completed two graduate programs. Graduate degrees were received in areas including education administration, sport management, business administration, public administration, athletic administration, economics, counselor education, and industrial relations. Note that the degrees are applicable to athletics and administration in some way.

- At least 5 of the 17 FBS athletic directors receiving graduate degrees completed a sport management graduate program (Barbour, De Carolis, Turner, Sterk, and Greenspan).

It is important to note, graduate school can be used to refine one's educational background to meet the needs/requirements of an athletic director. A growing number of institutions require or prefer the school's athletic administrators to hold graduate degrees. Consequently, the large number of athletic directors who hold graduate degrees reflects the general requirements commonly found in college athletics.

Table 55-2   Career Tracks: Big Ten Conference Athletic Directors (As of April 2008)

School: University of Illinois
Athletic Director: Ron Guenther[1]
Education: Undergraduate: University of Illinois (Physical Education)
Graduate: University of Illinois (Administration)
Career Path
High School Teacher and Football Coach:
Began career as a teacher and coach for two suburban Chicago high schools.
Boston College:
Landed a job as an offensive line coach at Boston College; worked in this capacity from 1971 to 1974.
North Central College:
Moved on to North Central College, where he spent 8 years (1975–1983); positions included director of admissions, associate head football coach, and vice president of development and public affairs.
University of Illinois:
From 1983 to 1987, served as assistant athletic director for Chicago operations.
Spent 3 years working as associate athletic director for development.
From 1988 to 1989, served as interim director of athletics for external operations.
Worked 2 years with the University of Illinois Foundation as director of major gifts.
Named University of Illinois athletic director in May 1992.
Notes: Played football while attending Illinois, lettering in 1965 and 1966. Team MVP in 1966.

School: Indiana University
Athletic Director: Rick Greenspan[2]
Education: Undergraduate: University of Maryland (Behavioral Science)
Graduate: Idaho State University (Physical Education with an Athletics Administration Emphasis)
Career Path
Universities of Wisconsin and New Hampshire:
At the beginning of his career, held positions in physical education and recreational sports at the University of Wisconsin at Milwaukee and the University of New Hampshire.
University of California at Berkeley:
Was at the University of California at Berkeley for 8 years, where he was associate athletics director for external affairs and also served as acting athletics director for 1 year.
University of Miami (FL):
Spent 1 year as senior associate athletics director at the University of Miami.
Illinois Southern University:
Appointed director of athletics at Illinois Southern University in 1993; worked there until 1999.
West Point Academy:
Served as director of athletics at West Point from 1999 to 2004.
Indiana University:
Hired as athletics director in September 2004.
Notes: Played baseball while attending the University of Maryland; 4-year letter winner.

School: University of Iowa
Athletic Director: Gary Barta[3]
Education: Undergraduate: North Dakota State University (Mass Communication and Broadcast Journalism)
Career Path
North Dakota State University:
Began his career at NDSU in 1988 as an associate director of development and later became the director of development.
During his time at NDSU, worked as a sportscaster for WDAY radio/television in Fargo, ND.
University of Northern Iowa:
Served as director of athletic development and external relations at the UNI from 1990–1996.
University of Washington:
From 1996 to 2003, served as Washington's senior associate athletic director for external relations and sports programs.
University of Wyoming:
Worked as the school's athletic director from 2003 to 2006.
University of Iowa:
Hired as University of Iowa athletic director in August 2006.
Notes: Played as option quarterback for North Dakota State Bison football squads that won the Division II NCAA National Championship in 1983, 1985, and 1986.

School: University of Michigan
Athletic Director: Bill Martin[4]
Education: Undergraduate: Wittenberg University
Graduate: University of Stockholm, Sweden (Economics); University of Michigan (MBA)
Career Path
First Martin Corporation:
In 1968, he founded First Martin Corp., a diversified real estate construction, development, and management firm.
Bank of Ann Arbor:
Founder and chairman of the board of Bank of Ann Arbor.
Washtenaw Land Conservancy:
Served as president of the Washtenaw Land Conservancy.
United States Sailing Foundation and Association:
Served as president of the United States Sailing Foundation, as well as the U.S. Sailing Association, the national governing body of the sport, from 1988 to 1991.
United States Olympic Committee:
Served as the president of the U.S. Olympic Committee, after having served on its board of directors for 8 years.
University of Michigan:
In February 1999, was one of four members of a committee appointed by former University of Michigan President Lee Bollinger to review the financial management of the athletic department.
Appointed interim director of intercollegiate athletics in March 2000.
Named the permanent athletic director in August 2000.
Notes: Currently on the board of directors for the U.S. Olympic Foundation, National Football Foundation, and College Hall of Fame, Inc.
Received the U.S. Olympic Committee General Douglas MacArthur Award, the organization's highest award, honoring his leadership as acting president of the USOC.

1. Miller, S., and Burson, D. (2006). 2005–2006 Illinois Women's Golf Media Guide, p. 22. Retrieved November 9, 2007, from http://grfx.cstv.com/photos/schools/ill/sports/w-golf/auto_pdf/06_wgolf.pdf.
2. Hoosier Athletics: Rick Greenspan Profile. (n.d.). Retrieved November 9, 2007, from http://iuhoosiers.cstv.com/genrel/greenspan_rick00.html.
3. Administration: Director of Athletics Gary Barta. (n.d.). Retrieved November 9, 2007, from http://hawkeyesports.cstv.com/administration/athletic-director.html.
4. William C. Martin: Director of Intercollegiate Athletics. (n.d.). Retrieved November 9, 2007, from http://www.mgoblue.com/document_display.cfm?document_id=3065.

Table 55-2   Continued

School: Michigan State University
Athletic Director: Mark Hollis[5]
Education: Undergraduate: Michigan State University
Graduate: University of Colorado (MBA)
Career Path
Western Athletic Conference:
Hired out of Michigan St. in 1985 as an administrative assistant and rose to the level of assistant commissioner.
University of Pittsburgh:
Worked as an assistant and then later an associate athletic director.
Oversaw Pitt's operations for external affairs, game day management, and university facilities. Also managed logistics and budgets of basketball and football programs.
Michigan State University:
Returned to Michigan State in 1995 to oversee the department's external affairs, which includes marketing, community relations, media relations, broadcasting, and corporate sponsorship
Named athletic director in September 2007, and officially assumed duties on January 2008.
Notes: Worked as a basketball team manager while an undergrad at Michigan State.
Named 2002 National Marketer of the Year by the National Association of Collegiate Marketing Administrators.

School: University of Minnesota
Athletic Director: Joel Maturi[6]
Education: Undergraduate: University of Notre Dame (Government)
Graduate: University of Wisconsin-Platteville (Educational Administration)
Career Path
High School Coach:
Started out coaching football, basketball, baseball, and track and field for 19 years at Edgewood High School in Madison, Wisconsin.
University of Wisconsin:
Began a 9-year career in the University of Wisconsin athletic department in 1987.
From 1992 to 1996, served as associate director of athletics.
University of Denver:
Moved to DU as the athletic director in 1996; worked in this capacity until 1998.
Miami University of Ohio:
Hired by Miami University of Ohio as the school's athletic director in 1998; worked there until 2002.
University of Minnesota:
Named athletic director at Minnesota in 2002.
Notes: Inducted into the Wisconsin Basketball Hall of Fame in 1992 (for his distinguished coaching career).

School: Northwestern University
Athletic Director: Jim Philips[7]
Education: Undergraduate: University of Illinois
Graduate: Arizona State University (Masters in Education)
Doctorate: University of Tennessee (Educational Administration)
Career Path
University of Illinois:
Worked as a student assistant for Illinois Athletic Department as an undergrad.
Arizona State University:
In 1990 he joined the Arizona State basketball coaching staff as a restricted earnings coach.
University of Tennessee:
Joined the University of Tennessee Athletic Department where he acted as an assistant athletic director for development.
University of Notre Dame:
Hired by Norte Dame in 2000 as an associate athletic director. He was later promoted to senior associate director of athletics for external affairs, handling development, sponsorships, and ticketing.
Northern Illinois University:
Named athletic director of Husky athletics beginning in 2004, where he served until he was hired by Northwestern.
Northwestern University:
Hired as athletic director in 2008.
Notes: Member of the NCAA Women's Basketball Committee.

School: Ohio State University
Athletic Director: Gene Smith[8]
Education: Undergraduate: University of Notre Dame (Business Administration)
Career Path
University of Notre Dame:
Following graduation, joined the Notre Dame coaching staff under Dan Devine and remained in that capacity until 1981.
IBM:
Left Notre Dame following the 1981 season to accept a marketing position with IBM.
Eastern Michigan University:
Returned to college athletics in April 1983 as assistant athletic director at Eastern Michigan University.
In 1985, he was appointed as interim director of athletics.
Was awarded the director position on a full-time basis in 1986.
Iowa State University:
In 1993, he was named athletics director at ISU.
Arizona State University:
Moved to ASU in 2000, as the school's athletic director.
Ohio State University:
Hired as Ohio State's athletic director in March 2005.
Notes: Attended Notre Dame on a football scholarship and played 4 years as defensive end.
Past president of the National Association of Collegiate Directors of Athletics (NACDA) and was that organization's first African American president.
In total, he has over 23 years of AD experience.

5. Mark Hollis Named MSU Athletics Director-Designate. (2007, Sep. 12). *MSUSpartans.com*. Retrieved April 25, 2008, from http://msuspartans.cstv.com/genrel/091207aab.html.
6. Athletics Director Joel Maturi. (n.d.). Retrieved November 9, 2007, from http://www.gophersports.com/ViewArticle.dbml?DB_OEM_ID=8400&KEY=&ATCLID=293874.
7. Jim Phillips Profile. (n.d.). Retrieved April 2, 2008, from http://nusports.cstv.com/school-bio/nw-athdir.htlm.
8. Gene Smith: Director of Athletics. (n.d.). Retrieved November 9, 2007, from http://www.ohiostatebuckeyes.com/ViewArticle.dbml?&DB_OEM_ID=17300&ATCLID=1051911.

Table 55-2 Continued

School: Penn State University
Athletic Director: Tim Curley[9]
Education: Undergraduate: Penn State University (Health and Physical Education)
Graduate: Penn State University (Counselor Education)
Career Path
Penn State University:
Served a year as a graduate assistant coach while pursuing his master's degree.
Named the Nittany Lions' first full-time football recruiting coordinator in 1978.
In 1981, was named assistant to the athletic director.
Named director of athletics in December 1993.
Notes: Played basketball and football at State College Area High School.
Walked on as a football player at Penn State, only to have his career cut short by injuries.
In 2007, served as president of the National Association of Collegiate Directors of Athletics (NACDA).

School: Purdue University
Athletic Director: Morgan Burke[10]
Education: Undergraduate: Purdue University (Industrial Management)
Graduate: Purdue University (Industrial Relations)
Law School: John Marshall Law School
Career Path
Inland Steel Company:
Pursued a successful career with Inland Steel Co. after law school, moving through 13 positions in an 18-year span.
Was vice president when he departed Inland Steel.
Purdue University:
Named athletics director in January 1993.

School: University of Wisconsin
Athletic Director: Barry Alvarez[11]
Education: Undergraduate: University of Nebraska
Graduate: University of Nebraska
Career Path
High School Coach:
Coaching career began at the high school level, serving as an assistant at Lincoln (NE) Northeast High from 1971 to 1973.
Took over as head coach at Lexington (NE) High from 1974 to 1975.
Last prep coaching stop was at Mason City (Iowa) High where he was head coach from 1976 to 1978.
University of Iowa:
Hired as an assistant coach in 1979.
University of Notre Dame:
Left Iowa after the 1986 season to become linebackers coach at Notre Dame.
Promoted to defensive coordinator and then again to assistant head coach.
University of Wisconsin:
Hired as head football coach of the Badgers in 1990.
Added administrative duties to his job description in 2000 when he was named associate athletic director.
Performed dual coaching and athletic director duties in 2004 and 2005.
Following the 2005 season, stepped down as Wisconsin's football coach; maintained AD position.
Notes: Starred as a prep linebacker and went on to play at Nebraska (1965–1967).
The 1993 National Coach of the Year, Alvarez is a two-time (1993 and 1998) Big Ten Conference Coach of the Year.

9. Tim Curley Profile. (n.d.). Retrieved November 9, 2007, from http://gopsusports.cstv.com/genrel/curley_tim00.html.
10. Athletics Director Morgan J. Burke. (n.d.). Retrieved November 9, 2007, from http://purduesports.cstv.com/school-bio/pur-morgan-burke.html.
11. Barry Alvarez. (n.d.). Retrieved November 9, 2007, from http://www.uwbadgers.com/bios/?staffid=100.

Two of the 21 FBS athletic directors (Burke and Garrett) completed law school:

- Burke obtained a graduate degree in addition to his law degree and was included in the graduate degree analysis above.

- Garrett obtained only a law degree.

How did the FBS athletic directors begin their careers?

- Subsequent to any collegiate playing career, the 21 FBS athletic directors began their careers in a variety of manners, as follows:
  - Ten ADs began in the coaching ranks:
    - Five ADs (Livengood, Love, Guenther, Maturi, and Alvarez) started out as high school coaches.
    - Five ADs (Barbour, De Carolis, Phillips, Smith, and Curely) started out as college coaches.

- Seven ADs (Bowlsby, Guerrero, Turner, Sterk, Greenspan, Hollis, and Barta) began in college athletics administration.

- Three ADs (Kilkenny, Martin, and Burke) started out in nonsports, business positions.

- Two ADs (Garrett and Murphy) started out as a professional football player in the NFL.

Do athletic directors have nonsports, business experience?

- Only 5 of the 21 FBS athletic directors appear to have experience outside of the sports industry:
  - Kilkenny, Mason, and Burke established themselves as business leaders before making the transition into college athletics administration. They hold the most extensive nonsports, business experience among the 21 athletic directors.

- Following his NFL playing career, Garrett worked outside of the sports industry.
- Smith worked for IBM for 2 years during his transition from college coach to college athletics administrator.

Although many business skills are transferable, extensive nonsports, business experience does not appear to be the likely path to an athletic director position.

The 21 FBS athletic directors also appear to have very little sport management experience outside of college athletics (i.e., experience working for professional teams, sports marketing agencies, etc.). Martin is the one exception, having worked for U.S. Sailing and the USOC.

How many colleges has the typical FBS athletic director worked for during his or her career?

- On average, each FBS athletic director has worked for 3.38 different colleges during his or her career. Greenspan and Sterk lead the pack, working for seven schools and six schools, respectively.
- The high number of average schools indicates a need to be mobile in order to advance one's career. For instance, if a person is ready to move from an assistant AD position to an associate AD position (or possibly even an AD position), this often requires a move to a school with an opening at that level.
- It appears that 5 of the 21 athletic directors (Kilkenny, Garrett, Martin, Curley, and Burke) have worked exclusively for only one college. With the exception of Curley, each of these individuals got into college athletics administration later in their career.

Do FBS athletic directors get more than one opportunity to be an athletic director?

- On average, each FBS athletic director has held two athletic director positions in his or her career. Turner, Greenspan, and Smith have each held four AD positions.
- Nine of the 21 FBS athletic directors have held only one AD position.
- Although almost half of the FBS athletic directors have held only one AD position, there does appear to be an opportunity to hold more than one AD position during one's career.

IS THERE A PATTERN IN THE CAREER TRACKS?

Four viable career tracks stand out from the analysis of the athletic directors—the "athlete" track, the "coach" track, the "business leader" track, and the "entry-level administration" track. There is also an important trend to note, which can appropriately be called the "alumni connection."

The Athlete Track

At least 13 of the 21 athletic directors played sports at the collegiate level, and two of these individuals went on to play professionally. Each of these 13 athletes arrived at their athletic director positions in a different way, but the common connection of being an athlete is important.

During a person's college athletic playing career, one is able to witness firsthand how a college athletic department operates and to understand the challenges of being a student-athlete. A person with no such college playing experience will have to learn about duplicating this experience and knowledge. Therefore, college athletic administrators often look favorably at previous playing experience when looking to hire new employees. This can improve a former athlete's chances of landing a college athletic administration position (i.e., it can help get one's foot in the door).

In addition to valuable playing experience, college athletes are also likely to have stronger network connections than nonathletes. For example, an athlete may develop connections with his or her coach, members of the school's athletic administration, or prominent alumni. Such connections can play an important role in one's job search in college athletics.

It is important to note that 7 of the 13 athletes took coaching positions following their playing careers. Their playing experience likely aided in their pursuit of a coaching position. They then made a transition from coaching to college athletics administration. These individuals are included in a separate career track (the coach track), discussed in the following section.

If you are a former athlete, current athlete, or someone looking to follow the athlete career track, look at the career tracks of Greenspan, Barta, Bowlsby, Guerrero, Garrett, and Sterk. Each provides an example of how an athlete can make the transition from athlete to college athletics administrator. In addition, the career tracks of Guenther, Smith, Curley, Alvarez, Love, Barbour, and De Carolis provide insight into how an athlete can transition first into coaching and then into college athletic administration.

The Coach Track

As noted previously, 10 of the 21 athletic directors have coaching experience at the college level, high school level, or both. Although at least seven of these coaches also were athletes prior to becoming a coach (see the athlete track in the previous section), their coaching experience is significant enough to warrant a separate coach career track.

One's coaching experience is likely to play a significant role in the pursuit of a career in college athletics administration for a number of reasons. For example, the experience of working hands on with athletes, assistant coaches, and college athletic administrators can be invaluable. Another reason may be the transferability of leadership skills that are required of both a successful coach and an athletic director. A coach is also likely to have strong network connections to college athletics, which can aid in one's transition into an administrative position. To some extent, the 10 former coaches turned athletic directors likely utilized these aspects in starting their careers in college athletics administration.

The 10 coaches had a wide variety of coaching experiences ranging from a few years to 30+ years. Each of the 10 coaches was able to transition from a coaching position to a college administration position; however, each did so in a slightly different manner. For example, Livengood and Maturi had short-lived coaching careers and made the leap from high school coach to college athletic administrator. Following their coaching careers, they took entry-level positions in college athletics and worked their way up through the athletic departments of multiple schools (similar to the entry-level administration track described later in this chapter). In contrast, Mason and Alvarez had long, distinguished college coaching careers, and both made the transition from coach to college athletics administration later in their careers. For the most part, they started their careers in college athletics administration at a much higher level in comparison to Livengood and Maturi.

If you have coaching experience, or plan to follow the coaching track into college athletics administration, look at the career tracks of Livengood, Love, Barbour, De Carolis, Guenther, Phillip, Maturi, Smith, Curley, and Alvarez. Each provides a unique twist on the coach track, providing insight into how you might try to map your own career path.

The Business Leader Track

The business leader track represents an additional athletic director career track. Kilkenny, Martin, and Burke all obtained extensive experience outside of college sports and established themselves as business leaders. They then were able to make a transition from business leader to college athletics administrator. Each did so in a different manner, so if you are planning to follow the business leader career track, review these individuals carefully.

A business leader will typically have a strong connection with a particular school, and this connection may become an important factor in the person becoming the school's athletic director. This interest could result from a number of reasons; for example, the person could have previously attended the school, the person could live and/or work in the school's community, or the person could know the school's president, chancellor, and/or prominent alumni. Without the aid of previous athletic administration experience, collegiate playing experience, or coaching experience, a business leader is likely to rely on a connection and a strong and established business record to move into college athletics.

Sandy Barbour, director of athletics at the University of California-Berkeley, speaks at a recent National Association of Collegiate Directors of Athletics (NACDA) meeting. Sandy is one of the few female athletic directors of a Bowl Championship Series school.

The Entry-Level Administration Track

Only 2 of the 21 athletic directors (Turner and Hollis) followed a pure entry-level administration track, but the track is a viable path to an AD position, nonetheless. The entry-level administration track is one in which a person without playing or coaching experience obtains an entry-level position within a college athletic department. This person then works his or her way up through the ranks, eventually earning an athletic director position. This type of path requires a great deal of on-the-job training, which may be supplemented with a graduate school education. The person generally takes an entry-level position, such as an internship or a position in a ticket office, to get his or her foot in the door. They stick with it because they find the work to be enjoyable. Over time, they receive promotions, with the likely order of higher-level positions being assistant athletic director, associate athletic director, and then athletic director. Moving into higher positions may require the person to move from school to school to find suitable openings.

Former athletes and coaches, once they get their start in college athletics, may also follow a track similar to the entry-level administration track. They may use their playing/coaching experience to get their foot in the door, but once they are in, they start at the bottom of the athletic department and work their way up. In addition, it's quite possible their playing/coaching experience may result in a speedier ascent to higher positions within an athletic department. Livengood and Maturi are two examples of coaches who followed an entry-level administration track once they got their start in college athletics. Furthermore, Bowlsby, Guerrero, Sterk, Greenspan, and Barta are all former athletes who followed their own variation of the entry-level administration track.

Table 56-1   Career Tracks: New England Small College Athletic Conference (NESCAC) Athletic Directors (As of June 2007)

School: Amherst College
Athletic Director: Suzanne Coffey[1]
Education: Undergraduate: University of New Hampshire (Studio Art)
Graduate: University of Southern Maine (Public Policy)
Career Path
University of New Hampshire:
Coached at UNH for 2 years.
Bowdoin College:
Coached at Bowdoin College for 2 years.
Bates College:
In 1985, was hired by Bates as the school's associate director of athletics, assistant professor of physical education, and head coach of the women's lacrosse team.
Promoted to associate professor in 1985.
Served as interim athletic director in 1990.
Appointed athletic director in 1991.
Amherst College:
Hired as athletic director in 2006.
Notes: Attended UNH on a lacrosse and field hockey scholarship.

School: Bates College
Athletic Director: Kevin McHugh[2]
Education: Undergraduate: Columbia University (Latin American Studies)
Graduate: University of Massachusetts (Sport Management)
Career Path
University of Massachusetts:
While attending graduate school at UMass, served as an assistant wrestling coach and junior varsity football coach.
Yale University:
From 1979 to 1983, served as operations and facilities manager at Yale University.
Bowling Green:
Served as assistant athletic director at Bowling Green for 4 years.
The College of New Jersey:
Hired in 1987 as the school's athletic director.
Also served as executive director for student development and campus programs and was head of the department of campus activities.
Bates College:
In April 2007, named director of athletics and chair of the department of physical education.
A 4-year varsity wrestler at Columbia, McHugh was a two-time captain who twice earned All-Ivy honors at 134 pounds. He was named Columbia's Most Outstanding Wrestler his last 2 years and earned All-American honors from *National Mat News*.
Notes: Was inducted into the National Wrestling Coaches Association Division III Wrestling Hall of Fame as a contributor to the sport.

School: Bowdoin College
Athletic Director: Jeff Ward[3]
Education: Undergraduate: Dartmouth College (American Studies)
Graduate: Columbia University (Higher Education)
Career Path
United States Military Academy at West Point:
Ward was a member of the U.S. Military Academy athletic staff in a variety of positions including personnel oversight for the department.
Served as assistant head coach for the West Point men's swimming team from 1978 to 1982.
Columbia University:
Led the women's swim team as head coach when the program was established in 1982.
Ward was assistant athletic director for eligibility and recruiting from 1986 to 1990.
Also served as assistant director for fund-raising from 1986 to 1987.
Brown University:
Served as assistant director of Brown Athletics from 1990 to 1997.
Bowdoin College:
Hired as the school's athletic director in 1998.
Notes: Was a varsity letter winner in swimming at Dartmouth College.

School: Colby College
Athletic Director: Marcella Zalot[4]
Education: Undergraduate: Smith College (Economics)
Graduate: University of Massachusetts (Sport Management)
Career Path
University of Massachusetts:
While attending UMass, served as a graduate assistant coach in women's basketball.
National Collegiate Athletic Association (NCAA):
Spent 3 years working for the NCAA as an eligibility representative.
Harvard University:
Hired by Harvard in 1992 as an assistant athletic director overseeing compliance issues. She remained at Harvard until 1997.
Colby College:
Arrived at Colby in 1997 to serve as an associate athletics director and senior women's athletics administrator.
Promoted to the athletic director position in 2001.
Notes: While at Smith, Zalot was a goalkeeper on the soccer team that went to the first-ever NCAA Division III women's soccer tournament and was a 1,000-point scorer and 2-year captain in basketball.

1. Coffey Named Athletic Director at Amherst. (2006, June 15). NESCAC. Retrieved November 28, 2007, from http://www.nescac.com/Releases/2005-06/Amherst_Coffey_061506.htm.
2. Kevin McHugh Appointed Director of Athletics at Bates College. (2007, Apr. 16). Bates College. Retrieved November 28, 2007, from http://www.bates.edu/x158175.xml.
3. Bowdoin Names Ward Athletic Director. (1998, Feb. 15). Bowdoin College. Retrieved November 28, 2007, from http://www.bowdoin.edu/news/archives/1bowdoincampus/000498.shtml.
4. Colby Athletic Director Marcella Zalot. (n.d.). Colby College. Retrieved November 28, 2007, from http://www.colby.edu/athletics_cs/staff/ad.cfm.

Table 56-1   Continued

School: Connecticut College
Athletic Director: Francis Shields[5]
Education: Undergraduate: St. Lawrence University
Career Path

Connecticut College:

Served as men's lacrosse coach for 23 years.

Also served as an adjunct professor of physical education.

Named assistant athletic director in 1994.

Appointed athletic director in 2003.

Also holds the title of chair of the physical education department.

Notes: During his senior year at St. Lawrence, earned All-American honors as a lacrosse player.

Inducted into the St. Lawrence University Athletic Hall of Fame in 1994 and the Geneva, New York Sports Hall of Fame in 1997.

School: Hamilton College
Athletic Director: Jon Hind[6]
Education: Undergraduate: Hamilton College (Mathematics and Economics)
Graduate: Kent State University (Athletic Administration)
Career Path

High School Teacher and High School/College Coach:

Taught math and religion at St. Mary's School in Clinton, New York, from 1980 to 1981. During this same time, Hind also served as a part-time assistant coach for football and men's lacrosse at Hamilton.

From 1981 to 1985, Hind was a math instructor and an assistant coach for football, wrestling, and men's lacrosse at Henninger High School (New York).

Returned to Clinton in the fall of 1985 to teach math at Clinton High School and to be an assistant coach for Hamilton's football and lacrosse teams.

College of Wooster:

In 1986, moved to the College of Wooster (D-III) as the school's men's lacrosse coach.

Also served as offensive coordinator and assistant football coach at Wooster.

Butler University:

Started at Butler University in 1991 as the men's lacrosse coach.

Left coaching to become an athletic administrator in 1999.

Assumed management and marketing responsibilities in 2005.

Served as interim athletic director in 2006.

Hind's last position at Butler was associate athletic director for operations.

Hamilton College:

Returned to his alma mater as athletic director in 2007.

Notes: Played lacrosse and football at Hamilton. He was a 4-year letter winner and two-time captain as a defenseman on the lacrosse team, and lettered in football as a sophomore.

School: Middlebury College
Athletic Director: Erin Quinn[7]
Education: Undergraduate: Middlebury College
Graduate: Tufts University (Teaching)
Career Path

Middlebury College:

Began his coaching career at Middlebury, working with the lacrosse and football programs in 1987.

Tufts University:

While completing his graduate degree, Quinn was an assistant coach in lacrosse and football at Tufts.

Lake Forest College:

After 2 years at Tufts, Quinn landed his first head coaching job, heading up the men's lacrosse program at Lake Forest College in Illinois.

Middlebury College:

After 1 year at Lake Forest College, Quinn returned to Middlebury in 1990 as an assistant coach in lacrosse and football.

Named head coach of the lacrosse team in 1991, while still maintaining his football duties.

After leading the lacrosse team for 15 years, Quinn moved in athletics administration. He was appointed the school's athletic director in July 2006.

While attending Middlebury, was a member of the football team.

Notes: Quinn is a five-time winner of the NEILA (New England Intercollegiate Lacrosse Association) Division III Coach of the Year award, earning the College Lacrosse USA Division III National Coach of the Year award in 2001.

Quinn was elected to the New England Lacrosse Hall of Fame in 2003.

School: Trinity College
Athletic Director: Richard Hazleton[8]
Education: Undergraduate: Marietta College (Concentrations in Business, Economics, and History)
Graduate: University of Massachusetts (Sport Management)
Career Path

High School Teacher and Coach:

Taught history and was an assistant football coach at Lancaster High School in Ohio from 1969 to 1973.

Amherst College:

Become the head freshman football coach at Amherst College in 1973.

Trinity College:

In 1974, Hazelton came to Trinity as an assistant professor of physical education, head track and field coach, and assistant football coach.

In 1982, he assumed the duties as the acting associate athletic director when the school's AD took a sabbatical leave; subsequently appointed to the athletic director position on a full-time basis.

In 1989, Hazelton was also awarded the position of professor of physical education.

---

5. Francis J. Shields. (n.d.). Connecticut College. Retrieved November 28, 2007, from http://www.conncoll.edu/academics/web_profiles/shields.html.

6. Hind '80 Named Hamilton College Athletic Director. (2007, Mar. 20). Hamilton College. Retrieved November 28, 2007, from http://www.hamilton.edu/news/more_news/display.cfm?id=11964.

7. Erin Quinn. (n.d.). Middlebury College. Retrieved November 28, 2007, from http://www.middlebury.edu/athletics/staff/admin/quinn.htm.

8. Athletics Staff Information: Richard J. Hazelton. (n.d.). Trinity College. Retrieved November 28, 2007, from http://www.trincoll.edu/athletics/main.aspx?mode=asBio&r_id=2.

Table 56-1   Continued

School: Tufts University
Athletic Director: Bill Gehling[9]
Education: Undergraduate: Tufts University (Child Studies)
Graduate: Tufts University (Education)
Career Path
Tufts University:
Was a volunteer assistant coach for the Tufts men's soccer team while teaching in local schools.

Following the enactment of Title IX in 1979, Gehling was asked to head up a new women's soccer program at Tufts.

Also served as the head golf coach and assistant women's basketball coach.

Spent 12 years as an assistant and associate athletic director for the school.

In 1999, Gehling was named the school's athletic director.

Notes: While attending Tufts, Gehling was twice a New England All-Star and four times a Greater Boston League All-Star in soccer.

School: Wesleyan University
Athletic Director: John Biddiscombe[10,11]
Education: Undergraduate: Springfield College
Graduate: Slippery Rock State University (Education)
Career Path
Wesleyan University:
Began career at Wesleyan in 1974 as a three-sport coach.

Coached the wrestling team from 1974 to 1989.

Named athletic director and chair of the physical education department in 1988.

In addition to his athletic administration duties, Biddiscombe also serves as an adjunct professor.

Notes: Named New England Coach of the Year in 1984 and 1989, and was inducted into the New England Wrestling Hall of Fame in 2004.

School: Williams College
Athletic Director: Harry Sheehy[12]
Education: Undergraduate: Williams College
Career Path
Williams College:
Returned to his alma mater in the fall of 1983 to coach basketball. Served in this position until being named athletic director in 2001.

Notes: Sheehy was a two-time All-American in basketball for Williams College. He later went on to become the all-time leader in rebounds and points for Athletes in Action.

Inducted into the New England Basketball Hall of Fame in 2002.

9. Bill Gehling: Taking Jumbo Pride in Tufts. (n.d.). Tuftonia. Retrieved November 28, 2007, from http://www.tufts.edu/alumni/tuftonia/archives/fall99/newsworthy.shtml.
10. John S. Biddiscombe. (n.d.). Wesleyan. Retrieved November 28, 2007, from http://www.wesleyan.edu/alumni/shasha/2006/speakers.html.
11. Wesleyan Athletics Director John Biddiscombe Inducted into New England College Conference Wrestling Hall of Fame. (2004, Feb. 24). Wesleyan. Retrieved November 28, 2007, from http://www.wesleyan.edu/athletics/sportsinfo/news/staff/newsbiddieneccwahoff0304.html.
12. Williams' Harry Sheehy Named to New England Basketball Hall of Fame Inaugural Class. (2002, July 11). NESCAC. Retrieved November 28, 2007, from http://www.nescac.com/Releases/Williams_SheehyHallofFame.htm.

- In addition to their college coaching experience, Hind and Hazelton also have had experience coaching high school athletes.
- It is important to note that at least 10 of the 14 coaches were also collegiate athletes (analyzed above). Information about the collegiate playing experience of the remaining four former coaches was not readily available.

What type of education do Division III athletic directors have?

- All 19 Division III athletic directors completed a 4-year undergraduate program. Majors included studio art, Latin American studies, American studies, economics, mathematics, business, history, child study, physical education, journalism, government, and English. The diversity in degrees indicates that athletic directors have a variety of educational backgrounds.
  - None of the 19 athletic directors completed a sport management undergraduate program; however, at least two ADs received an undergraduate degree in physical education.
- Sixteen of the 19 Division III athletic directors completed a graduate program. Graduate degrees were received in areas including public policy, sport management, higher education, athletic administration, teaching, education, social sciences, physical education, and business administration. Note that, compared to the undergraduate degrees, the graduate degrees are focused primarily on athletics and administration/education.
  - At least 6 of the 19 Division III athletic directors receiving graduate degrees completed a sport management/athletic administration graduate program (McHugh, Zalot, Hind, Hazelton, Diles, and VanderZwaag).
  - It is important to note that graduate school can be used to refine one's educational background to meet the needs/requirements of an athletic director. A growing number of institutions require or prefer the school's athletic administrators to hold graduate degrees. Consequently, the high number of graduate degrees found in this group of athletic directors reflects the general requirements commonly found in college athletics. This is also consistent with the analysis of FBS athletic directors, which found 17 of 21 athletic directors to have at least one graduate degree.
- Two of the 19 Division III athletic directors completed a doctoral program:
  - Diles received a PhD in education.
  - Weingartner received a PhD in education administration.
- One of the 19 Division III athletic directors (Downes) completed law school. Although a law background can certainly aid an athletic director, it has not been a preferred or common route for Division III ADs.

Table 56-2 Career Tracks: University Athletic Association (UAA) Athletic Directors (As of June 2007)

School: Brandeis University
Athletic Director: Sheryl Sousa[1]
Education: Undergraduate: Brandeis University (American Studies)
Graduate: Binghamton University (Social Sciences)
Career Path
Eastern College Athletics Conference:
Worked as an administrative intern in 1990–1991.
Ithaca College:
Took a position as assistant director of athletics and senior women's administrator.
Binghamton University:
In 1992, Sousa was appointed assistant marketing director and volleyball coach at Binghamton University.
Promoted to associate director of athletics at Binghamton in 1994 and served in that position until 1998.
Served as acting athletic director in 1998.
Brandeis University:
Hired as associate athletic director and women's volleyball coach in 1998.
Promoted to athletic director in 2004.
Notes: Was a 4-year letter winner at Brandeis in softball and volleyball, serving as captain of both teams in both her junior and senior years.

School: Carnegie Mellon University
Athletic Director: Susan Bassett[2]
Education: Undergraduate: Ithaca College (Physical Education)
Graduate: Indiana University (Physical Education)
Career Path
William Smith College:
Began her athletic career as head swimming and diving coach at William Smith College. She was also an assistant lacrosse and field hockey coach.
Union College:
Served as the head men's and women's swimming coach at Union College.
William Smith College:
Returned to William Smith as the school's director of athletics. She served in this capacity for 10 years.
During her time at William Smith, Bassett was also an associate professor of physical education at the coordinate colleges of Hobart and William Smith.
Carnegie Mellon University:
Named Carnegie Mellon University's director of athletics, physical education, and recreation in July 2005.
Notes: Became a member of the Ithaca College Athletic Hall of Fame in 2005.
Elected to the Union College Athletic Hall of Fame in 2006.

School: Case Western Reserve University
Athletic Director: Dave Diles[3]
Education: Undergraduate: Ohio University (Journalism)
Graduate: Ohio University (Sports Administration)
PhD: University of Michigan (Education)
Career Path
New England Patriots (NFL):
Worked as a marketing intern for the Patriots in 1984.
New York Jets (NFL):
Worked as the team's assistant director of public relations.
University of Michigan:
Was an administrative assistant at the University of Michigan from 1985 to 1987.
Dexter Community Schools:
From 1987 to 1989, served as the director of athletics at Dexter Community Schools.
Central Michigan University:
He was hired as an assistant athletic director in 1989 and served in this capacity until 1991.
Auburn University:
Served as an assistant athletic director at Auburn from 1991 to 1994.
St. Bonaventure University:
Worked at St. Bonaventure from 1994 to 1999, serving as the school's athletic director.
Central Michigan University:
Hired as the school's athletic director in 1999, staying in this role until 2005.
Case Western Reserve University:
Named the school's athletic director in April 2006.
Notes: Son of longtime national sports broadcaster and writer Dave Diles, Sr.

School: University of Chicago
Athletic Director: Tom Weingartner[4]
Education: Undergraduate: Stanford University
Graduate: Northwestern University
PhD: Northwestern University (Education Administration)
Career Path
Northwestern University:
Began his college athletics career at Northwestern University, where he served as director of intramural, recreational, and club sports from 1974 to 1979.
St. Mary's College (MD):
From 1979 to 1985, served as the athletics director and an assistant professor of human development at St. Mary's.
Manhattanville College:
Served as athletic director and associate professor of human development at Manhattanville (NY) College from 1985 to 1990.
University of Chicago:
Hired as the school's athletic director in 1990.
Notes: Was a linebacker on the Stanford football team.

1. Sousa '90 Named Director of Athletics. (2004, May 19). Brandeis. Retrieved November 28, 2007, from http://my.brandeis.edu/news/item?news_item_id=102756&show_release_date=1.
2. Susan Bassett—Director of Athletics. (n.d.). Carnegie Mellon. Retrieved November 28, 2007, from http://www.cmu.edu/athletics/staff/sbassett.html.
3. Case Attracts New Athletic Director from Division I. (2005, Apr. 26). Case Western Reserve University. Retrieved November 28, 2007, from http://www.case.edu/athletics/varsity/news/2004-05/pr4_26_05.htm.
4. Information obtained via e-mail from the University of Chicago Sports Information Office.

Table 56-2   Continued

School: Emory University
Athletic Director: Tim Downes[5]
Education: Undergraduate: Dartmouth College (Government and English)
Law School: Washington and Lee School of Law
Career Path
Washington and Lee University:
While attending law school, served as assistant coach for the lacrosse and soccer programs.
Also served as a student representative on the University Athletic Committee.
Patriot League:
From 1993 to 1995, worked in the Patriot League office as assistant executive director for compliance and championships.
Johns Hopkins University:
Served as associate athletic director at Johns Hopkins University in Baltimore, MD from 1995 to 1999.
California Institute of Technology:
From 1999 to 2004, served as director of athletics, physical education, and recreation at Caltech.
Southern California Intercollegiate Athletic Conference:
In addition to his Caltech duties, Downes served as the first commissioner for the Southern California Intercollegiate Athletic Conference from 2001 to 2004.
Franklin and Marshall College:
Served as the school's athletic director from 2004 to 2007.
Emory University:
Appointed Emory University's director of athletics and recreation in July 2007.
Notes: Was a 4-year starter on the Dartmouth lacrosse team and was named to the All–New England team as a senior.

School: New York University
Athletic Director: Christopher Bledsoe[6]
Education: Undergraduate: Fairfield University
Graduate: Pace University (MBA)
Career Path
Pace University:
Upon graduating from Fairfield, Bledsoe joined the Pace athletics staff in 1980 as an assistant to the director.
Subsequently served as assistant athletic director and sports information director.
Promoted to director of athletics and intramurals in 1988; served in this capacity until 1996.
Earned his MBA from Pace in 1992.
During his years at Pace, Bledsoe also served as chair of the New York Collegiate Athletic Conference (NYCAC), and as president of the Mideast Collegiate Conference, the Liberty Football Conference, and the Big Apple Basketball Conference.
New York University:
Became New York University's director of athletics, intramurals, and recreation in September 1996.

School: University of Rochester
Athletic Director: George VanderZwaag[7]
Education: Undergraduate: Trinity College (Economics)
Graduate: University of Massachusetts (Sport Management)
Career Path
University of Massachusetts:
At UMass, VanderZwaag was a research assistant and graduate assistant in the athletic business office.
Tulane University:
From 1989 to 1991, served as an assistant to the athletic director for student services and operations at Tulane.
Princeton University:
Named assistant athletic director at Princeton in 1991.
In 1995, promoted to associate director of athletics. Within 2 years, was promoted to the position of senior associate director of athletics.
University of Rochester:
Hired in 1991 as the school's director of athletics and recreation.
Notes: Played varsity football while attending college, and was a member of the Trinity golf team.

School: Washington University (St. Louis)
Athletic Director: John Schael[8]
Education: Undergraduate: Miami University of Ohio (Physical Education)
Graduate: Miami University of Ohio (Administration and Physical Education)
Career Path
University of Chicago:
Worked at the University of Chicago from 1968 to 1978 as the school's wrestling coach.
Also served as the associate director of physical education and athletics from 1974 to 1978.
Washington University (St. Louis):
Hired by Washington in 1978 as the school's athletic director; has held the position for 30 years.
Notes: While attending Miami, lettered 4 years in wrestling and 1 year in baseball.
Inducted into Miami's Sports Hall of Fame in 1983.
Inducted into Washington University's Sports Hall of Fame in 2006

---

5. Tim Downes, Director of Athletics and Recreation. (n.d.). Emory Athletics. Retrieved November 28, 2007, from http://www.go.emory.edu/Coach_Bios/Staff/Downes.html.
6. Athletics Directory, Christopher Bledsoe. (n.d.). NYU Athletics. Retrieved November 28, 2007, from http://www.nyu.edu/athletics/directory/4.

7. VanderZwaag Named Director of Athletics and Recreation. (1999, Mar. 24). Rochester Athletics. Retrieved November 28, 2007, from http://www.rochester.edu/news/show.php?id=215.
8. John Schael, Director of Athletics. (n.d.). Washington University. Retrieved November 28, 2007, from http://bearsports.wustl.edu/staff/schael.html.

How did the Division III athletic directors begin their careers?

Subsequent to any collegiate playing career, the 19 Division III athletic directors began their careers in a variety of manners, as follows:

- Fourteen athletic directors started out coaching:
  - Hind started out as an assistant college coach and high school teacher.
  - Gehling started out as a volunteer assistant college coach and local school teacher.
  - Hazelton started out as an assistant high school coach and teacher.
  - Coffey, McHugh, Ward, Zalot, Shields, Quinn, Biddiscombe, Sheehy, Bassett, Downes, and Schael started out as college coaches at various levels (i.e., graduate assistant coach, assistant coach, or head coach).
- Four athletic directors started out in entry-level administration positions within college athletics:
  - Weingartner, Bledsoe, and VanderZwaag got their start at the school level.
  - Sousa got her start at the conference level.
- One athletic director, Diles, got his start working as an intern for the New England Patriots (NFL). He spent less than 2 years working in professional sports before transitioning into college athletics administration.

Do Division III athletic directors have nonsports business experience?

None of the 19 Division III athletic directors has significant nonsports business experience. Although many business skills are transferable to the college environment, obtaining extensive nonsports business experience has not been a common career path for Division III athletic directors.

The 19 athletic directors also appear to have very little sports experience outside of college athletics (i.e., experience working for professional teams, sports marketing agencies, etc.).

How many colleges has the typical Division III athletic director worked for during his or her career?

- On average, each Division III athletic director has worked for 2.95 different colleges during his or her career. Diles and Downes lead the pack, working for five schools each.
  - The high number of average schools indicates a need to be mobile in order to advance one's career. For instance, if a person is ready to move from an assistant AD position to an associate AD position (or possibly even an AD position), this often requires a move to a school with an opening at that level.

- It appears that 4 of the 19 Division III athletic directors (Shields, Gehling, Biddiscombe, and Sheehy) have worked exclusively for one college. It is important to note that Shields, Biddiscombe, and Sheehy all had extensive coaching careers at their respective schools and made the transition into college athletics administration later in their careers.

Do Division III athletic directors get more than one opportunity to be an athletic director?

- On average, each Division III athletic director has held 1.47 athletic director positions in his or her career. Diles, Weingartner, and Downes have each held three AD positions.
- Twelve of the 19 athletic directors have held only one AD position.
- Although more than half of the athletic directors have held only one AD position, there does appear to be an opportunity to hold more than one AD position during one's career.

IS THERE A PATTERN IN THE CAREER TRACKS?

Three viable career tracks stand out from the analysis of the Division III athletic directors—the "athlete track," the "coach track," and the "entry-level administration track." These tracks are all similar in nature to the FBS athletic director tracks discussed in Chapter 55. Notably absent: none of the Division III athletic directors in the sample of 19 followed the "business leader" track discussed in that chapter. This is not to say a business leader could not make the transition from the business world into a Division III athletic director position, however. In addition, the "alumni connection" noted in Chapter 55 also is present in this group of Division III athletic directors.

The Athlete Track

At least 14 of the 19 Division III athletic directors are former college athletes. The career tracks of these 13 individuals provide examples of how an athlete can work to become an athletic director. Specifically, the career tracks of Sousa, Weingartner, and VanderZwaag provide examples of how one can make the transition from athlete to athletic director, without being a coach. In addition, the career tracks of McHugh, Ward, Zalot, Shields, Hind, Quinn, Gehling, Coffey, Sheehy, Downes, and Schael provide examples of how one can make the transition first from athlete to coach, and then from coach to athletic director.

The path that former athletes can take to obtain an athletic director position was previously discussed in Chapter 55, in conjunction with the analysis of FBS athletic directors. Review this information for more details about the athlete track.

Table 57-1   Career Tracks: NCAA Football Bowl Subdivision (FBS) Conference Commissioners (As of August 2007)

Conference: Atlantic Coast Conference (ACC)
Commissioner: John Swofford[1]
Education: Undergraduate: University of North Carolina
Graduate: Ohio University (Athletics Administration)
Career Path
University of Virginia:
Began as an intern at UVA.
Hired as UVA's athletic ticket manager and assistant to the director of athletic facilities and finance in the fall of 1973.
University of North Carolina:
Returned to UNC in May 1976 as assistant athletic director and business manager.
Named executive vice president of the educational foundation in 1979.
Became UNC's athletic director in May 1980, at the age of 31 (youngest major college AD at the time).
Atlantic Coast Conference:
Appointed commissioner of the ACC in 1997.
Notes: Two-time all-state football player and three-sport MVP in football, basketball, and track at Wilkes Central High School.
Played quarterback and defensive back for North Carolina from 1969 to 1971.

Conference: Big 12 Conference
Commissioner: Dan Beebe[2]
Education: Undergraduate: Cal Poly Pomona (Social Science)
Law School: University of California Hastings College
Career Path
NCAA:
Worked as an NCAA enforcement representative from 1982 to 1986.
Wichita State:
Hired as assistant director of athletics at Wichita State in 1986.
NCAA:
Worked as NCAA director of enforcement from 1987 to 1989.
Ohio Valley Conference:
Hired as commissioner of the Ohio Valley Conference in 1989; worked in this capacity for 14 years.
Big 12:
Hired as senior associate commissioner and chief operating officer of the Big 12 in 2003.
Named commissioner in 2007.
Notes: Lettered in football and was a team captain at Cal Poly Pomona.

Conference: Big East Conference
Commissioner: Michael Tranghese[3]
Education: Undergraduate: St. Michael's College (VT)
Career Path
American International College:
Career in college athletics began at American International College in the mid 1960s.
Providence College:
During the 1970s, he was the sports information director at Providence College.
Big East Conference:
In 1979, he helped establish the Big East Conference, becoming the conference's first full-time employee.
Served as associate commissioner of the Big East until 1990 when he assumed commissioner duties.
Notes:
Member of the St. Michael's golf team from 1962 to 1965.
Served as the basketball team's manager while attending St. Michael's.

Conference: Big Ten Conference
Commissioner: James Delany[4]
Education: Undergraduate: University of North Carolina (Political Science)
Law School: University of North Carolina
Career Path
Legal Experience:
After earning his law degree, served as counsel for the North Carolina Senate Judiciary Committee from 1973 to 1974, and was staff attorney for the North Carolina Justice Department from 1974 to 1975.
NCAA:
College athletics administration career began at the NCAA where he was employed as an enforcement representative from 1975 to 1979.
Ohio Valley Conference:
From 1979 to 1989, served as commissioner of the Ohio Valley Conference.
Big Ten Conference:
In 1989, Delany was appointed commissioner of the Big Ten.
Notes:
Member of the North Carolina varsity basketball team from 1967 to 1970. Served as team captain during his senior year.

Conference: Conference USA
Commissioner: Britton Banowsky[5]
Education: Undergraduate: University of Oklahoma (Business)
Law School: University of Oklahoma
Career Path
Legal Experience:
From 1986 to 1989, operated a private law practice.
Southland Conference:
From 1989 to 1991, worked as assistant commissioner of the Southland Conference.
Southwest Conference
From 1991 to 1993, worked as assistant commissioner of the Southwest Conference.
Southland Conference:
Returned to the Southland Conference in 1993 as the commissioner. Worked in this capacity until 1996.
Big 12 Conference:
In 1996, hired as the associate commissioner and general counsel for the Big 12 Conference.
Conference USA:
Appointed commissioner of Conference USA in 2002.

Conference: Mid-American Conference
Commissioner: Rick Chryst[6]
Education: Undergraduate: University of Notre Dame (Economics). Law School: Duke University
Career Path
United States Naval Academy:
Worked 3 years as the assistant sports information director at the United States Naval Academy in Annapolis, MD (1983–1986)
Duke University:
Following stint at Annapolis, entered Duke University School of Law.
Southwest Conference:
First entered conference administration with the Southwest Conference upon graduation from law school in May 1989.
Joined the ACC in May 1992.
Atlantic Coast Conference:
Worked 7 years as assistant commissioner with the ACC.
Responsible for marketing, television, corporate programs, legal affairs, special events, and community outreach programs.
Mid-American Conference:
Left the ACC for the MAC in 1999, where he was appointed commissioner.
Notes: Played baseball while attending Notre Dame. Father, George, was a long-time high school and college football coach and administrator in Wisconsin.
Chryst has two brothers working in football. Paul is the offensive co-coordinator at Wisconsin, and George (Geep) is the offensive quality control coach for the Carolina Panthers.
Geep has also coached professionally in the NFL with Arizona, Chicago, and San Diego.

Table 57-1 Continued

Conference: Mountain West Conference
Commissioner: Craig Thompson[7]
Education: Undergraduate: University of Minnesota (Journalism)
Career Path

Kansas State University:
Worked from 1978 to 1980 as assistant sports information director at Kansas State University.

Kansas City Kings:
Hired by the Kansas City Kings as director of public relations and promotions in 1980; worked in this capacity until 1983.

Metro Conference:
Transitioned back into college athletics administration in 1983, working for the Metro Conference as director of communications until 1987.

American South Conference:
Hired as commissioner in 1987; served in this capacity until 1991.

Sun Belt Conference:
Took over as commissioner of the Sun Belt Conference in 1991.

Mountain West Conference:
Hired to be the first commissioner of the newly formed Mountain West Conference in 1998.

Conference: Pacific-10 Conference
Commissioner: Thomas Hansen[8]
Education: Undergraduate: University of Washington
Career Path

Vancouver Columbian:
Worked as a sports reporter on the staff of the *Vancouver (WA) Columbian* from 1959 to 1960.

Pac-10 Conference:
Transitioned into the world of college athletics, moving to the Pac-10 Conference as public relations director in 1960; worked in this capacity for 7 years.

NCAA:
Hired by the NCAA in 1967 as the director of public relations.
Promoted to assistant executive director in 1971. Significant duties included being director of the NCAA football television program for 11 years, administrator of the NCAA Division I Basketball Tournament for 2 years, director of governmental affairs, administrator for the Committee on Women's Athletics, and director of media relations for many NCAA events.

Pac-10 Conference:
Returned to the Pac-10 in 1983 as conference commissioner.

Conference: Southeastern Conference (SEC)
Commissioner: Mike Slive[9]
Education: Undergraduate: Dartmouth College
Graduate: Georgetown (Masters in Law)
Law School: University of Virginia
Career Path

Dartmouth College:
Assistant director of athletics at Dartmouth College from 1968 to 1969.

Noncollege Athletics Law Experience:
Partner at Stebbins & Bradley, Hanover, NH, from 1969 to 1977.
Judge of Hanover (NH) District Court from 1972 to 1977.
Judicial master and clerk of Grafton County (NH) Superior Court from 1977 to 1979.

Pac-10 Conference:
Returned to college athletics, serving as the assistant executive director of the Pac-10 Conference from 1979 to 1981.

Cornell University:
Served as director of athletics for Cornell University from 1981 to 1983.

Noncollege Athletics Law Experience:
Founded the law offices of Michael L. Slive, located in Hanover, NH (1983–1986).
From 1986 to 1991, was a partner at Coffield, Ungaretti, & Harris (Chicago, IL).
From 1990 to 1991, Slive was also a senior partner and founder of Slive-Glazier Sports Group, located in Chicago, IL, and Kansas City, MS.

Great Midwest Conference:
Hired as commissioner of the Great Midwest Conference in 1991. Served in this capacity until 1995.

Conference USA:
Held the commissioner position for Conference USA from 1995 to 2002.

Southeastern Conference:
Hired in 2002 as commissioner of the SEC.

1. ACC Commissioner John Swofford. (n.d.). Atlantic Coast Conference. Retrieved November 12, 2007, from http://www.theacc.com/this-is/commissioner.html.

2. Dan Beebe Commissioner. (n.d.). Big 12 Conference. Retrieved November 12, 2007, from http://www.big12sports.com/aboutbig12/commissioner.html.

3. Big East Conference Staff. (n.d.). Big East Conference. Retrieved November 12, 2007, from http://www.bigeast.org/ViewArticle.dbml?&DB_OEM_ID=19400&ATCLID=1150051.

4. James E. Delany, Commissioner Big Ten Conference. (n.d.). Big Ten Conference. Retrieved November 12, 2007, from http://bigten.cstv.com/school-bio/delany-bio.html.

5. Commissioner Britton Banowsky. (n.d.). Conference USA. Retrieved November 12, 2007, from http://conferenceusa.cstv.com/ot/c-usa-banowsky.html.

6. Rick Chryst, Commissioner. (n.d.). Mid-Atlantic Conference. Retrieved November 12, 2007, from http://mac-sports.com/ViewArticle.dbml?DB_OEM_ID=9400&KEY=&ATCLID=323244.

7. Craig Thompson Profile. (n.d.). Mountain West Conference. Retrieved November 12, 2007, from http://themwc.cstv.com/staff/thompson.html.

8. Thomas C. Hansen Profile. (n.d.). Pac-10 Conference. Retrieved November 12, 2007, from http://www.pac-10.org/genrel/hansen_thomasc00.html.

9. Slive Named Southeastern Conference Commissioner. (2002, July 2). Southeastern Conference. Retrieved November 12, 2007, from http://www.secsports.com/new/local/commissioner_070202.

Table 57-1   Continued

Conference: Sunbelt Conference
Commissioner: Wright Waters[10]
Education: Undergraduate: Livingston University (Physical Education)
Graduate: Livingston University (Secondary Education)
Career Path
Livingston University:
Began his career in athletics as the head trainer and student assistant football coach at Livingston from 1972 to 1974.
Southern Mississippi University:
Served one season as an assistant trainer and equipment manager.
Vincent, AL, High School:
Worked one year as a teacher and football coach.
Southern Mississippi University:
In 1976, returned to Southern Mississippi as administrative assistant and academic director; served in this capacity until 1979.
University of Florida:
Hired as assistant athletic director in 1979. Worked in this capacity at UF until 1983.
University of Louisiana at Lafayette:
Worked as associate athletic director from 1983 to 1984.
Tulane University:
Worked as associate athletic director from 1984 to 1989.
Southeastern Conference:
Hired as assistant commissioner in 1989.
Southern Conference:
Named conference commissioner in 1991. Served as commissioner for 7 years.
Crimson Tide Sports Marketing:
Hired as general manager in 1998; worked for Crimson Tide Sports Marketing for 1 year.
Sunbelt Conference:
Appointed commissioner in 1999.

Conference: Western Athletic Conference (WAC)
Commissioner: Karl Benson[11]
Education: Undergraduate: Spokane Falls Community College and Boise State University (Physical Education)
Graduate: University of Utah (Athletics Administration)
Career Path
Fort Steilacoom Community College:
Served as baseball coach for 8 years.
Held the director of athletics position from 1979 to 1984.
University of Utah:
From 1984 to 1986, was an assistant baseball coach and an administrative assistant in the athletics department.
NCAA:
Joined the NCAA staff in 1986 as a compliance representative and was appointed assistant director of championships in 1987.
Promoted to director of championships in 1990.
Mid-American Conference:
Served as conference commissioner for 4 years (1990–1994).
Western Athletic Conference:
Appointed WAC commissioner in 1994.
Notes: Played baseball at both Spokane Falls Community College and Boise State University.

10. Wright Waters, Commissioner. (n.d.). Sunbelt Conference. Retrieved November 12, 2007, from http://www.sunbeltsports.org/ViewArticle.dbml?SPSID=22248&SPID=1817&DB_OEM_ID=4100&ATCLID=156835.
11. Karl Benson, WAC Commissioner. (n.d.). Western Athletic Conference. Retrieved November 12, 2007 from http://www.wacsports.com/ViewArticle.dbml?DB_OEM_ID=10100&KEY=&ATCLID=537091.

What type of education do FBS conference commissioners have?

- All 11 FBS conference commissioners have an undergraduate degree. Majors included social science, political science, business, economics, journalism, and physical education. The variety of degrees provides an indication that many different educational backgrounds can prepare someone for graduate school, because most FBS conference commissioners have a graduate degree.
- At least 8 of the 11 FBS commissioners hold some type of advanced degree:
  - Three commissioners hold master's degrees, four hold law degrees, and one holds both a master's degree and a law degree.
  - The four master's degrees include 1 masters of law, 1 masters of secondary education, and 2 masters of athletic administration.
- Education is an integral component of college athletics. As such, it is becoming more common for high-level college athletics administrators to hold advanced degrees. The high number of advanced degrees found

in this group of FBS conference commissioners reflects this.

How did current FBS conference commissioners get their start?

- Current FBS conference commissioners had a variety of starting positions in their professional careers:
  - Three commissioners (Tranghese, Chryst, and Thompson) started in a school's sports information department.
  - Two commissioners (Delaney and Banowsky) started out as lawyers in private practice.
  - Two commissioners (Waters and Benson) started out as a trainer or trainer/coach.
  - One commissioner (Beebe) started out working for the NCAA in enforcement.
  - One commissioner (Swofford) started out as an intern in college athletics.
  - One commissioner (Hansen) started out as a reporter.
- This demonstrates there are many different starting points for the people who are conference commissioners.

How many FBS conference commissioners worked as an athletic director or assistant athletic director?

- Of the 11 current FBS conference commissioners, three served as an athletic director prior to becoming a conference commissioner. This includes Benson, who served as an athletic director at a community college. Only two commissioners have experience as an NCAA athletic director—Swofford at the University of North Carolina and Slive at Cornell University.

    In addition, two FBS conference commissioners (Beebe and Waters) had previous assistant and/or associate athletic director experience prior to becoming a conference commissioner.

    This means that 5 out of the 11 current FBS conference commissioners had at least some athletic director or assistant/associate athletic director experience prior to being named conference commissioner. This represents 45% of the group.

How many FBS conference commissioners worked as an associate or assistant commissioner prior to becoming the commissioner?

- Six of the 11 current FBS conference commissioners (Beebe, Tranghese, Banowsky, Chryst, Slive, and Waters) worked at a conference office as either an associate commissioner or an assistant commissioner prior to becoming a commissioner.

- Of these six commissioners, three (Tranghese, Banowsky, and Chryst) had no previous athletic director or assistant/associate athletic director experience. This means that, in total, 8 out of the 11 commissioners (73%) did at least one of the following: worked as an athletic director, worked as an assistant or associate athletic director, or worked as an assistant or associate commissioner.

What about the other three FBS conference commissioners? What type of experiences do they have?

- The three FBS commissioners with no previous athletic director, assistant/associate athletic director, or assistant/associate commissioner experience are Delany, Thompson, and Hansen. Of this group, both Delaney and Hansen have significant experience working for the NCAA (Delaney in enforcement, Hansen in public relations). Thompson also brings considerable public relations experience, having worked for the NBA's Kansas City Kings (the only professional sports experience in the group) and the Metro Conference (as the director of communications).

- It should also be pointed out that in addition to Delaney and Hansen, Beebe and Benson also have significant NCAA experience. Beebe worked in enforcement, while Benson worked in both compliance and championships.

This means 4 out of the 11 commissioners, or 36%, worked for the NCAA at some point during their career.

Do FBS conference commissioners have extensive non-sports, business experience?

- Only three FBS conference commissioners appear to have significant work experience outside of the sports industry:
    - Delany, Banowsky, and Slive all gained nonsports legal experience prior to starting their careers in the sports industry.

Do FBS conference commissioners get more than one opportunity to be a conference commissioner?

- Seven of the 11 FBS commissioners have held more than one conference commissioner post, although only two (Slive and Benson) have been commissioner of more than one FBS conference. The other five (Banowsky, Beebe, Delany, Thompson, and Waters) served as commissioners of smaller conferences prior to obtaining their position as head of an FBS conference. Working as commissioner of a smaller conference can be viewed as good experience leading to a larger conference.

- It should be noted that both Thompson and Slive have each held three commissioner positions, while Beebe, Delaney, Banowsky, Waters, and Benson have each held two such posts.

IS THERE A PATTERN IN THE CAREER TRACKS?

The path toward an FBS conference commissioner position is typically long. On average, it took 11 years of work for each commissioner to obtain his or her *first* commissioner position, and 21 years of work to obtain his or her first *FBS conference* commissioner position. Although each of the commissioners took a slightly different path, all 11 FBS conference commissioners have one thing in common— they obtained their current position by working their way up through the ranks of college athletics administration. Some did so primarily at the school level, whereas others developed at the conference level. Also important, working directly for the NCAA played a significant developmental role for a few commissioners. These common trends can be summarized into the following career tracks—the "school" track, the "conference" track, the "school-conference" track, and the "NCAA" track.

The School Track

The school track can best be summarized as an individual who develops his or her skills and abilities at the school level, prior to making the transition into conference-level work. This can be accomplished in a number of different ways; for example, someone may spend time working as an athletic director at the school level before taking a conference commissioner position. Significant steps in one's development at the school level are likely to include assistant athletic director, associate athletic director, and athletic director positions.

Individuals following this track can make the transition from the school level to an FBS conference in one or two moves. The one-move process would include a direct jump from the school level to an FBS conference; the two-move process would first include a move to a smaller, non-FBS conference followed by a move from the non-FBS conference to an FBS conference. The career tracks of Swofford, Slive, and Waters are good examples of commissioners who followed a variation of the school track.

If you have an interest in the school track, you should also review the career tracks for athletic directors in Chapters 55 and 56. This will provide additional insight into how one can obtain an athletic director position, which can then be helpful in applying for a conference commissioner position.

The Conference Track

The conference track can best be summarized as an individual who developed his or her skills and abilities at lower-level conference positions prior to obtaining an FBS conference commissioner position. It is likely such individuals spent time as assistant or associate conference commissioners. In addition, these individuals may have previously worked as a conference commissioner at a smaller, non-FBS conference. The career track of Banowsky provides insight into how one can make the transition from an entry-level conference position into an FBS conference commissioner position.

The School-Conference Track

One's development does not need to be isolated solely to either a school or a conference. As a result, a hybrid school-conference track resulting from a combination of the school track and the conference track is also a possibility. Someone following such a track may have spent the early portion of his or her career at the school level, working his or her way up to a mid-level position. This person may have then made a lateral move from a school to a conference, moving from

one mid-level position to another. In such cases, the person's development process continues at the conference level. Tranghese, Chryst, and Thompson all started out at the school level and then made the transition to mid-level conference administration. Their career tracks provide good examples of the school-conference track.

The NCAA Track

Four of the 11 FBS conference commissioners spent time working directly for the NCAA. They then used this experience to land a conference commissioner position. The career tracks of Hansen and Benson demonstrate how one can make the transition from the NCAA directly into an FBS conference commissioner position. Beebe and Delany also made the leap from the NCAA to an FBS conference commissioner position, but they first held commissioner positions at smaller conferences before obtaining a commissioner position at an FBS conference. Review these career tracks to learn more about the impact that working at the NCAA can have on one's career in college athletics administration.

CREATING YOUR OWN TRACK

Although the analysis of the career tracks of the 11 FBS conference commissioners does not result in one *ideal* path to follow, it does provide multiple options. If you are interested in working as a conference commissioner at the FBS level, consider starting out in the athletic department at the school level, taking an entry-level position at the conference level, or obtaining a position at the NCAA. The success of the 11 FBS conference commissioners analyzed in this chapter demonstrates that any one of these paths can lead to this position.

A separate analysis has been conducted in Chapter 58 on commissioners of NCAA Football Championship Subdivision (FCS) conferences. Many FBS conference commissioners previously held commissioner positions at FCS conferences, so this information provides additional guidance in helping one to develop a career plan. The career tracks of FCS conference commissioners are similar to the career tracks discussed in this chapter.

CHAPTER FIFTY-EIGHT

NCAA Football Championship Subdivision Conference Commissioners

There are currently 15 NCAA Football Championship Subdivision (FCS) conferences led by 14 conference commissioners (the Missouri Valley Football Conference and Pioneer Football League share a commissioner). You can learn more about the duties and responsibilities of conference commissioners in Chapter 73. Furthermore, information about the NCAA and the make-up of its divisions can be found in Chapter 29.

   Table 58-1 provides the educational background and work experiences for all 14 FCS conference commissioners as of August 2007. The information was obtained from conference websites, media guides, articles in the popular press, and interviews. The information is as accurate and complete as these sources, and provides a general idea of how current conference commissioners came to obtain such high level positions. The purpose of the table and accompanying analysis is to provide ideas and insight on what a conference commissioner's career path might look like. This can then be used by someone hoping to become a conference commissioner to map out a potential career plan of his or her own. Note that a separate analysis of FBS conference commissioners can be found in Chapter 57.

BACKGROUNDS OF CURRENT FCS CONFERENCE COMMISSIONERS

What is the current make-up of conference commissioners at the FCS level? The following analysis provides some insight into answering this question.

How many FCS conference commissioners had a significant athletic career?

- At least 5 of the 14 FCS conference commissioners (Fullerton, Grom, Thomas, Steinbrecher, and Sharp)

participated in collegiate athletics. This represents about 36% of the group. In comparison, 54% of FBS conference commissioners are former athletes.

- None of the 14 FCS conference commissioners appears to have had a significant professional sports career.

- Although it is not a job *requirement* to have previous playing experience at the college level, such playing experience does seem to provide some benefit to people looking to work in college athletics. This benefit may come from first-hand knowledge gained during the person's athletic playing career, or it may come from networking opportunities with coaches, college administrators, and alumni.

How many FCS conference commissioners have coaching experience?

- It appears that only three FCS commissioners have previous coaching experience:

  - Fullerton coached at both the high school and college levels.

  - Thomas and Femovich coached at the college level.

What type of education do FCS conference commissioners have?

- All 14 FCS conference commissioners have an undergraduate degree. Majors include mathematics, physical education, journalism, communications, and Afro-American studies. The variety of degrees provides an indication that many different educational backgrounds can prepare someone for graduate school.

Table 58-1   Career Tracks: NCAA Football Championship Subdivision Conference Commissioners (As of August 2007)

Conference: Big Sky Conference
Commissioner: Doug Fullerton[1]
Education: Undergraduate: California Western University (Mathematics)
Graduate: Montana State University (Higher Education)
Career Path
High School Teaching and Coaching:
Worked in 1971 as a teacher and coach at Ennis High School.
In 1972, moved to Bozeman High School as a teacher and coach.
Montana State University:
Began his career at MSU in 1978; held various positions in the athletic department (including assistant basketball coach).
Appointed to assistant athletic director in 1981.
Named MSU athletic director in 1984.
Big Sky Conference:
Hired as conference commissioner in 1995.
Notes: While at California Western, was a three-time letter winner in baseball and two-time letter winner in basketball.

Conference: Big South Conference
Commissioner: Kyle Kallander[2]
Education: Undergraduate: University of Washington (Physical Education)
Graduate: University of Washington (Kinesiology)
Career Path
Seattle Seahawks (NFL):
Began career as a public relations assistant for the Seahawks.
Uniprint Printing Co.:
Served as sports coordinator at Uniprint Printing from 1983 to 1985.
University of Washington:
During his 7 years at Washington, worked as director of advertising and promotions and director of compliance (1985–1992).
Southwest Conference:
Hired by the Southwest Conference in 1992 as assistant commissioner.
Promoted to commissioner in 1995.
Big South Conference:
Named Big South commissioner in 1996.

Conference: Colonial Athletic Association (CAA)
Commissioner: Tom Yeager[3]
Education: Undergraduate: Springfield College, Mass.
Graduate: attended graduate school, but information on specific school could not be found
Career Path
Pregraduate School:
Prior to attending graduate school, Yeager served as a youth athletic director. He decided to attend graduate school with the hope of becoming a college athletics administrator.
NCAA:
Following graduate school, was hired to work in the NCAA's enforcement department in 1976.
Promoted in 1981 to the position of assistant director of legislative services.
In 1984, named director of legislative services.
Colonial Athletic Conference:
Hired as the conference's first commissioner in 1985.

Conference: Missouri Valley Football Conference
Commissioner: Patty Viverito[4]
Education: Undergraduate: Northern Illinois University
Graduate: University of Massachusetts (Sport Management)
Career Path
University of Texas:
Started out as special project director at UT in 1979.
Tidewater Tides (Minor League Baseball):
Worked in minor league baseball as an account executive with the Tidewater Tides starting in 1981.
Gateway Conference:
Hired as conference commissioner in 1982.
Missouri Valley Conference:
Hired by the Missouri Valley Conference in 1988 as a senior associate commissioner (championships, compliance); currently holds this position today.
Pioneer Football League:
Hired as conference commissioner in 1994; currently holds this position today.
Notes: Currently works for two conferences:
The Pioneer Football League (commissioner)
The Missouri Valley Conference (senior associate commissioner)
Husband, Frank, is the president and director of the St. Louis Sports Commission.

Conference: Great West Football Conference
Commissioner: Ed Grom[5]
Education: Undergraduate: University of Kansas (Journalism)
Career Path
Big Eight Conference (currently the Big 12 Conference):
Worked as an assistant on the league's service bureau.
University of Missouri–Kansas City:
Worked in sports information for 5 years.
Promoted to assistant athletic director.
Served as interim athletic director in 1998–1999.
Mid-Continent Conference (now the Summit League):
Hired in 1999; currently serves as an associate commissioner.
Great West Football Conference:
Hired in 2006 as conference commissioner.
Notes: Currently works for two conferences:
Great West Football Conference (commissioner)
The Summit League (associate commissioner)
While at Kansas, played on the Jayhawk golf squad, was the summer sports editor for the *University Daily Kansan*, and worked as a stringer for the *Wichita Eagle-Beacon*.

Conference: Ivy League
Commissioner: Jeff Orleans[6]
Education: Undergraduate: Yale University
Law School: Yale University
Career Path
Attorney, Office of Civil Rights:
Worked as an attorney in the Office of Civil Rights from 1971 to 1975.
University of North Carolina System:
Worked as a special assistant to the president in the UNC system from 1975 to 1984.
Ivy League:
Served as the executive director of Ivy League Athletics since 1984.
Notes: Was a principal author of the original implementing regulation for Title IX of the Education Amendments of 1972.

1. Commissioner Douglas Fullerton. (n.d.). Big Sky Conference. Retrieved November 13, 2007, from http://www.bigskyconf.com/article.asp?articleid=2385.
2. Kyle B. Kallander, Commissioner. (n.d.). Big South Conference. Retrieved November 13, 2007, from http://www.bigsouthsports.com/ViewArticle.dbml?DB_OEM_ID=4800&ATCLID=130906.
3. Scharff, A. (2006, May 12). Commish Yeager, CAA on the Rise. HofstraChronicle.com. Retrieved December 5, 2007, from http://media.www.hofstrachronicle.com/media/storage/paper222/news/2006/05/12/Sports/Commish.Yeager.Caa.On.The.Rise-1984285.shtml.
4. Patty Viverito. (n.d.). Missouri Valley Conference. Retrieved November 13, 2007, from http://www.mvc.org/mvc/bios.htm#viverito.
5. Ed Grom, Associate Commissioner. (n.d.). The Summit League. Retrieved November 13, 2007, from http://admin.xosn.com/ViewArticle.dbml?DB_OEM_ID=3900&ATCLID=919780.
6. Executive Director, Jeffrey Orleans. (n.d.). IvyLeagueSports.com. Retrieved November 13, 2007, from http://www.ivyleaguesports.com/schools/orleans.asp.

Table 58-1   Continued

Conference: Metro Atlantic Athletic Conference (MAAC)
Commissioner: Richard Ensor[7]
Education: Undergraduate: St. Peter's College
Graduate: University of Massachusetts (Sport Management)
Law School: Seton Hall University
St. Peter's College:
Started out as the assistant director of the Recreation Life Center at St. Peter's from 1975 to 1978.
St. Louis University:
Moved to St. Louis University as an assistant athletic director in 1978.
St. Peter's College:
Returned to St. Peter's in 1979 as the school's sports information director; served in this capacity until 1982 when he decided to attend graduate school.
Seton Hall University:
After completing graduate school, was hired by Seton Hall in 1985 as the assistant athletic director of marketing and promotions.
University of Massachusetts:
Took an assistant professor position in the UMass Sport Management department, where his concentration was on Sports Marketing and Sports Law.
MAAC Conference:
Hired as conference commissioner in 1988.

Conference: Mid-Eastern Athletic Conference (MEAC)
Commissioner: Dr. Dennis Thomas[8]
Education: Undergraduate: Alcorn State University
Graduate: University of Louisiana-Monroe
PhD: SUNY Buffalo
Career Path
Northeast Louisiana State University:
Began his career as an assistant football coach at Northeast Louisiana State.
Alcorn State University:
From 1985 to 1986, worked as assistant head football coach and defensive coordinator at Alcorn State.
South Carolina State University:
From 1986 to 1989, was the head football coach at South Carolina State.
Hampton University:
Hired by Hampton in 1989 as department chair of health, physical education, recreation, and dance.
Appointed athletic director in 1990; served in this capacity until 2002.
Mid-Eastern Conference:
Named conference commissioner in 2002.
Earned All-American status as a football student-athlete at Alcorn State.
Inducted into the SWAC Hall of Fame in 2003.

Conference: Northeast Conference (NEC)
Commissioner: Brenda Weare[9]
Education: Undergraduate: University of Wisconsin (Communications)
Graduate: University of Iowa (Athletic Administration)
Career Path
Mundelein College:
Worked as athletic director at Mundelein College in Chicago.
NCAA:
Worked in compliance services at the NCAA.
Great Midwest Conference:
Enjoyed a stint as assistant commissioner of the Great Midwest Conference.
Conference USA:
Served as the league's interim commissioner for a 5-month period in 2002.
Most recently served as senior associate commissioner of Conference USA.
Northeast Conference:
Appointed conference commissioner in August 2006.

Conference: Ohio Valley Conference (OVC)
Commissioner: Dr. Jon Steinbrecher[10]
Education: Undergraduate: Valparaiso University (Physical Education and Journalism)
Graduate: Ohio University (Sports Administration)
PhD: University of Indiana (Physical Education in Sports Administration)
Career Path
Various Colleges:
Served in athletic departments at Houston Baptist University, Indiana University, and Davidson College.
Mid-Continent Conference:
Worked at the Mid-Continent Conference from 1989 to 1994; positions included director of communications, director of marketing and communications, and assistant commissioner.
Served as the conference's commissioner from 1994 to 2003.
Ohio Valley Conference:
Appointed conference commissioner in 2003.
Notes: While attending Valparaiso, Steinbrecher was an all-conference and academic all-conference selection in football and a conference champion in tennis.

Conference: Patriot League
Commissioner: Carolyn Schlie Femovich[11]
Education: Undergraduate: Valparaiso University
Graduate: Indiana University
Career Path
Indiana University:
Career in intercollegiate athletics began in 1974 at Indiana University as a graduate teaching assistant.
Gettysburg College:
Served as head women's basketball and tennis coach from 1975 to 1982.
Added the responsibilities of coordinator of women's athletics from 1978 to 1982.
University of Pennsylvania:
Hired by Penn as associate athletic director (facilities) in 1982.
Served as interim athletic director in 1985.
Took the role of senior associate athletic director from 1986 to 1999.
Patriot League:
Hired as executive director of the Patriot League in 1999.

Conference: Pioneer Football League (PFL)
Commissioner: Patty Viverito
See information on Missouri Valley Football Conference.
In addition to her role as commissioner of the Pioneer Football League, Patty Viverito is also commissioner of the Gateway Conference. Her information has been presented above.

7. Richard J. Ensor, Commissioner. MAAC. Retrieved November 13, 2007, from http://www.maacsports.com/ViewArticle.dbml?&DB_OEM_ID=17400&ATCLID=939124&SPID=10427&SPSID=87819.
8. Dennis Thomas Named MEAC Commissioner. (2002, Aug. 2). *Onnidan Online.* Retrieved November 13, 2007, from http://www.onnidan.com/02-03/news/august/meac0802.htm.
9. Staff Directory, Brenda Weare. (n.d.). Northeast Conference. Retrieved November 13, 2007, from http://www.northeastconference.org/bio.asp?staffid=12.
10. Dr. Jon A. Steinbrecher. (n.d.). Ohio Valley Conference. Retrieved November 13, 2007, from http://www.ovcsports.com/ViewArticle.dbml?SPSID=31152&SPID=2453&DB_OEM_ID=6200&ATCLID=696640.
11. About Patriot League: Carolyn Schlie Femovich, Executive Director. (n.d.). Patriot League. Retrieved November 13, 2007, from http://patriotleague.cstv.com/school-bio/patr-school-bio-staff-femovich.html.

Table 58-1   Continued

Conference: Southern Conference (SOCON) **Commissioner:** John Iamarino[12] **Education:** Undergraduate: St. Bonaventure University (Journalism) **Career Path** *Georgetown University:* Entered the field of intercollegiate athletics as assistant sports information director at Georgetown from 1979 to 1981. *Jacksonville University:* Moved to Jacksonville as sports information director from 1981 to 1984. *Sun Belt Conference:* From 1984 to 1997, worked in a variety of publicity, compliance, and administrative positions at the Sun Belt Conference, rising to the level of associate commissioner. *Northeast Conference:* Served as commissioner of the Northeast Conference from 1997 to 2006. *Southern Conference:* Appointed commissioner of the Southern Conference in 2006.	**Conference:** Southland Conference **Commissioner:** Tom Burnett[13] **Education:** Undergraduate: Louisiana Tech University (Journalism) **Career Path** *Louisiana Tech University:* Got his start as a sports information assistant at Louisiana Tech from 1985 to 1988. Promoted to assistant sports information director in 1988. *American South Conference:* Moved to the American South Conference in 1989 as the co-director of the Service Bureau. Took on the role of director of communications in 1990. *Sun Belt Conference:* Hired by the Sun Belt Conference as director of communications in 1991. Promoted to assistant commissioner in 1995. Promoted to associate commissioner in 1999. *Southland Conference:* Named commissioner of the Southland Conference in 2002. **Notes:** While attending Louisiana Tech, spent one year as the sports editor of the school's student newspaper, *The Tech Talk*.	**Conference:** Southwestern Athletic Conference (SWAC) **Commissioner:** Duer Sharp[14] **Education:** Undergraduate: University of Wisconsin-Madison (Afro-American Studies) Graduate: University of Wisconsin-Madison (Afro-American Studies) **Career Path** *Big Ten Conference:* Started at the Big Ten Conference as an intern in 1997. Served as Big Ten Conference sport management administrator and coordinator for Big Ten and Chicago Public Schools SCORE (reading program) from 1998 to 2003. *Southwestern Athletic Conference:* Hired by the SWAC in 2003 as assistant commissioner. Promoted to associate commissioner in 2005. Named interim commissioner in 2007. **Notes:** Was a 4-year starter on the Wisconsin football team.

12. John Iamarino, Commissioner. (2007, July 21). The Southern Conference. Retrieved November 13, 2007, from http://www.soconsports.com/ViewArticle.dbml?&DB_OEM_ID=4000&ATCLID=222846.

13. Tom Burnett Named Southland Conference Commissioner. (2002, Dec. 23). I-AA.org. Retrieved November 13, 2007, from http://www.i-aa.org/article.asp?articleid=38882.

14. SWAC Staff, Duer Sharp. (n.d.). *SWAC*. Retrieved November 13, 2007, from http://www.swac.org/ssp/staff?s_id=19.

- At least 11 of the 14 FCS conference commissioners hold some type of advanced degree:
  - Seven commissioners hold master's degrees (Fullerton, Kallander, Yeager, Viverito, Weare, Femovich, and Sharp).
  - One commissioner holds both a master's degree and a law degree (Ensor).
  - One commissioner holds a law degree (Orleans).
  - Two commissioners hold both a master's degree and a doctorate degree (Thomas and Steinbrecher).
  - The master's degrees are in areas such as higher education, kinesiology, sport management, and Afro-American studies.
  - Education is an integral component of college athletics. As such, it is becoming more common for high-level college athletics administrators to hold advanced degrees. The high number of advanced degrees found in this group of FCS conference commissioners reflects this (and it is consistent with the analysis of FBS conference commissioners).

How did current FCS conference commissioners get their start?

- Current FCS conference commissioners had a variety of starting positions in their professional careers:
  - Six commissioners (Viverito, Ensor, Weare, Steinbrecher, Iamarino, and Burnett) started out in entry-level positions within a school's athletic department.
  - Two commissioners (Grom and Sharp) started out in entry-level positions with a conference.
  - Three commissioners started out as coaches at either the college (Thomas and Femovich) or high school (Fullerton) level.
  - One commissioner (Orleans) started out in legal practice.
  - One commissioner (Kallander) began his career working for a professional sports team in public relations.
  - One commissioner (Yeager) got his start by working as a youth sports director.
- This demonstrates there are many different starting points a person can choose to begin with, yet still obtain a position such as conference commissioner.

How many FCS conference commissioners worked as an athletic director or assistant athletic director?

- Of the 14 current FCS conference commissioners, 4 served as an athletic director prior to becoming a conference commissioner. Fullerton and Thomas both served as an athletic director on a full-time basis, while Grom and Femovich each held the position on an interim basis.

- In addition, prior to becoming a conference commissioner, Ensor had previous assistant athletic director experience (without reaching the level of athletic director).

- This means that 5 out of the 14 current FCS conference commissioners had at least some athletic director or assistant athletic director experience prior to being named conference commissioner. This represents almost 36% of the group.

How many FCS conference commissioners worked as an assistant or associate commissioner prior to becoming the commissioner?

- Eight of the 14 FCS conference commissioners (Kallander, Viverito, Grom, Weare, Steinbrecher, Iamarino, Burnett, and Sharp) worked at a conference office as either an assistant commissioner or an associate commissioner prior to becoming a commissioner.

- Of these eight commissioners, only one (Grom) had previous athletic director or assistant athletic director experience. This means that, in total, 12 out of the 14 FCS commissioners (almost 86%) did at least one of the following: worked as an athletic director, worked as an assistant athletic director, or worked as an assistant or associate commissioner.

What about the other two FCS conference commissioners? What type of experiences do they have?

- The two commissioners with no previous athletic director, assistant/associate athletic director, or assistant/associate commissioner experience are Yeager and Orleans.

  - Yeager had extensive experience working at the NCAA, which he used to obtain a commissioner position.

  - Prior to obtaining his commissioner position, Orleans had 5 years' experience working as an attorney and 10 years' experience working as a special assistant to the president of a major university.

Do FCS conference commissioners have extensive non-sports, business experience?

- Having spent 5 years as a practicing attorney, Orleans is the only FCS commissioner with significant experience outside of the sports industry. The remaining 13 commissioners have worked almost exclusively in sports-related entities, primarily in college athletics.

Do FCS conference commissioners get more than one opportunity to be a conference commissioner?

- Five of the 14 FCS commissioners have held more than one conference commissioner position:

  - Kallander, Steinbrecher, and Iamarino have each held two full-time commissioner positions.

  - Weare has held one interim commissioner position and one full-time commissioner position.

  - Viverito holds two commissioner positions simultaneously.

Patty Viverito, senior associate commissioner of the Missouri Valley Conference, at its recent media day. The Missouri Valley Conference is a Football Championship Subdivision (FCS) conference. In addition, Viverito also is the commissioner of the Pioneer Football League, the nation's only non-scholarship FCS conference. In 1982, Viverito became the first female FCS football commissioner.

IS THERE A PATTERN IN THE CAREER TRACKS?

The path toward an FCS conference commissioner position is likely to follow one of the four career tracks found in the analysis of FBS conference commissioners—the "school" track, the "conference" track, the "school-conference" track, and the "NCAA" track. (See Chapter 57 for explanations of the four tracks.)

Table 59-1   Career Track: ACC Marketing Professionals (As of July 2007)

School: Boston College **Name:** Jamie DiLoreto[1] **Title:** Associate athletics director, external operations **Education:** Undergraduate: University of Massachusetts (Sport Management) Graduate: Boston College (Administration) **Career Path** *Boston College:* Joined BC as a ticket office assistant in 1993; served in that position until 1999. Promoted to sports marketing manager in 1999. Assumed the head administrative duties in the external relations office on an interim basis in September 2001. Named assistant athletics director for external operations in 2002. Promoted to associate athletics director for external operations in May 2007.	**School:** Clemson University **Name:** John Seketa[2] **Title:** Assistant athletic director of event promotions **Education:** Undergraduate: Southern Illinois University (Business Administration) Graduate: Western Illinois University **Career Path** *University of Illinois:* Started as an intern in the Illinois athletic department. *Eastern Illinois University:* Worked as the promotions director at Eastern Illinois University, where he promoted all sports. *Clemson University:* Has been at Clemson for 21 years, and has worked his way up to his current position of assistant athletic director of event promotions.	**School:** Duke University **Name:** Mike Sobb[3] **Title:** Assistant athletic director, marketing **Education:** Undergraduate: Indiana University (Marketing) **Career Path** *Duke University:* Started at Duke in 1988 as an assistant in the sports information office. Took over as promotions director in 1990. In January 2001, was promoted to director of marketing. In May 2004, was promoted to his current position of assistant athletic director for marketing.
School: Florida State University **Name:** Jason Dennard[4] **Title:** Director of promotions and marketing **Education:** Undergraduate: Kennesaw State University (Sport Management) Graduate: Florida State University **Career Path** *Georgia Tech:* Started by volunteering at Georgia Tech for 3 months; this then turned into a marketing assistant position for 18 months. *Florida State University:* Moved to a marketing assistant position at Florida State for 9 months. Promoted to assistant director of promotions; served in this capacity for 18 months. Promoted to director of promotions and marketing in 2005.	**School:** Georgia Tech **Name:** Jennifer Pierce[5] **Title:** Director of promotions and events **Education:** Undergraduate: University of California-Berkley (Mass Communications) Graduate: University of South Carolina (Sports and Entertainment Management) **Career Path** *San Francisco 49ers (NFL):* Was a 49ers cheerleader and worked for the production company that oversaw the cheerleaders. *Public Relations Company:* Took an internship with a PR company working in a nonsports capacity. Worked her way up to an account manager after two years. *Television Station:* Moved to a television station where she was an assistant assignment editor. *Nonprofit Organization:* Worked at a nonprofit organization as an event planner in Colorado. *Air Force Academy:* While in Colorado, coached the Air Force cheerleaders. *University of South Carolina:* Decided to get back into sports full time by attending graduate school. Worked in the SC athletic department while in school. *Georgia Tech:* Took her current position at Georgia Tech upon completing the graduate program at SC.	**School:** North Carolina State University **Name:** Amy Baker[6] **Title:** Director of sales—Wolfpack Sports Marketing **Education:** Undergraduate: North Carolina State University (Communications) **Career Path** *North Carolina State University:* Worked several internships with the NC State Athletic Department while attending school. Upon graduation, started full-time as a sales assistant; worked in this capacity for 1 year. *Carolina Panthers (NFL) Radio Network:* Moved to the Carolina Panthers Radio Network, beginning as a sales assistant in 1997. From 1998 to 2000, worked as an account executive. *Jefferson Pilot Sports:* Hired as the director of sales at Jefferson Pilot Sports; worked there from 2000 to 2003. *North Carolina State University:* In 2003, returned to NC State working for Wolfpack Sports Marketing as an account executive. Promoted to director of sales in 2006.

1. Jamie DiLoreto Profile. (n.d.). Boston College Eagles Official Athletic Website. Retrieved November 12, 2007, from http://bceagles.cstv.com/genrel/diloreto_jamie00.html.
2. John Seketa Profile. (n.d.). Clemson Tigers. Retrieved November 12, 2007, from http://clemsontigers.cstv.com/genrel/seketa_john00.html.
3. Mike Sobb. (2005, July 22). GoDuke.com. Retrieved November 12, 2007, from http://www.goduke.com/ViewArticle.dbml?SPSID=22647&SPID=1841&DB_OEM_ID=4200&ATCLID=157706.
4. Information obtained via phone call with Jason Dennard.
5. Information obtained via phone call with Jennifer Pierce.
6. Information obtained via e-mail with Amy Baker.

Table 59-1   Continued

School: University of Maryland
Name: Brett Tillett[7]
Title: Director of marketing
Education: Undergraduate: St. Mary's College of Maryland (Economics)
Graduate: University of Massachusetts (Sport Management)
Career Path
Comcast SportsNet:
Got his start in sports as a production intern at Comcast SportsNet in Washington, DC; worked there for 1 year before going to graduate school.
University of Maryland:
After graduate school had an internship in the athletic department at Maryland.
In 2003–2004, became the assistant director of sports marketing.
Promoted to the associate director of sports marketing.
In 2006, was promoted to his current director of marketing position.

School: University of North Carolina
Name: Michael Beale[7]
Title: Assistant athletic director for marketing
Education: Undergraduate: Elon College (Leisure/Sport Management)
Graduate: Ohio University (Sports Administration)
Career Path
Wake Forest University:
Worked as an intern in the athletics department in 1993.
Ohio Sports Network/Ohio University:
Served as a marketing specialist from January to July 1995.
University of Kentucky:
Worked as an intern in the athletics department from 1995 to 1997.
Virginia Commonwealth University:
Hired as a staff assistant in the athletics department in 1997; worked in this capacity for 1 year.
University of North Carolina:
Began at UNC as a member of the ticket office staff in 1998.
Promoted to assistant director of marketing in 1999.
Has worked as UNC's assistant athletic director for marketing since 2001.

School: University of Virginia
Name: Todd Goodale[8]
Title: Associate athletic director for marketing and video services
Education: Undergraduate: University of Virginia
Career Path
Television:
Following his graduation from UVA, worked as a sports reporter and anchor for WVIR-TV in Charlottesville.
University of Virginia:
Began as a member of the Virginia Sports Marketing staff, serving as producer of the football and basketball coaches' television shows; also worked as an account executive.
From 1998 to 2004, worked as the creative director for Cavalier Sports Marketing.
Served as UVA's director of video services from 2004 to 2006.
Promoted to associate athletic director for marketing and video services in 2006.

School: Virginia Tech
Name: Jeremy Wells[9]
Title: Assistant director of athletics for sports marketing and promotions
Education: Undergraduate: Lynchburg College (Sport Management)
Career Path
Minor League Baseball:
Interned with two minor league baseball teams before working for the Richmond Braves (AAA) as manager of group sales; worked in this capacity for 2 years.
Promoted to head of marketing and promotions with the Braves.
Virginia Tech:
Moved to Virginia Tech as a marketing and promotions coordinator.
After 1 year, was promoted to director of marketing and promotions.
Worked his way up to executive director of marketing and promotions.
In 2007, was elevated to his current role of assistant director of athletics for sports marketing and promotions.

7. Information obtained via e-mail and phone call with Brett Tillett.
8. Todd Goodale. (2007, July 19). Virginia Cavaliers. Retrieved November 12, 2007, from http://admin.xosn.com/ViewArticle.dbml?&DB_OEM_ID=17800&ATCLID=1133804.

9. Information obtained via phone call with Jeremy Wells.

- Six of the 10 ACC marketers (DiLoreto, Seketa, Dennard, Pierce, Tillett, and Beale) completed a graduate program.
  - At least three of the six graduate degrees were from sport management programs (Pierce, Tillett, and Beale).
  - A growing number of institutions require or prefer the school's athletic administrators to hold graduate degrees. Consequently, the high number of graduate degrees found in this group of ACC marketers reflects the general requirements commonly found in college athletics. This is in sharp contrast to the low level of graduate degrees held by NBA marketers (see Chapter 53). Although a graduate degree can be helpful working in professional sports, it is less likely that advanced degrees will be required for such jobs.
- Detailed education information (such as undergraduate major) could be found for only 9 of the 10 ACC marketers. All nine received either an undergraduate or a graduate degree that directly relates to his or her current job (i.e., marketing, communications, business, or sport management). Although an education in marketing or business may not be required, this strong showing indicates it can be useful, and most collegiate marketers do have such an education.

How did ACC marketers begin their careers?

- Six of the 10 ACC marketers started their career in college athletics, usually in an entry-level position:
  - DiLoreto (ticket office) and Sobb (sports information) started out as assistants.
  - Dennard started out volunteering before receiving a marketing assistant position.
  - Seketa, Baker, and Beale started out as athletic department interns.
  - It appears that of these six, all but one (Baker) has worked exclusively in college athletics.
- The remaining four ACC marketers (not accounted for above) started in the sports industry, but outside of college athletics:
  - Pierce started out as a cheerleader for the San Francisco 49ers (NFL).
  - Tillett started out working as a production intern for Comcast SportsNet.
  - Goodale started out as a sports reporter.
  - Wells started out as an intern for the Richmond Braves.

Do ACC marketers have extensive nonsports, business experience?

- Only 1 of the 10 ACC marketers appears to have significant experience outside of the sports industry:
  - Pierce held a variety of jobs outside of the sports industry, working in public relations, television production, and event planning. She used graduate school as a means to transition into the sports industry.

How many colleges has the typical ACC marketer worked for during his or her career?

- On average, each ACC marketer has worked for 1.7 different colleges during his or her career. Beale and Seketa lead the pack, working for four schools and three schools, respectively.
- It appears that 6 of the 10 ACC marketers (DiLoreto, Sobb, Baker, Tillett, Goodale, and Wells) have worked exclusively for only one college.
  - Baker did work for NC State on two different occasions, mixing in 6 years of radio sports marketing work in between NC State positions.
  - Although they only worked for one college athletic department, Tillett, Goodale, and Wells did receive additional work experience at sports entities outside of college athletics.

IS THERE A PATTERN IN THE CAREER TRACKS?

Three viable career tracks stand out from the analysis of the ACC marketers—the "learn-on-the-job" track, the "graduate school" track, and the "lateral move." There is also an important trend to note, which can appropriately be called the "alumni connections."

The Learn-on-the-Job Track

Five of the 10 ACC marketers got their start in college athletics, and have remained there throughout their entire career. They started out in internships, assistant positions, and in one case, as a volunteer, and they stuck with it. They have learned on the job and developed their marketing skill set along the way. Each has worked his way up the ranks into his current position as head of their school's marketing department. The success of DiLoreto, Seketa, Sobb, Dennard, and Beale demonstrate the viability of following such a track.

The Graduate School Track

At least 2 of 10 the ACC marketers (Pierce and Tillett) used sport management graduate programs as a means to transition into college athletics.

Prior to graduate school, Pierce worked a variety of jobs (both sports- and nonsports-related) and pursued a sport management graduate degree as a way to get into sports full time. Pierce made the most of her time at South Carolina, working in the athletic department while attending graduate school. Upon completing SC's program, Pierce was able to use her previous work experience in conjunction with her sport management graduate education to land her current marketing position at Georgia Tech.

Tillett worked in television production for Comcast SportsNet prior to attending the sport management graduate program at the University of Massachusetts. Although he did gain sports experience at Comcast SportsNet, Tillett called upon his advanced degree in sport management to land an internship at the University of Maryland. With this start, Tillett worked his way up through the ranks in a manner similar to the learn-on-the-job track described in the previous section.

The success that Pierce and Tillett have enjoyed helps to demonstrate the impact a sport management graduate degree can have on someone looking to make a career change into college athletics.

The Lateral Move

Three of the 10 ACC marketers (Baker, Goodale, and Wells) followed a career track that may be categorized as a lateral move. They developed skills in non-college sports positions and then used those skills to land positions inside college athletics.

Although Baker began her career in college athletics, working for her alma mater North Carolina State upon her graduation, she ventured outside of college athletics for a significant portion of her career. Baker spent 6 years working for the Carolina Panthers Radio Network and Jefferson Pilot Sports in a marketing capacity. She then made a lateral move, returning to college athletics as a member of North Carolina State's marketing department.

Goodale started his career in television as a sports reporter and anchor. He then leveraged the skills he acquired in the television industry to land a production job with the University of Virginia, creating a lateral move into college athletics. Once he got started at UVA, Goodale was able to work his way up through the ranks of the athletic department, eventually landing his position as associate athletic director for marketing and video services.

Wells began his career in minor league baseball, working primarily in a marketing capacity. He was able to make the lateral move from marketing minor league baseball to marketing college athletics, obtaining a marketing coordinator position at Virginia Tech. During his time at Virginia Tech, Goodale followed a path similar to the learn-on-the-job track described previously.

The career tracks of Goodale and Wells demonstrate it is not necessary to start your career in college sports in order to obtain a prominent college marketing position. Furthermore, when looking at Baker, Goodale, and Wells, it is apparent that marketing skills obtained outside of college sports can be transferable into the college athletics marketing environment. This aspect of transferability makes lateral moves into college athletics marketing possible. Networking may be very helpful in making a lateral move into sports.

Alumni Connections

Although not constituting a career track in and of itself, the role that alumni connections have on a career should not be overlooked. Both DiLoreto and Dennard currently work for the same schools from which they received their graduate degrees, and Baker and Goodale work for the same schools from which they received their undergraduate degrees. This means 4 of the 10 ACC marketers currently work at schools they previously attended as a student, creating a seemingly strong alumni connection. It may be that these individuals used their time as students to develop personal connections with members of the athletic department or with prominent faculty members, or it could be that the school was simply interested in hiring one of its alums. Either way, it appears these individuals were able to use their alumni connections to land their positions.

CREATING YOUR OWN TRACK

If you have an interest in working in marketing for a college athletic department, a number of career tracks are available to you. You can start out in college athletics and work you way up, or you can gain experience outside of college athletics and then make a transition into your desired field. If you choose the latter route, you may want to consider graduate school as a tool to aid in the transition process. You should also keep in mind that graduate degrees are common in higher-level positions within college athletics administration.

If you have a strong interest in college athletics administration, be sure to review the career tracks for college athletic directors and conference commissioners in Chapters 55 through 58.

Section 4

Organizational Charts

Introduction to Organizational Charts

Much of the fascination and intrigue surrounding the business side of sports has to do with the unknown. The general public often is simply unaware of what takes place behind the scenes, and this creates interest—people want to know what is going on and who is doing it. In this section and the next, this book will attempt to shed some light on these areas. This information can be very helpful for people considering and planning their careers in the sports industry.

Section 4 includes various organizational charts from different sports industry segments. This section was included for a number of reasons, but most importantly to provide a sense of the types of job titles found in sports entities. Looking over the organizational charts will also shed light on the division of responsibility and reporting lines (meaning who reports to whom). This section should provide a basic understanding of the organization in which sport professionals work. This understanding should then provide a context in which to review the job descriptions found in Section 5.

It should also be pointed out that the information regarding reporting lines can help in developing a career plan. For example, let's say you are interested in becoming the head of public relations for a professional sports team. By studying the organizational charts for this type of entity, you will be able to see the entry-level position and the reporting lines to the head position. Generally speaking, this presents one possible path to follow for upward mobility. This can provide valuable direction for planning a career in a specific area.

The organizational charts included in this section are examples of recent charts from various sports entities. You should keep a few things in mind while reading this section. To begin with, organizational charts are not static objects. As people change jobs (through hirings, firings, promotions, etc.), an organization will often revise job duties and responsibilities (and sometimes job titles) to capitalize on the strengths of its employees. This ultimately results in changes to the entity's organizational chart.

Also, not all sports entities are set up in the same manner, so organizational charts can vary significantly from one entity to the next, even within the same industry segment. This is due in large part to the differing needs and priorities of the organizations. Some entities are owned by publicly traded corporations, whereas others are family-run operations. The organizational charts for each of these types of entities may look dramatically different from one another. For example, a sports team that is owned by a publicly traded company may be able to draw upon corporate or other resources that may not be available to a family-run organization. This may result in a team that is part of a publicly traded company having fewer dedicated employees working full time for the team, because the team can rely on corporate employees to fill some of their personnel needs. This is more likely to be found in nonsport-based functions such as human resources, information technology, accounting/finance, and possibly legal services. At a smaller, family-run team, such positions are more likely to be a direct part of the team's personnel structure, because there is no parent entity with which the team can share employees.

In addition, some entities are part of a consolidated group of companies within the sports industry (e.g., a parent company may own a professional team, a regional sports network, and an arena), whereas other entities operate on their own (e.g., a professional sports team without any ownership ties to other companies). An organizational chart for one consolidated example, Spurs Sports & Entertainment, is presented in Chapter 62. In addition to owning an NBA team, the owner of the San Antonio Spurs also owns a WNBA team and a minor league hockey team. Adding to the complexity, the owner also controls the operations of the facility in which the teams play. The ownership group of the Boston Celtics, on the other hand, does not have any of these things—it does not own any teams other than the Celtics, nor does it run the arena the Celtics play in. As you can imagine, the list of variations among different sport entities is endless, and each variation may result in a different organizational arrangement.

There are also general differences between leagues. For example, in the NFL there are likely to be fewer broadcast positions, because most broadcasting is done at the league level and, compared to the NBA, NHL, and MLB, each team has fewer games for which it has broadcast responsibilities. In contrast, there are many more NBA, NHL, and MLB broadcasts controlled at the team level and there are many more games to broadcast, so there may be more broadcasting jobs and opportunities at the team level in these leagues. Additionally, given its reduced schedule of games and strong league marketing presence, NFL teams may also hire fewer marketing professionals than teams in other leagues. These differences should be reflected in a team's organizational chart.

Organizational chart differences also can be generated by the physical design of the organizational chart itself. Some entities create very detailed organizational charts, accounting for every person in the organization. In contrast, other entities include only supervisory positions in their organizational charts. This results in a smaller, more simplified organizational chart, but it may not be truly reflective of the jobs in the organization.

Due to the fluid nature of organizational charts (within a particular entity) and the variation of organizational structures (within a particular industry segment), the charts included in this book are not meant to be a definitive guide to the organizational structure in that industry segment or even that particular team or organization. They are simply provided as examples of how certain sports entities are structured. Keep this in mind as you study the organizational charts.

In an attempt to provide a comprehensive view, this section includes a number of organizational charts from sports entities across a variety of industry segments. Within each industry segment, you will find a wide variety of functional areas covered. For instance, if you are interested in marketing, you will find organizational charts from colleges, professional teams, professional leagues, and agencies (among others) that include some type of marketing component. Studying the organizational charts from the marketing perspective should help you to get a better understanding of the types of marketing jobs available in the industry.

College Athletics

BOSTON COLLEGE

Boston College (BC) is a private school and a member of the Atlantic Coast Conference (ACC). BC's organizational chart (shown in **Figure 61-1**) is an example of the type of organizational structures in place at a private school that has a broad-based athletic program and is a member of a Bowl Championship Series Conference. Important to note, this is a complex organizational structure with a number of associate athletic directors and assistant athletic directors. The chart also goes into great detail, including not only supervisory positions, but also interns. The chart does a good job of illustrating how BC divides the roles and responsibilities among all of its employees. For more information on college athletics, please review the NCAA industry segment in Chapter 29.

UNIVERSITY OF MICHIGAN

The University of Michigan is a state school and a member of the Big Ten athletic conference. Two organizational charts for Michigan's athletic department (**Figures 61-2** and **61-3**) are presented here. The first chart, Figure 61-2, represents a top-level view of the athletic director and immediate associates and assistants. This provides a second look at how a major college athletic department divides roles and responsibilities among its leadership.

The second Michigan organizational chart, Figure 61-3, is a look at the university's marketing department and the supervisory roles that lie within this particular department. Each major department within Michigan's athletic department has its own organizational chart; the marketing department has been chosen as an example.

UNIVERSITY OF MASSACHUSETTS–AMHERST

Similar to Michigan, the University of Massachusetts–Amherst (UMass) is a state school, but is a member of the Atlantic 10 Conference, competing as an NCAA Football Championship Subdivision school (FCS, formerly Division I-AA). It is important to note that UMass's organizational chart (shown in **Figure 61-4**) contains far fewer positions than BC's chart. This difference is primarily due to the labor-intensive nature of football at the Bowl Subdivision level (FBS, formerly Division I-A). Schools such as BC (and Michigan) that compete in football at the FBS level typically employ more people in their athletic departments than schools that compete at lower levels of college football, such as UMass. The work at the FBS level is simply larger in scope and requires more people to carry out the operations. This inherently creates more opportunities for job seekers at schools at the FBS level.

UMass's organizational chart provides an example of how a school competing at the FCS level might structure its athletic department.

WESTFIELD STATE COLLEGE

Westfield State College, located in Westfield, Massachusetts, is a member of the NCAA Division III. The public school has a little over 4,000 students and competes in the Massachusetts State College Athletics Conference. In comparison to the aforementioned college athletic programs, Westfield State is a smaller athletic program, and its organizational chart (shown in **Figure 61-5**) reflects this. This chart is an example of how Division III college athletic departments are structured.

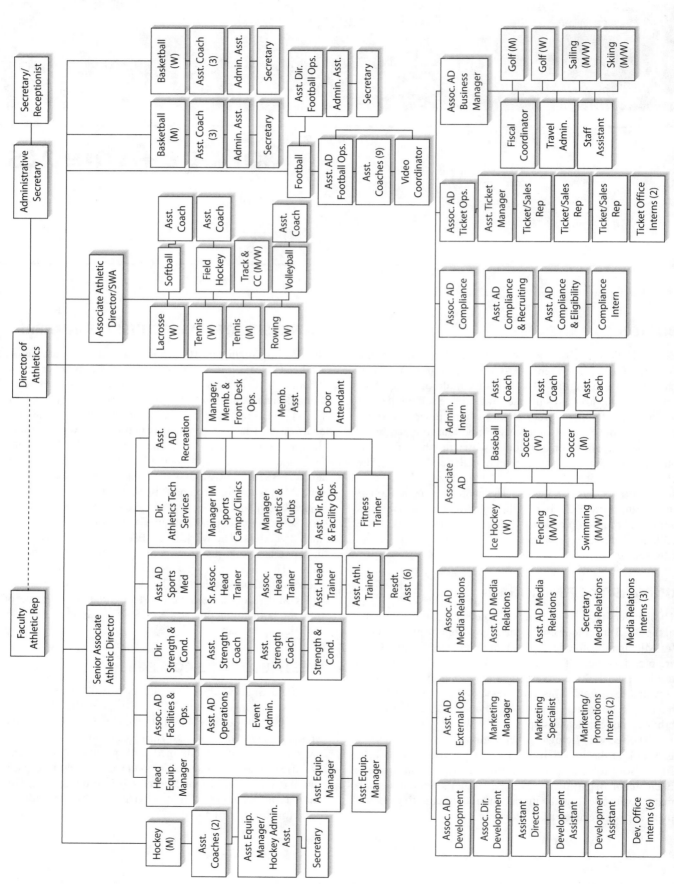

Figure 61-1   Boston College: Athletic Department

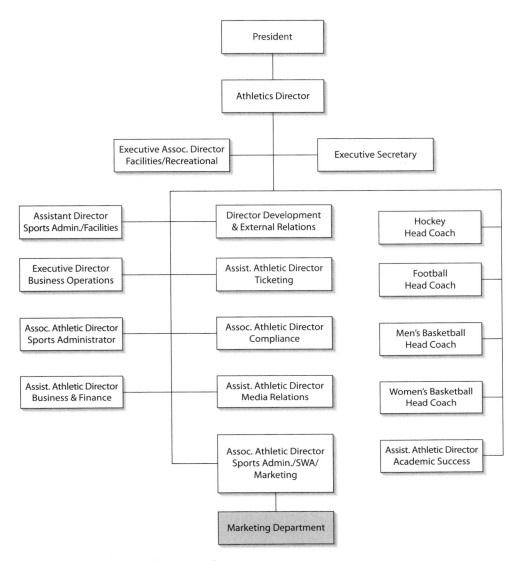

Figure 61-2   University of Michigan: Executive Structure

Figure 61-3   University of Michigan: Marketing Department

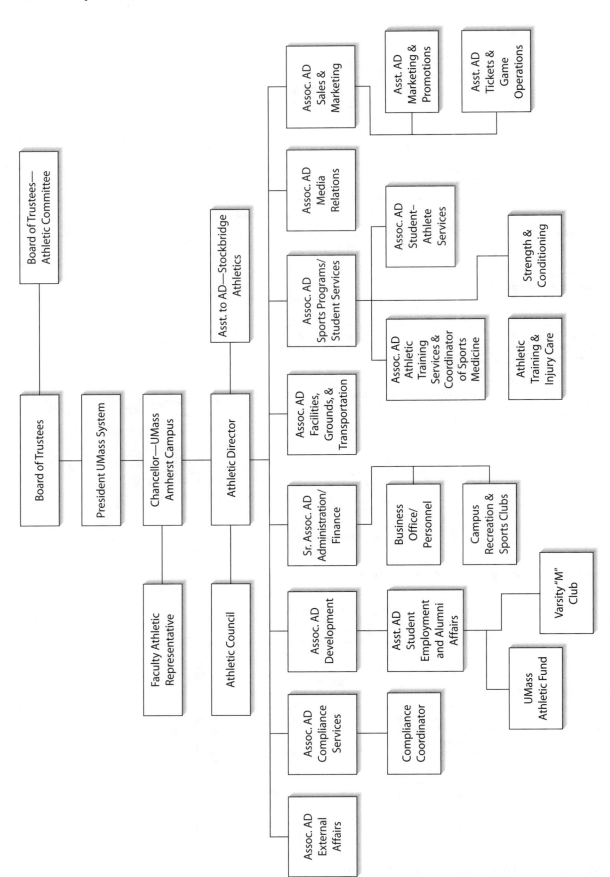

Figure 61-4 University of Massachusetts–Amherst: Athletic Department

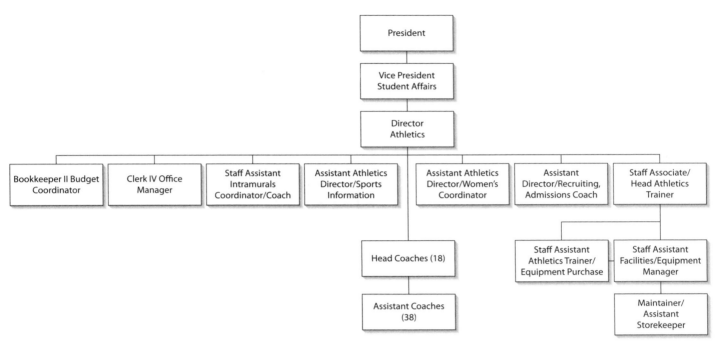

Figure 61-5   Westfield State College: Athletic Department

UNIVERSITY OF ST. THOMAS

St. Thomas is also an NCAA Division III school and a member of the Minnesota Intercollegiate Athletic Conference. This organizational chart (shown in **Figure 61-6**) provides a more detailed perspective on Division III college athletics (compared to the Westfield State chart presented in Figure 61-5). At St. Thomas, men and women compete in 20 varsity sports and nearly 40 club sports. Approximately 10,500 undergraduate and graduate students attend St. Thomas.

METRO ATLANTIC ATHLETIC CONFERENCE

With 10 full-time member schools, the Metro Atlantic Athletic Conference (MAAC) completed its 27th year of competition in the 2007-2008 academic year. The MAAC is not a BCS member. The organizational chart for the MACC (shown in **Figure 61-7**) displays the conference's relative smaller size when compared to that of a BCS conference office (shown in Figure 61-8). The MAAC conference members include Canisius College, Fairfield University, Iona College, Loyola College (MD), Manhattan College,

Marist College, Niagara University, Rider University, Saint Peter's College, and Siena College. In addition, a number of associate members field teams for specific sports such as football, baseball, and lacrosse. In total, the conference conducts 24 championships and supports 25 sports. The conference headquarters are located in Edison, New Jersey.

NCAA FOOTBALL BOWL SUBDIVISION AND BOWL CHAMPIONSHIP SERIES CONFERENCE

The organizational chart presented in **Figure 61-8** is for an NCAA Football Bowl Subdivision (FBS) and Bowl Championship Series (BCS) Conference. The conference asked to remain anonymous, so its name is not included with the chart. As an FBS/BCS conference, this particular conference represents "big-time" college athletics and is one of the most prominent conferences in college athletics. Note how the conference's chart in Figure 61-8 includes more positions than the MAAC chart (Figure 61-7), reflecting the more complicated nature of operating a larger BCS conference office with big time football and a conference run football playoff game.

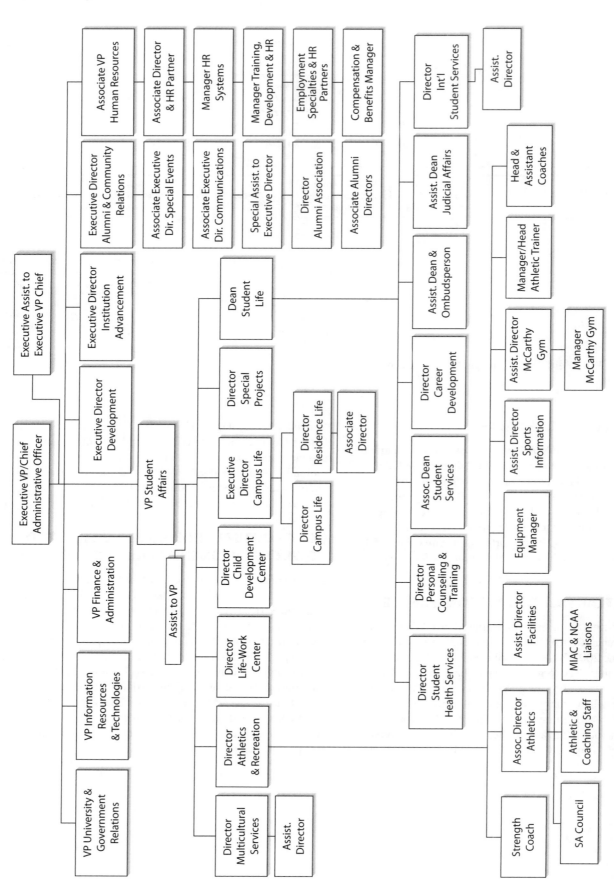

Figure 61-6   University of St. Thomas: Athletic Department

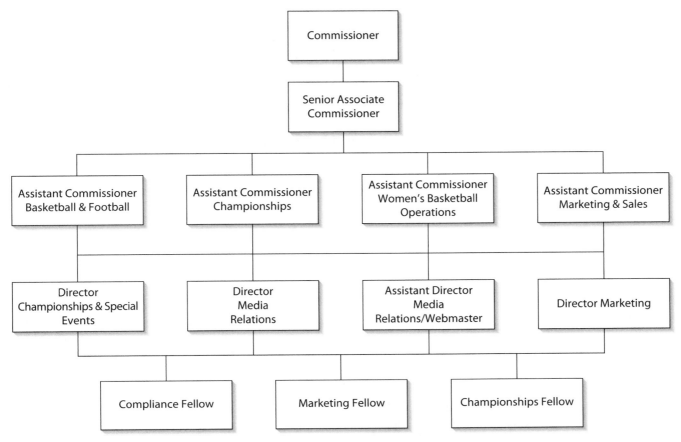

Figure 61-7   Metro Atlantic Athletic Conference

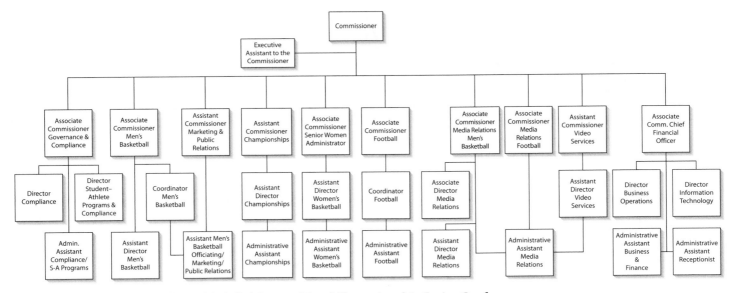

Figure 61-8   NCAA Football Bowl Subdivision and Bowl Championship Series Conference

CHAPTER SIXTY-TWO

Professional Sports Teams

For the purposes of this book, professional sports have been broken down into two areas—teams and leagues. Organizational charts for select teams are presented in this chapter, and organizational charts for select league entities can be found in Chapter 63.

Adonis ("Sporty") Geralds is the community relations coordinator of the Charlotte Bobcats Arena. Geralds was formerly general manager of the Charlotte Coliseum. He is also a very popular speaker and author of a motivational book, *The Champion in You*.

NFL FRANCHISE

An NFL franchise is depicted in this chapter's first organizational chart, but the organization asked to remain anonymous. Even without the specific team name attached, the organizational chart still provides excellent insight into how an NFL franchise is organized. Although other NFL franchisees may have some differences from this structure, the basic core structure is likely to be similar.

To make it easier to follow, the chart has been broken down into three smaller charts: one representing the executive structure (**Figure 62-1**), a second representing the football operations (**Figure 62-2**), and a third representing the business operations (**Figure 62-3**).

For more information on the NFL, please read the industry segment write-up for the NFL in Chapter 18.

Executive Structure

Figure 62-1, which shows the franchise's executive structure, indicates the team's operations are primarily broken down into three areas of focus—football operations, legal and human resources, and business operations. The team's president is responsible for managing the activities of all three departments, and he reports directly to the team's owner.

Football Operations

The football operations department of an NFL franchise is responsible for everything that takes place on the football field—from player acquisitions, to scouting and contract negotiations. Professionals employed in the football operations department include coaches, trainers, scouts, equipment managers, and security personnel. Together, these individuals work to ensure the team is successful from a performance (or playing) standpoint. The general manager usually oversees this department. The other important member of this department is the head coach, who holds a great deal of responsibility and decision-making power.

In reviewing the organizational chart (Figure 62-2), note that director or supervisory positions are presented in a box. These individuals are responsible for managing the positions listed below their box.

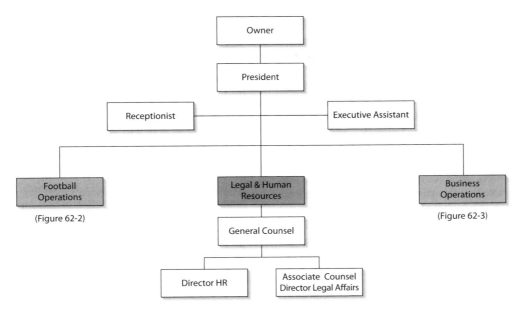

Figure 62-1   NFL Franchise: Executive Structure

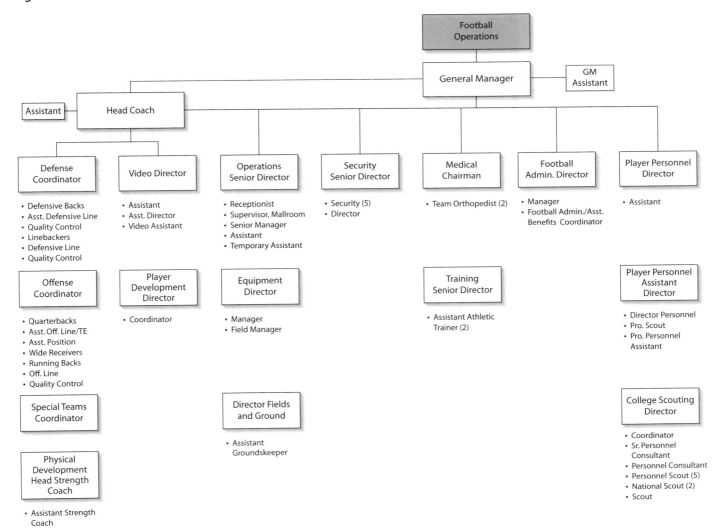

Figure 62-2   NFL Franchise: Football Operations

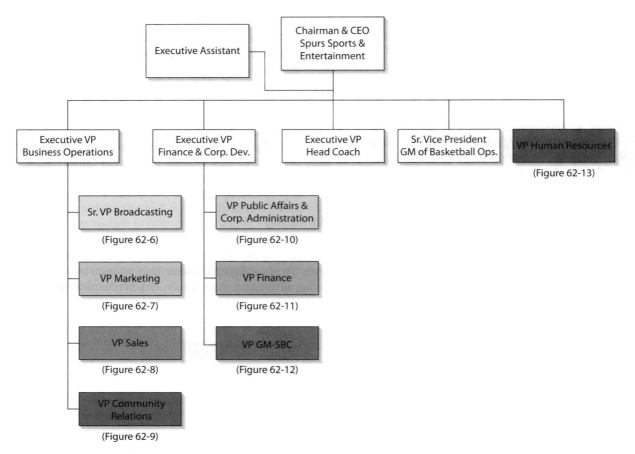

Figure 62-5   Spurs Sports & Entertainment: Executive Structure

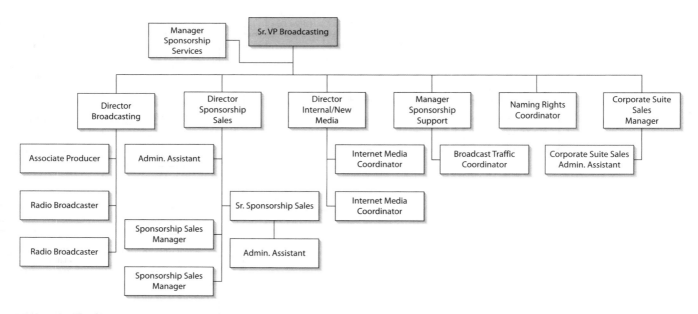

Figure 62-6   Spurs Sports & Entertainment: Broadcasting

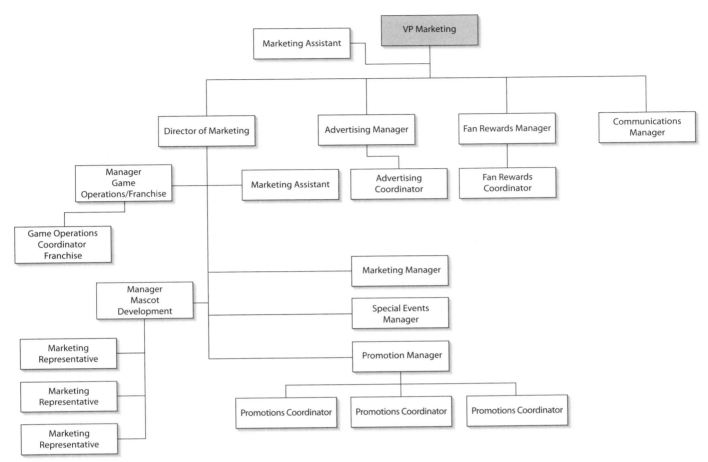

Figure 62-7   Spurs Sports & Entertainment: Marketing

Guest Services and Sales

Figure 62-8 represents the positions and responsibilities that fall under the direction of the vice president of sales for Spurs Sports & Entertainment. Included in this department are ticket operations, guest services, group sales, and sales.

Community Relations

Figure 62-9 represents the positions and responsibilities that fall under the direction of the vice president of community relations for Spurs Sports & Entertainment. Talent resources, events and donations, community relations, and education and recreation are all areas within this department.

External Affairs

Figure 62-10 represents the positions and responsibilities that fall under the direction of the vice president of public affairs and corporate administration for Spurs Sports & Entertainment. This is the smallest department within the company's structure.

Finance

Figure 62-11 represents the positions and responsibilities that fall under the direction of the executive vice president of finance for Spurs Sports & Entertainment. Within this department, the company has chosen to separate the accounting/finance duties of the AT&T Center from all other accounting/finance duties.

Community Arena Management

Figure 62-12 represents the positions and responsibilities that fall under the direction of the vice president/general manager of the community arena for Spurs Sports & Entertainment. This group of professionals is in charge of the day-to-day operations of the AT&T Center. The responsibilities have been divided into the following areas: audio/visual systems, information technology, event services, facility services, and bookings.

Human Resources

Figure 62-13 represents the positions and responsibilities that fall under the direction of the vice president of human

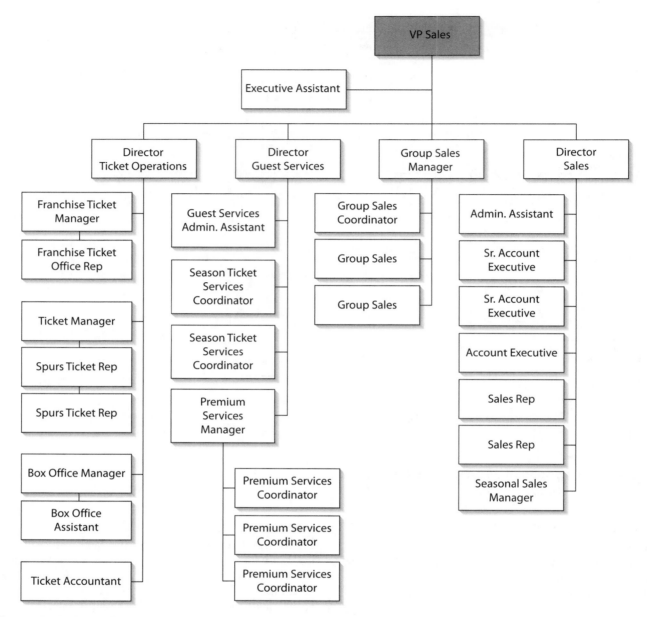

Figure 62-8   Spurs Sports & Entertainment: Guest Services and Sales

resources for Spurs Sports & Entertainment. This department handles personnel matters for the company.

PIRATE CITY: PITTSBURGH PIRATES FLORIDA OPERATIONS

This Pittsburgh Pirates play baseball in the National League of Major League Baseball. As part of the MLB schedule, teams play spring training games in the months of February and March. Thus, each spring, teams go to either Florida or Arizona to prepare for the upcoming season. In the case of the Pittsburgh Pirates, the team's spring training facilities are located in Bradenton, Florida, in a place referred to as

"Pirate City." Pirate City is also home to the team's minor league training facilities. **Figure 62-14** demonstrates the team's organizational structure and how its Florida operations relate to the rest of the franchise. For more information on MLB, please read the industry segment write-up for MLB in Chapter 19.

BASEBALL OPERATIONS FOR A MAJOR LEAGUE BASEBALL TEAM

Each MLB team allocates a great deal of time and money to the drafting, signing, and development of its players in a minor league system. Therefore, it is not surprising that

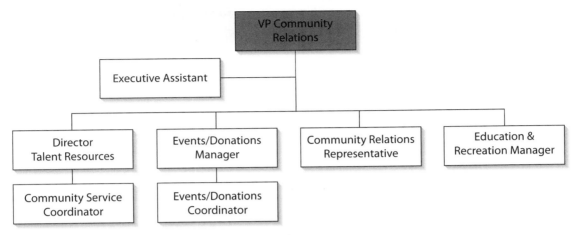

Figure 62-9   Spurs Sports & Entertainment: Community Relations

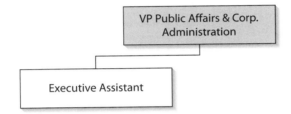

Figure 62-10   Spurs Sports & Entertainment: External Affairs

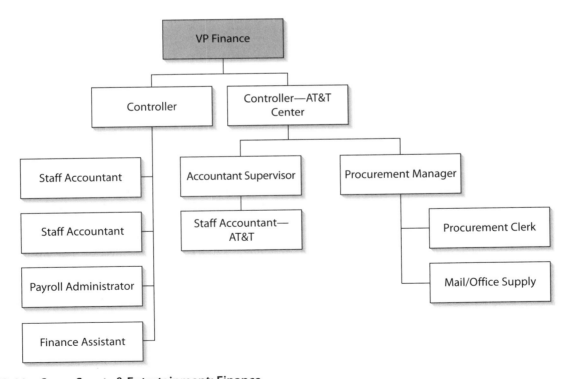

Figure 62-11   Spurs Sports & Entertainment: Finance

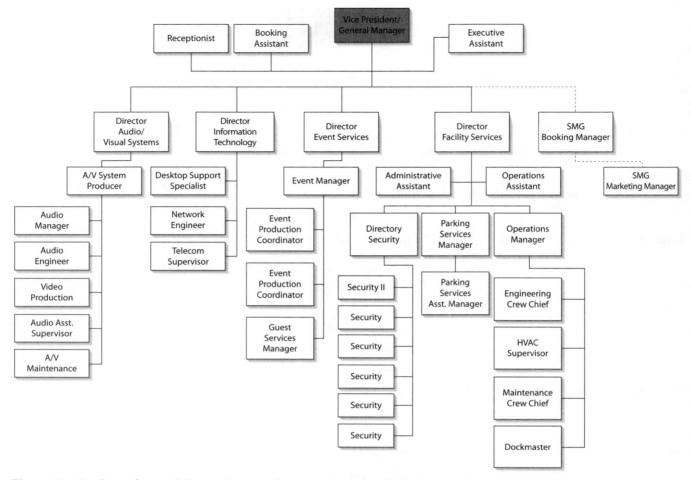

Figure 62-12   Spurs Sports & Entertainment: Community Arena Management

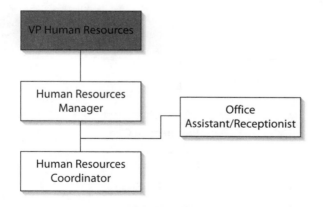

Figure 62-13   Spurs Sports & Entertainment: Human Resources

MLB teams employ an extensive baseball operations department. The organizational chart shown in **Figure 62-15** is an example structure of the baseball operations for a Major League Baseball team. This chart provides a good indication of the types of positions found in the player personnel and talent evaluation segments of the industry. Additionally, due to its minor league system, you can expect to find similar structures and positions at National Hockey League teams (but on a lesser scale). In contrast, NFL and NBA teams employ similar scouting structures, but are likely to have fewer positions for player development because there are no minor league systems in the NFL, and only the D-League in the NBA. The football operations organizational chart shown in Figure 62-2 provides insight into the types of scouting and talent evaluation positions commonly found in the NFL.

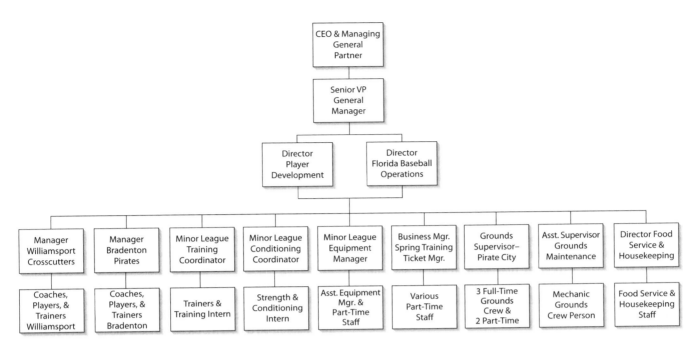

Figure 62-14   Pittsburgh Pirates: Florida Operations

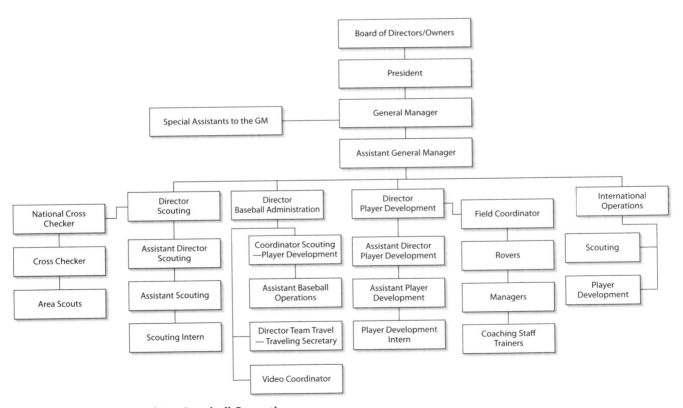

Figure 62-15   MLB Franchise: Baseball Operations

Professional Sport Leagues

Professional sport leagues make up a significant component of the professional sports landscape. Employees at a league office are in charge of overseeing the operations of all league-wide activity. This often entails coordinating activity among the league's teams and other constituents. Quite often, leagues hold a great deal of power and much of the operations are behind the scenes. Therefore, most leagues consider their organizational structure to be confidential and choose not to disclose this information to the general public.

PROFESSIONAL TEAM SPORT: LEAGUE OFFICE

As mentioned, some leagues would rather not see their organizational structure published for the public to view. The structure presented in **Figure 63-1** is one such case. Although the name of the league has been removed for confidentiality purposes, the chart still provides value. This is an organizational chart from one of the "Big Four" professional sport leagues in North America. Close examination of the chart reveals the types of roles, responsibilities, and divisions often found in league offices. Although not every league office is structured like this, the chart does provide a good example of what you might expect to see. Important to

note, the chart contains only top-level management positions, and is therefore a relatively simplified organizational structure. Under each of the positions reflected on the chart there is likely to be a department filled with various managers and staff members. For more information on the types of activities commonly carried out in a league office of a "Big Four" professional sport, please review the career tracks of league executives for the NBA and MLB in Section 3 of this book (Chapters 50, 51, 53, and 54).

NFL JAPAN

In today's ever-expanding global marketplace, it is not uncommon for entities to look for ways to increase revenues internationally. The NFL is no different in this regard, and it has created NFL Japan. In 1997, the league opened an office in Japan to help promote the league, as well as the game of football. As you can see from the recent organizational chart for the league's office in Japan (**Figure 63-2**), the promotion of the NFL is accomplished through television, sponsorship, licensing, fan development, and public relations. For more information on the NFL, please read the industry segment write-up for the NFL in Chapter 18.

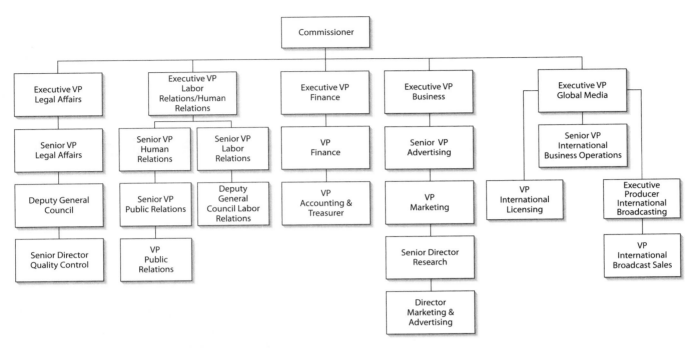

Figure 63-1   Professional Team Sport: League Office Structure

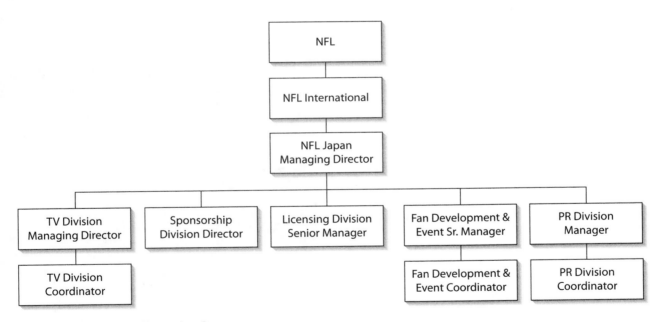

Figure 63-2   NFL Japan: Executive Structure

CHAPTER SIXTY-FOUR 64

Sport Associations and Events

Sport associations and events represent another aspect of the sports industry. Sports associations often function in a similar fashion to professional leagues in that they are responsible for managing and running sporting events and competitions. Due to the size and importance of certain events, entire departments of an association often are dedicated to managing one particular event. Examples of associations and events that fall into this category include the NCAA (Final Four), the United States Tennis Association (U.S. Open), the United States Golf Association (U.S. Open), and the National Thoroughbred Racing Association (Kentucky Derby). This chapter includes two example organizational structures for sports associations and events.

2007 U.S. OPEN GOLF CHAMPIONSHIP

The U.S. Open, one of the four major championships in men's professional golf, is the showcase event for the United States Golf Association (USGA). The event is held annually at different golf courses around the country. The organizational chart presented in **Figure 64-1** depicts the men and women who work to put on this event each year. One can expect to find similar structures for championship events throughout the sports industry, including tennis and college athletics. You will find more information on the USGA and the U.S. Open in Chapter 29.

NEW ENGLAND PGA

The PGA of America (Professional Golfers' Association) is a membership organization for all of the nation's club professionals. PGA professionals are instructors, businesspersons, and community leaders who are responsible for teaching the game and conducting the business of golf. The PGA is divided into geographic sections, and regional organizations help manage the day-to-day duties and

Wade Martin, president and general manager of AST Dew Tour. Martin spearheaded the creation and development of the AST Dew Tour, which started in 2005. It was the first ever season-long action sports tour. The tour features many well known action sports athletes such as Shaun White, Travis Pastrana, and Dave Mira. In 2008, Martin led the ground-breaking alliance between NBC Sports and MTV Networks, centered around the AST Dew Tour.

responsibilities in designated areas. In total, there are 41 sections nationwide; the New England PGA (**Figure 64-2**) is an example of one such section.

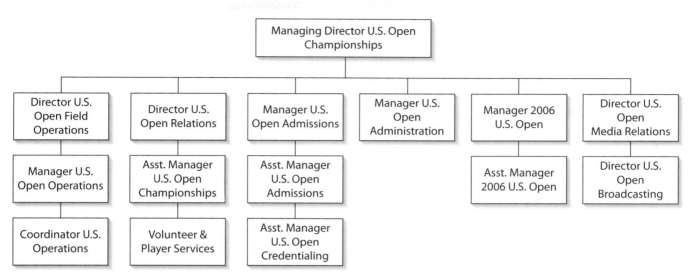

Figure 64-1   2007 U.S. Open Golf Championship: Executive Structure

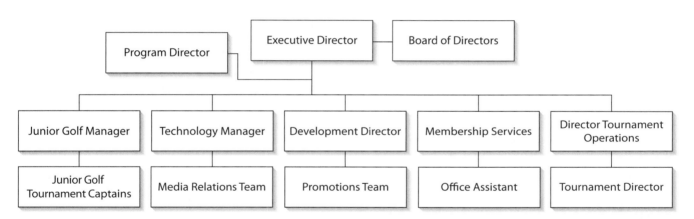

Figure 64-2   New England PGA: Executive Structure

The New England PGA is a nonprofit association dedicated to promoting the game of golf. The association consists of over 750 PGA class A golf professionals and over 240 PGA apprentices at over 450 golf facilities located in five states: Massachusetts, Maine, New Hampshire, Rhode Island, and Vermont. Designated facilities include public, private, and resort golf courses; teaching centers; and driving ranges. The association's offices are located in Boylston, Massachusetts. For more information on the PGA, please read the industry segment write-up on the PGA in Chapter 29.

CHAPTER SIXTY-FIVE

Unions

In a number of professional sports, unions play the important roles of representing the players and managing the owner-player relationship. The primary purpose of the union is to represent players in matters concerning wages, hours, working conditions and to protect their rights. The union achieves this by negotiating a collective bargaining agreement (CBA). In addition, unions represent players' interests in licensing rights and their intellectual property matters. This chapter includes two parts of a player's union in one of the "Big Four" professional sports leagues. For more information on the unions, please read the industry segment write-up for the unions in Chapter 43.

MLBPA: LABOR TEAM

The labor team of this union (**Figure 65-1**) is responsible for overseeing all labor-related matters for the union. Similar duties and roles would be found in other professional sports unions, such as the NFL Players Association and the National Basketball Players Association.

MLBPA: LICENSING TEAM

Licensing is another significant responsibility for some professional sport unions. The unions licensing team (**Figure 65-2**) is responsible for coordinating, managing, and maximizing the licensing rights and fees for professional players. Video game and trading card companies are two of the more prominent acquirers of player licensing rights.

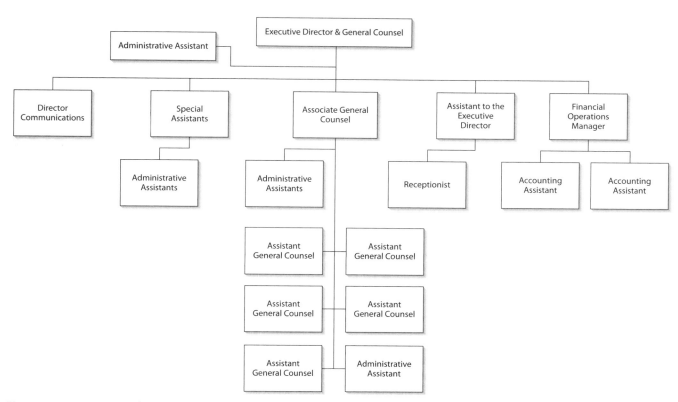

Figure 65-1   Union: Labor Team

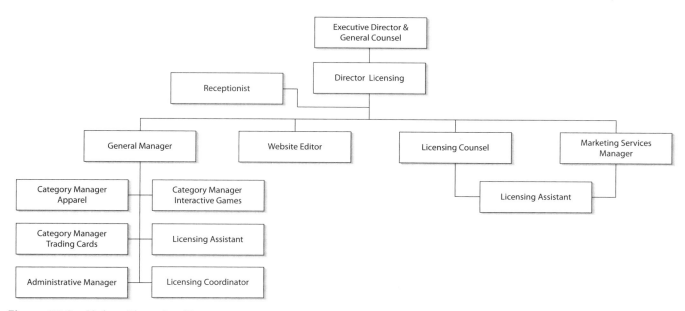

Figure 65-2   Union: Licensing Team

CHAPTER SIXTY-SEVEN

Facilities

Facilities play a significant role in a number of industry segments, including college and professional sports. Facilities provide a place to play the game, but they must also be run in a fiscally prudent manner. To describe this industry segment, this chapter includes two representative organizations.

MASSMUTUAL CENTER

The MassMutual Center, formerly known as the Springfield Civic Center, is located in Springfield, Massachusetts. The arena holds 6,677 guests for sporting events, concerts, and other gatherings. In addition, 40,000 square feet of exhibition space can also be found within the arena complex. The building is owned by the Commonwealth of Massachusetts through the Massachusetts Convention Center Authority (MCCA). In October 2005, MCCA contracted with a facility management company, Global Spectrum, to handle the management of the arena. Interesting to note, the Springfield Falcons (previously discussed in Chapter 62) play their home games at the arena.

The organizational chart depicted in **Figure 67-1** is representative of similar facilities in the arena management industry. It illustrates the working relationship between a building's owner and the outside management company. For more information on facility management, please read the facility management write-up in Chapter 31.

LARGE INDOOR ARENA

The second facility organizational chart is from a larger indoor arena that hosts NHL hockey games and NBA basketball games, as well as a variety of concerts, family shows, and other events. The facility's ownership group controls both the arena and the NHL franchise, but has no controlling interest in the local NBA team. This particular organization wishes not to disclose the arena's name for confidentiality purposes. The organizational chart for this entity is rather large and has been broken down into smaller subsections.

It is important to note that a large arena such as this employs more people than a smaller arena, such as the MassMutual Center. This difference in size is reflected in the organizational charts. The larger arena also has premium seating; therefore, there is a department for this. The organization allocates a number of full-time and part-time positions to the selling and servicing of the arena's premium areas, including club-level seats, luxury suites, and lounges. Notice that there are several employees (vice president of client relations/premium club, senior director of premium club, premium box office manager, etc.) managing this highly important area of business. These positions spread across multiple departments and some positions have multiple reporting lines, which add to the complexity of the charts for the larger arena.

The organizational charts provide a representative example of how large indoor arenas can be structured.

President's Office

This subsection of the large indoor arena's organizational chart (**Figure 67-2**) illustrates the structure found within the president's office. It shows the leaders and decision makers running the organization. Many of the positions included on this chart have departments reporting to them, which are shown on subsequent organizational charts.

Finance Department

The vice president of finance/CFO (included in Figure 67-2) is in charge of overseeing the finance and accounting functions of the arena. **Figure 67-3** presents the various positions in the finance department.

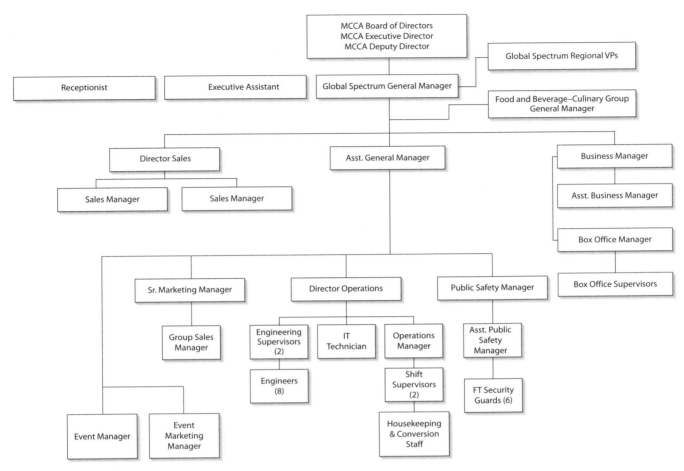

Figure 67-1   MassMutual Center: Facility Management Structure

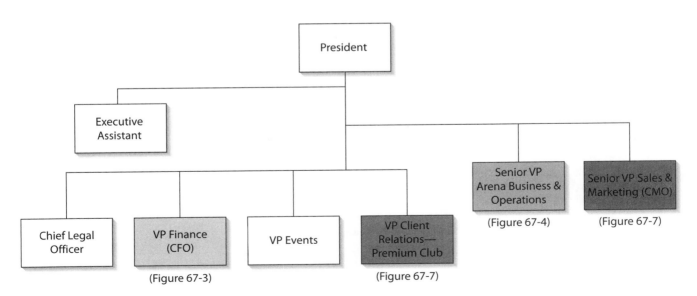

Figure 67-2   Large Indoor Arena: President's Office

Arena Business and Operations

The senior vice president of arena business and operations (included in Figure 67-2) oversees a number of vital operations, including retail merchandising, customer service, technology, building operations, and the box office. This position has a number of positions and departments reporting directly to it, which are illustrated in **Figure 67-4**. Departments such as technology and the box office have their own dedicated organizational charts, which are presented subsequently in the following sections.

Technology and eBusiness Department

The vice president of technology and e-business, also known as the chief technology officer (CTO), reports directly to the

senior vice president of arena business and operations, as shown in the chart in Figure 67-4. The organization's technology department chart (**Figure 67-5**) is specialized in nature. Rather than list all of the various positions found within the department, it instead lists the areas in which the department's activities are focused. This provides insight into the types of technology work needed in large arenas. Gaining specialized expertise in one of these areas may improve one's chances of getting an IT-related job at a large arena.

Box Office

The director of ticket operations (included in Figure 67-4) manages all box office–related activity for the arena. The organizational structure for the box office is illustrated in

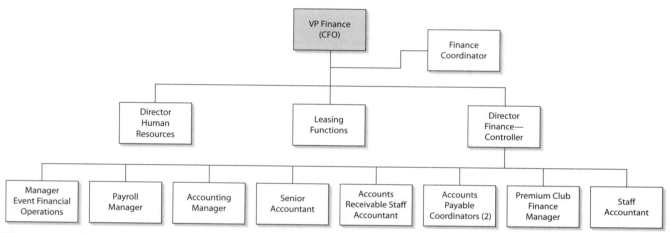

Figure 67-3   Large Indoor Arena: Finance Department

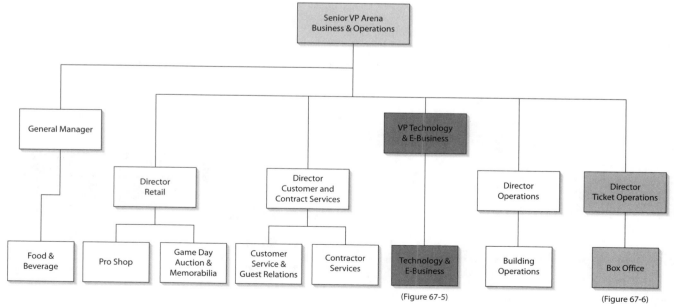

Figure 67-4   Large Indoor Arena: Arena Business and Operations

Figure 67-6. There are two important things to note about the organizational chart for the arena's box office department.

First, the director of ticket operations has some supervisory responsibilities over the premium box office manager, but does not have complete control (thus, the inclusion of the dashed line connecting these two positions in Figure 67-6). The premium box office manager also reports to the senior director of premium club, who is included in the sales department organizational chart (see the following section). Essentially, this means the premium box office manager has two supervisors, one located within the box office and one located within the sales department.

The second important thing to note about Figure 67-6 is that the arena has employees focusing exclusively on hockey ticketing operations. This is due to the arena's ownership control over the hockey club. If the arena held no such ownership interest, the arena would likely not employ people in such hockey-dedicated positions.

Sales Department

The sales department is run by the senior vice president of sales and marketing (in some organizations, the chief marketing officer). This position is an executive position and was included in the president's office organizational chart presented in Figure 67-2. The organizational chart for the sales department (**Figure 67-7**) illustrates the various positions that are under the control of the CMO. Important to note, premium seating is a subsection of the sales department, and has a separate chart presented in the next section. In addition, the vice president of client relations/premium club indirectly supervises the activities of the senior director of premium club and the senior director of the premium sales (as depicted by the dashed lines in the figure).

Premium Seating Department

The premium seating department (**Figure 67-8**) is a subsection of the sales department. The senior director of premium club is responsible for managing the activities of the department. Once again, this chart illustrates the dual reporting role of the premium box office manager, reporting directly to the senior director of premium club and indirectly to the director of ticket operations.

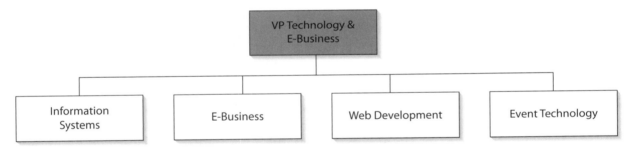

Figure 67-5   Large Indoor Arena: Technology and eBusiness Department

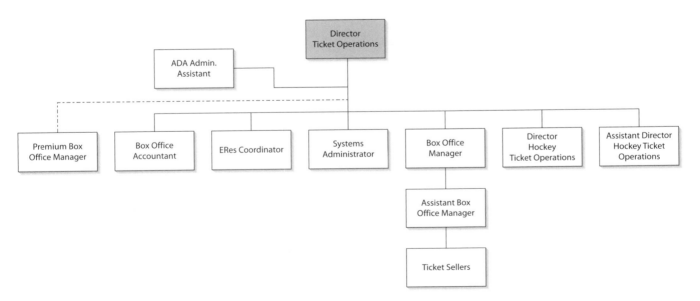

Figure 67-6   Large Indoor Arena: Box Office

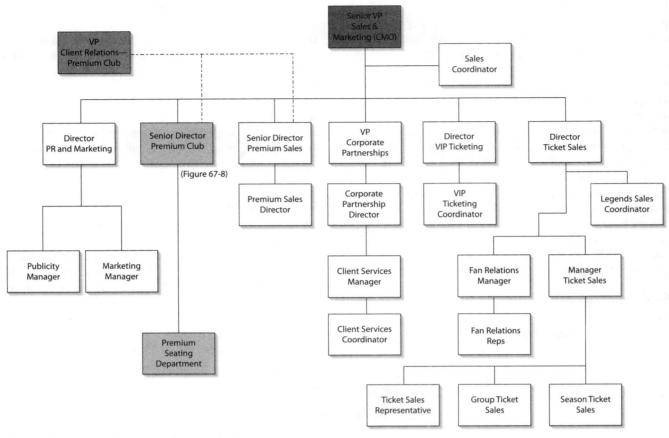

Figure 67-7   Large Indoor Arena: Sales Department

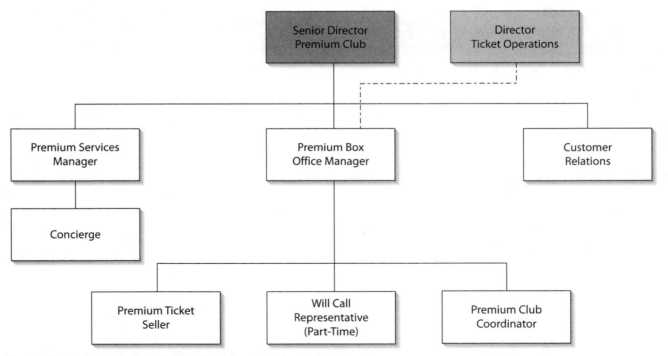

Figure 67-8   Large Indoor Arena: Premium Seating Department

CHAPTER SIXTY-EIGHT 68

Amateur Athletics

Throughout the United States, there are a large number of amateur athletic organizations. These organizations, which can range greatly in size and structure, may be responsible for creating and enforcing rules, organizing competitions, selecting national teams, and/or dealing with world sports organizations. For example, USA Swimming is responsible for implementing a standard set of swimming and eligibility rules across the country; interacting with the International Swimming Federation (FINA); and selecting which athletes will represent the United States in the Olympics and other international competitions. Other examples of amateur organizations include the Ultimate Players Association (Frisbee), the Professional Bowlers Association (PBA), USA Badminton, USRowing, and USA Wrestling. In addition, there are other amateur sports organizations, such as the Bourne Braves, whose main function is to operate a team on which amateurs can play. Included in this chapter, you will find organizational charts for two amateur athletic associations: USA Swimming and the Bourne Braves.

USA SWIMMING

USA Swimming is the national governing body (NGB) for the sport of swimming in the United States. The organization is headquartered in Colorado Springs, Colorado, and operates as a nonprofit entity. Most people are probably familiar with USA Swimming through the Olympic Games and other international competitions, at which U.S. swimmers, such as Michael Phelps, compete as part of the U.S. National Team. Although achieving competitive success is important, the responsibilities of USA Swimming go far beyond the National Team. The organization is also in charge of promoting the sport, aiding in the construction of new aquatic centers, organizing swimming events, administering competitive swimming, and managing the more than 300,000 members of USA Swimming. The following departments work to accomplish the objectives of the organization:

- Business Development: Acts as the promotions agency for the sport. Also helps to organize national events, such as the U.S. Open and Olympic Trials.

- Business Operations/Member Services: Manages the membership data for the organization's members. It also manages the technology within the sport and uses this technology to evaluate statistics and times to better assist coaches and athletes.

- Club Development: Works to support and strengthen the national infrastructure of club swimming in the United States. This department also assists with the planning and development of new aquatic centers.

- Financial Affairs: Manages the organization's finances.

- National Team: Prepares athletes and coaches for the highest level of international competition.

- Fundraising and Alumni: Acts as the fundraising arm of USA Swimming.

The organizational chart in **Figure 68-1** presents these departments and the specific positions found within each one. This provides a good example for how other NGBs (such as USA Soccer, USA Basketball, etc.) may be structured. Note that USA Swimming uses a director-manager-coordinator hierarchy for its positions.

BOURNE BRAVES

The Bourne Braves are 1 of 10 teams that compete in the Cape Cod Baseball League (CCBL). The CCBL is a wood-bat summer league for collegiate players, located on Cape Cod in Massachusetts. The organizational structure for the Bourne Braves (**Figure 68-2**) is a good example of a structure required to operate a nonprofit amateur sports entity. Most of the positions are on a volunteer basis, and no compensation is provided.

CHAPTER SEVENTY

Print and Media

Historically, much of sports media coverage was provided by newspapers and magazines. In recent years, the nature of sports coverage in newspapers and magazines has changed significantly. There are some magazines, such as *Sports Illustrated* and *ESPN: the Magazine*, that cover a wide range of sports topics while others, such as *SLAM* (basketball), *Baseball America,* and *Pro Football Weekly*, focus on a particular sport.

In addition to newspapers and magazines, there is a relatively new industry called "new media" that is increasingly important. The new media industry encompasses all media that can be distributed digitally, typically over the Internet but also via cell phone text messaging and e-mailing. One of the most popular forms for new media is the blog. A blog is a location on a website where people, called bloggers, regularly share their thoughts or ideas with others via the Internet. In this way, sports blogs are similar to a sports writer's newspaper column. However, one should be aware that the majority of sports blogs on the Internet are written in a casual manner by unpaid and non-affiliated writers. Therefore, blogs may be biased or incorrect in ways that one would not find in a newspaper. With that being said, many media companies such as ESPN and *Sports Illustrated* have begun hiring popular bloggers to provide material for their websites. To represent the print and media section of the industry, this chapter includes an organizational chart for *Sports Illustrated*.

SPORTS ILLUSTRATED

A detailed write-up on *Sports Illustrated* can be found in Chapter 37. The organizational chart depicted in **Figure 70-1** represents only the marketing functions of the company. Similar positions are likely to be found at other magazines as well as at newspapers.

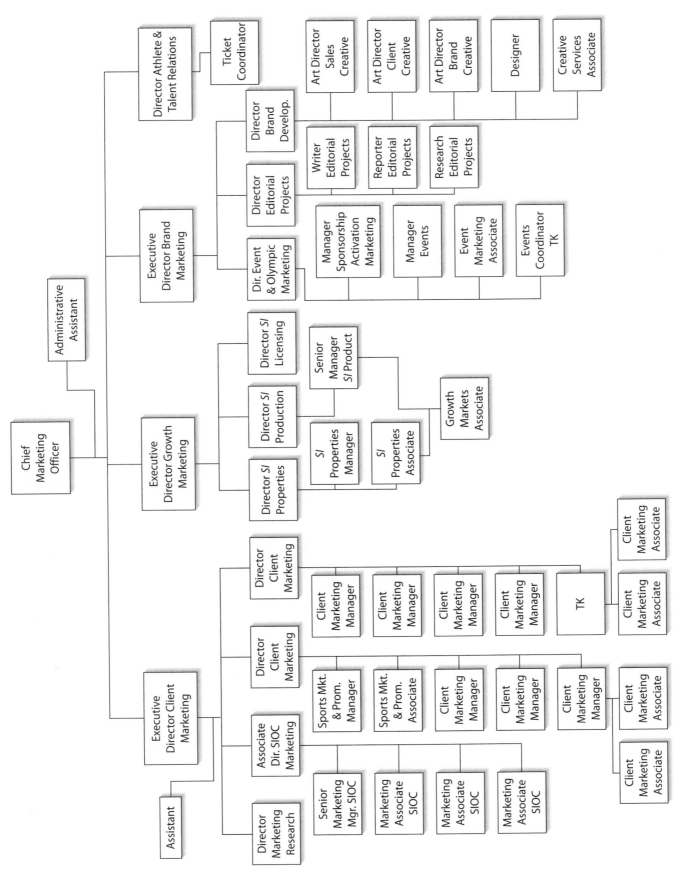

Figure 70-1 *Sports Illustrated:* **Marketing Department**

71

Sports Conglomerates

Sports conglomerates are becoming more prevalent throughout the sports industry. As ownership groups continue to acquire multiple assets in related lines of business, companies are growing more and more complex. To provide examples of such sports conglomerates, this chapter presents an organizational chart of Comcast Spectacor, which is a subsidiary of Comcast, and the top-level organizational chart of New England Sports Ventures.

COMCAST SPECTACOR

A self-proclaimed sports and entertainment firm, Comcast Spectacor owns the following sports-related assets:

- Professional sports teams:
  - Philadelphia Flyers of the NHL
  - Philadelphia 76ers of the NBA
  - Philadelphia Phantoms of the American Hockey League
- Event arenas, including:
  - Wachovia Center
  - Wachovia Spectrum
- A series of community skating rinks called the Flyers Skate Zone
- A facility management company called Global Spectrum
- A food service management company called Ovations
- A marketing consulting company called Front Row Marketing
- A full-service ticketing subsidiary called New Era Tickets

In addition, Comcast Spectacor's parent company controls and operates prominent sports cable channels, such as Versus, The Golf Channel, and Comcast SportsNet. The organizational chart presented in **Figure 71-1** illustrates how Comcast organizes all of these entities.

Peter Luukko, president and COO, and Edward M. Snider, founder and chairman of Comcast Spectacor. Comcast Spectacor was one of the first sports entertainment and management companies, and it remains at the forefront some 30 years later. It owns and manages franchises (the Philadelphia 76ers and the Philadelphia Flyers), facilities, marketing and ticketing agencies, and media properties.

More information on Global Spectrum can be found in Chapter 31, and more information on Comcast SportsNet can be found in Chapter 35.

NEW ENGLAND SPORTS VENTURES

New England Sports Ventures (NESV) is the parent company of the Boston Red Sox, Fenway Park, New England Sports Network, and the more recently established Fenway Sports Group. The setup neatly bundles an MLB baseball team, its ballpark, TV operations, and a growing sports marketing agency under one umbrella organization. In 2007, Fenway Sports Group also purchased a 50% equity stake in Roush Fenway Racing, listed by *Forbes* as NASCAR's most valuable rac-

ing team. The organizational chart presented in **Figure 71-2** is a top-level chart depicting the division of entities under the control of NESV. Some of the entities share employees, such as the Boston Red Sox and Fenway Sports Group. (According to *SportsBusiness Journal*, seven executives split time between the entities.)[1] This provides an indication that when working for a sports conglomerate there is a possibility of working on projects for more than one entity. More information on Fenway Sports Group can be found in Chapter 41.

Endnotes

1. Fisher, E. (2007, July 9–15). Fenway Sports Picks Up Speed in 4th Year. *Street & Smith's SportsBusiness Journal*, vol. 10, issue 11, p. 30.

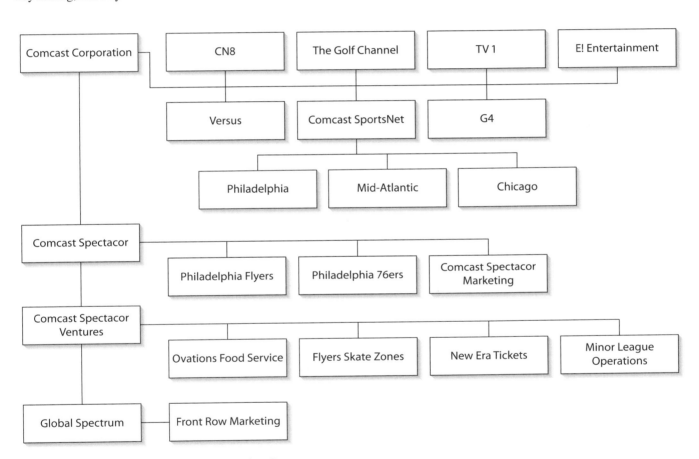

Figure 71-1 Comcast Spectacor: Executive Structure

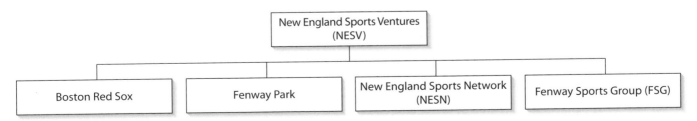

Figure 71-2 New England Sports Ventures: Executive Structure

Section 5

Job Announcements

and sponsorship combined into a single position). There are advantages and disadvantages to each type of position. Generally speaking, the more focused the position, the more opportunity there is for the employee to become an expert in that area. This may increase the employee's effectiveness and likelihood of success at his or her current position. In contrast, a broad-based position may provide a broader, more well-rounded experience that may be of more use if the employee decides to pursue more advanced positions in the future. Typically, the larger the organization, the more likely you are to find specialized positions.

In addition, there are subtle differences in job titles. Where one organization may have a director of public relations, another organization may choose to call a comparable position the director of communications (or possibly director of media relations). In cases such as this, most of the actual job *responsibilities* are likely to be very similar, but the job *titles* and some of the responsibilities may differ. Nonetheless, if you are going into an interview at a particular organization, it is good to know the descriptive title used by the organization.

As you read the various job descriptions, be on the lookout for key themes found in job descriptions within the same field. These are likely to be the most important skills and requirements for that particular field. If you decide to pursue a career in the field, devise a plan to obtain any such skills and/or requirements that you currently lack. For example, if you wish to work in marketing for a professional team, previous sales experience can be an important factor in getting a job. If you do not possess any sales experience, this is something you may want to work towards obtaining.

The job descriptions are arranged by functional departments, such as marketing, community relations, and so on, not by industry segment. What if you are unsure of what functional department you would like to work in, but you do know you are only interested in college athletics? Most functional departments presented in this book include job descriptions from multiple industry segments. If you are only interested in college athletics, focus on the job descriptions pertaining to this field.

Job announcements included in this section were primarily obtained from sources listed in Chapter 7. As you begin your job search in sports, use these valuable resources to learn about current job openings.

COMPENSATION

Compensation levels for sports positions are generally not well publicized and can vary significantly by position title, market, organization, assigned duties, level of previous experience, and level of education. To demonstrate these differences, consider the following:

- Comparing the heads of marketing for two NBA teams, one may have a job title of chief marketing officer (CMO), and the other may only have a title of vice president of marketing. In such a case, a CMO is likely to earn a larger salary than the VP of marketing, and the difference could be substantial (i.e., more than $100,000).

- Even though they may perform the same job duties for similar organizations, someone working in a larger market, such as New York, will typically earn more than someone working in a smaller market, such as Columbus, Ohio. This is also true of nonsports positions.

- The size and level of the organization matters. For example, someone who is the head of public relations for an MLB team is likely to earn more than someone who is the head of public relations for a Single-A minor league team. The same holds true for positions in college athletics—people employed at Division I athletic programs are likely to earn more than people employed at Division III athletic programs.

- Not all organizations place the same value on positions. As a result, some organizations simply pay more or pay less than other organizations for seemingly identical positions at otherwise similar organizations. This is a matter of priorities and perceived value within a particular organization.

- Despite having the same job title, someone working for an organization that owns both an NBA team and an NHL team, as well as the arena the teams play in, is likely to earn more than someone working for an organization that simply owns an NHL team. The increased level of compensation is due to the increased demands and greater responsibility that come with working for multiple sports properties simultaneously.

- Previous work experience can increase the level of compensation. For example, if a job has a pay range of $45,000 to $65,000, candidates with previous work experience are more likely to be on the higher end of the compensation range, whereas candidates with less work experience will likely be on the lower end.

- Particularly in college athletics, the level of completed education can influence one's level of compensation. For instance, someone with a doctoral degree may earn more than someone with a master's degree in a similar position.

Keep in mind, a position in the sports industry will often pay less than a comparable position in the business world. As previously noted in a subsection of Chapter 3 ("Show Me the Money!"), this is due to the supply and demand of positions within the sports industry.

Ideally, each of the job announcements presented in this section would include a compensation range. In reality, though, most sports organizations are hesitant to release such information, because it limits their ability to negotiate compensation packages with new hires. This situation is not isolated to the sports environment; it occurs in the business world as well. The few job announcements that did include a compensation range have been included in the job announcements presented in this section.

In an attempt to provide you with a better idea of the types of salary ranges you can expect to find working in the sports industry, compensation information from a variety of industry sources has been gathered. This information can be found at the beginning of most functional areas and includes compensation ranges for multiple levels of positions within those areas. The lack of compensation information for a particular functional area is not meant to be a judgment of that particular area; it means there was a lack of available information. The compensation estimates represent a reasonable salary range for an average-size organization in a mid-size market. Working for a larger organization or in a larger market may result in a salary slightly higher than the range given, and vice versa. The compensation estimates are only to be used to guide your expectations—they should not be relied upon as the actual figures for positions.

LANGUAGE OF THE INDUSTRY

Remember, these are the actual job announcements and descriptions used by the various sports organizations. Thus, they represent the language commonly found throughout the industry. If you find words or phrases that are unfamiliar to you (e.g. CRM, customer relationship management, may be a new term for you), this is where your homework comes in handy (see Chapter 2). By referring to sources such as *Street & Smith's SportsBusiness Journal* and other publications, you can learn about current industry trends and buzzwords. This should help you to better understand any new terms or phrases you come across as you read the job descriptions.

POSITION SPOTLIGHTS

Throughout this section of the book, *Position Spotlights* have been provided to enhance your understanding of select positions within the sports industry. The *Position Spotlights* are generalizations and summaries for a particular position with a greater emphasis on the job and its responsibilities (as compared to the job announcements, which typically focus more on a job's qualifications and requirements). You will find the *Position Spotlights* throughout Section 5, and they are placed near job announcements and descriptions for similar or comparable positions.

CHAPTER SEVENTY-THREE

Leadership Positions

"Success comes from knowing that you did your best to become the best that you are capable of becoming."

—John Wooden, former head basketball coach of the UCLA Bruins and member of the Basketball Hall of Fame

Leadership positions are found in every segment of the sports industry. Their primary role is to set the strategic direction of the organization and to oversee the management of the organization. Titles range from athletic director, to commissioner, to executive director, to president. In most cases, these are the most prominent and visible business professionals in a particular organization.

Not surprisingly, leadership positions are typically the highest paid business professionals within their respective organizations. Although compensation levels will vary significantly from organization to organization, the following can be expected:

- The commissioner of a major sports league or the executive director of a major sports union will typically range from $1 million to $20 million per year.

- The commissioner of a smaller sports league, such as the Arena Football League, will earn less, but still likely in the $100,000+ range.

- The conference commissioner of a Football Bowl Subdivision conference (formerly Division I-A) will likely earn between $350,000 and $2 million, depending on the conference.

- An athletic director of a Football Championship Subdivision school (formerly Division I-AA) will likely earn between $90,000 and $215,000 year; an AD at a larger Football Bowl Subdivision school will earn more and an AD at a smaller Division II or Division III school will earn less.

- For a few of the following positions, a specific salary has been presented. In such cases, this is the executive's actual compensation, as reported in recent news articles.

DIRECTOR OF ATHLETICS AND RECREATION, UNIVERSITY OF MASSACHUSETTS–DARTMOUTH

Industry Segment:	College Athletics, NCAA Division III
Functional Area:	Management
Experience:	Three years of senior-level experience required
Location:	Dartmouth, Massachusetts

The University of Massachusetts–Dartmouth is seeking nominations and applications for the position of director of athletics and recreation. Reporting directly to the vice chancellor for student affairs, the director of athletics and recreation is responsible for all aspects of the intercollegiate athletics, intramural, and fitness and recreation programs at the university. Located on the beautiful south coast of Massachusetts just an hour from Boston and 30 minutes from Newport and Providence, Rhode Island, the University of Massachusetts–Dartmouth serves about 8,700 students— 7,600 undergraduate students and 1,100 graduate students. Approximately 50% of the students reside on campus and about 90% are between the ages of 18 and 24. The university offers a high -quality academic experience in more than 60 major areas of study from five colleges, including arts and sciences, business, engineering, nursing, visual and performing arts, and a distinctive school for marine science and technology. UMass Dartmouth strives to be the university of choice for students seeking high-quality liberal arts and science programs as well as professional academic programs that build the foundation for civic responsibility, individual skills, and professional success. The *U.S. News and World Report* has ranked UMass–Dartmouth among its top northern public universities and UMass–Dartmouth offers a broad range of baccalaureate and graduate degrees vital to the economic, social, and cultural well-being of the region and commonwealth.

The successful candidate will possess a record of integrity and progressive advancement in intercollegiate athletics administration. The director is expected to manage the department of athletics and recreation with integrity, respecting the university's mission and its commitment to excellence. This individual should understand and value the philosophy of NCAA Division III intercollegiate athletics and its place within an academic community. The director bears principal responsibility for leading a competitive intercollegiate program, including varsity and club sports and a strong program of recreation, intramurals, and fitness/wellness that is open to all students and other members of the university community. The director also represents UMass–Dartmouth at the national and regional levels, serves in a leadership role in many areas including the efforts to achieve the university's gender equity and diversity goals, and manages the efficient use of fiscal resources and facilities. The director is responsible for compliance with all policies, rules, and regulations of UMass–Dartmouth and of the conferences and associations to which it belongs.

Qualifications

The ideal candidate will provide solid leadership for the program, will possess a comprehensive knowledge of athletics administration at the NCAA Division III level, and will guide both the internal and external operations of the program. He/she will have experience evaluating and mentoring personnel. The candidate should also have experience relevant to building relationships with different constituencies of the university. Highly desirable qualifications include a bachelor's degree, master's degree preferred, relevant background in athletics administration, and at least 3 years of senior-level experience in athletics administration.

ATHLETICS DIRECTOR, DELTA STATE UNIVERSITY

Industry Segment:	College Athletics, NCAA Division II
Functional Area:	Management
Experience:	Five years of experience required
Location:	Cleveland, Mississippi

Delta State University in Cleveland, Mississippi, invites applications and nominations for athletics director. This position is a full-time senior-level management position,

serving on the university cabinet and reporting directly to the president. Widely acknowledged as one of the leading NCAA Division II programs in the nation, Delta State's athletics program has a long and proud history of competitive programs, national championships, and academic excellence.

Responsibilities

The successful candidate must demonstrate a commitment to academic excellence for the student-athlete while promoting and sustaining a clear vision for competing at the highest level within the Gulf South Conference and the NCAA. The athletics director will develop and implement marketing and fundraising strategies to fund facility improvements, scholarship endowments, and operating budgets for all athletics programs. The individual should possess exceptional organizational skills, be capable of handling multiple tasks, and efficiently administer the day-to-day operations of the intercollegiate athletics program. In addition, it is essential that he/she have experience in planning and administering a departmental budget and the proven ability to maintain the fiscal integrity of the athletics program. The director will serve as the principal spokesperson for DSU athletics and will develop events in cooperation with various athletics constituencies, including the Green and White Fund and the DSU Foundation.

Qualifications

Master's degree is required. Doctorate preferred. The candidate will demonstrate successful experience in managing a complex financial organization, athletics fundraising, athletics marketing, student-athlete recruiting, and retention. Five years of relevant athletics administrative management or equivalent experience is required. Evidence of skills in fiscal planning, personnel management, effective written/oral communication, commitment to student-athletes, NCAA compliance and reporting systems, short/long range planning, public relations, and a commitment to diversity and gender equity must be reflected in each application.

DIRECTOR OF INTERCOLLEGIATE ATHLETICS, MICHIGAN STATE UNIVERSITY

Industry Segment:	College Athletics, NCAA Football Bowl Subdivision
Functional Area:	Management
Experience:	10+ years of experience required
Location:	East Lansing, Michigan

Michigan State University seeks an experienced, accomplished, innovative leader, with a commitment to inclusion and the highest ethical standards to serve as director of intercollegiate athletics.

Qualifications

Candidates must have a minimum of 10 years' experience as a NCAA Division I senior athletic administrator or possess senior corporate leadership experience, including a minimum of 5 years' experience in financial administration, fundraising, games operations, facility management, human resources policy, and public relations within a major athletic conference or corporate environment.

A demonstrated understanding and appreciation of the role of NCAA Division I athletics in the context of an academic environment, emphasizing the importance of the scholarly growth and development of student-athletes, is required. Candidates must possess excellent organizational, communication, and interpersonal skills and a capacity to develop a strong and inclusive leadership team. The highest level of personal integrity and ethical standards, including a commitment to and compliance with NCAA and Big Ten Conference rules, is required.

Candidates must have a demonstrated commitment to MSU's core values of quality, inclusion, and connectivity, as well as an ability to apply these values in leadership and management of the Department of Intercollegiate Athletics. The ability to develop and implement innovative approaches for revenue development in athletics is a must, as is the ability to conduct long-range strategic, financial, and facility planning and budgeting on behalf of the department.

Candidates must have a demonstrated ability to work collaboratively with senior university administration and other relevant university departments, and to communicate effectively with and command respect of coaches, student-athletes, and other internal athletic constituencies, across all intercollegiate sports. Additionally, candidates must be able to communicate effectively with media, alumni, donors, boosters, and other external constituencies.

The candidate selected must possess credentials appropriate for an institution of higher education. The director of intercollegiate athletics reports to the president. There are likely to be internal candidates for this position.

Michigan State University has been advancing knowledge and transforming lives through innovative teaching, research, and outreach for more than 150 years. It is known worldwide as a major public university with global reach and extraordinary impact. It offers more than 200 programs of study, many of them nationally ranked, which attract scholars worldwide who are interested in combining education with practical problem solving. Located in East Lansing, the beautiful 5,200-acre campus includes 660 buildings. More than 200 programs of study are offered to more than 45,000 students from all 83 counties in Michigan, all 50 states in the United States, and about 125 countries around the world. MSU has 25 varsity squads, 12 intercollegiate sports for men, and 13 intercollegiate sports for women.

MSU is committed to achieving excellence through cultural diversity. The university actively encourages applications and/or nominations of women, persons of color, veterans, and persons with disabilities.

EXECUTIVE DIRECTOR, USA WATER SKI

Industry Segment:	National Governing Body, Water Skiing
Functional Area:	Management
Experience:	Seven years of experience required
Location:	Polk City, Florida

USA Water Ski sanctions competitive water skiing events in the United States and promotes exciting disciplines like water skiing, wakeboarding, and more. The organization's mission also includes helping to ensure our waterways may be shared in a safe and fun manner. USA Water Ski also is recognized by the United States Olympic Committee as the national governing body for organized water skiing in the United States.

USA Water Ski consists of nine affiliate disciplines, which are supported by a full-time headquarters staff of 18. Offices are located in Polk City, Florida, just off I-4 halfway between Tampa and Orlando. Facilities include a recently completed world-class competition site. More information about USA Water Ski is available at www.USAWaterski.org.

The successful candidate will be a strategic leader capable of identifying and developing opportunities for increasing participation nationally through comprehensive program design and implementation. Must have a proven track record in staff management, budgeting, and financial administration.

Responsibilities

- Manage headquarters staff and the operation of USA Water Ski, Inc.

- Implement and maintain programs to develop and support participants and members

- Financial reporting to the association's president and executive committee

Qualifications

- Seven-plus years of business experience, including senior management

- Demonstrated history of the successful development and implementation of a strategic plan

- Strong financial management, budgeting, and administration skills

- Proven track record of motivating and managing key personnel

- Experience with not-for-profit organizations and national governing body is a plus

- Exceptional communications skills

- Bachelor's degree in business, sports management, or equivalent

Position Spotlight *NCAA Football Bowl Subdivision College Athletic Director*

The director of athletics (also known as the athletics director or AD) is the highest-ranking position in a university's athletic department. The person in this role is ultimately responsible for all the actions and decisions that relate to intercollegiate athletics at a university. Quite often, an AD's job is both very public and political in nature.

The demands at a Football Bowl Subdivision (FBS) school create unique challenges for athletic directors, because athletic departments at these schools maintain constant national visibility, manage budgets ranging from $10 million to over $70 million, and must field at least 14 total teams (a minimum of seven of which are in women's sports) while dispersing over $4 million in scholarships. This typically requires coordinating the efforts of 100+ full-time staff.

The FBS (formerly Division I-A) is also synonymous with "big-time" college football, which has its positives and negatives for a university. The top programs receive financial rewards from bowl games and television revenues, but the expense of a football program is typically a significant expense for athletic departments. At the Football Championship Subdivision level (FCS, formerly Division I-AA), similar pressures exist, but the football programs compete on a smaller scale and have less demanding NCAA requirements in terms of scholarship money and requisite attendance figures. FBS schools' expenses dwarf other divisions; the average FBS school's expenses are three times greater than those of FCS schools and 30 times greater than the average nonfootball Division III school. (For a thorough analysis of divisional differences, please see Chapter 29). Not surprisingly, managing an institution's football program is very time consuming for an FBS AD, often requiring 60- to 70-hour work weeks.

An AD's job can be divided into internal operations and external activities. The internal component enables the operation of the school's sports teams; management of coaches, compliance, facility management, and academic services for student-athletes are examples of internal areas of focus for an AD. The external activities provide financial support to the programs, through fundraising and sponsorships, and visibility for the university, through television exposure and merchandise licensing. As the head of the department, it is often the AD who meets with the media to speak on behalf of the athletic department. This requires well-developed public speaking skills. In order to fundraise effectively for the university, the AD must also have a strong development office and will often use the football and/or basketball teams to appeal to boosters and alumni.

The job requirements for an AD vary from institution to institution and even from one time period to another within the same school. One school may look to hire an AD with specialized experience in creating championship programs in Olympic sports, whereas another school's priority may lie with securing outside funding for the construction of new facilities. Another area of importance may be improving the graduation rates of the school's student-athletes. Even at the same school, priorities can shift between the hiring processes for consecutive athletic directors. For example, a university may have hired an AD initially because of his business acumen in office efficiency, but after a wave of recruiting scandals leads to the AD's resignation, the school looks to replace him or her with someone of undeniable integrity. In the first instance, the institution sought a candidate who came with a background in industry, whereas the next time the same school preferred someone with a track record for running clean programs.

One of the tasks for any AD is to select, organize, and manage a staff that meets the priorities of the job and complements the AD's strengths. In some systems, the AD may dedicate all his or her time to dealing with trustees, meeting with faculty and other nonathletic university personnel, and appealing to state politicians (particularly necessary at state-financed universities), in which case a member of the senior staff will run the operational components of the department. At all FBS schools, the department staff handles many operational elements autonomously, and thus this group must be skilled, trusted, dedicated, loyal, and hardworking. To form such a staff, when a new AD comes to a university, he or she often will bring some of his or her own people (i.e., those with whom the AD has worked with in previous jobs) to fill positions in the department. This is further reason to properly network, maintain a solid work ethic, and establish good relationships with friends and co-workers along the way through a career.

COMMISSIONER, MIDWEST CLASSIC CONFERENCE

Industry Segment: College Athletics, NAIA
Functional Area: Management
Experience: Unspecified
Location: Traveling

The Midwest Classic Conference (MCC) is accepting applications for the full-time position of commissioner. The commissioner shall work at the direction of the Council of Presidents and the Athletic Directors' Council as the league's chief operating officer and will provide leadership for the conference in the areas of strategic planning and membership. The commissioner would serve as the primary administrator, with a strong emphasis on marketing and increased exposure of the Midwest Classic Conference. The commissioner would serve as the budget officer.

The position of a conference commissioner is a paid position by the league. The term of employment shall be for a one-year term beginning on July 1 of the year of appointment. Appointment to the position and salary shall be

Position Spotlight *Conference Commissioner, College Athletics*

Universities and colleges are members of larger governing associations, usually the NCAA or NAIA (see Chapter 29 for additional information on college athletics), and most schools are also part of a smaller subset of schools, called a conference. Conferences consist of a number of schools (typically 8 to 12) with similar goals, interests, sizes, and/or geographic locations. Larger conferences have a league office in which administrators make operational decisions (e.g., scheduling games, assigning referees, securing television broadcasts, and other event management functions) on behalf of the conference's member institutions. The commissioner, the conference's highest-ranking member, serves as chief operating officer for the conference.

One of the commissioner's tasks is ensuring the fluid operation of activities within the conference's sports and the hiring of the conference's personnel. The commissioner hires a staff that will complement his or her own strengths and weaknesses while carrying out the mission of the conference. For example, if the conference goal is to enter the upper echelon of NCAA basketball, the commissioner may dedicate some of his or her time to negotiating with schools in his or her conference and with other conferences in order to encourage a more difficult out of conference schedule, which will create more nationally attractive games and increase television exposure. Therefore, the commissioner may hire someone or assign his or her operational tasks to other staff. In other cases, these jobs may be handled directly by the conference commissioner, and he or she will divide the other responsibilities to the rest of the staff. As with athletic directors, the staff with which the commissioner surrounds him- or herself is extremely important.

The actual responsibilities of a commissioner will differ greatly depending on the conference. The work in each conference varies, as do the long-term goals for the league. The size of conferences depends on the scale of the sports for which the conference is responsible; for instance, a Football Bowl Subdivision (formerly Division I-A) conference championship game requires considerable effort from the conference office, which is not required for conferences who have only regular season contests. In some cases, a conference will hire a commissioner not to increase revenues, but to cut costs associated with running the league. For example, the Metro Atlantic Athletic Conference (MAAC) found a venue to host its championships that absorbed the cost of producing the event, which saved the conference thousands of dollars annually. In such situations, a candidate whose background is in operational efficiencies and/or one who brings established relationships (i.e., contacts), creativity, or skills in negotiation may be more attractive than one with experience in a development office.

Most conferences seek to grow and/or improve, whether in terms of actual member schools, the financial bottom line, playing performance, or the recognition for the conference and its members. By cultivating relationships with others in the industry and implementing strategic initiatives, the commissioner works to achieve the conference's objectives. For example, negotiating with another conference to have annual games played between the two conferences' member schools will create exposure for both conferences in regions where they normally would not have visibility (e.g., the annual in-season basketball games between schools of the Big 10 and ACC).

Much of a commissioner's job involves high-level strategy, negotiation, and consensus building. Although the commissioner represents the interests of the member schools' presidents and athletic directors, he or she sets the conference's agenda and direction. If there is difference of opinion within the conference school's presidents (operating as the Council of Presidents), which is regularly the case, the commissioner must negotiate a consensus among the schools in order to advance the conference as a whole. The actual dynamics of conferences differ as well; some commissioners are very powerful within their league and influential with the NCAA. On the other hand, conferences where presidents and AD's control the agenda have commissioners whose power is much less.

The Bowl Championship Series for the NCAA Football Bowl Subdivision creates additional duties for the commissioners of BCS member conferences. Under its current format, the BCS is managed by the commissioners of the 11 NCAA FBS conferences, the director of athletics at the University of Notre Dame, and representatives of the bowl organizations. Current BCS conferences include the Atlantic Coast (ACC), Big East, Big Ten, Big 12, Conference USA, Mid-American, Mountain West, Sun Belt, Pacific-10, Southeastern (SEC), and Western Athletic (WAC). The conference commissioners work with the Notre Dame athletic director to make decisions regarding all BCS issues. Together, their work is done in consultation with an athletic director's advisory group and subject to the approval of a presidential oversight committee, whose members represent all 117 FBS programs. A conference commissioner also serves as BCS coordinator. For the 2006 and 2007 seasons, the coordinator was Mike Slive, commissioner of the Southeastern Conference.[4]

legally binding relationship between workers and owners in the National Football League, are met. It negotiates and monitors retirement and insurance benefits.

The NFLPA executive director spearheads the negotiations with the league on the aforementioned issues and assumes the leadership and provides direction to the association. The position is assigned through a vote from the representatives of the player's association.

Responsibilities

- Serves as chief negotiator for players for labor agreements (collective bargaining agreement) with the league
- Files grievances against the league on behalf of players
- Ensures all league policies that affect players are adhered to by the league
- Resolves disputes between the players and the league
- Acts as the public face of the union, requiring such things as testifying before Congress and addressing the media
- Manages the operations of the union office
- Sets the overall path and vision for the union
- Oversees agents and sets agent guidelines
- Handles pension activity

Qualifications

A bachelor's degree is required; typically, most executive directors have earned a law degree (JD). Ideal candidates will possess negotiation skills, leadership and management skills, strong communications skills, interpersonal skills, organizational skills, and creativity.

Experience

Most executive directors have practiced law in a corporate setting or as a general counsel for a union or have filled executive roles within the player's association. Those with no legal background usually have served on the bargaining committee of the player's association, either as a player or in an administrative capacity.

Associations and Trade Publications

- Associations
  - Sports Lawyers Association (SLA)
  - Black Entertainment and Sports Lawyers Association (BESLA)
- Trade publications
  - *The Sports Lawyer Journal* (annual journal, SLA)
  - *The Sports Lawyer* (electronic newsletter, SLA)
  - *Street & Smith's SportsBusiness Journal*

COMMISSIONER, NBA

Industry Segment:	Professional Sports, Basketball, NBA League Office
Functional Area:	Management
Experience:	Unspecified
Location:	New York
Compensation:	Estimated at around $10 million per year[5]
	Other commissioner salaries (per the leagues' recent tax filings, as reported by *Street & Smith's SportsBusiness Journal*):
	• Bud Selig (MLB): $15.06 million[5]
	• Roger Goodell (NFL): $11.2 million[5]
	• Gary Bettman (NHL): $5.9 million[5]
	• Tim Finchem (PGA): $3.6 million[6]
	• Dan Garber (MLS): $2.0 million[6]

The following is a general description detailing the types of responsibilities and requirements commonly found for this position. An actual job announcement was not available.

The commissioner implements and guides the overall direction and vision for the National Basketball Association (NBA) and is responsible for the overall health and viability of the league. In addition, the commissioner represents the team owners in key league-wide issues and negotiations including the collective bargaining agreement (CBA), which governs the practices of the league.

Responsibilities

- Represents all team owners and their interests in CBA negotiations and other league policies
- Positively promotes the NBA, the teams, and its players in order to broaden the fan base of the game
- Ensures the integrity, health, and success of the league is maintained
- Identifies and pursues alternative revenue streams through such avenues as the Internet, international business operations, the WNBA, and the D-League
- Strengthens current corporate alliances and forge novel business partnerships
- Administers punishment for teams and players that violate rules outlined in the CBA
- Resolves disputes between the owners and the player's union
- Oversees the negotiation of television rights deals, including the national television deal (currently with ABC/ESPN) and other cable deals (currently with TNT)

Qualifications

A bachelor's degree is required; an advanced degree in law (JD) or business (MBA) is typically necessary for the position. Ideal candidates will possess negotiation skills, leadership and management skills, strong communications skills, interpersonal skills, organizational skills, and creativity.

- The current commissioner (David Stern) earned a law degree and served as general counsel for the NBA prior to being named commissioner.

- Gary Bettman (NHL) also holds a law degree, resulting in two of the four current commissioners of the "Big 4" professional sports leagues (NBA, NFL, MLB, and NHL) holding law degrees. The previous commissioner of the NFL (Paul Tagliabue) also held a law degree.

Experience

Typically, commissioners have practiced law in a corporate setting or as a general counsel for a sports organization or have filled executive roles in a league office. The league's current commissioner, David Stern, worked for a law firm that represented the league and subsequently served as general counsel and as an executive vice president of the NBA.

Endnotes

1. Shaw, J. (2007, Dec. 10) Bivens Gets 45% Pay Increase in First Full Year. *Street & Smith's SportsBusiness Journal.* Retrieved October 17, 2008 from http://www.sportsbusinessjournal.com/article/57357.

2. Kaplan, D. (2007, July 9). Upshaw's Compensation at Least $6.7 Million. *Street & Smith's SportsBusiness Journal.* Retrieved April 29, 2008, from http://www.sportsbusinessjournal.com/article/55594.

3. NHLPA Offers Paul Kelly Five-Year, $10M Contract. (2007, Oct. 17). *Street and Smith's SportsBusiness Daily.* Retrieved April 29, 2008, from http://www.sportsbusinessdaily.com/article/115763.

4. Governance. (n.d.). *Bowl Championship Series.* Retrieved October 5, 2007, from http://www.bcsfootball.org/bcsfb/governance.

5. Fisher, E., & Kaplan, D. (2008, Mar. 10). Selig's Pay Climbs 4 Percent to $15.06 Million. *Street and Smith's SportsBusiness Daily.* Retrieved April 1, 2008, from http://www.sportsbusinessjournal.com/article/58312.

6. Mickle, T. (2007, June 11). Bettman, Daly Get $2M Raises. *Street & Smith's SportsBusiness Journal.* Retrieved August 21, 2008, from http://www.sportsbusinessjournal.com/article/55422.

Sales and Marketing

Sales and marketing in the sports industry can be far reaching. Naturally, it includes an entity's general marketing activities, but it can also include, depending on the particular organization, activities relating to tickets, sponsorships, promotions, and customer service. Ultimately, in most organizations, this is where you will find the revenue generators. They are responsible for bringing in the money, and thus play an important role within an organization.

As you read the job descriptions, you will find a wide variety of terms used to define sales positions. Inside sales, premium sales, season ticket sales, corporate sales, and sponsorship sales are a few of the more common terms used in the industry. Professionals employed in such positions are responsible for connecting people and businesses with the sports entity. This is accomplished by selling tickets, sponsorships, advertising, and promotions.

It also is important to note that making a sale is only part of the job. Once sales have been made, sports entities often spend a great deal of time and effort to provide service to their customers. For example, once a company has agreed to a sponsorship agreement with a sports entity, it is the responsibility of the sports entity to ensure that the terms and conditions of the sponsorship agreement are carried out. Fulfilling such obligations is what is commonly referred to as service. Some organizations combine sales and service responsibilities into one position, whereas others separate the two into different positions. As a general rule, the more money a person or company spends on tickets or sponsorship packages, the higher the demand for service. For example, a company leasing a suite at a sports stadium will demand (and ultimately receive) a higher level of service from the sports entity than an individual who purchases tickets to a single game. An example of a service provided to prominent customers is a team-hosted meet-and-greet with players, coaches, and team personnel. Such events allow team representatives to interact with fans, strengthening relationships and solidifying the fans' commitment to the team. Teams also often allow season ticket holders to purchase additional individual tickets to highly sought after games (such as Yankees–Red Sox or Cubs–Cardinals) before they go on sale to the general public. Although this may seem to slight the average fan who purchases only a handful of games each season, many teams have prioritized satisfying (and retaining) their very best and most profitable

---

Box 74-1   Definition of Key Sales Terms

Inside sales representatives: Sales representatives who sell a sports organization's products and services over the phone, the Internet, or other media from *inside* the company's office. They can either make outgoing calls to potential customers or receive incoming calls for new sales. These salespeople usually do not visit client sites for sales appointments.

Premium sales representatives: Sales representatives who focus exclusively on selling and servicing a sports organization's *premium* products. In a professional sports setting,

premium products include such things as luxury suites, club-level seats, and courtside seats.

Season ticket sales representatives: Sales representatives who focus exclusively on selling *season tickets*. These sales representatives typically do not focus on selling individual game tickets.

Corporate sales representatives: Sales representatives who focus exclusively on selling to *corporations*. Corporate sales can take on many different forms, including advertising, premium seating, naming rights, and sponsorships.

customers. Think of service as everything that takes place after a sale has been made. Such service can be an extremely important part of a team's operations, and can often be rewarded with retention bonuses (based on the percentage of season ticket holders who renew their account for the next season). Recognizing the distinction between sales and service will help make it easier to understand the positions described in this chapter.

COMPENSATION LEVELS

Industry compensation for marketing positions can vary tremendously depending on many factors, including the cost of the product. The following compensation levels are reasonable expectations for mid-sized organizations in mid-sized markets.

Professional Sports

- Entry level (account executive, coordinator, etc.): $25,000 to $35,000
- Manager level: $40,000 to $60,000
- Director level: $90,000 to $130,000
- Vice president of marketing: $125,000 to $175,000
- Chief marketing officer: $150,000 to $500,000

Facility Management

- Head of marketing for a large indoor arena: $150,000 to $175,000

College Athletics

- Assistant/associate athletic director of marketing for a Football Championship Subdivision school: $40,000 to $75,000
- Assistant commissioner for marketing for a Football Bowl Subdivision Conference: $55,000 to $120,000

This chapter includes more job descriptions than any other for a reason: This is an accurate reflection of the state of the industry. For the most part, sports entities are in the business of selling—whether it's tickets, merchandise, concessions, or experiences. Consequently, you are likely to find many more opportunities in sales and marketing than in other functional areas, due to a relatively larger number of positions. It should come as no surprise, then, that the most common way to break into the industry is through sales and marketing.

In the following job descriptions, you will find a representative sample of the types of sales and marketing positions available in the industry. Ticket and box office positions can be found in Chapter 75, immediately following the more general marketing positions presented here.

SALES INTERN, SEATTLE MARINERS

Industry Segment:	Professional Sports, Baseball, MLB Team
Functional Area:	Sales and Marketing
Experience:	Internship
Location:	Seattle, Washington
Compensation:	Unpaid; college credit received as compensation

The Seattle Mariners Baseball Club is recruiting to fill the position of sales intern. The sales department maintains interns in each of the following quarters* (approximate date range):

- Winter Quarter—Early January to mid-to-late March
- Spring Quarter—Late March to early June
- Summer Quarter—Early June to late August
- Fall Quarter—September to mid-December
  * Please indicate your preferred quarter in the letter of application.

Requirements

The Seattle Mariners internship program offers college students the opportunity to take the first step into the sporting industry. Interns with the Seattle Mariners are unpaid, so interns must be enrolled at an accredited 4- or 5-year college or university leading to a bachelor or advanced degree and must receive college/university credit for their internship. The student must be able to provide proof of their college/university credit prior to starting their assignment. Priority will be given to students who attend college in the northwest region or who have attended high school in Washington State. Internships may be full-time or part-time based on student availability and department needs. The Seattle Mariners front office is at Safeco Field in Seattle, Washington; interns will report to that location.

It is the Seattle Mariners' goal to hire the best students into its intern program. The Mariners accept both undergraduate and graduate students into this program. Students are eligible for an internship after completing their freshman year; however, our largest population of interns on record is junior level or above.

Qualifications

- Computer skills (word processing, spreadsheets, databases, e-mail)
- Excellent oral and written communication skills

- Detail oriented
- Interest in customer service and sales/marketing
- Aptitude for managing multiple projects
- Ability to problem solve

Job Duties

- Perform customer, market, and industry research
- Assist with mailings to current and potential customers
- Update customer database
- Respond to customer inquiries via phone and e-mail
- Perform database integrity projects
- Assist with various sales/customer service projects
- Participate in planning of customer events

MARKETING AND TEAM SERVICES INTERN, ECHL LEAGUE OFFICE

Industry Segment:	Professional Sports, Minor League Hockey, ECHL League Office
Functional Area:	Sales and Marketing
Experience:	Internship
Location:	Princeton, New Jersey
Compensation:	Likely to be unpaid, hourly wage, or small monthly stipend

To assist in all aspects of the ECHL's marketing and team services departments. Applicants should have strong verbal, analytical, and computer skills, with knowledge of Quark and Macintosh applications preferred, proficient in Microsoft Excel and Word. Must possess strong analytical skills and an eye for detail. Good planning and communications skills are a plus.

Duties and Responsibilities

- Assist in preparations for the 2007 ECHL marketing meetings
- Assist in creation and development of sponsor proposals
- Assist team services in tracking ticket sales results and analysis, best practices, and monitoring team websites
- Research potential marketing contacts
- Assist with the upkeep and facilitation of current licensees
- Research on prospective licensees

CORPORATE SALES AND SERVICE INTERNSHIP, PORTLAND TRAIL BLAZERS

Industry Segment:	Professional Sports, Basketball, NBA Team
Functional Area:	Sales and Marketing
Experience:	Internship
Location:	Portland, Oregon
Compensation:	Unpaid; college credit received as compensation

Length of internship is October through May. For college/graduate school credit only—nonpaid, instructor approval required. No other employee benefits; relocation expenses will not be covered.

Purpose

The internship position is designed to allow students to experience a professional work environment by assisting the corporate sales and service staff with a variety of independent and group projects relating to Trail Blazers sponsors.

Duties and Responsibilities

- Assist sponsorship team in developing, coordinating, and executing sponsor-related community retail promotions and employee incentive programs
- Help with set-up, storage, distribution, and collection of point-of-purchase materials and sort mail/entries for sponsor promotions
- Assist in hosting sponsor entertainment functions during games and other special events
- Assist Game Night intern with game responsibilities
- Coordinate with photographer the sponsor-related shots that need to be taken each home game
- Coordinate the VIP (Rose Room) passes and additional tickets for sponsor-related needs
- Coordinate the Rose Room activities for each home game
- Aid the sponsorship team in development and production of sponsor proposals/presentations
- Aid in mass mailings by mail merging database files for form letters; stuffing, labeling, and sealing envelopes; and posting for mail
- Coordinate with sponsors the setup, storage, distribution, and collection of handouts and other prizes for in-arena promotions
- Perform miscellaneous filing, copying, routing, and sending materials by messenger

Desired Competencies

- Integrity and values: Can be trusted to act in a manner that is truthful and values direct, honest communication at all levels of the organization

- Interpersonal confidence: Strong interpersonal skills; can effectively communicate and relate to all levels within and outside the organization; creates and builds positive and productive relationships

- Adaptability: Responds quickly and effectively to changing trends and circumstances; embraces change and welcomes fresh perspectives; learns from past mistakes and adjusts accordingly

- Managing processes: Ability to manage appropriate steps to get projects completed; has strong abilities to organize people and processes; can create a plan for resourceful workflow

- Organizational ability: Can manage people and resources to get projects completed; has a strong ability to multi-task and keep order

Qualifications

- Bachelor's degree (management/marketing preferred)
- Detail oriented
- One to 2 years database management experience
- Strong understanding of database development, database management, and e-marketing strategies
- A strong knowledge of online data collection and marketing initiatives
- Ability to work independently
- Previous special events experience
- Experience in special event planning and execution, as well as event marketing
- Strong verbal and written communication skills
- Required computer skills: Microsoft Word, Excel, PowerPoint
- Preferred skills: Microsoft Access, Adobe Photoshop, website development and design

CLIENT SERVICES MANAGER, WASHINGTON REDSKINS

Industry Segment:	Professional Sports, Football, NFL Team
Functional Area:	Sales and Marketing
Experience:	Two years of experience required
Location:	Ashburn, Virginia

Duties and Responsibilities

- Execute all elements of national sponsorship contracts, including TV and radio media, print advertising, stadium signage, special events, hospitality, and in-game promotions

- Facilitate the production and placement of all inventory after it is sold in coordination with ad agencies, media properties, broadcasters, publishers, and promotional vendors

- Assist in the detailed coordination of multiple high-profile events and game day experiences

- Develop and activate co-branded sponsorship platforms

Desired Competencies

- Professional demeanor, with ability to communicate clearly to executives at all levels (both internal and external)

- Detail oriented with ability to juggle various responsibilities and meet demanding deadlines

- Interest in industry-specific research and learning

- Ability to work independently, take initiative, recommend solutions, and make informed decisions

Qualifications

- College degree and 2 years' work experience in sports-related marketing, events, and/or media. Graduate degree and/or experience with professional sports considered a plus.

ACCOUNT MANAGER—CORPORATE SPONSOR SERVICES, CAROLINA PANTHERS

Industry Segment:	Professional Sports, Football, NFL Team
Functional Area:	Sales and Marketing
Experience:	Two years of experience required
Location:	Charlotte, North Carolina

Duties and Responsibilities

- Manage and service assigned sponsorship accounts; act as primary contact for all assigned sponsorship accounts

- Liaison between sponsor, Panthers sales rep, marketing, and broadcast departments; must assume responsibility for providing timely, appropriate responses to requests/suggestions/complaints or refer such comments to the sales rep and director and follow up accordingly

- Must have knowledge of every element and promotion in sponsor's package and implement each element accordingly; provide event coordinator with all available promotion information, per contract

- Be abreast of other Panthers opportunities that may be available to assigned sponsors; must be proactive in securing assigned sponsors a spot in as many in-house promotional avenues as available

- Work closely with sponsor event coordinator to ensure appropriate implementation of assigned sponsor events; open communication with coordinator is crucial

- Assist sponsor event coordinator with sponsor events, to include but not limited to Bank of America Flag Football, Miller Flag Football, Outback Kid's Clinics, and others; action plan will be developed and supervised by appropriate account manager

- Work with marketing department to coordinate and implement all game day sponsor events

- Responsible for coordinating all assigned sponsor artwork, print work, signage, etc.

Qualifications

- Bachelor's degree

- Two or more years of business experience with significant exposure to clients, customer service, and sales

- Must be flexible to work evenings, weekends, and some overnight travel

- Must possess excellent oral and written communication skills; exchange information with others clearly and concisely; ability to present ideas and facts

- Must be proficient in MS Word, Excel, PowerPoint, and Outlook

MARKETING COORDINATOR, DETROIT PISTONS/PALACE SPORTS & ENTERTAINMENT SERVICE COMPANY

Industry Segment:	Professional Sports, Basketball, NBA Team
Functional Area:	Sales and Marketing
Experience:	Two years of experience required
Location:	Auburn Hills, Michigan

Palace Sports & Entertainment Service Company has an immediate opening for a full-time marketing coordinator to work in our corporate marketing department.

Duties and Responsibilities

- Ensure all elements of sponsorship contracts are fulfilled

- Accurately obtain and maintain client information

- Provide efficient and timely sponsorship assistance

- Assist in various marketing efforts and client promotions

- Provide superb ongoing customer service skills

Qualifications

- Ideal candidates will have at least 1 to 2 years of professional experience.

- Candidates must be proficient in Microsoft Word, Excel, PowerPoint, and Outlook.

- Candidates must be able to work extended hours including evenings, weekends, and holidays as required.

- This is a business dress environment; candidates must be professional in appearance and communications.

- Ability to handle highly confidential information is required.

- Candidates must have the ability to receive directions and requests from multiple sources and effectively prioritize their work.

CORPORATE SALES EXECUTIVE, MEMPHIS REDBIRDS

Industry Segment:	Professional Sports, Minor League Baseball, Pacific Coast League Team (AAA)
Functional Area:	Sales and Marketing
Experience:	Two years of experience required
Location:	Memphis, Tennessee

Responsibilities

Responsibilities include developing, presenting, and selling advertising strategies and opportunities to current and prospective corporate partners. Emphasis is placed on the sale of ballpark signage, yearbook ads, radio, television, sponsorships and special promotions, season tickets, groups, and Foundation contributions all in a manner as is necessary to help the sales team meet and exceed the organization's forecasted sales goals. This position reports to the vice president of sales.

Other responsibilities include account management of existing partners, database entry, working selected trade shows, and game day public relations. This includes holding "meet and greets" for season ticket holders, advertising and promotional partners, group fans, and special guests.

A thorough knowledge of all sales inventory and the organization's not-for-profit message is expected to help promote to the corporate community. Ideal candidate will possess at least 2 years of sales experience.

Duties and Responsibilities

- Corporate sales: 60%
- Season tickets and group sales: 10%
- Account management including game day public relations: 20%
- Miscellaneous duties including preparing proposals, database, in-house committee and department meetings, representing Redbirds at out-of-office functions and club meetings, etc.: 10%

EVENT ADVERTISING AND PROMOTION MANAGER, U.S. SOCCER FEDERATION

Industry Segment:	National Governing Body, Soccer
Functional Area:	Sales and Marketing
Experience:	Two years of experience required
Location:	Chicago, Illinois

Key position in generating ticket sales for U.S. Soccer's Men's (MNT) and Women's National Team (WNT) events, including WNT preparation matches for the 2007 FIFA Women's World Cup and MNT games leading to the 2007 CONCACAF Gold Cup. The candidate will demonstrate a high level of skill, effectiveness, energy, and enthusiasm and work well within the events department team and with local partners for each event.

Duties and Responsibilities

Manage promotion of U.S. Soccer's National Team events, including:

- Advertising:
  - Guide development of advertising elements (print ads, posters, direct mail pieces, and other printed materials; scripts for radio/television ads)
  - Recommend advertising plan for each event, keeping within a budget framework
  - Negotiate media purchases and trade, when necessary
- Direct marketing:
  - Utilize and assist with development of ticket buyer e-mail and conventional mail lists
  - Execute direct mail and mass e-mail programs
  - Draft messages for e-mail-based ticket sales promotions

- Outreach programs:
  - Develop and execute sales promotions meant to generate ticket sales and widespread media attention
  - Enlist U.S. Soccer's local members to assist in the promotion of each event
  - Coordinate with marketing department for sponsor-related promotional opportunities (and develop ideas for such opportunities)
  - Instigate other grassroots promotional programs
- Managing and reporting:
  - Coordinate with local organizing committee counterpart for promotion of each event
  - Track and document all promotion placements and expenditures
  - Log post-event promotion reports after each game for marketing department use and events department analysis

Other Duties

- Manage all on-site promotion activities at each event, including name gathering program, halftime activities, and other elements that may be developed over time; assist with event presentation and event script development
- Oversee protocol-related functions at event site, when necessary

Qualifications

Professional-level writing ability required. Strong attention to detail is essential. Skills central to position include ability to guide creative process and evaluate design work of others to achieve a high level of quality. Bachelor's degree. Two years' experience minimum in media planning and/or buying. Knowledge of soccer structure at national and international levels a plus. Grass roots marketing experience helpful. Windows environment, Microsoft Office programs. Knowledge of foreign languages (particularly Spanish) a plus.

DIRECTOR OF SPORTS MARKETING, HIGH POINT UNIVERSITY

Industry Segment:	College Athletics, NCAA Football Championship Subdivision
Functional Area:	Sales and Marketing
Experience:	Two years of experience required
Location:	High Point, North Carolina

High Point University, an NCAA Division I institution, is seeking applications for the position of director of sports marketing. This is a full-time, 12-month position in the department of athletics reporting directly to the director of athletics.

Duties and Responsibilities

- Solicitation and management of sponsorship agreements
- Development and implementation of marketing and promotional plans to increase attendance at all home athletics events
- Oversight of licensing, retail relationships, and of newsprint, radio, and television advertisement
- Management of the Panther radio network
- Work with the Panther Club and Office of Institutional Advancement in fundraising
- Development and implementation of special events
- Development and management of an annual sports marketing budget

Qualifications

- Bachelor's degree required, master's degree preferred
- Minimum of 2 years' experience in marketing in NCAA intercollegiate athletics or a related field
- Excellent oral and written communication skills as well as interpersonal skills to work with administrative staff and head coaches
- Ability to work a flexible and irregular schedule and the ability to organize and complete multiple tasks and meet deadlines

MANAGER CORPORATE SALES AND SPONSORSHIPS, NEW YORK YANKEES

Industry Segment:	Professional Sports, Baseball, MLB Team
Functional Area:	Sales and Marketing
Experience:	Two years of experience required
Location:	New York

Responsible for prospecting and securing sponsorship and other new business opportunities for the New York Yankees in both the existing and new Yankee Stadium, scheduled to open for the 2009 season. Interact with all areas of the club, to ensure that the sponsors' deal elements are fulfilled and business objectives are met through their association with the Yankees.

Duties and Responsibilities

- Support existing staff by working on sales efforts for prospective current and new stadium partner opportunities, reporting to, and working closely with, department head
- Work on sponsor proposal documents and related projects
- Assist with select departmental gameday activities, specifically for client entertainment
- Must be able to work long hours and games, especially during the season
- Limited travel

Qualifications

- College degree and minimum 2 years' direct sales experience preferred. Must have strong organizational skills.
- Ability to:
  - Research categories, draft, present, and close deals
  - Interact with different departments within an organization
  - Handle pertinent tasks and a variety of projects simultaneously
  - Communicate effectively in both written and verbal form

CORPORATE SPONSORSHIP SALES EXECUTIVE, HOUSTON ROCKETS

Industry Segment:	Professional Sports, Basketball, NBA Team
Functional Area:	Sales and Marketing
Experience:	Three to five years of experience required
Location:	Houston, Texas

The corporate sponsorship sales executive is responsible for generating leads and closing advertising and sponsorship agreements for the team, as well as the ongoing servicing of accounts.

Duties and Responsibilities

- Identifies sponsorship leads and prepares and presents proposals
- Works closely with marketing to achieve cross-departmental revenue generation goals
- Works closely with the other corporate sales managers to ensure that broadcasting elements are incorporated into sponsorship packages
- Works with the corporate services department to ensure that all broadcast material is properly trafficked and that clients are provided with broadcast affidavits

- Works with the corporate services department in the servicing of accounts
- Manages expense budgets related to sales activities
- Manages revenue budgets to ensure appropriate allocation of sponsorship revenue
- Researches and writes business action plans to support new business directions
- Prepares weekly revenue reports
- Liaises with other departments on sponsored programs; departments to include game presentation, community relations, and ticketing
- Other related duties as required

Ideal Candidate

Ideal candidates will have at least 3 to 5 years of sponsorship or related sales experience. Strong existing advertising agency and client relationships are a plus. Excellent people skills, with the ability to interact effectively and in a professional, diplomatic, and mature manner with VIPs as well as internal and external clients at all levels are a must. High level of initiative and inner drive are preferred. Candidate must have excellent problem-solving skills as well as excellent communication and presentation skills. The ability to generate new and creative sales ideas is needed. Candidates must be able to meet tight deadlines and work effectively in a high-pressure environment. Computer literacy is preferred. The selected candidate must be able to work evenings, weekends, and holidays as required.

Qualifications

- Television broadcast sales experience
- Knowledge of the advertising business
- A degree or diploma in sports marketing or related field
- Proficiency in MS Word and MS Excel
- Knowledge of and passion for the sport

DIRECTOR OF SALES AND MARKETING, GLOBAL SPECTRUM CONVENTION CENTERS

Industry Segment:	Event Management, Convention Centers
Functional Area:	Sales and Marketing
Experience:	Three to five years of experience required
Location:	Multiple locations throughout the United States

To manage, supervise, and coordinate the activities and operations of the sales and marketing division for an assigned facility; to schedule and book facility events; and to provide highly responsible staff assistance to higher-level management staff. Position reports to general manager.

Duties and Responsibilities

- Assume management responsibility for all services and activities of the sales and marketing division including the scheduling and booking of all facility events
- Manage and participate in the development and implementation of goals, objectives, policies, and priorities of all sales and marketing programs and activities
- Monitor and evaluate the efficiency and effectiveness of service delivery methods and procedures; assess and monitor workload, administrative and support systems, and internal reporting relationships; identify opportunities for improvement and review with the facility manager; implement improvements
- Select, train, motivate, and evaluate all sales and marketing personnel; provide or coordinate staff training; work with employees to correct deficiencies; implement discipline and termination procedures
- Plan, direct, coordinate, and review the work plan for providing marketing, booking, and sales services; meet with staff to identify and resolve problems; assign work activities, projects, and programs; monitor work flow; review and evaluate work products, methods, and procedures
- Participate in the development and administration of the annual budget; forecast of additional funds needed for staffing, equipment, materials, and supplies; direct the monitoring of and approve expenditures; direct and implement adjustments as necessary
- Prepare written proposals; reevaluate potential business value of various events and clients; initiate contractual arrangement; finalize all booking arrangement; prepare contracts; negotiate rental and other rates as required
- Conduct tours of facility for potential licensees; answer questions and provide information regarding facility capabilities
- Direct and plan promotional projects and coordinate focused marketing programs; develop strategies for new markets and clients
- Oversee the development of all facility advertising and marketing materials; analyze facility rental rates, schedules, and labor rates and modify as necessary
- Participate on a variety of committees; attend and participate in professional group meetings
- Stay abreast of new trends and innovations in the field of sales and marketing

- Oversee the scheduling and booking of all facility events; serve as a liaison with outside promoters, permittees, and presenters as well as other departments and divisions; negotiate and resolve significant and controversial issues
- Provide responsible staff assistance to the facility director as necessary; prepare and present staff reports and other related correspondence
- Respond to and resolve difficult and sensitive inquiries and complaints
- Perform related duties and responsibilities as required

Accountabilities

- Operational characteristics, services, and activities of facility sales and marketing program
- Organizational and management practices as applied to the analysis and evaluation of programs, policies, and operational needs
- Modern and complex principles and practices of event scheduling and booking operations
- Principles and practices of accounting
- Principles and practices of budget preparation and control
- Principles of supervision, training, and performance evaluation
- Principles of crowd management
- Client needs as they apply to facility usage
- Pertinent federal, state, and local laws, codes, and regulations

Authority

- Manage, direct, and coordinate the work of professional and clerical personnel
- Select, supervise, train, and evaluate staff
- Plan, organize, and coordinate the technical operations of convention center
- Develop and implement comprehensive marketing and sales programs to promote facility use
- Provide administrative and professional leadership and direction for all technical services activities
- Recommend and implement goals, objectives, and practices for providing effective and efficient facility scheduling, booking, and marketing service
- Plan and organize facility events efficiently
- Negotiate and implement facility contracts for services
- Prepare and administer large and complex budgets

- Prepare clear and concise administrative and technical reports
- Analyze problems, identify alternative solutions, project consequences of proposed actions, and implement recommendations in support of goals
- Research, analyze, and evaluate new service delivery methods, procedures, laws, and regulations
- Interpret and apply federal, state, and local policies, procedures, laws, and regulations
- Perform responsible and difficult secretarial work involving the use of independent judgment and personal initiative
- Understand the organization and operation of the convention center and of the outside agencies as necessary to assume assigned responsibilities
- Interpret and apply administrative and departmental policies and procedures
- Establish and maintain effective working relationships with those contracted in the course of work

Qualifications

- Three to 5 years of increasingly responsible sales and marketing experience for a hotel with substantial meeting space, convention center, or performing arts facility including some supervisory responsibility
- Bachelor's degree from an accredited college or university with major coursework in marketing, public relations, business administration, sport management, or other related field
- Ability to work beyond normal business hours, including nights, weekends, and holidays as needed

MARKETING ANALYST TEAM MARKETING AND BUSINESS OPERATIONS, NBA LEAGUE OFFICE

Industry Segment:	Professional Sports, Basketball, NBA League Office
Functional Area:	Sales and Marketing
Experience:	Three to five years of experience required
Location:	New York

The marketing analyst leads the development and implementation of the league's (NBA, WNBA, & D-League) customer acquisition strategy. He or she is responsible for the strategic positioning, marketing, and management of all customer acquisition efforts across all NBA "touch points" (e.g., e-mail, mobile, partnership marketing, web, new media, etc.). He or she acts as a liaison across all NBA departments establishing the necessary processes and programs to help individual business units reach their target customer.

Duties and Responsibilities

- Acquisition Strategy:
  - Identify partners, programs, and platforms that best enable the NBA to reach individual fans at the right time, via the appropriate medium (online and offline) with a compelling value proposition to engage them into a direct relationship with the league
  - Evaluate the effectiveness of various consumer acquisition strategies including promotions/sweepstakes, viral campaigns, new media opportunities, loyalty marketing, and partnership/affinity marketing
  - Establish the program/campaign strategies, calculate return on investment (ROI), and analyze program performance to optimize and adjust as necessary
- Touch-Point Reporting and ROI Analysis:
  - Create methods to track and report effectiveness for each touch point and establish benchmarks for acquisition programs' success
  - Develop touch-point optimization recommendations based upon campaign/program analysis
  - Create model and metrics to determine ROI and cost management for acquisition efforts
- Business Development:
  - Lead team on all data acquisition partnership programs with external parties (e.g., ESPN, NBA Corporate Partners, etc.) to ensure optimal data capture
  - Develop potential partnership targets that extend beyond existing NBA partners/sponsors and explore "nontraditional" partnership opportunities with partners that are aligned with customer needs and behaviors
  - Team lead on development and management of all league data share and regulations

Qualifications

- A creative thinker with a strong analytic mind
- Desire to work in a fast-paced, evolving, growing, dynamic, and challenging environment
- Excellent communication and interpersonal skills, combined with the ability to build/lead teams and create consensus
- Ability to work within large organizations and across multiple divisions to identify internal and external opportunities
- Ability to problem solve at a tactical, as well as strategic level
- Ability to manage multiple parallel task streams and oversee the development of an internal consumer acquisition discipline
- Ability to extract intelligence and behavioral inferences from data and disseminate to stakeholders
- Knowledge of all e-mail/mobile and data capture regulations including CAN SPAM
- Degree from a top university/college
- MBA preferred

Experience

- Three to 5 years of relationship marketing, direct and/or new media experience with proven experience in developing effective customer acquisition programs for a leading consumer-facing business
- Proven track record in identifying effective co-marketing and partnership targets, establishing the strategy, rationale, and ROI
- Experience in using new media channels (web, e-mail, mobile) to create effective data and communication partnership programs
- Experience in managing multiple programs (across multiple channels) and establishing campaign communication calendars
- Experience in creating campaign briefs (proposition, content, functionality, placement), setting target performance metrics, and working with multiple divisions to implement
- Experience in using campaign analysis tools, database segmentation, and behavioral data to analyze and improve performance of programs/campaigns; mapping back to ROI
- Experience in monitoring industry (e-mail, web, mobile) best practices and incorporating into communication strategies
- Experience in recruiting talent, building a team, and developing personnel

SENIOR DIRECTOR OF MARKETING AND PROMOTIONS, FLORIDA PANTHERS AND BANKATLANTIC CENTER

Industry Segment:	Facilities and Professional Sports, Hockey, NHL Team
Functional Area:	Sales and Marketing
Experience:	Three to five years of experience required
Location:	Sunrise, Florida

Duties and Responsibilities

- Assist in the implementation of the marketing goals and objectives for all events at BankAtlantic Center

- Direct activities to ensure growth and expansion of services and to guarantee that marketing goals and objectives are met

- Supervise and manage staff and department efforts of website, fan development, promotions, mascot, game presentation, and youth hockey

- Serve as primary contact with advertising agency, local radio and television, and work closely involving daily decisions

- Assist in allocating budget among direct mail, newspaper, radio, television, and promotion expenses

- Establish and sustain personal relationships with media personnel, including newspaper, magazines, television, and radio

- Oversee and direct the development of e-marketing campaigns and database administration

- Oversee the development and implementation of all printed and electronic advertising and marketing materials, including, but not limited to radio, television, print, and new media advertising campaigns

- Develop media buying/brand management plans with our advertising agency, monitor trends across the sports and entertainment industries, and implement consumer research/survey tools to assist in marketing efforts and strategies

- Work with NHL to localize any NHL-wide initiatives and to use NHL sources, research, and personnel to assist the club's local marketing efforts

- Oversee the implementation of promotional events and ticket promotions within BankAtlantic Center including HockeyFest, Coolest Bars, Panthers University, and promotional tours

- Direct the scheduling and coordination of Panthers promotional tools: Inflatable Slap Shot Game, Inflatable Rink, and Border Patrol Rink

- Responsible for overseeing monthly reporting of the utilization of all promotional interactive tools

- Oversee team mascot and his involvements

- Participate and network within the community and industry; involvement in industry-related associations and community organizations

- Other duties as assigned

Qualifications

- BA in sports management, marketing, or business

- Three to 5 years' experience in marketing

- Minimum 2 years of supervisory experience

- Demonstrate knowledge of the principles, practices, and terminology of advertising, marketing, public relations programs, and public speaking

- Organize and prioritize work to meet deadlines; work effectively under pressure

- Strong organizational skills, written and oral communication skills, team-oriented

- Proficient with Windows, Word, Excel, Outlook, PowerPoint, etc.

- Ability to work nights, weekends, and holidays

CRM MARKETING MANAGER, NFL LEAGUE OFFICE

Industry Segment:	Professional Sports, Football, NFL League Office
Functional Area:	Sales/Marketing and Information Technology
Experience:	Three to five years of experience required
Location:	New York

The NFL Digital Media Group is seeking a customer relationship management (CRM) marketing manager who will contribute to the overall marketing initiatives of NFL.com and the Digital Media Group.

Duties and Responsibilities

- Ensure marketing initiatives and CRM technology decisions are in sync

- Develop, execute, and maintain data integrity strategy of league CRM/database policies

- Working in conjunction with the Digital Media team and other department to develop league-wide data policy and process for digital media CRM

- Oversee the creation, development, and maintenance of NFL.com database program with the technology team and further develop database CRM strategy for marketing and business development purposes

- Contribute in optimizing the overall performance of NFL.com as it relates to increasing traffic, registered users, web analytics, digital media commerce/subscription businesses, and all site marketing initiatives

- Responsible for managing and executing marketing research initiatives for the digital media group

- Schedule, produce, proof, test, and send HTML and text online newsletters and other e-mail communications

- Responsible for ensuring all privacy laws and regulations are met
- Report, summarize, and present results of the e-mail campaigns to the digital media group
- Work with tech team and third-party partners to incorporate NFL.com league-wide data policies and procedures
- Work with the analytics team to develop comprehensive site reporting analytics, digital subscription businesses, and e-mail programs
- Work with design, editorial, and technical teams during new feature/functionality development projects to understand analytical needs
- Provide sound feedback and suggestions for enhancing the user experience for the portal overall within the CRM and database strategy
- Track data, analyze results, and implement changes based on collected site data
- Contribute to any NFL.com initiatives required

Qualifications

- BS degree preferred, 3 to 5 years of marketing, CRM, and database experience preferred
- Understanding of the Internet and sports businesses—database, e-commerce, marketing, sponsorship, subscription products
- E-mail marketing experience with an understanding of the e-mail industry and performance metrics
- Understanding of the creative development process (particularly e-mail)
- Strong project management experience and database computer skills
- Responsible for managing and executing marketing research initiatives for the digital media group
- Clear understanding of the financial/business media landscape
- Strong organizational skills with the ability to simultaneously manage multiple projects
- Strong business writing skills including presentation development
- Search marketing experience
- Research and survey marketing experience
- Prior financial profit and loss responsibilities
- Familiarity with the development and execution of promotions
- Knowledge of business/financial media with background in marketing and the sales process towards this target audience
- Knowledge of web technologies at a strategic level including online advertising and media practices, online advertising measurement, website development process, website measurement, and search engine marketing
- Strong understanding of sports business time frames
- Ability to multitask and work under strict deadlines
- Understand new technologies and business pertaining to NFL.com growth

CO-MARKETING MANAGER, ESPN

Industry Segment:	Multimedia (Cable Television, Magazine, Website, etc.)
Functional Area:	Sales and Marketing
Experience:	Four years of experience required
Location:	New York

Duties and Responsibilities

- Manage the development and delivery of custom TV, magazine, and online advertiser solutions and concepts for CMS New York–based sales teams; solutions include:
  - Consumer promotions (on-air and off-channel)
  - Online sweepstakes and games
  - Co-branded advertising and content
  - Fantasy games
  - Wireless promotions
  - Sponsored polls
  - Advertorials
  - Innovative custom ideas
- Manage in-house creative and production teams on the development of on-air and online advertising campaigns to support promotional programs
  - Lead the development of program recaps and case studies to support future sales efforts
  - Assist in the development and sale of promotion and co-marketing concepts to current and potential advertising partners
  - Work with advertisers to extend promotions off-channel through retail, on-premise, online, and print
  - Some travel required

Qualifications

- College degree preferred with 4+ years of promotional and/or marketing experience required
- Must have experience managing the development and execution of promotional and/or advertising creative
- Excellent organization, communication, computer management, and presentation skills necessary

Desired Qualifications

- Promotion agency experience a plus
- Working knowledge of PowerPoint, Word, Excel, HTML, Photoshop, Illustrator, and ImageReady a plus

ASSISTANT COMMISSIONER FOR MARKETING AND SALES, METRO ATLANTIC ATHLETIC CONFERENCE

Industry Segment:	College Athletics, NCAA Football Championship Subdivision
Functional Area:	Sales/Marketing and Broadcasting
Experience:	Unspecified
Location:	Edison, New Jersey
Compensation:	$45,000

Duties and Responsibilities

- Create, manage, and fulfill million-dollar marketing, sales, and broadcast budget for the MAAC
- Cash sales goals for the position are subject to yearly review but are minimally projected for the 2007–08 fiscal year as $700,000; the fiscal year runs from July 1 to June 30
- Oversee and direct the MAAC marketing staff (director of marketing, MAAC marketing fellow, etc.) and work directly with the MAAC commissioner on all marketing initiatives
- Recruit, confirm, and implement new sponsors at various levels
- Service and renew (at an increased level) existing MAAC sponsors
- Grow scope, status, and standing of the MAAC within the collegiate community
- Develop marketable elements (e.g., website, rotating signage, live streaming, radio, etc.) in conjunction with the MAAC staff and the MAAC Marketing & TV committee
- Clear broadcast packages and syndication efforts with regional and national sports networks and Internet platforms in conjunction with the commissioner, the MAAC Marketing & TV committee, and ESPN Regional Television
- Produce broadcasts on-site with the director of marketing, MAAC staff, and the conference's production company, currently ESPN Regional Television
- Coordinate the production and sales of the MAAC Basketball Championship game program with the MAAC's vendor, IMG College.

- Interact with the MAAC staff on all production elements for the program and media guide related to marketing efforts
- Utilize all functions of IMG College as it relates to national print sales
- Coordinate placement of sponsor ads and related elements with MAAC's Internet vendor, XOS, Inc.
- Emphasize and focus on sales and the elimination of operating deficits for the MAAC marketing operation
  - Provide leadership and overview for MAAC marketing operations
- Develop and present an annual budget for MAAC marketing operations to the MAAC Marketing & TV committee
  - Prepare monthly sales and expense reports to the commissioner and senior associate commissioner for finance and compliance, and quarterly reports for the MAAC Marketing committee
  - Submit travel and entertainment expense reports on a timely basis, within budget parameters, and have all major expenditures approved by the commissioner or senior associate commissioner
- Maintain continuous and open lines of communications with all MAAC institutions, institutional marketing directors (via quarterly conference calls), and the MAAC Marketing & Television committee including all on-campus operational elements of sponsorships and broadcasts
- Ensure all elements of sponsorships are thoroughly fulfilled and implemented
- Act as a liaison between the MAAC and host arenas (Times Union Arena, Sovereign Bank Arena, Arena at Harbor Yard, etc.) and championship sites (Disney Sports Attractions, Trenton Thunder Stadium, USTA Complex, etc.) to develop sponsorships; fulfill MAAC sponsorship elements, etc. within existing contracts between the MAAC and these host facilities
- Implement contract, advertising sales, and transportation/setup of Dorna signage for all MAAC broadcasts per sponsorship contracts
- Attend NACMA-sponsored seminars and meetings as budgeted
- Other duties as assigned by commissioner

This position reports to the MAAC commissioner. The term of employment is July 1 to June 30. Compensation for the term is $45,000. If cash sales goal of $700,000 reached during term, promotion to associate commissioner for sales and marketing for the following term at base salary of $60,000. Position includes Guardian Phs Plan and dental insurance. Pension of 8%, you may match up to 8% supplemental TIAA-CREF. Employee will receive 20 days of vacation accruing in accordance with MAAC policy, to be used during the term. There will be no cash out for unused vacation time at the end of the term, or if your employment ends before the term expires. The office operating schedule is Monday–Friday, 9 AM to 5 PM. Position will require additional evening and weekend hours, plus travel to broadcast sites, championships, and meetings.

MANAGER TEAM MARKETING AND BUSINESS OPERATIONS, NBA LEAGUE OFFICE

Industry Segment:	Professional Sports, Basketball, NBA League Office
Functional Area:	Sales and Marketing
Experience:	Unspecified
Location:	New York

This person is responsible for working closely with NBA/WNBA/NBDL teams to collect, create, and disseminate best practices in loyalty and customer service, in order to improve teams' fan satisfaction, loyalty, and retention levels.

Duties and Responsibilities

- Continuously evaluate, measure, and report on the critical drivers of fan satisfaction, loyalty, and retention
- Benchmark loyalty best practices across industries to help teams optimize retention programs, processes, and perks
- Catalogue season ticket holder retention practices per team
- Visit NBA/WNBA/NBDL arenas to evaluate service experiences
- Assist in development of analysis, recommendations, and presentations to teams

Required Skills/Knowledge

- Analytical skills, including experience with regression analysis
- Presentation and facilitation skills
- Service operations management

Qualifications

- Management consulting and/or financial services experience a must
- Loyalty marketing, customer relationship management, and/or hospitality experience a plus
- Bachelor's degree
- MBA a plus

VICE PRESIDENT OF SALES, SAN JOSE GRAND PRIX

Industry Segment:	Motor Sports, Champ Car World Series
Functional Area:	Sales and Marketing
Experience:	Five to seven years of experience required
Location:	San Jose, California

We are looking for an energetic, motivated, and persistent vice president of sales who possesses the ability to work in a fast-paced environment with a proven track record of meeting or exceeding revenue goals. This position reports directly to the president.

Duties and Responsibilities

- Establishing and achieving overall sales goals
- Sponsorship sales for all aspects of the sports and entertainment event to local and regional companies including all business categories
- Develop sponsorship packages and pricing
- Develop proposals, presentations, and collateral materials for potential partners
- Establish and cultivate relationships with industry professionals within the Bay Area
- Selling to major clients; participate in account solicitation and closings
- Will work independently and with other team members to close sales opportunities
- Aggressively identify, prioritize, and manage corporate partnerships with a targeted set of large strategic partners that have global and multi-market reach to create measurable business results for each partner
- Provide leadership in managing, motivating, and coordinating corporate partnerships, hospitality management, public, and group ticket sales and sales campaigns
- Establish sales goals, objectives, and quotas
- Develop strategic sales plan including execution plans, client profiling, and sales budgeting and forecasting
- Sales management and coordination of sales reporting, meeting coordination, and other forms of business development
- Works closely with the hospitality team to coordinate sponsors' hospitality packages
- At the conclusion of the 2007 race, conduct a customer satisfaction survey and begin the renewal process for 2008
- Perform other duties and responsibilities as assigned

Qualifications

- BA in relevant field; 5 to 7 years' experience in selling sport and entertainment event elements, including the packaging of sponsor and media elements
- Demonstrated ability to integrate sponsor initiatives with media partners and promotional campaigns in an event environment
- Demonstrate ability to acquire and manage existing accounts
- Proven sales record
- "Performance" driven/metrics
- Self-starter who is capable of working independently and following through
- Excellent written and verbal communication skills, professional demeanor, and the ability to engage prospective clients are required
- Ability to work within absolute deadlines and maintain composure in stressful situations
- Passionate about the sports industry
- Previous experience with sales budgeting and forecasting
- Salesforce.com experience a plus
- Some evenings and weekend work will be required
- Computer knowledge is a must

DIRECTOR OF SPONSORSHIP AND BUSINESS DEVELOPMENT, USA DIVING

Industry Segment:	National Governing Body, Diving
Functional Area:	Sales and Marketing
Experience:	Five to ten years of experience required
Location:	Indianapolis, Indiana

The director of sponsorship and business development will be responsible for the development of new sponsor partnerships for USA Diving. He or she will be responsible for business development plans, sponsor solicitation, proposal development, and contract execution to fully enhance sponsor and business development strategies for revenue growth and membership development. This position will report directly to the CEO.

Duties and Responsibilities

- Establish program strategies and revenue goals in coordination with the CEO and director of marketing
- Develop strategies to solicit and cultivate sponsors
- Create, manage, and implement sponsorship sales program to achieve strategic goals

- Provide regular reports to the CEO
- Work closely with the director of marketing and communications coordinator to ensure maximum brand awareness and media exposure
- Assist with the implementation of sponsorship agreements as needed

Qualifications

- Bachelor's degree, preferably in business, marketing, or sports management; master's or MBA preferred
- Five to 10 years in a sponsorship sales or marketing-related position
- Ability to develop partnership relationships with top-level corporate decision makers
- Superior prospecting, selling, and negotiating skills with proven experience closing deals
- Strategic planning experience with proven results
- Strong communication (both verbal and written) and presentation skills
- Ability to travel

VICE PRESIDENT OF MARKETING, ST. LOUIS BLUES

Industry Segment:	Professional Sports, Hockey, NHL Team
Functional Area:	Sales/Marketing and Community Relations
Experience:	Five to ten years of experience required
Location:	St. Louis, Missouri

This position requires a dynamic, professional, energetic, creative marketing leader with a successful track record (preferred) in collegiate, minor league, and/or professional sports. Direct all marketing activities, such as in-game entertainment, advertising, communications, promotions, digital media, and community outreach efforts, to maximize ticket and sponsorship revenue and enhance the St. Louis Blues and Scottrade Center's image in the community and industry.

Duties and Responsibilities

- Lead strategy for advertising, promotions, communications, and publicity for the St. Louis Blues and Scottrade Center
  - Ensure that these efforts are in line with the organization's budgets and goals

Position Spotlight   *Director of Sponsorship*

The primary job of a professional team's director of sponsorships is to increase revenues attained through corporate partnerships. Companies often use the popularity of professional sports teams as a medium through which they can cultivate potential customers. By putting signage in the playing venue, offering store discounts to customers with game ticket stubs, or giving free chicken wings to the fan with the funniest hat, a company brand can be intertwined within the overall game experience. The sponsorship director negotiates sponsorship arrangements on behalf of the team and/or venue while coordinating the sponsoring companies' promotional efforts.

Corporate sponsorship of sports is nothing new; for example, the Green Bay Packers were given their nickname because the Indian Packing Company funded the team jerseys and provided athletic fields. Team sponsorship departments have spawned then-revolutionary ideas such as putting the sponsoring company logo under the ice in a hockey rink, naming an event after a sponsor (e.g., Pilot Pen Invitational [tennis], Outback Bowl [college football]), and placing advertisements behind the batter in a baseball game. Thanks to these creative marketing tactics, teams were able to create additional partnerships and product placements to capitalize fully on the sponsorship market.

In hiring a director of sponsorships, organizations not only will look at educational backgrounds, but also will probably put greater weight on previous work experience and recommendations. Consequently, a successful track record in sales and marketing is critical to obtaining this position. The director utilizes sales expertise and consummate interpersonal skills to nurture current relationships and develop new partnerships. Retaining existing sponsors is a job that many consider as important as, if not more important than, attracting new clientele. Continuing to offer sponsors positive return on their investment keeps those customers loyal while allowing the team to predict future revenue streams and adjust its budgets accordingly. (Accurate budgeting allows teams to devote financial resources to player salaries, which can lead to a better team on the field.). This part of the job often requires the director to function in a social capacity while providing a good product. Entertaining clients at box seats, on golf courses, or over nice dinners may be a perk to some job candidates, but it also means working many nights and weekends.

In addition to relating well with clients, the director must use excellent communication and diplomatic skills in working with other departments in the organization. For every way in which the Director of Sponsorship integrates a sponsor into the team, he or she must obtain approval from a coworker within the organization. For example, to have a shooting contest at halftime of a basketball game, the sponsorships director works with the operations manager; for access to the locker room, he or she must coordinate with the personnel director; or to have the radio announcer mention a sponsor's product as part of the broadcast, he or she works with the director of media relations. Each of these departments has its own assignments and responsibilities, so the director of sponsorships must be particularly tactful when working with the other directors and convincing them of the value behind his or her sponsorship idea.

- Leverage corporate and media resources to extend communications reach and integration of consistent messaging among all programs, publications, and initiatives

- Collaborate with current and potential business partners to synergistically develop customized promotional programs that leverage each other's assets

- Create and manage all in-game entertainment for Blues games and other events

  - Manage staff responsible for event production, Blue Crew, Ice Girls, and fan development efforts

- Manage staff responsible for technical and creative aspects of digital media such as websites

  - Utilize digital media to enhance the team and building's image in the community and industry as well as maximize sponsorship and ticket revenue

- Manage community relations staff and establish goals and programs to enhance the team's image in the community

- Responsible for all marketing department goals and budgets

- Coordinate with other executives to fully integrate the team's ticket sales and sponsorship with all marketing efforts

- Provide leadership, support, and activation for business partners

- Represent the properties by attending or speaking at member and industry events as well as other professional organizations

- Other duties as assigned by the CEO, St. Louis Blues Enterprises

Qualifications

To perform this job successfully, an individual must be able to perform each essential duty satisfactorily. The requirements listed below are representative of the knowledge, skill, and/or ability required. Reasonable accommodations may be made to enable individuals with disabilities to perform the essential functions.

- Bachelor's degree in marketing-, sales-, or business-related field
- Five to 10 years' related experience managing an organization's public image and communications, preferably in a professional sports setting
- Consumer marketing experience, preferably in business to consumer (b-to-c) brands that have touched the sports, events, or entertainment industry, with a particular emphasis in experiential marketing
- Familiarity with consumer promotional programs, retail promotional programs
- Prior management experience of a marketing staff
- Must have experience in the successful development and implementation of core event marketing activities
- Effective leader with strong people skills
- Passion for sports and entertainment business, sales, and marketing
- Prior success with managing and performing in a multitasking environment
- Experience with tight deadlines for managing projects
- Creative problem solving
- High integrity and confidentiality
- Effective communication skills
- Team-oriented with a healthy and positive attitude
- Possesses excellent verbal and written skills
- Experience developing planning tools, budgets, projections, etc.
- Confidence in presenting plans and projections to senior management/ownership
- Ability to build strong relationships with outside vendors and possess strong negotiation skills
- Demonstrated sound organizational and coordination skills for delegating tasks

MARKETING ACCOUNT EXECUTIVE, PORTLAND TRAIL BLAZERS

Industry Segment:	Professional Sports, Basketball, NBA Team
Functional Area:	Sales and Marketing
Experience:	Seven years of experience required
Location:	Portland, Oregon
Compensation:	$48,762 to $73,144

The account executive is responsible for guiding the development and execution of marketing plans and programs for all new ticket sales and retention of current ticket customers. Through experience, organization, and tenacity, the AE is instrumental in working with all departments to conceive, develop, and create materials, promotional concepts, events, programs, and initiatives that drive revenue for tickets. The AE is also responsible for ensuring that work is produced on time and on brand.

Duties and Responsibilities

- Proactive, strategic development and execution of marketing plans, programs, events, and initiatives for ticket sales and retention
- Write creative media briefs providing clear direction on all campaigns and events
- Work closely with creative team from concept through completion
- Develop media plans for advertising campaigns and work with media buyer to ensure goals are met
- Lead cross-functional teams through the planning and execution of events
- Develop and maintain a keen understanding of our customers and market
- Identify changes in the marketplace and adjust marketing plans accordingly to meet objectives and fall within budget
- Identify synergies and opportunities across functions to achieve revenue and build the brand
- Continual communication with department heads to understand and discuss the products, services, and marketing requirements of each particular product/internal client
- Liaise with, and act as the link between, the sales, service, and marketing functions internally and NBA externally by maintaining regular contact with all, ensuring that communication flows effectively and teamwork remains strong
- Help sales and service staff meet individual goals by working with them to build and implement marketing plans and activities
- Be available to assist with projects and tasks, at all levels, to meet deadlines and sell
- Work closely with fellow account strategy team to achieve overall company objectives

Qualifications

- Excellent project manager
- Proficient at crafting and implementing integrated marketing plans

- Act as main point of contact with marketing partner organizations with regards to event and hospitality opportunities
- Play primary role in preserving long-term relationship with marketing partner

Internal

- Reports to vice president of advancement
- Works closely with the president/CEO, vice president of finance and operations, vice president of marketing and sales, and vice president of guest experience and programming
- Works to ensure client presentations are consistent with goals of Office of Advancement initiatives
- Works with trustees to establish relationships and leads

External

- Develops relationships with current and potential regional and national marketing partners
- Aggressively works sports business media
- Prominent public representative of the Basketball Hall of Fame
- Works with representatives of Hall of Fame licensed projects (e.g., HHX, Game 7 Sports Marketing, National Sports Museum, etc.)

Qualifications

- Minimum 7 to 10 years of responsibility in the sales and execution aspects of a similar property
- Experience with sponsorship/marketing partnership sales and activation/integration programs to *Fortune* 100 companies required
- Exposure to a nonprofit environment a plus
- Budget management experience required
- Established list of corporate relationships a significant plus

The Naismith Memorial Basketball Hall of Fame is a 501(c)3 organization. Salary is commensurate with qualifications and experience. Excellent benefits package included.

MANAGER OF CLUB CONSULTING AND SERVICES, NHL LEAGUE OFFICE

Industry Segment:	Professional Sports, Hockey, NHL League Office
Functional Area:	Sales and Marketing
Experience:	Unspecified
Location:	New York

Responsible to work with various club consulting and services department personnel to facilitate the communication and sharing of best practices between the NHL league office and its member clubs, for the purpose of helping build club revenue through ticket and sponsorship sales and service, marketing, advertising, and promotion.

Duties and Responsibilities

- Management of various departmental resources and applications, and associated staff support of each, including the league-wide communications intranet, NHL Link
- Oversight of club compliance with various league guidelines including all local club premium licensing
- Management of department support staff in the performance of various department duties, including sales and marketing information/material gathering, aggregation, and dissemination between and among member clubs
- Responsible for coordination of league initiatives by member clubs including All-Star Fan Balloting, season opener, and playoff campaigns
- Assist with the execution of and participate in league-wide meetings, workshops, trade shows, and conference calls

Ideal Candidate

The ideal candidate must be self-motivated, have the ability to handle multiple tasks, and be able to establish daily work priorities in a high-energy atmosphere. Must have excellent written and verbal communication skills. Must be computer literate and be able to work with Microsoft Word, Excel, and PowerPoint. Must have the ability to travel. An undergraduate degree is required. Professional sports league or team experience is a plus.

VICE PRESIDENT OF SPONSORSHIP SALES, AVP PRO BEACH VOLLEYBALL TOUR

Industry Segment:	Professional Sports, AVP Pro Beach Volleyball
Functional Area:	Sales and Marketing
Experience:	Eight to ten years of experience required
Location:	Los Angeles, California

The vice president of sponsorship sales is responsible for securing national AVP sponsorships. The position reports to the general manager of events and partnerships. The AVP Pro Beach Volleyball Tour (AVP) is the premier professional beach volleyball tour. AVP athletes include past Olympic Gold, Silver, and Bronze medal winners. All AVP events are televised on network or cable media.

Duties and Responsibilities

- Develop and manage a target list of potential sponsors
- Sell fully integrated national sponsorships packages, including bundled packages of rights, assets, and media
- Identify and develop new sponsorable assets and sales opportunities related to the AVP platform
- Frequent travel on sales calls and to AVP events is required

Qualifications

- Minimum of 8 to 10 years of sponsorship sales experience is required
- Sales experience with touring sports or entertainment properties is preferred
- Strong MS Outlook, MS Excel, MS PowerPoint, and computer system skills
- Ability to develop relationships and work well with others in a fast-paced, dynamic environment
- Take initiative and ability to manage multiple projects with strong follow-through
- Detail oriented with strong organizational skills
- Excellent oral and written communication skills

DIRECTOR MARKETING AND MEDIA, NBA LEAGUE OFFICE

Industry Segment:	Professional Sports, Basketball, NBA League Office
Functional Area:	International Sales and Marketing
Experience:	Eight years of experience required
Location:	New York

Position will work in close coordination with the NBA's China offices on the management of locally based marketing partnerships and development/implementation of marketing programs (games, events, and grassroots properties).

Duties and Responsibilities

- Responsible for strategic planning, program development, budget management, and implementation of international marketing properties (e.g., All-Star balloting) and events (e.g., China Games, grassroots programs)
- Work with appropriate account teams to manage implementation of partner contractual benefits including financial allocations, event sponsorships, promotional obligations, and media advertising
- Coordinate with appropriate account teams on activation by global marketing partners in China

- Support business development efforts through the creation of sales materials as well as participating in sales pitches
- Support and guide China marketing partnership negotiations
- Seek opportunities for growth through increasing size and scope of marketing programs as well as finding new sources of revenue
- Constantly seek synergy and expansion opportunities between U.S. and China programs/partnerships including regular sharing of information between the China and U.S. offices
- Work with key NBA business divisions to integrate objectives/strategies into promotional and marketing programs in China where possible
- Oversee the internal review and approval process on creative and promotional submissions
- Work with events and entertainment groups and/or regional offices to maintain event budgets
- Directly manage New York–based employees with dotted-line accountability to account management teams in NBA China offices

Qualifications

- Candidate must be self-directed with experience working in a dynamic, matrixed environment, preferably in an advertising agency
- Demonstrated creativity and expertise in the development and implementation of strategic marketing plans (for both partnerships and properties)
- Experience in contract negotiations
- Strong written and verbal communication skills
- Strong project management skills a must
- Minimum of 8 years' relevant business experience
- Experience living and/or working in China
- Agency experience preferred
- Oral and written fluency in Mandarin
- Undergraduate degree; MBA is a plus

DIRECTOR OF MARKETING, PROFESSIONAL SPORTS TEAM

Industry Segment:	Professional Sports, Teams in Multiple Leagues
Functional Area:	Sales and Marketing
Experience:	Five to ten years of experience required
Location:	Multiple locations throughout the United States

The following is a general description detailing the types of responsibilities and requirements commonly found for this position. An actual job announcement was not available.

Duties and Responsibilities

- Marketing plan to sell tickets
  - Prepare advertisements touting the team, players, and/or slogans
- This can be done within the team's in-house marketing department or in conjunction with an outside advertising agency
  - Put ads on billboards, in print media, in direct mailings, on consumer products, in television spots, on the Internet, or anywhere else an impression would generate attention
- Ticket packages
  - Create and promote ticket plans for various segments of fans in conjunction with the director of ticketing
  - Collaborate with the director of ticketing and director of sponsorships to ensure proper framing of advertisements and their use in the correct medium
- Ticket packages aimed at families are marketed much differently than luxury suite seats that are of interest to wealthy fans or businesses
- There should be a proper fit between the ticket package and its target audience
- In-game entertainment
  - Create an entertaining environment regardless of team performance
  - Coordinate promotional activities and giveaways during breaks in game play
- Run contests involving fans (e.g., racing miniature go-carts, launching rubber chickens into laundry baskets, running around the stadium while in a bratwurst costume)
  - Schedule live entertainment acts to fill gaps in play (e.g., magicians, acrobats, or dancers)
  - Consider arrangements negotiated through the director of sponsorships for in-game endorsement of a sponsor's brand; for example, a contestant might have to hit a shot from half-court in order to win roundtrip airfare on JetBlue, who is also the official airline of the home team
- Manage staff
- Lead and develop those on the marketing team, including account executives, managers, and interns
- Direct game day personnel

Education

- Minimum: bachelor's degree
- Preferred: master's degree
- Most common degrees of those in the field: marketing, business, sports management, communications, or a related combination of education and experience

Experience

- Minimum:
  - Five to 10 years' experience in the fields of marketing, promotions, and/or ticketing
  - Some jobs may require 5 years or more of experience in sports or live entertainment
- Preferred:
  - Prior management experience expected
  - Knowledge of budgeting
  - Management and budgeting experiences need not be sports or marketing related

Skills

- Required expertise:
  - Marketing-specific knowledge:
    - Advertisement design strategies
    - Market research/survey tactics
    - Understandings of fan behavior and interests
    - Familiarity with trends in the marketplace
- Required proficiency:
  - Business acumen
    - Management of finances and people
    - Negotiating skills to work out deals with marketing channels
  - Creativity
    - Needed to formulate unique mechanisms to use in order to reach customers
- Preferred skills:
  - Knowledge of the local community
    - Especially valuable for minor league teams, where the sponsors are more likely to be smaller, regional businesses

Career Progression

Most who reach the level of director do so through advancement from lower-level positions in the marketing, promotions, sponsorship, and ticketing fields. Internships in marketing and promotions are some of the most prevalent in the industry, and thus are more available to someone looking to pursue this career path. The experience does not have to start with a professional sports organization either, because marketing internships are available in many collegiate athletic departments, particularly at the Division I level. Starting in sales can also be a springboard to a marketing job, in part because the two departments work together so closely that networking could open up a career move.

The director of marketing position has a greater degree of "transferability" than many other positions in sports. Those in this position will frequently move from one sport league to another, something that cannot be done as easily for positions such as the director of scouting. In addition, many candidates gain experience outside the sports field, though as mentioned previously, some teams will require a sport-specific background.

Associations and Trade Publications

- Associations
  - American Marketing Association
  - Sport Marketing Association

- National Sports Marketing Network
- Delta Epsilon Chi: network of college and high school students interested in marketing
- Trade publications
  - Advertising specific:
    - *Advertising Age*
    - *Team Marketing Report* newsletter (and annual *Sport Sponsor FactBook*)
  - Academic sports marketing journals:
    - *International Journal of Sports Marketing and Sponsorship*
    - *International Journal of Sports Management and Marketing*
    - *Sports Marketing Quarterly*
  - Sports/business related:
    - *SportsBusiness Journal*
    - *SportsBusiness Daily*
    - *The Wall Street Journal*

Position Spotlight   *Director of Marketing for a Professional Sports Team*

The director of marketing (or comparable title) is the highest-level marketing position in a professional sports team's front office. The two primary goals of a director of marketing are to maintain/increase demand for the viewing of a team's games, both in attendance and with multimedia, and to create a positive association of the team's brand with its fans. The first goal involves creating a good atmosphere at the game (the "game experience" or "game presentation"), a significant portion of which is accomplished through promotional efforts and marketing the team in a way that makes viewers want to tune in and be connected to the franchise. The second goal, of building brand equity (customer knowledge), drives team popularity and can increase the fan base and merchandise sales.

In trying to reach fans, the director of marketing determines which media will be the most effective method(s) of communication, the timing of marketing efforts, and how to allocate resources to the various approaches. He or she considers inputs such as past experiences, focus groups, market research studies, and Nielsen ratings in allocating financial resources. He or she will also look to the experiences of other teams in the league and other sports entities. This process may include apportioning resources to fund additional research studies if necessary.

Like any other consumer good, there must be a demand for the specific sport product in order for it to succeed. Several factors determine consumer preference for a sports team, some of which the marketing director can influence (e.g., entertainment value, media coverage) and others he or she cannot (e.g., geographic location, star player, other sports industry competition). These factors combine to shape the perceived quality of the entire sport product (i.e., team, in-game experience, logo, venue, etc.) and determine the degree to which fans are loyal to the brand. Proper marketing can raise awareness for a nascent franchise or further demand for an already popular team. As the team attracts more fans, the team can sell more tickets (both season tickets and for individual games), tickets at a higher cost, more apparel, and concessions and sponsorships. The team develops a larger television fan base, perhaps even expanding outside its regional market, which has the potential for lucrative contracts with specialized cable/satellite networks. The volume of fans attracts sponsorship investment from businesses seeking to reach these fans and become associated with the popular team. A director of marketing who possesses a creative vision, strong management skills, and interpersonal competence can be critical in driving this demand.

SENIOR VICE PRESIDENT OF MARKETING, NFL NETWORK

Industry Segment: Broadcasting, League-Owned Cable
                   Television Channel
Functional Area: Sales and Marketing
Experience: Unspecified
Location: Culver City, California

Duties and Responsibilities

The overall marketing of NFL Network including consumer, on-air promotions, affiliate marketing, and marketing research.

On-Air Promotions

Responsible for driving audience tune-in through development of promotional spots for individual programs, interstitials, and IDs, executed in a style that distinguishes the network. Develop daily on-air plan (time/day/date specific) to drive awareness and tune-in, including planning and scheduling on-air inventory, topical in-show mentions, ticker copy, and league assets.

Affiliate Marketing

Provide overall marketing to NFL Network affiliates, including:

- Current affiliates: Initiatives that drive affiliate revenue including LAS (local ad sales) and subscriber acquisition (upgrades)

- System launch: Develop and execute plans with affiliated systems to launch NFL Network subscribers

- Demand: Develop plans targeting specific systems to create demand for NFL Network

- Video-on-demand: Market VOD platform as point of differentiation for NFL Network affiliates

Audience Analysis

Analyze audience viewing dynamics (Nielsen minute-by-minute, dial-testing, etc.) to identify source/causes behind audience viewing behavior with particular attention to audience tune-out; work with programming, production, and marketing to find solutions to build audience. Support all network departments (programming, production, sales and marketing) with daily, weekly, and monthly ratings analysis. Provide programming ratings estimates for use in scheduling the network, program acquisition, and building ad sales rate cards and audience estimates.

Custom Research: Support all network functions to provide custom research to address business issues including:

- Pilot testing (give input on potential of show concepts)
- Current show testing (identify opportunities to improve current shows)
- Talent testing (consumer evaluation of individual talent)
- Assessment of distribution issues such as pricing/switching
- Audience tracking
- Other custom research as necessary to drive/support business

Marketing Synergy

Work with NFL League departments (such as marketing, research, events) to take advantage of unique marketing opportunities to drive the business and consumer insights to improve performance.

CHIEF MARKETING OFFICER, PROFESSIONAL SPORTS TEAM

Industry Segment: Professional Sports, Teams in Multiple
                   Leagues
Functional Area: Sales and Marketing
Experience: Seven to ten years of experience
                   required
Location: Multiple locations throughout the
                   United States
Compensation: $150,000 to $500,000+, depending on
                   the organization

The following is a general description detailing the types of responsibilities and requirements commonly found for this position. An actual job announcement was not available.

The chief marketing officer plans and implements an organization's business strategy, which is designed to create brand awareness, drive revenue growth, and develop brand equity.

Duties and Responsibilities

- Lead, manage, and coordinate the functions of the marketing division through:
  - Media
  - Public relations
  - Promotional activities
  - Marketing materials
  - Sponsorships
- Drive revenue growth through the creation of novel (new) sellable marketing programs, identification of sales target, and development of sales strategies

- Attract new clients through creative marketing initiatives
- Develop and maintain relationships with new and existing clients
- Conceptualize and design annual marketing plans
- Build and maintain the reputation of the team, company, or league's brand
- Plan and oversee all promotion activity
- Work along with the corporate partnership department to help devise value-added promotional concepts and strategies during the packaging and sales processes
- Develop advertising for radio and television broadcasts
- Prepare and produce reports on:
  - Public relations progress
  - Marketing efforts/results
  - Demographics
  - Economic trends
  - Creative services
  - Research initiatives
  - Fan relations

Education

- Minimum:
  - Bachelor's degree from an accredited college or university with major course work in marketing, business administration, or a related field
- Preferred:
  - Master's in marketing, sport management, or a related field preferred
  - MBA preferred, with a focus in marketing

Qualifications

- Experience: Several years (varies, but typically at least 7 to 10 years) of increasingly responsible sales and marketing experience, preferably in the sports industry
- Required expertise: Proficient knowledge of Word, Excel, PowerPoint, Publisher, Adobe Photoshop, or equivalent desktop publishing program
- Preferred skills:
  - Strong communication skills, both oral and written
  - Superior presentation skills
  - Ability to multitask
  - Strong organizational skills
  - Creativity
  - Good management/leadership skills

Associations and Trade Publications

- Associations
  - National Sports Marketing Network
- Trade publications
  - *Street & Smith's SportsBusiness Journal*
  - *SportsBusiness Daily*
  - *Sales & Marketing Management*
  - *Marketing News*
  - *Advertising Age*
  - *Sports Business Research Network*
  - *Migala Report*

Owls Athletics Marketing, the official marketing representative of Florida Atlantic University Athletics, has an immediate opening for two aggressive ticket sales interns. Position is a 12-month, OPS position (nonsalaried and does not include benefits), and compensation is $1,200/month plus commission.

Primary responsibilities of this position include generating ticket sales for football, men's and women's basketball, softball, and baseball through season, mini-plan, group, and single game sales to create long-term loyalty with the FAU fan base. Sales assistants will be provided sales goals and evaluated regularly on level of performance.

These positions require individuals with initiative, persistence, and the ability to pay attention to detail. The positions will also be responsible for assisting with all ticket operations, database management, pregame hospitality logistics, on-field promotions and/or ticket sales functions, and any other areas as assigned.

Qualifications

Minimum one year of ticket sales experience. Must be well organized and demonstrate an ability to manage multiple tasks with minimal supervision. Willing to work long hours and weekends. Bachelor's degree required in related field. Master's degree preferred. Must possess strong written and verbal communication skills and creativity. Knowledge of graphics-related software a plus.

TICKET OFFICE REPRESENTATIVE, NEW ENGLAND PATRIOTS

Industry Segment:	Professional Sports, Football, NFL Team
Functional Area:	Tickets/Box Office Sales and Service
Experience:	Entry level
Location:	Foxboro, Massachusetts

The Gillette Stadium ticket office is hiring part-time employees to work at Gillette Stadium events. Events include: New England Patriots football games, New England Revolution soccer games, stadium concerts, and trade shows.

- Employees will be required to work one or more of the following positions on an event day: ticket seller, customer service, advanced booth, or will call.

- Prior experience with Archtics and Ticketmaster ticketing systems is preferred, but not required.

- All candidates are required to have excellent communications and organizational skills, strong accountancy skills, and computer skills.

- Applicants are expected to be dedicated, hard-working, self-motivated individuals who can function productively in a challenging environment.

Position Spotlight   *Ticketing Assistant*

A ticketing assistant works in a ticket office, typically with several other employees (4 to 8) and at the direction of a ticketing director. Several ticketing assistants may work alongside each other in comparable positions where each dedicates most of his or her time to a particular area (or two). For example, there may be a ticketing assistant for each of the following: group sales, customer relations, season ticket sales, individual game sales, and luxury and/or premium seat sales.

The ticketing assistant's primary responsibility is to sell tickets for the organization. This involves calling past clients, prospecting new leads, and cultivating relationships with local groups and organizations. These duties change on game days, however, when the ticketing assistant's role becomes much more customer-service oriented. The ticketing assistant may be asked to solve problems for customers, such as lost tickets or tickets for the wrong game. The assistant could perform a similar function at the "will call" or reserved ticket window, where he or she would handle tickets left for someone by a player or someone in the organization or tickets purchased online or via phone. He or she may also be assigned to assist in the box office, where

he or she will help sell tickets, distribute tickets, and/or solve ticket problems.

The responsibilities of the job may also include ticketing situations such as selling/distributing playoff tickets, assigning seats to season ticket holders (including at a secondary home venue, if necessary), selling the allotment of tickets to away games, and working with an external ticket company (e.g., Ticketmaster or XOS).

The ticketing assistant must able to handle several detail-oriented tasks, ranging from properly processing ticket orders to preparing reports, such as individual game reports or season-ticket-holder reports, to tracking all interactions with actual or potential ticket buyers. Properly documenting conversations, and being able to reference them later, is an important skill for creating stronger personal relationships with customers.

Work is not confined to the ticketing office; the ticketing assistant also collaborates with representatives from marketing, sponsorship, and/or customer service for various initiatives. He or she may go into the community as part of a grassroots program or develop a source-code system on flyers to track the effectiveness of a promotional campaign.

- Employees will be expected to work nights and weekends when an event is scheduled.

- Applicants must be 18 years of age or older.

- Employee must have his or her own source of transportation.

TICKET OPERATIONS COORDINATOR, BOSTON CELTICS

Industry Segment:	Professional Sports, Basketball, NBA Team
Functional Area:	Tickets/Box Office Sales and Service
Experience:	Entry level
Location:	Boston, Massachusetts

Duties and Responsibilities

- Reconciliation of payment batches with finance department

- Processing ticket payments

- Billing and collection of outstanding receivables

- Fulfillment of online ticket purchases through Archtics

- Serve as primary contact and track all customer service issues

- Provide operational support relating to all season and group sales accounts

- Resolve and answer all client concerns or issues relating to their account or the TD Banknorth Garden

- Assist in responding to all aspects of Fan Service touchpoints (e-mail, fan mail, phone, etc.)

- Responsible for quarterly touchpoints (e-mail, fan mail, phone, etc.) with assigned accounts

- Assist in upgrade process and refund process of season ticket holders

- Resolve game day ticket information (paid and printed)

- Maintain computerized records of all season and group ticket accounts

- Handle box office and/or customer service duties on game nights

- Assist with various ticket promotions, community events, and social and civic activities or requests

Qualifications

- Bachelor's degree

- Strong time management and organizational skills

- Ability to communicate effectively with the public

- Excellent customer service skills

- Strong computer skills including Ticketmaster Archtics

- High-energy, people person

- Ability to interact with other departments under many circumstances

- Ability to work long/flexible hours, including evenings, weekends, and holidays

TICKET SALES REPRESENTATIVE, MINNESOTA TIMBERWOLVES

Industry Segment:	Professional Sports, Basketball, NBA Team
Functional Area:	Tickets/Box Office Sales and Service
Experience:	Entry level
Location:	Minneapolis, Minnesota

The primary focus of this position is selling season full and partial season tickets for the Timberwolves via telemarketing, electronic mail, face-to-face meetings, and special events. This position has no supervisory responsibilities.

Duties and Responsibilities

- Cold call area businesses, local groups/organizations, and individuals

- Generate outside and inside appointments each week

- Participate in sales/promotional and team events outside normal business hours

- Deliver quality customer service to maximize season ticket base

- Implement sales promotion programs and literature as well as assist the organization in other various special events, promotions, and social/civic activities

- Handle additional sales and sales and marketing objectives as assigned by the VP of premium seating and ticket sales and/or senior director of sales

- Other duties as assigned

Qualifications

- Four-year college degree required

- Must have NBA/WNBA knowledge

- Ticket sales, customer service, and promotions background preferred

- Ability to work flexible, demanding hours including evenings, weekends, and holidays

- Must have own or access to transportation for outside meetings and events

- Ability to lift and carry up to 10 pounds

- Prospects new business clients via investigative appointments; initiates discussions with key decision makers
- Delivers effective presentations that satisfy prospects' needs through various combinations of hospitality including suites, season tickets, club seating, VIP seating, party packages, partial plans, employee group nights, banquet space, etc.
- Develops new and exciting inventory to meet the specific needs of each prospect/client
- Reacts to and overcomes problems or objections; executes contract and administers billing process
- Implements all aspects of the client relationship; assists and directs the implementation of hospitality usage by offering expertise and experience from other client relationships
- Follows up on all deadlines to ensure all materials are on time and ensures proper delivery times of all hospitality programs
- Coordinates details of group nights (books dinners, arranges speakers, coordinates personnel, etc.)
- Attends client meetings to educate support staff on programs
- Submits timely reports to management, including weekly sales revenue reports
- Entertains and nurtures relationships with current and prospective clients
- Services and renews existing business

Qualifications

College degree, preferably in communications or marketing. A minimum 1 year of experience in sports, media, and/or direct sales is preferred. Must possess good computer skills and have the ability to work independently. Must have excellent communication skills. Must be available to work all home games of Cleveland's new professional hockey team, set to begin play in the fall of 2007.

INSIDE SALES MANAGER, DELRAY BEACH INTERNATIONAL TENNIS CHAMPIONSHIPS

Industry Segment:	Professional Sports, ATP Tennis Tournament
Functional Area:	Tickets/Box Office Sales and Service
Experience:	Unspecified
Location:	Delray Beach, Florida
Compensation:	Hourly wage, plus commission

Delray Beach International Tennis Championships (ITC) invites you to join us for an intriguing opportunity, available September 2007–February 2008. Match Point, Inc. owns and operates the $437,000 Delray Beach International Tennis Championships (Feb. 11–17, 2008), one of only 16 men's professional ATP tennis tournaments in the United States. Players in previous years have included Andre Agassi, Andy Roddick, Tommy Haas, Robby Ginepri, Lleyton Hewitt, Mardy Fish, and many more.

Overall Purpose

The position's primarily responsibility is to manage an inside sales department.

Duties and Responsibilities

- Assist in training of new inside sales staff
- Supervise sales representatives and provide continued training to maximize ticket revenue
- Ensure staff work well together as a team
- Create systems to gauge individual staff members' performance
- Oversee daily ticket orders submitted by staff
- Sell series packages, individual session, special events, and group tickets to database of qualified contacts
- Compile reporting for all relevant sales data
- Provide customer service to existing ticket buyers, prospective ticket buyers, and the public
- Oversee all staff scheduling

Qualifications

- Experience in leading an inside sales department or telemarketing sales team
- Proven track record of meeting or exceeding sales goals
- Possesses good communication skills
- Has the ability to perform multiple tasks simultaneously
- Shows an ability to create innovative ways to achieve sales goals

Managers will receive hourly wage plus commission, and may have the opportunity to work full time with the corporate partnerships department.

GUEST EXPERIENCE REPRESENTATIVE FOR SEASON TICKETS, MIAMI DOLPHINS

Industry Segment:	Professional Sports, Football, NFL Team
Functional Area:	Tickets/Box Office Sales and Service
Experience:	One year of experience required
Location:	Miami, Florida

Perform all duties relating to the service and renewal of assigned Miami Dolphins season ticket accounts.

Duties and Responsibilities

- Proactively communicate with assigned season ticket accounts via telephone, e-mail, direct mail, and face-to-face meetings
- Field and respond to all inbound season ticket holder inquiries and requests
- Act as guest relations liaison during all Miami Dolphins home games and major Dolphin Stadium events
- Assist with season ticket retention by securing renewal commitments
- Work with the Dolphin Stadium ticket office by gathering and fulfilling season ticket holder upgrade requests
- Facilitate the usage of Miami Dolphins season tickets via charitable contributions, employee incentive programs, and ticket forwarding system
- Plan, facilitate, and execute exclusive season ticket holder events throughout the calendar year

Other Responsibilities

- Involvement in game day activities and promotions for all department events
- Facilitate special projects as assigned
- Additional related duties as assigned

Qualifications

- College graduate, 4-year degree preferred
- Minimum of 1 year of customer relations experience in sports or entertainment industry preferred
- Strong customer service and interpersonal skills
- Archtics ticketing system experience preferred
- Bilingual (English/Spanish) a plus
- Excellent written and oral communications skills
- Ability to handle heavy phone volume, both outbound and inbound
- Ability to work weekends, nights, and holidays as dictated by events
- MS Word, Excel, PowerPoint, and Outlook computer skills

SENIOR GROUP TICKET SALES AND SERVICE EXECUTIVE, ATLANTA THRASHERS/ATLANTA SPIRIT LLC

Industry Segment:	Professional Sports, Hockey, NHL Team
Functional Area:	Tickets/Box Office Sales and Service
Experience:	Two years of experience required
Location:	Atlanta, Georgia

Position reports to Director, group sales and service and manager, group sales and service

Duties and Responsibilities

- Writing new business while maximizing sales, including referrals, to current Hawks, Thrashers, and Philips Arena customers via:
  - Making an established number of prospecting calls per week
  - Setting up face-to-face appointments with prospects and clients
  - Developing, planning, and executing established and new group and theme nights
  - Answering incoming inquiries on lead day
- Perform senior-level sales duties including assisting with training, helping develop group programs, and advising new sales team members
- Act as a role model, creating a positive sales culture in the department by providing an example of a successful sales executive for the less experienced group sales ticket sales and service staff
- Reach established sales goals via ticket sales to corporations, schools, churches, youth sports leagues, scouts, civic organizations, charity organizations, community nights, etc.
- Service current group sales customers via phone calls, e-mails, and visiting clients at games
- Compliance with formatted phone presentations and group sales approach
- Compliance with data entry
- Assist with large group mailings
- Participate in various sales, team, and community events and social and civic activities

- Assist with other departments in the sales division
- Network at outside events including business after-hours, clinics, talks, etc.
- Market group programs including, but not limited to, individual party/hospitality suites, picnics, birthday parties, preliminary games, etc.
- Perform additional duties as assigned

Work Product

- Sell established tickets according to goals

Performance Measurements

- Reaching established monthly group sales goals
- Implementation of successful group nights throughout the year
- Increase in number of repeat and return buyers
- Attaining established number of referrals

Qualifications

- Minimum of 2 years of successful sales and/or event planning experience
- Bachelor's degree, business or sport management preferred

DIRECTOR OF TICKET OPERATIONS, UNIVERSITY OF CENTRAL FLORIDA

Industry Segment:	College Athletics, NCAA Football Bowl Subdivision School
Functional Area:	Tickets/Box Office Sales and Service
Experience:	Two years of experience required
Location:	Orlando, Florida

UCF Athletics Association, Inc. at the University of Central Florida, an NCAA Division I institution and Conference USA member, is seeking applications for the position of director of ticket operations. The selected candidate will oversee the management of the athletics ticket office, responsible for the administration of all operations related to ticketing, supervision of athletics ticket office staff, maintenance on internal controls to ensure proper accounting procedures, and operation of Archtics Ticketing System.

Qualifications

Master's degree in an appropriate area of specialization; or a bachelor's degree in an appropriate area of specialization and 2 years of appropriate experience. Prefer 2 years or ticketing experience at the NCAA Division I level and experience with computer ticketing system.

As a UCFAA, Inc. staff member, the selected candidate will be a person of integrity and character who shares a commitment for knowing and complying with NCAA, conference, and institutional rules as they apply to the UCF Athletics program. The person selected for this position will be employed by the UCFAA, which is a separate entity from the University of Central Florida.

ASSISTANT TICKET MANAGER, ARMY ATHLETIC ASSOCIATION

Industry Segment:	College Athletics, NCAA Football Bowl Subdivision School
Functional Area:	Tickets/Box Office Sales and Service
Experience:	Two to five years of experience required
Location:	West Point, New York

Duties and Responsibilities

Provides management support for all phases of the activity. The area of responsibility includes, but is not limited to, coordination and assignment of seating, ticket printing, and ticket distribution; management and implementation of the "will call" and complimentary ticket list; auditing, selling, and accounting for tickets; and customer service. Coordinates with various activities such as marketing and promotions and the Athletic Club to maximize team sale objectives, customer retention, and service. Manages the automated ticket system to increase sales revenue and customer satisfaction; staff training; and program evaluation.

Qualifications

Bachelor's degree in sports management or related field required. Two to 5 years of related working experience, preferably at the NCAA Division I level. Working knowledge of Paciolan or similar ticketing system. Excellent verbal and written communications skills.

TICKET SALES MANAGER, HOUSTON COMETS

Industry Segment:	Professional Sports, Basketball, WNBA Team
Functional Area:	Tickets/Box Office Sales and Service
Experience:	Unspecified
Location:	Houston, Texas

Responsibilities

The ticket sales manager is responsible for overseeing all ticket sales efforts of the team, including:

- Setting, achieving, and reporting ticket sales goals
- Daily and weekly reporting of new ticket sales
- Ongoing sales training
- Direct market activities related to sales goals
- Planning and executing group sales activities
- Preparation of business plans
- Budget preparation and expense management
- Management of sales staff

Qualifications

- Service orientation and commitment to winning relationships
- Superb communication, prioritization, and organizational skills
- Excellent problem-solving skills
- Must be able to work a flexible schedule
- Must have ticket sales management experience for a professional sports team
- College graduate

ASSISTANT BOX OFFICE MANAGER, SMG PENSACOLA CIVIC CENTER

Industry Segment:	Facility Management, Civic Center
Functional Area:	Tickets/Box Office Sales and Service
Experience:	Unspecified
Location:	Pensacola, Florida

SMG, the leader in privately managed public assembly facilities, has an excellent and immediate opening for an assistant box office manager at the Pensacola Civic Center. The assistant box office manager assists with the day-to-day operation of the box office. This position is responsible for selling tickets on a computerized ticketing system, reconciling ticket sales with daily reports, handling and processing ticket requests and group sales orders, and coordinating manifest and event info with Ticketmaster personnel. In addition, this position schedules, trains, and supervises part-time ticket sellers with the direct supervision of the box office manager.

Duties and Responsibilities

- Sells tickets to patrons on daily and event basis on computerized Ticketmaster system
- Schedules, trains, supervises, and interviews part-time ticket sellers

- Handles ticket requests and processes accessible seating requests
- Opens and closes the box office independently
- Updates telephone ticket information and upcoming events
- Prints daily audits for Civic Center events; inputs data on spreadsheets; prints daily sales reports; prints end of day reports
- Oversees all ticketing accounting regarding daily receipts, deposits, cash handling, etc.
- Ability to work flexible hours, based on events, with core hours of 8:00 AM to 5:00 PM; schedule will include evenings, weekends, and holidays as needed
- Assists in working with event promoter and appropriate personnel to establish ticket pricing and seating configuration
- Assists in coordinating the house scale for all ticket events
- Maintains communication with Ticketmaster representatives for updates and/or revisions in computer operations
- Monitors daily ticket sales for all upcoming events and communicates information to the director and promoter representative
- Maintains accurate record of daily balance of cash received, tickets sold, and change bank/vault
- Demonstrates excellent customer service skills, responds promptly to customer needs, responds to accessible seating requests for service and assistance, able to work independently and handle most box office questions without assistance
- Other duties as assigned

Qualifications

- Demonstrated knowledge of ticket selling/box office operation
- Knowledge of cash handling
- Knowledge of supervisory principles and practices
- Able to coordinate and schedule staff
- Knowledge of problem-solving techniques
- Demonstrated public relations skills
- Previous box office experience in similar environment preferred
- Reasonable accommodations will be considered for those with disabilities

SUITE SALES MANAGER, ATLANTA BRAVES

Industry Segment:	Professional Sports, Baseball, MLB Team
Functional Area:	Tickets/Box Office Sales and Service
Experience:	Five years of experience required
Location:	Atlanta, Georgia

Duties and Responsibilities

- Sales:
  - Researching and analyzing industry trends and potential new clients
  - Networking
  - Cold calling prospective companies
  - Customizing sales proposals
  - Delivering effective sales presentations
  - Communicating on a timely basis through close of sale
- Marketing:
  - Devising and executing marketing strategies to achieve objective in selling suites
- Game day duties:
  - Include customer service for suite holders, researching any problems within the suites, resolving ticket complaints or problems, and assisting guests with any ticketing questions
- Account management:
  - Ensuring that all aspects of suite agreements are executed; working with other departments to ensure all parking, tickets, etc. are handled appropriately
- Ability to collaborate, coordinate, and communicate with various departments throughout the organization such as ticketing and corporate sales

Qualifications

- Bachelor's degree in business or sports administration
- Five years of team or sports facility sales experience
- Proven track record in selling season tickets/luxury suites
- Excellent verbal and written communication skills
- Ability to represent company effectively in a variety of settings and with diverse communities
- Ability to work effectively and independently with diverse groups of people, all levels of employees, including internal and external high profile individuals
- High standard of work ethic and ability to maintain confidentiality
- Demonstrated understanding of and appreciation for diverse cultures
- Must be proficient in PowerPoint, Microsoft Office programs
- Position requires some game day duty, and must be able to work long hours, weekends, and holidays

76

Public Relations

An organization's public relations (or media relations) department plays a crucial role in establishing, maintaining, and enhancing a team's relationship with the media. Serving as intermediaries between the team (players, coaches, and management) and the public, professionals in public relations roles must cultivate and maintain a strong relationship with the media in an effort to promote a sports organization's public image and brand.

Public relations professionals are responsible for dealing with members of the media of various forms, including print, television, radio, and the Internet. They handle "newsworthy" events surrounding the actual games, such as lineups, injuries, statistics, and applicable team/league records. On game days, information is compiled both at home and on the road, and certain statistics are tabulated and distributed during the game (i.e., after each quarter or at halftime). Public relations professionals also handle newsworthy events relating to the team in general, such as announcing a trade via a press conference or press release, or speaking on behalf of the organization in responding to press inquiries regarding contract discussions, trades, coaching changes, or legal troubles regarding the team's athletes.

Public relations professionals are also given the sometimes-challenging task of deciding media access for events. There is limited space for media members at an event, and thus it is the job of the public relations department to determine which media outlets will receive permission to view the contest from the media section of the facility. The media section varies depending on the event (e.g., the press generally sits close to the court in basketball games, but up in the press box at football games), but it will typically offer a good view of the action and the necessary amenities (such as power plugs and network jacks for laptops, and television monitors for replays). The rise of the Internet as a consumption mechanism for sports news creates challenges in differentiating between true online media sources and personal bloggers. One issue teams and the media relations personnel are dealing with is when/how much/whether to allow media access to bloggers.

There may be a close working relationship between a sports entity and the media. Media outlets need "inside access" to team affairs and personnel in order to create content to both satisfy and attract their audience. Likewise, the media's portrayal of a team has long been a crucial element to the public's perception of a team. The public learns about team activities primarily through media channels, and thus a team of media relations personnel must work hard to present its best side. Managing this sometimes complex dynamic is one of the responsibilities of the people employed in positions similar to those listed in this chapter.

In the college athletics setting, similar tasks are conducted by a school's sports information department or media relations department, which are typically run by the sports information director (SID) or media relations director. In addition to managing relationships with the media, the SID or media relations director may also be responsible for activities such as printing and designing schedules and programs, submitting scores to the appropriate governing bodies, and developing and managing the sports and athletics department's website.

Also important to note, individual athletes often hire publicists who work to manage the media coverage for that particular athlete. Such work can play a role in creating a positive public perception for the athlete, which, when done effectively, can maintain and/or lead to endorsement opportunities. Organizations that run individual sport competitions and tours (such as tennis and golf) also employ public relations personnel to manage the media coverage on behalf of the collective organization of individual athletes (e.g., Professional Golfer's Association (PGA) or Women's Tennis Association (WTA)).

- A proven record of media placement and effectively working with media
- Strong written and verbal communication skills
- Ability to make decisions independently
- Ability to multitask
- Must be creative, organized, and enthusiastic
- Must be a team player

HISPANIC PUBLIC RELATIONS MANAGER, HOMESTEAD-MIAMI SPEEDWAY

Industry Segment:	Motor Sports, Multi-Use Track
Functional Area:	Public Relations
Experience:	Unspecified
Location:	Miami, Florida

The Hispanic public relations manager is responsible for managing all phases of Hispanic PR, media, community relations, and publicity related to Homestead-Miami Speedway.

Key responsibilities include creating PR initiatives tied to the promotion and ticket selling of the Speedway's major events, which include Ford Championship Weekend, highlighted by the season finales of the NASCAR Sprint Cup, and Busch and Craftsman Truck Series; and the SpeedJam/Indy 300 weekend, featuring the IRL IndyCar Series and Grand Am Rolex Sports Car Series.

The Hispanic public relations manager is responsible for building new and existing relationships with local, regional, and national Hispanic media. Candidate must be fluent in Spanish with the ability to translate oral and written material. Media outreach and public awareness of all year-round track activities (more than 250 events annually) are also major facets of this position.

Position is responsible for media relations and event management at the Speedway through the management of the media center, press box, TV, and radio broadcasts, as well as media-specific programs (press conferences, special events, etc.).

The Hispanic public relations manager must possess very proactive and creative outreach skills—this position extends beyond a reactive "manage the media" position.

Duties and Responsibilities

- Work closely with the Speedway staff to develop PR initiatives related to the promotion and ticket selling of the Speedway's major events
- Excellent writing skills (bilingual), to contribute to editorial content both on- and off-line

- Aggressively generate fresh, creative story angles and sources to provide to both local and national media across multiple beats (motorsports, lifestyle, business, entertainment)
- Actively contribute to staff sales and marketing meetings new ideas integrating PR efforts aimed at increasing both media coverage and ticket sales
- Coordinate and execute press conferences and releases
- Manage on- and off-site events tied to track and event promotion
- Manage and supervise interns and volunteer staff, assigning tasks and projects, and communicating consistent expectations; manage projects to successful completion
- Compile and manage media and video files/archive library related to track

Qualifications

- Journalism: excellent writing skills; familiarity with AP style
- Proactive and creative PR outreach skills
- Highly organized, resourceful, and able to manage multiple projects simultaneously
- Ability to adjust, adapt, and resolve unforeseen situations under pressure
- Ability to work well with different personalities in a fast-paced environment
- Enterprising and self-starter with the ability to work with minimal supervision
- Knowledge of motorsports (NASCAR, IndyCar, etc.), with a thirst to learn more
- Ability to handle highly sensitive and confidential information
- Exceptional interpersonal and telephone skills
- Knowledge of Microsoft Word/Excel
- Exceptional guest and client service capabilities
- Available to work nontraditional hours in conjunction with events

SPORTS INFORMATION DIRECTOR, CORNELL COLLEGE

Industry Segment:	College Athletics, NCAA Division III School
Functional Area:	Public Relations: Sports Information
Experience:	One to three years of experience required
Location:	Mount Vernon, Iowa

Cornell College is a nationally known, private undergraduate liberal arts college featuring an active, close-knit community of nearly 1,200 residential students. An NCAA Division III institution and a competitive member of the Iowa Intercollegiate Athletic Conference (IIAC), Cornell is seeking applications for the position of sports information director in the department of athletics. This is a full-time, 12-month position (including frequent evenings and weekends) that reports to the director of athletics. The sports information director is responsible for compiling, distributing, and archiving information for all 19 intercollegiate programs. Promotes Cornell athletics to the media and maintains athletics website. Writes for and helps produce athletic print and online publications, including publications distributed by the Alumni and College Advancement Office.

Qualifications

Expertise in webpage maintenance, demonstrated excellence in writing, and knowledge of sport statistics software is essential. Must be able to work independently; the ability to shoot photos of athletic competition is desirable. Minimum qualifications include a bachelor's degree and a commitment to the values, standards, and expectations of NCAA Division III athletics and a liberal arts college.

Experience

Candidates must have 1 to 3 years of experience in sports media or sports information (preferably at the collegiate level), excellent communication skills, strong organizational and leadership skills, and proficiency with software applications including Stat Crew, Adobe Photoshop, and a Web content management system.

To apply, submit a letter of application, résumé, and contact information for three references. Finalists will be required to submit three published writing samples.

PUBLIC RELATIONS ASSISTANT/ COORDINATOR, MILWAUKEE BUCKS

Industry Segment:	Professional Sports, Basketball, NBA Team
Functional Area:	Public Relations
Experience:	Two to three years of experience required
Location:	Milwaukee, Wisconsin

The public relations assistant/coordinator will work closely with the department's director, manager, and intern to help meet and exceed the organization's public relations goals. The primary roles of the public relations assistant/coordinator will be to handle game notes during the NBA season; work with players, coaches, staff, and media to handle various interview requests; and serve as the primary contact and

editor for many of the team's annual publications, including the media guide.

The ideal candidate will have strong people skills, solid experience, a willingness to work until the job is done, a desire to bring about positive change to the organization, and an ability to work well and thrive in a team environment.

Qualifications

- Must be a college graduate, preferably with a degree in a related field (journalism, communication, English, or sports administration)
- Two to three years of relevant experience; NBA experience helpful
- Strong writing skills, both technical and creative
- Ability to handle multiple, time-sensitive tasks simultaneously
- Willingness to work nontraditional work hours (including nights and weekends)

MANAGER OF SOCCER COMMUNICATIONS, MISL LEAGUE OFFICE

Industry Segment:	Professional Sports, Indoor Soccer, MISL League Office
Functional Area:	Public Relations
Experience:	Two to three years of experience required
Location:	Westport, Connecticut

Position reports to vice president, marketing and communications. Job purpose is to assist in the coordination, management, and promotion of the Major Indoor Soccer League through internal and external communications.

Duties and Responsibilities

- Manage the league's day-to-day media relations efforts, including media outreach with local, regional, and national outlets
- Compile the league's weekly release; assist with the coordination and production of league publications, including league media guide and other printed materials
- Assist with content development and management of MISL.net, the official website of the Major Indoor Soccer League
- Attend select MISL events to assist league and team staffs in the processing and presentation of information for league and media use
- Other duties as assigned

- Plan annual e-mail schedule, assess effectiveness of each message, and make changes to increase open and click-through rates
- Create and execute promotions and sweepstakes designed to grow the registered user base and Sox Pride On-Line Fan Club
- Execute offline sales initiatives online
- Oversee maintenance of loswhitesox.com and Spanish-language e-newsletter
- Assess effectiveness of all efforts, monitor site traffic, and manage responses to fan questions sent through the site

Qualifications

- College degree in communications, marketing, or related field
- Five to 7 years of experience in integrated communications
- Three years of supervisory experience, with a demonstrated ability to manage departments with a diverse range of responsibility
- Must be an excellent communicator, with the ability to manage multiple tasks

DIRECTOR, MEDIA RELATIONS AND PUBLIC RELATIONS, BOSTON NLL TEAM

Industry Segment:	Professional Sports, National Lacrosse League Team
Functional Area:	Public Relations
Experience:	Unspecified
Location:	Boston, Massachusetts

Boston Lacrosse seeks an experienced director, media relations to maximize mainstream PR coverage for the team, as well as seek out new PR opportunities in the corporate, youth lacrosse, and target market communities. The director will be responsible for writing and implementing a PR business plan, which will be an integral part of the overall sales and marketing plan. This position must also maximize production and efforts of direct report staff, game day volunteers, and interns.

Duties and Responsibilities

- Oversees production writing and distribution of all organization press releases
  - Press release areas of focus include, but are not limited to, team, community, corporate, youth development, business, and games

- Work closely with the management staff to develop a fully integrated PR plan, which will be an integral part of the overall sales and marketing plan
- Serve as the managing editor for editorial content on the Internet
  - Responsible for hiring and recruiting writers and assigning feature stories on players and team
  - Works with guest columnists, providing editorial support
- Responsible for aggressive new story generation and pitching story ideas to NLL Boston beat writers to propose story angles
  - Pitches to include stories on team, players, supporters groups, mascots, and broadcast commentators
- Responsible for pitching story ideas to "nontraditional" media such as health, fitness, fashion, lifestyle, business, and entertainment
- Responsible for pitching stories and maximizing opportunities for the new NLL franchise, creating a timeline for announcements and biweekly newsletters on franchise progress
- Direct management and supervision of part-time PR position, full-time interns, and game day staff; assign tasks and projects and communicate consistent expectations of each
- Actively contribute in staff meetings, sales meetings, and marketing meetings
- Contribute new ideas to integrate PR efforts within the most important areas of the business, which are ticket sales and marketing
- Coordinate and execute all press conferences, stadium announcements, and other team-related functions
- Oversee an organized photo/video archive library of files and delegate duties within the department
- Manage all aspects of game day preparation and delegate duties accordingly, meeting all PR needs and logistics including credentialing, parking, and game day staff assignment
- Work closely with other NLL teams to coordinate away game road trip travel and investigate ways to maximize all PR opportunities during away game road trips
- Organize and coordinate off-season player PR training in full cooperation with president/CEO and head coach to train players on the new franchise and general marketing strategies for the new season
- Manage four key media distribution lists: mainstream, business, youth lacrosse, and local community media outlets

Supportive Functions

- Ability to read, listen, and communicate effectively in English, both verbally and in writing is a must
- Ability to access and accurately input information using a moderately complex computer system
- Knowledge of Microsoft Word/Excel required

Qualifications

- Must be highly organized, resourceful, a quick learner, and able to handle multiple projects simultaneously
- Exceptional guest and client service capabilities
- Enterprising and self-starter with the ability to work with minimal supervision
- Ability to work well with different personalities in a fast-paced environment
- Ability to handle highly sensitive and confidential information
- Exceptional interpersonal and telephone skills
- Ability to work evenings and weekends

VICE PRESIDENT OF COMMUNICATIONS, MALOOF SPORTS AND ENTERTAINMENT (MS&E)

Industry Segment:	Facilities and Professional Sports, Basketball, NBA and WNBA
Functional Area:	Public Relations
Experience:	Seven years of experience required
Location:	Sacramento, California

Develop, coordinate, and direct public relations and community service activities for MS&E; ensure that MS&E is proactively responsive to critical local issues and needs while maintaining a visible and positive community presence by performing the following duties personally or through subordinate supervisors.

Duties and Responsibilities

The following lists the primary essential functions of this position. This description may not be all-inclusive. Other duties may be assigned as needed.

- Represent MS&E to the press and public by acting as chief corporate spokesperson for all nonbasketball-related issues
- Field and direct responses to all nonbasketball media-related inquiries
- Plan and implement MS&E's public relations strategies, policies, and procedures for all nonbasketball-related issues

- Research and write copy for corporate promotional materials
- Develop contacts and relationships with media representatives to create opportunities for keeping the company and its products or services in front of the public and the trade
- Maintain database of public relations contacts
- Advise on the preparation and presentation of product or service information at trade shows, displays, and exhibits
- Develop ideas and opportunities for feature articles, interviews, presentations, and other public relations activities that promote awareness of the company and its products or services
- Assist and coach MS&E staff with public speaking engagements, presentations, and preparation of articles for publication
- Work with marketing and advertising personnel to coordinate public relations activities with promotional and sales activities
- Advise management on community service projects and activities
- Develop and manage public relations and community service department and budget
- Help develop and conduct customer opinion surveys and manage public relations aspects of customer testing programs
- Provide leadership for all public relations and community service department team members
- Supervise public relations department team members and community services director
  - Includes: hiring, coaching, counseling, performance management, growth, and development

Qualifications

- Minimum 7 years' experience in corporate communications and crisis management
- Experience with company website content management preferred
- BA/BS in public relations, communications, business, or related field
- Professional public relations certification preferred

Required Computer Skills

- All Microsoft Office products

Other Required Skills and Abilities

- Outstanding written and oral communication skills; outstanding interpersonal skills
- Proven track record in developing relationship with the media

- Strong leadership and people development skills
- Comfortable, confident, friendly on-camera presentation skills

VICE PRESIDENT, PUBLIC RELATIONS, CHAMP CAR WORLD SERIES

Industry Segment:	Motor Sports, Champ Car Racing
Functional Area:	Public Relations
Experience:	Unspecified
Location:	Indianapolis, Indiana

Champ Car seeks a senior-level executive who will be responsible for creating and crafting a comprehensive communications and public relations strategy for the series, which will include reaching out across all lines of communications from website strategy to general media and including all forms of communications, as in bloggers, broadcast media, print media, grassroots marketing, and help position the series around the United States and around the world as a major force in sports, particularly motorsports. Ideally, Champ Car seeks someone with at least 15 years of media experience (with preferably an automotive company/agency servicing the automotive industry or motorsports) and who has exhibited a strong and successful strategic approach to communications, not merely developing relationships and servicing those relationships with media personnel. This kind of a "strategic campaign manager" will be determining the timing and placement of key personnel and the kinds of stories and information to generate maximum interest in the sport, drivers, owners, and sponsors.

Duties and Responsibilities

- Responsible for building the brand through the development and implementation of the Champ Car public relations and communications strategies; this includes strategies and plans to promote the series and its athletes' reputations through internal communications, public relations, community relations, and media relations
- Provides leadership and direction as well as development of functional area managers
- Develops proactive public relations stories and leads to generate an overall interest in and positive reputation for the Champ Car
- Works closely with local event media, national media, and international media in promoting the Champ Car Series, the teams, individual drivers, and executives
- Develops communications channels locally, nationally, and internationally for disseminating news and publicity regarding the Champ Car
- Serves as an advisor to senior management

- Collaborates with other functional areas to improve internal communication and generate enthusiasm for the series
- Serves as a spokesperson for the series

SENIOR MANAGER, CORPORATE COMMUNICATIONS, NHL LEAGUE OFFICE

Industry Segment:	Professional Sports, Hockey, NHL League Office
Functional Area:	Public Relations
Experience:	Seven years of experience required
Location:	New York

A management position responsible for framing the communication strategy and public relations tactics supporting the business platforms of NHL Enterprises and NHL.com, including NHL ICE, Broadcasting, and Digital Media.

Work with the senior vice president of communications and the entire communications staff to plan the pubic relations strategy and develop the message points for the league's marketing programs, sponsor and consumer product partners, as well as new media relationships. The ideal candidate will develop message points and press materials to aggressively pitch to the business media, broadcast media, and technology media. Additional responsibilities will include assisting in all aspects of media relations, media services, editorial services, and league event management for print and electronic business outlets. Other miscellaneous department duties as assigned.

Duties and Responsibilities

- Assist NHL Enterprises in the development of a plan to create a stronger presence in the business and sponsorship community

Qualifications

- A proven track record in pitching and placement in business and new media
- Strong written and oral communication skills
- Experience in speech writing and strong editorial skills
- Proven ability to organize individual and multiple projects simultaneously
- Ability to build and maintain a team attitude among staff members
- Proven ability in media placement and crisis management
- BA/BS minimum degree; graduate degree in journalism a plus
- Minimum 7 years' public relations experience required
- A background in web-based media a plus

Community Relations

Whereas an organization's public relations department controls what you know about an organization, it's up to community relations professionals to manage how you *feel* about an organization. Through their work, they hope to evoke a positive emotional reaction from the general public toward the organization. This is accomplished through the management of an organization's community relations activities.

Whether it's Read to Achieve, Stay in School, D.A.R.E (the anti-drug program), or the United Way, it is not uncommon to see sports entities and athletes giving back to the community. Such activity is meant to develop relationships with new fans, as well as strengthen relationships with existing fans. Player appearances, hospital visits, and fundraising activities (such as charity auctions) are also common community relations activities. Teams also get involved by hosting mascot appearances and player autograph sessions in conjunction with events such as charity carnivals and dinners.

One example of community relations conducted by a professional sports team is the Eagles Youth Partnership (EYP) and their association with the Philadelphia Eagles. EYP uses the brand power of the Eagles to raise money to run programs that improve the health and education of children in the greater Philadelphia area. Their two main programs are the Eagles Eye Mobile and the Eagles Book Mobile that travel to area schools and recreation centers to give children eyeglasses and books, respectively. They estimate that they help 50,000 children every year through their efforts. During their free time, players often ride along on the buses to help brighten a child's day. In addition to these programs, EYP supports after-school chess clubs; a yearly playground build that all team players, coaches, and staff participate in; and an award ceremony for local scholar football players.

The main source of revenue for EYP is the annual Eagles Carnival and Auction, which raises approximately 50% of the program's $2 million annual budget. The carnival takes place during the preseason at Lincoln Financial Field. Every player, coach, and cheerleader is in attendance to interact with the public, whether through autographs or helping to run an activity. Some former players also show up to sign autographs and help the cause. In addition, prior to the event, an auction is held in conjunction with a local radio station that sells unique experience items with some of the Eagles players, such as a fishing trip or a round of golf. At the carnival, a silent auction is held that features items signed by Eagles players and also stars from other sports teams. Fans get a unique opportunity to interact with their favorite athletes and money is raised for a good cause. In the end, both sides benefit.

By having a positive impact on the community through community relations, sports teams are able to solidify their presence within their community. Employees in the positions listed in this chapter are responsible for coordinating and managing similar efforts on behalf of their respective organizations.

COMPENSATION LEVELS

Industry compensation for community relations positions can very tremendously depending on the factors explained. The following compensation levels are reasonable expectations for mid-sized organizations in mid-sized markets:

Professional Sports

- Entry level: $30,000 to $35,000
- Manager level: $50,000 to $70,000
- Director or coordinator level: $90,000 to $120,000

Mike Tamburro, president of the Pawtucket Red Sox of the International League (AAA), is speaking to young fans at a PawSox clinic. Tamburro has been with the PawSox since 1979, and has served as both the president and general manager. Tamburro has been selected as the International League's Executive of the Year five times.

COMMUNITY RELATIONS INTERN, HOUSTON DYNAMO

Industry Segment:	Professional Sports, Soccer, MLS Team
Functional Area:	Community Relations
Experience:	Intern
Location:	Houston, Texas
Compensation:	Likely to be unpaid, hourly wage, or monthly stipend

Duties and Responsibilities

- Assist with all game day events and activities
- Support community relations programs, events, and appearances (Score at School, Kicks for Kids, etc.)
- Aid in the implementation of Dynamo Charities events and fundraisers (golf tournament, overnight soccer tournament, etc.)

Supportive Functions

In addition to performance of the essential functions, this position may be required to perform a combination of the following supportive functions, with the percentage of time performing each function to be determined solely by the supervisor based upon the particular requirements of the company.

- Setup of game day booths and activities
- Assist other Dynamo departments as needed

Specific Required Job Knowledge, Skills, and Abilities

The individual must possess the following knowledge, skills, and abilities and be able to explain and demonstrate that he or she can perform the essential functions of the job, with or without reasonable accommodation, using some other combination of skills and abilities.

- Must commit to work all Dynamo home games plus Dynamo Charities fundraisers and special events
- May be asked to do office work 1 to 2 days a week
- Excellent writing, telephone, and communication and interpersonal skills
- Proficient in Microsoft Word and Excel

Qualifications

Any combination of education and experience equivalent to graduation from high school or any other combination of education, training, or experience that provides the required knowledge, skills, and abilities. College diploma or degree in progress preferred.

COMMUNITY RELATIONS ASSISTANT, DETROIT PISTONS/PALACE SPORTS & ENTERTAINMENT SERVICE COMPANY

Industry Segment:	Professional Sports, Basketball, NBA Team
Functional Area:	Community Relations
Experience:	Unspecified
Location:	Auburn Hills, Michigan

Palace Sports & Entertainment Service Company is looking for a community relations assistant. This position will contribute in various aspects of the community relations department, including planning and development of programming, event management, the Pistons-Palace Foundation, fundraising, and assisting the department with general day-to-day responsibilities.

Duties and Responsibilities

- NBA Pistons/WNBA Shock programming and event management:
  - Assist with all programming and events, including planning and development
  - Assist with secondary programming, including planning and development
  - Manage and/or assist with all department drives (i.e., coat drive, mitten drive, and book drive)
  - Point-person for charitable donation programs, including drafting responses, communicating with community ambassadors, and fulfilling incoming requests

- Point-person for charitable ticket donations for sales blitz tickets, player tickets, sponsor tickets, and family show tickets
- Maintain database of all items donated through community relations charitable merchandise program
- Develop and maintain partnerships with nonprofit and local organizations
- Schedule and execute on-court presentations as necessary
- Assist with monitoring department inventory (e.g., autographed items)
- Pistons-Palace Foundation:
  - Assist within special event fundraisers and general efforts as needed
  - Assist with all in-arena and online auction activity
  - Responsible for data entry related to the foundation
  - Assist with launch of foundation programming (i.e., grant and scholarship programs)
- Miscellaneous:
  - Handle day-to-day administrative duties
  - Assist with increasing and enhancing player imaging locally and nationally
  - Contribute to community relations in support of group sales efforts
  - Support community relations staff in the training and supervising of interns, streamlining responsibilities appropriately including research assignments, website copy, incoming foundation calls, special projects, and miscellaneous
  - Join boards, committees, and other external organizations as necessary
  - Other responsibilities as assigned

Qualifications

- A college degree from a 4-year accredited university
- Prior experience within community relations/nonprofit
- Candidates must be able to work extended hours including evenings, weekends, and holidays as required
- Candidates must be proficient in Microsoft Office programs, particularly Excel
- Candidates must have the ability to receive directions and requests from multiple sources and effectively prioritize and complete their work in a timely manner
- Must have excellent communication skills, both verbal and written
- Ability to handle highly confidential information is compulsory

COMMUNITY RELATIONS COORDINATOR, WASHINGTON CAPITALS

Industry Segment:	Professional Sports, Hockey, NHL Team
Functional Area:	Community Relations
Experience:	Unspecified
Location:	Washington, DC

Duties and Responsibilities

- Manage and fulfill all external donation requests and answer fan mail
- Assist with the implementation of the Capitals' Reading Is Cool program
- Assist on the development and execution of game-night drives and fundraisers; help coordinate game-night logistics for those initiatives
- Secure prizing and donations for and assist in the planning and execution of the Caps Care Classic golf tournament
- Coordinate ticket distribution and Olympia riders for Olie's All-Stars and Ovechkin's Crazy 8's and distribute promotional items to participants
- Help create and develop game-night fundraising events and activities to further promote Washington Capitals Charities
- Assist with autograph sessions and player appearances
- Help manage and monitor the nontraditional sports media contact list with the aim of increasing awareness of the Washington Capitals' players, coaches, community relations projects, and the organization's brand
- Assist in the writing, editing, and publication of community relations material, including certificates, general correspondence, and requests
- Support in the layout and design of Capitals community relations publications, including collateral items and game-night signage
- Assist in the maintenance of community page on website; review and select recent photos from events/programs to include
- Work with in-house creative in the development of collateral items needed to execute community programs; assist in ordering and corresponding with suppliers
- Assist with special projects and events relating to the communications and marketing departments
- Distribute incoming faxes and mail to department staff
- Alert communications coordinator to nontraditional sports stories and/or news clippings on Capitals organization for daily distribution and help update media log
- Related duties as assigned

BUSINESS DEVELOPMENT AND STRATEGY INTERN, ORLANDO MAGIC

Industry Segment:	Professional Sports, Basketball, NBA Team
Functional Area:	New Business and Media Development
Experience:	Internship
Location:	Orlando, Florida
Compensation:	$750 monthly stipend

To assist the business development and strategy department with projects, ongoing research, analysis, and strategic planning.

Duties and Responsibilities

- Assist with projects for business strategy and development, including but not limited to research and preparation of presentations
- Assist business development managers as required with project schedules and progress tracking
- Perform detailed research on new business strategies (via Internet and/or other resources)
- Assist business development manager and business strategy manager with both long- and short-term strategic planning for the Orlando Magic
- Assist in maintaining business development and strategy office in an organized and efficient manner:
  - Maintain project files
  - Update appropriate research folders
  - Formulate correspondence
  - Maintain communication with internal and external stakeholders
- Provide daily industry updates for business development–related projects
- Arrange, maintain, and update vendor-supplied information
- Help business development manager and business strategy manager in organizing and summarizing all project communication
- Assist business development managers with website maintenance
- Attend community and business development–related meetings as needed by the business development manager and provide detailed executive reports
- Game night responsibilities vary depending on the scope of current projects
- Perform all other duties as assigned

Qualifications

- Graduate-level student or recent college graduate
- Business, sport management, or related major
- Strong accounting and budgeting skills
- Ability to work independently and demonstrate initiative
- Ability to handle multiple tasks and prioritize goals
- Excellent communication skills, both oral and written
- Proficient in Microsoft Word, Excel, and PowerPoint

MANAGER: WEBSITE AND NEW MEDIA, NEW YORK RED BULLS

Industry Segment:	Professional Sports, Soccer, MLS Team
Functional Area:	New Business and Media Development
Experience:	Two to four years of experience required
Location:	Secaucus, New Jersey

Position is in the communications department and reports to the vice president of marketing and sales.

Position Purpose

The manager of www.newyorkredbulls.com is responsible for overseeing design, implementation, and maintenance of the team's website, including assisting with the identification of new media strategies.

Required Duties and Responsibilities

- Works with each department to develop specific Internet strategies designed to further business objectives and goals
- Works with each department to ensure necessary materials desired to be posted on the website are delivered in an appropriate format and monitored for accuracy and timeliness
- Works with the director of communications to manage writing, editing, and production of content on a daily basis for inclusion on the website
- Manages and utilizes the content publishing tool to update the site
- Coordinates with internal departments to ensure that the website (including advertising and sponsorship inventory) is complete, accurate, and user friendly
- Continuously works to ensure the website is using cutting edge technology

- Manages online streaming video, podcasts, cell phone downloads, etc.
- Liaises with the MLS League Office on all league-related online issues
- Maintains fan and customer e-mail database
- Coordinates and distributes departmental messages and press releases to e-mail subscribers
- Works with other departments to develop and implement linkage strategies
- Monitors related third-party sites (e.g., players, broadcasters, sponsors, etc.) to ensure compliance with team and league guidelines
- Liaises with MIS department to ensure systems are maintained for effective and reliable Internet service
- Works closely with Red Bull Salzburg to maintain consistency between web properties

Specific Required Job Knowledge, Skills, and Abilities

The individual must possess the following knowledge, skills, and abilities and be able to explain and demonstrate that he or she can perform the essential functions of the job, with or without reasonable accommodation, using some other combination of skills and abilities.

- Ideal candidate ought to be professional, motivated, and enthusiastic
- Must have excellent interpersonal and external communication skills, possess a strong customer service orientation, and have the ability to maintain smooth working relationships with all internal staff and management
- Knowledge of and passion for the sport
- Bilingual (English and Spanish)
- Excellent oral, written, and proofreading skills
- Must be proficient with the following computer programs and languages: Java, CSS, Flash, HTML, DHTML, Photoshop
- Knowledge of web content/publishing interface and HTML

Qualifications

- Education: Any combination of education and experience equivalent to graduation from college or any other combination of education, training, or experience in the field of marketing, communications, and business that provides the required knowledge, skills, and abilities
- Experience: At least 2 to 4 years of marketing and/or communications experience with 1 to 3 years of web-page design and desktop publishing experience; experience working for a team, athletic department, or entertainment venue/event requested

Other

Regular attendance in conformance with the standards set by New York Red Bulls is essential to the successful performance of this position. Employees with irregular attendance will be subject to disciplinary action, up to and including termination of employment. Due to the cyclical nature of the sports and entertainment industry, the employee may be required to work varying schedules to reflect the business needs of the company.

INTERACTIVE SPECIALIST, PORTLAND TRAIL BLAZERS

Industry Segment:	Professional Sports, Basketball, NBA Team
Functional Area:	New Business and Media Development
Experience:	Three years of experience required
Location:	Portland, Oregon
Compensation:	$48,758 to $64,062

You're *energetic*, *responsible*, and love working in a *team environment*. Flash is your interactive weapon of choice, and you're not afraid to use it. You walk around with a laptop tied to your hip and are constantly trying to find new ways to make your website load faster and be as cross-browser friendly as possible. You want to push electronic marketing to new heights via e-mail, social networking, text messaging, and good old-fashioned website interaction. You constantly push the electronic envelope to help engage and sell events and experiences. You will be infecting your ideas on *rosequarter.com*, *trailblazers.com*, and *iamatrailblazersfan.com*.

Sounds good to you? Would you like to become the interactive specialist for the Portland Trail Blazers? Read on!

Description

The interactive specialist is responsible for the daily posting of events, promotions, and contests on rosequarter.com. Also designs and develops interactive Flash applications to be used on both rosequarter.com and trailblazers.com. These applications utilize video, photos, and XML to help drive event revenue, retention, and sponsorship revenue. One intern will report to the interactive specialist.

Duties and Responsibilities

- Post new events, contests, and promotional information on rosequarter.com
- Develop, create, send, and report on e-mail campaigns and graphics for rosequarter.com and trailblazers.com
- Flash development for rosequarter.com and trailblazers.com

- At least 2 years of supervisory responsibility and working as part of a team environment
- Excellent interpersonal, verbal/written communication, and organizational skills
- Superior customer service skills
- Ability to work nights, weekends, and holidays required as needed
- Ability to prioritize and handle multiple assignments under pressure

VICE PRESIDENT OF INTERNET STRATEGY AND DEVELOPMENT, VERSUS

Industry Segment:	Media
Functional Area:	New Business and Media Development
Experience:	Minimum of seven years required
Location:	Philadelphia, Pennsylvania

This position reports to the president of Versus and is responsible for running the business side of operations and driving the creative material for Versus online.

Duties and Responsibilities

- Responsible for network Internet strategy, content, and traffic to maximize potential of the website as it relates to branding, support of network programming, viewer loyalty, and network sales and affiliate support
- In collaboration with Versus programming and production team, develop and implement creative, brand-driven video and editorial content across multiple sports and competition genres, including but not limited to the NHL, mixed martial arts, collegiate sports, professional bull riding, professional cycling, hunting, and fishing
- Develop strategies for integrating Versus' digital assets into network website
- Manage website operations including day-to-day edit and technical
- Marketing of website using network resources to meet traffic growth targets
- Directly responsible for preparation of and adhering to website budget
- Responsible for acquiring and publishing network online video for broadband channel

- Work with CNS setting Internet sales budgets, assisting in developing ad packages, and managing all online advertising operations
- Monetize broadband assets online where rights allow
- Manage online relationships including overseeing legal agreements
- Liaison with Comcast.net in support of major network initiatives including supplying video content

Represent network's online initiatives with press and within industry

- Bachelor's degree; master's degree preferred
- More than 7 years of related experience in Internet production and editorial (including video) management with sports background
- More than 3 years in senior management role and ability to function as a senior strategist with key members of Versus management team
- Creative instinct, experience, skills, and initiative to deliver compelling editorial and content
- Demonstrated leadership and interpersonal skills and proven ability to motivate and manage creative and editorial staff
- Solid analytical skills to build and track Internet department budgets
- Strong management orientation with significant experience setting and achieving time-sensitive goals and developing and implementing multiple projects
- Excellent verbal, written, communication, and presentation skills
- Working knowledge of legal and technical aspects of website development and operations
- Internet advertising sales experience a plus

Endnotes

1. Hohler, B. (2007, Aug. 4). NFL Limits Web. *The Boston Globe*. Retrieved August 21, 2008, from http://www.boston.com/sports/articles/2007/08/04/nfl_limits_web.

Game Operations and Production

Game operations and production staff are responsible for overseeing the actual events that take place on the day of a sporting event. They control the scoreboards, video boards, music, and any announcements made to the audience. The following are two examples of such positions in the sports industry.

DIRECTOR OF GAME OPERATIONS, IOWA ENERGY

Industry Segment:	Professional Sports, Basketball, NBDL Team
Functional Area:	Game Operations and Production
Experience:	One to two years preferred
Location:	Des Moines, Iowa

The director of game operations is responsible for programming all arena announcements, music, promotions, message center text and graphics, implementation, and execution of all game day operations.

Duties and Responsibilities

- Management of team and arena personnel to accomplish the desired arena atmosphere

- Serve as liaison between team and arena management and personnel

- Responsible for the production of all arena signage and budget to accomplish the same

- Responsible for game promotion budget

- In charge of seasonal employees such as public address announcer, message board operator, and all operations personnel provided by the arena

Qualifications

Must demonstrate a high degree of leadership, time management, and organizational skills. Candidate must have experience directing and managing game operations. Must have proven ability to work with both team and arena personnel. Computer literacy is a plus. The ideal candidate must be a self-starter as well as a team player. The ability to work year-round long hours is preferred.

DIGITAL MEDIA COORDINATOR, BOSTON CELTICS

Industry Segment:	Professional Sports, Basketball, NBA Team
Functional Area:	Game Operations and Production
Experience:	Entry level
Location:	Boston, Massachusetts

Position reports to the director of game operations and events.

Duties and Responsibilities

- Coordinate day-to-day video and graphic needs for game operations department and other departments as needed

- Responsible for operating and coordinating in-house HD cameras, and light and sound equipment

- Primary contact for all video needs, in-house camera, and logo requests

- Shoot and produce player appearance and event videos as requested

- Shoot and produce mascot skit and event videos as requested

- Edit and produce in-game videos, including but not limited to player highlight videos, mascot skits, player CR videos, player messaging videos, and sponsor videos
- Assist in the coordination and production of Media Day shoot
- Help create LED animations for all LED boards in arena
- Produce in-game sponsor animations and graphics
- Provide game presentation video web content
- Assist with setup and breakdown of team press conferences
- Primary contact between arena and game operations department on game days for all technical issues
- Candidate will be a part of all game-day production and entertainment meetings

Qualifications

- Candidate must have a bachelor's degree
- Video editing experience on either Adobe Premiere or Final Cut Pro
- Experience in Photoshop and Adobe After Effects
- TV video production experience preferable

Player Personnel

Player personnel is arguably the most visible nonplaying aspect of the team-sports industry. It's up to these professionals to assemble the team you see on the field or court. They make the trades, free agent signings, and draft selections that grab headlines quite frequently. Their duties can range from scouting and statistical analysis to contract negotiations and trade discussions.

There is currently a growing movement in MLB toward younger, more business-oriented player personnel professionals. As John Schuerholz, the 67-year-old GM of the Atlanta Braves, stated in *USA Today*, "I introduce myself to anyone who looks my son's age, just in case they're a GM. . . . I feel like Obi-Wan Kenobi."[1] This movement is most apparent in examining the appointment of Jon Daniels, Theo Epstein, and Andy Friedman as general managers (for the Texas Rangers, Boston Red Sox, and Tampa Bay Rays, respectively). All three of these people were named GM in their late 20s, and all three brought a nontraditional business background to the baseball world.

Although not all teams are choosing to go the younger route in hiring new GMs, the trend is worth noting. Just as important, though, is the seemingly higher value that some teams place on business skills rather than baseball experience. Take Jon Daniels, for instance. He possessed just 4 years of baseball experience prior to becoming a GM. This is in sharp contrast to Wayne Krivsky, general manager for the Cincinnati Reds, who worked 27 years in scouting and development before receiving his current position as GM. Why the change? As Stuart Sternberg, part owner of the Tampa Bay Rays, noted, "With the prices of franchises, you've got to have someone who understands the pocketbook, the brand and what it takes to grow it. . . . Given all the needs, I need someone with a broader set [of skills]."[2]

As you can imagine, the path to becoming a general manager is quite varied. Section 2 of this book provides greater insight into the paths people have taken to become general manager in MLB, including how the young superstars of the baseball world ascended to such a lofty position at such an early age. If you are interested in a career in player personnel, make sure to take a look at Chapter 19.

The job descriptions included in this chapter will provide insight into the types of duties and responsibilities that player personnel professionals throughout the sports world encounter on a daily basis. If this segment of the industry is of particular interest to you, take a look at the organizational chart in Figure 62-15 in Chapter 62, which depicts the player personnel positions of a sample major league baseball team, and Figure 62-2, which depicts the player personnel positions of an NFL franchise.

COMPENSATION LEVELS

Industry compensation for player personnel positions can very tremendously depending on the factors explained. Many of the positions included in this chapter are player personnel positions in baseball. For these positions, compensation estimates have been provided with each job description. To provide additional compensation information, the following salary ranges can be found in professional football. Similar ranges can be expected in professional basketball and hockey, as well.

Professional Sports

- Entry level: $30,000 to $35,000
- Manager level: $50,000 to $70,000
- Director level: $90,000 to $125,000
- Executive level: $150,000+

FOOTBALL OPERATIONS INTERNSHIP, SAN FRANCISCO 49ERS

Industry Segment:	Professional Sports, Football, NFL Team
Functional Area:	Player Personnel
Experience:	Internship
Location:	Santa Clara, California
Compensation:	Likely to be unpaid, hourly wage, or monthly stipend

The San Francisco 49ers football operations department is currently seeking an intern to assist in the performance analysis of professional and collegiate football players. This internship will be during the season (September–December 2007) working part time, 15–20 hours/week, and will be located at our Santa Clara facility.

Duties and Skills

The majority of the internship will be spent watching film and tracking player performance. The ability to recognize blocking assignments and defensive schemes is important. Football playing and/or coaching experience is heavily recommended, though not required. Basic knowledge of Microsoft Excel is a plus.

BASKETBALL OPERATIONS INTERNSHIP, ORLANDO MAGIC

Industry Segment:	Professional Sports, Basketball, NBA Team
Functional Area:	Player Personnel
Experience:	Internship
Location:	Orlando, Florida
Compensation:	$750 monthly stipend

Assist the basketball operations department with day-to-day responsibilities that involve the various branches of the department.

Job Relationships

- Reports to: executive assistant to head coach/player services coordinator
- Supervises: N/A

Duties and Responsibilities

- Assist with all daily administrative functions, which include sorting mail, answering phones, coordinating player mail room and distributing mail/phone messages, filing, scheduling, etc.
- Assist other branches of department as needed—video, player services, scouting office, general manager's office, etc.
- Responsible for taking/typing minutes in basketball operations meetings
- Assist in maintaining and distributing department calendars, such as scouting, vacation, and practice court calendars
- Assist with game night responsibilities—work approximately 35 Magic home games
- Other duties as assigned

Qualifications

- Ability to communicate efficiently and effectively with internal and external clients
- Excellent verbal and written skills
- Ability to multitask and maintain confidential information
- Ability to work on projects independently
- Proficient in Microsoft Office
- Maintain a professional image

Physical Demands

- Be able to work long hours and most weekends during the NBA season

AREA SCOUT SUPERVISORS (NORTHERN TX, OK, KS, NE), ST. LOUIS CARDINALS

Industry Segment:	Professional Sports, Baseball, MLB Team
Functional Area:	Player Personnel
Experience:	Unspecified
Location:	Dallas, Texas, or Tulsa, Oklahoma
Compensation:	Unspecified in announcement. Amateur scouts can expect to earn: • Part-time area scout: $15,000 to 25,000 • Full-time area scout: $40,000+ • National cross-checker: $80,000+

Duties and Responsibilities

- Responsible for all players that have professional potential, with special emphasis on high school and junior college players
- Maintain a top-50 draft-eligible player list
- Write scouting reports on all draft-eligible players with professional potential
- Understand and interpret analytical information on all players
- Maintain efficient travel schedule throughout the year to adhere to budget
- Prepare expense reports for individual travel costs
- Responsible for understanding and knowing each player's make-up
- Understand players' market value, talent, and appropriate draft round
- Participate in and prepare for the annual amateur draft
- Conduct workouts and tryouts in your area
- Assist in special projects, team projects, task forces, etc.
- Complete assigned summer responsibility—pro coverage, college summer league, high school tournaments and showcases, etc.

Qualifications

- Willing to relocate—likely to Dallas or Tulsa
- Undergraduate degree
- Experience in baseball strongly preferred (player, scout, front office, coach, or industry)
- Working knowledge of MS Office suite—expert with MS Excel
- Strong Internet research skills
- Strong interpersonal skills
- Attention to detail
- Willing to work on weekends and holidays

Position reports to the regional supervisor.

DIRECTOR OF PLAYER PERSONNEL, HOUSTON ROCKETS

Industry Segment:	Professional Sports, Basketball, NBA Team
Functional Area:	Player Personnel
Experience:	Unspecified
Location:	Houston, Texas

This position will be responsible for evaluation of NBA, minor league, NCAA, and international players. The evaluations will be used for free agent, draft, and trade purposes. Position reports to the general manager and vice president of player personnel.

Duties and Responsibilities

- Evaluate players from all ranks: NBA, NCAA, minor league, and international play
- In-person evaluation of players: practice, games, camps, and workouts
- Video evaluation of players
- Statistical evaluation of players
- Gather background information concerning a prospect's character
- Written reports to be entered into Rocket database—postevaluations
- Attend postseason college camps (PIT and Orlando Pre-Draft)
- Attend and participate in free-agent and predraft workouts
- Attend free-agent and/or mini-camps conducted by Rockets
- Participate in the development of summer league roster with GM and VP of Player Personnel
- Attend summer league contests, as well as other summer leagues
- Travel domestically and internationally as requested by the GM and/or VP of Player Personnel
- Develop working relationships with coaching staff, personnel staff, support staff, players
- Other duties as assigned

DIRECTOR OF SCOUTING, MAJOR LEAGUE BASEBALL TEAM

Industry Segment:	Professional Sports, Baseball, MLB Team
Functional Area:	Player Personnel
Experience:	Seven to ten years of experience required
Location:	Multiple locations throughout the United States
Compensation:	$100,000 to $150,000

The following is a general description detailing the types of responsibilities and requirements commonly found for this position. An actual job announcement was not available.

Duties and Responsibilities

The primary role of the scouting director is to oversee the organization's scouting department and procure talent for the Major League club. Tasks include, but are not limited to, the following:

- Evaluate talent at the amateur, professional, and international level and report to the GM and assistant GM on a daily basis
- Prepare for and select players during the Rule IV: June Amateur Draft
- Negotiate contracts with selected players from the Rule IV draft, as well as international free agents
- Oversee the signing of domestic amateur players (U.S., Canada, Puerto Rico) and international players (located throughout the world)
- Develop and manage the scouting budget
- Hire and manage a scouting staff
- Advise the general manager in player acquisitions throughout the season on trades, free agents, the draft, etc.

Education

A bachelor's degree is almost necessary, and some scouting directors have master's degrees, although this is not as prevalent.

Experience

Many scouting directors are former players, managers, and staff members. Previous talent evaluation experience is typically necessary.

Special Skills

- Baseball knowledge such as scouting and player evaluation.
- People skills are essential to the job.
- Organizational skills, accounting and budgeting skills, and negotiating skills are helpful.
- Foreign language skills are preferred (Spanish, Japanese, etc.).

Career Progression

- Typically start as a scout, then move through the ranks to advanced scout, cross-checker (regional or national), and then assistant director of scouting

Trade Publications

- *Baseball America* (online and print editions)
- *Baseball Prospectus*
- *Baseball Digest*
- *Baseball Weekly*
- *Sporting News*
- *Collegiate Baseball Newspaper*
- *USA Today Baseball Weekly*

DIRECTOR OF PLAYER DEVELOPMENT, MAJOR LEAGUE BASEBALL TEAM

Industry Segment:	Professional Sports, Baseball, MLB Team
Functional Area:	Player Personnel
Experience:	Five to ten years of experience typically required
Location:	Multiple locations throughout the United States
Compensation:	$100,000 to $150,000

The following is a general description detailing the types of responsibilities and requirements commonly found for this position. An actual job announcement was not available.

Duties and Responsibilities

The primary role of the director of player development is to oversee development and instructional training of players in a team's farm system. Tasks may include, but are not limited to, the following:

- Assign, develop, and evaluate minor league players
- Teach, train, guide, and prepare players to play at the major league level
- Implement specific organizational strategies and operational philosophies throughout the farm system that are consistent with the parent club (i.e., methods of hitting, pitching, fielding, throwing, rehabbing, strength and conditioning, etc.)
- Manage rosters at each affiliate club
- Schedule and plan all nonseason operations, such as spring training, fall leagues, winter leagues, instructional leagues, and mini-camps

- Coordinate all player moves (transactions, releases, free agent signings, etc.)
- Manage field and front office personnel
- Maintain working relationships with affiliates and their respective GMs
- Hire minor league coordinators (rovers), on-field staff, and front office staff within department
- Plan and manage player development budget
- Conduct player and staff evaluations
- Monitor coaches and managers throughout the organization
- Travel to affiliates throughout the season to monitor and help improve player development
- Reports to the general manager

Education

- Minimum:
  - A college degree is not necessary, but can be beneficial when dealing with complex organizational structures and strategies.
- Preferred:
  - A business degree (BA or BS in business administration) may be helpful if the director of player development has to manage the minor league baseball operations budget and/or deal with budgetary constraints.

Experience

- Minimum:
  - Playing experience is crucial to understanding how to teach and improve players' abilities.
  - Previous coaching/managing experience is also helpful.
- Preferred:
  - Typically have experience in baseball operations (front office) as assistant to director of minor league operations, assistant to scouting director, or assistant to general manager.

Required Special Skills

- Player evaluation skills, including monitoring development and assessing players' strengths and weaknesses
- Must have teaching/training skills, because this position works with developing players on a daily basis

- Patience and people skills are needed, because developing players takes time
- Must be dedicated and hardworking; with the various fall and winter leagues, this is a year-round job
- Must be adaptable, because every day brings something new
- Foreign language skills are preferred (Spanish, Japanese, etc.)
- Negotiating skills and some accounting/budgeting skills are needed
- Tough/competitive nature

Career Progression

- There is no set path and progression can vary immensely:
  - Former players often begin in coaching jobs or become assistants in player development, and then progress into a director's position.
  - Minor league coaches and managers can transition into player development and work up to a director's position.
  - Some work their way through the scouting ranks, starting as a scout, then advanced scout, and then move into a player development role within the front office, eventually working up to a director's position.

Trade Publications

- *Baseball America* (online and print editions)
- *Baseball Prospectus*
- *Baseball Digest*
- *Baseball Weekly*
- *Sporting News*
- *USA Today Baseball Weekly*

ASSISTANT GENERAL MANAGER, MAJOR LEAGUE BASEBALL TEAM

Industry Segment:	Professional Sports, Baseball, MLB Team
Functional Area:	Player Personnel
Experience:	Seven to ten years of experience required
Location:	Multiple locations throughout the United States
Compensation:	$150,000 to $300,000

Position Spotlight   *Farm Director (Director of Player Development, Director of Minor League Operations)*

The term *farm director* is an older description that is still used by some MLB organizations; however, it is more common to see director of player development or director of minor league operations as the title for this position. Depending on the organization, the responsibilities for this position vary among the different titles; however, there are some constants shared by all clubs. The director of player development is mainly responsible for teaching, guiding, and developing players within the organization, both personally and professionally, in order to prepare them for the major leagues. Additionally, directors of player development are responsible for hiring and managing the minor league coaches and instructors who will work with the players on a daily basis within the assigned affiliate. Therefore, the director of player development is responsible for putting the minor league system in place. Directors of player development should have a well-thought-out, highly structured strategy. Therefore, it is crucial to be an organized, driven manager with a great knowledge of the game who knows how to teach and improve players' abilities.

The director of player development is a very challenging job, for several reasons. For instance, each director of player development is responsible for integrating or synthesizing his philosophy among all affiliates so that when players move from one team to another, every coach knows the players' strengths and weaknesses, and also what the players need to work on to improve. Then, he must be able to continually develop that player for the next level in a relatively short period of time. Thus, vertical integration is a key element in player development. Another challenge to the job is that every day is different, which requires the director of player development to be adaptable. For instance, there may be a player that a director of player development has been working with for a long time and developing into a great, talented, major-league-ready player who is unexpectedly traded away. That connection with the player is then lost, and now the director of player development must concentrate and focus on another area in the organization. It is an ongoing process of improvement and development that requires attention year round, especially with all the leagues that are played overseas during the off-season.

Directors of player development enjoy working within an organization and find it very rewarding to see players from within the system succeed at the major league level. However, though it may be a rewarding position, there is a little room to grow beyond it within an organization, so many successful directors of player development have moved on from this position to become assistant GM's or GM's of a major league club.

The following is a general description detailing the types of responsibilities and requirements commonly found for this position. An actual job announcement was not available.

Duties and Responsibilities

The primary role of the assistant GM is to work directly with the general manager in all facets of baseball operations, some of which include, but are not limited to:

- Player acquisitions
- Contract negotiations, in particular Minor League free agents and players with 0 to 3 years of major league service
- Interpreting and adhering to the Basic Agreement and Major League and Minor League Transaction Rules
- Player evaluation
- Scouting and player development, both domestic and international
- Salary arbitration
- Media relations

In addition to daily baseball operations responsibilities, assistant GMs may also be in charge of the hiring of front office staff. Along with the director of player development and the scouting director, assistant GMs will also assist in the hiring of scouts and field personnel. Some assistant GMs may be responsible for managing the baseball operations budget and team payroll.

Education

- Minimum:
  - A college degree is typically necessary.
- Preferred:
  - A business degree (BA or BS in business administration) may be helpful in dealing with budget issues.
  - It is common to find graduate degrees such as an MBA, an MS in sport management, or a law degree (JD).

Preferred Experience

- Can vary immensely; typically have experience in baseball operations, in either scouting or player development
- May also have playing and/or coaching experience

Required Special Skills

- Baseball knowledge, such as scouting and player evaluation, is essential.
- Negotiation skills, leadership skills, people skills, and some accounting/budgeting skills are necessary for success.
- Must be highly organized and detail-oriented.

Trade Publications

- *Baseball America* (online and print editions)
- *Baseball Prospectus*
- *Baseball Digest*
- *Baseball Weekly*
- *Sporting News*
- *USA Today Baseball Weekly*

GENERAL MANAGER, MAJOR LEAGUE BASEBALL TEAM

Industry Segment:	Professional Sports, Baseball, MLB Team
Functional Area:	Player Personnel
Experience:	See career track in Chapter 50
Location:	Multiple locations throughout the United States
Compensation:	Depends on team, $300,000 to $5 million+

The following is a general description detailing the types of responsibilities and requirements commonly found for this position. An actual job announcement was not available.

A general manager of a Major League Baseball team is ultimately the decision maker who usually has the power to assemble a ball club to compete at the major league level. Many factors influence how a general manager operates within a franchise (the most dominant of which is money), and those factors will dictate how much influence the GM will have on managing the team.

Duties and Responsibilities

- Create and manage a 40-player roster
- Manage the team's salary budget
- Execute and negotiate players' contracts
- Monitor player development and scouting throughout the organization
- Respond to reporters, beat writers, and team media
- Advise and select amateur players in the annual draft, in consultation with the scouting director and other front office personnel
- Analyze the free agent market and prospective players throughout the league and international markets
- Interact with players, coaches, and scouts
- Hire and manage front office personnel
- Report to the team president

Education

- Varies from high school graduates, to graduates of 4-year colleges, to graduates of master's programs and law schools
- See Chapter 50 for a more detailed analysis of the educational background of current GMs

Preferred Experience

- Player development and scouting experience are extremely helpful.
- Nearly all GMs have gone up through the front office baseball operations system in some capacity.
- See Chapter 50 for a more detailed analysis of the previous experience for current GMs.

Required Special Skills

- Communication and public speaking skills are critical
- Must have well-developed negotiation and leadership skills
- An ability to analyze and evaluate talent is essential
- Must have dedication and a desire to compete

Trade Publications

- *Baseball America* (online and print editions)
- *Baseball Digest*
- *Street & Smith's SportsBusiness Journal*
- *MLB Advanced Media (mlb.com)*
- *The Sporting News*
- *Baseball Prospectus*
- *Sports Illustrated*

- Book flights (travel) for player moves, families, front office, and staff
- Create travel itinerary for all road trips
- Coordinate travel to winter and general manager meetings
- Responsible for applying for and obtaining Canadian work visas
- Assist foreign players with U.S. immigration issues
- Make accommodations for rehabbing injured players
- Handle daily ticket requests for players and staff—regular season, postseason, and All-Star Game
- Work with local and state police to establish team escort
- Maintain player contact information
- Develop and manage travel budget
- Maintain team travel petty cash and checking account
- Assist players and field staff with personal issues, such as making dinner reservations, obtaining tickets to events, etc.
- Manage all travel accounting, including:
  - Hotel invoices
  - Charter fees
  - Manager and coaches expenses
  - Bus and truck invoices
  - Player reimbursement and expense
  - Payroll deductions
  - Per diem for players and staff
  - Team credit card billing
- Coordinate Spring Training activity, including:
  - Manage weekly meal money
  - Coordinate players, staff, and admin travel to and from Spring Training
  - Handle daily ticket requests
  - Coordinate hotels and car rentals
  - Reserve bus to Spring Training games
  - Complete player and staff payroll paperwork
  - Coordinate moving trucks (supplies, equipment, etc.)
  - Other duties as assigned

Education

Bachelor's degree is strongly preferred, and some have graduate degrees such as an MBA

Qualifications

- Communication skills, people skills, and accounting/budgeting skills are critical
- Must have an ability to multi-task
- Need to be detail-oriented and organized
- Foreign language skills are preferred (Spanish, Japanese, etc.)

TEAM PRESIDENT/GENERAL MANAGER, SCRANTON/WILKES-BARRE YANKEES

Industry Segment:	Professional Sports, Baseball, International League Team (AAA)
Functional Area:	Administration
Experience:	Unspecified, likely to require seven to ten years of experience
Location:	Scranton, Pennsylvania

The team president/general manager is responsible for the overall operation of the organization. This includes oversight and direct involvement in sponsorship sales, ticket sales, entertainment, media relations, broadcasting, marketing and promotions, stadium operations, office administration, accounting, organization infrastructure, and human resources.

Duties and Responsibilities

- Overall operation of the organization
- Prepare and submit of fiscal year budgets
- Financial reporting
- Sell key sponsorships
- Respond to all legal matters
- Handle team insurance issues
- Oversee office administration
- Oversee human resources
- Liaison with city/county/other governmental groups
- Liaison with Major League affiliate
- Liaison with the league
- Liaison with the National Association of Professional Baseball Leagues
- Liaison with Mandalay Sports corporate office
- Liaison with concessionaire

Position Spotlight   *Minor League General Manager*

The job of a minor league general manager is much different from a major league general manager. The primary responsibilities of a minor league GM are operational and business-related. His or her responsibilities are more closely aligned today with a businessperson in the major league front office. The decisions on talent, such as the selection, drafting, signing, and placement of players on teams, are the responsibility of the major league team. Therefore, the minor league GM has the players who are assigned to the team he or she is running.

The minor league general manager is responsible for hiring, supervising, and managing the front office staff. The size of the staff varies depending on the level of team (A, AA, AAA). The higher-level leagues generally require more staff because there are more fans and a higher profile. As a result, there are more ticket sales, more media contacts, and more operational responsibilities on game day. Another factor determining the size of the front office staff is whether the facility is run by the team or by the owner (such as the city). If the team operates the facility, more staff will be needed for the team's games (and also if there are other events or activities held in the stadium).

During the season, much of the time the GM will be focused on the operational aspects of overseeing the games and maximizing the revenues from ticket sales and concessions. The GM has the overall responsibility of supervising the full-time staff to ensure that the facility is in good condition and fully operational. For many minor league teams, this starts with field and facility maintenance, but also includes setting up signage, ticket sales, concessions, media rooms, and promotional activities.

The off-season (outside the regular season) is not an off-season from working. It is only an off-season from playing games. The nature of the work changes. It may include capital projects like stadium improvements, upgrades, and expansion. It may include maintenance, such as painting and repairs. Much of the sales and marketing work is done in the off-season. Renewal ad sales of sponsorship are done in the off-season. In addition, the corporate, group, and season ticket sales are started and often completed in the off-season. This includes the renewals of existing customers, as well as sales to new customers. The game promotional activities are also planned, and then developed and agreed to with the partners. In addition, publications such as the program and media guide are developed in the off-season. The GM will also work with full-time, part-time, and internship staff members in the off-season as well as during the season.

To be a successful minor league GM, one needs excellent communication and people skills, an ability to multi-task, strong networking skills, an ability to lead, an ability to generate sales and marketing opportunities, and budgeting/financial analysis skills.

- Responsible for leads on stadium construction and/or capital projects
- Responsible for leads on stadium management
- Oversee community relations for organization
- Help develop public image and Mandalay Baseball Properties brand
- Handle trademarks and copyrights of franchise name, marks, and logo
- High level of involvement with ticketing and sponsorship sales strategies
- Oversee sponsorship sales
- Oversee marketing campaigns
- Coordinate issues relative to stadium lease
- Manage and control budgeted revenues and expenses for entire organization
- Oversee the ticketing, sponsor sales, entertainment, and media relations departments

GENERAL MANAGER/PRESIDENT, ECHL TEAM MEMBER

Industry Segment:	Professional Sports, Hockey, ECHL Team
Functional Area:	Administration
Experience:	Unspecified, likely to require seven to ten years of experience
Location:	Unidentified

A member team of the ECHL is currently seeking qualified candidates for a general manager/president. This long-established team with a great history and past success on and off the ice has a great opportunity for an energetic individual to come in and make their mark in the ECHL.

The president/general manager is responsible for overseeing all business development, sales growth, and day-to-day operations of the team including the adherence to all league mandates, payroll issues, schedule coordination,

Position Spotlight   *Major League Baseball Team President and CEO*

It is the role of the president/CEO of a major league base-ball team to provide leadership to all parts of the organiza-tion, including both the business and baseball operations of the organization. With the sport's recent explosion of revenue, a president's job has grown more complex. The president is responsible for overseeing not only the base-ball aspects of the team, but also local TV and radio deals, stadium deals, sponsorship, marketing, ticket sales, com-munity service—all the way down to concessions and mer-chandise. Stan Kasten, president of the Washington Nationals, was quoted as saying, "I see three areas where the CEO and president has to be prominent: (1) to organize and connect, put together the right structure; (2) putting the right people in the right boxes; (3) making sure they have the resources, whether its money or direct support."[1]

Ultimately, a baseball organization is a corporation like any other business, and the role of a baseball president/CEO is not that different from the role of a CEO in the busi-ness world. A team's president is charged with establishing a winning tone throughout the organization—both on and off the field—and making sure everyone is held account-able for achieving the team's goals. He or she is held responsible for the results of all facets of the organization, and must manage the team's available resources to maxi-mize their return on investment. Although the daily duties of a team president are vast and too numerous to list here, the following list provides examples of the types of tasks some team presidents encounter:

- Interview general manager and manager candidates
- Work with the general manager to set an overarching team philosophy to govern player transactions and the minor league system
- If the team plays in an older stadium, find ways to gen-erate new revenue streams from the existing structure or explore the possibility of building a new facility
- If a new facility is needed/desired, the president will work to secure stadium financing, and failing this, may possibly explore relocation options
- Make decisions regarding facility upgrades, such as remodeling stadium suites, building bunker suites, or enhancing the scoreboard
- Establish customer service policies and training pro-grams for team employees
- Maintain a close working relationship with the team's owner(s) and other outside constituents

- Supervise and help coordinate the team's marketing, sponsorship, and advertising departments
- Conduct interviews with various television, radio, and print media
- Manage the team's community service efforts
- Negotiate concession contracts with outside conces-sionaires
- Represent the team's interests in league meetings

There are generally two different prevailing thoughts on who makes a good president/CEO of an MLB team. Some owners prefer an experienced business executive with little or no baseball experience. Such people often bring considerable management expertise and business skills. Baseball franchises are worth millions of dollars, and some owners seek the comfort of knowing their investment is being managed by a more-traditional business profes-sional. As an example, in 2005, the Tampa Bay Rays hired Matt Silverman as their president/CEO. At the time, Matt had worked the two previous years for the Rays as the team's vice president of planning and development. Prior to this position, though, Matt had no experience working in baseball (in either the business or baseball operations). What Matt did bring was a Harvard degree and business experience from Wall Street.

In contrast, some owners prefer a president/CEO with an extensive baseball background that complements their business acumen. Such owners are generally of the mind-set that an organization's success begins with its success on the field, so it is only natural to hire a president/CEO who has a solid understanding of the baseball side of the industry. Often, a baseball background lends credibility to a president's decisions that impact player personnel and baseball operations.

As of August 2007, there were only seven presidents/CEOs who possessed considerable baseball experience (typically as a former GM): Andy McPhail of the Orioles, Sandy Alderson of the Padres, Jeff Moorad of the Dia-mondbacks, Tal Smith of the Astros, Stan Kasten of the Nationals, Larry Lucchino of the Red Sox, and Dave Dom-browski of the Tigers (who also happens to be the team's general manager). It will be interesting to see if more teams will decide in the coming years that baseball experience is a prerequisite of a suitable president/GM candidate.

marketing/sales collateral materials, and employee supervision. The general manager/president's primary objectives are to strengthen the team's brand to drive ticket sales and corporate sponsorship revenues while managing the financial and operational aspects of the team. This individual will work in tandem with ownership and their arena to execute the business plan.

Duties and Responsibilities

- Develop business and sales strategies to increase revenue
- Expand, prospect, and generate new corporate partnerships through interaction in the community
- Plan and manage the financial and operational aspects of the team
- Equipment and inventory control management
- Assure compliance with all league requirements
- Work with hockey personnel on player trades and roster moves
- Interface with departments to assist in the development, implementation, and analysis of marketing and sales campaigns
- Coordinate event and game schedule with arena and visiting team personnel

- Foster and maintain relationships with various media outlets and other promotional partners
- Assist with development and execution of game day promotions and game presentation
- Assist with development and administration of customer retention programs

Qualifications

- Experience in successfully developing and generating ticket and/or sponsorship revenues
- A history of sales success and the ability to build and lead a sales-driven and customer-focused organization
- Experience overseeing financial reports and budgets
- Strong analytical skills and business acumen
- Proven leadership and management abilities
- Strong communication and teambuilding skills
- A bachelor's degree in finance, business, or related field

Endnotes

1. Cafardo, N. (2007, June 24). McPhail Game for the Job. *Boston Globe*, p. F4.

CHAPTER EIGHTY-TWO

Accounting and Finance

An organization's accounting and finance department is responsible for all fiscal matters related to a sports organization. Historically, this department focused primarily on day-to-day accounting, simple tracking of revenues and expenses, and paying the necessary bills. Today, the department's role has increased significantly. Professionals employed in an organization's accounting and finance department are involved with short-term and long-term budgeting, capital structuring, cash flow management, forecasting, communicating the entity's financial position, and setting the overall strategic financial direction. This change corresponds to the increased complexity of organizations and the greater focus on revenue maximization and the bottom line.

Nonetheless, accounting and finance in the sports industry is similar in nature to accounting and finance outside of the sports industry. The essential duties and responsibilities (cash management, capital budgeting, risk management, financial reporting, etc.) are the same; just the underlying subject matter is different. Therefore, it is not uncommon to see job postings for accounting and finance positions requiring (or preferring) candidates to have related experience from nonsports entities (such as experience at large, national public accounting firms). Another common preference is for candidates to hold a CPA license. This is one functional area in which it is more common to see professionals make the jump from nonsports entities to sports entities, although a significant pay decrease typically accompanies such a move.

Industry compensation for accounting and finance positions can vary tremendously depending on the factors explained in Chapter 72. The following compensation levels are reasonable expectations for mid-sized organizations in mid-sized markets.

Professional Sports

- Staff accountant or analyst, entry level: $25,000 to $35,000

- Senior accountant or analyst: $45,000 to $65,000
- Controller or accounting manager: $60,000 to $80,000
- Vice president or director: $90,000 to $150,000
- Executive VP or CFO: $150,000+

College Athletics

- Business manager, NCAA Football Championship Subdivision school: $40,000 to $60,000
- Assistant or associate athletic director business/finance, NCAA Football Championship Subdivision school: $40,000 to $75,000

Professionals hired into the following positions are given the responsibility of assisting with, overseeing, or managing their organization's financial well-being.

FINANCE INTERN, OAKLAND ATHLETICS

Industry Segment:	Professional Sports, Baseball, MLB Team
Functional Area:	Accounting and Finance
Experience:	Internship
Location:	Oakland, California
Compensation:	Likely to be unpaid, hourly wage, or monthly stipend

Duties and Responsibilities

The finance intern's primary responsibilities will be assisting the department with various administrative duties. Primary duties will include, but are not limited to, the following:

- Enter A/P checks for various bank accounts into accounting software

- Enter complimentary merchandise forms into accounting software to allocate to appropriate department
- Enter monthly postage allocations across departments
- Work with merchandising department to investigate novelty chargebacks/NSF checks
- Assist in distribution of monthly departmental budget information
- Various tasks, projects, etc.

Qualifications

- Qualified applicants must have excellent communication, organizational, and highly interpersonal skills
- Must be detail oriented and have excellent written and verbal skills
- Proficiency in Excel
- Have taken accounting and/or finance classes

STAFF ACCOUNTANT, BALTIMORE RAVENS

Industry Segment:	Professional Sports, Football, NFL Team
Functional Area:	Accounting and Finance
Experience:	Entry level, zero to two years of experience preferred
Location:	Owings Mills, Maryland

Prepares journal entries, account reconciliations, and financial analyses for the Baltimore Ravens. Responsibilities also include analyzing revenues, expenses, financial trends, and financial commitments to explain actual operating results and predict future activities. Reports financial data to management and offers suggestions to maximize financial and operation efficiencies and effectiveness.

Duties and Responsibilities

- Monitor organizational cash position and forecast future cash inflows/outflows
- Oversee all accounting and reporting aspects of fixed assets; track all additions, disposals, and depreciations in fixed asset subledger
- Oversee all accounting and reporting aspects of concessions/novelties
- Serve as a financial liaison to third-party providers
- Oversee the accounting and invoicing of miscellaneous receivables (e.g., mascot/cheerleader appearances, event reimbursements, etc.)
- Post journal entries and prepare monthly account analyses
- Reconcile operating and controlled disbursement bank accounts

- Prepare and monitor profit-loss statements for stadium concerts and various sporting events
- Coordinate fleet vehicle program
- Maintain all prepaid expense activity and related amortization
- Assist in the annual organizational budget process
- Assist in procuring and administering corporate and workers' compensation insurance polices
- Assist in the preparation of schedules for a variety of audits
- Prepare property tax returns
- Prepare employee relocation summary reports on a monthly basis
- Perform special financial projects, as deemed necessary

Required Education and/or Experience

Bachelor's degree in accounting and 0 to 2 years of experience in public or private accounting. Experience with financial reporting and financial statements a plus. Knowledge of commonly used concepts, practices, and procedures.

Qualifications

- Organizational and analytical skills, detail oriented, customer focus, drive for results, effective communication and passion for sports, manage multiple tasks/projects
- Ability to assess processes, pinpoint areas of improvement, and execute changes to achieve efficiencies
- Experience with Great Plains accounting software a plus
- Strong Microsoft Excel/Word/Outlook skills
- Must have passion for sports and be a team player!

FINANCIAL ANALYST, NFL LEAGUE OFFICE

Industry Segment:	Professional Sports, Football, NFL League Office
Functional Area:	Accounting and Finance
Experience:	Three years of experience required
Location:	New York

The financial analyst works very closely with the senior vice president of finance, director, and management council/league office business managers. The primary functions of this role include analyzing and driving financial performance for the league office and management council departments. In addition, this position will also have responsibility for performing proper technical analysis of accounts, implementation of accounting policies, and compliance with technical standards of accounting. A successful candidate should have solid finance and accounting skills; excellent

- This function includes the following: (1) the formulation of accounting policy; (2) the coordination of systems and procedures; and (3) the preparation of operating data, regular reports, and special analyses as required.

- Coordinate with senior management the long-range strategic planning initiatives for the team, assess the financial requirements implicit in those plans, evaluate potential return on investment, and develop alternative ways to satisfy those financial requirements

- Assist all segments of management in evaluating means of maximizing profits and minimizing losses throughout the business operation

- Manage all federal, state, and local tax compliance for all applicable tax liabilities and contingent tax exposures with respect to both ongoing operations and other organic transactions

- Assure protection of assets of the business through internal control, internal auditing, and proper insurance coverage

- Coordinate with and manage all outside audit requirements, including external auditor and special audit projects

- Oversee all finance/accounting-related information technology issues for the organization

- Provide strong leadership, coaching, and mentoring for all staff in an environment that is based upon teamwork, diversity, nondiscrimination, fairness, and balance

- Support the team's mission, vision, and values by exhibiting excellence, competence, collaboration, innovation, respect, empowerment of others, commitment to community, accountability, and ownership of work

- The VP, finance, will conduct the above job responsibilities under the guidance and direction of the president of the Tampa Bay Rays.

Required Knowledge and Experience

- Must possess a broad and practical knowledge of finance, accounting, and information technology in addition to mature and sound judgment

- Solid experience in entertainment/sports and/or a related industry, such as retail or hospitality, is strongly preferred; MLB experience is preferred, but not essential

- Demonstrated success in implementing financial procedures and controls in a similarly sized organization is strongly preferred

- Strong analytical and writing skills are required, as are excellent written and verbal communication skills

- Ability to maintain confidentiality and exercise discretion is essential

- Fluency with general office PC applications (i.e., word processing, spreadsheets, and databases) in addition to an understanding of standard budgeting software packages (e.g., Microsoft Great Plains) is required

Education and Formal Training

- Bachelor's degree
- Master's degree preferred
- Finance and accounting background strongly preferred

Experience

- A minimum of 5 years of experience directly relevant to the above tasks and responsibilities with demonstrated record of accomplishment

BUSINESS MANAGER, UNIVERSITY OF COLORADO

Industry Segment:	College Athletics, NCAA Football Bowl Subdivision School
Functional Area:	Accounting and Finance
Experience:	Seven years of experience required
Location:	Boulder, Colorado

The University of Colorado at Boulder is currently accepting qualified applicants for the position of business manager. Under the general direction of the director of intercollegiate athletics, this position has a broad range of responsibilities that are essential to the financial success and internal efficiency of the athletics department including management of the administrative, financial affairs, human resources, and information technology support for the department of intercollegiate athletics.

Required Qualifications

- Bachelor's degree in accounting, business administration, public administration, or closely related field

- Minimum of 7 years of progressive financial management, accounting, and business planning experience, including 3 years of experience in process and/or systems analysis and development

- Demonstrated excellence in addressing financial and technological issues and ability to establish and maintain strong working relationships within a highly diverse organization

Preferred Qualifications

- Master's degree in business administration, accounting, finance, or public administration, or a CPA

- Experience in an athletics or sports entertainment environment

- Strong interpersonal and conflict resolution skills

- Demonstrated ability in effective management, supervision, and team building

The business manager in a collegiate athletic department is primarily responsible for all finance-related matters in the department. Tracking expenses, forecasting budgets, and purchasing equipment are all tasks accomplished through the business office.

An important purpose of the business office is the support it provides to teams, whose coaches and managers typically lack the fiscal familiarity necessary to manage all the financial elements of a team. The coaches are very skilled at their job, and by allowing an office to handle the financial matters for several teams, the department can realize economies of scale and leave the money matters to the financial experts. For example, for all small-scale (non-capital) purchases of equipment, a team will submit an order through the business office, which in turn will do the actual purchasing. In the case where a coach purchases items on his or her own, he or she will still submit paperwork to the business office detailing the expenditure and the rationale for its need. In order to capitalize on economies of scale, the business manager negotiates purchasing contracts on behalf of the department. Several teams may need training equipment, and it is the business manager's role to purchase the equipment in bulk or establish a relationship with a supplier willing to provide a regular discount. He or she also works with the college's purchasing department in order to take advantage of contracts reached on a school-wide level.

A sometimes unpopular part of the business manager's job is as "watchdog" for the department's finances. The business office ensures that teams follow protocol and, along with the administrator in charge of the team, determines how to allocate discretionary funds. Although following set procedures often may seem like needless paperwork or bureaucracy, doing so is important to keeping costs low for the department and providing transparency to operations. As a nonprofit institution, a university receives tax breaks on its purchases, which requires specific documentation. In addition, information on state universities' spending is publicly available, and thus must be justifiable under public scrutiny. Although high ethical standards are important for any career, some business manager job descriptions explicitly request this characteristic for applicants.

In many schools the business manager will assist with the event operations for varsity competitions. Like other members of the athletic department, this requires a flexible schedule and the willingness to do some work in the evenings and on weekends.

DIRECTOR OF FINANCE, AEG LIVE

Industry Segment:	Event Management
Functional Area:	Accounting and Finance
Experience:	Ten years of experience required
Location:	Los Angeles, California

AEG Live seeks a director of finance to administer financial and administrative policies and procedures.

Duties and Responsibilities

• Report to CFO

• Hands-on experience in preparation of consolidated financial statements in accordance with GAAP including foreign currency translation

• Supervise transaction processing team (direct daily activities; enforce deadlines related to financial statement closing schedule; assess performance)

• Manage the annual budget process including the preparation of the consolidated budget

• Other responsibilities include coordinating efforts related to internal audit and year-end audit regarding corporate division, check-signing, budget preparation with involvement through business line controllers, preparation of monthly self-insurance analyses, maintaining JDE chart of accounts and add and delete business units as necessary, liaising with parent company systems support and accounting departments, handling all requested additions to JDE vendor master file, maintaining Rapid Decision and Crystal Reports packages, and implementing reports as requested by business line controllers

• Support outside firm in preparation of state, federal, and Canadian income tax returns; assure compliance with artist withholding requirements and supervise the preparation of monthly and annual business tax returns

• Act as subject matter expert for JDE, Rapid Decision, and Crystal Report packages

Qualifications

• College degree, accounting major

• CPA with an MBA a plus, but not required

• Ten years of minimum experience; entertainment industry experience preferred (personal service side, not TV or movie production)

• Strong analytical skills

• Confident user with demonstrated expertise in MS Office, JD Edwards One World version XE, Business Objects version X1R2 ("Rapid Decision"), and Crystal Reports

CHIEF FINANCIAL OFFICER, ARENA FOOTBALL LEAGUE

Industry Segment:	Professional Sports, Football, AFL League Office
Functional Area:	Accounting and Finance
Experience:	Ten to fifteen years of experience required
Location:	Chicago, Illinois

The chief financial officer (CFO) has the overall responsibility for the accounting, financial analysis, financial reporting, financing administration, and tax requirements of the Arena Football League. The position is also responsible for assisting, and in certain instances leading, various strategic initiatives, major agreements, and contract negotiations including, but not limited to, equity/debt financing and new business ventures. The ideal candidate will possess the following attributes: strength of character, sharp and quick intellect, abundance of energy, a passion for the Arena Football League, and an innate ability to have fun.

Duties and Responsibilities

- Oversee all financial, operations, and administrative areas of the Arena Football League

- Manage the league's and its affiliates' annual operating budget, projections, cash flow analysis, and financing ventures

- Monitor teams' compliance with standard AFL reporting and information sharing

- Work with senior management to research and analyze the financial implications (e.g., ROI, valuation, etc.) of potential business opportunities and major alliances

- Work with all segments of management within the organization with profit and loss responsibility as it pertains to the attainment of business objectives and the effectiveness of policies, organization structure, and procedures

- Manage all federal, state, and local tax compliance for all applicable tax liabilities and contingent tax exposures with respect to both ongoing operations and other organic transactions

- Collect and review team audited financial statements; ensure team compliance with league-wide credit facility financial statement reporting deadlines

- Coordinate with senior management the long-range strategic planning initiative for the league, assess the financial requirements implicit in those plans, evaluate potential return on investment, and develop alternative ways to satisfy those financial requirements

- Responsible for providing strong leadership, coaching, and mentoring for all staff in an environment that is based upon teamwork, diversity, nondiscrimination, fairness, and balance

- Responsible for supporting the Arena Football League's mission, vision, and values by exhibiting excellence, competence, collaboration, innovation, respect, empowerment of others, commitment to community, accountability, and ownership of work

- Serve as the league representatives with AFL's finance committee and board of directors

- Additional responsibilities as assigned by the commissioner and the deputy commissioner of the Arena Football League

Qualifications

- Five to 7 years of industry experience, preferably within team sports, media, or entertainment, demonstrating progressive growth in responsibility

- Ten to 15 years of total experience, including 4 to 6 in a managerial capacity

- Solid experience in the entertainment/sports industry, corporate environment, and business affairs and not-for-profit/association

- Significant, successful, similar, and compatible experience or business experience preferred

- Demonstrated analytical and writing skills are required

- Possesses a broad and practical knowledge of finance, accounting, information technology, and human resources fields

- Must have mature and sound judgment

- Must have strong presentation skills and be able to communicate effectively with owners and top management

- Proven to maintain confidentiality and exercise discretion

- Relevant experience in negotiating contracts

- Proven effective management of multiple related areas

- Demonstrated ability and experience developing and coordinating multi-faceted plans and issues

- Proficiency with general office PC applications (i.e., word processing, spreadsheets, databases)

- Demonstrated sound organizational, coordinating, and personal interface skills

- Demonstrated excellent written and verbal communication skills

- Proven job reliability, diligence, dedication, and attention to detail

Facility Management

In conjunction with a long, continuing period of growth in the sports industry, sports facilities have also become larger, more extravagant, and thus more expensive. Facilities currently found in the industry include small indoor facilities (such as a small college basketball arena with a seating capacity of only a few thousand), large indoor facilities (such as a domed NFL stadium with a seating capacity of 70,000+), small outdoor facilities (such as a college soccer field with a seating capacity of only a few hundred), and large outdoor facilities (such as an outdoor college football stadium with a seating capacity of 100,000+). Adding further complication to the available options, you will also find retractable roof stadiums, which eliminate the element of weather from a stadium's operations, but also introduce a new level of complexity and expense. As you can imagine, the duties and responsibilities of facility managers at each of these locations will vary tremendously.

The sports industry has seen a recent move toward more specialized outdoor stadiums. Look at the sports of baseball and football, for example. Thirty years ago, a city would build one multi-purpose stadium for a baseball and football team to share. Such practice is no longer common, with baseball teams and football teams requiring single-purpose stadiums to meet the revenue-generating demands of their sport, as well as the comfort demands of their fan bases. In 2007, three MLB teams (Marlins, Twins, and A's) shared facilities with NFL teams, while a number of other teams (such as the Nationals and Mets) played in stadiums that were originally intended to be multi-purpose stadiums. All of these teams, with the exception of the Marlins, have plans to build a new, baseball-only stadium within the next 5 years. Interestingly, this level of specialization has not made a significant impact on the NBA or NHL, where teams housed in the same city are more apt to share arenas. This is largely due to the fact that a specialized basketball arena does not vary significantly from a specialized hockey arena, eliminating the need to build two separate facilities.

Major League Soccer is another sport in which a specialized stadium craze has taken hold. In the league's initial seasons, teams typically played matches in stadiums built for NFL or NCAA college football teams. Unable to draw crowds to fill the stadiums and stuck in poor lease deals, MLS teams looked to build soccer-only stadiums. As of 2008, seven MLS teams (out of 14 total teams) played in stadiums built specifically for soccer, three other teams have plans to build such stadiums (due to be completed before 2010), and another four teams have proposed building soccer-specific stadiums.

In an effort to maximize revenues, sports facilities have also recently increased the number of music concerts and other entertainment options in their schedule of activities. Even historic ballparks, such as Wrigley Field and Fenway Park, have recently hosted concerts by such acts as the Rolling Stones, Jimmy Buffet, Dave Matthews Band, and the Police. This increased activity can create problems for sports teams in terms of damage to the playing surface, as evidenced by a 2007 Police concert at Wrigley Field. Following the concert, the Chicago Cubs were forced to resod areas of the outfield and even painted some of the grass green to remove any signs of concert damage. Ultimately, facility managers must balance the need for increased revenues against the need to maintain the integrity and condition of the playing surface.

Professionals employed in the types of positions listed in this chapter are responsible for managing the facilities used throughout the sports industry. It is their job to make sure the facilities are fully utilized to host sporting and entertainment events of every type and size. These are the people who work behind the scenes to create an enjoyable experience for everything from a sporting event to a concert.

Industry compensation for facility management positions can vary tremendously depending on the factors explained in Chapter 72. The following compensation levels are reasonable expectations for mid-sized organizations in mid-sized markets:

Facility Management

- Entry level: $30,000 to 35,000
- Assistant operations manager: $75,000 to $105,000
- Event coordinator: $75,000 to $105,000
- Director of operations: $95,000 to $130,000
- General manager (small arena): $80,000 to $150,000
- General manager (large arena): $165,000 to $190,000+

College Athletics

- Facilities coordinator, NCAA Football Championship Subdivision school: $30,000 to $50,000
- Assistant athletic director of facilities and operations, NCAA Football Championship Subdivision school: $35,000 to $70,000

OPERATIONS INTERN, SPRINT CENTER

Industry Segment:	Facility Management
Functional Area:	Facility Management
Experience:	Intern
Location:	Kansas City, Missouri
Property:	New 18,000-seat indoor arena opening in 2007
Compensation:	Unpaid, college credit must be received

Kansas City's newest arena, Sprint Center, seeks an intern who is interested in learning about all aspects of the arena operations including, but not limited to, music tours, concerts promotion, marketing, public relations, ticketing, and finance.

Duties and Responsibilities

- Event services:
  - Answer phone calls and provide clients with assistance
  - Assist with administrative duties such as faxing and filing
  - Gather and research information for the touring department on a regular basis
  - Provide efficient special event support through behind the scenes prep work

- Marketing and public relations:
  - Organize advertising print ads, tearsheets, and articles into a well-designed high-end notebook
  - Assist and create marketing presentations
  - Assemble and distribute press kits and PR materials
  - Spearhead annual clip book (photocopy print clips, dub television hits, etc.)
  - Handle nonprofit requests and donations
  - Help field media requests and press ticket requests
  - General administrative duties
  - Assist with any upcoming and various Sprint Center projects

Required Job Knowledge, Skills, and Abilities

- Detail-oriented with excellent written and verbal communication skills
- Proficient in the Internet as well as Word, Excel, and PowerPoint software applications
- Knowledge of different art media, different types and formats of printing and art techniques
- Good organizational skills with general knowledge of marketing/advertising
- Currently enrolled in a college or university working towards an undergraduate degree; have completed (a minimum) 60 hours of college-level coursework
- Proactive and able to work independently
- Professional in both appearance and attitude

Qualifications

This internship is for school credit only. Interested applicants must be enrolled full time and must be able to verify that he or she will receive course credit for the internship. Interns must provide verification of school enrollment and credit prior to starting the internship with our organization.

ASSISTANT MANAGER OF FACILITIES AND ENGINEERING, BOSTON BRUINS/TD BANKNORTH GARDEN

Industry Segment:	Facility Management and Professional Sports (NHL Team)
Functional Area:	Facility Management
Experience:	Unspecified
Location:	Boston, Massachusetts
Property:	19,600-seat indoor arena, home to the NBA's Boston Celtics and the NHL's Boston Bruins

Assists manager of facilities and engineering in directing and managing all facility operational functions and personnel related to environment, preventive maintenance, energy management, maintenance projects and repair, and capital projects at TD Banknorth Garden to ensure an efficient and safe environment for co-workers and guests.

Duties and Responsibilities

- Ensure compliance with building specifications and budget
- Manage outside contractors and coordinate scheduling of daily projects
- Oversee various tradespersons
- Assist in formation and planning of cost savings and efficiency measures
- Other duties as assigned

Expectations

Strong organizational skills, strong computer skills, strong communications skills, strong interpersonal skills, strong technical skills, and strong analytical skills. Familiarity with building systems including HVAC, electrical, plumbing, emergency power systems, and fire suppression and alarm systems. Knowledge of AutoCAD a plus.

EVENT MANAGER—ROSE QUARTER, GLOBAL SPECTRUM

Industry Segment:	Facility Management
Functional Area:	Facility Management
Experience:	Unspecified
Location:	Portland, Oregon
Property:	Multiple indoor facilities, including the 20,000-seat Rose Garden (home of the NBA's Portland Trailblazers), the 12,000-seat Memorial Coliseum, the 6,500-seat Theater of the Clouds, the 40,000-square-foot Exhibit Hall, and the Rose Quarter Commons

Duties and Responsibilties

Responsible for the planning and execution of events at Portland Arena Management (PAM) facilities. Primary client contact and serves as the liaison between all facility users and the arena staff.

Work long and varied hours in a fast-paced environment. Ability to establish solid relationships with promoters/clients, multiple departments, and franchises in our facilities. Interpret contracts and work closely with sales staff to ensure client's expectations/contract obligations are met. Coordinate with internal and external contractors/vendors/departments and other services. Serve as event lead at event. Serve as liaison between client and arena staff. Approve all staffing levels and additional expenses for each event. Calculate, prepare, and submit all settlement estimates and final settlement of event. Prepare written evaluations of events. Prepare financials and settlements for each event. Maintain accurate and complete event files.

Qualifications

Global Spectrum at the Rose Quarter is looking for an event manager with strong management, motivational, organizational, interpersonal, and communication skills. Knowledge of Microsoft Office, the Internet, New Era Ticketing, and www.EventBooking.com are required and/or preferred. Must have an ability to make decisions independently in a high-pressure environment. College degree preferred, equivalent work experience will be considered.

BOOKING MANAGER, DOLPHIN STADIUM

Industry Segment:	Facility Management
Functional Area:	Facility Management
Experience:	Three to five years of experience required
Location:	Miami, Florida
Property:	76,500-seat outdoor stadium, home to the NFL's Miami Dolphins and MLB's Florida Marlins

Duties and Responsibilities

- Responsible for booking nontenant events, including but not limited to events less than 10,000 patrons
- Reconciliation of actual event expenses, contract fulfillment, and budget
- Responsible for dissemination of event-related requests and working with the operations manager on event set-up and execution
- Serves as on-site contact for nontenant events
- Coordination of Dolphins, Marlins, Orange Bowl, and concert special events (i.e., tailgate parties, hospitality events, family nights, Sports Town, Super Saturdays, pregame and half-times, others as assigned).
- Liaison between sales/marketing and stadium operations for all promotions and special events

Qualifications

- Good communication skills
- Professional demeanor
- Ability to work with a wide range of people
- Good problem-solving skills and ability to adapt to change quickly and positively

Excellent work ethic needed along with ability to work long hours at different times during the year. This is a 12-month position with full benefits and reports to the assistant AD/business. Bachelor's degree required; master's degree preferred.

ASSISTANT ATHLETIC DIRECTOR—FACILITIES AND INTERNAL OPERATIONS, ILLINOIS STATE UNIVERSITY

Industry Segment:	College Athletics, NCAA Football Championship Subdivision
Functional Area:	Facility Management
Experience:	Unspecified
Location:	Normal, Illinois
Property:	All facilities on Illinois State University campus

Illinois State University invites applications for the position of assistant athletics director—facilities/internal operations.

Duties and Responsibilities

- Serving as the liaison to university facility management personnel, architects, and contractors regarding general construction, expansion, enhancement, and modification of existing and proposed athletic facilities
- Scheduling, operations, fiscal management, maintenance, and repair of all athletic facilities
- Supervising event, facilities, and operational staff
- Contract negations and signing of contracts for special events

Qualifications

Bachelor's degree required. Master's degree preferred. In addition, must acquire the necessary understanding of NCAA, board of trustees, university, and state regulations and policies to assure control and compliance.

GENERAL MANAGER, GLOBAL SPECTRUM CONVENTION CENTER

Industry Segment:	Facility Management
Functional Area:	Facility Management
Experience:	Four years of experience required
Location:	Various locations throughout the United States
Property:	Varies by location

Responsible for overall management, promotion, and operation of the facility, including construction, purchasing, policy formulation, booking, marketing, finance, food and beverage, box office, advertising, security, production, maintenance, and related operations. Gives direction to each department, as needed, through each department's director. Reports to Global Spectrum regional vice president. Supervises directors of each department, business manager, and administrative assistant.

Duties and Responsibilities

- Evaluate existing policies and procedures and recommend improvements that will better reflect the needs of the facility and/or improve the efficiency and safety of operations
- Plan, organize, coordinate, and direct all activities and personnel engaged in maintaining and operating the facility
- Conduct marketing, budgeting, and weekly staff meetings
- Prepare, implement, and monitor a detailed program budget
- Responsible for recruiting, training, supervising, and evaluating administrative and supervisory staff
- Establish and maintain effective working relationships with civic organizations, city personnel, media, lessees, employees, and the general public
- Aggressively promote the use of the facility to maximize its utilization and negotiates lease agreements as determined necessary and in the best interests of the facility
- Responsible for the development of standard operating procedures for all operational functions of the facility (e.g., marketing, finance, box office, parking, maintenance, administration, food and beverage, and related areas)

- Prepare and maintain required and necessary reports/records for the city and/or corporate
- Prepare a projected program cost analysis
- Supervise the cost accounting required of assigned events to include facility rental, box office fees, house equipment rental, supplies and services purchased, event supervision, ushers, ticket takers, ticket sellers, door guards, announcers, guest services, traffic control, parking attendants, and other related support staff
- Perform other duties as assigned

Required Special Characteristics and Knowledge

- Thorough knowledge of the principles and practices used in the successful management of a public assembly facility
- Ability to anticipate problems and implement immediate corrective action
- Ability to manage a large enterprise operation
- Considerable knowledge of event solicitation and presentation, maintenance, custodial and safety requirements, public relations, advertising and media relations, box office operations, personnel, and office management
- Ability to work simultaneously with a broad variety of vested interest groups and to foster a cooperative environment, including simultaneous consumer/banquet events
- Ability to achieve quality results with a minimum of resources
- Ability to perform effectively under significant pressure typically associated with meeting the demands and timetables of the entertainment industry
- Thorough knowledge of governmental administration and responsibilities
- Ability to communicate clearly and concisely, orally and in writing

Qualifications

- Graduation from a 4-year accredited college or university with major course work in business, facility management, public administration, or related fields
- A minimum of 4 years of experience in senior management of a public assembly facility
- Active member of the International Association of Assembly Managers (preferred)
- Combination of education and experience will be evaluated

DIRECTOR OF STADIUM GROUNDS, COLUMBUS CREW

Industry Segment:	Professional Sports, Soccer, MLS Team
Functional Area:	Facility Management
Experience:	Five years of experience required
Location:	Columbus, Ohio
Property:	22,500-seat, outdoor, soccer-specific stadium, home to MLS's Columbus Crew

Columbus Crew Stadium is seeking a self-motivated, quality-focused, professional sports turf field manager to maintain and manage the organization's world class playing surfaces and grounds. The work environment is primarily outdoors and in all weather conditions.

Duties and Responsibilities

- Overseeing and maintaining the playing surfaces at Crew Stadium and the Crew training facility
- Overseeing and maintaining the common and landscaped areas around Crew Stadium
- Supervising a grounds crew of full-time and part-time seasonal workers
- Responsible for the ordering, purchasing, and maintaining of all grounds products and equipment
- Developing and managing the stadium and team grounds and landscaping budgets
- Working closely with other departments for event set-up and/or turn around
- Position reports directly to the VP, operations

Qualifications

- Bachelor's degree in agronomy, turf grass science, or similar field of study
- At least 5 years of experience in the field
- Experience with sand base systems
- Demonstrates ability to perform moderate to heavy physical labor for extended periods of time
- Equivalent combination of training and/or experience

DIRECTOR OF OPERATIONS, PRUDENTIAL CENTER

Industry Segment:	Facility Management
Functional Area:	Facility Management
Experience:	Five to seven years of experience required
Location:	Newark, New Jersey
Property:	New 18,000-seat indoor arena opening in 2007, future home of the NHL's New Jersey Devils and Seton Hall men's basketball

The director of operations will have the opportunity to develop and implement material and personnel resource plans that will ensure the provision of this state of the art facility as well as ensure the comfort and security of guests for all events. This person will also be responsible for the maintenance and housekeeping of the venue, including the purchase and inventory of all supplies used in maintenance and housekeeping of the facility.

Duties and Responsibilities

- Schedule, negotiate, and oversee all aspects of event operations, including set-up and breakdown, facility maintenance, housekeeping, broadcasting, and landscaping

- Prepare annual operations budgets to ensure costs are within budget; provide recommendations for budget changes, expenditures, and revisions; prepare monthly budget variance reports for GM; provide planning and design with cost estimates on construction projects

- Review operational budget and monitor expenses

- Monitor and evaluate performance of contracted housekeeping and cleaning services, initiating corrective measures where required

- Monitor operational aspects of minor and major rentals, comply with lease agreement for special events such as concerts

- Prepare and negotiate contracts for AV, housekeeping, and concessions to ensure staffing for all events

- Responsible for overseeing the purchasing, repair, and maintenance of all facility equipment; responsible for controlling inventory of building tools, furniture, keys, machinery, cleaning supplies, and related building equipment

- Schedule off-season maintenance and preventive maintenance projects, and secures competitive bids for facility maintenance and repair projects

- Maintain accurate and timely maintenance records

- Continuously review current building needs and makes recommendations to the GM

- Prepare for the GM the weekly schedule and report of facility operations

- Work cooperatively with the GM on all construction, renovation, and equipment changes and/or purchases

- Oversee the cleanliness of the arena, equipment, and mechanical areas

- Assure the cleanliness of spectator and public areas regularly

- Update and supervise the completion of the maintenance and repair manual

- Oversee the Illness Prevention Program, attend safety meetings, and review matters related to general health concerns

- Maintain security, safety, and service of guests and employees during all arena events

- Manage the hiring, supervision, and training of operations, facility maintenance, housekeeping, and broadcasting staff

- Assume responsibility for keeping records on all maintenance and repairs to facility machinery and equipment

- Supervise the assistant director operations and superintendent/chief engineer; oversee weekly projects

- Recruit, contract with, and monitor qualified professionals for the various operations and maintenance responsibilities

- Supervise custodial training program to maintain an adequate supply of back-up custodians

Required Job-Specific Knowledge, Skills, and Abilities

- Must be proficient with MS Office Excel

- Must have a valid NJ driver's license and clean DMV record

- Must have excellent management and leadership skills

- Must have extensive working knowledge of heating, ventilation, electrical, and security systems

- Knowledge of the functions, operations, and equipment of a multi-purpose sports facility (outdoor sports facility preferred)

- Must have working knowledge of HVAC systems, plumbing, electrical, and computer energy management systems

- Knowledge and ability to train employees on safety practices and all applicable safety standards for public facilities

- Ability to plan, coordinate, and supervise the operational activities with full-time managers and part-time operations staff
- Ability to record, communicate, and function as a manager in the facility
- Knowledge of current first aid and safety procedures
- Ability to establish and maintain effective working relationships with supervisors, subordinates, and the public

Qualifications

- College degree or equivalent required; degree in sports management or facilities management preferred
- Five to 7 years of previous operations management experience required, preferably at a major sports and/or entertainment facility that includes supervising a large group of employees
- Operations experience at an indoor sports/recreation venue preferred
- Previous experience in staging major events at an indoor arena required
- *Please note:* Due the nature of the sports and entertainment industry, this position requires a flexible work schedule, which will include evenings, weekends, and holidays.

VICE PRESIDENT OF BALLPARK OPERATIONS, WASHINGTON NATIONALS

Industry Segment:	Professional Sports, Baseball, MLB Team
Functional Area:	Facility Management
Experience:	Unspecified
Location:	Washington, DC
Property:	41,000-seat outdoor baseball stadium, future home of MLB's Washington Nationals

The vice president of ballpark operations will be responsible for the oversight and management of guest services, grounds, event and building security, special event operations, office services, and warehouse operations of the Nationals Ballpark, and associated parking garages. Interface with the DCSEC, facility manager, food service and retail vendors, cleaning contractor, and parking service, while providing all necessary oversight of each area. Work closely with the executive vice president to ensure the ballpark operates in a first class manner operationally and through superior customer service.

Duties and Responsibilities

- Oversee the management of the event operations staff including the guest services staff, customer service, ushers, ticket-takers, parking staff, emergency medical services/first aid, grounds crew, law enforcement, and event security; plan and implement all required resources and staff to efficiently prepare, execute, and close out all events
- Responsible for the facilitation and approval of sponsorship sales, in-game activation, as well as coordinating with the marketing and broadcasting departments to provide resources and direct event operations in order to meet the needs of sponsors and various promotional activities
- Develop and maintain close working relationships with local officials and vendors including the Metropolitan Police and Fire Departments, neighborhood groups, ADA advocacy groups, Department of Emergency Management, District Department of Transportation, Department of Public Works, WMATA, and other related entities
- Interface with the DCSEC in order to plan and facilitate their contractually based special events as well as working in tandem with regard to neighborhood issues and concerns
- Interface with food service general manager to coordinate game day operation as well as oversight of their responsible alcohol sales management and other relevant ballpark policies
- Oversee the mailroom, warehouse, and shipping/receiving operations of the ballpark
- Manage office services and switchboard/receptions functions
- Oversee and manage energy conservation programs
- Responsible for the preparation of the departmental budget and the management and tracking of all associated expenses
- Interface and provide oversight of the facility, maintenance, and engineering manager in order to ensure the highest level of standards within Major League Baseball
- Oversee the 24/7 ballpark control room and all building security
- Establish event staffing levels, which are necessary to achieve the highest level of customer service and appropriate level of security within approved budget parameters
- Establish the standards of customer service as well as event staff policies and procedures, while ensuring that all manuals and training programs are appropriately supportive

- Manage the contract with the housekeeping provider in order to consistently attain the cleanness benchmarks that have been established by comparable venues within the industry

- Manage the contract with the parking service provider and all associated customer service concerns and issues

- Develop collateral materials for employees and fans such as Accessibility Guide, Event Handbook, and Guest Information Guide

- Other duties as assigned

The previous statement reflects the general details necessary to describe the principle functions of the occupation described and shall not be construed as a detailed description of all the work requirements that may be inherent in the occupation.

Required Knowledge, Skills, and Abilities

- Demonstrated effective leadership skills and prior management experience

- Strong background in budget preparation and budget management

- Understanding of general building codes, permits, and OSHA-related requirements

- Demonstrated ability and experience to multi-task and delegate

- Proficiency with general office PC applications (i.e., word processing, spreadsheets, databases)

- Experience in making sound business decisions

- Creative focus regarding problem-solving

- Team-oriented with healthy and positive attitude

- Knowledge in determining and coordinating logistical needs to support large public events, preferably in a large sports arena or event facility

- Demonstrated sound organizational, coordinating, and personal interface skills

- Demonstrated excellent written and verbal communication skills

- Proven job reliability, diligence, dedication, and attention to detail

- Must be flexible with working nights, weekends, and holidays

Qualifications

The employee is required to have a valid driver's license in good standing and operate a company-owned vehicle.

Physical Demands

The physical demands described here are representative of those that must be met by an employee to successfully perform the essential functions of this job. Reasonable accommodations may be made to enable individuals with disabilities to perform the essential functions. While performing the duties of this job, the employee is regularly required to stand or walk; use hands to finger, handle, or feel objects, tools, or controls; and reach with hands and arms. Must have clear vision at 20 inches or less. The employee is occasionally required to stoop, kneel, crouch, sit, or crawl. The employee must occasionally lift and/or move up to 45 pounds.

Information Technology

Similar to the rest of the business world, sports entities rely on technology to conduct business each and every day. This is a new facet of the sports industry, truly emerging in the last 5 to 10 years. You will find that much of the work relies on technical skills and expertise in the areas of information technology, computer networking, database management, and website development/maintenance. In addition, if technology is utilized in scouting or game analysis (which is becoming more and more common), greater importance is then placed on a sports background or education.

Although their duties may be similar to professionals employed outside the sports industry, people employed in the positions listed in this chapter are responsible for meeting the technology demands of today's sports entities.

Industry compensation for information technology positions can vary tremendously depending on the factors explained in Chapter 72. The following compensation levels are reasonable expectations for mid-sized organizations in mid-sized markets.

Professional Sports

- Entry level: $30,000 to $35,000
- Manager level: $50,000 to $80,000
- Director level: $90,000 to $150,000
- Executive level: $150,000+

INFORMATION TECHNOLOGY INTERN, TAMPA BAY LIGHTNING

Industry Segment:	Professional Sports, Hockey, NHL Team
Functional Area:	Information Technology
Experience:	Internship
Location:	Tampa, Florida
Compensation:	Unpaid

The St. Pete Times Forum is looking for outstanding sophomore, junior, and senior students majoring in management information systems (MIS) to join our internship program based on business needs. The purpose of the internship is to provide meaningful, professional hands-on experience to students with proven academic performance. This is a non-paid position focusing on the learning experience throughout the internship. Ten to 20 hours per week would be required.

Duties and Responsibilities

- Documentation
- Validation
- Workstation installation and support
- Help desk support
- Network security
- LAN/wireless network support

The successful candidate will provide users an exemplary level of service and be prepared to interface with all levels of management and employees.

- *Off-Season*: During the off-season, the core responsibilities of this position are to provide regular maintenance and administration of the servers on the network. The candidate will also troubleshoot and resolve network issues, install software to client configuration, and interface with users. You must have experience with supporting a Windows 2000/2003 server environment. The SA will also be required to research, order, and deploy new equipment as necessary. The successful candidate must possess the ability to analyze, understand, and troubleshoot a wide array of systems problems. In addition to the above duties, the SA will likely also manage a given number of smaller IT projects as directed by IT management.

- *In-Season:* The SA will continue to maintain his or her role providing support to users and perform regular maintenance and administration to servers and the network. In addition, the SA will assist in game day preparations and testing (during the week of home games), as well as game day support for various systems (e.g., POS system).

Qualifications

- Education:
  - Minimum 2 years of experience with Windows Workstation and Server required
  - Four-year college degree in information systems, computer science, or engineering preferred
  - Industry-recognized IT certifications are preferred
- Professional experience:
  - Hardware/software support, configuration, and installation for PC and Mac
  - Windows LAN administration
  - Blackberry support
- Responsibilities:
  - Plan for deployment of new hardware and software
  - Answer support calls from help desk and track problems in database
  - Have the ability to handle a wide variety of IT projects and responsibilities
  - Be highly organized, dependable, analytical, detail-oriented, a quick study, and able to communicate well to both senior management and front-line workers both verbally and in writing
  - Be a team player and willing to pitch in on the task at hand as necessary

- Be able to accommodate the flexible, dynamic schedule of a professional sports team
- Be able to work well in a high pressure, dynamic, fast-paced environment
- Preferred experience:
  - SharePoint experience a plus
  - POS administration
  - Requirements analysis
  - Systems experience with an MS/Cisco environment
  - Telecomm experience

The Washington Redskins' work environment can be very demanding and fast-paced and often requires employees to rapidly refocus and modify priorities. It also provides a rapid learning curve to a wide variety of IT projects and responsibilities that can significantly expand the right candidate's skill set.

VICE PRESIDENT OF INFORMATION TECHNOLOGY, ARIZONA DIAMONDBACKS

Industry Segment:	Professional Sports, Baseball, MLB Team
Functional Area:	Information Technology
Experience:	Unspecified
Location:	Phoenix, Arizona

The information technology department of the Arizona Diamondbacks was formerly a shared service with the Phoenix Suns and Dodge Theatre. It operated mostly as a service function, providing management, supervision, and support of the IT systems at the Arizona Diamondbacks.

The VP of IT will manage a director, network manager, and systems administrator to continue to service the functions of the business, but will also work to fulfill the new vision of the IT department: *To be the most innovative and technologically advanced team in Major League Baseball.*

This vision will be achieved across three main areas:

- Providing fans with cutting-edge, interactive content, information, and experiences
- Providing advanced tools for baseball operations to improve performance and decision making
- Providing reliable business tools that are relevant, increase productivity, and assist in driving business results

Duties and Responsibilities

- Extensive experience in integrating, managing, planning, and coordinating information technology with a high degree of expertise involving Microsoft Windows operating system

- Troubleshooting problems that may occur on the computer servers and systems, network devices, Active Directory network environment, e-mail, CRM, and other IT systems

- Work with management and employees to manage the purchase, protection, licensing, maintenance, and replacement of information technology hardware devices and software systems

- Establish and implement IT policies, procedures, and standards and ensure their conformance with the technology goals and procedures

- Monitor the reporting and resolution of IT problems that occur within the Arizona Diamondbacks IT structure

- Target sponsor opportunities and work with VP, corporate partnerships to drive technological innovation in a cost-effective manner

- Focus on reliability, relevance, and customer service with each internal department considered a key customer

- Develop a 3-year departmental plan that outlines architecture and key areas of improvement and prioritizes allocation of resources utilizing the following steps:
  - Maintenance: Maintaining current level of functionality and reliability without hiccups, including:
    - Determine "must have" priorities for next 6 months
    - Determine "will need" priorities for 6 to 18 months out
    - Create 18-month maintenance execution plan
  - Improvements: Creating IT department short-term wins for the organization, including:
    - Determine all areas of opportunity
    - Prioritize by usefulness and practicality
    - Select top priorities and create execution plan with timelines and goals
  - Innovation:
    - Determine long-range goals and objectives
    - Create timeline and metrics to achieve those goals

Qualifications

- Impeccable integrity and professional maturity

- Excellent business judgment

- Strategic thinker with ability to conceptualize big picture while at the same time possessing necessary attention to detail

- Strong communicator in both personal and group settings

- Collaborative management style—advocate of team concept

- Positive influencer, comfortable with ambiguity and change

- Excellent oral and written communication skills

- Fundamental technical and strategic understanding of technology architecture development

- Working knowledge of PC software and hardware, including MS Office, MS Windows XP Pro, and MS 2003 Server Pro

- Working knowledge of MS Active Directory network

- Working knowledge of MS Exchange Server

- Working knowledge of MS SQL database operations and concepts

- Familiarity with the operations and management of local area networks

- Bachelor's degree required; master's degree preferred

CHAPTER EIGHTY-FIVE

Human Resources

The duties and responsibilities of human resources (HR) professionals employed by sports organizations are quite similar to those employed by nonsports organizations. Human resources professionals are placed in charge of an organization's personnel needs, including the recruitment, hiring, retention, and termination of employees, as well as handling all employment issues, compensation, and employment policies. Twenty years ago, you would have great difficulty finding an HR department at sports organizations. Now, both league offices and individual teams sport human resources departments, supporting the growing complexity of sports organizations over the last two decades. You may also encounter a situation where the sports organization's parent company handles the HR duties. For example, if you were interested in working for the Big Ten Network (the new sports channel for the Big Ten Conference), you would need to apply through the human resources department of Fox Sports, which is part owner of the network.

Ultimately, even if you do not want to work in human resources, this department should hold great importance to you, because virtually all job and internship hires will go through here. Employees hired into the positions included in this chapter manage the day-to-day human resources needs for their respective organizations.

Industry compensation for human resources positions can vary tremendously depending on the factors explained in Chapter 72. The following compensation levels are reasonable expectations for mid-sized organizations in mid-sized markets.

Professional Sports

- Entry level: $30,000 to $35,000
- Manager level: $50,000 to $70,000
- Director level: $90,000 to $150,000+

HUMAN RESOURCES MANAGER, CLEVELAND CAVALIERS

Industry Segment:	Professional Sports, Basketball, NBA Team
Functional Area:	Human Resources
Experience:	Five years of experience required
Location:	Cleveland, Ohio

The human resources manager is responsible for coordinating HR policies and programs, with emphasis in, but not limited to, recruitment and employment, recordkeeping and compliance, and team member relations. Works closely with director in developing, implementing, and evaluating ongoing HR policies, programs, functions, and activities. Leads human resources coordinator (in collaborative fashion), and may lead human resources assistant for certain tasks/functions.

Duties and Responsibilities

- Assist the director in the daily administration of HR services as assigned, including but not limited to recruitment and selection, promotions, transfers, contract negotiation and administration, EEO compliance, job classification, performance evaluation, and team member relations

- Manage recruitment and employment activities and human resources coordinator's workload as it pertains to those duties

- Develop and manage orientation and follow-up program for new team members to assure understanding of the organization and its culture; support HR coordinator in presentation of program; maintains company organizational charts and directories

- Maintain and assist with the further development of HR information system records (Abra) and develop, prepare, generate, and analyze regular and special reports from database, including but not limited to issues such as staffing levels, turnover, absenteeism, recruitment, applicant tracking, compensation, promotions, etc.

- Assist in development, implementation, and maintenance of personnel policies and procedures and team member handbook, and communicates same through use of company intranet and other communication vehicles

- Maintain and expand knowledge and understanding of existing and proposed federal and state laws/regulations affecting HR management

- Participate in the investigation and resolution of ongoing team member relations problems, anticipates problems whenever possible, and develops, recommends, and initiates appropriate steps for resolution

- Participate in company committees as requested, particularly those that support team member relations; coordinates annual service awards program and United Way campaign

- Assure benefits administrator receives appropriate information that might affect team member benefits; maintains familiarity with benefits, worker's compensation, and unemployment responsibilities in order to answer team member inquiries, as needed

- Participate in developing department goals, objectives, and systems; recommend new approaches and policies/procedures to support continual improvements in department efficiency and services

- Has access to and is involved with confidential matters on a regular basis; may deal with information related to collective bargaining

- Perform basic office duties as needed, including correspondence composition and typing, filing, answering phones, and receiving visitors

- Assist with special projects as requested, and performs other duties as assigned

Qualifications

- Education and formal training: Bachelor's degree, preferably with special focus in human resource management or related field, or knowledge of specialized principles and techniques equivalent to what would normally be obtained through a formal 4-year, college-level academic program or specialized training program in human resources; Professional in Human Resources (PHR) certification is a plus

- Experience: At least 5 years of experience in an administrative, preferably human resources, position required, with employment and/or employee relations experience highly desirable

- Other qualifications and skills:

  - Working knowledge of basic principles and practices of HR administration, as well as regulatory requirements, particularly relative to employment/employee relations

  - Solid computer skills and ability to learn Abra HRIS system and Crystal Reports

  - Familiarity with ADP Payroll (or other payroll systems) a plus

  - Proficiency in word processing and spreadsheet software (Word and Excel preferred)

  - Strong analytical and problem-solving skills

  - Superior interpersonal skills essential

  - Ability to work effectively with all levels of staff, including management and ownership, as well as outside applicants

  - Strong verbal/written communication and presentation skills

  - Knowledge and understanding of benefits administration, plan design, and recordkeeping is a plus

  - Familiarity with state and federal regulations that affect benefits (e.g., COBRA, FMLA, ERISA) is a plus

  - Must be able to work independently and exercise initiative and good judgment; deal effectively with time pressures despite numerous interruptions; organize and prioritize work to handle more than one project at a time; demonstrate flexibility in adapting to frequent changes; and maintain the highly confidential nature of personnel work

HUMAN RESOURCES MANAGER, WMG CORPORATE

Industry Segment:	Sports Agencies
Functional Area:	Human Resources
Experience:	Seven years of experience required
Location:	Los Angeles, California

Duties and Responsibilities

- Serve as the human resources business partner to designated units within the company, providing a single point of contact to employees for all general human resources issues

- Provide advice and counsel on such matters as employee relations, performance management, disciplinary measures, complaints, suggestions, benefits, promotion, salary proposals, and other related issues

- Research, develop, and administer employee training and development programs with the objective of increasing bench strength and developing a succession plan

- Investigate opportunity for a tuition reimbursement program and presents business case to management

- Continually monitor targeted training needs and keeps the training program fresh, relevant, and compelling

- Administer the company's performance management and salary review program

- Work with managers in the establishment of employee goals and counsels management on proper ways to evaluate and communicate job performance to employees

- Assist in the development of performance improvement plans as necessary

- Work closely with other members of human resources team and corporate marketing to increase and improve communication throughout the company

- Such initiatives may include, but are not limited to, developing a guest speaker series, contributing to the newsletter, leveraging videoconference and webcasting opportunities, arranging executive/employee lunches, conducting employee surveys, and making periodic visits to the company satellite offices

- Attend the staff meeting of designated business units to remain abreast of current and future departmental activities and generally understand the objectives of the business

- Serve an integral role in preparation for strategic acquisitions and in the integration of new employees resulting from such acquisitions

- Continually investigate ways in which to provide additional and improved employee services that are both meaningful to employees and cost-effective

- Follow up with the new employees within a month of hire to ensure they have a rich initial employment experience and to assist them with any challenges they may be experiencing

- Counsel management in preparation for employee terminations and participates in termination meetings

- Conduct exit interviews with departing employees; build and maintain a database of termination information, analyze and report data, and work with management to reduce unwanted turnover

Qualifications

- Bachelor's degree required

- Seven years in a human resource generalist role

- Experience developing and implementing HR policies and procedures

- Proven ability to succeed in an entrepreneurial, service-oriented environment with multiple office locations

- Strong communication, organization, and computer skills

Event Management

Sporting events can be large and complex. As such, they often require a number of people to plan, manage, and execute them in order to run as smoothly as possible. Event management professionals take on this responsibility. Industry compensation for event management positions can vary tremendously depending on the factors explained in Chapter 72. As an example, an assistant commissioner for championships at a Football Bowl Subdivision conference (discussed below) can expect to earn $65,000 to $95,000.

ASSISTANT COMMISSIONER FOR CHAMPIONSHIPS, COLONIAL ATHLETIC ASSOCIATION

Industry Segment:	College Athletic, NCAA Football Championship Subdivision
Functional Area:	Event Management
Experience:	Unspecified
Location:	Richmond, Virginia

Located in Richmond, the Colonial Athletic Associations is an NCAA Division I conference. This is one of two assistant commissioners for championships positions with shared responsibilities for the conference's 21-sport championship program. The position reports to the senior associate commissioner for marketing/development, the deputy commissioner for basketball, and the commissioner.

Duties and Responsibilities

- Serving as the primary administration liaison including pre-event planning, game management, marketing, and merchandising of assigned championship sports

- Serve as the liaison with the coaches of assigned championship sports including processing recommendations to the Competition Committee and athletic directors

- Supervise and coordinate the production of schedules in assigned sports

- Responsible for the supervision of officials' coordinators in assigned sports

- Other duties as assigned

Qualifications

The successful candidate must have an earned bachelor's degree and a minimum of 3 years of administrative experience, preferably in event management. The individual should have an outgoing personality stressing innovation, creativity, and excellent interpersonal and written communication skills with the ability to work within specific deadlines in sometimes stressful situations.

DIRECTOR OF CHAMPIONSHIPS, METRO ATLANTIC ATHLETIC CONFERENCE

Industry Segment:	College Athletic, NCAA Football Championship Subdivision
Functional Area:	Event Management
Experience:	Unspecified
Location:	Edison, New Jersey
Compensation:	$27,500, plus benefits

The Metro Atlantic Athletic Conference (MAAC), an NCAA Division I conference located in Edison, is accepting applications for the position of director of championships.

Duties and Responsibilities

- Plan and conduct conference sports, championships, and special events including on-site management and follow-up for these events
- Assist with the development of league schedules for sports other than basketball
- Assist in the development of in-season and championship policies and administrative agreements
- Conduct coaches meetings for sports assigned, and assist with league meeting preparations for athletic directors, senior woman administrators, and other groups as assigned
- Coordinate public relations program for conference championships with MAAC director of media relations and MAAC webmaster
- Coordinate MAAC merchandise and sales program
- Coordinate Student-Athlete Advisory Committee (SAAC) events
- Staff liaison to MAAC Sportsmanship Committee
- Coordinate MAAC Championships hosted at Disney Sports
- Coordinate hosting of NCAA Championship for cross country and other nonbasketball championships
- Other duties as assigned by commissioner

Qualifications

- BA degree
- Computer experience
- Excellent oral and written skills

Broadcasting

Broadcasting in the sports industry can take on many forms, including live game coverage, taped studio shows (such as ESPN's *SportCenter*), and original entertainment (such as ESPN's *Playmakers*). In recent years, there has been a proliferation of sports cable channels, including the expansion of ESPN (into ESPN2, ESPNews, and ESPNU), the advent of the NFL Network, the increased growth of regional sports networks, and the emergence of the Big Ten Network. This has resulted in new opportunities for broadcasting professionals looking to work in the sports industry. The following are a small sample of jobs that fall within the broadcasting classification of the sports industry. These jobs focus on the business side of broadcasting, rather than the "talent" side of the industry (i.e., the broadcaster).

BROADCAST COMMUNICATIONS INTERN, LOS ANGELES GALAXY

Industry Segment:	Professional Sports, Soccer, MLS Team
Functional Area:	Broadcasting
Experience:	Internship
Location:	Carson, California
Compensation:	Likely to be unpaid, hourly wage, or monthly stipend

The broadcast communications intern(s) will assist the Los Angeles Galaxy communications department in its day-to-day duties and game day media operations while learning the daily workings and intricacies of a professional soccer club's communications department.

Weekly Duties

- Assist with the production of all of the club's printed materials; this includes writing and editing of any text
- Maintaining the communications department archives through the cataloging of photos and press clippings
- Assist with all PR efforts and initiatives at training sessions, including handling media requests and supplying credentialed media with the necessary information
- Serving as the Galaxy communications representative at select community functions, taking pictures, shooting video, conducting interviews, and writing recaps as necessary

Game Day Duties

- Assist with the day's media operations, including:
  - Preparation of all press box materials
  - The setup of the press box
  - Staffing media will-call
  - Assisting the official team photographer
  - Assisting with in-game press box management
  - Postgame interviews and quote collection
  - Special projects that will utilize proficient video shooting and editing capabilities

Required Job Knowledge, Skills, and Abilities

- Strong written and verbal communication skills; bilingual is a plus
- Proficiency with Microsoft Office software; other programs, such as Adobe Photoshop, are a plus

- Ability to work in a professional environment
- Ability to work under pressure and tight deadlines
- Knowledge of the sport of soccer and MLS

Qualifications

- Education: This internship is for qualified candidates who can gain course credit with an accredited academic institution
- Other: Must maintain professional appearance and demeanor

PRODUCER/EDITOR, NFL DIGITAL MEDIA GROUP

Industry Segment:	Professional Sports, Football, NFL League Office
Functional Area:	Broadcasting
Experience:	One to three years of experience required
Location:	Culver City, California

The NFL Digital Media Group is seeking a producer/editor to create, edit, post, and apply metadata to video produced daily for NFL.com.

Duties and Responsibilities

- Responsible for video production, working closely with the NFL Network/NFL Films to produce original content and to repurpose content for distribution across NFL.com
- Work closely with editorial team to create video packages to enhance coverage of games and other events
- Responsible for executing projects defined by the senior producer/editor and coordinating producer
- Work with editorial team to develop multimedia content packages to feature daily
- Develop content promotion on all website home pages and channel homepages
- Edit, post, and apply metadata to all video content that is featured across NFL.com

Qualifications

- One to 3 years of experience in video production, with experience in digital media preferred
- Bachelor's degree in journalism, broadcast media, or web production, or related field preferred
- Knowledge of content management systems
- Extensive experience working with video encoding platforms and tools
- Understanding of all facets of video production

- Proficiency in Final Cut Pro and other video production suites preferred
- Working knowledge of HTML
- Experience with Flash, Photoshop, and Illustrator preferred
- Experience and understanding of sports industry preferred

PROGRAMMING MANAGER, BIG TEN NETWORK—FOX SPORTS

Industry Segment:	Broadcasting, Cable Sports Network
Functional Area:	Broadcasting
Experience:	Unspecified
Location:	Chicago, Illinois

Big Ten Network (BTN) is seeking a manager, programming who will be responsible for managing the planning, creation, and distribution of the monthly programming schedule for the network. This position is located in Chicago.

Duties and Responsibilities

- Collaborate with the vice president of programming to manage all aspects of programming including scheduling, acquisitions, and development for BTN; assist in the creation, development, and distribution of the weekly program schedule
- Take part in the negotiations with third party programming suppliers for the acquisition of content and to meet revenue goals
- Perform various projects for senior management and other departments regarding future scheduling
- Other duties and projects as necessary

Qualifications

- Must have a strong interest and thorough knowledge of sports, and preferably the Big Ten Conference and member institutions
- BA/BS degree in business, communications, or related area
- Previous program scheduling experience is preferred, including experience dealing with vendors and customers, as well as negotiating supplier deals
- Superior oral and written communication skills are required, including good negotiating skills
- Overall understanding of the sports and television business, including knowledge of the cable industry, is highly preferred
- Ability to multi-task and work effectively under daily time constraints in a high pressure environment is essential
- Strong computer skills including file management software knowledge with programs such as Filemaker Pro

Licensing

The names, logos, and symbols associated with sports organizations have become very marketable and valuable items. Their primary purpose has historically been to create an identifiable image through which an athletic organization can promote the sale of its product or service. More recently, however, the sales of a name, logo, and/or symbol in association with caps, pennants, T-shirts, jerseys, and other souvenirs have become a significant revenue generator for an athletic organization. As a result, organizations put forth great effort to retain the exclusive right to determine who will put their name, logo, or symbol on these profit-making items. The process of awarding the right to use a team's trademarks is called licensing.

Sports licensing is big business. In 2006, total retail sales of licensed sports products in North America was an estimated $13.9 billion.[1] Most professional sports leagues have developed licensing programs to capitalize on the public demand. College athletic departments, conferences, and the NCAA itself, as well as other organizations such as the U.S. Olympic Committee and the U.S. Tennis Association, have done likewise.

In professional sports leagues, the league generally has the right to control team marks. The leagues (such as Major League Baseball, the National Football League, the National Basketball Association, and the National Hockey League) formed separate entities, often known as a "properties" division, that primarily deal with the licensing of the league and club trademarks (including teams and league names and logos) to vendors. The vendors manufacture products featuring these marks and, in turn, sell these products to retailers and to the general public. The merchandising revenue is then divided among the teams, usually on an equal or pro rata basis.

Like the leagues, players associations have formed entities that handle licensing issues for athletes. For example, the NFL Players Association (NFLPA) formed Players Inc., which is the licensing arm of the NFLPA. Players Inc. provides marketing and licensing services to companies interested in using names and likenesses of current and past NFL players. Any program involving six or more NFL players requires a Players Inc. license. The revenues received from this licensing is then distributed, pro rata, to the players and used for other association needs. These revenues can be quite significant; for example, it has been reported that the licensing revenues for each MLB player are over $30,000 per year.

With such significant dollars at stake, organizations have turned to professionals with legal expertise in intellectual property law to protect the organization's legal rights in its trademarks. The following jobs are a sample of the types of positions you can find in the field of sports licensing.

LICENSING ASSISTANT, PLAYERS INC.

Industry Segment:	Professional Sports, Football, NFL Players Union
Functional Area:	Licensing
Experience:	Entry level
Location:	Washington, DC
Compensation:	$25,000 to $35,000

Established in 1956, the National Football League Players Association is the union for professional football players in the National Football League. In 1993, the NFLPA was officially recognized as the union representing the players, and its current collective bargaining agreement governs the sport at least until 2008. Players Inc. is the NFLPA's for-profit licensing and marketing subsidiary. The purpose of this position is to provide assistance to the executive vice president/COO and vice president, corporate marketing.

- Provides year-end staff evaluation
- Participates in the hiring of department staff
- Conducts weekly staff meetings
- Prepares departmental monthly status reports
- Facilitates and plans with corporate marketing department to create and execute license participation in integrated marketing programs for Players Inc. properties and events, including retail promotions, advertising, and sponsorships
- Works closely with licensees and player marketing department to create player marketing opportunities

- Business development/strategy/planning:
  - Responsible for business development and creating new channel revenue opportunities
  - Prepares and develops department business plans and strategic initiatives
  - Prepares annual business reports for the various departments
  - Develops and creates licensing and promotional strategy
  - Creates and implements premium and promotional programs with current and potential partners
  - Develops retail and consumer promotions for licensed products in conjunction with category managers
  - Defines and implements growth strategies for Fantasy Football and multimedia category
  - Cultivates and builds current partner relationships while developing new licensing retail and multimedia relationships
  - Serves as company liaison at licensing industry events

- Budget/financial reporting:
  - Responsible for budget preparation, analysis, and management
  - Provides annual revenue and growth projections by category
  - Responsible for department royalty books and payments
  - Reconciles monthly budget statements (actual vs. budget)

- Negotiation/partner agreements:
  - Evaluates licensing applications, negotiates terms, oversees product development and quality control, and manages royalty reporting and payments for categories
  - Negotiates contract business terms with partners and handles all renewals
  - Prepares year-end deal analysis and review
  - Prepares term sheets for approval by COO
  - Prepares license agreements utilizing approved contract language
  - Consults with staff counsel regarding license agreement drafting and changes in contract language
  - Oversees license agreement compliance
  - Develops and builds key relationships with partner managers and staff

- Communications:
  - Works with licensees to ensure Players Inc. brand awareness and brand continuity by developing consistent packaging and labeling, logo placement, and strategic product placement
  - Provides effective internal communication of key plans, initiatives, and projects
  - Builds internal relationships and creates cross-departmental partnerships
  - Polices marketplace for unlicensed product
  - Serves as the main contact for all departmental licensees on all relevant topics/issues
  - Acts as the point person for department PR and marketing efforts
  - Serves as a liaison with the NFL consumer products and marketing group
  - Represents Players Inc. as board member on the board of the Fantasy Sports Association

Endnotes

1. Lefton, T. (2007, June 25). Licensed Products Aren't Hitting the Wall, SGMA President Says. *Street & Smith's SportsBusiness Journal*. Retrieved September 9, 2008, from http://www.sportsbusinessjournal.com/article/55559.

Legal Services

Sports entities often find themselves in need of legal counsel due to the publicity and the business nature of sports. From this, a field of sports law and sports lawyers has emerged. These professionals are experts in the law as it pertains to the sports industry.

Lawyers practicing in sports primarily fall into two categories—inside counsel and outside counsel. Someone working as inside counsel works as an employee of the organization and manages the legal aspects of the organization's activities from within (i.e., "inside") the entity. In contrast, outside counsel provides legal advice and services on a consultant basis from "outside" the organization. Outside counsel are not considered employees of the organization, and may be experts in such matters as contract law, antitrust law, or labor law. An organization's inside counsel typically works with and uses outside counsel for complex legal matters that require a certain level of expertise not possessed by the inside counsel.

The job descriptions found in this chapter provide an idea of the type of work legal professionals can find within sports organizations. These positions are all considered inside counsel–type positions.

Industry compensation for legal services positions can vary tremendously depending on the factors explained in Chapter 72. The following compensation levels are reasonable expectations for the industry.

Professional Sports Union

- Associate general counsel: $150,000 to $300,000
- General counsel: $250,000 to $650,000

LEGAL ASSISTANT, NFL PLAYERS ASSOCIATION AND PLAYERS INC.

Industry Segment:	Professional Sports, Football, NFL Players Union
Functional Area:	Legal Services
Experience:	Entry level
Location:	Washington, DC
Compensation:	$25,000 to $35,000

Duties and Responsibilities

- Screens and/or handles all incoming phone calls, mail, and visitors for general counsel and department
- Records, logs, and files personal conduct policy violations and appeals
- Prepares letters to players regarding eligibility for termination pay; files letters regarding player contract status; copies salary cap and agent admin department on player contract status letters
- Sends copies of grievances and fine appeals to players and agents as requested; schedules and coordinates appeal hearings, as directed by staff counsels
- Types, mails, and files letters and other correspondence for general counsel and staff counsels, including preparing P-1 Visa petition letters for foreign NFL players
- Sets up conference calls for general counsel and staff counsels

- Schedules daily appointments, meetings, and travel arrangements for general counsel
- Tracks schedules of staff counsels
- Assists in maintaining appropriate departmental filing system
- Performs other legal department duties when primary duties listed above do not demand full-time attention
- Prepares and compiles all correspondence for NFLCA and Arena Football League grievances; maintains a computerized database for all grievances

Job Specifications

Type 60–70 WPM; ability to operate (or learn to operate) copiers, postage meter, facsimile, Dictaphone, and word and data processors, including Microsoft Office Suite

PARALEGAL, ATLANTA BRAVES

Industry Segment:	Professional Sports, Baseball, MLB Team
Functional Area:	Legal Services
Experience:	Three to five years of experience required
Location:	Atlanta, Georgia

Duties and Responsibilities

- Assist general counsel (GC) in preparing and reviewing major commercial agreements, including sponsorship, marketing, advertising, and other contractual arrangements
- Assist GC in preparing, reviewing, and negotiating other contractual arrangements, including vendor agreements, ticketing and hotel agreements, leases, independent contractor, consulting, and any other business arrangements of the company
- Assist GC in monitoring and managing all litigation and presuit disputes, including complex commercial matters, class actions, civil rights lawsuits, wage and hour claims, personal injury, employee benefits claims, and significant internal investigations
- Assist GC in providing day-to-day legal support for various business divisions and areas of the company, including minor league team operations
- Assist GC with management and monitoring of all legal affairs of the company including preparing key dates and contract summaries, project reports, and client educational materials and seminars

- Research and review relevant league and statutory rules and laws that govern the business and assist in the interpretation of such laws, as well as preparation of memos and correspondence regarding the research findings
- Position reports to the vice president and general counsel

Qualifications

- Minimum requirements include a BS or BA and a paralegal certification or equivalent
- Three to 5 years of experience as a paralegal in a corporate in-house setting or law firm environment
- Specific experience in contract drafting and review, legal research and writing, litigation management, and project management skills are desired
- Sports or entertainment experience is preferred
- Highly effective interpersonal and communication skills (written and verbal), in addition to analytical and independent thinking in a fast-paced environment
- Proactive, organized, and detail-oriented person who can effectively prioritize and multi-task projects
- An understanding and appreciation for diverse cultures and an ability to work effectively and relate well with individuals of diverse backgrounds at all levels of the company
- Self-motivated individual with high degree of responsibility, sense of urgency, and accountability
- Microsoft Office (Word, Outlook, Excel, and PowerPoint) proficiency
- Able to work long hours, weekends, and holidays
- Background check and drug screen required

SENIOR COUNSEL, TURNER BROADCASTING

Industry Segment:	Broadcasting, Cable Sports Networks
Functional Area:	Legal Services
Experience:	Five years of experience required
Location:	Atlanta, Georgia

Duties and Responsibilities

The Turner legal department in Atlanta is looking for an experienced attorney to handle legal matters for Turner Sports and Turner Sports Interactive, Inc., including all television rights agreements, talent agreements, content licensing and syndication agreements, programming clearance and development, review of marketing and promotional initiatives, and management of legal staff.

Qualifications

Candidate must have practiced law for at least 5 years at a reputable law firm, network, and/or media company, with a minimum of 3 years of actual, hands-on experience representing a media entity. Candidate must have excellent academic credentials and references, solid drafting and negotiating skills, strong interpersonal skills, and be collaborative and teamwork oriented. Must be able to work under pressure with strong attention to detail, effectively juggle competing priorities, have a strong work ethic and excellent analytical and organizational skills, and possess excellent judgment and the ability to interact effectively with other attorneys and staff, in-house client groups, and opposing counsel and agents.

ATTORNEY, LPGA

Industry Segment:	Professional Sports, Golf, LPGA Headquarters
Functional Area:	Legal Services
Experience:	Six years of experience required
Location:	Daytona, Florida

The Ladies Professional Golf Association (LPGA), located in Daytona Beach, Florida, seeks an attorney to assist in all facets of its legal affairs, including contract drafting/advice (sponsorships, tournaments, and media), corporate governance, and intellectual property protection.

Qualifications

Ideal candidate will have at least 6 years of law firm or sports organization experience, experience in corporate and commercial transactions, trademark and copyright law experience, and experience with technology and media rights.

ASSISTANT GENERAL COUNSEL, NFL MANAGEMENT COUNCIL

Industry Segment:	Professional Sports, Football, NFL League Office
Functional Area:	Legal Services
Experience:	Eight to ten years of experience required
Location:	New York

The primary responsibility of the assistant general counsel (as part of the labor relations counsel) is to give legal advice to the league and its clubs and to represent them, together or individually, in all collective bargaining and employment law matters involving the NFL, players, and officials. Such advice and counsel should result in the resolution, through arbitration, trial, or settlement, of over 75 grievances each year involving financial exposure of over $50 million on terms most favorable to the party represented. Additionally, such responsibilities may entail administration of NFL policies of substance abuse, steroids, and conduct and/or participation in designated joint owner/player committees (e.g., Player Safety Committee), which should result in effectuation of league interests in these areas.

This position also requires the ability to prepare and present cases for arbitration and to assess the qualification of arbitrators serving under the CBA along with those in other industries. This includes making determination of when to terminate the services of appointed arbitrators and to select new arbitrators when vacancies occur.

Duties and Responsibilities

- Prepare legal advice memoranda for clubs regarding all labor relations matters

- Evaluate arbitrator performance in injury and noninjury grievance context and terminate and replace them where appropriate

- Review all legal positions to be taken in arbitration and court hearings and briefs by labor relations counsel; modify and coordinate when necessary in order to assure uniformity of legal positions and best use of historical precedent

- Advise vice president of operations and compliance and director of player personnel of legal matters associated with their departments

- Draft suggested contract language for player contracts, and consult with clubs regarding the use thereof

- Prepare and make a presentation at the annual labor seminar relating to contract negotiations and processing of grievance for club personnel

- Prepare materials and presentations to update owners at meetings of Council Executive Committee and other relevant NFL committees

- Work internally with and support attorneys in other departments of the NFL in areas of mutual interest, including litigation support, development of NFL policy, and advising clubs on areas involving the intersection of labor policy and other substantive areas of concern

- Exchange and receive current information from counsel in other NFL departments in bi-monthly staff meetings

- Evaluate job-related performance of certain Management Council employees

- Prepare presentations and participate in various academic and professional seminars and symposia on sports law issues

- Communicate and work with counsel in other professional sports regarding contract negotiations, collective bargaining issues, and other areas of mutual concern

- Represent NFL Management Council and clubs in administering the collective bargaining agreement; specifically, arbitration proceedings including injury, noninjury, special master, impartial arbitrator cases, and grievances filed by NFL officials

- Represent or aid in representation of NFL and clubs in state and federal court or administrative actions involving disputes arising under EEOC, labor, or antitrust laws

- Administer NFL policies on steroids, substance abuse, and personal conduct, requiring administration of budgeting; oversight of testing protocols; supervision of NFL medical advisors; preparation for hearings; and representation of the league in player discipline appeal hearings

- Give legal counsel to clubs and the league regarding interpretation of collective bargaining agreements and their rights, duties, and obligations there under

- Aid in drafting and negotiation of collective bargaining proposals involving player discipline, dispute resolution procedures, and other player work rules

- Negotiate and implement NFL officials' collective bargaining agreement

- Advise league on workplace policies relating to league employees; provide legal review and analysis of player policies regarding domestic violence, gambling, and gun possession

Requirements

The requirements for this position call for a law degree and 8 to 10 years of sports/entertainment litigation experience. Qualified candidates will also have an extensive academic background and familiarity with NFL and other sports' labor relations history and CBAs. Working knowledge of various computer applications and strong communication skills are also highly important to the success of this position. The position involves extensive travel for hearings and depositions. This position, as with many legal positions, is demanding mentally and physically, requiring a great deal of stamina. The position reports directly to the senior vice president and general counsel.

SENIOR VICE PRESIDENT AND GENERAL COUNSEL, NFL MANAGEMENT COUNCIL

Industry Segment:	Professional Sports, Football, NFL League Office
Functional Area:	Legal Services
Experience:	Ten years of experience required
Location:	New York

The general counsel is responsible for all matters of a legal nature related to labor relations or personnel, including advice and counsel to league and club executives on such matters, and representation in litigation of labor or personnel matters before arbitrators, administrative agencies, and state or federal courts. The general counsel also participates in negotiating and drafting all provisions of the collective bargaining agreement, which covers all NFL players from their draft or first contract through postretirement. CBA provisions regulate all employee working conditions and control over $2.9 billion of employee costs per year, the largest single expense of the league, and results in a competitively balanced, profitable professional sport with a positive public image.

Duties and Responsibilities

- Responsible for $4 to $8 million legal budget and all legal affairs relating to players, officials, and other employee groups

- Responsible for hiring and supervision of in-house and outside legal counsel, resulting in quality legal representation of clubs and the league in arbitration or grievances and federal court and administrative litigation (e.g., National Labor Relations Board)

- Advise league and 30 member clubs on labor and employment law matters

- Supervise staff of five attorneys who represent clubs in 75 arbitration proceedings each year involving exposure of over $50 million per year

- Participate in negotiation and drafting of all player and game official work rules and costs through collective bargaining

- Responsible for crisis management through development and implementation of strategy for dealing with labor disruption (strike, replacement players, etc.)

- Advise member clubs and league office of rights and responsibilities under CBA

- Supervise and aid in administration of NFL Drugs of Abuse and Alcohol Program resulting in drug treatment for players in need and imposition of fines and suspensions where appropriate

- Supervise and aid in administration of Personal Conduct Program

- Supervise administration of player benefits, including advice to owner trustees on Taft-Hartley trust boards set up to provide retirement and disability benefits, supplemental disability benefits, and club/player 401(k) investments and distributions

- Act as alternate trustee and fiduciary on Taft-Hartley boards as required

- Supervise player insurance providers and negotiate premiums and plan changes

- Aid in preparation and presentation of reports to Management Council Executive Committee and owners

- Prepare and present to owners for approval Management Council resolutions as required by Management Council Constitution and By-Laws

Qualifications

- Education: College and law school degrees, admission to a state bar

- Experience: 10 years of labor law and/or litigation experience

- Abilities and skills:

  - Ability to recognize and address complex legal issues

  - Familiarity with ERISA and methods of appropriate investment of trust funds and hiring of investment managers

  - Negotiation skills

  - Ability to supervise professional staff and manage outside counsel

  - Outstanding verbal and written communication skills

The position requires extensive travel, in excess of 100 nights per year. Negotiation periods involve continuous 15 to 20 hour days for months at various locations throughout the country. The position reports to the executive vice president and chairmen of the Management Council Executive Committee (CEC).

CHAPTER NINETY

Compliance

The National Collegiate Athletic Association (NCAA) is a voluntary association composed of colleges and universities, conferences, organizations, and individuals, totaling over 1,200 members. Member schools agree to be bound by NCAA rules and regulations, and are obligated to administer their athletic programs in accordance with the NCAA rules. The NCAA does not offer membership to individual student-athletes. Instead, it operates under the principle of institutional control. In essence, this means that the NCAA deals only with a school's administration, and the school is responsible for monitoring the activities of individual student-athletes.

Compliance is a unique aspect of college athletics. Each year, there are highly publicized cases of NCAA rules violations. Violations can include such things as academic fraud, recruiting violations, improper payments to players (including both money and benefits), eligibility violations, and unauthorized practice sessions. When these violations involve a student-athlete, the NCAA informs the school of its findings and requests that the school declare the student-athlete ineligible. If the school does not comply with the request, the NCAA may invoke sanctions against all or any part of the institution's athletic program. Schools may also be sanctioned by the NCAA if they are found to lack institutional control.

The NCAA is structured in such a way that the entire compliance responsibility does not lie within the NCAA national office. Instead, the NCAA is divided into conferences, based primarily on geographic location. Each conference is responsible for regulating its member institutions and ensuring that the minimum standards, as outlined in the *NCAA Manual*, are not violated. Each conference has a detailed set of rules and regulations, and a mechanism to enforce those rules. These regulations cover eligibility standards, dispute resolution mechanisms, sportsmanship rules, championship guidelines, and player/coach conduct. It is important to remember that each conference is still governed by the NCAA; therefore, no conference rule may be contradictory to an NCAA rule.

It is the role of compliance officers, such as those listed in this chapter, to monitor a school's adherence to school, conference, and NCAA rules. Compliance-related work can be found at colleges and universities, athletic conferences, and the NCAA national office.

Industry compensation for compliance positions can vary tremendously depending on the factors explained in Chapter 72. The following compensation levels are reasonable expectations for mid-sized organizations in mid-sized markets.

College Athletics

- Compliance coordinator/specialist: $25,000 to $35,000
- Head compliance officer, Division II (asst./assoc. AD or director): $25,000 to $35,000
- Head compliance officer, FCS/I-AA school (asst./assoc. AD or director): $45,000 to $55,000
- Head compliance officer, FBS/I-A school (asst./assoc. AD or director): $90,000 to $110,000
- Director of compliance, FBS/I-A conference: $48,000 to $80,000
- Associate commissioner of compliance, FBS/I-A conference: $100,000 to $165,000

ATHLETIC COMPLIANCE SPECIALIST, CLEVELAND STATE UNIVERSITY

Industry Segment:	College Athletics, NCAA Football Championship Subdivision
Functional Area:	Compliance
Experience:	Unspecified
Location:	Cleveland, Ohio

Cleveland State University is accepting applications and nominations for the position of athletic compliance specialist. This is a full-time, 12-month appointment.

Duties and Responsibilities

Assists the compliance office in NCAA and conference-related matters. Maintains a thorough understanding of and keeps current with NCAA policies and legislative interpretations as they pertain to NCAA Division I status. Implements and ensures staff adherence to all conference policies as they pertain to membership in good standing. Interacts professionally with all internal and external customers using strong interpersonal skills.

Minimum Qualifications

Bachelor's degree and experience in a student services environment. Familiarity with NCAA and conference-related policies, procedures, and legislation. Must possess excellent written, verbal, and interpersonal communication skills. Ability to work effectively with diverse populations.

Preferred Qualifications

Advanced degree in sports administration or higher education related to counseling/advising on career/academic issues. Experience working in an NCAA Division I athletics department. Experience working in athletic compliance. This is a grade position with salary commensurate with experience. Send letter of interest; résumé; and names, addresses, phone numbers, and e-mail addresses of at least three professional references.

SPECIAL ASSISTANT TO GENERAL COUNSEL FOR NCAA COMPLIANCE, FLORIDA INTERNATIONAL UNIVERSITY–MIAMI

Industry Segment:	College Athletics, NCAA Football Bowl Subdivision
Functional Area:	Compliance
Experience:	Unspecified
Location:	Miami, Florida

Florida International University in Miami is seeking applications for the position of special assistant to the general counsel for NCAA compliance. FIU is a member of the Sun Belt Conference and offers 17 NCAA Division I sports programs. The successful candidate will analyze and apply NCAA, Sun Belt Conference, and campus regulations in a consistent and uniform manner. Requires detailed knowledge of athletic legislation, campus academic and financial aid policies, administrative procedures, and relevant state and federal regulations, and the ability to apply and comply with these regulations with a high level of expertise and accuracy in a timely manner.

Duties and Responsibilities

- Implement and oversee all processes, procedures, and systems necessary to assist the university in complying with National Collegiate Athletic Association (NCAA) and Sun Belt Conference rules and regulations for 17 NCAA Division I men's and women's intercollegiate sports (Division I-A in football)

- Coordinate NCAA rules education programs for administrators, coaches, support staff, student-athletes, and booster groups

- Serve as legislative liaison to the Sun Belt Conference and the NCAA; work with admissions office, financial aid office, and registrar's office on the appropriate implementation of policies and procedures to ensure compliance with NCAA and conference regulations; handle all appeal and waiver requests at both the conference and NCAA level

- Investigate and report rules violations in conformity with NCAA and conference policy; supervise the university's associate athletics director for compliance, director of athletic eligibility and oversee the preparation of NCAA squad lists and eligibility certifications

- Serve as liaison to the NCAA initial-eligibility clearinghouse; facilitate annual eligibility/educational meetings with each intercollegiate athletics squad and administer the NCAA student-athlete statement

- Oversee completion and submission of required NCAA reports and surveys including the institution's NCAA APR report

- Oversee NCAA compliance for the department's summer camps and clinics

SENIOR MAJOR GIFT OFFICER FOR THE DEPARTMENT OF ATHLETICS, UNIVERSITY OF CALIFORNIA, BERKELEY

Industry Segment:	College Athletics, NCAA Football Bowl Subdivision
Functional Area:	Development
Experience:	Unspecified
Location:	Los Angeles, California
Compensation:	$80,000 to $95,000

The University of California, Berkeley is the preeminent public university in the country. We're also one of the leading employers in the San Francisco Bay Area. We are currently seeking a senior major gift officer for the department of athletics. Under the supervision of the director of development, the senior major gift officer (SMGO) is responsible for the identification, cultivation, solicitation, and stewardship of major gift-level prospective donors—defined as individuals capable of contributing $250,000 or more to the department of athletics. The SMGO develops and manages department relationships with its top prospects and donors and ensures that these relationships are nurtured and maintained for the benefit of the department over time. The SMGO will be assigned a specific portfolio of prospects that have the potential to give to the department at the major gift level. He or she is also expected to qualify major gift prospects and solicit gifts directly.

This is a 2-year, contract position located in Los Angeles, California, and requires weekly travel to the Bay Area for meetings and possibly some additional travel to meet with prospects. This is a field fundraising position and the SMGO will be expected to be out of the office making calls on prospects at least 3 days per week. It is possible that this person will reside in Southern California, but will be responsible for regular meetings at the UC campus in Berkeley.

Duties and Responsibilities

- Help meet the fundraising objectives of the department
- Develop and implement long- and short-term plans to secure major and annual gifts from alumni, friends, volunteers, corporations, foundations, and other entities in support of the department's mission and priorities
- Formulate marketing plans and strategies to reach annual fundraising goals and capital campaign strategies
- Build a volunteer program for alumni and friends while centralizing the Booster Club activities
- Manage a portfolio of 100–125 major gift prospects, the bulk of whom have the capacity to give $250,000 or more

- Oversee the annual campaign and stewardship of donors at the $10,000 level and below
- Originate a minimum of 25 contacts per month
- Raise a minimum of $2 million per year once established with an appropriate portfolio
- Identify additional annual goals, including numbers of solicitations made and gifts closed
- Apply knowledge and understanding of the department of athletics, its traditions, programs, campus issues, needs, and priorities to the development process
- Motivate administrators, faculty, staff, and volunteers to participate in the identification, cultivation and solicitation of major gifts
- Assist with the structure and development of the department's fundraising efforts, including the development of new fundraising strategies, new ways to structure gifts, and new fundraising marketing materials
- Facilitate communication among administrators, faculty, donors, prospects, and volunteers
- Manage collaborative working relationships with fundraising colleagues in university relations, and other campus schools and units, in order to develop strategies for joint solicitation and to negotiate differences

Qualifications

- Bachelor's degree
- Experience with identifying, cultivating, and directly soliciting major gifts in an academic setting
- Ability to use quantitative and qualitative assessments to draw conclusions
- Experience with intercollegiate athletic administration or development
- Ability to maintain strict confidentiality and exhibit professionalism
- Experience with developing and structuring complex major gifts
- Ability to accomplish specific outcomes and maintain self-confidence in order to act decisively
- Understanding of tax guidelines governing charitable giving
- Knowledge of fundraising campaigns and experience with guiding and motivating volunteers
- Ability to interact effectively with volunteers, prospects, and senior campus officials
- Ability to oversee multiple projects and quickly discern complex and competing interests

- Proficiency with computer skills in basic office software, such as Microsoft Office, and the ability to quickly learn function-specific software
- Ability to persuasively discuss academic programs, needs, and priorities with prospective donors and volunteers
- Flexibility to travel and attend weekend and evening events
- Ability to work comfortably with prominent and wealthy individuals
- Excellent verbal and written communication skills
- Ability to encourage a participative process and work well in teams; master's degree preferred

Endnotes

1. Giving to the University of Michigan. (n.d.). University of Michigan. Retrieved September 29, 2007, from http://www.giving.umich.edu/where/units/athletics.htm.

2. Athletic Development—Supporting University of Alabama Athletics. (n.d.). Rolltide.com, The Official Site of University of Alabama Athletics. Retrieved September 29, 2007, from http://www.rolltide.com/ViewArticle.dbml? DB_OEM_ID=8000&ATCLID= 242777.

- Intermediate-level Microsoft Word and Excel experience and beginner-level PowerPoint experience required

- Ability to handle multiple tasks with keen attention to detail and thorough follow-through

- Flexible, willing to work nontraditional hours, including some nights and weekends

- Social, outgoing; able to network, develop, and maintain relationships

- Ability to travel and commit to schedule before program launch

- Comfortable working with liquor and in the nightclub environment

- Bachelor's degree in communications or marketing is preferred but not required

ACCOUNT EXECUTIVE, WASSERMAN MEDIA GROUP—MARKETING

Industry Segment:	Sports Agencies
Functional Area:	Marketing and Consulting
Experience:	Two to four years of experience required
Location:	Los Angeles, California

Work as member of T-Mobile account team with primary focus on the development and implementation of youth-oriented sponsorship and promotions programs.

Duties and Responsibilities

- Working with various entities (clients, teams, leagues, other brands, agencies, internal field marketing services group, merchandise companies, promotion website/fulfillment companies, etc.) to execute and activate promotional relationships

- Compiling, maintaining, and presenting client status reports, program recaps, and overall presentations

- Researching and keeping up on wireless and related industries and demonstrating an understanding of those specific industries and competitive landscapes

- Maintaining a system for reviewing incoming sponsorship proposals and assessing viability of potential relationships

Qualifications

- All candidates must have 2 to 4 years of sponsorship/promotions/marketing experience at an agency or on a brand

- College degree

- Strong verbal and communication skills

- Experience in creation and delivery of presentations

- Strong interpersonal skills

- Thrive in a team-oriented environment

- Ability to mentor and motivate co-workers

- Detail oriented with strong organizational skills

- Ability to multi-task in a fast-paced environment

ACCOUNT SUPERVISOR, PARAGON

Industry Segment:	Sports Agencies
Functional Area:	Marketing and Consulting
Experience:	Four years of experience required
Location:	Skokie, Illinois

The account supervisor will be responsible for planning, managing, and overseeing the activities and operations for assigned Paragon account teams as they relate to the clients' marketing and promotional initiatives. The account supervisor will function as the liaison between the client and account management teams, as well as between the account management team and Paragon management. The account supervisor will also provide general assistance and support to account management initiatives.

Duties and Responsibilities

- Oversee and manage client communications, cultivating communication across all channels, including day-to-day contact and account team communication

- Evaluate and negotiate relationships with sponsorship properties

- Initiate research and construct strategic recommendations

- Augment and manage relations with all sponsorship properties

- Participate in preparation and establishment of budget, and assist in budget management

- Manage, motivate, and evaluate account team members for career progression while promoting a team atmosphere

Qualifications

- Minimum 4 years of experience in corporate sponsorships, preferably in sports and entertainment industry

- Staff management experience and demonstrated leadership ability in team work environment

- Excellent communication and interpersonal skills, as well as a high comfort level giving presentations

- The ability to handle multiple projects and adapt to changing conditions

- Must be able to travel, have a valid driver's license, and have the ability to do light physical work

ACCOUNT MANAGER—GOLF, IMG

Industry Segment:	Sports Agencies
Functional Area:	Marketing and Consulting
Experience:	Experience preferred, no requirement specified
Location:	Cleveland, Ohio

IMG Golf is looking for an account manager who will have two primary areas of responsibility: one with IMG Golf's management of the Bank of America relationship and the other through the coordination and management of various sponsorships related to the AT&T National PGA Tour event.

Duties and Responsibilities

- Assist team by coordinating fulfillment activities for the World Points platform, and attending various experiences for Bank of America's Ultimate Access program
- Manage various events, experiences, and memorabilia engagements
- Work with the UA team and outside contacts to create opportunities, assist with the acquisition of desired assets from those outside entities, and facilitate the development of marketing materials to highlight the programs to UA customers
- Manage the hospitality and marketing programs for various sponsors of the AT&T National PGA Tour event, held each July in Washington, DC.
- Produce invitations, manage the sponsor's invitee database, develop on-site programming, and manage most of the logistics surrounding the event (hotel, transportation, catering, etc.)
- On-site presence during the week of the event to manage all functions described above, with appropriate follow-up at the conclusion of the event

The desired candidate needs to be able to handle multiple functions in a fast-paced work environment. Prior account management, hospitality, or marketing experience highly preferred. Position requires periods of extensive travel.

PROJECT DIRECTOR, IEG

Industry Segment:	Sports Agencies
Functional Area:	Sponsorship Consulting
Experience:	Three to five years of experience required
Location:	Chicago, Illinois

IEG, Inc. is the world leader in sponsorship marketing information, with publishing, education, measurement, consulting, and training divisions.

Duties and Responsibilities

- Serve as client liaison/team member, concentrating on property audits
- Create sponsorship strategies and proposals for diverse cross-section of rights holders
- Prepare competitive research for select audits
- Serve as presenter, concentrating on audits, custom training sessions, and speeches
- Manage support staff on select processes: information gathering, research, and valuation
- Provide editorial support on consulting and custom research projects, as well as speeches

Qualifications

- Strong strategic orientation and problem-solving skills
- Knowledge of research fundamentals
- Strong written and verbal communication skills
- Excellent project management skills and ability to effectively handle multiple projects simultaneously
- Strong proofing skills and detail orientation
- Able to work independently and as part of a team
- Proficient in Microsoft Office, especially Word, Excel, and PowerPoint
- Three to 5 years of sponsorship experience

VICE PRESIDENT VALUATION SERVICES, IEG

Industry Segment:	Sports Agencies
Functional Area:	Sponsorship Consulting
Experience:	Five to seven years of experience required
Location:	Chicago, Illinois

Primary responsibilities are generating new business opportunities through face-to-face meetings and conference calls with qualified leads and carrying those leads through to closure.

Duties and Responsibilities

- Understand the sponsorship issues and reasons for purchasing IEG Sponsorship Services with each prospect
- Apply knowledge of market and market trends to identify key prospects and obtain meetings with key decision makers and to close business

- Develop and implement strategies that result in client relationship development and revenue generation

- Meet assigned activity and revenue targets on a monthly basis

- Craft compelling sales approaches and deliver successful presentations to key targets; apply knowledge of IEG competitive differentiators in sales situations

- Conduct research on and follow up with new prospects, cold calls, networked referral calls, e-mail, mail, and call-in inquiries

- Attend/present at meetings in high volume, including IEG events and targeted industry-related conferences

Qualifications

- Industry and subject-matter expertise, possessing an in-depth understanding of emerging trends

- Proven track record of developing and closing new account business and meeting sales objectives

- Five to seven years of sales experience with several years successfully selling consulting services to senior-level executives

- Understanding of the basic sales principles such as lead generation, opportunity qualification, proposal development, follow-up, contract negotiation, and closure

- Strong verbal and presentation skills

- Proficiency in MS Word, Excel, PowerPoint, and Outlook

- Ability to work independently and deal effectively with others, both internally and externally

DIRECTOR SPONSORSHIP CONSULTING, VELOCITY SPORTS & ENTERTAINMENT

Industry Segment:	Sports Agencies
Functional Area:	Marketing and Consulting
Experience:	Six to eight years of experience required
Location:	Norwalk, Connecticut

Velocity Sports & Entertainment is seeking a director to lead one of our premiere client accounts. Ideal candidates must be experienced sports marketing professionals with a minimum of 6 to 8 years of marketing experience, including leading a piece of business for an agency. Ideal candidates also possess experience and professional knowledge in the technology industry. Critical skill sets include strategic planning and creation of activation programs for corporate sponsors. Exceptional client service, strategic thinking, leadership, negotiation skills, and a track record of growing

business are all mandatory. Candidate will work on multiple projects within an account and therefore should have very strong organizational skills and work ethic. Position will be located in our Norwalk headquarters.

ASSOCIATE VICE PRESIDENT, STRATEGIC GROUP

Industry Segment:	Sports Agencies
Functional Area:	Marketing and Consulting
Experience:	Seven years of experience required
Location:	New York

As part of our continuing evolution into one of the most influential sports and entertainment marketing agencies in the industry, we are seeking an associate vice president, group account director (or potentially VP) capable of delivering flawless strategy while managing relationships with some of our most critical clients. Possessing 7+ years of experience in the sports marketing, integrated sponsorship consulting, or brand building businesses dealing with top brands, the ideal candidate will be a hybrid talent capable of delivering impeccable customer service and growing the bottom line through both expanding existing client programs and acquiring new business. Property relations experience and established relationships (teams and leagues) are a serious plus. An existing Rolodex whose focus is on established relationships with category leaders is a plus as is experience in the entertainment and lifestyle sponsorship fields. A strong existing team with smoothly functioning process is already in place needing a leader to provide top-line strategy and take their potential to the next level. Strong presentation skills are necessary and the ability to function in a fast-paced, dynamic office environment is a must. This is an opportunity for a star to rise to the next level in this industry as a top member of one of its most quickly growing firms. Compensation commensurate with experience and supplemented by performance incentives.

SPORTS AGENT, ATHLETE REPRESENTATION

Industry Segment:	Sports Agencies
Functional Area:	Athlete Representation
Experience:	No minimum required
Location:	Throughout the United States
Compensation:	Varies greatly from agent to agent: • Start-up agents: $25,000+ • Well-established agents: $1,000,000+ (Boras, Tellum, Steinberg, Rosenhaus, etc.) Agents typically receive 3% of their clients' on-field earnings and 15% to 25% of their marketing income

Position Spotlight *Sports Agent*

One very simple definition of an agent is a person who has a player for a client. A legal definition of an agent is one who is authorized to act for or in the place of another.

The requirements of being an agent have changed significantly since the 1970s, when sport agency first gained in popularity. At that time, the simple definition of an agent (one who has a client) was a truism. The need for oversight developed as agents became commonplace and the amount of money associated with the profession escalated. The modern agent must be aware of state and federal legislation regulating agents, such as the Uniform Athlete Agents Act (passed in 34 states) that requires agents to register and follow specific guidelines. The agent may also have to adhere to the players' association rules for the league in which his client plays. For example, in order to be a certified contract advisor of a National Football League player, the agent must register, be certified, pass an exam, pay a registration fee, and attend regular meetings. In addition, the NFLPA has specific rules about number and frequency with which agents must negotiate a player contract in order to remain on the active list of agents.

The responsibilities of agents vary significantly. Some agents, typically those with legal backgrounds, specialize only in contract negotiations for the players. At the other end of the spectrum are "full-service" agents who may be involved with every facet of an athlete's life. Many of the issues will be sport-related, such as negotiating contracts, arranging marketing endorsements, and managing tax liabilities. Agents also provide legal representation for cases of salary arbitration (baseball and hockey), injury grievance (football), or general grievance (e.g., drug testing, discipline, and contract interpretation). For off-the-field matters, agents may handle (or coordinate with these services) personal finances, investments, legal problems (divorce, estate planning, wills, purchasing of homes, child support, or criminal charges), family travel to games, summer camps, and/or any number of other life aspects.

With the increases in salaries and endorsements (for some athletes), there is quite a bit of work for a full-service agent of a superstar. The athlete becomes a small business with many different issues requiring different areas of expertise to service this type of athlete. Some agents are sole practitioners who will handle some of the work and then use a network of people to provide various services. In other cases, the athlete's relationship will be with a large agency (such as IMG, Octagon, or CAA) that provides most of the services from different departments within the organization. For example, the marketing, media, and legal departments each handle the various issues within their areas of expertise for a number of clients. Some agents focus on one sport, such as Scott Boras, whose specialty is baseball. There are also mid-size firms with different leading agents focusing on different sports, which is how, at one time, Leigh Steinberg (football) and Jeff Moorad (baseball) were partners. The large representation firms seek to represent athletes in several major team sports, but these firms also may represent many high-profile athletes in individual sports, such as golf or tennis. In fact, most of IMG's original clients were golfers, including Arnold Palmer and Gary Player.

In the Tom Cruise movie *Jerry Maguire*, one of the famous lines is, "Show me the money!" Although the athlete said this phrase, it also may be applied to the agent. One attraction for agents is the financial compensation of the job. Agents usually charge on a percentage basis that ranges from 1% to 5% depending on the sport, athlete, situation, and guidelines of the players' association. With multiyear contract packages as high as $100 million, the resulting fee can be quite lucrative for the agent (for instance, an 8-year, $14 million per year contract will result in $420,000 annually for an agent earning 3% over the life of the contract). In addition to this, the agent usually receives 15% to 20% of marketing contracts signed by the athlete. Other attractions to the job for some include the association with highly visible/popular athletes and just being involved with the sports industry.

One downside to the agent business is that it is very competitive, and sometimes unethical. It is also difficult to break into, because there are not many clients relative to the number of people who would like to represent the athletes.

Agents don't work only for athletes. Other individuals in the industry need representation too, including coaches, media members (e.g., broadcasters, studio analysts), and athletic directors. Agents may also represent companies in brokering deals with sport properties; for example, a firm may hire an agency to help maximize the return on investment from a sponsorship deal, or an owner may hire someone to facilitate the sale of a team.

The following is a general description detailing the types of responsibilities and requirements commonly found for this position. An actual job announcement was not available.

Duties and Responsibilities

- Advising and providing guidance to professional athletes as well as amateur athletes with potential for professional careers
- Negotiating client contracts, including drafted players
- Representing clients in arbitration hearings with league and/or team personnel
- Representing player in league and team grievance procedures
- Interpreting the league's rules and regulations for clients
- Thorough understanding of the following:
  - Collective bargaining agreement for all leagues in which athletes are represented

- League by-laws
- Standard player contract
- League salary information
- Managing client's finances (financial planning/money management)
- Handling client's marketing and public relations
- Counseling the athlete during troubled times
- Providing legal advice for medical compensation/worker's compensation and insurance
- Must gain certification through players' association

Education

- Minimum:
  - Bachelor's degree
- Preferred:
  - Law degree
  - MBA
  - Master's degree in sport management
- Preferred and/or Helpful Experience:
  - Playing background
  - Previous legal work with an emphasis on labor law and contracts
  - Need to have established a strong network to obtain clients

Type of Employment

- Some agents work in large agencies (IMG, Octagon, WMG)
- Some run their own business (Boras)

Required Special Skills

- Negotiation skills, leadership skills, patience, competitiveness, analytical skills, player evaluation skills, statistical analysis, communication skills, people skills, and networking skills all play a vital role in the success of a sports agent.

Associations

- Must be certified under the league's union
- Trade publications:
  - *Baseball America*
  - *Sports Illustrated*
  - *Street & Smith's SportsBusiness Journal*
  - *Street & Smith's SportsBusiness Daily*

Corporate Sponsorship

There are often three sides to every sponsorship agreement—the property (usually a sporting event, team, or league), the sponsor, and a marketing agency. The sponsor pays the property to be a sponsor, but relies on the marketing agency to maximize the use of the sponsorship rights. This relationship is visible everywhere you turn. For example, a company like Home Depot wants to connect to a certain age demographic that happens to watch college football. Through the help of a marketing agency, *ESPN's College Game Day Built by the Home Depot* was created.

Due to the growing complexity and financial implications of sports sponsorship, corporate sponsors must maintain and manage relationships with both the property and their marketing agency. Companies that are major players in the sports sponsorship game (such as Coca-Cola, Pepsi, Sprint/Nextel, etc.) typically hire employees to manage their sports sponsorship activities. The job description in this chapter is what Wells Fargo Bank looks for in hiring someone into its corporate sponsorship department.

Industry compensation for corporate sponsorship positions can vary tremendously depending on the factors explained in Chapter 72. The following compensation levels (before bonuses or commissions) are reasonable expectations for mid-sized organizations in mid-sized markets.

Sponsor Properties

- Manager: $50,000 to $60,000
- Director: $100,000 to $125,000
- Senior or executive vice president: $125,000 to $150,000+

SPONSORSHIP MARKETING MANAGER, WELLS FARGO BANK

Industry Segment:	Corporate Sponsorship
Functional Area:	Sales and Marketing (Sponsorship)
Experience:	Five years of experience required
Location:	San Francisco, California

The sponsorship consultant will play a key role in managing the Wells Fargo sponsorship proposal review and evaluation process as well as supporting the development of an enterprise marketing sponsorship marketing strategy. The sponsorship consultant will also be a resource to regional marketing management, line of business, and product group personnel.

Day-to-day responsibilities include, but are not limited to, managing vendor relationships with Sponsor Direct, the online sponsorship application software provider, and Millsport (Wells Fargo's sponsorship agency).

In the Sponsor Direct relationship, the sponsorship consultant will perform administrative duties that ensure efficient and effective operation of the Sponsor Direct automated online sponsorship review process for regional marketing consultants. As the liaison with regional marketing managing the Millsport relationship, the sponsorship consultant will direct the communications between regional marketing personnel and the agency. The sponsorship consultant will supervise Millsport personnel as they evaluate sponsorships and create value-added marketing ideas for the Wells Fargo regional marketing personnel.

In managing both vendor relationships, the sponsorship consultant will ensure all sponsorship reports, monthly and quarterly evaluations, and invoicing occur in a timely manner.

Duties and Responsibilities

- Manage the day-to-day operation of the Wells Fargo Sponsor Direct online sponsorship evaluation process

- Supervise Millsport's management of the Wells Fargo sponsorship evaluation process

- Maintain communications and work flow to ensure agreed-to key performance indicators are met on a consistent basis

- Build excellent sustainable regional marketing, line of business, and product group relationships

Qualifications

- Four-year college degree, in a related field

- Five-plus years of sponsorship marketing experience with a leading sponsorship agency

- Demonstrated project management skills

- Demonstrated ability to work in a team environment

- Potential to manage sponsorships in the future

- Experience with cause-related marketing programs a plus

Sporting Goods and Apparel

The sporting goods and apparel industry plays a role in the life of most people. Whether you are lacing up your sneakers or heading to the gym for a workout, most of us have contact with these companies. This chapter includes three sample job descriptions that provide an indication of the types of opportunities available in this field. If you have a strong interest level in sporting goods and apparel, you will likely need additional resources. Most prominent sporting goods and apparel companies have job boards on the Internet, and you should take a look at those for additional information. (*Helpful hint*: To quickly find a company's job board, do an Internet search using the company's name and jobs, such as "Nike jobs" or "jobs at Reebok." This should point you in the right direction.)

ASSOCIATE PROMOTION SPECIALIST, REEBOK

Industry Segment:	Sporting Goods and Apparel
Functional Area:	Promotions and Product Management
Experience:	Four years of experience required
Location:	Canton, Massachusetts

The sports licensing division is looking for an associate promotion specialist to properly and accurately place orders of all promo uniforms that fall within the NBA umbrella. This role also requires consultation with team entities on custom make requests and budget maintenance, and is a key contact between brand and team equipment managers.

Duties and Responsibilities

- Manage order placement of all NBA and NBA All-Star and special event team uniform orders with factories; volume approximately $5 million in cost

- Consult with clients on nonteam-related custom orders to determine appropriate uniform category (procut, swingman, replica, etc.) and production path that will best fit client's needs and timelines; clients may include community relations, PR, and marketing departments from each team; player agents; league offices; and Adidas/Reebok marketing/advertising

- Police order requests to ensure that uniforms being manufactured are in compliance with league restrictions, in concurrence with Adidas goals, and do not wrongfully infringe on player or franchise proprietary rights

- Maintain the team uniform budget tracking on a seasonal basis for over 58 teams, league, and Adidas; responsibilities include invoicing and collection

- Develop ordering plan, payment agreement, and timeline for special event uniforms; explain process to teams with follow-up to ensure process is executed and uniforms are delivered on time

- Communicate with factories on a daily basis to prioritize production orders

Qualifications

- Bachelor's degree

- Four years of project management responsibility

95

Internship Programs

Rather than sporadically hiring interns, some sport organizations choose to bring in a group of interns (sometimes referred to as an internship class) as part of a formal internship program. There are advantages and disadvantages of working in such a program. You gain an opportunity to build camaraderie with the other members of your internship class (which may make for a more enjoyable internship experience), but you also face increased competition to stand out in the eyes of the organization. This may make it more difficult to obtain a full-time position at the end of the internship period. The following listings are two examples of internship programs at major professional sports teams and one example of an internship program at the NFL Players Association.

INTERNSHIP OPPORTUNITIES, HOUSTON ASTROS

Industry Segment:	Professional Sports, Baseball, MLB Team
Functional Area:	Various
Experience:	Internship
Location:	Houston, Texas
Compensation:	Likely to be unpaid, hourly wage, or monthly stipend

Please read the list of Fall internships within the Houston Astros Internship Program. After you review, you will be asked to pick three departments of interest and rank them in order. These are full-time internship opportunities, which require interns to work a 32- to 40-hour workweek. Specific duties and responsibilities will vary based upon the department but this is a "hands on" internship opportunity. If there is a requirement such as fluency or computer program

knowledge, you must meet that requirement before selecting that as a department of interest.

The following are qualifications for the Internship Program:

- Energetic and enthusiastic
- Outgoing, positive attitude and personality
- Must be a "team player"
- Interested in more than just working in a high profile environment
- Ability to multi-task and work in a fast-paced environment
- Willing to offer ideas and suggestions
- Punctual and professional

Ballpark Entertainment/Production

The ballpark entertainment intern will be responsible for recording, tape logging, and dubbing highlight clips from Astros games. The selected individual will also be responsible for supporting both the community development and conference center departments through its various events and player appearances. This includes operating video cameras, editing, and other production responsibilities. Other duties include creating graphics such as headshots. The internship is more suited for an individual who possesses experience in computer-based programs, such as Avid, Final Cut Pro, After Effects, and Photoshop. The intern candidate should want to pursue a career in sports production. The intern candidate must be able to work all games (which may include day, night, weekend, and holiday games). This intern will assume additional roles on an as-needed basis. A media production major is recommended for this internship.

Baseball Operations

This intern will assist with general administrative and clerical duties, which include answering phones, filing, faxing, copying, organizing archive files, sorting mail internally, and helping with staff mailings. The selected individual will copy and distribute winterball statistics weekly and assist with playoff preparation and other special projects/reports as needed. This intern will also support with meeting preparations, work comp and player insurance, MVP ceremony preparation, free agent preparation, Rule V draft preparation, and airport and doctor visits. This intern will assume additional roles on an as-needed basis and must be proficient in Excel and Word. Fluency in Spanish is preferred and a plus.

Broadcasting

The broadcasting intern will manage program logs and traffic instructions from the advertising department. The selected individual is responsible for log times/affidavits of when spots ran, as well as mailing this information to the sponsors to ensure timely payment. This intern will have a close working relationship with the traffic departments at advertising agencies as well as personnel in charge of traffic at larger companies. This intern will also process ticket requests for radio affiliates and send them via UPS. The intern will assume additional roles on an as-needed basis. Radio and TV major is recommended, but public relations/marketing is also a good major for this intern.

Business Development

The selected individual will establish contact with leads, make proposals, and put together PowerPoint presentations; set up meetings with the potential sponsors; and assist in the closing of the sale. This intern will have the opportunity to see a sale from beginning to end and assist throughout the entire process. The intern will have pregenerated leads presented to them and will also be expected to make phone calls in order to solicit ads for the organization. Other duties will include researching other companies from the generated leads and selling billboards throughout the ballpark. This intern may also assist with press conferences and will assume additional roles on an as-needed basis. Preferred majors include business management, marketing, or sports management. Must be proficient in Word and PowerPoint and must be a detail-oriented professional at all times.

Community Development

The community development intern will be strongly involved with the community and is responsible for promoting a good charitable name for the organization. The selected individual is responsible for processing and responding to donation and group ticket requests as well as mailing out or delivering the approved donations/tickets. This intern will be responsible for setting up and coordinat-

ing programs such as Grand Slam for Youth Program, Astros Buddies, and other charitable programs. The intern will assist in scheduling and coordinating engagement photos, first pitches, and other events that may take place during the designated semester, as well as schedule community events with local children and the players. The intern will have direct involvement with elementary and middle schools to assist in projects such as honor roll, perfect attendance, and other programs. The selected intern will assume additional roles on an as-needed basis. Must be proficient in Excel, Word, and Outlook and be able to work all games (which may include day, night, weekend, and holiday games).

Engineering

The engineering intern is responsible for an array of tasks, which include hands-on engineering duties as well as office and clerical work. The selected individual will place orders with contractors, meet the contractors on the job site to show the problem, and process all paperwork relating to the problem. This intern may assist the engineering crew while they fix motors, reassemble gears, check piping, and take apart and put together all types of machinery. This intern should have a firm grasp on engineering techniques and be proficient in Excel. The selected individual will provide customer service and deal with clients on a daily basis. The selected individual will need to handle and satisfy all customer needs within the conference center in a professional manner. The intern will hook up all audio/visual equipment for the clients (which may include laptops, projectors, mixing boards, etc.) and may be required to run through a tutorial to show the clients how to use each piece of equipment. Another major responsibility of this intern is being familiar with the setup for press conferences. Recommended majors include engineering, sports management, and A/V, and proficiency in Excel and Word is required. Knowledge of Auto-Cad is a plus. This intern will assume additional roles on an as-needed basis.

Finance

The primary goal of the finance internship is to offer the intern candidate entry-level accounting and finance work experience within the organization. The intern will assume the role as a staff accountant and will work closely with the accounts payable and accounts receivable departments on a daily basis. The intern duties include processing checks and preparing bank deposits, account reconciliations, processing vendor invoices for payment, spreadsheet analysis, and some clerical work. The intern may also be asked to assist with special projects on an as-needed basis. Strong organizational and analytical skills are important as well as a working knowledge of Excel. Candidate must be an accounting or finance major and be eligible to receive college credit for the internship.

Graphics

This intern will work closely with marketing and other departments in creating a wide range of print graphics, including but not limited to ballpark signage, promotional items, brochures, posters, flyers, postcards, and invitations. In addition, they will help create print ads and interact with various print publications, uploading to their FTP sites and performing other functions on an as-needed basis. Candidates must have an extensive working knowledge of Adobe InDesign, Illustrator, and Photoshop on a Mac operating system. Must be able to handle multiple projects under flexible and extreme deadlines. Strong understanding of the printing process and web design a plus.

Groundskeeping

This intern's main responsibility will be to learn and assist with the maintenance of the field and ballpark grounds, ensuring the field is game- and camera-ready. This may include stripping the infield, keeping the dirt moist, learning fertilizer calculations, patching infield holes, leveling home plate, trimming trees outside the ballpark, picking up trash, edging the infield, and many other related duties on an as-needed basis. This intern will also assist with the maintenance of all equipment as well as help set up pregame activities such as batting practice. The intern will assume additional roles on an as-needed basis. The selected intern should have familiarization with mowers, blowers, and tractors and must be a hard worker and team player. Please note—this intern will work on the field at all times.

Guest Services

The guest services intern plays an integral role in ballpark operations on game day and helps oversee a staff of approximately 250 ushers, ticket takers, and ballpark supervisors. Candidates should have strong interpersonal and communication skills, demonstrate initiative, and be prepared to work extended hours and weekends. The selected individual manages lost and found by maintaining a log and addressing messages/inquiries left by guests. Other responsibilities include responding to fan feedback e-mails on a daily basis, updating personnel files, and generating staffing sheets. The guest services intern will also be in charge of staffing for conference center needs, such as tours, parties, and other events. The guest services intern regularly networks with a variety of departments within the organization as well as external business partners and will assume additional roles on an as-needed basis. Must be proficient in all Office programs, particularly Excel.

Human Resources

The human resources intern will play an integral role in the recruiting efforts of future interns and other part-time staff positions. This intern will perform administrative and clerical duties, which include filing, faxing, processing paper-work, making phone calls, prepping letters, organizing and creating personnel files, and other necessary functions. Other duties include helping create termination reports and other reports with a strong emphasis on using Excel. The selected individual assists in the issuance of stadium credentials/badges year round. Desired major for this intern is human resources, but it is not required. The selected individual must be professional and able to handle a large amount of confidential information. This individual must feel comfortable asking questions, interviewing, and passing along information in a professional and confidential manner. This intern will assume additional roles on an as-needed basis.

Market Development

The market development department's primary goal is the development of niche marketing programs targeted at continuously expanding the ball club's fan base. The department works in such areas as Spanish-language marketing and community programs, special niche and general market-sponsored events, team website content development, as well as Spanish television and radio broadcast. Please visit our Spanish website at www.astrosdehouston.com for more information. The market development intern will assist in keeping track of all Astros international media efforts, including print publications, radio and TV broadcast spots, and the Spanish website; developing programs to increase traffic to the Spanish website; and serving as a liaison with sponsors via e-mail and phone and may sometimes include in-person meetings. This intern will also assist in the editing and publishing of articles for the team's Spanish publication, *Cronicas de los Astros*, and with the supervision of the Spanish radio broadcast. Other responsibilities include translating all game recaps into Spanish in a timely manner for dissemination among the Astros' extensive international media database. The intern is also responsible for keeping an up-to-date clippings file to keep track of the Astros' international media coverage. At times, the selected intern will interview players in Spanish as well as translate press releases into Spanish. Other duties include organizing bilingual baseball clinics and other Spanish community initiatives by coordinating and logistically planning the events with the players. The intern will assume additional roles on an as-needed basis. Must be fluent in both Spanish and English (writing, speaking, and translating) and have extensive copywriting knowledge. Majors for this intern may include marketing, sports management, and Spanish.

Marketing

This intern will serve as the main point of contact for all scoreboard messages that come in via the website. This particular intern will help coordinate and research special events, which may require contacting outside vendors and/or researching other teams' events. This intern will primarily assist with theme nights, special events, and promotions.

A major responsibility of this intern is to draft the radio promotions for game day broadcasting as well as reporting a recap of all media exposure for sponsors. This intern will also assist with pregame activities such as the national anthem, first pitch, and others, and will also schedule the street team intern's events throughout the city. The intern will assume additional roles on an as-needed basis. This intern must act as a professional at all times and be able to work all games (which may include day, night, weekend, and holiday games). Must have both excellent written and oral communication skills and be proficient in Excel and Word, and must also be an excellent copywriter as they may need to develop copy.

Media Relations

The media relations intern will deal exclusively with the media, for both internal and external purposes. The selected individual will sort through all newspaper sites, package all pertinent clips, and distribute it throughout the office or to media personnel. This intern will also run the minor league reports and recap all the games from the previous day. Other duties include running stat packets for media and internal use. This intern will set up the press box for media personnel prior to the games, as well as pass out media credentials on game days. This intern must be proficient in Word, Excel, and PageMaker and be able to work all games (which may include day, night, weekend, and holiday games). Recommended majors include anything in the communication field, particularly journalism, public relations, and marketing. This intern will assume additional roles on an as-needed basis.

Risk Management/Information Technology

The risk management/IT intern will provide basic clerical assistance such as filing, preparing monthly in-house vendor First Aid reporting for billing purposes, data entry, preparing monthly statistical reports, and updating and maintaining in-house medical worker's comp payments. This intern will also aid in litigation research in preparation for responses to interrogatories, maintain certificate of insurance system, assist in repricing medical bills, and assist with various research projects, building walk-through inspections, and worker's comp Q&A with TPA regarding research information. The selected individual will generate certificate of insurance letters to vendors, contractors, and subcontractors regarding renewal certificates and assist with IT and risk management projects with database/incident/statistical reporting. This intern will assume additional roles on an as-needed basis.

Special Events/Conference Center

This intern will work with the special events/conference center department to handle all nonbaseball game events and meetings held at Minute Maid Park. Our business is 85% corporate and is wide-reaching to include business meetings, galas, trade shows, batting practice and softball games, holiday parties, corporate events, wedding receptions, and bar mitzvahs. The internship requires a responsible self-starter who loves a fast-paced, team-oriented environment. They will be relied on heavily to assist our dynamic department meet our day-to-day operational goals. This person must be a strong communicator with above-average computer skills. They will be responsible for administrative tasks such as contract generation, filing, answering the phone, disseminating information, and taking detailed messages as well as database upkeep. This person will also assist in the sales and event management process. Duties will include selling and coordinating all engagement and bridal photo shoots at Minute Maid Park, sending out detailed audiovisual requests and internal event sheets on various meetings and events, maintaining department promotional item inventory, assisting with client site visits, and assisting in the management of events and meetings held at Minute Maid Park. The special events/conference center intern will work with many departments within the Astros organization as well as our partners in ARAMARK Facility Services and ARAMARK Catering. They will also deal with our corporate and social clients. Ideal intern candidates will possess maturity and poise to deal with all these entities. This internship may require working additional hours during the week and some weekends.

Advertising/Sales/Sponsorship

The intern will work extensively with contracts and proposals for sponsorship accounts. This includes making ledgers from existing contracts and composing new business proposals to sell sponsorships/billboards throughout the park. This intern may deal with large sponsors and therefore must be professional at all times. The selected individual will have pregame activities and may be required to assist with hosting sponsors and events before and during games. These interns must be able to work all games (which may include day, night, weekend, and holiday games), and must be proficient in PowerPoint for editing purposes. The interns will assume additional roles on an as-needed basis. Recommended majors for this intern are marketing and public relations.

Ticket Sales and Service

By joining the Astros ticket services staff, the intern will leave with experience in both sales and operations. This intern will actually sell Astros season, group, individual, and suite tickets throughout the duration of their internship. For an intern intrigued by a career in the sales industry, this is the ideal opportunity. During the season, this intern will be responsible for the MVP phone line handling all season tickets, suites, and other special seating. The selected individual will also participate in a rotating box office shift with the other interns in this department that will consist of walk up

- Qualifications:
  - College student with study emphasis in sports administration, marketing, or a related field; student must receive college credit for the internship
  - Must have excellent oral and written communication skills
  - Computer literacy is required, especially in Microsoft Office applications (Word, Excel, etc.); experience in PowerPoint a plus
  - Must be able to absorb and deal with several tasks effectively despite numerous interruptions
  - Must be professional, personable, and neat in appearance
  - Must be available to work Cavaliers home games

Facility Operations Intern

At the direction of the department's team leaders, will observe the operations and learn the functions of the facility operations team, specifically, and Cavaliers Holdings Company, generally, by assisting with various projects.

- Duties and responsibilities:
  - Event coordination: Assist with event planning and coordination, including meetings, move-ins, rehearsals, concerts, basketball/hockey games, and other special services and support for Quicken Loans Arena ("The Q") events
    - Once acclimated, help coordinate The Q events, including event opening and closing activities, assisting event personnel with various functions, and troubleshooting/problem-solving during events as required
- Facilities services: Assist with administrative functions of the facility operations team, including budgeting, cost control, equipment inventory, preventive maintenance, record controls, safety reports, event follow-up, and payroll functions
- Technical services: Assist with administrative and daily technical support functions of the department, including parking, sound systems, lighting, heating, cooling, staging, video presentation, and ventilation
- Interns also assist with any special project(s) related to The Q and its event planning that are assigned to the department
  - Examples have included energy management reviews, structural steel comparisons, concert staffing, emergency evacuation planning, fire safety programs, handicapped accessibility reviews, computerized equipment controls analysis, and technical manual review and analysis

- Qualifications:
  - College student with study emphasis in facility management or a related field; student must receive college credit for the internship
  - Computer literacy is required; experience in Microsoft Office applications (Word, Excel, etc.) is preferred; exposure to CAD software is a plus
  - Must be organized, flexible, and able to accept direction and constructive criticism, as necessary, and to absorb and work on multiple projects
  - Must be responsible; maturity and the ability to distinguish between ordinary and out-of-the-ordinary events and/or circumstances are essential
  - Previous "hands-on" experience in a similar environment is helpful
  - Must be available to work arena events

Marketing Intern

At the direction of the department's team leaders, will observe the operations and learn the functions of the marketing team, specifically, and Cavaliers Holdings Company, generally, by assisting with special projects, game/event operations, publications, promotions, and fan development.

- Duties and responsibilities:
  - Assists in coordinating events based on seasonal projects within the marketing team
  - Assists with other special projects as assigned
    - Examples of special projects/duties include: market research and distribution, game day activities and promotions, Cavaliers Caravan appearances, Fan-Fest, NBA Draft Day parties, Hoop-It-Up events, special team appearances, and seasonal giveaways
- Qualifications:
  - College student with study emphasis in marketing, sports administration, or a related field; student must receive college credit for the internship
  - Must have excellent oral and written communication skills
  - Computer literacy with experience in Microsoft Office applications (Word, Excel, etc.) is required
  - Must be organized and detail-oriented; must take responsibility seriously and be independently motivated
  - Must be flexible, able to accept direction and constructive criticism, as necessary, and have the ability to work efficiently on multiple projects
  - Must be available to work Cavaliers home games

Sales Intern

At the direction of the department's team leaders, will observe the operations and learn the functions of the sales team, specifically, and Cavaliers Holdings Company, generally, by assisting with various projects.

- Duties and responsibilities:
  - Participate in all sales administrative activities, including mailings, flyer creation, etc.
  - Assist in the coordination/implementation of special events, based on current need
    - Events may include Cavaliers Charities Golf Classic, Season Ticket Holder Parties, and Ticket Prospect Nights
- Assist in game day activities
- Compile sales reports and help sales team with projects related to various marketing/sales activities, as well as demographic studies, filing, administrative projects, VIP ticket order processing, and more
- Assist with other projects as assigned
- Qualifications:
  - College student with study emphasis in sports administration, marketing, or a related field; student must receive college credit for the internship
  - Must have excellent oral and written communication skills
  - Computer literacy is required; experience in Microsoft Office applications (Word, Excel, etc.) is necessary
  - Past experience in accounting, ticketing, and/or office procedures is helpful
  - Must be organized and enjoy detail; must be flexible, able to accept direction and constructive criticism, as necessary, and to absorb and work on multiple projects
  - Maturity and the ability to distinguish between ordinary and out-of-the-ordinary events and/or circumstances are essential
  - Must be self-motivated and disciplined
  - Must be available to work Cavaliers home games

INTERNSHIP PROGRAM, NFLPA

Industry Segment:	Professional Sports, Football, NFL Players Union
Functional Area:	Various
Experience:	Internship
Location:	New York
Compensation:	$11 per hour.

Goals

- Assist colleges and universities that require or allow internships in degree preparation by providing appropriate opportunities
- Provide work experience to students requiring on-the-job training for graduation
- Provide additional resources to the NFL Players Association and Players Inc.
- To be considered, prospective interns must meet the following requirements:
  - Students must be entering their junior or senior year of study in an undergraduate program, graduate students, or have completed their degree within the past 6 months
  - Candidates seeking a legal internship must be currently enrolled in law school or have received their JD within the past 6 months
  - All potential interns must submit a résumé, cover letter, application, transcript, letters of recommendation, and a writing sample to the manager of human resources; all materials must be received for consideration

Availability of Internships

We currently offer a highly competitive and very limited number of internships. Depending on the season, there will be a maximum of six positions available.

Compensation and Travel

Intern will be paid a compensation rate of $11 per hour. The intern will be provided with reasonable daily travel expenses to and from our office at 2021 L Street, NW.

Terms

The NFL Players Association/Players Inc. Intern Program is conducted on a year-round basis and positions are filled each Winter, Spring, Summer, and Fall term. Each internship is no more than 90 calendar days.

Job descriptions and work expectations will be reviewed and explained by the intern's supervisor on the first day of the internship. NFLPA/Players Inc. office hours are 9:00 AM to 5:30 PM Monday through Friday. On occasion, interns may be expected to work evenings or weekends.

Index